PENGUIN CLASSICS

PENGUIN ENGLISH POETS
GENERAL EDITOR: CHRISTOPHER RICKS

JOHN DONNE
The Complete English Poems

JOHN DONNE was born into a Catholic family in 1572. After a conventional education at Hart Hall, Oxford, and Lincoln's Inn, he took part in the Earl of Essex's expedition to the Azores in 1597. He secretly married Anne More in December 1601, and was imprisoned by her father, Sir George, in the Fleet two months later. He was ordained priest in January 1615, and proceeded to a Doctorate of Divinity at Cambridge in April of that year. In 1621 he was made Dean of St Paul's in London, a post which he held until his death in 1631. He is famous for the sermons he preached in his later years as well as for his poems.

A. J. SMITH was Professor Emeritus of the University of Southampton. His books include *Literary Love* (1983), *The Metaphysic of Love* (1985) and *Metaphysical Wit* (1992). He died in Salisbury in 1991.

John Donne
The Complete English Poems

EDITED BY A. J. SMITH

PENGUIN BOOKS

PENGUIN BOOKS

Published by the Penguin Group
Penguin Books Ltd, 80 Strand, London WC2R 0RL, England
Penguin Putnam Inc., 375 Hudson Street, New York, New York 10014, USA
Penguin Books Australia Ltd, 250 Camberwell Road, Camberwell, Victoria 3124, Australia
Penguin Books Canada Ltd, 10 Alcorn Avenue, Toronto, Ontario, Canada M4V 3B2
Penguin Books India (P) Ltd, 11 Community Centre, Panchsheel Park, New Delhi – 110 017, India
Penguin Books (NZ) Ltd, Cnr Rosedale and Airborne Roads, Albany, Auckland, New Zealand
Penguin Books (South Africa) (Pty) Ltd, 24 Sturdee Avenue, Rosebank 2196, South Africa

Penguin Books Ltd, Registered Offices: 80 Strand, London WC2R 0RL, England

www.penguin.com

First published 1971
Reprinted with corrections 1976
Reprinted in Penguin Books 1986
Reprinted with revised Further Reading, 1996
37

Set in Ehrhardt Monotype
Printed in England by Clays Ltd, St Ives plc

ISBN-13: 978–0–140– 42209–2

www.greenpenguin.co.uk

Contents

Preface 13
Table of Dates 17
Further Reading 26
A Note on the Metre 33

Songs and Sonnets

Air and Angels 41
The Anniversary 41
The Apparition 42
The Bait 43
The Blossom 44
Break of Day 45
The Broken Heart 46
The Canonization 47
Community 48
The Computation 49
Confined Love 49
The Curse 50
The Damp 51
The Dissolution 52
The Dream 52
The Ecstasy 53
The Expiration 56
Farewell to Love 56
A Fever 57

6 CONTENTS

The Flea   58
The Funeral   59
The Good Morrow   60
The Indifferent   61
A Jet Ring Sent   61
A Lecture upon the Shadow   62
The Legacy   63
Lovers' Infiniteness   64
Love's Alchemy   65
Love's Deity   65
Love's Diet   66
Love's Exchange   67
Love's Growth   69
Love's Usury   69
The Message   70
Negative Love   71
A Nocturnal upon S. Lucy's Day   72
The Paradox   73
The Primrose   74
The Prohibition   75
The Relic   75
Self Love   76
Song (Go, and catch a falling star)   77
Song (Sweetest love, I do not go)   78
Sonnet. The Token   79
The Sun Rising   80
The Triple Fool   81
Twicknam Garden   82
The Undertaking   83
A Valediction: forbidding Mourning   84
A Valediction: of the Book   85
A Valediction: of my Name in the Window   87

7 CONTENTS

A Valediction: of Weeping 89
The Will 90
Witchcraft by a Picture 91
Woman's Constancy 92

Elegies

1 Jealousy 95
2 The Anagram 96
3 Change 97
4 The Perfume 98
5 His Picture 100
6 Oh, let me not serve so 101
7 Nature's lay idiot 102
8 The Comparison 103
9 The Autumnal 105
10 The Dream 106
11 The Bracelet 107
12 His Parting from Her 110
13 Julia 113
14 A Tale of a Citizen and his Wife 114
15 The Expostulation 116
16 On his Mistress 118
17 Variety 119
18 Love's Progress 122
19 To his Mistress Going to Bed 124
20 Love's War 126
    Sappho to Philaenis 127

Epithalamions or Marriage Songs

Epithalamion Made at Lincoln's Inn   133
An Epithalamion, or Marriage Song on the Lady Elizabeth
and Count Palatine being Married on
St Valentine's Day   135
Eclogue   1613. December 26   139
Epithalamion   142

Epigrams

Hero and Leander   149
Pyramus and Thisbe   149
Niobe   149
A Burnt Ship   149
Fall of a Wall   149
A Lame Beggar   150
Cales and Guiana   150
Sir John Wingfield   150
A Self Accuser   150
A Licentious Person   150
Antiquary   151
Disinherited   151
Phryne   151
An Obscure Writer   151
Klockius   151
Raderus   151
Mercurius Gallo-Belgicus   152
Ralphius   152
The Liar   152
Manliness   152

Satires

1 Away thou fondling motley humourist 155
2 Sir; though (I thank God for it) I do hate 158
3 Kind pity chokes my spleen 161
4 Well; I may now receive, and die 164
5 Thou shalt not laugh in this leaf, Muse 170
Upon Mr Thomas Coryat's Crudities 173

The Progress of the Soul (Metempsychosis) 176

Verse Letters

The Storm 197
The Calm 199
To Mr B. B. 200
To Mr C. B. 201
To Mr S. B. 202
To Mr E. G. 202
To Mr I. L. (Blessed are your north parts) 203
To Mr I. L. (Of that short roll of friends) 203
To Mr R. W. (If, as mine is, thy life a slumber be) 204
To Mr R. W. (Kindly I envy thy song's perfection) 205
To Mr R. W.
(Muse not that by thy mind thy body is led) 205
To Mr R. W.
(Zealously my Muse doth salute all thee) 206
To Mr Rowland Woodward 206
To Mr T. W. (All hail, sweet poet) 207
To Mr T. W. (At once, from hence) 208
To Mr T. W. (Haste thee harsh verse) 209
To Mr T. W. (Pregnant again with th' old twins) 209
To Sir Henry Goodyer 210

A Letter Written by Sir H. G. and J. D.
alternis vicibus   212

To Sir Henry Wotton (Here's no more news)   213

To Sir Henry Wotton (Sir, more than kisses)   214

To Sir Henry Wotton,
at his going Ambassador to Venice   216

H. W. *in Hibernia Belligeranti*   217

To Sir Edward Herbert, at Juliers   218

To Mrs M. H.   219

To the Countess of Bedford at New Year's Tide   221

To the Countess of Bedford
(Honour is so sublime perfection)   223

To the Countess of Bedford
(Reason is our soul's left hand)   225

To the Countess of Bedford (Though I be dead)   226

To the Countess of Bedford (To have written then)   227

To the Countess of Bedford (You have refined me)   229

To the Lady Bedford   231

Epitaph on Himself   233

A Letter to the Lady Carey, and Mistress Essex Rich,
from Amiens   234

To the Countess of Huntingdon (Man to God's image)   236

To the Countess of Huntingdon
(That unripe side of earth)   238

To the Countess of Salisbury   242

Epicedes and Obsequies

Elegy on the L. C.   247

Elegy on the Lady Markham   247

Elegy on Mistress Boulstred   249

An Elegy upon the Death of Mistress Boulstred   251

Elegy upon the Untimely Death of the Incomparable
Prince Henry   253

Obsequies to the Lord Harrington, Brother to the Lady
Lucy, Countess of Bedford 256
An Hymn to the Saints, and to Marquis Hamilton 263

The Anniversaries

An Anatomy of the World: The First Anniversary 269
To the Praise of the Dead, and the Anatomy 269
An Anatomy of the World 270
A Funeral Elegy 283
Of the Progress of the Soul: The Second Anniversary 286
The Harbinger to the Progress 286
Of the Progress of the Soul 287

Divine Poems

To E. of D. with Six Holy Sonnets 305
To Mrs Magdalen Herbert: of St Mary Magdalen 305
Holy Sonnets 306
La Corona 306
Divine Meditations 309
1 Thou hast made me 309
2 As due by many titles 309
3 O might those sighs and tears 310
4 Oh my black soul! 310
5 I am a little world 310
6 This is my play's last scene 311
7 At the round earth's imagined corners 311
8 If faithful souls be alike glorified 312
9 If poisonous minerals 312
10 Death be not proud 313
11 Spit in my face ye Jews 313
12 Why are we by all creatures waited on? 313
13 What if this present were the world's last night? 314
14 Batter my heart, three-personed God 314
15 Wilt thou love God, as he thee? 315
16 Father, part of his double interest 315

17 Since she whom I loved 316
18 Show me dear Christ 316
19 Oh, to vex me 316

A Litany 317
The Cross 326
Resurrection, imperfect 327
Upon the Annunciation and Passion falling
upon one day. 1608 328
Good Friday, 1613. Riding Westward 329
To Mr Tilman after he had taken orders 331
Upon the Translation of the Psalms by Sir Philip
Sidney, and the Countess of Pembroke his Sister 332
The Lamentations of Jeremy, for the most part
according to Tremellius 334
A Hymn to Christ, at the Author's last going
into Germany 346
Hymn to God my God, in my Sickness 347
A Hymn to God the Father 348

Notes 351
Index of Titles 669
Index of First Lines 675

Preface

No editor of Donne's poems can be confident that he is printing just what Donne wrote. With a few possible exceptions Donne's own drafts of his poems never reached the press, and only one copy of an English poem in his own hand has survived. Indeed the evidence is that even the best of the early manuscript collections and printed editions we have stand at several removes from the original copies, and multiply copying errors or select by accident from the several versions of a poem that Donne himself had put about.

None the less these seventeenth-century documents are our one means to an accurate knowledge of Donne's poems. We now have the verse letter to the Lady Carey and Mistress Essex Rich as Donne sent it. Some forty-five manuscripts which bring together poems by Donne survive from Donne's own day. Seven of his poems and a bit of another were published singly in his lifetime. And there were seven printed editions of the body of his verse from 1633 to 1669. The early collections fall into definite groups, according to the sources they drew on, and they are not equally important. Of the seventeenth-century editions in particular only one has the authority of the best manuscript collections. The 1633 edition is a valuable text because it was printed from manuscripts fairly near to Donne's original copies, while the subsequent editors, including Donne's son in 1650, drew on sources further from the originals than some versions we already have or on material already in print. But the only known text of Donne's verse which has paramount authority is that of the autograph verse letter; and in general a student often needs to have in front of him all the readings of a line which the early versions offer.

My aim in the present edition is to provide a text which is closely faithful to the early versions without being archaic. I have mod-

ernized spelling throughout, but never the words themselves, and
the punctuation only in a very few instances where the old pointing
will confuse a modern reader. I have followed no single copy text,
and don't pretend to a scientific definitiveness; this is simply an
attempt, wide open to question as it must be, to offer the richest
and most pointed readings of Donne's poems that have good
authority in the early versions. My debt to previous editors of
Donne is as great as it is obvious, no less where we differ over a
reading; and I have benefited from commentaries by Mark Roberts
and other recent students of the text.

The order of the poems here is not that in which Donne com-
posed them. A straight chronological disposition of Donne's
poetry would be illuminating, though inconvenient. But it is not
remotely possible, for we only rarely know just when he wrote this
poem or that. The 1635 editor's arrangement of the poems in
groups according to their kind is the only practicable one, and it
does suggest the broad rhythm of Donne's career. Even so, it
imposes an arbitrary and perhaps distorting pattern upon the
writing; there would be some danger of misinterpreting Donne if
one followed Izaac Walton in taking these groups for distinct
categories of his life and thought, or as marking a clear-cut pro-
gression. If Walton's own evidence is worth anything then Donne
would have composed several love lyrics while he was finishing
The First Anniversary and some years after he wrote the greater
part of the Holy Sonnets. In the spring of 1613 he appears to have
written in succession the erotic St Valentine's Day Epithalamion,
the pious meditation Good Friday, 1613. Riding Westward and The
Primrose. Much of his best religious poetry comes from his time at
Mitcham when he was still desperately working to catch the eye of
influential people at Court and refusing to take holy orders.

The three Epithalamions run typically athwart our ordering of
them. One of them is probably an early poem, while the other two
must be among the last pieces Donne wrote before he became a
priest; yet we perforce group them together and place them with
the erotic writings of his early manhood. What matters much
more than any harm to these particular poems is the possibility
that a concern with genre may oversimplify the variegated texture
of the poet's thought and work, and itself subvert our search for

the coherence of Donne's poetic vision behind its apparent discontinuities.

Early collections of Donne's poetry include a number of poems that are not certainly his or that he probably did not write. Modern editors have differed sharply about which poems they accept as Donne's, which they reject, and which relegate to a section of *dubia*. For this edition I see no advantage in a category of doubtful poems. It seemed right simply to exclude the poems that Donne is unlikely to have written and to put in the main body of the text all the poems that he might well have written, with due warning to the reader both there and in the notes when Donne's authorship has been questioned. I do not feel equally confident that Donne wrote all the doubtful poems I include. But where the circumstances leave it open to question it is a matter of critical opinion whether Donne could have written this poem or that, and my concern was to make it possible for the reader to judge.

The purpose of this edition is to make an old and difficult author as intelligible as is now possible to readers of today. So my one steady concern in the notes is to explain the lines and the poems themselves. With Donne that regularly means making clear the unfamiliar or special senses in which he uses words. Textual variants help our understanding of this poet in particular, for they can show one not only the several readings of a line that are possible, but what readers near Donne's own day made or failed to make of his subtle complexities of syntax and of thought. The notes aim to give such variant readings as might bear upon the sense, but they do not record all the differences between the early versions. They do not provide information which would serve only readers who can assess the relative standing of the early versions and have access to them; so they name a manuscript only where there is some question of the authority of a reading or the placing of a poem. Nor do they make critical judgements. And what they do offer puts me again much in debt to other students of Donne: H. J. C. Grierson, R. C. Bald, I. A. Shapiro, W. Milgate and, above all, Helen Gardner.

Table of Dates

·

1572 *Between January and June* Born in Bread Street, London, the third of six children.

Father, John. A thriving London merchant, leading member of the Ironmongers' Company; claimed descent from the Welsh family Dwn, of Kidwelly, Carmarthenshire.

Mother, Elizabeth. A lifelong Catholic; daughter of John Heywood, epigrammatist and interlude writer, granddaughter of John Rastell, interlude writer, greatniece of Sir Thomas More. Family history of devotion to the memory of More, and of suffering and exile for the Catholic faith under Elizabeth. Her brothers Ellis and Jasper Heywood (translator of Seneca) became Jesuits in exile; and Jasper headed the clandestine Jesuit mission in England 1581–3, was then caught, sentenced to death, imprisoned and exiled.

1576 *?January* Father dies, aged about forty-three.
?July Mother marries Dr John Syminges of Trinity Lane, London, a well-off widower with three children, sometime President of the Royal College of Physicians.

1577 Elizabeth Donne (sister) dies.

1581 *November* Mary and Katherine Donne (sisters) die.

1583 Family move to St Bartholomew's Close, London (stepfather probably practising at St Bartholomew's Hospital).

1584 *October* Matriculates from Hart Hall, Oxford, with Henry Donne (brother).

1588 *July* Dr John Syminges (stepfather) dies.

1588–9   ?At Cambridge.

1589–91   ?Travels abroad.

1590–91   Mother marries Richard Rainsford, a Catholic gentle-
          man.

1591   Enters Thavies Inn.

1592   *May*   Admitted to Lincoln's Inn (in the tradition of
          his mother's family).

1593   *February*   Master of the Revels at Lincoln's Inn.
          June   Receives part of his share in his father's estate.
          Henry Donne (brother) dies of plague in Newgate
          Prison while held for harbouring a seminary priest.

1594   *April*   Receives part of his brother's share in their in-
          heritance. At Lincoln's Inn.

1595   Engages a servingman, so living as a gentleman of
          means.

1596   *June*   Sails from Plymouth as a gentleman adventurer
          in the English expedition to Cadiz under Essex and
          Raleigh.
          21 June   Cadiz attacked, captured and looted.
          August   Reaches England, with the English fleet.

1597   *July*   Sails on the 'Islands' expedition for Ferrol and
          the Azores. Ships caught in a storm and return to
          Plymouth.
          August   Sails with the expedition to the Azores.
          9–10 September   Ships becalmed off the Azores.
          October   Fleet returns to England.

1597–8   Enters service of Sir Thomas Egerton, the Lord Keeper
          of England, at York House, Strand.

1599   Swordbearer at the funeral of Sir Thomas Egerton's
          son (killed in Ireland under Essex) at Chester.
          ?Meets Mrs Magdalen Herbert.

1600   In lodgings near the Savoy.

1601   *October–December*   Enters Parliament as MP for
          Brackley.
          December   Secretly marries Ann More, daughter of

Sir George More (Sir Thomas Egerton's brother-in-law).

1602   *February*   Confesses the marriage to his wife's father. Imprisoned in the Fleet, and Egerton dismisses him from his post.
April   The Court of Audiences upholds the validity of the marriage. Moves to Pyrford, Surrey, to live as a guest with his wife's cousin, Sir Francis Wolley.

1603   Daughter Constance born.

1604   Son John born.

1605   ?Travels in France and Italy.
Son George born.

1606   *April*   Returns to England. Moves to Mitcham, with his family.

1606–7   Son Francis born.
Takes lodgings in the Strand.
June   Unsuccessfully seeks employment in the Queen's household. Latin verses on *Volpone* published.

1606–10   ?Assisting Thomas Morton, chaplain to the Earl of Rutland, in polemical writings against the Church of Rome.

1607   Morton made Dean of Gloucester and urges Donne to take holy orders; Donne replies that he is unworthy.

1608   Daughter Lucy born. Baptized 8 August with Lucy Countess of Bedford as godmother.
November   Unsuccessfully seeks secretaryship in Ireland.

1609   *February*   Unsuccessfully seeks secretaryship with the Virginia Company.
The Expiration published in Ferrabosco's *Airs*.
Daughter Bridget born.

1610   *January*   *Pseudo-Martyr* published.
April   Honorary M A from Oxford.

1611   *January*   Daughter Mary born.
Ignatius his Conclave published.

Upon Mr Thomas Coryat's Crudities published in *Coryat's Crudities*.

November   Sets out for the Continent with Sir Robert Drury's party, leaving his wife and family with her brother-in-law in the Isle of Wight.

December   At Amiens.

An Anatomy of the World (The First Anniversary) published.

1612   *The First and Second Anniversaries* published.

January   Goes to Paris with the Drurys; ill there.

Wife gives birth to a still-born child.

April–August   Travels in Germany and Belgium with the Drurys.

September   Returns to England.

Moves with his family to a house on the Drury estate, Drury Lane.

Break of Day published in Corkine's *Second Book of Airs*.

6 November   Death of Prince Henry.

1613   *14 February*   Marriage of Princess Elizabeth and the Elector Palatine.

March–April   Visits Sir Henry Goodyer at Polesworth, Warwickshire.

April   Visits Sir Edward Herbert at Montgomery Castle.

July–August   Son Nicholas born.

Elegy upon . . . Prince Henry published in the third edition of J. Sylvester's *Lachrymae Lachrymarum*.

Ill, with his family.

1614   *April–June*   Sits as MP for Taunton (a seat in the gift of Sir Edward Phelips). Serves on various select committees.

May   Daughter Mary dies.

Unsuccessful attempts to find state employment.

November   Son Francis dies.

1615   *23 January*   Ordained deacon and priest at St Paul's

Cathedral. Appointed a royal chaplain, and attends James I to Cambridge.

March   Honorary DD from Cambridge (given at the King's command).

April   Daughter Margaret born.

30 April   Preaches before the Queen at Greenwich (the first of Donne's sermons which has survived).

June   Preaches at Camberwell and the Inner Temple.

1616   *January*   Granted rectory of Keyston, Huntingdonshire.

April   Preaches to the Court at Whitehall.

July   Presented with the rectory of Sevenoaks, Kent.

October   Appointed Divinity Reader at Lincoln's Inn.

1617   Preaches at Paul's Cross, Sevenoaks, Whitehall, Denmark House (before the Queen), Knole (before the Earl of Dorset).

10 August   Wife Ann gives birth to a still-born child.

15 August   Wife dies.

1618   *February–April*   Preaches at Court, and at Lincoln's Inn.

1619   Preaches at Court, to the Countess of Montgomery, to the Lords (during the King's serious illness), at Lincoln's Inn (a sermon of valediction before leaving for the Continent).

May   Leaves for Germany as Chaplain with Viscount Doncaster's embassy of mediation to the Princes of Germany and Bohemia.

June–July   Preaches at Heidelberg to the Prince and Princess Palatine.

December   Preaches at The Hague on the journey home.

1620   *January*   Returns to London with Doncaster's embassy.

January–August   Preaches at Lincoln's Inn, at Court, at Camberwell, etc.

1621   Preaches at Harrington House (to the Countess of Bedford), at Court, etc.

The Anniversaries republished.

Resigns from living of Keyston.

22 November   Elected Dean of St Paul's, and installed.

25 December   Preaches the Christmas Day sermon in St Paul's.

1622   Preaches at Lincoln's Inn, at Court, St Paul's, the Spital Cross, Camberwell, Hanworth (to the Earl of Carlisle and his guests), to the Virginia Company, etc.

February   Resigns Readership at Lincoln's Inn.

April   Instituted as rector of Blunham, Bedfordshire.

Justice of the Peace for Kent and Bedfordshire.

May–July   Made honorary member of the Virginia Company and of its Council.

28 June   Appointed Judge in the Court of Delegates.

August   Granted prebend of Chiswick.

Two sermons published.

Various short prose writings published in Overbury's *A Wife*.

October   Hearing a case in the Court of Delegates.

1623   Preaches at Court, St Paul's, Lincoln's Inn (the sermon of dedication of the new chapel), and for the Law Sergeants' Feast.

January–March   Hearing a case in the Court of Delegates, attending Council meetings of the Virginia Company, etc.

Three sermons published.

November–December   Seriously ill with relapsing fever.

December   Constance Donne (daughter) marries Edward Alleyn.

1624   *February   Devotions upon Emergent Occasions* published.

March   Appointed vicar of St Dunstan's.

Preaches at St Paul's, St Dunstan's, St John's (to the Earl of Exeter), etc.

Four sermons republished.

1625   Preaches at St Dunstan's, St Paul's, at Court, Denmark House, etc.

Open breach with Alleyn over financial matters arising out of Constance Donne's marriage.

?*March*   Writes his last poem (*An Hymn to the Saints, and to Marquis Hamilton*).

27 March   King James I dies.

3 April   Preaches the first sermon to King Charles I, which is then published.

26 April   Preaches to the Court at Denmark House, for King James's lying in state.

June   Ill.

Four sermons published.

The Anniversaries republished.

July–December   Plague in London; retires to Sir John Danvers' house at Chelsea (Lady Magdalen Danvers' son, George Herbert, was also there).

1626   Preaches at St Dunstan's, St Paul's, Court (before the King), at the funeral of Sir William Cokayne, etc.

February   Chosen Prolocutor of Convocation.

2 February   Charles I crowned.

24 February   Preaches to the King at Court, and the sermon then published.

Breakdown of Constance Donne's marriage with Alleyn (Alleyn dies later in the year).

July–October   Judging cases in the Court of Delegates.

Appointed governor of the Charterhouse.

Appointed Justice of the Peace for Bedfordshire.

Ignatius his Conclave republished.

Four sermons published.

1627   *January*   Lucy Donne (daughter) dies.

Preaches at St Paul's, Court, Paul's Cross, St Dunstan's, Chelsea, for the marriage of the Earl of Bridgewater's daughter, etc.

February–November   Hearing cases in the ecclesiastical courts.

18 March   Sir Henry Goodyer (close friend) dies.

21 May   Lucy Countess of Bedford (patroness and friend) dies.

June Lady Magdalen Danvers (formerly Mrs Magdalen Herbert) dies, and Donne preaches her funeral sermon which is then published.
Devotions upon Emergent Occasions republished.

1628   Preaches at St Paul's, Court, St Dunstan's, etc.
February Christopher Brooke (lifelong friend) dies.
Attending and hearing cases in the ecclesiastical courts; attending meetings of the governors of the Charterhouse, etc.

1629   Preaches at St Paul's, Court, Paul's Cross, etc.
Attends various hearings of ecclesiastical courts, meetings of governors of the Charterhouse, etc.

1630   Preaches at St Paul's, Court, etc.
January–May Hears cases in the ecclesiastical courts, attends meetings of governors of the Charterhouse, etc.
24 June Constance Donne marries Samuel Harvey of Aldborough Hatch.
In line for promotion to a bishopric.
The Broken Heart and part of *Song* (Go, and catch a falling star) published in *A Help to Memory and Discourse*.
Autumn Taken seriously ill while visiting daughter Constance at Aldborough Hatch. During illness, writes out his old sermons from notes.
13 December Makes will.

1631   *January* Mother dies aged about eighty-six.
25 February Last sermon at Court (published posthumously as *Death's Duel*).
26 February Attends meeting of governors of the Charterhouse.
February–March Poses for a drawing of himself in his shroud.
21 March Transacts last Cathedral business.
31 March Dies.
3 April Buried in St Paul's.

1632   Memorial statue erected in St Paul's (carved from the drawing of him in his shroud), with a Latin epitaph probably composed by himself.

1633   *Poems, by J. D. with Elegies on the Author's Death*, printed by M. F. for John Marriot (the first collected edition of Donne's verse).

1635   *Poems, by J. D. . . .*

1639   *Poems, by J. D. . . .*

1640   *LXXX Sermons* published, with Walton's *Life of Dr John Donne*.

1649   *Poems, by J. D. . . .*
       L Sermons published.

1650   *Poems, by J. D. . . .* (prepared by John Donne the younger).

1654   *Poems, by J. D. . . .* printed by J. Flesher (for) John Sweeting.

1658   Walton's *Life of Donne*, in an enlarged edition.

1660   *XXVI Sermons* published.

1669   *Poems, and etc. by John Donne late Dean of St Pauls . . .* printed by T. N. for Henry Herringman.

1670   Walton's *Lives of Donne, Wotton, Hooker and Herbert* published.

1675   Walton's *Lives* reprinted.

Further Reading

ABBREVIATIONS

CQ	Critical Quarterly
EC	Essays in Criticism
ELH	English Literary History
HLQ	Huntingdon Library Quarterly
JEGP	Journal of English and Germanic Philology
KR	Kenyon Review
MLR	Modern Language Review
MP	Modern Philology
OED	Oxford English Dictionary
PQ	Philological Quarterly
PMLA	Publications of the Modern Language Association of America
REL	Review of English Literature
RES	Review of English Studies
SP	Studies in Philology
TLS	The Times Literary Supplement

POEMS

Standard Editions

John Donne: Poems 1633, Scolar Press, 1969 (facsimile edition).

Helen Gardner (ed.), *John Donne: The Divine Poems*, 2nd edn, Clarendon Press, 1978.

Helen Gardner (ed.), *John Donne: The Elegies and The Songs and Sonnets*, Clarendon Press, 1965.

Herbert J. C. Grierson (ed.), *The Poems of John Donne*, Clarendon Press, 1912.

Frank Manley (ed.), *John Donne: The Anniversaries*, Johns Hopkins Press, 1963.

W. Milgate (ed.), *John Donne: The Satires, Epigrams and Verse Letters*, Clarendon Press, 1967.

W. Milgate (ed.), *John Donne: The Epithalamions, Anniversaries, and Epicedes*, Clarendon Press, 1978.

Gary A. Springer (ed.), *The Variorum Edition of the Poetry of John Donne*, Vol. 6. *The Anniversaries and Epicedes and Obsequies*, Indiana University Press, 1995.

Gary A. Springer (ed.), *The Variorum Edition of the Poetry of John Donne*, Vol. 8. *The Epigrams, Epithalamions, Epitaphs, Inscriptions, and Miscellaneous Poems*, Indiana University Press, 1995.

Other Useful Editions

John Carey (ed.), *The Oxford Authors: John Donne*, Oxford University Press, 1990 ('Virtually all' Donne's English poetry, and selected prose).

John Hayward (ed.), *John Donne: Complete Poetry and Selected Prose*, Nonesuch Press, 1929.

Frank Kermode (ed.), *The Poems of John Donne* (selection), Limited Editions Club, Cambridge, 1968.

C. A. Patrides (ed.), *The Complete English Poems of John Donne*, Everyman's Library, 1985.

Theodore Redpath (ed.), *The Songs and Sonnets of John Donne*, 2nd edn, St. Martin's Press, 1983.

Seventeenth-century musical settings of Donne's poems are given in *Poemes de Donne, Herbert et Crashaw mis en musique par leurs contemporains*, introduction by J. Jacquot, Centre National de la Recherche Scientifique, 1961, and in Appendix B of Helen Gardner's edition of *The Elegies and The Songs and Sonnets*.

There is a facsimile of the 1611 edition of *The First Anniversary* by the Roxburghe Club, 1961.

PROSE

Selected Editions

Ignatius His Conclave, Amsterdam, Theatrum Orbis Terrarum, 1977 (facsimile edition).

Helen Gardner and Timothy Healy (eds.), *John Donne: Selected Prose* (chosen by Evelyn M. Simpson), Clarendon Press, 1967.

Timothy Healy (ed.), *Ignatius His Conclave*, Clarendon Press, 1969.

M. Thomas Hester (introd.), *Letters to Severall Persons of Honour*, Scholars' Facsimiles and Reprints, 1977 (facsimile edition).

Helen Peters (ed.), *John Donne: Paradoxes and Problems*, Clarendon Press, 1980.

George R. Potter and Evelyn M. Simpson (eds.), *The Sermons of John Donne*, University of California Press, 1953–61.

Anthony Raspa (ed.), *John Donne: Devotions upon Emergent Occasions*, McGill-Queen's University Press, 1975.

Neil Rhodes (ed.), *John Donne: Selected Prose*, Penguin Books, 1987.

E. Savage (ed.), *John Donne's Devotions upon Emergent Occasions*, Salzburg, Institut für Englische Sprache und Literatur, 1975.

John Sparrow (ed.), *Devotions upon Emergent Occasions*, Cambridge University Press, 1923.

Evelyn M. Simpson (ed.), *Essays in Divinity*, Clarendon Press, 1952.

Ernest W. Sullivan, II (ed.), *Biathanatos*, University of Delaware Press, 1984.

Gosse's *Life and Letters of John Donne* and Hayward's edition of the *Complete Poetry and Selected Prose* also give selections from Donne's letters.

BIBLIOGRAPHIES AND CONCORDANCE

Lloyd E. Berry, *A Bibliography of Studies in Metaphysical Poetry 1939–1960*, University of Wisconsin Press, 1964.

Douglas Bush, *English Literature in the Earlier Seventeenth Century*, 2nd edn, Clarendon Press, 1962.

H. C. Combs and Z. R. Sullens, *Concordance to the English Poems of John Donne*, Packard, 1940.

Geoffrey Keynes, *A Bibliography of Dr. John Donne*, 4th edn, Clarendon Press, 1973.

John R. Roberts (ed.), *John Donne: An Annotated Bibliography of Modern Criticism*, 1912–1967, University of Missouri Press, 1973.

John R. Roberts (ed.), *John Donne: An Annotated Bibliography of Modern Criticism*, 1968–1978, University of Missouri Press, 1982.

BIOGRAPHIES

R. C. Bald, *John Donne: A Life*, Clarendon Press, 1970. (The standard life.)

R. C. Bald, *Donne and the Drurys*, Cambridge University Press, 1959.

John Carey, *John Donne: Life, Mind, and Art*, 2nd edn, Faber and Faber, 1990.

Edmund Gosse, *The Life and Letters of John Donne*, Dodd Mead, 1899.

M. Thomas Hester (ed.), *Letters to Severall Persons of Honour* (facsimile 1651 edn), Delmar, New York, 1977.

George Parfitt, *John Donne: A Literary Life*, Macmillan, 1989.

Izaac Walton, *Life of Dr. John Donne* [1640] (ed. G. Saintsbury), Oxford University Press, 1927. (See also David Novarr, *The Making of Walton's 'Lives'*, Cornell University Press, 1958.)

SOME CRITICAL STUDIES

N. J. C. Andreasen, *John Donne: Conservative Revolutionary*, Princeton University Press, 1967.

James S. Baumlin, *John Donne and the Rhetorics of Renaissance Discourse*, University of Missouri Press, 1991.

Joan Bennett, *Four Metaphysical Poets*, Cambridge University Press, 1934; revised as *Five Metaphysical Poets*, Cambridge University Press, 1963.

Joan Bennett, 'The Love Poetry of John Donne', in J. Dover Wilson (ed.), *Seventeenth-Century Studies Presented to Sir Herbert Grierson*, Clarendon Press, 1938.

David Blair, 'Inferring Gender in Donne's *Songs and Sonnets*', *Essays in Criticism* XLV, 1995.

Louis I. Bredvold, 'The Naturalism of Donne in Relation to Some Renaissance Traditions', *JEGP* XXII (1923).

Louis I. Bredvold, 'The Religious Thought of Donne in Relation to Medieval and Later Traditions', in *Studies in Shakespeare, Milton and Donne*, University of Michigan Press, 1925.

Cleanth Brooks, *The Well-Wrought Urn*, Reynal & Hitchcock, 1949; Dennis Dobson, 1949.

M. L. Browne, *Donne and the Politics of Conscience in Early Modern England*, E. J. Brill, 1995.

Charles Monroe Coffin, *Donne and the New Philosophy*, Columbia University Press, 1937.

Rosalind L. Colie, 'The Rhetoric of Transcendence', *PQ* XLIII, 1964. (*The Anniversaries.*)

J. E. V. Crofts, 'John Donne', in *Essays and Studies by Members of the English Association* XXII, Clarendon Press, 1937.

Patrick Cruttwell, *The Shakespearean Moment*, Chatto & Windus, 1954.

Patrick Cruttwell, 'The Love Poetry of John Donne: Pedantique Weeds or Fresh Invention?', in Malcolm Bradbury and D. Palmer (eds.), *Metaphysical Poetry*, Arnold, 1970.

T. S. Eliot, 'Donne in our Time', in T. Spencer (ed.), *A Garland for John Donne*, Harvard University Press, 1931.

T. S. Eliot, 'The Metaphysical Poets' (1921), in *Selected Essays*, Faber, 1932.

Robert Ellrodt, *Les Poètes métaphysiques anglais*, vol. I, 2nd edn, Librairie José Corti, 1960.

William Empson, *Seven Types of Ambiguity*, Chatto & Windus, 1930, ch.4.

William Empson, *Essays on Renaissance Literature*, vol. I *Donne and His New Philosophy*, John Haffenden (ed.), Cambridge University Press, 1993.

Barbara Everett, *Donne: A London Poet*, Oxford University Press, 1972.

Peter Amadeus Fiore (ed.), *Just So Much Honour*, Pennsylvania State University Press, 1972.

Dennis Flynn, *John Donne and the Ancient Catholic Nobility*, Indiana University Press, 1995.

Raymond-Jean Frontain and Frances M. Malpezzi, *John Donne's Religious Imagination: Essays in Honor of John T. Shawcross*, UCA Press, 1995.

Helen Gardner, 'The Argument about *The Ecstasy*', in Herbert Davis and Helen Gardner (eds.), *Elizabethan and Jacobean Studies Presented to F. P. Wilson*, Clarendon Press, 1959.

Helen Gardner, *The Business of Criticism*, Clarendon Press, 1959.

Helen Gardner (ed.), *Twentieth-Century Views: John Donne*, Prentice-Hall, 1962.

K. W. Gransden, *John Donne*, Archon Books, 1969.

Achsah Guibbory, '"Oh, Let Mee Not Serve So": The Politics of Love in Donne's *Elegies*,' *ELH* LVII, 1990.

Dayton Haskin, 'Reading Donne's *Songs and Sonnets* in the Nineteenth Century', *John Donne Journal* IV, 1985.

M. T. Hester and R. V. Young (eds.), *John Donne Journal*, North Carolina State University, from 1982 (published twice a year).

Merritt Y. Hughes, 'The Lineage of *The Ecstasy*' *MLR* XXVII, 1932.

Merritt Y. Hughes, 'Kidnapping Donne', in *Essays in Criticism, University of California Studies in English* IV, University of California Press, 1934.

Merritt Y. Hughes, 'Some of Donne's "Ecstasies"', *PMLA* LXXV, 1960.

Samuel Johnson, 'Cowley', [1783] in George Birkbeck Hill (ed.), *Lives of the English Poets*, Clarendon Press, 1905.

William R. Keast (ed.), *Seventeenth-Century English Poetry*, Oxford University Press, 1962.

Frank Kermode, *John Donne*, Longman, 1957.

Frank Kermode (ed.), *Discussions of John Donne*, Heath, 1962.

Frank Kermode (ed.), *The Metaphysical Poets*, Fawcett Publications, 1969.

Frank Kermode, *Shakespeare, Spenser, Donne*, Routledge and Kegan Paul, 1971.

Frank Kermode and A. J. Smith, 'The Metaphysical Poets', in Alan Sinfield (ed.), *English Poetry*, Sussex Books, 1976.

John Klause, 'Donne and the Wonderful', *ELR* XVII, 1987.

John Klause, 'Hope's Gambit: The Jesuitical, Protestant, Skeptical Origins of Donne's Heroic Ideal', *SP* XCI, 1994.

F. R. Leavis, 'The Line of Wit', in *Revaluation*, Chatto & Windus, 1936.

Pierre Legouis, *Donne the Craftsman*, Henri Didier, 1928.

J. B. Leishman, *The Monarch of Wit*, Hutchinson, 1951.

C. S. Lewis, 'Donne and Love Poetry in the Seventeenth Century' in J. Dover Wilson (ed.), *Seventeenth-Century Studies Presented to Sir Herbert Grierson*, Clarendon Press, 1938.

Deborah H. Lockwood, 'Donne's Idea of Woman in the *Songs and Sonnets*', *Essays in Literature* XIV, 1987.

Julian Lovelock (ed.), *Donne: Songs and Sonnets: A Casebook*, Macmillan, 1973.

Anthony Low, 'Donne and the Reinvention of Love', *ELR* XX, 1990.

M. M. Mahood, *Poetry and Humanism*, Cape, 1950.

Arthur F. Marotti, *John Donne, Coterie Poet*, University of Wisconsin Press, 1986.

Louis L. Martz, *The Poetry of Meditation*, Yale University Press, 1954.

Louis L. Martz, *The Wit of Love: Donne, Carew, Crashaw, Marvell*, University of Notre Dame Press, 1969.

Earl Miner, *The Metaphysical Mode from Donne to Cowley*, Princeton University Press, 1969.

Michael Francis Moloney, *John Donne: His Flight from Mediaevalism*, University of Illinois, 1944.

David Norbrook, 'The Monarchy of Wit and the Republic of Letters: Donne's Politics', in Elizabeth D. Harvey and Katherine Eisaman Maus (eds.), *Soliciting Interpretation: Literary Theory and Seventeenth-Century English Poetry*, University of Chicago Press, 1990.

David Novarr, *The Disinterred Muse*, Cornell University Press, 1980.

A. C. Partridge, *John Donne: Language and Style*, André Deutsch, 1978.

Ted-Larry Pebworth, 'John Donne, Coterie Poetry, and the Text as Performance', *SEL* XXIX, 1989.

Douglas L. Peterson, 'John Donne's *Holy Sonnets* and the Anglican Doctrine of Contrition', *SP* LVI, 1959.

Mario Praz, *Secentismo e Marinismo in Inghilterra*, Società An. Editrice 'La Voce', 1925.

Mario Praz, 'Donne and the Poetry of his Time', in T. Spencer (ed.), *A Garland for John Donne*, Harvard University Press, 1931; reprinted in *The Flaming Heart*, Doubleday, 1958.

Mario Praz, *John Donne*, Editrice S.A.I.E., 1958.

Mary Ann Radzinowicz, 'The Politics of John Donne's Silences', *John Donne Journal* VII, 1988.

Mary Paton Ramsay, *Les Doctrines médiévales chez Donne*, Humphrey Milford, 1917.

Robert H. Ray, *A John Donne Companion*, Garland, 1990.

Christopher Ricks, 'Donne after Love', in Elaine Scarry (ed.), *Literature and the Body*, Johns Hopkins University Press, 1988. Reprinted as 'Donne: "Farewell to Love!"' in *Essays in Appreciation*, Oxford University Press, 1996.

John R. Roberts (ed.), *Essential Articles for the Study of John Donne's Poetry*, Archon Books, 1975.

Mark Roberts, 'If It Were Done When 'Tis Done . . .', *EC* XVI, 1966. (The text.)

Murray Roston, *The Soul of Wit*, Clarendon Press, 1974.

M. Rowe, *I Launch at Paradise*, Epworth Press, 1964. (The religious poetry.)

Milton Allan Rugoff, *Donne's Imagery*, Corporate Press, 1939.

Wilbur Sanders, *John Donne's Poetry*, Cambridge University Press, 1971.

John T. Shawcross, 'The Arrangement and Order of John Donne's Poems', in Neil Fraistat (ed.), *Poems in their Place: The Intertextuality and Order of Poetic Collections*, University of North Carolina Press, 1986.

Terry G. Sherwood, *Fulfilling the Circle: A Study of John Donne's Thought*, University of Toronto Press, 1984.

A. J. Smith, *John Donne: The Songs and Sonnets*, Arnold, 1964.

A. J. Smith, 'Donne's Poetry', in *The Sphere History of Literature in English* II, Sphere Books, 1970.

A. J. Smith, (ed.), *John Donne: Essays in Celebration*, Methuen, 1972.

A. J. Smith (ed.), *John Donne: The Critical Heritage*, Routledge and Kegan Paul, 1975.

A. J. Smith, *Metaphysical Wit*, Cambridge University Press, 1991.

James Smith, 'On Metaphysical Poetry', *Scrutiny* II, 1933.

Theodore Spencer (ed.), *A Garland for John Donne*, Harvard University Press, 1931.

Arnold Stein, *John Donne's Lyrics*, University of Minnesota Press, 1962; Oxford University Press, 1962.

Richard Strier, 'John Donne Awry and Squint: The "Holy Sonnets" 1608–1610', *MP* LXXXVI, 1989.

Gary A. Stringer (ed.), *New Essays on Donne*, University of Salzburg, 1977.

Claude Summers and Ted Larry Pebworth (eds.), *The Eagle and the Dove: Reassessing John Donne*, University of Missouri Press, 1986.

Claude J. Summers and Ted-Larry Pebworth (eds.), *'Bright Shootes of Everlastingnesse': The Seventeenth Century Religious Lyric*, University of Missouri Press, 1987.

Edward Tayler, *Donne's Idea of a Woman: Structure and Meaning in The Anniversaries*, Columbia University Press, 1991.

Kathleen Tillotson, 'Donne's Poetry in the Nineteenth Century', in H. Davis and Helen Gardner (eds.), *Elizabethan and Jacobean Studies Presented to F. P. Wilson*, Clarendon Press, 1959.

Rosamund Tuve, *Elizabethan and Metaphysical Imagery*, University of Chicago Press, 1947.

Leonard Unger, *Donne's Poetry and Modern Criticism*, Regnery, 1950.

Helen C. White, *The Metaphysical Poets*, Macmillan Co., 1936.

George Williamson, *The Donne Tradition*, Harvard University Press, 1930.

George Williamson, 'Donne's *Farewell to Love*', *MP* XXVI, 1939.

George Williamson, *Seventeenth-Century Contexts*, Faber, 1960.

George Williamson, 'The Design of Donne's Anniversaries', *MP* LX, 1963.

Richard B. Wollman, 'The "Press and the Fire": Print and Manuscript Culture in Donne's Circle', *SEL* XXXIII, 1993.

R. V. Young, '"O my America, my new-found land": Pornography and Imperial Politics in Donne's *Elegies*', *South Carolina Review* IV, 1987.

W. Zunder, *The Poetry of John Donne*, Harvester Press, 1982.

A Note on the Metre

Donne's rhythms depend upon colloquial speech-forms which he himself notated when he wrote out his poems, and copyists of his manuscripts tried to preserve. Early printed editions of his poetry indicate somewhat haphazardly, by apostrophe or by contraction, where vowels are to be slurred or elided – 'To'other', 'thou'rt', 'we'are met', 'blest', 'faln', 'swoln', 'gainst', 'Twere', 'scatt'ring'.

The present text reproduces these or equivalent marks only where a modern reader might otherwise mistake an accent at first. It assumes a readiness to slur or elide, without the signal of an apostrophe, such forms as a final vowel or 'y' followed by an initial vowel or 'h' – 'Like the other foot', 'We had never met', 'By occasion', 'They are', 'sinew and vein', 'claims I have made', 'Country of Courts'. But an elision is always indicated where failure to observe it might disrupt the rhythm of a line, or obscure the sense, or destroy the rhyme – 'That we'have no Reason', 'early'into'heaven', 'th'usual', 'fall'n', 'thou'rt', 'complain'st'; 'to'intergraft'; 'pray'th' (to rhyme with 'faith'). In general Donne's rhythms require that a definite article is almost always elided with a following vowel, and that 'to' or 'thou' is frequently elided with a following vowel. But the only sure guide to them is the accent of the speaking voice in rendering a particular sense.

Words which need to be stressed in an unfamiliar way are not marked in the text but accented in the notes. The following words are sometimes stressed in an unfamiliar way:

accénts (noun)   Made of th'accents, and best phrase of all these,
               (*Satire* 4, line 37)

aspéct   That but from his aspect and exercise,
               (*Elegy upon ... Prince Henry,* line 41)

blasphémous	And vile blasphemous conjurors to call (*Divine Meditations* 8, line 10)
captíved	But is captived, and proves weak or untrue, (*Divine Meditations* 14, line 8)
cément	The cement which did faithfully compact (*The First Anniversary*, line 49)
commérce	If this commerce 'twixt heaven and earth were not (*The First Anniversary*, line 399)
cónfessors	A virgin squadron of white confessors, (*A Litany*, line 92)
constéllate	What artist now dares boast that he can bring Heaven hither, or constellate anything, (*An Anatomy of the World, The First Anniversary*, lines 391–2)
controvérsies	A hundred controversies of an ant (*The Second Anniversary*, line 282)
extrácts (noun)	Kept hot with strong extracts, no bodies last: (*To the Countess of Bedford at New Year's Tide*, line 20)
éxtreme	But extreme sense hath made them desperate; (*An Elegy upon the Death of Mistress Boulstred*, line 8) (The modern pronunciation, 'extréme', is more frequent in Donne as in *Air and Angels*, line 22: nor in things Extreme, and scatt'ring bright, can love inhere;)
illústrate	Illustrate them who come to study you. (*To the Countess of Salisbury*, line 74)
medicinal (méd' cinal)	But they, yea ashes too, are medicinal, (*The First Anniversary*, line 404)
meláncholy	Weaved in my low devout melancholy, (*La Corona* 1, line 2)
óbnoxious	Think but how poor thou wast, how obnoxious; (*The Second Anniversary*, line 163)

pedantry (pedántery)	When wilt thou shake off this pedantry, (*The Second Anniversary*, line 291)
perfúme (noun and verb)	A loud perfume, which at my entrance cried (*Elegy* 4, line 41)
persévered	Had she persevered just, there would have been (*Elegy on Mistress Boulstred*, line 61)
réclused	Widowed and reclused else, her sweets she enshrines (*To the Countess of Bedford*, 'You have refined me', line 17)
recórd (noun)	I find you all record, all prophecy. (*To the Countess of Bedford*, 'You have refined me', line 52)
siníster	Deliver us from the sinister way. (*A Litany*, line 198)
sojoúrn	The straw, which doth about our hearts sojourn. (*To Mr Rowland Woodward*, line 24)
substántiál	Though you be much loved in the prince's hall, There, things that seem, exceed substantial. (*Elegy* 4, lines 63–4)
súrrounded	Blasted with sighs, and surrounded with tears, (*Twicknam Garden*, line 1)
triúmph	Thyself, and to triumph, thine army lost. (*Elegy on Mistress Boulstred*, line 68)

A rhythm may frequently depend upon our pronouncing separately all the syllables in a word, and sometimes the rhyme depends upon it too. The following suffixes are usually to be pronounced as two separate syllables:

-ean   ocean (*Elegy on the Lady Markham*, line 1. Pronounced as three syllables, to rhyme with 'man'.)

-eon   dungeon (*The Lamentations of Jeremy*, line 251. Three syllables, to rhyme with 'stone'.)

-eous   righteous (*Divine Meditations* 6, line 13. Three syllables.)

-ial   essential (*The Second Anniversary*, line 384. Four syllables, to rhyme with 'fall'.)

-ia   alleluias (*A Litany*, line 202. Five syllables, to rhyme with 'prays'.)

-ian   Egyptians (*The Lamentations of Jeremy*, line 359. Four syllables.)

-ient   ancient (*La Corona* 1, line 4. Three syllables.)

-ion   commission (*Obsequies to the Lord Harrington*, line 227. Four syllables, to rhyme with 'every one'.)

precipitation (*The First Anniversary*, line 98. Six syllables, to rhyme with 'upon'.)

religion (*The First Anniversary*, line 188. Four syllables, to rhyme with 'on'.)

proportion (*The First Anniversary*, line 250. Four syllables, to rhyme with 'gone'.)

-ious   spacious (*The First Anniversary*, line 123. Three syllables.)

Some groups of vowels may need to be read as two syllables wherever they occur in a word:

earnest (three First swear by thy best love in earnest
syllables)   (*Satire* 1, line 13)

The participial ending *-ed* is sometimes to be sounded as a separate syllable, sometimes not:

bishoped   (*To Mr B.B.*, line 28. Three syllables.)

covered   (*Elegy* 1, line 4. Three syllables, to rhyme with 'bed'.)

distempered   (*To Mr R.W.*, 'Muse not', line 2. Four syllables, to rhyme with 'led'.)

fashioned   (*A Litany*, line 8. Three syllables, to rhyme with 'dead'.)

ravished   (*Divine Meditations* 17, line 3. Three syllables, to rhyme with 'dead'.)

summoned   (*Divine Meditations* 4, line 1. Three syllables, to rhyme with 'fled'.)

But:

coffined   (Satire 1, line 4. Two syllables.)

caged   (*Elegy* 1, line 22. One syllable.)

ragged   (*Good Friday*, 1613, line 28. One syllable.)

Early versions of the poems show by a mark of elision which *–ed* endings are not to be pronounced as an extra syllable – 'coffin'd'. The distinction has not been kept in the present text because the rhythm of the line itself usually makes it clear which pronunciation is called for. The notes indicate words that might be mispronounced even so.

In the early versions of the poems the following words sometimes occur in a colloquial form for the sake of the rhyme:

anchorite   Given as 'anchorit' (*The Second Anniversary*, line 169)

been   Given as 'bin' (*Elegy on Mistress Boulstred*, line 61)

lose   Given as 'leese' (*Satire* 5, line 86)

then   Given as 'than' (*The First Anniversary*, line 25)

waste   Given as 'wast' (*The Lamentations of Jeremy*, line 80)

when   Given as 'whan' (*The Second Anniversary*, line 51)

In the present text these words have their modern form, but the early form is given in the notes wherever it matters.

Songs and Sonnets

Air and Angels

Twice or thrice had I loved thee,
Before I knew thy face or name;
So in a voice, so in a shapeless flame,
Angels affect us oft, and worshipped be;
   Still when, to where thou wert, I came,
Some lovely glorious nothing I did see,
   But since my soul, whose child love is,
Takes limbs of flesh, and else could nothing do,
   More subtle than the parent is
10 Love must not be, but take a body too,
    And therefore what thou wert, and who
      I bid love ask, and now
That it assume thy body, I allow,
And fix itself in thy lip, eye, and brow.

Whilst thus to ballast love, I thought,
And so more steadily to have gone,
With wares which would sink admiration,
I saw, I had love's pinnace overfraught,
   Every thy hair for love to work upon
20 Is much too much, some fitter must be sought;
   For, nor in nothing, nor in things
Extreme, and scatt'ring bright, can love inhere;
   Then as an angel, face and wings
Of air, not pure as it, yet pure doth wear,
   So thy love may be my love's sphere;
     Just such disparity
As is 'twixt air and angels' purity,
'Twixt women's love, and men's will ever be.

The Anniversary

   All kings, and all their favourites,
   All glory of honours, beauties, wits,
The sun itself, which makes times, as they pass,
Is elder by a year, now, than it was

When thou and I first one another saw:
All other things, to their destruction draw,
   Only our love hath no decay;
This, no tomorrow hath, nor yesterday,
Running it never runs from us away,
10 But truly keeps his first, last, everlasting day.

   Two graves must hide thine and my corse,
    If one might, death were no divorce,
Alas, as well as other princes, we,
(Who prince enough in one another be,)
Must leave at last in death, these eyes, and ears,
Oft fed with true oaths, and with sweet salt tears;
   But souls where nothing dwells but love
(All other thoughts being inmates) then shall prove
This, or a love increased there above,
20 When bodies to their graves, souls from their graves remove.

   And then we shall be throughly blessed,
    But we no more, than all the rest.
Here upon earth, we are kings, and none but we
Can be such kings, nor of such subjects be;
Who is so safe as we? where none can do
Treason to us, except one of us two.
   True and false fears let us refrain,
Let us love nobly, and live, and add again
Years and years unto years, till we attain
30 To write threescore, this is the second of our reign.

The Apparition

When by thy scorn, O murderess, I am dead,
And that thou think'st thee free
From all solicitation from me,
Then shall my ghost come to thy bed,
And thee, feigned vestal, in worse arms shall see;
Then thy sick taper will begin to wink,
And he, whose thou art then, being tired before,

Will, if thou stir, or pinch to wake him, think
    Thou call'st for more,
10 And in false sleep will from thee shrink,
And then poor aspen wretch, neglected thou
Bathed in a cold quicksilver sweat wilt lie
    A verier ghost than I;
What I will say, I will not tell thee now,
Lest that preserve thee; and since my love is spent,
I had rather thou shouldst painfully repent,
Than by my threatenings rest still innocent.

The Bait

Come live with me, and be my love,
And we will some new pleasures prove
Of golden sands, and crystal brooks,
With silken lines, and silver hooks.

There will the river whispering run
Warmed by thy eyes, more than the sun.
And there the'enamoured fish will stay,
Begging themselves they may betray.

When thou wilt swim in that live bath,
10 Each fish, which every channel hath,
Will amorously to thee swim,
Gladder to catch thee, than thou him.

If thou, to be so seen, be'st loth,
By sun, or moon, thou darkenest both,
And if myself have leave to see,
I need not their light, having thee.

Let others freeze with angling reeds,
And cut their legs, with shells and weeds,
Or treacherously poor fish beset,
20 With strangling snare, or windowy net:

Let coarse bold hands, from slimy nest
The bedded fish in banks out-wrest,
Or curious traitors, sleavesilk flies
Bewitch poor fishes' wandering eyes.

For thee, thou need'st no such deceit,
For thou thyself art thine own bait,
That fish, that is not catched thereby,
Alas, is wiser far than I.

The Blossom

Little think'st thou, poor flower,
　Whom I have watched six or seven days,
And seen thy birth, and seen what every hour
Gave to thy growth, thee to this height to raise,
And now dost laugh and triumph on this bough,
　　　Little think'st thou
That it will freeze anon, and that I shall
Tomorrow find thee fall'n, or not at all.

Little think'st thou, poor heart
10　　That labour'st yet to nestle thee,
And think'st by hovering here to get a part
In a forbidden or forbidding tree,
And hop'st her stiffness by long siege to bow:
　　　Little think'st thou,
That thou tomorrow, ere that sun doth wake,
Must with this sun, and me a journey take.

But thou which lov'st to be
　Subtle to plague thyself, wilt say,
Alas, if you must go, what's that to me?
20　Here lies my business, and here I will stay:
You go to friends, whose love and means present
　　　Various content
To your eyes, ears, and tongue, and every part.
If then your body go, what need you a heart?

Well then, stay here; but know,
When thou hast stayed and done thy most;
A naked thinking heart, that makes no show,
Is to a woman, but a kind of ghost;
How shall she know my heart; or having none,
30   Know thee for one?
Practice may make her know some other part,
But take my word, she doth not know a heart.

Meet me at London, then,
    Twenty days hence, and thou shalt see
Me fresher, and more fat, by being with men,
Than if I had stayed still with her and thee.
For God's sake, if you can, be you so too:
      I would give you
There, to another friend, whom we shall find
40 As glad to have my body, as my mind.

Break of Day

'Tis true, 'tis day, what though it be?
O wilt thou therefore rise from me?
Why should we rise, because 'tis light?
Did we lie down, because 'twas night?
Love which in spite of darkness brought us hither,
Should in despite of light keep us together.

Light hath no tongue, but is all eye;
If it could speak as well as spy,
This were the worst, that it could say,
10 That being well, I fain would stay,
And that I loved my heart and honour so,
That I would not from him, that had them, go.

Must business thee from hence remove?
Oh, that's the worst disease of love,
The poor, the foul, the false, love can
Admit but not the busied man.

He which hath business, and makes love, doth do
Such wrong, as when a married man doth woo.

The Broken Heart

He is stark mad, who ever says,
   That he hath been in love an hour,
Yet not that love so soon decays,
   But that it can ten in less space devour;
Who will believe me, if I swear
That I have had the plague a year?
   Who would not laugh at me, if I should say,
   I saw a flask of powder burn a day?

Ah, what a trifle is a heart,
10   If once into Love's hands it come!
All other griefs allow a part
   To other griefs, and ask themselves but some,
They come to us, but us Love draws,
He swallows us, and never chaws:
   By him, as by chain-shot, whole ranks do die,
   He is the tyrant pike, our hearts the fry.

If 'twere not so, what did become
   Of my heart, when I first saw thee?
I brought a heart into the room,
20   But from the room, I carried none with me;
If it had gone to thee, I know
Mine would have taught thy heart to show
   More pity unto me: but Love, alas,
   At one first blow did shiver it as glass.

Yet nothing can to nothing fall,
   Nor any place be empty quite,
Therefore I think my breast hath all
   Those pieces still, though they be not unite;
And now as broken glasses show
30   A hundred lesser faces, so

My rags of heart can like, wish, and adore,
But after one such love, can love no more.

The Canonization

For God's sake hold your tongue, and let me love,
  Or chide my palsy, or my gout,
My five grey hairs, or ruined fortune flout,
  With wealth your state, your mind with arts improve,
    Take you a course, get you a place,
    Observe his Honour, or his Grace,
Or the King's real, or his stamped face
  Contemplate; what you will, approve,
  So you will let me love.

10 Alas, alas, who's injured by my love?
  What merchant's ships have my sighs drowned?
Who says my tears have overflowed his ground?
  When did my colds a forward spring remove?
    When did the heats which my veins fill
    Add one more to the plaguy bill?
Soldiers find wars, and lawyers find out still
  Litigious men, which quarrels move,
  Though she and I do love.

Call us what you will, we are made such by love;
20   Call her one, me another fly,
We are tapers too, and at our own cost die,
  And we in us find the eagle and the dove,
    The phoenix riddle hath more wit
    By us; we two being one, are it.
So to one neutral thing both sexes fit
  We die and rise the same, and prove
  Mysterious by this love.

We can die by it, if not live by love,
  And if unfit for tombs and hearse
30 Our legend be, it will be fit for verse;

And if no piece of chronicle we prove,
   We'll build in sonnets pretty rooms;
   As well a well wrought urn becomes
The greatest ashes, as half-acre tombs,
   And by these hymns, all shall approve
   Us canonized for love:

And thus invoke us; 'You whom reverend love
   Made one another's hermitage;
You, to whom love was peace, that now is rage;
40   Who did the whole world's soul contract, and drove
     Into the glasses of your eyes
     (So made such mirrors, and such spies,
That they did all to you epitomize,)
   Countries, towns, courts: beg from above
   A pattern of your love!'

Community

Good we must love, and must hate ill,
For ill is ill, and good good still,
   But there are things indifferent,
Which we may neither hate, nor love,
But one, and then another prove,
   As we shall find our fancy bent.

If then at first wise Nature had
Made women either good or bad,
   Then some we might hate, and some choose,
10 But since she did them so create,
That we may neither love, nor hate,
   Only this rests, All, all may use.

If they were good it would be seen,
Good is as visible as green,
   And to all eyes itself betrays:
If they were bad, they could not last,
Bad doth itself, and others waste,
   So, they deserve nor blame, nor praise.

But they are ours, as fruits are ours,
20 He that but tastes, he that devours,
    And he that leaves all, doth as well:
Changed loves are but changed sorts of meat,
And when he hath the kernel eat,
    Who doth not fling away the shell?

The Computation

For the first twenty years, since yesterday,
    I scarce believed, thou couldst be gone away,
For forty more, I fed on favours past,
    And forty on hopes, that thou wouldst, they might last.
Tears drowned one hundred, and sighs blew out two,
    A thousand, I did neither think, nor do,
    Or not divide, all being one thought of you;
    Or in a thousand more, forgot that too.
Yet call not this long life; but think that I
10 Am, by being dead, immortal; can ghosts die?

Confined Love

Some man unworthy to be possessor
Of old or new love, himself being false or weak,
    Thought his pain and shame would be lesser,
If on womankind he might his anger wreak,
        And thence a law did grow,
        One should but one man know;
        But are other creatures so?

    Are sun, moon, or stars by law forbidden,
To smile where they list, or lend away their light?
10   Are birds divorced, or are they chidden
If they leave their mate, or lie abroad a-night?
        Beasts do no jointures lose
        Though they new lovers choose,
        But we are made worse than those.

Who e'er rigged fair ship to lie in harbours
And not to seek new lands, or not to deal withal?
   Or built fair houses, set trees, and arbours,
Only to lock up, or else to let them fall?
      Good is not good, unless
20   A thousand it possess,
      But doth waste with greediness.

The Curse

Whoever guesses, thinks, or dreams he knows
Who is my mistress, wither by this curse;
     His only, and only his purse
     May some dull heart to love dispose,
And she yield then to all that are his foes;
   May he be scorned by one, whom all else scorn,
   Forswear to others, what to her he hath sworn,
   With fear of missing, shame of getting, torn:

Madness his sorrow, gout his cramps, may he
10 Make, by but thinking, who hath made him such:
     And may he feel no touch
     Of conscience, but of fame, and be
Anguished not that 'twas sin, but that 'twas she:
   In early and long scarceness may he rot,
   For land which had been his, if he had not
   Himself incestuously an heir begot:

May he dream treason, and believe, that he
Meant to perform it, and confess, and die,
     And no record tell why:
20   His sons, which none of his may be,
Inherit nothing but his infamy:
   Or may he so long parasites have fed,
   That he would fain be theirs, whom he hath bred,
   And at the last be circumcised for bread:

The venom of all stepdames, gamesters' gall,
What tyrants, and their subjects interwish,
    What plants, mines, beasts, fowl, fish,
    Can contribute, all ill which all
Prophets, or poets spake; and all which shall
30 Be annexed in schedules unto this by me,
    Fall on that man; for if it be a she
    Nature before hand hath out-cursed me.

The Damp

When I am dead, and doctors know not why,
    And my friends' curiosity
Will have me cut up to survey each part,
When they shall find your picture in my heart,
    You think a sudden damp of love
    Will through all their senses move,
And work on them as me, and so prefer
Your murder, to the name of massacre.

Poor victories; but if you dare be brave,
10   And pleasure in your conquest have,
First kill th' enormous giant, your Disdain,
And let th' enchantress Honour, next be slain,
    And like a Goth and Vandal rise,
    Deface records, and histories
Of your own arts and triumphs over men,
And without such advantage kill me then.

For I could muster up as well as you
    My giants, and my witches too,
Which are vast Constancy, and Secretness,
20 But these I neither look for, nor profess;
    Kill me as woman, let me die
    As a mere man; do you but try
Your passive valour, and you shall find then,
Naked you have odds enough of any man.

The Dissolution

She is dead; and all which die
   To their first elements resolve;
And we were mutual elements to us,
   And made of one another.
   My body then doth hers involve,
And those things whereof I consist, hereby
In me abundant grow, and burdenous,
   And nourish not, but smother.
   My fire of passion, sighs of air,
10 Water of tears, and earthy sad despair,
     Which my materials be,
But near worn out by love's security,
She, to my loss, doth by her death repair,
   And I might live long wretched so
But that my fire doth with my fuel grow.
     Now as those active kings
   Whose foreign conquest treasure brings,
Receive more, and spend more, and soonest break:
This (which I am amazed that I can speak)
20   This death, hath with my store
     My use increased.
And so my soul more earnestly released,
Will outstrip hers; as bullets flown before
A latter bullet may o'ertake, the powder being more.

The Dream

Dear love, for nothing less than thee
Would I have broke this happy dream,
    It was a theme
For reason, much too strong for phantasy,
Therefore thou waked'st me wisely; yet
My dream thou brok'st not, but continued'st it;

Thou art so true, that thoughts of thee suffice,
To make dreams truths, and fables histories;
Enter these arms, for since thou thought'st it best,
10 Not to dream all my dream, let's act the rest.

As lightning, or a taper's light,
Thine eyes, and not thy noise waked me;
      Yet I thought thee
(For thou lov'st truth) an angel, at first sight,
But when I saw thou saw'st my heart,
And knew'st my thoughts, beyond an angel's art,
When thou knew'st what I dreamed, when thou knew'st
    when
Excess of joy would wake me, and cam'st then,
I must confess, it could not choose but be
20 Profane, to think thee anything but thee.

Coming and staying showed thee, thee,
But rising makes me doubt, that now,
      Thou art not thou.
That love is weak, where fear's as strong as he;
'Tis not all spirit, pure, and brave,
If mixture it of fear, shame, honour, have.
Perchance as torches which must ready be,
Men light and put out, so thou deal'st with me,
Thou cam'st to kindle, goest to come; then I
30 Will dream that hope again, but else would die.

The Ecstasy

Where, like a pillow on a bed,
  A pregnant bank swelled up, to rest
The violet's reclining head,
  Sat we two, one another's best;

Our hands were firmly cemented
  With a fast balm, which thence did spring,
Our eye-beams twisted, and did thread
  Our eyes, upon one double string;

So to' intergraft our hands, as yet
10   Was all our means to make us one,
And pictures in our eyes to get
    Was all our propagation

As 'twixt two equal armies, Fate
    Suspends uncertain victory,
Our souls, (which to advance their state,
    Were gone out), hung 'twixt her, and me.

And whilst our souls negotiate there,
    We like sepulchral statues lay;
All day, the same our postures were,
20   And we said nothing, all the day.

If any, so by love refined,
    That he soul's language understood,
And by good love were grown all mind,
    Within convenient distance stood,

He (though he knew not which soul spake
    Because both meant, both spake the same)
Might thence a new concoction take,
    And part far purer than he came.

This ecstasy doth unperplex
30   (We said) and tell us what we love,
We see by this, it was not sex,
    We see, we saw not what did move:

But as all several souls contain
    Mixture of things, they know not what,
Love, these mixed souls doth mix again,
    And makes both one, each this and that.

A single violet transplant,
    The strength, the colour, and the size,
(All which before was poor, and scant,)
40   Redoubles still, and multiplies.

When love, with one another so
    Interinanimates two souls,
That abler soul, which thence doth flow,
    Defects of loneliness controls.

We then, who are this new soul, know,
    Of what we are composed, and made,
For, th' atomies of which we grow,
    Are souls, whom no change can invade.

But O alas, so long, so far
50   Our bodies why do we forbear?
They are ours, though they are not we, we are
    The intelligences, they the sphere.

We owe them thanks, because they thus,
    Did us, to us, at first convey,
Yielded their forces, sense, to us,
    Nor are dross to us, but allay.

On man heaven's influence works not so,
    But that it first imprints the air,
So soul into the soul may flow,
60   Though it to body first repair.

As our blood labours to beget
    Spirits, as like souls as it can,
Because such fingers need to knit
    That subtle knot, which makes us man:

So must pure lovers' souls descend
    T' affections, and to faculties,
Which sense may reach and apprehend,
    Else a great prince in prison lies.

To our bodies turn we then, that so
70   Weak men on love revealed may look;
Love's mysteries in souls do grow,
    But yet the body is his book.

And if some lover, such as we,
   Have heard this dialogue of one,
Let him still mark us, he shall see
   Small change, when we'are to bodies gone.

The Expiration

So, so, break off this last lamenting kiss,
   Which sucks two souls, and vapours both away,
Turn thou ghost that way, and let me turn this,
   And let ourselves benight our happiest day,
We asked none leave to love; nor will we owe
   Any, so cheap a death, as saying, Go;

Go; and if that word have not quite killed thee,
   Ease me with death, by bidding me go too.
Oh, if it have, let my word work on me,
10   And a just office on a murderer do.
Except it be too late, to kill me so,
   Being double dead, going, and bidding, go.

Farewell to Love

   Whilst yet to prove,
I thought there was some deity in love
   So did I reverence, and gave
Worship; as atheists at their dying hour
Call, what they cannot name, an unknown power,
   As ignorantly did I crave:
      Thus when
Things not yet known are coveted by men,
   Our desires give them fashion, and so
10 As they wax lesser, fall, as they size, grow.

     But, from late fair
His highness sitting in a golden chair,
   Is not less cared for after three days

By children, than the thing which lovers so
Blindly admire, and with such worship woo;
   Being had, enjoying it decays:
       And thence,
What before pleased them all, takes but one sense,
   And that so lamely, as it leaves behind
20 A kind of sorrowing dullness to the mind.

     Ah cannot we,
As well as cocks and lions jocund be,
   After such pleasures? Unless wise
Nature decreed (since each such act, they say,
Diminisheth the length of life a day)
   This; as she would man should despise
      The sport,
Because that other curse of being short,
   And only for a minute made to be
30 Eager, desires to raise posterity.

    Since so, my mind
Shall not desire what no man else can find,
   I'll no more dote and run
To pursue things which had endamaged me.
And when I come where moving beauties be,
   As men do when the summer's sun
      Grows great,
Though I admire their greatness, shun their heat;
   Each place can afford shadows. If all fail,
40 'Tis but applying worm-seed to the tail.

A Fever

Oh do not die, for I shall hate
   All women so, when thou art gone,
That thee I shall not celebrate,
   When I remember, thou wast one.

But yet thou canst not die, I know,
    To leave this world behind, is death,
But when thou from this world wilt go,
    The whole world vapours with thy breath.

Or if, when thou, the world's soul, go'st,
10   It stay, 'tis but thy carcase then,
The fairest woman, but thy ghost,
    But corrupt worms, the worthiest men.

Oh wrangling schools, that search what fire
    Shall burn this world, had none the wit
Unto this knowledge to aspire,
    That this her fever might be it?

And yet she cannot waste by this,
    Nor long bear this torturing wrong,
For much corruption needful is
20   To fuel such a fever long.

These burning fits but meteors be,
    Whose matter in thee is soon spent.
Thy beauty, and all parts, which are thee,
    Are unchangeable firmament.

Yet 'twas of my mind, seizing thee,
    Though it in thee cannot perséver.
For I had rather owner be
    Of thee one hour, than all else ever.

The Flea

Mark but this flea, and mark in this,
How little that which thou deny'st me is;
Me it sucked first, and now sucks thee,
And in this flea, our two bloods mingled be;
Confess it, this cannot be said
A sin, or shame, or loss of maidenhead,
    Yet this enjoys before it woo,

    And pampered swells with one blood made of two,
    And this, alas, is more than we would do.

10 Oh stay, three lives in one flea spare,
    Where we almost, nay more than married are.
    This flea is you and I, and this
    Our marriage bed, and marriage temple is;
    Though parents grudge, and you, we'are met,
    And cloistered in these living walls of jet.
      Though use make you apt to kill me,
      Let not to this, self murder added be,
      And sacrilege, three sins in killing three.

    Cruel and sudden, hast thou since
20 Purpled thy nail, in blood of innocence?
    In what could this flea guilty be,
    Except in that drop which it sucked from thee?
    Yet thou triumph'st, and say'st that thou
    Find'st not thyself, nor me the weaker now;
      'Tis true, then learn how false, fears be;
      Just so much honour, when thou yield'st to me,
      Will waste, as this flea's death took life from thee.

The Funeral

Whoever comes to shroud me, do not harm
      Nor question much
That subtle wreath of hair, which crowns my arm;
The mystery, the sign you must not touch,
      For 'tis my outward soul,
Vicerory to that, which then to heaven being gone,
      Will leave this to control,
And keep these limbs, her provinces, from dissolution.

For if the sinewy thread my brain lets fall
10   Through every part,
Can tie those parts, and make me one of all;
These hairs which upward grew, and strength and art
      Have from a better brain,

Can better do it; except she meant that I
      By this should know my pain,
As prisoners then are manacled, when they are condemned
  to die.

Whate'er she meant by it, bury it with me,
      For since I am
Love's martyr, it might breed idolatry,
20 If into others' hands these relics came;
      As 'twas humility
To afford to it all that a soul can do,
      So, 'tis some bravery,
That since you would save none of me, I bury some of you.

The Good Morrow

I wonder by my troth, what thou, and I
      Did, till we loved? were we not weaned till then,
But sucked on country pleasures, childishly?
      Or snorted we in the seven sleepers' den?
'Twas so; but this, all pleasures fancies be.
If ever any beauty I did see,
Which I desired, and got, 'twas but a dream of thee.

And now good morrow to our waking souls,
      Which watch not one another out of fear;
10 For love, all love of other sights controls,
      And makes one little room, an every where.
Let sea-discoverers to new worlds have gone,
Let maps to others, worlds on worlds have shown,
Let us possess one world, each hath one, and is one.

My face in thine eye, thine in mine appears,
      And true plain hearts do in the faces rest,
Where can we find two better hemispheres
      Without sharp north, without declining west?
What ever dies, was not mixed equally;
20 If our two loves be one, or, thou and I
Love so alike, that none do slacken, none can die.

The Indifferent

I can love both fair and brown,
Her whom abundance melts, and her whom want betrays,
Her who loves loneness best, and her who masks and plays,
Her whom the country formed, and whom the town,
Her who believes, and her who tries,
Her who still weeps with spongy eyes,
And her who is dry cork, and never cries;
I can love her, and her, and you and you,
I can love any, so she be not true.

10 Will no other vice content you?
Will it not serve your turn to do, as did your mothers?
Have you old vices spent, and now would find out others?
Or doth a fear, that men are true, torment you?
Oh we are not, be not you so,
Let me, and do you, twenty know.
Rob me, but bind me not, and let me go.
Must I, who came to travail thorough you,
Grow your fixed subject, because you are true?

Venus heard me sigh this song,
20 And by love's sweetest part, variety, she swore,
She heard not this till now; and that it should be so no more.
She went, examined, and returned ere long,
And said, 'Alas, some two or three
Poor heretics in love there be,
Which think to establish dangerous constancy.
But I have told them, "Since you will be true,
You shall be true to them, who are false to you." '

A Jet Ring Sent

Thou art not so black, as my heart,
Nor half so brittle, as her heart, thou art;

What wouldst thou say? shall both our properties by thee be
    spoke,
  Nothing more endless, nothing sooner broke?

    Marriage rings are not of this stuff;
  Oh, why should aught less precious, or less tough
Figure our loves? Except in thy name thou have bid it say,
  I am cheap, and naught but fashion, fling me away.

    Yet stay with me since thou art come,
10   Circle this finger's top, which didst her thumb.
Be justly proud, and gladly safe, that thou dost dwell with
  me,
  She that, oh, broke her faith, would soon break thee.

A Lecture upon the Shadow

Stand still, and I will read to thee
A lecture, love, in love's philosophy.
    These three hours that we have spent,
    Walking here, two shadows went
Along with us, which we ourselves produced;
But, now the sun is just above our head,
    We do those shadows tread;
    And to brave clearness all things are reduced.
  So whilst our infant loves did grow,
10 Disguises did, and shadows, flow,
  From us, and our care; but, now 'tis not so.

That love hath not attained the high'st degree,
Which is still diligent lest others see.

Except our loves at this noon stay,
We shall new shadows make the other way.
    As the first were made to blind
    Others; these which come behind
Will work upon ourselves, and blind our eyes.
If our loves faint, and westwardly decline;
20   To me thou, falsely, thine,

      And I to thee mine actions shall disguise.
The morning shadows wear away,
But these grow longer all the day,
But oh, love's day is short, if love decay.

Love is a growing, or full constant light;
And his first minute, after noon, is night.

The Legacy

When I died last, and, dear, I die
   As often as from thee I go,
   Though it be an hour ago,
And lovers' hours be full eternity,
I can remember yet, that I
   Something did say, and something did bestow;
Though I be dead, which sent me, I should be
Mine own executor and legacy.

I heard me say, 'Tell her anon,
10   That my self', that is you, not I,
   'Did kill me,' and when I felt me die,
I bid me send my heart, when I was gone;
But I alas could there find none,
   When I had ripped me, and searched where hearts should
      lie;
It killed me again, that I who still was true,
In life, in my last will should cozen you.

Yet I found something like a heart,
   But colours it, and corners had,
   It was not good, it was not bad,
20 It was entire to none, and few had part.
As good as could be made by art
   It seemed; and therefore for our losses sad,
I meant to send this heart instead of mine,
But oh, no man could hold it, for 'twas thine.

Lovers' Infiniteness

If yet I have not all thy love,
Dear, I shall never have it all,
I cannot breathe one other sigh, to move,
Nor can entreat one other tear to fall.
All my treasure, which should purchase thee,
Sighs, tears, and oaths, and letters I have spent,
Yet no more can be due to me,
Than at the bargain made was meant.
If then thy gift of love were partial,
10 That some to me, some should to others fall,
    Dear, I shall never have thee all.

Or if then thou gavest me all,
All was but all, which thou hadst then;
But if in thy heart, since, there be or shall
New love created be, by other men,
Which have their stocks entire, and can in tears,
In sighs, in oaths, and letters outbid me,
This new love may beget new fears,
For, this love was not vowed by thee.
20 And yet it was, thy gift being general,
  The ground, thy heart is mine; whatever shall
    Grow there, dear, I should have it all.

Yet I would not have all yet,
He that hath all can have no more,
And since my love doth every day admit
New growth, thou shouldst have new rewards in store;
Thou canst not every day give me thy heart,
If thou canst give it, then thou never gav'st it:
Love's riddles are, that though thy heart depart,
30 It stays at home, and thou with losing sav'st it:
  But we will have a way more liberal,
  Than changing hearts, to join them, so we shall
    Be one, and one another's all.

Love's Alchemy

Some that have deeper digged love's mine than I,
Say, where his centric happiness doth lie:
      I have loved, and got, and told,
But should I love, get, tell, till I were old,
I should not find that hidden mystery;
      Oh, 'tis imposture all:
And as no chemic yet the elixir got,
      But glorifies his pregnant pot,
      If by the way to him befall
10 Some odoriferous thing, or medicinal,
    So, lovers dream a rich and long delight,
    But get a winter-seeming summer's night.

Our ease, our thrift, our honour, and our day,
Shall we, for this vain bubble's shadow pay?
      Ends love in this, that my man,
Can be as happy as I can; if he can
Endure the short scorn of a bridegroom's play?
      That loving wretch that swears,
'Tis not the bodies marry, but the minds,
20   Which he in her angelic finds,
      Would swear as justly, that he hears,
In that day's rude hoarse minstrelsy, the spheres.
Hope not for mind in women; at their best
    Sweetness and wit, they are but mummy, possessed.

Love's Deity

I long to talk with some old lover's ghost,
    Who died before the god of love was born:
I cannot think that he, who then loved most,
    Sunk so low, as to love one which did scorn.
But since this god produced a destiny,

And that vice-nature, custom, lets it be;
   I must love her, that loves not me.

Sure, they which made him god, meant not so much,
   Nor he, in his young godhead practised it.
10 But when an even flame two hearts did touch,
   His office was indulgently to fit
Actives to passives. Correspondency
Only his subject was; it cannot be
   Love, till I love her, that loves me.

But every modern god will now extend
   His vast prerogative, as far as Jove.
To rage, to lust, to write to, to commend,
   All is the purlieu of the god of love.
Oh were we wakened by this tyranny
20 To ungod this child again, it could not be
   I should love her, who loves not me.

Rebel and atheist too, why murmur I,
   As though I felt the worst that love could do?
Love might make me leave loving, or might try
   A deeper plague, to make her love me too,
Which, since she loves before, I am loth to see;
Falsehood is worse than hate; and that must be,
   If she whom I love, should love me.

Love's Diet

To what a cumbersome unwieldiness
And burdenous corpulence my love had grown,
   But that I did, to make it less,
   And keep it in proportion,
Give it a diet, made it feed upon
That which love worst endures, discretion.

Above one sigh a day I allowed him not,
Of which my fortune, and my faults had part;
   And if sometimes by stealth he got

10   A she sigh from my mistress' heart,
And thought to feast on that, I let him see
'Twas neither very sound, nor meant to me.

If he wrung from me a tear, I brined it so
With scorn or shame, that him it nourished not;
    If he sucked hers, I let him know
    'Twas not a tear, which he had got,
His drink was counterfeit, as was his meat;
For, eyes which roll towards all, weep not, but sweat.

Whatever he would dictate, I writ that,
20   But burnt my letters; when she writ to me,
    And that that favour made him fat,
    I said, 'If any title be
Conveyed by this, ah, what doth it avail,
To be the fortieth name in an entail?'

Thus I reclaimed my buzzard love, to fly
At what, and when, and how, and where I choose;
    Now negligent of sport I lie,
    And now as other falconers use,
I spring a mistress, swear, write, sigh and weep:
30   And the game killed, or lost, go talk, and sleep.

Love's Exchange

    Love, any devil else but you,
Would for a given soul give something too.
    At Court your fellows every day,
Give th' art of rhyming, huntsmanship, and play,
    For them who were their own before;
    Only I have nothing which gave more,
But am, alas, by being lowly, lower.

    I ask not dispensation now
To falsify a tear, or sigh, or vow,
10   I do not sue from thee to draw
A *non obstante* on nature's law,

These are prerogatives, they inhere
In thee and thine; none should forswear
Except that he Love's minion were.

Give me thy weakness, make me blind,
Both ways, as thou and thine, in eyes and mind;
  Love, let me never know that this
Is love, or, that love childish is.
  Let me not know that others know
20 That she knows my pain, lest that so
A tender shame make me mine own new woe.

If thou give nothing, yet thou'art just,
Because I would not thy first motions trust;
  Small towns which stand stiff, till great shot
Enforce them, by war's law condition not.
  Such in love's warfare is my case,
  I may not article for grace,
Having put Love at last to show this face.

This face, by which he could command
30 And change the idolatry of any land,
  This face, which wheresoe'er it comes,
Can call vowed men from cloisters, dead from tombs,
  And melt both poles at once, and store
  Deserts with cities, and make more
Mines in the earth, than quarries were before.

For this Love is enraged with me,
Yet kills not. If I must example be
  To future rebels; if th' unborn
Must learn, by my being cut up, and torn:
40 Kill, and dissect me, Love; for this
  Torture against thine own end is,
Racked carcases make ill anatomies.

Love's Growth

I scarce believe my love to be so pure
    As I had thought it was,
    Because it doth endure
Vicissitude, and season, as the grass;
Methinks I lied all winter, when I swore,
My love was infinite, if spring make it more.
But if this medicine, love, which cures all sorrow
With more, not only be no quintessence,
But mixed of all stuffs, paining soul, or sense,
And of the sun his working vigour borrow,
Love's not so pure, and abstract, as they use
To say, which have no mistress but their Muse,
But as all else, being elemented too,
Love sometimes would contemplate, sometimes do.

And yet not greater, but more eminent,
    Love by the spring is grown;
    As, in the firmament,
Stars by the sun are not enlarged, but shown,
Gentle love deeds, as blossoms on a bough,
From love's awakened root do bud out now.
If, as in water stirred more circles be
Produced by one, love such additions take,
Those like so many spheres, but one heaven make,
For, they are all concentric unto thee,
And though each spring do add to love new heat,
As princes do in times of action get
New taxes, and remit them not in peace,
No winter shall abate the spring's increase.

Love's Usury

For every hour that thou wilt spare me now,
    I will allow,

Usurious God of Love, twenty to thee,
When with my brown, my grey hairs equal be;
Till then, Love, let my body reign, and let
Me travel, sojourn, snatch, plot, have, forget,
Resume my last year's relict: think that yet
    We had never met.

Let me think any rival's letter mine,
10   And at next nine
Keep midnight's promise; mistake by the way
The maid, and tell the Lady of that delay;
Only let me love none, no, not the sport;
From country grass, to comfitures of Court,
Or city's quelque-choses, let report
    My mind transport.

This bargain's good; if when I am old, I be
    Inflamed by thee,
If thine own honour, or my shame, or pain,
20 Thou covet, most at that age thou shalt gain.
Do thy will then, then subject and degree,
And fruit of love, Love, I submit to thee,
Spare me till then, I'll bear it, though she be
    One that loves me.

The Message

Send home my long strayed eyes to me,
Which (oh) too long have dwelt on thee,
Yet since there they have learned such ill,
    Such forced fashions,
    And false passions,
      That they be
      Made by thee
Fit for no good sight, keep them still.

Send home my harmless heart again,
10 Which no unworthy thought could stain,

But if it be taught by thine
　　To make jestings
　　Of protestings,
　　　　And cross both
　　　　Word and oath,
Keep it, for then 'tis none of mine.

Yet send me back my heart and eyes,
That I may know, and see thy lies,
And may laugh and joy, when thou
20　　Art in anguish
　　And dost languish
　　　　For some one
　　　　That will none,
Or prove as false as thou art now.

Negative Love

I never stooped so low, as they
Which on an eye, cheek, lip, can prey,
　Seldom to them, which soar no higher
　Than virtue or the mind to admire,
For sense, and understanding may
　Know, what gives fuel to their fire:
My love, though silly, is more brave,
For may I miss, whene'er I crave,
If I know yet what I would have.

10　If that be simply perfectest
Which can by no way be expressed
　But negatives, my love is so.
　To all, which all love, I say no.
If any who decipher best,
　What we know not, ourselves, can know,
Let him teach me that nothing; this
As yet my ease, and comfort is,
Though I speed not, I cannot miss.

A Nocturnal upon S. Lucy's Day, being the shortest day

'Tis the year's midnight, and it is the day's,
Lucy's, who scarce seven hours herself unmasks,
   The sun is spent, and now his flasks
   Send forth light squibs, no constant rays;
      The world's whole sap is sunk:
The general balm th' hydroptic earth hath drunk,
Whither, as to the bed's-feet, life is shrunk,
Dead and interred; yet all these seem to laugh,
Compared with me, who am their epitaph.

10 Study me then, you who shall lovers be
At the next world, that is, at the next spring:
   For I am every dead thing,
   In whom love wrought new alchemy.
      For his art did express
A quintessence even from nothingness,
From dull privations, and lean emptiness
He ruined me, and I am re-begot
Of absence, darkness, death; things which are not.

All others, from all things, draw all that's good,
20 Life, soul, form, spirit, whence they being have;
   I, by love's limbeck, am the grave
   Of all, that's nothing. Oft a flood
      Have we two wept, and so
Drowned the whole world, us two; oft did we grow
To be two chaoses, when we did show
Care to aught else; and often absences
Withdrew our souls, and made us carcases.

But I am by her death (which word wrongs her)
Of the first nothing, the elixir grown;
30   Were I a man, that I were one,
   I needs must know; I should prefer,

> If I were any beast,
> Some ends, some means; yea plants, yea stones detest,
> And love; all, all some properties invest;
> If I an ordinary nothing were,
> As shadow, a light, and body must be here.
>
> But I am none; nor will my sun renew.
> You lovers, for whose sake, the lesser sun
>   At this time to the Goat is run
40   To fetch new lust, and give it you,
>   Enjoy your summer all;
> Since she enjoys her long night's festival,
> Let me prepare towards her, and let me call
> This hour her vigil, and her eve, since this
> Both the year's, and the day's deep midnight is.

The Paradox

> No lover saith, I love, nor any other
>   Can judge a perfect lover;
> He thinks that else none can, nor will agree
>   That any loves but he:
> I cannot say I loved, for who can say
>   He was killed yesterday?
> Love with excess of heat, more young than old,
>   Death kills with too much cold;
> We die but once, and who loved last did die,
10   He that saith twice, doth lie:
> For though he seem to move, and stir a while,
>   It doth the sense beguile.
> Such life is like the light which bideth yet
>   When the light's life is set,
> Or like the heat, which fire in solid matter
>   Leaves behind, two hours after.
> Once I loved and died; and am now become
>   Mine epitaph and tomb.
> Here dead men speak their last, and so do I;
20   Love-slain, lo, here I lie.

The Primrose

      Upon this primrose hill,
      Where, if heaven would distil
A shower of rain, each several drop might go
To his own primrose, and grow manna so;
And where their form, and their infinity
      Make a terrestrial galaxy,
      As the small stars do in the sky:
I walk to find a true love; and I see
That 'tis not a mere woman, that is she,
But must, or more, or less than woman be.

      Yet know I not, which flower
      I wish; a six, or four;
For should my true love less than woman be,
She were scarce anything; and then, should she
Be more than woman, she would get above
      All thought of sex, and think to move
      My heart to study her, not to love;
Both these were monsters; since there must reside
Falsehood in woman, I could more abide,
She were by art, than nature falsified.

      Live primrose then, and thrive
      With thy true number, five;
And women, whom this flower doth represent,
With this mysterious number be content;
Ten is the farthest number; if half ten
      Belong unto each woman, then
      Each woman may take half us men;
Or if this will not serve their turn, since all
Numbers are odd, or even, and they fall
First into this, five, women may take us all.

The Prohibition

Take heed of loving me,
At least remember, I forbade it thee;
  Not that I shall repair my unthrifty waste
Of breath and blood, upon thy sighs, and tears,
  By being to thee then what to me thou wast;
But, so great joy, our life at once outwears,
  Then, lest thy love, by my death, frustrate be,
  If thou love me, take heed of loving me.

Take heed of hating me,
10 Or too much triumph in the victory.
  Not that I shall be mine own officer,
And hate with hate again retaliate;
  But thou wilt lose the style of conqueror,
If I, thy conquest, perish by thy hate.
  Then, lest my being nothing lessen thee,
  If thou hate me, take heed of hating me.

Yet, love and hate me too,
So, these extremes shall neither's office do;
  Love me, that I may die the gentler way;
20 Hate me, because thy love's too great for me;
  Or let these two, themselves, not me decay;
So shall I live thy stage, not triumph be;
  Lest thou thy love and hate and me undo,
  To let me live, Oh love and hate me too.

The Relic

When my grave is broke up again
Some second guest to entertain,
(For graves have learned that woman-head
To be to more than one a bed)
  And he that digs it, spies

A bracelet of bright hair about the bone,
   Will he not let us alone,
And think that there a loving couple lies,
Who thought that this device might be some way
10 To make their souls, at the last busy day,
Meet at this grave, and make a little stay?

   If this fall in a time, or land,
   Where mis-devotion doth command,
   Then, he that digs us up, will bring
   Us, to the Bishop, and the King,
    To make us relics; then
Thou shalt be a Mary Magdalen, and I
    A something else thereby,
All women shall adore us, and some men;
20 And since at such time, miracles are sought,
I would have that age by this paper taught
What miracles we harmless lovers wrought.

   First, we loved well and faithfully,
   Yet knew not what we loved, nor why,
   Difference of sex no more we knew,
   Than our guardian angels do;
    Coming and going, we
Perchance might kiss, but not between those meals;
    Our hands ne'er touched the seals,
30 Which nature, injured by late law, sets free:
These miracles we did; but now alas,
All measure, and all language, I should pass,
Should I tell what a miracle she was.

Self Love

He that cannot choose but love,
 And strives against it still,
Never shall my fancy move;
 For he loves 'gainst his will;

Nor he which is all his own,
    And can at pleasure choose,
When I am caught he can be gone,
    And when he list refuse.

Nor he that loves none but fair,
10   For such by all are sought;
Nor he that can for foul ones care,
    For his judgement then is naught:

Nor he that hath wit, for he
    Will make me his jest or slave;
Nor a fool, for when others . . .
    He can neither . . . .

Nor he that still his mistress pays,
    For she is thralled therefore:
Nor he that pays not, for he says
20   Within she's worth no more.

Is there then no kind of men
    Whom I may freely prove?
I will vent that humour then
    In mine own self love.

Song

Go, and catch a falling star,
    Get with child a mandrake root,
Tell me, where all past years are,
    Or who cleft the Devil's foot,
Teach me to hear mermaids singing,
    Or to keep off envy's stinging,
            And find
            What wind
Serves to advance an honest mind.

10 If thou be'est born to strange sights,
        Things invisible to see,

Ride ten thousand days and nights,
    Till age snow white hairs on thee,
Thou, when thou return'st, wilt tell me
All strange wonders that befell thee,
        And swear
        No where
Lives a woman true, and fair.

If thou find'st one, let me know,
    Such a pilgrimage were sweet,
20 Yet do not, I would not go,
    Though at next door we might meet,
Though she were true, when you met her,
And last, till you write your letter,
        Yet she
        Will be
False, ere I come, to two, or three.

Song

Sweetest love, I do not go,
    For weariness of thee,
Nor in hope the world can show
    A fitter love for me;
        But since that I
Must die at last, 'tis best,
To use my self in jest
    Thus by feigned deaths to die.

Yesternight the sun went hence,
10   And yet is here today,
He hath no desire nor sense,
    Nor half so short a way:
        Then fear not me,
But believe that I shall make
Speedier journeys, since I take
    More wings and spurs than he.

O how feeble is man's power,
   That if good fortune fall,
Cannot add another hour,
20   Nor a lost hour recall!
      But come bad chance,
And we join to it our strength,
And we teach it art and length,
    Itself o'er us to advance.

When thou sigh'st, thou sigh'st not wind,
   But sigh'st my soul away,
When thou weep'st, unkindly kind,
   My life's blood doth decay.
    It cannot be
30 That thou lov'st me, as thou say'st,
If in thine my life thou waste,
   Thou art the best of me.

Let not thy divining heart
   Forethink me any ill,
Destiny may take thy part,
   And may thy fears fulfil;
    But think that we
Are but turned aside to sleep;
They who one another keep
40   Alive, ne'er parted be.

Sonnet. The Token

Send me some token, that my hope may live,
   Or that my easeless thoughts may sleep and rest;
Send me some honey to make sweet my hive,
   That in my passions I may hope the best.
I beg no riband wrought with thine own hands,
   To knit our loves in the fantastic strain
Of new-touched youth; nor ring to show the stands
   Of our affection, that as that's round and plain,
So should our loves meet in simplicity;

10   No, nor the corals which thy wrist enfold,
Laced up together in congruity,
    To show our thoughts should rest in the same hold;
No, nor thy picture, though most gracious,
    And most desired, because best like the best;
Nor witty lines, which are most copious,
    Within the writings which thou hast addressed.

Send me nor this, nor that, to increase my store,
But swear thou think'st I love thee, and no more.

The Sun Rising

      Busy old fool, unruly sun,
      Why dost thou thus,
Through windows, and through curtains call on us?
Must to thy motions lovers' seasons run?
      Saucy pedantic wretch, go chide
      Late school-boys, and sour prentices,
    Go tell court-huntsmen, that the King will ride,
    Call country ants to harvest offices;
Love, all alike, no season knows, nor clime,
10 Nor hours, days, months, which are the rags of time.

      Thy beams, so reverend, and strong
      Why shouldst thou think?
I could eclipse and cloud them with a wink,
But that I would not lose her sight so long:
      If her eyes have not blinded thine,
      Look, and tomorrow late, tell me,
    Whether both th'Indias of spice and mine
    Be where thou left'st them, or lie here with me.
Ask for those kings whom thou saw'st yesterday,
20 And thou shalt hear, All here in one bed lay.

      She'is all states, and all princes, I,
      Nothing else is.
Princes do but play us; compared to this,

All honour's mimic; all wealth alchemy.
  Thou sun art half as happy as we,
  In that the world's contracted thus;
 Thine age asks ease, and since thy duties be
 To warm the world, that's done in warming us.
Shine here to us, and thou art everywhere;
30 This bed thy centre is, these walls, thy sphere.

The Triple Fool

 I am two fools, I know,
For loving, and for saying so
 In whining poetry;
But where's that wiseman, that would not be I,
 If she would not deny?
Then as th'earth's inward narrow crooked lanes
Do purge sea water's fretful salt away,
 I thought, if I could draw my pains
Through rhyme's vexation, I should them allay.
10 Grief brought to numbers cannot be so fierce,
For, he tames it, that fetters it in verse.

 But when I have done so,
Some man, his art and voice to show,
 Doth set and sing my pain,
And, by delighting many, frees again
 Grief, which verse did restrain.
To love and grief tribute of verse belongs,
But not of such as pleases when 'tis read,
 Both are increased by such songs:
20 For both their triumphs so are published,
And I, which was two fools, do so grow three;
Who are a little wise, the best fools be.

Twicknam Garden

Blasted with sighs, and surrounded with tears,
  Hither I come to seek the spring,
  And at mine eyes, and at mine ears,
Receive such balms, as else cure everything;
  But O, self traitor, I do bring
The spider love, which transubstantiates all,
  And can convert manna to gall,
And that this place may thoroughly be thought
  True paradise, I have the serpent brought.

10 'Twere wholesomer for me, that winter did
  Benight the glory of this place,
  And that a grave frost did forbid
These trees to laugh, and mock me to my face;
  But that I may not this disgrace
Endure, nor yet leave loving, Love, let me
  Some senseless piece of this place be;
Make me a mandrake, so I may groan here,
  Or a stone fountain weeping out my year.

Hither with crystal vials, lovers come,
20 And take my tears, which are love's wine,
And try your mistress' tears at home,
For all are false, that taste not just like mine;
  Alas, hearts do not in eyes shine,
Nor can you more judge woman's thoughts by tears,
  Than by her shadow, what she wears.
O perverse sex, where none is true but she,
  Who's therefore true, because her truth kills me.

The Undertaking

I have done one braver thing
    Than all the Worthies did,
And yet a braver thence doth spring,
    Which is, to keep that hid.

It were but madness now t'impart
    The skill of specular stone,
When he which can have learned the art
    To cut it, can find none.

So, if I now should utter this,
10   Others (because no more
Such stuff to work upon, there is,)
    Would love but as before.

But he who loveliness within
    Hath found, all outward loathes,
For he who colour loves, and skin,
    Loves but their oldest clothes.

If, as I have, you also do
    Virtue attired in woman see,
And dare love that, and say so too,
20   And forget the He and She;

And if this love, though placed so,
    From profane men you hide,
Which will no faith on this bestow,
    Or, if they do, deride:

Then you have done a braver thing
    Than all the Worthies did,
And a braver thence will spring,
    Which is, to keep that hid.

A Valediction: forbidding Mourning

As virtuous men pass mildly away,
    And whisper to their souls, to go,
Whilst some of their sad friends do say,
    The breath goes now, and some say, no:

So let us melt, and make no noise,
    No tear-floods, nor sigh-tempests move,
'Twere profanation of our joys
    To tell the laity our love.

Moving of th' earth brings harms and fears,
10   Men reckon what it did and meant,
But trepidation of the spheres,
    Though greater far, is innocent.

Dull sublunary lovers' love
    (Whose soul is sense) cannot admit
Absence, because it doth remove
    Those things which elemented it.

But we by a love, so much refined,
    That our selves know not what it is,
Inter-assured of the mind,
20   Care less, eyes, lips, and hands to miss.

Our two souls therefore, which are one,
    Though I must go, endure not yet
A breach, but an expansion,
    Like gold to aery thinness beat.

If they be two, they are two so
    As stiff twin compasses are two,
Thy soul the fixed foot, makes no show
    To move, but doth, if th'other do.

And though it in the centre sit,
30   Yet when the other far doth roam,
It leans, and hearkens after it,
    And grows erect, as that comes home.

Such wilt thou be to me, who must
    Like th' other foot, obliquely run;
Thy firmness makes my circle just,
    And makes me end, where I begun.

A Valediction: of the Book

I'll tell thee now (dear love) what thou shalt do
    To anger destiny, as she doth us,
    How I shall stay, though she esloign me thus,
And how posterity shall know it too;
        How thine may out-endure
        Sibyl's glory, and obscure
        Her who from Pindar could allure,
    And her, through whose help Lucan is not lame,
And her, whose book (they say) Homer did find, and name.

10 Study our manuscripts, those myriads
        Of letters, which have past 'twixt thee and me,
        Thence write our annals, and in them will be
    To all whom love's subliming fire invades,
            Rule and example found;
            There, the faith of any ground
            No schismatic will dare to wound,
        That sees, how Love this grace to us affords,
    To make, to keep, to use, to be these his records.

    This book, as long lived as the elements,
20   Or as the world's form, this all-graved tome
        In cypher write, or new made idiom;
    We for Love's clergy only are instruments,
            When this book is made thus,
            Should again the ravenous

Vandals and Goths inundate us,
Learning were safe; in this our universe
Schools might learn sciences, spheres music, angels verse.

Here Love's divines (since all divinity
Is love or wonder) may find all they seek,
30   Whether abstract spiritual love they like,
Their souls exhaled with what they do not see,
Or, loth so to amuse
Faith's infirmity, they choose
Something which they may see and use;
For, though mind be the heaven, where love doth sit,
Beauty a convenient type may be to figure it.

Here more than in their books may lawyers find,
Both by what titles mistresses are ours,
And how prerogative these states devours,
40   Transferred from Love himself, to womankind,
Who though from heart, and eyes,
They exact great subsidies,
Forsake him who on them relies,
And for the cause, honour, or conscience give,
Chimeras, vain as they, or their prerogative.

Here statesmen, (or of them, they which can read,)
May of their occupation find the grounds,
Love and their art alike it deadly wounds,
If to consider what 'tis, one proceed,
50   In both they do excel
Who the present govern well,
Whose weakness none doth, or dares tell;
In this thy book, such will their nothing see,
As in the Bible some can find out alchemy.

Thus vent thy thoughts; abroad I'll study thee,
As he removes far off, that great heights takes;
How great love is, presence best trial makes,
But absence tries how long this love will be;
To take a latitude
60   Sun, or stars, are fitliest viewed

At their brightest, but to conclude
Of longitudes, what other way have we,
But to mark when, and where the dark eclipses be?

A Valediction: of my Name in the Window

My name engraved herein,
Doth contribute my firmness to this glass,
  Which, ever since that charm, hath been
  As hard, as that which graved it, was;
Thine eye will give it price enough to mock
    The diamonds of either rock.

'Tis much that glass should be
As all confessing, and through-shine as I,
  'Tis more, that it shows thee to thee,
  And clear reflects thee to thine eye.
But all such rules, love's magic can undo,
    Here you see me, and I am you.

As no one point, nor dash,
Which are but accessory to this name,
  The showers and tempests can outwash,
  So shall all times find me the same;
You this entireness better may fulfil,
    Who have the pattern with you still.

Or if too hard and deep
This learning be, for a scratched name to teach,
  It, as a given death's head keep
  Lovers' mortality to preach,
Or think this ragged bony name to be
    My ruinous anatomy.

Then, as all my souls be
Emparadised in you, (in whom alone
  I understand, and grow and see,)
  The rafters of my body, bone

Being still with you, the muscle, sinew, and vein,
30   Which tile this house, will come again.

Till my return repair
And recompact my scattered body so,
   As all the virtuous powers which are
   Fixed in the stars, are said to flow
Into such characters, as graved be
      When these stars have supremacy,

So since this name was cut
When love and grief their exaltation had,
   No door 'gainst this name's influence shut;
40   As much more loving, as more sad,
'Twill make thee; and thou shouldst, till I return,
      Since I die daily, daily mourn.

When thy inconsiderate hand
Flings ope this casement, with my trembling name,
   To look on one, whose wit or land,
   New battery to thy heart may frame,
Then think this name alive, and that thou thus
      In it offend'st my Genius.

And when thy melted maid,
50 Corrupted by thy lover's gold, and page,
   His letter at thy pillow hath laid,
   Disputed it, and tamed thy rage,
And thou begin'st to thaw towards him, for this,
      May my name step in, and hide his.

And if this treason go
To an overt act, and that thou write again;
   In superscribing, this name flow
   Into thy fancy, from the pane.
So, in forgetting thou rememberest right,
60   And unaware to me shalt write.

But glass, and lines must be
No means our firm substantial love to keep;
   Near death inflicts this lethargy,

And this I murmur in my sleep;
Impute this idle talk, to that I go,
  For dying men talk often so.

A Valediction: of Weeping

  Let me pour forth
My tears before thy face, whilst I stay here,
For thy face coins them, and thy stamp they bear,
And by this mintage they are something worth,
  For thus they be
  Pregnant of thee;
Fruits of much grief they are, emblems of more,
When a tear falls, that thou falls which it bore,
So thou and I are nothing then, when on a divers shore.

10 On a round ball
A workman that hath copies by, can lay
An Europe, Afric, and an Asia,
And quickly make that, which was nothing, all,
  So doth each tear,
  Which thee doth wear,
A globe, yea world by that impression grow,
Till thy tears mixed with mine do overflow
This world, by waters sent from thee, my heaven dissolved so.

  O more than moon,
20 Draw not up seas to drown me in thy sphere,
Weep me not dead, in thine arms, but forbear
To teach the sea, what it may do too soon;
  Let not the wind
  Example find,
To do me more harm, than it purposeth;
Since thou and I sigh one another's breath,
Whoe'er sighs most, is cruellest, and hastes the other's death.

The Will

Before I sigh my last gasp, let me breathe,
Great Love, some legacies; here I bequeath
Mine eyes to Argus, if mine eyes can see,
If they be blind, then Love, I give them thee;
My tongue to fame; to ambassadors mine ears;
   To women or the sea, my tears.
Thou, Love, hast taught me heretofore
By making me serve her who had twenty more,
That I should give to none, but such, as had too much before.

10   My constancy I to the planets give;
My truth to them, who at the Court do live;
Mine ingenuity and openness,
To Jesuits; to buffoons my pensiveness;
My silence to any, who abroad hath been;
   My money to a Capuchin.
Thou Love taught'st me, by appointing me
To love there, where no love received can be,
Only to give to such as have an incapacity.

My faith I give to Roman Catholics;
20   All my good works unto the schismatics
Of Amsterdam; my best civility
And courtship, to an university;
My modesty I give to soldiers bare;
   My patience let gamesters share.
Thou Love taught'st me, by making me
Love her that holds my love disparity,
Only to give to those that count my gifts indignity.

I give my reputation to those
Which were my friends; mine industry to foes;
30   To schoolmen I bequeath my doubtfulness;
My sickness to physicians, or excess;
To Nature, all that I in rhyme have writ;

And to my company my wit.
Thou Love, by making me adore
Her, who begot this love in me before,
Taught'st me to make, as though I gave, when I did but
restore.

To him for whom the passing bell next tolls,
I give my physic books; my written rolls
Of moral counsels, I to Bedlam give;
40   My brazen medals, unto them which live
In want of bread; to them which pass among
All foreigners, mine English tongue.
Thou, Love, by making me love one
Who thinks her friendship a fit portion
For younger lovers, dost my gifts thus disproportion.

Therefore I'll give no more; but I'll undo
The world by dying; because love dies too.
Then all your beauties will be no more worth
Than gold in mines, where none doth draw it forth;
50   And all your graces no more use shall have
Than a sundial in a grave.
Thou Love taught'st me, by making me
Love her, who doth neglect both me and thee,
To invent, and practise this one way, to annihilate all three.

Witchcraft by a Picture

I fix mine eye on thine, and there
Pity my picture burning in thine eye,
My picture drowned in a transparent tear,
When I look lower I espy;
Hadst thou the wicked skill
By pictures made and marred, to kill,
How many ways mightst thou perform thy will?

But now I have drunk thy sweet salt tears,
And though thou pour more I'll depart;
10   My picture vanished, vanish fears,

That I can be endamaged by that art;
    Though thou retain of me
One picture more, yet that will be,
Being in thine own heart, from all malice free.

Woman's Constancy

Now thou hast loved me one whole day,
Tomorrow when thou leav'st, what wilt thou say?
Wilt thou then antedate some new made vow?
        Or say that now
We are not just those persons, which we were?
Or, that oaths made in reverential fear
Of Love, and his wrath, any may forswear?
Or, as true deaths, true marriages untie,
So lovers' contracts, images of those,
Bind but till sleep, death's image, them unloose?
        Or, your own end to justify,
For having purposed change, and falsehood, you
Can have no way but falsehood to be true?
Vain lunatic, against these 'scapes I could
        Dispute, and conquer, if I would,
        Which I abstain to do,
For by tomorrow, I may think so too.

Elegies

Elegy 1 *Jealousy*

Fond woman, which wouldst have thy husband die,
And yet complain'st of his great jealousy;
If swoll'n with poison, he lay in his last bed,
His body with a sere-bark covered,
Drawing his breath, as thick and short, as can
The nimblest crocheting musician,
Ready with loathsome vomiting to spew
His soul out of one hell, into a new,
Made deaf with his poor kindred's howling cries,
10 Begging with few feigned tears, great legacies,
Thou wouldst not weep, but jolly, and frolic be,
As a slave, which tomorrow should be free;
Yet weep'st thou, when thou seest him hungerly
Swallow his own death, heart's-bane jealousy.
O give him many thanks, he is courteous,
That in suspecting kindly warneth us.
We must not, as we used, flout openly,
In scoffing riddles, his deformity;
Nor at his board together being sat,
20 With words, nor touch, scarce looks adulterate.
Nor when he swoll'n, and pampered with great fare,
Sits down, and snorts, caged in his basket chair,
Must we usurp his own bed any more,
Nor kiss and play in his house, as before.
Now I see many dangers; for that is
His realm, his castle, and his diocese.
But if, as envious men, which would revile
Their prince, or coin his gold, themselves exile
Into another country, and do it there,
30 We play in another house, what should we fear?
There we will scorn his household policies,
His silly plots, and pensionary spies,
As the inhabitants of Thames' right side
Do London's Mayor; or Germans, the Pope's pride.

Elegy 2 *The Anagram*

Marry, and love thy Flavia, for, she
Hath all things, whereby others beauteous be,
For, though her eyes be small, her mouth is great,
Though they be ivory, yet her teeth are jet,
Though they be dim, yet she is light enough,
And though her harsh hair fall, her skin is rough;
What though her cheeks be yellow, her hair is red,
Give her thine, and she hath a maidenhead.
These things are beauty's elements, where these
10 Meet in one, that one must, as perfect, please.
If red and white and each good quality
Be in thy wench, ne'er ask where it doth lie.
In buying things perfumed, we ask, if there
Be musk and amber in it, but not where.
Though all her parts be not in th' usual place,
She hath yet an anagram of a good face.
If we might put the letters but one way,
In the lean dearth of words, what could we say?
When by the gamut some musicians make
20 A perfect song, others will undertake,
By the same gamut changed, to equal it.
Things simply good, can never be unfit.
She's fair as any, if all be like her,
And if none be, then she is singular.
All love is wonder; if we justly do
Account her wonderful, why not lovely too?
Love built on beauty, soon as beauty, dies,
Choose this face, changed by no deformities.
Women are all like angels; the fair be
30 Like those which fell to worse; but such as she,
Like to good angels, nothing can impair:
'Tis less grief to be foul, than to have been fair.
For one night's revels, silk and gold we choose,
But, in long journeys, cloth, and leather use.

Beauty is barren oft; best husbands say
There is best land, where there is foulest way.
Of what a sovereign plaster will she be,
If thy past sins have taught thee jealousy!
Here needs no spies, nor eunuchs; her commit
40 Safe to thy foes; yea, to a marmoset.
When Belgia's cities, the round countries drown,
That dirty foulness guards, and arms the town:
So doth her face guard her; and so, for thee,
Which, forced by business, absent oft must be,
She, whose face, like clouds, turns the day to night,
Who, mightier than the sea, makes Moors seem white,
Who, though seven years, she in the stews had laid,
A nunnery durst receive, and think a maid,
And though in childbed's labour she did lie,
50 Midwives would swear, 'twere but a tympany,
Whom, if she accuse herself, I credit less
Than witches, which impossibles confess,
Whom dildoes, bedstaves, and her velvet glass
Would be as loth to touch as Joseph was:
One like none, and liked of none, fittest were,
For, things in fashion every man will wear.

Elegy 3 *Change*

Although thy hand and faith, and good works too,
Have sealed thy love which nothing should undo,
Yea though thou fall back, that apostasy
Confirm thy love; yet much, much I fear thee.
Women are like the arts, forced unto none,
Open to all searchers, unprized, if unknown.
If I have caught a bird, and let him fly,
Another fowler using these means, as I,
May catch the same bird; and, as these things be,
10 Women are made for men, not him, nor me.
Foxes and goats, all beasts change when they please,
Shall women, more hot, wily, wild than these,

Be bound to one man, and did Nature then
Idly make them apter to endure than men?
They are our clogs, and their own; if a man be
Chained to a galley, yet the galley is free;
Who hath a plough-land, casts all his seed corn there,
And yet allows his ground more corn should bear;
Though Danuby into the sea must flow,
20   The sea receives the Rhine, Volga, and Po.
By nature, which gave it, this liberty
Thou lov'st, but Oh! canst thou love it and me?
Likeness glues love: then if so thou do,
To make us like and love, must I change too?
More than thy hate, I hate it, rather let me
Allow her change, than change as oft as she,
And so not teach, but force my opinion
To love not any one, nor every one.
To live in one land, is captivity,
30   To run all countries, a wild roguery;
Waters stink soon, if in one place they bide,
And in the vast sea are worse putrefied:
But when they kiss one bank, and leaving this
Never look back, but the next bank do kiss,
Then are they purest; change is the nursery
Of music, joy, life and eternity.

Elegy 4 *The Perfume*

Once, and but once found in thy company,
All thy supposed escapes are laid on me;
And as a thief at bar, is questioned there
By all the men, that have been robbed that year,
So am I, (by this traitorous means surprised)
By thy hydroptic father catechized.
Though he had wont to search with glazed eyes,
As though he came to kill a cockatrice,
Though he have oft sworn, that he would remove
10   Thy beauty's beauty, and food of our love,

Hope of his goods, if I with thee were seen,
Yet close and secret, as our souls, we have been.
Though thy immortal mother which doth lie
Still buried in her bed, yet will not die,
Takes this advantage to sleep out day-light,
And watch thy entries, and returns all night,
And, when she takes thy hand, and would seem kind,
Doth search what rings, and armlets she can find,
And kissing notes the colour of thy face,
20   And fearing lest thou art swoll'n, doth thee embrace;
To try if thou long, doth name strange meats,
And notes thy paleness, blushing, sighs, and sweats;
And politicly will to thee confess
The sins of her own youth's rank lustiness;
Yet love these sorceries did remove, and move
Thee to gull thine own mother for my love.
Thy little brethren, which like faery sprites
Oft skipped into our chamber, those sweet nights,
And kissed, and ingled on thy father's knee,
30   Were bribed next day, to tell what they did see:
The grim eight-foot-high iron-bound serving-man,
That oft names God in oaths, and only then,
He that to bar the first gate, doth as wide
As the great Rhodian Colossus stride,
Which, if in hell no other pains there were,
Makes me fear hell, because he must be there:
Though by thy father he were hired to this,
Could never witness any touch or kiss.
But Oh, too common ill, I brought with me
40   That, which betrayed me to mine enemy:
A loud perfume, which at my entrance cried
Even at thy father's nose, so we were spied.
When, like a tyrant king, that in his bed
Smelt gunpowder, the pale wretch shivered.
Had it been some bad smell, he would have thought
That his own feet, or breath, that smell had wrought.
But as we in our isle imprisoned,
Where cattle only, and diverse dogs are bred,

The precious unicorns, strange monsters call,
50 So thought he good, strange, that had none at all.
I taught my silks, their whistling to forbear,
Even my oppressed shoes, dumb and speechless were,
Only, thou bitter sweet, whom I had laid
Next me, me traitorously hast betrayed,
And unsuspected hast invisibly
At once fled unto him, and stayed with me.
Base excrement of earth, which dost confound
Sense, from distinguishing the sick from sound;
By thee the silly amorous sucks his death
60 By drawing in a leprous harlot's breath;
By thee, the greatest stain to man's estate
Falls on us, to be called effeminate;
Though you be much loved in the prince's hall,
There, things that seem, exceed substantial.
Gods, when ye fumed on altars, were pleased well,
Because you were burnt, not that they liked your smell;
You are loathsome all, being taken simply alone,
Shall we love ill things joined, and hate each one?
If you were good, your good doth soon decay;
70 And you are rare, that takes the good away.
All my perfumes, I give most willingly
To embalm thy father's corse; What? will he die?

Elegy 5 *His Picture*

Here take my picture, though I bid farewell;
Thine, in my heart, where my soul dwells, shall dwell.
'Tis like me now, but I dead, 'twill be more
When we are shadows both, than 'twas before.
When weather-beaten I come back; my hand,
Perhaps with rude oars torn, or sun-beams tanned,
My face and breast of haircloth, and my head
With care's rash sudden hoariness o'erspread,
My body a sack of bones, broken within,
10 And powder's blue stains scattered on my skin;

If rival fools tax thee to have loved a man,
So foul, and coarse, as oh, I may seem then,
This shall say what I was: and thou shalt say,
Do his hurts reach me? doth my worth decay?
Or do they reach his judging mind, that he
Should now love less, what he did love to see?
That which in him was fair and delicate,
Was but the milk, which in love's childish state
Did nurse it: who now is grown strong enough
20 To feed on that, which to disused tastes seems tough.

Elegy 6

Oh, let me not serve so, as those men serve
Whom honours' smokes at once fatten and starve;
Poorly enriched with great men's words or looks;
Nor so write my name in thy loving books
As those idolatrous flatterers, which still
Their prince's styles, with many realms fulfil
Whence they no tribute have, and where no sway.
Such services I offer as shall pay
Themselves, I hate dead names: oh then let me
10 Favourite in ordinary, or no favourite be.
When my soul was in her own body sheathed,
Nor yet by oaths betrothed, nor kisses breathed
Into my purgatory, faithless thee,
Thy heart seemed wax, and steel thy constancy.
So, careless flowers strowed on the water's face,
The curled whirlpools suck, smack, and embrace,
Yet drown them; so, the taper's beamy eye
Amorously twinkling, beckons the giddy fly,
Yet burns his wings; and such the devil is,
20 Scarce visiting them, who are entirely his.
When I behold a stream, which, from the spring,
Doth with doubtful melodious murmuring,
Or in a speechless slumber, calmly ride
Her wedded channel's bosom, and then chide

And bend her brows, and swell if any bough
Do but stoop down, to kiss her upmost brow:
Yet, if her often gnawing kisses win
The traitorous bank to gape, and let her in,
She rusheth violently, and doth divorce
30 Her from her native, and her long-kept course,
And roars, and braves it, and in gallant scorn,
In flattering eddies promising return,
She flouts the channel, who thenceforth is dry;
Then say I: that is she, and this am I.
Yet let not thy deep bitterness beget
Careless despair in me, for that will whet
My mind to scorn; and Oh, love dulled with pain
Was ne'er so wise, nor well armed as disdain.
Then with new eyes I shall survey thee, and spy
40 Death in thy cheeks, and darkness in thine eye.
Though hope bred faith and love; thus taught, I shall
As nations do from Rome, from thy love fall.
My hate shall outgrow thine, and utterly
I will renounce thy dalliance: and when I
Am the recusant, in that resolute state,
What hurts it me to be excommunicate?

Elegy 7

Nature's lay idiot, I taught thee to love,
And in that sophistry, oh, thou dost prove
Too subtle: Fool, thou didst not understand
The mystic language of the eye nor hand:
Nor couldst thou judge the difference of the air
Of sighs, and say, this lies, this sounds despair:
Nor by the'eye's water call a malady
Desperately hot, or changing feverously.
I had not taught thee then, the alphabet
10 Of flowers, how they devisefully being set
And bound up, might with speechless secrecy
Deliver errands mutely, and mutually.

Remember since all thy words used to be
To every suitor, *Ay, if my friends agree*;
Since, household charms, thy husband's name to teach,
Were all the love-tricks, that thy wit could reach;
And since, an hour's discourse could scarce have made
One answer in thee, and that ill arrayed
In broken proverbs, and torn sentences.
20 Thou art not by so many duties his,
That from the world's common having severed thee,
Inlaid thee, neither to be seen, nor see,
As mine: who have with amorous delicacies
Refined thee into a blissful paradise.
Thy graces and good words my creatures be;
I planted knowledge and life's tree in thee,
Which oh, shall strangers taste? Must I alas
Frame and enamel plate, and drink in glass?
Chafe wax for others' seals? break a colt's force
30 And leave him then, being made a ready horse?

Elegy 8 *The Comparison*

As the sweet sweat of roses in a still,
As that which from chafed musk cat's pores doth trill,
As the almighty balm of th' early east,
Such are the sweat drops of my mistress' breast.
And on her neck her skin such lustre sets,
They seem no sweat drops, but pearl carcanets.
Rank sweaty froth thy mistress' brow defiles,
Like spermatic issue of ripe menstruous boils,
Or like that scum, which, by need's lawless law
10 Enforced, Sanserra's starved men did draw
From parboiled shoes, and boots, and all the rest
Which were with any sovereign fatness blessed,
And like vile lying stones in saffroned tin,
Or warts, or weals, they hang upon her skin.
Round as the world's her head, on every side,
Like to the fatal ball which fell on Ide,

Or that whereof God had such jealousy,
As for the ravishing thereof we die.
Thy head is like a rough-hewn statue of jet,
20 Where marks for eyes, nose, mouth, are yet scarce set;
Like the first Chaos, or flat seeming face
Of Cynthia, when th' earth's shadows her embrace.
Like Proserpine's white beauty-keeping chest,
Or Jove's best fortune's urn, is her fair breast.
Thine's like worm-eaten trunks, clothed in seal's skin,
Or grave, that's dust without, and stink within.
And like that slender stalk, at whose end stands
The woodbine quivering, are her arms and hands.
Like rough-barked elmboughs, or the russet skin
30 Of men late scourged for madness, or for sin,
Like sun-parched quarters on the city gate,
Such is thy tanned skin's lamentable state.
And like a bunch of ragged carrots stand
The short swoll'n fingers of thy gouty hand.
Then like the chemic's masculine equal fire,
Which in the limbeck's warm womb doth inspire
Into th' earth's worthless dirt a soul of gold,
Such cherishing heat her best loved part doth hold.
Thine's like the dread mouth of a fired gun,
40 Or like hot liquid metals newly run
Into clay moulds, or like to that Etna
Where round about the grass is burnt away.
Are not your kisses then as filthy, and more,
As a worm sucking an envenomed sore?
Doth not thy fearful hand in feeling quake,
As one which gathering flowers, still fears a snake?
Is not your last act harsh, and violent,
As when a plough a stony ground doth rent?
So kiss good turtles, so devoutly nice
50 Are priests in handling reverent sacrifice,
And such in searching wounds the surgeon is
As we, when we embrace, or touch, or kiss.
Leave her, and I will leave comparing thus,
She, and comparisons are odious.

Elegy 9 *The Autumnal*

No spring, nor summer beauty hath such grace,
    As I have seen in one autumnal face.
Young beauties force your love, and that's a rape,
    This doth but counsel, yet you cannot scape.
If 'twere a shame to love, here 'twere no shame,
    Affection here takes reverence's name.
Were her first years the Golden Age; that's true,
    But now she's gold oft tried, and ever new.
That was her torrid and inflaming time,
10   This is her tolerable tropic clime.
Fair eyes, who asks more heat than comes from hence,
    He in a fever wishes pestilence.
Call not these wrinkles, graves; if graves they were,
    They were Love's graves; for else he is no where.
Yet lies not Love dead here, but here doth sit
    Vowed to this trench, like an anachorit.
And here, till hers, which must be his death, come,
    He doth not dig a grave, but build a tomb.
Here dwells he, though he sojourn everywhere,
20   In Progress, yet his standing house is here.
Here, where still evening is; not noon, nor night;
    Where no voluptuousness, yet all delight.
In all her words, unto all hearers fit,
    You may at revels, you at council, sit.
This is Love's timber, youth his underwood;
    There he, as wine in June, enrages blood,
Which then comes seasonabliest, when our taste
    And appetite to other things is past.
Xerxes' strange Lydian love, the platan tree,
30   Was loved for age, none being so large as she,
Or else because, being young, nature did bless
    Her youth with age's glory, barrenness.
If we love things long sought, age is a thing
    Which we are fifty years in compassing.

If transitory things, which soon decay,
    Age must be loveliest at the latest day.
But name not winter-faces, whose skin's slack;
    Lank, as an unthrift's purse; but a soul's sack;
Whose eyes seek light within, for all here's shade;
40   Whose mouths are holes, rather worn out, than made;
Whose every tooth to a several place is gone,
    To vex their souls at Resurrection;
Name not these living death's-heads unto me,
    For these, not ancient, but antiques be.
I hate extremes; yet I had rather stay
    With tombs, than cradles, to wear out a day.
Since such love's natural lation is, may still
    My love descend, and journey down the hill,
Not panting after growing beauties, so,
50   I shall ebb out with them, who homeward go.

Elegy 10 *The Dream*

Image of her whom I love, more than she,
    Whose fair impression in my faithful heart,
Makes me her medal, and makes her love me,
    As kings do coins, to which their stamps impart
The value: go, and take my heart from hence,
    Which now is grown too great and good for me:
Honours oppress weak spirits, and our sense
    Strong objects dull; the more, the less we see.

When you are gone, and reason gone with you,
10   Then fantasy is queen and soul, and all;
She can present joys meaner than you do;
    Convenient, and more proportional.

So, if I dream I have you, I have you,
    For, all our joys are but fantastical.
And so I 'scape the pain, for pain is true;
    And sleep which locks up sense, doth lock out all.

After a such fruition I shall wake,
  And, but the waking, nothing shall repent;
And shall to love more thankful sonnets make,
20   Than if more honour, tears, and pains were spent.

But dearest heart, and dearer image stay;
  Alas, true joys at best are dream enough;
Though you stay here you pass too fast away:
  For even at first life's taper is a snuff.

Filled with her love, may I be rather grown
Mad with much heart, than idiot with none.

Elegy 11 *The Bracelet*

UPON THE LOSS OF HIS MISTRESS' CHAIN,
FOR WHICH HE MADE SATISFACTION

Not that in colour it was like thy hair,
For armlets of that thou mayst let me wear;
Nor that thy hand it oft embraced and kissed,
For so it had that good, which oft I missed;
Nor for that silly old morality,
That as those links are tied, our love should be;
Mourn I that I thy sevenfold chain have lost,
Nor for the luck sake; but the bitter cost.
  Oh shall twelve righteous angels, which as yet
10 No leaven of vile solder did admit,
Nor yet by any way have strayed or gone
From the first state of their creation,
Angels, which heaven commanded to provide
All things to me, and be my faithful guide,
To gain new friends, to appease great enemies,
To comfort my soul, when I lie or rise;
Shall these twelve innocents, by thy severe
Sentence (dread judge) my sins' great burden bear?
Shall they be damned, and in the furnace thrown,
20 And punished for offences not their own?

They save not me, they do not ease my pains
When in that hell they are burnt and tied in chains.
    Were they but crowns of France, I cared not,
For, most of these, their natural country rot
I think possesseth, they come here to us,
So pale, so lame, so lean, so ruinous.
And howsoe'er French kings most Christian be,
Their crowns are circumcised most Jewishly.
Or were they Spanish stamps, still travelling,
30 That are become as Catholic as their king,
Those unlicked bear-whelps, unfiled pistolets
That, more than cannon shot, avails or lets,
Which, negligently left unrounded, look
Like many-angled figures in the book
Of some great conjurer, that would enforce
Nature, as these do justice, from her course;
Which, as the soul quickens head, feet and heart,
As streams, like veins, run through th' earth's every part,
Visit all countries, and have slily made
40 Gorgeous France, ruined, ragged and decayed,
Scotland, which knew no State, proud in one day,
And mangled seventeen-headed Belgia:
Or were it such gold as that wherewithal
Almighty chemics from each mineral
Having by subtle fire a soul out-pulled,
Are dirtily and desperately gulled:
I would not spit to quench the fire they were in,
For, they are guilty of much heinous sin.
But, shall my harmless angels perish? Shall
50 I lose my guard, my ease, my food, my all?
Much hope, which they should nourish, will be dead.
Much of my able youth, and lustihead
Will vanish, if thou love let them alone,
For thou wilt love me less when they are gone.
    Oh be content that some loud squeaking crier
Well-pleased with one lean threadbare groat, for hire,
May like a devil roar through every street,
And gall the finder's conscience, if they meet.

Or let me creep to some dread conjurer,
60 That with fantastic schemes fills full much paper,
Which hath divided heaven in tenements,
And with whores, thieves, and murderers stuffed his rents,
So full, that though he pass them all in sin,
He leaves himself no room to enter in.
But if, when all his art and time is spent,
He say 'twill ne'er be found; yet be content;
Receive from him that doom ungrudgingly,
Because he is the mouth of destiny.
      Thou say'st (alas) the gold doth still remain,
70 Though it be changed, and put into a chain.
So in the first fall'n angels, resteth still
Wisdom and knowledge, but, 'tis turned to ill;
As these should do good works, and should provide
Necessities, but now must nurse thy pride.
And they are still bad angels; mine are none,
For form gives being, and their form is gone.
Pity these angels yet; their dignities
Pass Virtues, Powers, and Principalities.
      But thou art resolute; thy will be done.
80 Yet with such anguish as her only son
The mother in the hungry grave doth lay,
Unto the fire these martyrs I betray.
Good souls, for you give life to everything,
Good angels, for good messages you bring,
Destined you might have been to such a one
As would have loved and worshipped you alone,
One that would suffer hunger, nakedness,
Yea death, ere he would make your number less.
But I am guilty of your sad decay,
90 May your few fellows longer with me stay.
      But Oh thou wretched finder whom I hate
So, that I almost pity thy estate;
Gold being the heaviest metal amongst all,
May my most heavy curse upon thee fall.
Here fettered, manacled, and hanged in chains
First mayst thou be, then chained to hellish pains;

Or be with foreign gold bribed to betray
Thy country, and fail both of that and thy pay.
May the next thing thou stoop'st to reach, contain
100 Poison, whose nimble fume rot thy moist brain;
Or libels, or some interdicted thing,
Which negligently kept, thy ruin bring.
Lust-bred diseases rot thee; and dwell with thee
Itchy desire and no ability.
May all the evils that gold ever wrought,
All mischiefs that all devils ever thought,
Want after plenty, poor and gouty age,
The plagues of travellers, love and marriage
Afflict thee, and at thy life's latest moment
110 May thy swoll'n sins themselves to thee present.
    But I forgive; repent thee honest man:
Gold is restorative, restore it then.
But if from it thou be'st loth to depart,
Because 'tis cordial, would 'twere at thy heart.

Elegy 12 *His Parting from Her*

Since she must go, and I must mourn, come night,
Environ me with darkness, whilst I write:
Shadow that hell unto me, which alone
I am to suffer when my love is gone.
Alas the darkest magic cannot do it,
Thou and great Hell to boot are shadows to it.
Should Cynthia quit thee, Venus, and each star,
It would not form one thought dark as mine are.
I could lend thee obscureness now, and say,
10 Out of my self, there should be no more day,
Such is already my felt want of sight,
Did not the fires within me force a light.
    O Love, that fire and darkness should be mixed,
Or to thy Triumphs so strange torments fixed!
Is't because thou thyself art blind, that we
Thy martyrs must no more each other see?

Or tak'st thou pride to break us on the wheel,
And view old chaos in the pains we feel?
Or have we left undone some mutual rite,
20 Through holy fear, that merits thy despite?
No, no. The fault was mine, impute it me,
Or rather to conspiring destiny,
Which (since I loved for form before) decreed,
That I should suffer when I loved indeed:
And therefore now, sooner than I can say
I saw the golden fruit, 'tis rapt away.
Or as I had watched one drop in a vast stream,
And I left wealthy only in a dream.
Yet Love, thou'rt blinder than thyself in this,
30 To vex my dove-like friend for my amiss:
And, where my own glad truth may expiate
Thy wrath, to make her fortune run my fate.
So blinded Justice doth, when favourites fall,
Strike them, their house, their friends, their followers all.
Was't not enough that thou didst dart thy fires
Into our bloods, inflaming our desires,
And mad'st us sigh and glow, and pant, and burn,
And then thy self into our flame didst turn?
Was't not enough, that thou didst hazard us
40 To paths in love so dark, so dangerous:
And those so ambushed round with household spies,
And over all, thy husband's towering eyes
That flamed with oily sweat of jealousy:
Yet went we not still on with constancy?
Have we not kept our guards, like spy on spy?
Had correspondence whilst the foe stood by?
Stol'n (more to sweeten them) our many blisses
Of meetings, conference, embracements, kisses?
Shadowed with negligence our most respects?
50 Varied our language through all dialects,
Of becks, winks, looks, and often under-boards
Spoke dialogues with our feet far from our words?
Have we proved all these secrets of thy art,
Yea, thy pale inwards, and thy panting heart?

And, after all this passed purgatory,
Must sad divorce make us the vulgar story?
First let our eyes be riveted quite through
Our turning brains, and both our lips grow to:
Let our arms clasp like ivy, and our fear
60 Freeze us together, that we may stick here,
Till Fortune, that would rive us, with the deed
Strain her eyes open, and it make them bleed.
For Love it cannot be, whom hitherto
I have accused, should such a mischief do.
    O Fortune, thou'art not worth my least exclaim
And plague enough thou hast in thy own shame.
Do thy great worst, my friend and I have arms,
Though not against thy strokes, against thy harms.
Rend us in sunder, thou canst not divide
70 Our bodies so, but that our souls are tied,
And we can love by letters still and gifts,
And thoughts and dreams; love never wanteth shifts.
I will not look upon the quickening sun,
But straight her beauty to my sense shall run;
The air shall note her soft, the fire most pure;
Water suggest her clear, and the earth sure.
Time shall not lose our passages; the spring
Shall tell how fresh our love was in beginning;
The summer how it ripened in the ear;
80 And autumn, what our golden harvests were.
The winter I'll not think on to spite thee,
But count it a lost season, so shall she.
    And dearest friend, since we must part, drown night
With hope of day, burthens well borne are light.
Though cold and darkness longer hang somewhere,
Yet Phoebus equally lights all the sphere.
And what he cannot in like portions pay,
The world enjoys in mass, and so we may.
Be then ever yourself, and let no woe
90 Win on your health, your youth, your beauty: so
Declare yourself base fortune's enemy,
No less by your contempt than constancy:

That I may grow enamoured on your mind,
When my own thoughts I there reflected find.
For this to the comfort of my dear I vow,
My deeds shall still be what my words are now;
The poles shall move to teach me ere I start;
And when I change my love, I'll change my heart;
Nay, if I wax but cold in my desire,
100 Think, heaven hath motion lost, and the world, fire:
Much more I could, but many words have made
That, oft, suspected which men would persuade;
Take therefore all in this: I love so true,
As I will never look for less in you.

Elegy 13 *Julia*

Hark news, O envy, thou shalt hear descried
My Julia; who as yet was ne'er envied.
To vomit gall in slander, swell her veins
With calumny, that hell itself disdains,
Is her continual practice; does her best,
To tear opinion even out of the breast
Of dearest friends, and (which is worse than vilde)
Sticks jealousy in wedlock; her own child
Scapes not the showers of envy; to repeat
10 The monstrous fashions, how, were alive to eat
Dear reputation. Would to God she were
But half so loth to act vice, as to hear
My mild reproof. Lived Mantuan now again,
That female-mastix, to limn with his pen
This she chimera, that hath eyes of fire,
Burning with anger, anger feeds desire,
Tongued like the night-crow, whose ill-boding cries
Give out for nothing but new injuries,
Her breath like to the juice in Tenarus
20 That blasts the springs, though ne'er so prosperous,
Her hands, I know not how, used more to spill
The food of others, than herself to fill.

But oh her mind, that Orcus, which includes
Legions of mischiefs, countless multitudes
Of formless curses, projects unmade up,
Abuses yet unfashioned, thoughts corrupt,
Misshapen cavils, palpable untroths,
Inevitable errors, self-accusing loaths:
These, like those atoms swarming in the sun,
30 Throng in her bosom for creation.
I blush to give her half her due; yet say,
No poison's half so bad as Julia.

Elegy 14 *A Tale of a Citizen and his Wife*

I sing no harm good sooth to any wight,
To lord or fool, cuckold, beggar or knight,
To peace-teaching lawyer, proctor, or brave
Reformed or reduced captain, knave,
Officer, juggler, or justice of peace,
Juror or judge; I touch no fat sow's grease,
I am no libeller, nor will be any,
But (like a true man) say there are too many.
I fear not *ore tenus*; for my tale,
10 Nor Count nor counsellor will red or pale.
    A citizen and his wife the other day
Both riding on one horse, upon the way
I overtook, the wench a pretty peat,
And (by her eye) well fitting for the feat.
I saw the lecherous citizen turn back
His head, and on his wife's lip steal a smack,
Whence apprehending that the man was kind,
Riding before, to kiss his wife behind,
To get acquaintance with him I began
20 To sort discourse fit for so fine a man:
I asked the number of the Plaguy Bill,
Asked if the Custom Farmers held out still,
Of the Virginian plot, and whether Ward
The traffic of the Midland seas had marred,

Whether the Britain Bourse did fill apace,
And likely were to give th' Exchange disgrace;
Of new-built Aldgate, and the Moorfield crosses,
Of store of bankrupts, and poor merchants' losses
I urged him to speak; But he (as mute
30   As an old courtier worn to his last suit)
Replied with only yeas and nays; at last
(To fit his element) my theme I cast
On tradesmen's gains; that set his tongue a-going:
Alas, good sir (quoth he) 'There is no doing
In Court nor City now'; she smiled and I,
And (in my conscience) both gave him the lie
In one met thought: but he went on apace,
And at the present time with such a face
He railed, as frayed me; for he gave no praise,
40   To any but my Lord of Essex' days;
Called those the age of action; 'true' (quoth he)
'There's now as great an itch of bravery,
And heat of taking up, but cold lay down,
For, put to push of pay, away they run;
Our only City trades of hope now are
Bawd, tavern-keeper, whore and scrivener;
The much of privileged kingsmen, and the store
Of fresh protections make the rest all poor;
In the first state of their creation,
50   Though many stoutly stand, yet proves not one
A righteous paymaster.' Thus ran he on
In a continued rage: so void of reason
Seemed his harsh talk, I sweat for fear of treason.
And (troth) how could I less? when in the prayer
For the protection of the wise Lord Mayor,
And his wise brethren's worships, when one pray'th,
He swore that none could say Amen with faith.
To get him off from what I glowed to hear,
(In happy time) an angel did appear,
60   The bright sign of a loved and well-tried inn,
Where many citizens with their wives have been
Well used and often; here I prayed him stay,

To take some due refreshment by the way.
Look how he looked that hid the gold (his hope)
And at return found nothing but a rope,
So he on me, refused and made away,
Though willing she pleaded a weary day:
I found my miss, shook hands, yet prayed him tell
(To hold acquaintance still) where he did dwell;
70 He barely named the street, promised the wine.
But his kind wife gave me the very sign.

Elegy 15 *The Expostulation*

To make the doubt clear, that no woman's true,
   Was it my fate to prove it strong in you?
Thought I, but one had breathed purest air,
   And must she needs be false because she's fair?
Is it your beauty's mark, or of your youth,
   Or your perfection, not to study truth?
Or think you heaven is deaf, or hath no eyes?
   Or those it hath, smile at your perjuries?
Are vows so cheap with women, or the matter
10   Whereof they are made, that they are writ in water,
And blown away with wind? Or doth their breath
   (Both hot and cold) at once make life and death?
Who could have thought so many accents sweet
   Formed into words, so many sighs should meet
As from our hearts, so many oaths, and tears
   Sprinkled among (all sweeter by our fears
And the divine impression of stolen kisses,
   That sealed the rest) should now prove empty blisses?
Did you draw bonds to forfeit? sign to break?
20   Or must we read you quite from what you speak,
And find the truth out the wrong way? or must
   He first desire you false, would wish you just?

O I profane, though most of women be
   This kind of beast, my thought shall except thee;

My dearest love, though froward jealousy,
  With circumstance might urge thy inconstancy,
Sooner I'll think the sun will cease to cheer
  The teeming earth, and that forget to bear,
Sooner that rivers will run back, or Thames
30 With ribs of ice in June would bind his streams,
Or Nature, by whose strength the world endures,
  Would change her course, before you alter yours.

But O that treacherous breast to whom weak you
  Did trust our counsels, and we both may rue,
Having his falsehood found too late, 'twas he
  That made me cast you guilty, and you me,
Whilst he, black wretch, betrayed each simple word
  We spake, unto the cunning of a third.
Cursed may he be, that so our love hath slain,
40 And wander on the earth, wretched as Cain,
Wretched as he, and not deserve least pity;
  In plaguing him, let misery be witty;
Let all eyes shun him, and he shun each eye,
  Till he be noisome as his infamy;
May he without remorse deny God thrice,
  And not be trusted more on his soul's price;
And after all self torment, when he dies,
  May wolves tear out his heart, vultures his eyes,
Swine eat his bowels, and his falser tongue
50 That uttered all, be to some raven flung,
And let his carrion corse be a longer feast
  To the King's dogs, than any other beast.

Now I have cursed, let us our love revive;
  In me the flame was never more alive;
I could begin again to court and praise,
  And in that pleasure lengthen the short days
Of my life's lease; like painters that do take
  Delight, not in made work, but whiles they make;
I could renew those times, when first I saw
60 Love in your eyes, that gave my tongue the law

To like what you liked; and at masks and plays
   Commend the self-same actors, the same ways;
Ask how you did, and often with intent
   Of being officious, be impertinent;
All which were such soft pastimes, as in these
   Love was as subtly catched, as a disease;
But being got it is a treasure sweet,
   Which to defend is harder than to get:
And ought not be profaned on either part,
70   For though 'tis got by chance, 'tis kept by art.

Elegy 16 *On his Mistress*

By our first strange and fatal interview,
By all desires which thereof did ensue,
By our long starving hopes, by that remorse
Which my words' masculine persuasive force
Begot in thee, and by the memory
Of hurts, which spies and rivals threatened me,
I calmly beg: but by thy father's wrath,
By all pains, which want and divorcement hath,
I conjure thee; and all the oaths which I
10 And thou have sworn to seal joint constancy,
Here I unswear, and overswear them thus,
Thou shalt not love by ways so dangerous.
Temper, O fair love, love's impetuous rage,
Be my true mistress still, not my feigned page;
I'll go, and, by thy kind leave, leave behind
Thee, only worthy to nurse in my mind
Thirst to come back; oh, if thou die before,
From other lands my soul towards thee shall soar,
Thy (else almighty) beauty cannot move
20 Rage from the seas, nor thy love teach them love,
Nor tame wild Boreas' harshness; thou hast read
How roughly he in pieces shivered
Fair Orithea, whom he swore he loved.
Fall ill or good, 'tis madness to have proved

Dangers unurged; feed on this flattery,
That absent lovers one in th' other be.
Dissemble nothing, not a boy, nor change
Thy body's habit, nor mind's; be not strange
To thy self only; all will spy in thy face
30 A blushing womanly discovering grace;
Richly clothed apes, are called apes, and as soon
Eclipsed as bright we call the moon the moon.
Men of France, changeable chameleons,
Spitals of diseases, shops of fashions,
Love's fuellers, and the rightest company
Of players, which upon the world's stage be,
Will quickly know thee, and know thee; and alas
Th' indifferent Italian, as we pass
His warm land, well content to think thee page,
40 Will hunt thee with such lust, and hideous rage,
As Lot's fair guests were vexed. But none of these
Nor spongy hydroptic Dutch shall thee displease,
If thou stay here. Oh stay here, for, for thee
England is only a worthy gallery,
To walk in expectation, till from thence
Our greatest King call thee to his presence.
When I am gone, dream me some happiness,
Nor let thy looks our long-hid love confess,
Nor praise, nor dispraise me, nor bless nor curse
50 Openly love's force, nor in bed fright thy nurse
With midnight's startings, crying out, 'Oh, oh
Nurse, O my love is slain, I saw him go
O'er the white Alps alone; I saw him, I,
Assailed, fight, taken, stabbed, bleed, fall, and die.'
Augur me better chance, except dread Jove
Think it enough for me to have had thy love.

Elegy 17 *Variety*

The heavens rejoice in motion, why should I
Abjure my so much loved variety,

And not with many youth and love divide?
Pleasure is none, if not diversified:
The sun that sitting in the chair of light
Sheds flame into what ever else seems bright,
Is not contented at one sign to inn,
But ends his year and with a new begins.
All things do willingly in change delight,
10 The fruitful mother of our appetite:
Rivers the clearer and more pleasing are,
Where their fair spreading streams run wide and far;
And a dead lake that no strange bank doth greet,
Corrupts itself and what doth live in it.
Let no man tell me such a one is fair,
And worthy all alone my love to share.
Nature in her hath done the liberal part
Of a kind mistress, and employed her art
To make her lovable, and I aver
20 Him not humane that would turn back from her:
I love her well, and would, if need were, die
To do her service. But follows it that I
Must serve her only, when I may have choice?
The law is hard, and shall not have my voice.
The last I saw in all extremes is fair,
And holds me in the sun-beams of her hair;
Her nymph-like features such agreements have
That I could venture with her to the grave:
Another's brown, I like her not the worse,
30 Her tongue is soft and takes me with discourse.
Others, for that they well descended are,
Do in my love obtain as large a share;
And though they be not fair, 'tis much with me
To win their love only for their degree.
And though I fail of my required ends,
The attempt is glorious and itself commends.
How happy were our sires in ancient time,
Who held plurality of loves no crime!
With them it was accounted charity
40 To stir up race of all indifferently;

Kindreds were not exempted from the bands:
Which with the Persian still in usage stands.
Women were then no sooner asked than won,
And what they did was honest and well done.
But since this title honour hath been used
Our weak credulity hath been abused;
The golden laws of nature are repealed,
Which our first Fathers in such reverence held;
Our liberty's reversed, our charter's gone,
50 And we made servants to opinion,
A monster in no certain shape attired,
And whose original is much desired,
Formless at first, but growing on it fashions,
And doth prescribe manners and laws to nations.
Here Love received immedicable harms,
And was despoiled of his daring arms,
A greater want than is his daring eyes,
He lost those awful wings with which he flies;
His sinewy bow, and those immortal darts
60 Wherewith he is wont to bruise resisting hearts.
Only some few strong in themselves and free
Retain the seeds of ancient liberty,
Following that part of Love although depressed,
And make a throne for him within their breast,
In spite of modern censures him avowing
Their sovereign, all service him allowing.
Amongst which troop although I am the least,
Yet equal in perfection with the best,
I glory in subjection of his hand,
70 Nor ever did decline his least command:
For in whatever form the message came
My heart did open and receive the flame.
But time will in his course a point descry
When I this loved service must deny,
For our allegiance temporary is,
With firmer age returns our liberties.
What time in years and judgement we reposed,
Shall not so easily be to change disposed,

Nor to the art of several eyes obeying;
80 But beauty with true worth securely weighing,
Which being found assembled in some one,
We'll love her ever, and love her alone.

Elegy 18 *Love's Progress*

Whoever loves, if he do not propose
The right true end of love, he's one that goes
To sea for nothing but to make him sick.
And love's a bear-whelp born, if we o'er-lick
Our love, and force it new strange shapes to take,
We err, and of a lump a monster make.
Were not a calf a monster that were grown
Faced like a man, though better than his own?
Perfection is in unity: prefer
10 One woman first, and then one thing in her.
I, when I value gold, may think upon
The ductileness, the application,
The wholesomeness, the ingenuity,
From rust, from soil, from fire ever free,
But if I love it, 'tis because 'tis made
By our new nature, use, the soul of trade.
    All these in women we might think upon
(If women had them) and yet love but one.
Can men more injure women than to say
20 They love them for that, by which they're not they?
Makes virtue woman? must I cool my blood
Till I both be, and find one, wise and good?
May barren angels love so. But if we
Make love to woman, virtue is not she,
As beauty's not, nor wealth. He that strays thus
From her to hers, is more adulterous
Than if he took her maid. Search every sphere
And firmament, our Cupid is not there.
He's an infernal god and underground
30 With Pluto dwells, where gold and fire abound.

Men to such gods, their sacrificing coals
Did not in altars lay, but pits and holes.
Although we see celestial bodies move
Above the earth, the earth we till and love:
So we her airs contemplate, words and heart,
And virtues; but we love the centric part.
   Nor is the soul more worthy, or more fit
For love than this, as infinite as it.
But in attaining this desired place
40 How much they stray, that set out at the face!
The hair a forest is of ambushes,
Of springes, snares, fetters and manacles;
The brow becalms us when 'tis smooth and plain,
And when 'tis wrinkled, shipwrecks us again;
Smooth, 'tis a paradise, where we would have
Immortal stay, and wrinkled 'tis our grave.
The nose like to the first meridian runs
Not 'twixt an east and west, but 'twixt two suns;
It leaves a cheek, a rosy hemisphere
50 On either side, and then directs us where
Upon the Islands Fortunate we fall,
(Not faint Canary, but ambrosial)
Her swelling lips; to which when we are come,
We anchor there, and think ourselves at home,
For they seem all: there sirens' songs, and there
Wise Delphic oracles do fill the ear;
There in a creek where chosen pearls do swell,
The remora, her cleaving tongue doth dwell.
These, and the glorious promontory, her chin
60 O'erpast; and the strait Hellespont between
The Sestos and Abydos of her breasts,
(Not of two lovers, but two loves the nests)
Succeeds a boundless sea, but yet thine eye
Some island moles may scattered there descry;
And sailing towards her India, in that way
Shall at her fair Atlantic navel stay;
Though thence the current be thy pilot made,
Yet ere thou be where thou wouldst be embayed,

Thou shalt upon another forest set,
70 Where many shipwreck, and no further get.
When thou art there, consider what this chase
Misspent by thy beginning at the face.
  Rather set out below, practise my art,
Some symmetry the foot hath with that part
Which thou dost seek, and is thy map for that
Lovely enough to stop, but not stay at:
Least subject to disguise and change it is;
Men say the Devil never can change his.
It is the emblem that hath figured
80 Firmness; 'tis the first part that comes to bed.
Civility, we see, refined the kiss
Which at the face begun, transplanted is
Since to the hand, since to the imperial knee,
Now at the papal foot delights to be.
If kings think that the nearer way, and do
Rise from the foot, lovers may do so too;
For as free spheres move faster far than can
Birds, whom the air resists, so may that man
Which goes this empty and ethereal way,
90 Than if at beauty's elements he stay.
Rich Nature hath in women wisely made
Two purses, and their mouths aversely laid;
They then, which to the lower tribute owe,
That way which that exchequer looks, must go.
He which doth not, his error is as great,
As who by clyster gave the stomach meat.

Elegy 19 *To his Mistress Going to Bed*

Come, Madam, come, all rest my powers defy,
Until I labour, I in labour lie.
The foe oft-times having the foe in sight,
Is tired with standing though they never fight.
Off with that girdle, like heaven's zone glistering,
But a far fairer world encompassing.

Unpin that spangled breastplate which you wear,
That th' eyes of busy fools may be stopped there.
Unlace yourself, for that harmonious chime
10 Tells me from you, that now 'tis your bed time.
Off with that happy busk, which I envy,
That still can be, and still can stand so nigh.
Your gown going off, such beauteous state reveals,
As when from flowery meads th' hill's shadow steals.
Off with that wiry coronet and show
The hairy diadem which on you doth grow;
Now off with those shoes, and then safely tread
In this love's hallowed temple, this soft bed.
In such white robes heaven's angels used to be
20 Received by men; thou angel bring'st with thee
A heaven like Mahomet's paradise; and though
Ill spirits walk in white, we easily know
By this these angels from an evil sprite,
Those set our hairs, but these our flesh upright.
    Licence my roving hands, and let them go
Before, behind, between, above, below.
O my America, my new found land,
My kingdom, safeliest when with one man manned,
My mine of precious stones, my empery,
30 How blessed am I in this discovering thee!
To enter in these bonds, is to be free;
Then where my hand is set, my seal shall be.
    Full nakedness, all joys are due to thee.
As souls unbodied, bodies unclothed must be,
To taste whole joys. Gems which you women use
Are like Atlanta's balls, cast in men's views,
That when a fool's eye lighteth on a gem,
His earthly soul may covet theirs, not them.
Like pictures, or like books' gay coverings made
40 For laymen, are all women thus arrayed;
Themselves are mystic books, which only we
Whom their imputed grace will dignify
Must see revealed. Then since I may know,
As liberally, as to a midwife, show

Thyself: cast all, yea, this white linen hence,
Here is no penance, much less innocence.
   To teach thee, I am naked first, why then
What needst thou have more covering than a man.

Elegy 20 *Love's War*

Till I have peace with thee, war other men,
And when I have peace, can I leave thee then?
All other wars are scrupulous; only thou
O fair free city, mayst thyself allow
To any one. In Flanders, who can tell
Whether the master press, or men rebel?
Only we know, that which all idiots say,
They bear most blows which come to part the fray.
France in her lunatic giddiness did hate
10 Ever our men, yea and our God of late;
Yet she relies upon our angels well,
Which ne'er return; no more than they which fell.
Sick Ireland is with a strange war possessed
Like to an ague, now raging, now at rest,
Which time will cure, yet it must do her good
If she were purged, and her head-vein let blood.
And Midas' joys our Spanish journeys give,
We touch all gold, but find no food to live.
And I should be in that hot parching clime,
20 To dust and ashes turned before my time.
To mew me in a ship, is to enthral
Me in a prison, that were like to fall;
Or in a cloister, save that there men dwell
In a calm heaven, here in a swaggering hell.
Long voyages are long consumptions,
And ships are carts for executions.
Yea they are deaths; is't not all one to fly
Into another world, as 'tis to die?
Here let me war; in these arms let me lie;
30 Here let me parley, batter, bleed, and die.

Thine arms imprison me, and mine arms thee,
Thy heart thy ransom is, take mine for me.
Other men war that they their rest may gain,
But we will rest that we may fight again.
Those wars the ignorant, these th' experienced love,
There we are always under, here above.
There engines far off breed a just true fear,
Near thrusts, pikes, stabs, yea bullets hurt not here.
There lies are wrongs, here safe uprightly lie;
40 There men kill men, we'will make one by and by.
Thou nothing; I not half so much shall do
In these wars, as they may which from us two
Shall spring. Thousands we see which travel not
To wars, but stay swords, arms, and shot
To make at home; and shall not I do then
More glorious service, staying to make men?

Sappho to Philaenis

Where is that holy fire, which verse is said
    To have? is that enchanting force decayed?
Verse, that draws Nature's works, from Nature's law,
    Thee, her best work, to her work cannot draw.
Have my tears quenched my old poetic fire;
    Why quenched they not as well, that of desire?
Thoughts, my mind's creatures, often are with thee,
    But I, their maker, want their liberty.
Only thine image, in my heart, doth sit,
10   But that is wax, and fires environ it.
My fires have driven, thine have drawn it hence;
    And I am robbed of picture, heart, and sense.
Dwells with me still mine irksome memory,
    Which, both to keep, and lose, grieves equally.
That tells me how fair thou art: thou art so fair,
    As, gods, when gods to thee I do compare,
Are graced thereby; and to make blind men see,
    What things gods are, I say they are like to thee.

For, if we justly call each silly man
20   A little world, what shall we call thee then?
Thou art not soft, and clear, and straight, and fair,
    As down, as stars, cedars, and lilies are,
But thy right hand, and cheek, and eye, only
    Are like thy other hand, and cheek, and eye.
Such was my Phao awhile, but shall be never,
    As thou wast, art, and, oh, mayst thou be ever.
Here lovers swear in their idolatry,
    That I am such; but grief discolours me.
And yet I grieve the less, lest grief remove
30   My beauty, and make me unworthy of thy love.
Plays some soft boy with thee, oh there wants yet
    A mutual feeling which should sweeten it.
His chin, a thorny hairy unevenness
    Doth threaten, and some daily change possess.
Thy body is a natural paradise,
    In whose self, unmanured, all pleasure lies,
Nor needs perfection; why shouldst thou then
    Admit the tillage of a harsh rough man?
Men leave behind them that which their sin shows,
40   And are as thieves traced, which rob when it snows.
But of our dalliance no more signs there are,
    Than fishes leave in streams, or birds in air.
And between us all sweetness may be had;
    All, all that Nature yields, or Art can add.
My two lips, eyes, thighs, differ from thy two,
    But so, as thine from one another do;
And, oh, no more; the likeness being such,
    Why should they not alike in all parts touch?
Hand to strange hand, lip to lip none denies;
50   Why should they breast to breast, or thighs to thighs?
Likeness begets such strange self flattery,
    That touching myself, all seems done to thee.
Myself I embrace, and mine own hands I kiss,
    And amorously thank myself for this.
Me, in my glass, I call thee; but alas,
    When I would kiss, tears dim mine eyes, and glass.

O cure this loving madness, and restore
  Me to me; thee, my half, my all, my more.
So may thy cheeks' red outwear scarlet dye,
60   And their white, whiteness of the galaxy,
So may thy mighty, amazing beauty move
  Envy in all women, and in all men, love,
And so be change, and sickness, far from thee,
  As thou by coming near, keep'st them from me.

Epithalamions or Marriage Songs

Epithalamion Made at Lincoln's Inn

The sun-beams in the east are spread,
Leave, leave, fair Bride, your solitary bed,
   No more shall you return to it alone,
It nurseth sadness, and your body's print,
Like to a grave, the yielding down doth dint;
     You and your other you meet there anon;
       Put forth, put forth that warm balm-breathing thigh,
Which when next time you in these sheets will smother
There it must meet another,
10   Which never was, but must be, oft, more nigh;
Come glad from thence, go gladder than you came,
Today put on perfection, and a woman's name.

Daughters of London, you which be
Our golden mines, and furnished treasury,
   You which are angels, yet still bring with you
Thousands of angels on your marriage days,
Help with your presence, and device, to praise
     These rites, which also unto you grow due;
       Conceitedly dress her, and be assigned,
20 By you, fit place for every flower and jewel,
Make her for love fit fuel
       As gay as Flora, and as rich as Ind;
So may she fair and rich, in nothing lame,
Today put on perfection, and a woman's name.

And you frolic patricians,
Sons of these senators' wealth's deep oceans,
   Ye painted courtiers, barrels of others' wits,
Ye country men, who but your beasts love none,
Ye of those fellowships whereof he's one,
30   Of study and play made strange hermaphrodites,
       Here shine; this Bridegroom to the Temple bring.
Lo, in yon path which store of strewed flowers graceth,
The sober virgin paceth;
       Except my sight fail, 'tis no other thing;

Weep not nor blush, here is no grief nor shame,
Today put on perfection, and a woman's name.

Thy two-leaved gates fair Temple unfold,
And these two in thy sacred bosom hold,
 Till, mystically joined, but one they be;
40 Then may thy lean and hunger-starved womb
Long time expect their bodies and their tomb,
 Long after their own parents fatten thee.
  All elder claims, and all cold barrenness,
All yielding to new loves be far for ever,
Which might these two dissever,
  Always, all th'other may each one possess;
For, the best Bride, best worthy of praise and fame,
Today puts on perfection, and a woman's name.

Oh winter days bring much delight,
50 Not for themselves, but for they soon bring night;
 Other sweets wait thee than these diverse meats,
Other disports than dancing jollities,
Other love tricks than glancing with the eyes,
 But that the sun still in our half sphere sweats;
  He flies in winter, but he now stands still,
Yet shadows turn; noon point he hath attained,
His steeds nill be restrained,
  But gallop lively down the western hill;
Thou shalt, when he hath run the world's half frame,
60 *Tonight put on perfection, and a woman's name.*

The amorous evening star is rose,
Why then should not our amorous star inclose
 Herself in her wished bed? Release your strings
Musicians, and dancers take some truce
With these your pleasing labours, for great use
 As much weariness as perfection brings;
  You, and not only you, but all toiled beasts
Rest duly; at night all their toils are dispensed;
But in their beds commenced
70   Are other labours, and more dainty feasts;

She goes a maid, who, lest she turn the same,
Tonight puts on perfection, and a woman's name.

Thy virgin's girdle now untie,
And in thy nuptial bed (love's altar) lie
  A pleasing sacrifice; now dispossess
Thee of these chains and robes which were put on
T' adorn the day, not thee; for thou, alone,
  Like virtue and truth, art best in nakedness;
    This bed is only to virginity
80 A grave, but, to a better state, a cradle;
Till now thou wast but able
    To be what now thou art; then that by thee
No more be said, *I may be*, but, *I am*,
Tonight put on perfection, and a woman's name.

Even like a faithful man content,
That this life for a better should be spent:
  So, she a mother's rich style doth prefer,
And at the Bridegroom's wished approach doth lie,
Like an appointed lamb, when tenderly
90   The priest comes on his knees t' embowel her;
    Now sleep or watch with more joy; and O light
Of heaven, to morrow rise thou hot, and early;
This sun will love so dearly
    Her rest, that long, long we shall want her sight;
Wonders are wrought, for she which had no maim,
Tonight puts on perfection, and a woman's name.

*An Epithalamion, or Marriage Song on the Lady
Elizabeth and Count Palatine being Married on
St Valentine's Day*

Hail Bishop Valentine, whose day this is,
    All the air is thy diocese,
    And all the chirping choristers
And other birds are thy parishioners,
    Thou marriest every year

The lyric lark, and the grave whispering dove,
The sparrow that neglects his life for love,
The household bird, with the red stomacher,
  Thou mak'st the blackbird speed as soon,
10 As doth the goldfinch, or the halcyon;
The husband cock looks out, and straight is sped,
And meets his wife, which brings her feather-bed.
This day more cheerfully than ever shine,
This day, which might enflame thyself, old Valentine.

Till now, thou warmed'st with multiplying loves
  Two larks, two sparrows, or two doves,
  All that is nothing unto this,
For thou this day couplest two phoenixes,
  Thou mak'st a taper see
20 What the sun never saw, and what the Ark
(Which was of fowls, and beasts, the cage, and park,)
Did not contain, one bed contains, through thee,
  Two phoenixes, whose joined breasts
Are unto one another mutual nests,
Where motion kindles such fires, as shall give
Young phoenixes, and yet the old shall live.
Whose love and courage never shall decline,
But make the whole year through, thy day, O Valentine.

Up then fair phoenix Bride, frustrate the sun,
30   Thyself from thine affection
  Takest warmth enough, and from thine eye
All lesser birds will take their jollity.
  Up, up, fair Bride, and call,
Thy stars, from out their several boxes, take
Thy rubies, pearls, and diamonds forth, and make
Thyself a constellation, of them all,
  And by their blazing, signify,
That a great Princess falls, but doth not die;
Be thou a new star, that to us portends
40 Ends of much wonder; and be thou those ends.
Since thou dost this day in new glory shine,
May all men date records, from this thy Valentine.

Come forth, come forth, and as one glorious flame
    Meeting another, grows the same,
    So meet thy Frederick, and so
To an unseparable union grow.
    Since separation
Falls not on such things as are infinite,
Nor things which are but one, can disunite.
You are twice inseparable, great, and one;
    Go, then to where the Bishop stays,
To make you one, his way, which divers ways
Must be effected; and when all is past,
And that you are one, by hearts and hands made fast,
You two have one way left, yourselves to entwine,
Besides this Bishop's knot, or Bishop Valentine.

But oh, what ails the sun, that here he stays,
    Longer today, than other days?
    Stays he new light from these to get?
And finding here such store, is loth to set?
    And why do you two walk,
So slowly paced in this procession?
Is all your care but to be looked upon,
And be to others spectacle, and talk?
    The feast, with gluttonous delays,
Is eaten, and too long their meat they praise,
The masquers come late, and I think, will stay,
Like fairies, till the cock crow them away.
    Alas, did not antiquity assign
A night, as well as day, to thee, O Valentine?

They did, and night is come; and yet we see
    Formalities retarding thee.
    What mean these ladies, which (as though
They were to take a clock in pieces,) go
    So nicely about the Bride;
A Bride, before a good night could be said,
Should vanish from her clothes, into her bed,
As souls from bodies steal, and are not spied.
    But now she is laid; what though she be?

80   Yet there are more delays, for, where is he?
He comes, and passes through sphere after sphere:
First her sheets, then her arms, then any where,
Let not this day, then, but this night be thine,
Thy day was but the eve to this, O Valentine.

Here lies a she sun, and a he moon here,
     She gives the best light to his sphere,
     Or each is both, and all, and so
They unto one another nothing owe,
     And yet they do, but are
90   So just and rich in that coin, which they pay,
That neither would, nor needs forbear nor stay,
Neither desires to be spared, nor to spare,
     They quickly pay their debt, and then
Take no acquittances, but pay again;
They pay, they give, they lend, and so let fall
No such occasion to be liberal.
More truth, more courage in these two do shine,
Than all thy turtles have, and sparrows, Valentine.

And by this act of these two phoenixes
100   Nature again restored is,
     For since these two are two no more,
There's but one phoenix still, as was before.
     Rest now at last, and we
As satyrs watch the sun's uprise, will stay
Waiting, when your eyes opened, let out day,
Only desired, because your face we see;
     Others near you shall whispering speak,
And wagers lay, at which side day will break,
And win by observing, then, whose hand it is
110   That opens first a curtain, hers or his;
This will be tried tomorrow after nine,
Till which hour, we thy day enlarge, O Valentine.

Eclogue 1613. December 26

ALLOPHANES finding IDIOS in the country in Christmas time, reprehends his absence from court, at the marriage of the Earl of Somerset. IDIOS gives an account of his purpose therein, and of his absence thence.

ALLOPHANES
Unseasonable man, statue of ice,
    What could to country's solitude entice
Thee, in this year's cold and decrepit time?
    Nature's instinct draws to the warmer clime
Even small birds, who by that courage dare,
    In numerous fleets, sail through their sea, the air.
What delicacy can in fields appear,
    Whilst Flora herself doth a frieze jerkin wear?
Whilst winds do all the trees and hedges strip
10   Of leaves, to furnish rods enough to whip
Thy madness from thee; and all springs by frost
    Have taken cold, and their sweet murmur lost;
If thou thy faults or fortunes wouldst lament
    With just solemnity, do it in Lent;
At Court the spring already advanced is,
    The sun stays longer up; and yet not his
The glory is, far other, other fires.
    First, zeal to Prince and State; then love's desires
Burn in one breast, and like heaven's two great lights,
20   The first doth govern days, the other nights.
And then that early light, which did appear
    Before the sun and moon created were,
The Prince's favour, is diffused o'er all,
    From which all fortunes, names, and natures fall;
Then from those wombs of stars, the Bride's bright eyes,
    At every glance, a constellation flies,
And sows the Court with stars, and doth prevent
    In light and power, the all-eyed firmament;

First her eyes kindle other ladies' eyes,
30   Then from their beams their jewels' lustres rise,
And from their jewels torches do take fire,
    And all is warmth, and light, and good desire;
Most other Courts, alas, are like to hell,
    Where in dark plots, fire without light doth dwell;
Or but like stoves, for lust and envy get
    Continual, but artificial heat;
Here zeal and love grown one, all clouds digest,
    And make our Court an everlasting east.
And canst thou be from thence?

IDIOS
                No, I am there.
40   As heaven, to men disposed, is everywhere,
So are those Courts, whose Princes animate,
    Not only all their house, but all their State.
Let no man think, because he is full, he hath all.
    Kings (as their pattern, God) are liberal
Not only in fullness, but capacity,
    Enlarging narrow men, to feel and see,
And comprehend the blessings they bestow.
    So, reclused hermits oftentimes do know
More of heaven's glory, than a worldling can.
50   As man is of the world, the heart of man,
Is an epitome of God's great book
    Of creatures, and man need no farther look;
So is the country of Courts, where sweet peace doth
    As their one common soul, give life to both,
I am not then from Court.

ALLOPHANES
              Dreamer, thou art,
    Think'st thou fantastic that thou hast a part
In the East-Indian fleet, because thou hast
    A little spice, or amber in thy taste?
Because thou art not frozen, art thou warm?
60   Seest thou all good because thou seest no harm?

The earth doth in her inward bowels hold
   Stuff well disposed, and which would fain be gold,
But never shall, except it chance to lie,
   So upward, that heaven gild it with his eye;
As, for divine things, faith comes from above,
   So, for best civil use, all tinctures move
From higher powers; from God religion springs,
   Wisdom, and honour from the use of kings.
Then unbeguile thyself, and know with me,
70   That angels, though on earth employed they be,
Are still in heaven, so is he still at home
   That doth, abroad, to honest actions come.
Chide thyself then, O fool, which yesterday
   Mightst have read more than all thy books bewray;
Hast thou a history, which doth present
   A Court, where all affections do assent
Unto the King's, and that, that King's are just?
   And where it is no levity to trust.
Where there is no ambition, but to obey,
80   Where men need whisper nothing, and yet may;
Where the King's favours are so placed, that all
   Find that the King therein is liberal
To them, in him, because his favours bend
   To virtue, to the which they all pretend.
Thou hast no such; yet here was this, and more,
   An earnest lover, wise then, and before.
Our little Cupid hath sued livery,
   And is no more in his minority,
He is admitted now into that breast
90   Where the King's counsels and his secrets rest.
What hast thou lost, O ignorant man?

IDIOS
                        I knew
All this, and only therefore I withdrew.
To know and feel all this, and not to have
   Words to express it, makes a man a grave
Of his own thoughts; I would not therefore stay

At a great feast, having no grace to say.
And yet I 'scaped not here; for being come
    Full of the common joy, I uttered some.
Read then this nuptial song, which was not made
100   Either the Court or men's hearts to invade,
But since I am dead, and buried, I could frame
    No epitaph, which might advance my fame
So much as this poor song, which testifies
    I did unto that day some sacrifice.

Epithalamion

The Time of the Marriage

Thou art reprieved, old year, thou shalt not die,
Though thou upon thy death-bed lie,
    And shouldst within five days expire,
Yet thou art rescued by a mightier fire,
    Than thy old soul, the sun,
110   When he doth in his largest circle run.
The passage of the west or east would thaw,
And open wide their easy liquid jaw
To all our ships, could a Promethean art
Either unto the northern pole impart
The fire of these inflaming eyes, or of this loving heart.

Equality of Persons

But undiscerning Muse, which heart, which eyes,
    In this new couple, dost thou prize,
    When his eye as inflaming is
As hers, and her heart loves as well as his?
120   Be tried by beauty, and then
The Bridegroom is a maid, and not a man.
If by that manly courage they be tried,
Which scorns unjust opinion; then the Bride
Becomes a man. Should chance or envy's art
Divide these two, whom nature scarce did part?
Since both have both th' inflaming eyes, and both the loving
        heart.

Raising of the Bridegroom

Though it be some divorce to think of you
    Singly, so much one are you two,
    Yet let me here contemplate thee,
130 First, cheerful Bridegroom, and first let me see,
    How thou prevent'st the sun,
And his red foaming horses dost outrun,
How, having laid down in thy Sovereign's breast
All businesses, from thence to reinvest
Them, when these triumphs cease, thou forward art
To show to her, who doth the like impart,
The fire of thy inflaming eyes, and of thy loving heart.

Raising of the Bride

But now, to thee, fair Bride, it is some wrong,
    To think thou wert in bed so long,
140   Since soon thou liest down first, 'tis fit
Thou in first rising shouldst allow for it.
    Powder thy radiant hair,
Which if without such ashes thou wouldst wear,
Thou, which to all which come to look upon,
Art meant for Phoebus, wouldst be Phaëton.
For our ease, give thine eyes th' unusual part
Of joy, a tear; so quenched, thou mayst impart,
To us that come, thy inflaming eyes, to him, thy loving
    heart.

Her Apparelling

Thus thou descend'st to our infirmity,
150   Who can the sun in water see.
    So dost thou, when in silk and gold,
Thou cloud'st thyself; since we which do behold,
    Are dust, and worms, 'tis just
Our objects be the fruits of worms and dust;
Let every jewel be a glorious star,
Yet stars are not so pure, as their spheres are.

And though thou stoop, to appear to us in part,
Still in that picture thou entirely art,
Which thy inflaming eyes have made within his loving heart.

Going to the Chapel

160 Now from your easts you issue forth, and we,
    As men which through a cypress see
      The rising sun, do think it two,
So, as you go to Church, do think of you,
    But that veil being gone,
By the Church rites you are from thenceforth one.
The Church Triumphant made this match before,
And now the Militant doth strive no more.
Then, reverend priest, who God's Recorder art,
Do, from his dictates, to these two impart
170 All blessings, which are seen, or thought by angel's eye or
    heart.

The Benediction

Blessed pair of swans, oh may you interbring
    Daily new joys, and never sing,
      Live, till all grounds of wishes fail,
Till honour, yea till wisdom grow so stale,
    That, new great heights to try,
It must serve your ambition, to die;
Raise heirs, and may here, to the world's end, live
Heirs from this King, to take thanks, yours, to give,
Nature and grace do all, and nothing art,
180 May never age, or error overthwart
With any west, these radiant eyes, with any north, this
    heart.

Feasts and Revels

But you are over-blessed. Plenty this day
    Injures; it causeth time to stay;
      The tables groan, as though this feast

Would, as the flood, destroy all fowl and beast.
    And were the doctrine new
That the earth moved, this day would make it true;
For every part to dance and revel goes.
They tread the air, and fall not where they rose.
190 Though six hours since, the sun to bed did part,
The masks and banquets will not yet impart
A sunset to these weary eyes, a centre to this heart.

The Bride's Going to Bed

What mean'st thou, Bride, this company to keep?
    To sit up, till thou fain wouldst sleep?
    Thou mayst not, when thou art laid, do so.
Thyself must to him a new banquet grow,
    And you must entertain
And do all this day's dances o'er again.
Know that if sun and moon together do
200 Rise in one point, they do not set so too.
Therefore thou mayst, fair Bride, to bed depart,
Thou art not gone, being gone, where e'er thou art,
Thou leav'st in him thy watchful eyes, in him thy loving
    heart.

The Bridegroom's Coming

As he that sees a star fall, runs apace,
    And finds a jelly in the place,
    So doth the Bridegroom haste as much,
Being told this star is fall'n, and finds her such.
    And as friends may look strange,
By a new fashion, or apparel's change,
210 Their souls, though long acquainted they had been,
These clothes, their bodies, never yet had seen.
Therefore at first she modestly might start,
But must forthwith surrender every part,
As freely, as each to each before, gave either eye or heart.

The Good-night

Now, as in Tullia's tomb, one lamp burnt clear,
    Unchanged for fifteen hundred year,
    May these love-lamps we here enshrine,
In warmth, light, lasting, equal the divine.
    Fire ever doth aspire,
220 And makes all like itself, turns all to fire,
But ends in ashes, which these cannot do,
For none of these is fuel, but fire too.
This is joy's bonfire, then, where love's strong arts
Make of so noble individual parts
One fire of four inflaming eyes, and of two loving hearts.

IDIOS

As I have brought this song, that I may do
    A perfect sacrifice, I'll burn it too.

ALLOPHANES

No Sir. This paper I have justly got,
    For, in burnt incense, the perfume is not
230 His only that presents it, but of all;
    Whatever celebrates this festival
Is common, since the joy thereof is so.
    Nor may yourself be priest: but let me go
Back to the Court, and I will lay it upon
    Such altars, as prize your devotion.

Epigrams

Hero and Leander

Both robbed of air, we both lie in one ground,
Both whom one fire had burnt, one water drowned.

Pyramus and Thisbe

Two, by themselves, each other, love and fear
Slain, cruel friends, by parting have joined here.

Niobe

By children's birth, and death, I am become
So dry, that I am now made mine own tomb.

A Burnt Ship

Out of a fired ship, which, by no way
But drowning could be rescued from the flame,
Some men leaped forth, and ever as they came
Near the foes' ships, did by their shot decay;
So all were lost, which in the ship were found,
    They in the sea being burnt, they in the burnt ship
        drowned.

Fall of a Wall

Under an undermined, and shot-bruised wall
A too-bold captain perished by the fall,
Whose brave misfortune, happiest men envied,
That had a town for tomb, his bones to hide.

A Lame Beggar

I am unable, yonder beggar cries,
To stand, or move; if he say true, he *lies*.

Cales and Guiana

If you from spoil of th' old world's farthest end
To the new world your kindled valours bend,
What brave examples then do prove it true
That one thing's end doth still begin a new.

Sir John Wingfield

Beyond th' old Pillars many have travelled
Towards the sun's cradle, and his throne, and bed.
A fitter pillar our Earl did bestow
In that late island; for he well did know
Farther than Wingfield no man dares to go.

A Self Accuser

Your mistress, that you follow whores, still taxeth you:
'Tis strange she should confess it, though it be true.

A Licentious Person

Thy sins and hairs may no man equal call,
For, as thy sins increase, thy hairs do fall.

Antiquary

If in his study he hath so much care
To hang all old strange things, let his wife beware.

Disinherited

Thy father all from thee, by his last will,
Gave to the poor; thou hast good title still.

Phryne

Thy flattering picture, Phryne, is like thee,
Only in this, that you both painted be.

An Obscure Writer

Philo, with twelve years' study, hath been grieved
To be understood; when will he be believed?

Klockius

Klockius so deeply hath sworn, ne'er more to come
In bawdy house, that he dares not go home.

Raderus

Why this man gelded Martial I muse,
Except himself alone his tricks would use,
As Katherine, for the Court's sake, put down stews.

Mercurius Gallo-Belgicus

Like Aesop's fellow-slaves, O Mercury,
Which could do all things, thy faith is; and I
Like Aesop's self, which nothing; I confess
I should have had more faith, if thou hadst less;
Thy credit lost thy credit: 'tis sin to do,
In this case, as thou wouldst be done unto,
To believe all: change thy name: thou art like
Mercury in stealing, but liest like a Greek.

Ralphius

Compassion in the world again is bred:
  Ralphius is sick, the broker keeps his bed.

The Liar

Thou in the fields walk'st out thy supping hours
  And yet thou swear'st thou has supped like a king;
Like Nebuchadnezzar perchance with grass and
    flowers,
  A salad worse than Spanish dieting.

Manliness

Thou call'st me effeminate, for I love women's joys;
I call not thee manly, though thou follow boys.

Satires

Satire 1

Away thou fondling motley humorist,
Leave me, and in this standing wooden chest,
Consorted with these few books, let me lie
In prison, and here be coffined, when I die;
Here are God's conduits, grave divines; and here
Nature's secretary, the Philosopher;
And jolly statesmen, which teach how to tie
The sinews of a city's mystic body;
Here gathering chroniclers, and by them stand
10 Giddy fantastic poets of each land.
Shall I leave all this constant company,
And follow headlong, wild uncertain thee?
First swear by thy best love in earnest
(If thou which lov'st all, canst love any best)
Thou wilt not leave me in the middle street,
Though some more spruce companion thou dost meet,
Not though a captain do come in thy way
Bright parcel gilt, with forty dead men's pay,
Nor though a brisk perfumed pert courtier
20 Deign with a nod, thy courtesy to answer.
Nor come a velvet Justice with a long
Great train of blue coats, twelve, or fourteen strong,
Wilt thou grin or fawn on him, or prepare
A speech to court his beauteous son and heir.
For better or worse take me, or leave me:
To take, and leave me is adultery.
Oh monstrous, superstitious puritan,
Of refined manners, yet ceremonial man,
That when thou meet'st one, with inquiring eyes
30 Dost search, and like a needy broker prize
The silk, and gold he wears, and to that rate
So high or low, dost raise thy formal hat:
That wilt consort none, until thou have known
What lands he hath in hope, or of his own,
As though all thy companions should make thee
Jointures, and marry thy dear company.

Why shouldst thou (that dost not only approve,
But in rank itchy lust, desire, and love
The nakedness and barrenness to enjoy,
40 Of thy plump muddy whore, or prostitute boy)
Hate virtue, though she be naked, and bare?
At birth, and death, our bodies naked are;
And till our souls be unapparelled
Of bodies, they from bliss are banished.
Man's first blessed state was naked, when by sin
He lost that, yet he was clothed but in beast's skin,
And in this coarse attire, which I now wear,
With God, and with the Muses I confer.
But since thou like a contrite penitent,
50 Charitably warned of thy sins, dost repent
These vanities, and giddinesses, lo
I shut my chamber door, and come, let's go.
But sooner may a cheap whore, that hath been
Worn by as many several men in sin,
As are black feathers, or musk-colour hose,
Name her child's right true father, 'mongst all those:
Sooner may one guess, who shall bear away
The Infanta of London, heir to an India;
And sooner may a gulling weather spy
60 By drawing forth heaven's scheme tell certainly
What fashioned hats, or ruffs, or suits next year
Our subtle-witted antic youths will wear;
Than thou, when thou depart'st from me, canst show
Whither, why, when, or with whom thou wouldst go.
But how shall I be pardoned my offence
That thus have sinned against my conscience?
Now we are in the street; he first of all
Improvidently proud, creeps to the wall,
And so imprisoned, and hemmed in by me
70 Sells for a little state his liberty;
Yet though he cannot skip forth now to greet
Every fine silken painted fool we meet,
He them to him with amorous smiles allures,
And grins, smacks, shrugs, and such an itch endures,

As 'prentices, or school-boys which do know
Of some gay sport abroad, yet dare not go.
And as fiddlers stop lowest, at highest sound,
So to the most brave, stoops he nigh'st the ground.
But to a grave man, he doth move no more
80 Than the wise politic horse would heretofore,
Or thou O elephant or ape wilt do,
When any names the King of Spain to you.
Now leaps he upright, jogs me, and cries, 'Do you see
Yonder well-favoured youth?' 'Which?' 'Oh, 'tis he
That dances so divinely'; 'Oh,' said I,
'Stand still, must you dance here for company?'
He drooped, we went, till one (which did excel
Th' Indians, in drinking his tobacco well)
Met us; they talked; I whispered, 'Let us go,
90 'T may be you smell him not, truly I do.'
He hears not me, but, on the other side
A many-coloured peacock having spied,
Leaves him and me; I for my lost sheep stay;
He follows, overtakes, goes on the way,
Saying, 'Him whom I last left, all repute
For his device, in handsoming a suit,
To judge of lace, pink, panes, print, cut, and pleat
Of all the Court, to have the best conceit.'
'Our dull comedians want him, let him go;
100 But Oh, God strengthen thee, why stoop'st thou so?'
'Why? he hath travelled.' 'Long?' 'No, but to me
(Which understand none), he doth seem to be
Perfect French, and Italian'; I replied,
'So is the pox'; he answered not, but spied
More men of sort, of parts, and qualities;
At last his love he in a window spies,
And like light dew exhaled, he flings from me
Violently ravished to his lechery.
Many were there, he could command no more;
110 He quarrelled, fought, bled; and turned out of door
Directly came to me hanging the head,
And constantly a while must keep his bed.

Satire 2

Sir; though (I thank God for it) I do hate
Perfectly all this town, yet there's one state
In all ill things so excellently best,
That hate, towards them, breeds pity towards the rest.
Though poetry indeed be such a sin
As I think that brings dearths, and Spaniards in,
Though like the pestilence and old fashioned love,
Riddlingly it catch men; and doth remove
Never, till it be starved out, yet their state
10 Is poor, disarmed, like papists, not worth hate.
One (like a wretch, which at Bar judged as dead,
Yet prompts him which stands next, and cannot read,
And saves his life) gives idiot actors means
(Starving himself) to live by his laboured scenes;
As in some organ, puppets dance above
And bellows pant below, which them do move.
One would move love by rhymes; but witchcraft's charms
Bring not now their old fears, nor their old harms:
Rams, and slings now are silly battery,
20 Pistolets are the best artillery.
And they who write to lords, rewards to get,
Are they not like singers at doors for meat?
And they who write, because all write, have still
That excuse for writing, and for writing ill.
But he is worst, who (beggarly) doth chaw
Others' wits' fruits, and in his ravenous maw
Rankly digested, doth those things out spew,
As his own things; and they are his own, 'tis true,
For if one eat my meat, though it be known
30 The meat was mine, th' excrement is his own.
But these do me no harm, nor they which use
To outdo dildoes, and out-usure Jews;
To out-drink the sea, to outswear the Litany;
Who with sins' all kinds as familiar be

As confessors; and for whose sinful sake,
Schoolmen new tenements in hell must make:
Whose strange sins, canonists could hardly tell
In which commandment's large receipt they dwell.
    But these punish themselves; the insolence
40 Of Coscus only breeds my just offence,
Whom time (which rots all, and makes botches pox,
And plodding on, must make a calf an ox)
Hath made a lawyer, which was alas of late
But a scarce poet; jollier of this state,
Than are new beneficed ministers, he throws
Like nets, or lime-twigs, wheresoe'er he goes,
His title of barrister, on every wench,
And woos in language of the Pleas, and Bench:
'A motion, Lady'; 'Speak Coscus'; 'I have been
50 In love, ever since *tricesimo* of the Queen,
Continual claims I have made, injunctions got
To stay my rival's suit, that he should not
Proceed'; 'Spare me'; 'In Hilary term I went,
You said, if I returned next 'size in Lent,
I should be in remitter of your grace;
In th' interim my letters should take place
Of affidavits'; words, words, which would tear
The tender labyrinth of a soft maid's ear,
More, more, than ten Sclavonians scolding, more
60 Than when winds in our ruined abbeys roar.
When sick with poetry, and possessed with Muse
Thou wast, and mad, I hoped; but men which choose
Law practice for mere gain, bold soul, repute
Worse than embrothelled strumpets prostitute.
Now like an owl-like watchman, he must walk
His hand still at a bill, now he must talk
Idly, like prisoners, which whole months will swear
That only suretyship hath brought them there,
And to every suitor lie in everything,
70 Like a king's favourite, yea like a king;
Like a wedge in a block, wring to the bar,
Bearing like asses, and more shameless far

Than carted whores, lie, to the grave judge; for
Bastardy abounds not in kings' titles, nor
Simony and sodomy in churchmen's lives,
As these things do in him; by these he thrives.
Shortly (as the sea) he will compass all our land;
From Scots, to Wight; from Mount, to Dover strand.
And spying heirs melting with luxury,
80   Satan will not joy at their sins, as he.
For as a thrifty wench scrapes kitchen stuff,
And barrelling the droppings, and the snuff,
Of wasting candles, which in thirty year
(Relic-like kept) perchance buys wedding gear;
Piecemeal he gets lands, and spends as much time
Wringing each acre, as men pulling prime.
In parchments then, large as his fields, he draws
Assurances, big, as glossed civil laws,
So huge, that men (in our time's forwardness)
90   Are Fathers of the Church for writing less.
These he writes not; nor for these written pays,
Therefore spares no length; as in those first days
When Luther was professed, he did desire
Short *Pater nosters*, saying as a friar
Each day his beads, but having left those laws,
Adds to Christ's prayer, the power and glory clause.
But when he sells or changes land, he impairs
His writings, and (unwatched) leaves out, *ses heires*,
As slily as any commenter goes by
100 Hard words, or sense; or in Divinity
As controverters, in vouched texts, leave out
Shrewd words, which might against them clear the doubt.
Where are those spread woods which clothed heretofore
Those bought lands? not built, nor burnt within door.
Where's th' old landlord's troops, and alms? In great halls
Carthusian fasts, and fulsome bacchanals
Equally I hate; means bless; in rich men's homes
I bid kill some beasts, but no hecatombs,
None starve, none surfeit so; but oh we allow,
110 Good works as good, but out of fashion now,

Like old rich wardrobes; but my words none draws
Within the vast reach of the huge statute laws.

Satire 3

Kind pity chokes my spleen; brave scorn forbids
Those tears to issue which swell my eye-lids,
I must not laugh, nor weep sins, and be wise,
Can railing then cure these worn maladies?
Is not our mistress fair religion,
As worthy of all our soul's devotion,
As virtue was to the first blinded age?
Are not heaven's joys as valiant to assuage
Lusts, as earth's honour was to them? Alas,
10 As we do them in means, shall they surpass
Us in the end, and shall thy father's spirit
Meet blind philosophers in heaven, whose merit
Of strict life may be imputed faith, and hear
Thee, whom he taught so easy ways and near
To follow, damned? O if thou dar'st, fear this;
This fear great courage, and high valour is.
Dar'st thou aid mutinous Dutch, and dar'st thou lay
Thee in ships' wooden sepulchres, a prey
To leaders' rage, to storms, to shot, to dearth?
20 Dar'st thou dive seas, and dungeons of the earth?
Hast thou courageous fire to thaw the ice
Of frozen north discoveries? and thrice
Colder than salamanders, like divine
Children in th'oven, fires of Spain, and the line,
Whose countries limbecks to our bodies be,
Canst thou for gain bear? and must every he
Which cries not, 'Goddess!' to thy mistress, draw,
Or eat thy poisonous words? courage of straw!
O desperate coward, wilt thou seem bold, and
30 To thy foes and his (who made thee to stand
Sentinel in his world's garrison) thus yield,
And for forbidden wars, leave th'appointed field?

Know thy foes: the foul Devil, he, whom thou
Strivest to please, for hate, not love, would allow
Thee fain, his whole realm to be quit; and as
The world's all parts wither away and pass,
So the world's self, thy other loved foe, is
In her decrepit wane, and thou loving this,
Dost love a withered and worn strumpet; last,

40 Flesh (itself's death) and joys which flesh can taste,
Thou lovest; and thy fair goodly soul, which doth
Give this flesh power to taste joy, thou dost loathe.
    Seek true religion. O where? Mirreus
Thinking her unhoused here, and fled from us,
Seeks her at Rome, there, because he doth know
That she was there a thousand years ago,
He loves her rags so, as we here obey
The statecloth where the Prince sate yesterday.
Crants to such brave loves will not be enthralled,

50 But loves her only, who at Geneva is called
Religion, plain, simple, sullen, young,
Contemptuous, yet unhandsome; as among
Lecherous humours, there is one that judges
No wenches wholesome, but coarse country drudges.
Graius stays still at home here, and because
Some preachers, vile ambitious bawds, and laws
Still new like fashions, bid him think that she
Which dwells with us, is only perfect, he
Embraceth her, whom his godfathers will

60 Tender to him, being tender, as wards still
Take such wives as their guardians offer, or
Pay values. Careless Phrygius doth abhor
All, because all cannot be good, as one
Knowing some women whores, dares marry none.
Gracchus loves all as one, and thinks that so
As women do in divers countries go
In divers habits, yet are still one kind,
So doth, so is religion; and this blind-
ness too much light breeds; but unmoved thou

70 Of force must one, and forced but one allow;

And the right; ask thy father which is she,
Let him ask his; though truth and falsehood be
Near twins, yet truth a little elder is;
Be busy to seek her, believe me this,
He's not of none, nor worst, that seeks the best.
To adore, or scorn an image, or protest,
May all be bad; doubt wisely, in strange way
To stand inquiring right, is not to stray;
To sleep, or run wrong is. On a huge hill,
80 Cragged, and steep, Truth stands, and he that will
Reach her, about must, and about must go;
And what the hill's suddenness resists, win so;
Yet strive so, that before age, death's twilight,
Thy soul rest, for none can work in that night,
To will, implies delay, therefore now do.
Hard deeds, the body's pains; hard knowledge too
The mind's endeavours reach, and mysteries
Are like the sun, dazzling, yet plain to all eyes.
Keep the truth which thou hast found; men do not stand
90 In so ill case here, that God hath with his hand
Signed kings blank-charters to kill whom they hate,
Nor are they vicars, but hangmen to Fate.
Fool and wretch, wilt thou let thy soul be tied
To man's laws, by which she shall not be tried
At the last day? Or will it then boot thee
To say a Philip, or a Gregory,
A Harry, or a Martin taught thee this?
Is not this excuse for mere contraries,
Equally strong; cannot both sides say so?
100 That thou mayest rightly obey power, her bounds know;
Those past, her nature, and name is changed; to be
Then humble to her is idolatry.
As streams are, power is; those blessed flowers that dwell
At the rough stream's calm head, thrive and prove well,
But having left their roots, and themselves given
To the stream's tyrannous rage, alas are driven
Through mills, and rocks, and woods, and at last, almost
Consumed in going, in the sea are lost:

So perish souls, which more choose men's unjust
110 Power from God claimed, than God himself to trust.

Satire 4

Well; I may now receive, and die; my sin
Indeed is great, but I have been in
A purgatory, such as feared hell is
A recreation, and scant map of this.
My mind, neither with pride's itch, nor yet hath been
Poisoned with love to see, or to be seen.
I had no suit there, nor new suit to show,
Yet went to Court; but as Glaze which did go
To a Mass in jest, catched, was fain to disburse
10 The hundred marks, which is the Statute's curse,
Before he 'scaped, so it pleased my destiny
(Guilty of my sin of going), to think me
As prone to all ill, and of good as forget-
ful, as proud, as lustful, and as much in debt,
As vain, as witless, and as false as they
Which dwell at Court, for once going that way.
Therefore I suffered this; towards me did run
A thing more strange than on Nile's slime the sun
E'er bred, or all which into Noah's Ark came:
20 A thing, which would have posed Adam to name:
Stranger than seven antiquaries' studies,
Than Afric's monsters, Guiana's rarities,
Stranger than strangers; one, who for a Dane,
In the Danes' Massacre had sure been slain,
If he had lived then; and without help dies,
When next the 'prentices 'gainst strangers rise.
One, whom the watch at noon lets scarce go by,
One, to whom, the examining Justice sure would cry,
'Sir, by your priesthood tell me what you are.'
30 His clothes were strange, though coarse; and black, though
      bare;
Sleeveless his jerkin was, and it had been

Velvet, but 'twas now (so much ground was seen)
Become tufftaffaty; and our children shall
See it plain rash awhile, then naught at all.
This thing hath travelled, and saith, speaks all tongues
And only knoweth what to all states belongs,
Made of th' accents, and best phrase of all these,
He speaks one language; if strange meats displease,
Art can deceive, or hunger force my taste,
40 But pedant's motley tongue, soldier's bombast,
Mountebank's drugtongue, nor the terms of law
Are strong enough preparatives, to draw
Me to bear this, yet I must be content
With his tongue: in his tongue, called compliment:
In which he can win widows, and pay scores,
Make men speak treason, cozen subtlest whores,
Out-flatter favourites, or out-lie either
Jovius, or Surius, or both together.
He names me, and comes to me; I whisper, 'God!
50 How have I sinned, that thy wrath's furious rod,
This fellow, chooseth me?' He sayeth, 'Sir,
I love your judgement; whom do you prefer,
For the best linguist?' And I sillily
Said, that I thought Calepine's Dictionary;
'Nay but of men, most sweet Sir'. Beza then,
Some Jesuits, and two reverend men
Of our two Academies, I named. There
He stopped me, and said; 'Nay, your Apostles were
Good pretty linguists, and so Panurge was;
60 Yet a poor gentleman, all these may pass
By travail.' Then, as if he would have sold
His tongue, he praised it, and such wonders told
That I was fain to say, 'If you had lived, Sir,
Time enough to have been interpreter
To Babel's bricklayers, sure the Tower had stood.'
He adds, 'If of Court life you knew the good,
You would leave loneness.' I said, 'Not alone
My loneness is; but Spartan's fashion,
To teach by painting drunkards, doth not last

70 Now; Aretine's pictures have made few chaste;
No more can princes' Courts, though there be few
Better pictures of vice, teach me virtue';
He, like to a high stretched lute string squeaked, 'O Sir,
'Tis sweet to talk of kings.' 'At Westminster,'
Said I, 'the man that keeps the Abbey tombs,
And for his price doth with whoever comes,
Of all our Harrys, and our Edwards talk,
From king to king and all their kin can walk:
Your ears shall hear naught, but kings; your eyes meet
80 Kings only; The way to it, is King Street.'
He smacked, and cried, 'He's base, mechanic, coarse,
So are all your Englishmen in their discourse.
Are not your Frenchmen neat?' 'Mine? as you see,
I have but one Frenchman, look, he follows me.'
'Certes they are neatly clothed. I of this mind am,
Your only wearing is your grogaram.'
'Not so Sir, I have more.' Under this pitch
He would not fly; I chaffed him; but as itch
Scratched into smart, and as blunt iron ground
90 Into an edge, hurts worse: so, I (fool) found,
Crossing hurt me; to fit my sullenness,
He to another key his style doth dress,
And asks, 'What news?' I tell him of new plays.
He takes my hand, and as a still, which stays
A semi-breve 'twixt each drop, he niggardly,
As loth to enrich me, so tells many a lie,
More than ten Holinsheds, or Halls, or Stows,
Of trivial household trash he knows; he knows
When the Queen frowned, or smiled, and he knows what
100 A subtle statesman may gather of that;
He knows who loves; whom; and who by poison
Hastes to an office's reversion;
He knows who hath sold his land, and now doth beg
A licence, old iron, boots, shoes, and egg-
Shells to transport; shortly boys shall not play
At span-counter, or blow-point, but they pay
Toll to some courtier; and wiser than all us,

He knows what lady is not painted; thus
He with home-meats tries me; I belch, spew, spit,
110   Look pale, and sickly, like a patient; yet
He thrusts on more; and as if he undertook
To say *Gallo-Belgicus* without book
Speaks of all states, and deeds, that have been since
The Spaniards came, to the loss of Amiens.
Like a big wife, at sight of loathed meat,
Ready to travail: so I sigh, and sweat
To hear this Macaron talk: in vain; for yet,
Either my humour, or his own to fit,
He like a privileged spy, whom nothing can
120   Discredit, libels now 'gainst each great man.
He names a price for every office paid;
He saith, our wars thrive ill, because delayed;
That offices are entailed, and that there are
Perpetuities of them, lasting as far
As the last day; and that great officers,
Do with the pirates share, and Dunkirkers.
Who wastes in meat, in clothes, in horse, he notes;
Who loves whores, who boys, and who goats.
I more amazed than Circe's prisoners, when
130   They felt themselves turn beasts, felt myself then
Becoming traitor, and methought I saw
One of our giant Statutes ope his jaw
To suck me in; for hearing him, I found
That as burnt venomed lechers do grow sound
By giving others their sores, I might grow
Guilty, and he free: therefore I did show
All signs of loathing; but since I am in,
I must pay mine, and my forefathers' sin
To the last farthing; therefore to my power
140   Toughly and stubbornly I bear this cross; but the hour
Of mercy now was come; he tries to bring
Me to pay a fine to 'scape his torturing,
And says, 'Sir, can you spare me'; I said, 'Willingly';
'Nay, Sir, can you spare me a crown?' Thankfully I
Gave it, as ransom; but as fiddlers, still,

Though they be paid to be gone, yet needs will
Thrust one more jig upon you; so did he
With his long complimental thanks vex me.
But he is gone, thanks to his needy want,
150 And the prerogative of my crown: scant
His thanks were ended, when I, (which did see
All the Court filled with more strange things than he)
Ran from thence with such or more haste, than one
Who fears more actions, doth make from prison.
   At home in wholesome solitariness
My precious soul began, the wretchedness
Of suitors at Court to mourn, and a trance
Like his, who dreamed he saw hell, did advance
Itself on me, such men as he saw there,
160 I saw at Court, and worse, and more; low fear
Becomes the guilty, not the accuser; then,
Shall I, none's slave, of high-born, or raised men
Fear frowns? And, my mistress Truth, betray thee
To th' huffing braggart, puffed nobility?
No, no, thou which since yesterday hast been
Almost about the whole world, hast thou seen,
O sun, in all thy journey, vanity,
Such as swells the bladder of our Court? I
Think he which made your waxen garden, and
170 Transported it from Italy to stand
With us, at London, flouts our Presence, for
Just such gay painted things, which no sap, nor
Taste have in them, ours are; and natural
Some of the stocks are, their fruits, bastard all.
   'Tis ten a-clock and past; all whom the mews,
Balloon, tennis, diet, or the stews,
Had all the morning held, now the second
Time made ready, that day, in flocks, are found
In the Presence, and I, (God pardon me).
180 As fresh, and sweet their apparels be, as be
The fields they sold to buy them; 'For a King
Those hose are,' cry the flatterers; and bring
Them next week to the theatre to sell;

Wants reach all states; me seems they do as well
At stage, as Court; all are players; whoe'er looks
(For themselves dare not go) o'er Cheapside books,
Shall find their wardrobe's inventory. Now,
The ladies come; as pirates, which do know
That there came weak ships fraught with cochineal,
190 The men board them; and praise, as they think, well,
Their beauties; they the men's wits; both are bought.
Why good wits ne'er wear scarlet gowns, I thought
This cause: these men, men's wits for speeches buy,
And women buy all reds which scarlets dye.
He called her beauty lime-twigs, her hair net;
She fears her drugs ill laid, her hair loose set.
Would not Heraclitus laugh to see Macrine,
From hat, to shoe, himself at door refine,
As if the Presence were a moschite, and lift
200 His skirts and hose, and call his clothes to shrift,
Making them confess not only mortal
Great stains and holes in them, but venial
Feathers and dust, wherewith they fornicate;
And then by Dürer's rules survey the state
Of his each limb, and with strings the odds tries
Of his neck to his leg, and waist to thighs.
So in immaculate clothes, and symmetry
Perfect as circles, with such nicety
As a young preacher at his first time goes
210 To preach, he enters, and a lady which owes
Him not so much as good will, he arrests,
And unto her protests protests protests
So much as at Rome would serve to have thrown
Ten Cardinals into the Inquisition;
And whispered 'By Jesu', so often, that a
Pursuivant would have ravished him away
For saying of our Lady's psalter; but 'tis fit
That they each other plague, they merit it.
But here comes Glorius that will plague them both,
220 Who, in the other extreme, only doth
Call a rough carelessness, good fashion;

Whose cloak his spurs tear; whom he spits on
He cares not, his ill words do no harm
To him; he rusheth in, as if 'Arm, arm,'
He meant to cry; and though his face be as ill
As theirs which in old hangings whip Christ, still
He strives to look worse, he keeps all in awe;
Jests like a licensed fool, commands like law.
 Tired, now I leave this place, and but pleased so
230 As men which from gaols to execution go,
Go through the great chamber (why is it hung
With the seven deadly sins?). Being among
Those Ascaparts, men big enough to throw
Charing Cross for a bar, men that do know
No token of worth, but Queen's man, and fine
Living, barrels of beef, flagons of wine,
I shook like a spied spy. Preachers which are
Seas of wit and arts, you can, then dare,
Drown the sins of this place, for, for me
240 Which am but a scarce brook, it enough shall be
To wash the stains away; though I yet
With Maccabees' modesty, the known merit
Of my work lessen: yet some wise man shall,
I hope, esteem my writs canonical.

Satire 5

Thou shalt not laugh in this leaf, Muse, nor they
Whom any pity warms; he which did lay
Rules to make courtiers, (he being understood
May make good courtiers, but who courtiers good?)
Frees from the sting of jests all who in extreme
Are wretched or wicked: of these two a theme
Charity and liberty give me. What is he
Who officers' rage, and suitors' misery
Can write, and jest? If all things be in all,
10 As I think, since all, which were, are, and shall
Be, be made of the same elements:

Each thing, each thing implies or represents.
Then man is a world; in which, officers
Are the vast ravishing seas; and suitors,
Springs; now full, now shallow, now dry; which, to
That which drowns them, run: these self reasons do
Prove the world a man, in which, officers
Are the devouring stomach, and suitors
The excrements, which they void. All men are dust,
20 How much worse are suitors, who to men's lust
Are made preys. O worse than dust, or worm's meat,
For they do eat you now, whose selves worms shall eat.
They are the mills which grind you, yet you are
The wind which drives them; and a wasteful war
Is fought against you, and you fight it; they
Adulterate law, and you prepare their way
Like wittols; th' issue your own ruin is.
　　Greatest and fairest Empress, know you this?
Alas, no more than Thames' calm head doth know
30 Whose meads her arms drown, or whose corn o'erflow:
You Sir, whose righteousness she loves, whom I
By having leave to serve, am most richly
For service paid, authorized, now begin
To know and weed out this enormous sin.
　　O age of rusty iron! Some better wit
Call it some worse name, if aught equal it;
The Iron Age that was, when justice was sold, now
Injustice is sold dearer far; allow
All demands, fees, and duties; gamesters, anon
40 The money which you sweat, and swear for, is gone
Into other hands: so controverted lands
'Scape, like Angelica, the strivers' hands.
If law be in the judge's heart, and he
Have no heart to resist letter, or fee,
Where wilt thou appeal? power of the courts below
Flow from the first main head, and these can throw
Thee, if they suck thee in, to misery,
To fetters, halters; but if the injury
Steel thee to dare complain, alas, thou go'st

50   Against the stream, when upwards: when thou art most
Heavy and most faint; and in these labours they,
'Gainst whom thou shouldst complain, will in the way
Become great seas, o'er which, when thou shalt be
Forced to make golden bridges, thou shalt see
That all thy gold was drowned in them before;
All things follow their like, only who have may have more.
Judges are gods; he who made and said them so,
Meant not that men should be forced to them to go,
By means of angels; when supplications
60   We send to God, to Dominations,
Powers, Cherubins, and all heaven's courts, if we
Should pay fees as here, daily bread would be
Scarce to kings; so 'tis. Would it not anger
A stoic, a coward, yea a martyr,
To see a pursuivant come in, and call
All his clothes, copes; books, primers; and all
His plate, chalices; and mistake them away,
And ask a fee for coming? Oh, ne'er may
Fair Law's white reverend name be strumpeted,
70   To warrant thefts: she is established
Recorder to Destiny, on earth, and she
Speaks Fate's words, and but tells us who must be
Rich, who poor, who in chairs, who in gaols:
She is all fair, but yet hath foul long nails,
With which she scratcheth suitors; in bodies
Of men, so in law, nails are th' extremities,
So officers stretch to more than Law can do,
As our nails reach what no else part comes to.
Why barest thou to yon officer? Fool, hath he
80   Got those goods, for which erst men bared to thee?
Fool, twice, thrice, thou hast bought wrong, and now
    hungerly
Begg'st right; but that dole comes not till these die.
Thou hadst much, and law's Urim and Thummim try
Thou wouldst for more; and for all hast paper
Enough to clothe all the Great Carrack's pepper.
Sell that, and by that thou much more shalt leese,

Than Haman, when he sold his antiquities.
O wretch that thy fortunes should moralize
Aesop's fables, and make tales, prophecies.
90 Thou'rt the swimming dog whom shadows cozened,
And div'st, near drowning, for what vanished.

Upon Mr Thomas Coryat's Crudities

Oh to what height will love of greatness drive
Thy leavened spirit, sesqui-superlative?
Venice' vast lake thou hadst seen, and wouldst seek then
Some vaster thing, and found'st a courtesan.
That inland sea having discovered well,
A cellar gulf, where one might sail to hell
From Heidelberg, thou longed'st to see; and thou
This book, greater than all, producest now.
Infinite work, which doth so far extend,
10 That none can study it to any end.
'Tis no one thing, it is not fruit nor root;
Nor poorly limited with head or foot.
If man be therefore man, because he can
Reason, and laugh, thy book doth half make man.
One half being made, thy modesty was such,
That thou on th' other half wouldst never touch.
When wilt thou be at full, great lunatic?
Not till thou exceed the world? Canst thou be like
A prosperous nose-born wen, which sometimes grows
20 To be far greater than the mother-nose?
Go then; and as to thee, when thou didst go,
Munster did towns, and Gesner authors show,
Mount now to *Gallo-Belgicus*; appear
As deep a statesman, as a gazetteer.
Homely and familiarly, when thou com'st back,
Talk of *Will Conqueror*, and *Prester Jack*.
Go bashful man, lest here thou blush to look
Upon the progress of thy glorious book,
To which both Indies sacrifices send;

30 The West sent gold, which thou didst freely spend,
   (Meaning to see 't no more) upon the press.
   The East sends hither her deliciousness;
   And thy leaves must embrace what comes from thence,
   The myrrh, the pepper, and the frankincense.
   This magnifies thy leaves; but if they stoop
   To neighbour wares, when merchants do unhoop
   Voluminous barrels; if thy leaves do then
   Convey these wares in parcels unto men;
   If for vast tons of currants, and of figs,
40 Of medicinal and aromatic twigs,
   Thy leaves a better method do provide,
   Divide to pounds, and ounces sub-divide;
   If they stoop lower yet, and vent our wares,
   Home-manufactures, to thick popular fairs;
   If omni-pregnant there, upon warm stalls,
   They hatch all wares for which the buyer calls;
   Then thus thy leaves we justly may commend,
   That they all kind of matter comprehend.
   Thus thou, by means which th'Ancients never took,
50 A pandect makest, and universal book.
   The bravest heroes, for public good
   Scattered in divers lands their limbs and blood.
   Worst malefactors, to whom men are prize,
   Do public good, cut in anatomies;
   So will thy book in pieces; for a lord
   Which casts at portescues, and all the board,
   Provide whole books; each leaf enough will be
   For friends to pass time, and keep company.
   Can all carouse up thee? no, thou must fit
60 Measures; and fill out for the half-pint wit.
   Some shall wrap pills, and save a friend's life so,
   Some shall stop muskets, and so kill a foe.
   Thou shalt not ease the critics of next age
   So much, at once their hunger to assuage.
   Nor shall wit-pirates hope to find thee lie
   All in one bottom, in one library.
   Some leaves may paste strings there in other books,

And so one may, which on another looks,
Pilfer, alas, a little wit from you,
70 But hardly* much; and yet I think this true;
As Sibyl's was, your book is mystical,
For every piece is as much worth as all.
Therefore mine impotency I confess,
The healths which my brain bears must be far less;
Thy giant wit o'erthrows me, I am gone;
And rather than read all, I would read none.

IN EUNDEM MACARONICON

Quot, dos haec, **Linguists** perfetti, *Disticha* fairont,
Tot cuerdos **States-men,** *hic* livre fara *tuus.*
80 Es *sat* a my l'honneur estre hic inteso; Car **I leave**
L'honra, de personne n'estre creduto, *tibi.*

Explicit Joannes Donne.

*I mean from one page which shall paste strings in a book. [Donne's side-note.]

The Progress of the Soul

Infinitati Sacrum

16 AUGUSTI 1601

Metempsychosis

POÊMA SATYRICON

EPISTLE

Others at the porches and entries of their buildings set their
arms; I, my picture; if any colours can deliver a mind
so plain, and flat, and through light as mine. Naturally at
a new author, I doubt, and stick, and do not say quickly,
good. I censure much and tax; and this liberty costs me
more than others, by how much my own things are worse
than others. Yet I would not be so rebellious against
myself, as not to do it, since I love it; nor so unjust to
others, to do it *sine talione*. As long as I give them as
10 good hold upon me, they must pardon me my bitings. I
forbid no reprehender, but him that like the Trent Council
forbids not books, but authors, damning whatever such a
name hath or shall write. None writes so ill, that he gives
not some thing exemplary, to follow, or fly. Now when I
begin this book, I have no purpose to come into any man's
debt; how my stock will hold out I know not; perchance
waste, perchance increase in use; if I do borrow any thing
of antiquity, besides that I make account that I pay it to
posterity, with as much and as good: you shall still find me
20 to acknowledge it, and to thank not him only that hath
digged out treasure for me, but that hath lighted me a candle
to the place. All which I will bid you remember, (for I would
have no such readers as I can teach) is, that the Pytha-
gorean doctrine doth not only carry one soul from man to
man, nor man to beast, but indifferently to plants also: and
therefore you must not grudge to find the same soul in an
emperor, in a post-horse, and in a mushroom, since no

unreadiness in the soul, but an indisposition in the organs
works this. And therefore though this soul could not move
30 when it was a melon, yet it may remember, and now tell me,
at what lascivious banquet it was served. And though it
could not speak, when it was a spider, yet it can remember,
and now tell me, who used it for poison to attain dignity.
However the bodies have dulled her other faculties, her
memory hath ever been her own, which makes me so seriously
deliver you by her relation all her passages from her first
making when she was that apple which Eve eat, to this
time when she is he, whose life you shall find in the end of
this book.

THE PROGRESS OF THE SOUL

FIRST SONG

1

I sing the progress of a deathless soul,
Whom Fate, which God made, but doth not control,
Placed in most shapes; all times before the law
Yoked us, and when, and since, in this I sing.
And the great world to his aged evening,
From infant morn, through manly noon I draw.
What the gold Chaldee, or silver Persian saw,
Greek brass, or Roman iron, is in this one;
A work to outwear Seth's pillars, brick and stone,
10   And (holy writ excepted) made to yield to none.

2

Thee, eye of heaven, this great soul envies not,
By thy male force, is all we have, begot.
In the first east, thou now begin'st to shine,
Suck'st early balm, and island spices there,
And wilt anon in thy loose-reined career
At Tagus, Po, Seine, Thames, and Danow dine,
And see at night thy western land of mine,
Yet hast thou not more nations seen than she,

That before thee, one day began to be,
20 And thy frail light being quenched, shall long, long outlive
    thee.

3
Nor, holy Janus, in whose sovereign boat
The Church, and all the monarchies did float;
That swimming college, and free hospital
Of all mankind, that cage and vivary
Of fowls, and beasts, in whose womb, Destiny
Us, and our latest nephews did instal
(From thence are all derived, that fill this all),
Didst thou in that great stewardship embark
So diverse shapes into that floating park,
30 As have been moved, and informed by this heavenly
    spark.

4
Great Destiny the commissary of God,
That hast marked out a path and period
For every thing; who, where we offspring took,
Our ways and ends seest at one instant; thou
Knot of all causes, thou whose changeless brow
Ne'er smiles nor frowns, O vouch thou safe to look
And show my story, in thy eternal book;
That (if my prayer be fit) I may understand
So much myself, as to know with what hand,
40 How scant, or liberal this my life's race is spanned.

5
To my six lustres almost now outwore,
Except thy book owe me so many more,
Except my legend be free from the lets
Of steep ambition, sleepy poverty,
Spirit-quenching sickness, dull captivity,
Distracting business, and from beauty's nets,
And all that calls from this, and t'other whets,
O let me not launch out, but let me save

Th' expense of brain and spirit; that my grave
50   His right and due, a whole unwasted man may have.

6

But if my days be long, and good enough,
In vain this sea shall enlarge, or enrough
Itself; for I will through the wave, and foam,
And shall in sad lone ways, a lively sprite
Make my dark heavy poem light, and light.
For though through many straits, and lands I roam,
I launch at paradise, and I sail towards home;
The course I there began, shall here be stayed,
Sails hoisted there, struck here, and anchors laid
60   In Thames, which were at Tigris, and Euphrates weighed.

7

For the great soul which here amongst us now
Doth dwell, and moves that hand, and tongue, and brow,
Which as the moon the sea, moves us, to hear
Whose story, with long patience you will long;
(For 'tis the crown, and last strain of my song)
This soul to whom Luther and Mahomet were
Prisons of flesh; this soul which oft did tear,
And mend the wracks of th' Empire, and late Rome,
And lived when every great change did come,
70   Had first in paradise, a low, but fatal room.

8

Yet no low room, nor than the greatest, less,
If (as devout and sharp men fitly guess)
That Cross, our joy, and grief, where nails did tie
That all, which always was all, everywhere,
Which could not sin, and yet all sins did bear;
Which could not die, yet could not choose but die;
Stood in the self same room in Calvary,
Where first grew the forbidden learned tree,
For on that tree hung in security
80   This soul, made by the Maker's will from pulling free.

9

Prince of the orchard, fair as dawning morn,
Fenced with the law, and ripe as soon as born
That apple grew, which this soul did enlive,
Till the then climbing serpent, that now creeps
For that offence, for which all mankind weeps,
Took it, and to her whom the first man did wive
(Whom and her race, only forbiddings drive)
He gave it, she to her husband, both did eat;
So perished the eaters, and the meat:

90   And we (for treason taints the blood) thence die and
      sweat.

10

Man all at once was there by woman slain,
And one by one we 're here slain o'er again
By them. The mother poisoned the well-head,
The daughters here corrupt us, rivulets,
No smallness 'scapes, no greatness breaks their nets,
She thrust us out, and by them we are led
Astray, from turning to whence we are fled.
Were prisoners judges, 'twould seem rigorous,
She sinned, we bear; part of our pain is, thus

100   To love them, whose fault to this painful love yoked us.

11

So fast in us doth this corruption grow,
That now we dare ask why we should be so.
Would God (disputes the curious rebel) make
A law, and would not have it kept? Or can
His creatures' will, cross his? Of every man
For one, will God (and be just) vengeance take?
Who sinned? 'twas not forbidden to the snake
Nor her, who was not then made; nor is 't writ
    That Adam cropped, or knew the apple; yet

110   The worm and she, and he, and we endure for it.

12

But snatch me, heavenly Spirit, from this vain
Reckoning their vanities, less is the gain

Than hazard still, to meditate on ill,
Though with good mind; their reasons, like those toys
Of glassy bubbles, which the gamesome boys
Stretch to so nice a thinness through a quill
That they themselves break, do themselves spill:
Arguing is heretics' game, and exercise
As wrestlers, perfects them; not liberties
120   Of speech, but silence; hands, not tongues, end heresies.

13

Just in that instant when the serpent's gripe,
Broke the slight veins, and tender conduit-pipe,
Through which this soul from the tree's root did draw
Life, and growth to this apple, fled away
This loose soul, old, one and another day.
As lightning, which one scarce dares say, he saw,
'Tis so soon gone, (and better proof the law
Of sense, than faith requires) swiftly she flew
To a dark and foggy plot; her, her fate threw
130   There through th' earth's pores, and in a plant housed her anew.

14

The plant thus abled, to itself did force
A place, where no place was; by nature's course
As air from water, water fleets away
From thicker bodies, by this root thronged so
His spongy confines gave him place to grow,
Just as in our streets, when the people stay
To see the Prince, and have so filled the way
That weasels scarce could pass, when she comes near
They throng and cleave up, and a passage clear,
140   As if, for that time, their round bodies flattened were.

15

His right arm he thrust out towards the east,
Westward his left; th' ends did themselves digest
Into ten lesser strings, these fingers were:
And as a slumberer stretching on his bed,

This way he this, and that way scattered
His other leg, which feet with toes upbear;
Grew on his middle parts, the first day, hair,
To show, that in love's business he should still
A dealer be, and be used well, or ill:
150   His apples kindle, his leaves, force of conception kill.

16

A mouth, but dumb, he hath; blind eyes, deaf ears,
And to his shoulders dangle subtle hairs;
A young Colossus there he stands upright,
And as that ground by him were conquered
A leafy garland wears he on his head
Enclased with little fruits, so red and bright
That for them you would call your love's lips white;
So, of a lone unhaunted place possessed,
Did this soul's second inn, built by the guest,
160   This living buried man, this quiet mandrake, rest.

17

No lustful woman came this plant to grieve,
But 'twas because there was none yet but Eve:
And she (with other purpose) killed it quite;
Her sin had now brought in infirmities,
And so her cradled child, the moist red eyes
Had never shut, nor slept since it saw light,
Poppy she knew, she knew the mandrake's might,
And tore up both, and so cooled her child's blood;
Unvirtuous weeds might long unvexed have stood;
170   But he's short-lived, that with his death can do most
      good.

18

To an unfettered soul's quick nimble haste
Are falling stars, and heart's thoughts, but slow-paced:
Thinner than burnt air flies this soul, and she
Whom four new coming, and four parting suns
Had found, and left the mandrake's tenant, runs
Thoughtless of change, when her firm destiny

Confined, and enjailed her, that seemed so free,
Into a small blue shell, the which a poor
Warm bird o'erspread, and sat still evermore,
180   Till her enclosed child kicked, and picked itself a door.

19

Out crept a sparrow, this soul's moving inn,
On whose raw arms stiff feathers now begin,
As children's teeth through gums, to break with pain,
His flesh is jelly yet, and his bones threads,
All a new downy mantle overspreads,
A mouth he opes, which would as much contain
As his late house, and the first hour speaks plain,
And chirps aloud for meat. Meat fit for men
His father steals for him, and so feeds then
190   One, that within a month, will beat him from his hen.

20

In this world's youth wise nature did make haste,
Things ripened sooner, and did longer last;
Already this hot cock in bush and tree
In field and tent o'erflutters his next hen,
He asks her not, who did so taste, nor when,
Nor if his sister, or his niece she be,
Nor doth she pule for his inconsistancy
If in her sight he change, nor doth refuse
The next that calls; both liberty do use;
200   Where store is of both kinds, both kinds may freely
    choose.

21

Men, till they took laws which made freedom less,
Their daughters, and their sisters did ingress;
Till now unlawful, therefore ill, 'twas not.
So jolly, that it can move, this soul is,
The body so free of his kindnesses,
That self-preserving it hath now forgot,
And slackeneth so the soul's, and body's knot
Which temperance straitens; freely on his she friends

He blood, and spirit, pith, and marrow spends,
210   Ill steward of himself, himself in three years ends.

22

Else might he long have lived; man did not know
Of gummy blood, which doth in holly grow,
How to make bird-lime, nor how to deceive
With feigned calls, hid nets, or enwrapping snare,
The free inhabitants of the pliant air.
Man to beget, and woman to conceive
Asked not of roots, nor of cock-sparrows, leave:
Yet chooseth he, though none of these he fears,
Pleasantly three, than straitened twenty years
220   To live, and to increase his race, himself outwears.

23

This coal with overblowing quenched and dead,
The soul from her too active organs fled
To a brook; a female fish's sandy roe
With the male's jelly, newly leavened was,
For they had intertouched as they did pass,
And one of those small bodies, fitted so,
This soul informed, and abled it to row
Itself with finny oars, which she did fit,
Her scales seemed yet of parchment, and as yet
230   Perchance a fish, but by no name you could call it.

24

When goodly, like a ship in her full trim,
A swan, so white that you may unto him
Compare all whiteness, but himself to none,
Glided along, and as he glided watched,
And with his arched neck this poor fish catched.
It moved with state, as if to look upon
Low things it scorned, and yet before that one
Could think he sought it, he had swallowed clear
This, and much such, and unblamed devoured there
240   All, but who too swift, too great, or well armed were.

25

Now swam a prison in a prison put,
And now this soul in double walls was shut,
Till melted with the swan's digestive fire,
She left her house the fish, and vapoured forth;
Fate not affording bodies of more worth
For her as yet, bids her again retire
To another fish, to any new desire
Made a new prey; for, he that can to none
Resistance make, nor complaint, sure is gone.
250   Weakness invites, but silence feasts oppression.

26

Pace with her native stream, this fish doth keep,
And journeys with her, towards the glassy deep,
But oft retarded, once with a hidden net
Though with great windows, for when need first taught
These tricks to catch food, then they were not wrought
As now, with curious greediness to let
None 'scape, but few, and fit for use to get,
As, in this trap a ravenous pike was ta'en,
Who, though himself distressed, would fain have slain
260   This wretch; so hardly are ill habits left again.

27

Here by her smallness she two deaths o'erpast,
Once innocence 'scaped, and left the oppressor fast;
The net through-swum, she keeps the liquid path,
And whether she leap up sometimes to breathe
And suck in air, or find it underneath,
Or working parts like mills, or limbecks hath
To make the water thin and airlike, faith
Cares not, but safe the place she's come unto
Where fresh, with salt waves meet, and what to do
270   She knows not, but between both makes a board or
        two.

28

So far from hiding her guests, water is
That she shows them in bigger quantities
Than they are. Thus doubtful of her way,
For game and not for hunger a sea pie
Spied through this traitorous spectacle, from high,
The silly fish where it disputing lay,
And to end her doubts and her, bears her away,
Exalted she is, but to the exalter's good,
As are by great ones, men which lowly stood.
280   It's raised, to be the raiser's instrument and food.

29

Is any kind subject to rape like fish?
Ill unto man, they neither do, nor wish:
Fishers they kill not, nor with noise awake,
They do not hunt, nor strive to make a prey
Of beasts, nor their young sons to bear away;
Fowls they pursue not, nor do undertake
To spoil the nests industrious birds do make;
Yet them all these unkind kinds feed upon,
To kill them is an occupation,
290   And laws make Fasts, and Lents for their destruction.

30

A sudden stiff land-wind in that self hour
To sea-ward forced this bird, that did devour
The fish; he cares not, for with ease he flies,
Fat gluttony's best orator: at last
So long he hath flown, and hath flown so fast
That many leagues at sea, now tired he lies,
And with his prey, that till then languished, dies:
The soul's no longer foes, two ways did err,
The fish I follow, and keep no calendar
300   Of the other; he lives yet in some great officer.

31

Into an embryon fish, our soul is thrown,
And in due time thrown out again, and grown

To such vastness as, if unmanacled
From Greece, Morea were, and that by some
Earthquake unrooted, loose Morea swum,
Or seas from Afric's body had severed
And torn the hopeful promontory's head,
This fish would seem these, and, when all hopes fail,
A great ship overset, or without sail
310   Hulling, might (when this was a whelp) be like this
        whale.

32
At every stroke his brazen fins do take,
More circles in the broken sea they make
Than cannons' voices, when the air they tear:
His ribs are pillars, and his high arched roof
Of bark that blunts best steel, is thunder-proof:
Swim in him swallowed dolphins, without fear,
And feel no sides, as if his vast womb were
Some inland sea, and ever as he went
He spouted rivers up, as if he meant
320   To join our seas, with seas above the firmament.

33
He hunts not fish, but as an officer,
Stays in his court, as his own net, and there
All suitors of all sorts themselves enthral;
So on his back lies this whale wantoning,
And in his gulf-like throat, sucks every thing
That passeth near. Fish chaseth fish, and all,
Flyer and follower, in this whirlpool fall;
O might not states of more equality
Consist? and is it of necessity
330   That thousand guiltless smalls, to make one great,
        must die?

34
Now drinks he up seas, and he eats up flocks,
He jostles islands, and he shakes firm rocks.
Now in a roomful house this soul doth float,

And like a Prince she sends her faculties
To all her limbs, distant as provinces.
The sun hath twenty times both crab and goat
Parched, since first launched forth this living boat.
'Tis greatest now, and to destruction
Nearest; there's no pause at perfection.
340   Greatness a period hath, but hath no station.

35
Two little fishes whom he never harmed,
Nor fed on their kind, two not throughly armed
With hope that they could kill him, nor could do
Good to themselves by his death: they did not eat
His flesh, nor suck those oils, which thence outstreat,
Conspired against him, and it might undo
The plot of all, that the plotters were two,
But that they fishes were, and could not speak.
How shall a tyrant wise strong projects break,
350   If wretches can on them the common anger wreak?

36
The flail-finned thresher, and steel-beaked sword-fish
Only attempt to do, what all do wish.
The thresher backs him, and to beat begins;
The sluggard whale yields to oppression,
And to hide himself from shame and danger, down
Begins to sink; the swordfish upward spins,
And gores him with his beak; his staff-like fins,
So well the one, his sword the other plies,
That now a scoff, and prey, this tyrant dies,
360   And (his own dole) feeds with himself all companies.

37
Who will revenge his death? or who will call
Those to account, that thought, and wrought his fall?
The heirs of slain kings, we see are often so
Transported with the joy of what they get,
That they, revenge and obsequies forget,
Nor will against such men the people go,

Because he's now dead, to whom they should show
Love in that act. Some kings by vice being grown
So needy of subjects' love, that of their own
370   They think they lose, if love be to the dead Prince
      shown.

38

This soul, now free from prison, and passion,
Hath yet a little indignation
That so small hammers should so soon down beat
So great a castle. And having for her house
Got the strait cloister of a wretched mouse
(As basest men that have not what to eat,
Nor enjoy aught, do far more hate the great
Than they, who good reposed estates possess)
This soul, late taught that great things might by less
380   Be slain, to gallant mischief doth herself address.

39

Nature's great masterpiece, an elephant,
The only harmless great thing; the giant
Of beasts; who thought, no more had gone, to make one
    wise
But to be just, and thankful, loth to offend,
(Yet nature hath given him no knees to bend)
Himself he up-props, on himself relies,
And foe to none, suspects no enemies,
Still sleeping stood; vexed not his fantasy
Black dreams, like an unbent bow, carelessly
390   His sinewy proboscis did remissly lie:

40

In which as in a gallery this mouse
Walked, and surveyed the rooms of this vast house,
And to the brain, the soul's bedchamber, went,
And gnawed the life cords there; like a whole town
Clean undermined, the slain beast tumbled down,
With him the murderer dies, whom envy sent
To kill, not 'scape; for, only he that meant

To die, did ever kill a man of better room,
And thus he made his foe, his prey, and tomb:
400   Who cares not to turn back, may any whither come.

41
Next, housed this soul a wolf's yet unborn whelp,
Till the best midwife, Nature, gave it help,
 ɔ issue. It could kill, as soon as go:
Abel, as white, and mild as his sheep were,
(Who in that trade of Church, and kingdoms, there
Was the first type) was still infested so
With this wolf, that it bred his loss and woe;
And yet his bitch, his sentinel attends
The flock so near, so well warns and defends,
410   That the wolf, (hopeless else) to corrupt her, intends.

42
He took a course, which since, successfully,
Great men have often taken, to espy
The counsels, or to break the plots of foes,
To Abel's tent he stealeth in the dark,
On whose skirts the bitch slept; ere she could bark,
Attached her with strait grips, yet he called those,
Embracements of love; to love's work he goes
Where deeds move more than words; nor doth she show,
Nor much resist, nor needs he straiten so
420   His prey, for, were she loose, she would nor bark, nor
       go.

43
He hath engaged her; his, she wholly bides;
Who not her own, none other's secrets hides.
If to the flock he come, and Abel there,
She feigns hoarse barkings, but she biteth not,
Her faith is quite, but not her love forgot.
At last a trap, of which some every where
Abel had placed, ends all his loss, and fear,
By the wolf's death; and now just time it was
That a quick soul should give life to that mass
430   Of blood in Abel's bitch, and thither this did pass.

44

Some have their wives, their sisters some begot,
But in the lives of emperors you shall not
Read of a lust the which may equal this;
This wolf begot himself, and finished
What he began alive, when he was dead,
Son to himself, and father too, he is
A riddling lust, for which schoolmen would miss
A proper name. The whelp of both these lay
In Abel's tent, and with soft Moaba,
440   His sister, being young, it used to sport and play.

45

He soon for her too harsh, and churlish grew,
And Abel (the dam dead) would use this new
For the field. Being of two kinds thus made,
He, as his dam, from sheep drove wolves away,
And as his sire, he made them his own prey.
Five years he lived, and cozened with his trade,
Then hopeless that his faults were hid, betrayed
Himself by flight, and by all followed,
From dogs, a wolf; from wolves, a dog he fled;
450   And, like a spy to both sides false, he perished.

46

It quickened next a toyful ape, and so
Gamesome it was, that it might freely go
From tent to tent, and with the children play,
His organs now so like theirs he doth find,
That why he cannot laugh, and speak his mind,
He wonders. Much with all, most he doth stay
With Adam's fifth daughter Siphatecia,
Doth gaze on her, and, where she passeth, pass,
Gathers her fruits, and tumbles on the grass,
460   And wisest of that kind, the first true lover was.

47

He was the first that more desired to have
One than another; first that e'er did crave

Love by mute signs, and had no power to speak;
First that could make love faces, or could do
The vaulter's somersaults, or used to woo
With hoiting gambols, his own bones to break
To make his mistress merry; or to wreak
Her anger on himself. Sins against kind
They easily do, that can let feed their mind
470   With outward beauty, beauty they in boys and beasts
      do find.

48

By this misled, too low things men have proved,
And too high; beasts and angels have been loved;
This ape, though else through-vain, in this was wise,
He reached at things too high, but open way
There was, and he knew not she would say nay;
His toys prevail not, likelier means he tries,
He gazeth on her face with tear-shot eyes,
And up lifts subtly with his russet paw
Her kidskin apron without fear or awe
480   Of Nature; Nature hath no gaol, though she have law.

49

First she was silly and knew not what he meant,
That virtue, by his touches, chafed and spent,
Succeeds an itchy warmth, that melts her quite,
She knew not first, now cares not what he doth,
And willing half and more, more than half loth,
She neither pulls nor pushes, but outright
Now cries, and now repents; when Tethlemite
Her brother, entered, and a great stone threw
After the ape, who, thus prevented, flew.
490   This house thus battered down, the soul possessed
      a new.

50

And whether by this change she lose or win,
She comes out next, where the ape would have gone in.
Adam and Eve had mingled bloods, and now

Like chemics' equal fires, her temperate womb
Had stewed and formed it: and part did become
A spongy liver, that did richly allow,
Like a free conduit, on a high hill's brow,
Life-keeping moisture unto every part,
Part hardened itself to a thicker heart,
500   Whose busy furnaces life's spirits do impart.

51

Another part became the well of sense,
The tender well-armed feeling brain, from whence,
Those sinewy strings which do our bodies tie,
Are ravelled out, and fast there by one end,
Did this soul limbs, these limbs a soul attend,
And now they joined: keeping some quality
Of every past shape, she knew treachery,
Rapine, deceit, and lust, and ills enow
To be a woman. Themech she is now,
510   Sister and wife to Cain, Cain that first did plough.

52

Whoe'er thou be'st that read'st this sullen writ,
Which just so much courts thee, as thou dost it,
Let me arrest thy thoughts, wonder with me,
Why plowing, building, ruling and the rest,
Or most of those arts, whence our lives are blessed,
By cursed Cain's race invented be,
And blessed Seth vexed us with astronomy.
There's nothing simply good, nor ill alone,
Of every quality comparison,
520   The only measure is, and judge, opinion.

Verse Letters

The Storm

TO MR CHRISTOPHER BROOKE

Thou which art I, ('tis nothing to be so)
Thou which art still thyself, by these shalt know
Part of our passage; and, a hand, or eye
By Hilliard drawn, is worth an history,
By a worse painter made; and (without pride)
When by thy judgement they are dignified,
My lines are such: 'tis the pre-eminence
Of friendship only to impute excellence.
England to whom we owe, what we be, and have,
10   Sad that her sons did seek a foreign grave
(For, Fate's, or Fortune's drifts none can soothsay,
Honour and misery have one face and way)
From out her pregnant entrails sighed a wind
Which at th' air's middle marble room did find
Such strong resistance, that itself it threw
Downward again; and so when it did view
How in the port, our fleet dear time did leese,
Withering like prisoners, which lie but for fees,
Mildly it kissed our sails, and, fresh and sweet,
20   As to a stomach starved, whose insides meet,
Meat comes, it came; and swole our sails, when we
So joyed, as Sara her swelling joyed to see.
But 'twas but so kind, as our countrymen,
Which bring friends one day's way, and leave them then.
Then like two mighty kings, which dwelling far
Asunder, meet against a third to war,
The south and west winds joined, and, as they blew,
Waves like a rolling trench before them threw.
Sooner than you read this line, did the gale,
30   Like shot, not feared till felt, our sails assail;
And what at first was called a gust, the same
Hath now a storm's, anon a tempest's name.
Jonas, I pity thee, and curse those men,
Who when the storm raged most, did wake thee then;

Sleep is pain's easiest salve, and doth fulfil
All offices of death, except to kill.
But when I waked, I saw, that I saw not.
I, and the sun, which should teach me had forgot
East, west, day, night, and I could only say,
40   If the world had lasted, now it had been day.
Thousands our noises were, yet we 'mongst all
Could none by his right name, but thunder call:
Lightning was all our light, and it rained more
Than if the sun had drunk the sea before.
Some coffined in their cabins lie, equally
Grieved that they are not dead, and yet must die.
And as sin-burdened souls from graves will creep,
At the last day, some forth their cabins peep:
And tremblingly ask what news, and do hear so,
50   Like jealous husbands, what they would not know.
Some sitting on the hatches, would seem there,
With hideous gazing to fear away fear.
Then note they the ship's sicknesses, the mast
Shaked with this ague, and the hold and waist
With a salt dropsy clogged, and all our tacklings
Snapping, like too high stretched treble strings.
And from our tottered sails, rags drop down so,
As from one hanged in chains, a year ago.
Even our ordnance placed for our defence,
60   Strive to break loose, and 'scape away from thence.
Pumping hath tired our men, and what's the gain?
Seas into seas thrown, we suck in again;
Hearing hath deafed our sailors; and if they
Knew how to hear, there's none knows what to say.
Compared to these storms, death is but a qualm,
Hell somewhat lightsome, and the Bermuda calm.
Darkness, light's elder brother, his birth-right
Claims o'er this world, and to heaven hath chased light.
All things are one, and that one none can be,
70   Since all forms, uniform deformity
Doth cover, so that we, except God say
Another *Fiat*, shall have no more day.

So violent, yet long these furies be,
That though thine absence starve me, I wish not thee.

The Calm

Our storm is past, and that storm's tyrannous rage,
A stupid calm, but nothing it, doth 'suage.
The fable is inverted, and far more
A block afflicts, now, than a stork before.
Storms chafe, and soon wear out themselves, or us;
In calms, heaven laughs to see us languish thus.
As steady as I can wish, that my thoughts were,
Smooth as thy mistress' glass, or what shines there,
The sea is now. And, as those Isles which we
10 Seek, when we can move, our ships rooted be.
As water did in storms, now pitch runs out
As lead, when a fired church becomes one spout.
And all our beauty, and our trim, decays,
Like courts removing, or like ended plays.
The fighting place now seamen's rags supply;
And all the tackling is a frippery.
No use of lanthorns; and in one place lay
Feathers and dust, today and yesterday.
Earth's hollownesses, which the world's lungs are,
20 Have no more wind than the upper vault of air.
We can nor lost friends, nor sought foes recover,
But meteor-like, save that we move not, hover.
Only the calenture together draws
Dear friends, which meet dead in great fishes' jaws:
And on the hatches as on altars lies
Each one, his own priest, and own sacrifice.
Who live, that miracle do multiply
Where walkers in hot ovens, do not die.
If in despite of these, we swim, that hath
30 No more refreshing, than our brimstone bath,
But from the sea, into the ship we turn,
Like parboiled wretches, on the coals to burn.

Like Bajazet encaged, the shepherd's scoff,
Or like slack-sinewed Samson, his hair off,
Languish our ships. Now, as a myriad
Of ants, durst th' Emperor's loved snake invade,
The crawling galleys, sea-gaols, finny chips,
Might brave our pinnaces, now bed-rid ships.
Whether a rotten state, and hope of gain,
40   Or, to disuse me from the queasy pain
Of being beloved, and loving, or the thirst
Of honour, or fair death, out pushed me first,
I lose my end: for here as well as I
A desperate may live, and a coward die.
Stag, dog, and all which from, or towards flies,
Is paid with life, or prey, or doing dies.
Fate grudges us all, and doth subtly lay
A scourge, 'gainst which we all forget to pray,
He that at sea prays for more wind, as well
50   Under the poles may beg cold, heat in hell.
What are we then? How little more alas
Is man now, than before he was! he was
Nothing; for us, we are for nothing fit;
Chance, or ourselves still disproportion it.
We have no power, no will, no sense; I lie,
I should not then thus feel this misery.

To Mr B. B.

Is not thy sacred hunger of science
   Yet satisfied? Is not thy brain's rich hive
   Fulfilled with honey which thou dost derive
From the arts' spirits and their quintessence?
Then wean thyself at last, and thee withdraw
   From Cambridge thy old nurse, and, as the rest,
   Here toughly chew, and sturdily digest
Th' immense vast volumes of our common law;
And begin soon, lest my grief grieve thee too,
10   Which is, that that which I should have begun

In my youth's morning, now late must be done;
And I as giddy travellers must do,
    Which stray or sleep all day, and having lost
    Light and strength, dark and tired must then ride post.

If thou unto thy Muse be married,
    Embrace her ever, ever multiply,
    Be far from me that strange adultery
To tempt thee and procure her widowhead.
My Muse (for I had one,) because I am cold,
20   Divorced herself: the cause being in me,
    That I can take no new in bigamy,
Not my will only but power doth withhold.
Hence comes it, that these rhymes which never had
    Mother, want matter, and they only have
    A little form, the which their father gave;
They are profane, imperfect, oh, too bad
    To be counted children of poetry
    Except confirmed and bishoped by thee.

To Mr C. B.

Thy friend, whom thy deserts to thee enchain,
    Urged by this inexcusable occasion,
    Thee and the saint of his affection
Leaving behind, doth of both wants complain;
And let the love I bear to both sustain
    No blot nor maim by this division,
    Strong is this love which ties our hearts in one,
And strong that love pursued with amorous pain;
But though besides thyself I leave behind
10   Heaven's liberal, and earth's thrice-fairer sun,
    Going to where stern winter aye doth won,
Yet, love's hot fires, which martyr my sad mind,
    Do send forth scalding sighs, which have the art
    To melt all ice, but that which walls her heart.

To Mr S. B.

O thou which to search out the secret parts
   Of the India, or rather paradise
   Of knowledge, hast with courage and advice
Lately launched into the vast sea of arts,
Disdain not in thy constant travailing
   To do as other voyagers, and make
   Some turns into less creeks, and wisely take
Fresh water at the Heliconian spring;
I sing not, siren like, to tempt; for I
   Am harsh; nor as those schismatics with you,
   Which draw all wits of good hope to their crew;
But seeing in you bright sparks of poetry,
   I, though I brought no fuel, had desire
With these articulate blasts to blow the fire.

To Mr E. G.

Even as lame things thirst their perfection, so
The slimy rhymes bred in our vale below,
Bearing with them much of my love and heart,
Fly unto that Parnassus, where thou art.
There thou o'erseest London: here I have been
By staying in London too much overseen.
Now pleasure's dearth our city doth possess,
Our theatres are filled with emptiness;
As lank and thin is every street and way
As a woman delivered yesterday.
Nothing whereat to laugh my spleen espies
But bearbaitings or law exercise.
Therefore I'll leave it, and in the country strive
Pleasure, now fled from London, to retrieve.
Do thou so too: and fill not like a bee
Thy thighs with honey, but as plenteously

As Russian merchants, thyself's whole vessel load,
And then at winter retail it here abroad.
Bless us with Suffolk's sweets; and as that is
20 Thy garden, make thy hive and warehouse this.

To Mr I. L.

Blessed are your north parts, for all this long time
  My sun is with you, cold and dark is our clime;
Heaven's sun, which stayed so long from us this year,
  Stayed in your north (I think) for she was there,
And hither by kind nature drawn from thence,
  Here rages, chafes and threatens pestilence;
Yet I, as long as she from hence doth stay,
  Think this no south, no summer, nor no day.
With thee my kind and unkind heart is run,
10   There sacrifice it to that beauteous sun:
And since thou art in paradise and needst crave
  No joy's addition, help thy friend to save.
So may thy pastures with their flowery feasts,
  As suddenly as lard, fat thy lean beasts;
So may thy woods oft polled, yet ever wear
  A green, and when thee list, a golden hair;
So may all thy sheep bring forth twins; and so
  In chase and race may thy horse all outgo;
So may thy love and courage ne'er be cold;
20   Thy son ne'er ward; thy loved wife ne'er seem old;
But mayst thou wish great things, and them attain,
  As thou tell'st her, and none but her my pain.

To Mr I. L.

Of that short roll of friends writ in my heart
  Which with thy name begins, since their depart,
Whether in the English Provinces they be,
  Or drink of Po, Sequan, or Danuby,

There 's none that sometimes greets us not, and yet
   Your Trent is Lethe; that past, us you forget.
You do not duties of societies,
   If from the embrace of a loved wife you rise,
View your fat beasts, stretched barns, and laboured fields,
10   Eat, play, ride, take all joys which all day yields,
And then again to your embracements go:
   Some hours on us your friends, and some bestow
Upon your Muse, else both we shall repent,
   I that my love, she that her gifts on you are spent.

To Mr R. W.

If, as mine is, thy life a slumber be,
   Seem, when thou read'st these lines, to dream of me,
Never did Morpheus nor his brother wear
   Shapes so like those shapes, whom they would appear,
As this my letter is like me, for it
   Hath my name, words, hand, feet, heart, mind and wit;
It is my deed of gift of me to thee,
   It is my will, myself the legacy.
So thy retirings I love, yea envy,
10   Bred in thee by a wise melancholy,
That I rejoice, that unto where thou art,
   Though I stay here, I can thus send my heart,
As kindly as any enamoured patient
   His picture to his absent love hath sent.

All news I think sooner reach thee than me;
   Havens are heavens, and ships winged angels be,
The which both gospel, and stern threatenings bring;
   Guiana's harvest is nipped in the spring,
I fear; and with us (methinks) Fate deals so
20   As with the Jews' guide God did; he did show
Him the rich land, but barred his entry in:
   Oh, slowness is our punishment and sin.
Perchance, these Spanish business being done,
   Which as the earth between the moon and sun

Eclipse the light which Guiana would give,
  Our discontinued hopes we shall retrieve:
But if (as all th' all must) hopes smoke away,
  Is not almighty virtue an India?
If men be worlds, there is in every one
30   Something to answer in some proportion
All the world's riches: and in good men, this
  Virtue, our form's form and our soul's soul, is.

To Mr R. W.

Kindly I envy thy song's perfection
  Built of all th' elements as our bodies are:
  That little of earth that'is in it, is a fair
Delicious garden where all sweets are sown.
In it is cherishing fire which dries in me
  Grief which did drown me: and half quenched by it
  Are satiric fires which urged me to have writ
In scorn of all: for now I admire thee.
  And as air doth fulfil the hollowness
10   Of rotten walls; so it mine emptiness,
Where tossed and moved it did beget this sound
Which as a lame echo of thine doth rebound.
  Oh, I was dead; but since thy song new life did give,
I recreated even by thy creature live.

To Mr R. W.

Muse not that by thy mind thy body is led:
For by thy mind, my mind's distempered.
So thy care lives long, for I bearing part
It eats not only thine, by my swoll'n heart.
And when it gives us intermission
We take new hearts for it to feed upon.
But as a lay man's genius doth control
Body and mind; the Muse being the soul's soul

Of poets, that methinks should ease our anguish,
10 Although our bodies wither and minds languish.
Write then, that my griefs which thine got may be
Cured by thy charming sovereign melody.

To Mr R. W.

Zealously my Muse doth salute all thee
Inquiring of that mystic trinity
Whereof thou and all to whom heavens do infuse
Like fire, are made; thy body, mind, and Muse.
Dost thou recover sickness, or prevent?
Or is thy mind travailed with discontent?
Or art thou parted from the world and me,
In a good scorn of the world's vanity?
Or is thy devout Muse retired to sing
10 Upon her tender elegiac string?
Our minds part not, join then thy Muse with mine
For mine is barren thus divorced from thine.

To Mr Roland Woodward

Like one who in her third widowhood doth profess
Herself a nun, tied to retiredness,
So affects my Muse now, a chaste fallowness,

Since she to few, yet to too many hath shown
How love-song weeds, and satiric thorns are grown
Where seeds of better arts, were early sown.

Though to use, and love poetry, to me,
Betrothed to no one art, be no adultery;
Omissions of good, ill, as ill deeds be.

10 For though to us it seem, and be light and thin,
Yet in those faithful scales, where God throws in
Men's works, vanity weighs as much as sin.

If our souls have stained their first white, yet we
May clothe them with faith, and dear honesty,
Which God imputes, as native purity.

There is no virtue, but religion:
Wise, valiant, sober, just, are names, which none
Want, which want not vice-covering discretion.

Seek we then ourselves in ourselves; for as
20 Men force the sun with much more force to pass,
By gathering his beams with a crystal glass;

So we, if we into ourselves will turn,
Blowing our sparks of virtue, may outburn
The straw, which doth about our hearts sojourn.

You know, physicians, when they would infuse
Into any oil, the soul of simples, use
Places, where they may lie still warm, to choose.

So works retiredness in us; to roam
Giddily, and be everywhere, but at home,
30 Such freedom doth a banishment become.

We are but farmers of our selves, yet may,
If we can stock our selves, and thrive, uplay
Much, much dear treasure for the great rent day.

Manure thy self then, to thy self be approved,
And with vain outward things be no more moved,
But to know, that I love thee and would be loved.

To Mr T. W.

All hail, sweet poet, more full of more strong fire,
    Than hath or shall enkindle any spirit,
    I loved what nature gave thee, but this merit
Of wit and art I love not but admire;
Who have before or shall write after thee,
Their works, though toughly laboured, will be

Like infancy or age to man's firm stay,
Or early and late twilights to midday.

Men say, and truly, that they better be
10   Which be envied than pitied: therefore I,
Because I wish thee best, do thee envy:
O wouldst thou, by like reason, pity me,
But care not for me, I, that ever was
In Nature's, and in Fortune's gifts, (alas,
  Before thy grace got in the Muses' school)
  A monster and a beggar, am now a fool.

Oh how I grieve, that late born modesty
  Hath got such root in easy waxen hearts,
  That men may not themselves, their own good parts
20 Extol, without suspect of surquedry,
For, but thyself, no subject can be found
Worthy thy quill, nor any quill resound
  Thy worth but thine; how good it were to see
  A poem in thy praise, and writ by thee.

Now if this song be too harsh for rhyme, yet, as
  The painters' bad god made a good devil,
  'Twill be good prose, although the verse be evil,
If thou forget the rhyme as thou dost pass.
Then write, that I may follow, and so be
30 Thy debtor, thy echo, thy foil, thy zany.
  I shall be thought, if mine like thine I shape,
  All the world's lion, though I be thy ape.

To Mr T. W.

At once, from hence, my lines and I depart,
I to my soft still walks, they to my heart;
I to the nurse, they to the child of art;

Yet as a firm house, though the carpenter
Perish, doth stand: as an ambassador
Lies safe, howe'er his king be in danger:

So, though I languish, pressed with melancholy,
My verse, the strict map of my misery,
Shall live to see that, for whose want I die.

10 Therefore I envy them, and do repent,
That from unhappy me, things happy are sent;
Yet as a picture, or bare sacrament,
    Accept these lines, and if in them there be
    Merit of love, bestow that love on me.

To Mr T. W.

Haste thee harsh verse as fast as thy lame measure
    Will give thee leave, to him, my pain and pleasure.
I have given thee, and yet thou art too weak,
    Feet, and a reasoning soul and tongue to speak.
Plead for me, and so by thine and my labour,
    I am thy Creator, thou my Saviour.
Tell him, all questions, which men have defended
    Both of the place and pains of hell, are ended;
And 'tis decreed our hell is but privation
10   Of him, at least in this earth's habitation:
And 'tis where I am, where in every street
    Infections follow, overtake, and meet:
Live I or die, by you my love is sent,
    And you'are my pawns, or else my testament.

To Mr T. W.

Pregnant again with th' old twins hope, and fear,
Oft have I asked for thee, both how and where
Thou wert, and what my hopes of letters were;

As in the streets sly beggars narrowly
Watch motions of the giver's hand and eye,
And evermore conceive some hope thereby.

And now thy alms is given, thy letter is read,
The body risen again, the which was dead,
And thy poor starveling bountifully fed.

10 After this banquet my soul doth say grace,
And praise thee for it, and zealously embrace
Thy love, though I think thy love in this case
 To be as gluttons, which say 'midst their meat,
 They love that best of which they most do eat.

To Sir Henry Goodyer

Who makes the past, a pattern for next year,
 Turns no new leaf, but still the same things reads,
Seen things, he sees again, heard things doth hear,
 And makes his life but like a pair of beads.

A palace, when 'tis that, which it should be,
 Leaves growing, and stands such, or else decays:
But he, which dwells there, is not so; for he
 Strives to urge upward, and his fortune raise;

So had your body her morning, hath her noon,
10 And shall not better; her next change is night:
But her fair larger guest, to whom sun and moon
 Are sparks, and short-lived, claims another right.

The noble soul by age grows lustier,
 Her appetite and her digestion mend,
We must not starve, nor hope to pamper her
 With women's milk, and pap unto the end.

Provide you manlier diet; you have seen
 All libraries, which are schools, camps, and courts;
But ask your garners if you have not been
20 In harvests, too indulgent to your sports.

Would you redeem it? then yourself transplant
   A while from hence. Perchance outlandish ground
Bears no more wit, than ours, but yet more scant
   Are those diversions there, which here abound.

To be a stranger hath that benefit,
   We can beginnings, but not habits choke.
Go; whither? Hence; you get, if you forget;
   New faults, till they prescribe in us, are smoke.

Our soul, whose country's heaven, and God her father,
30   Into this world, corruption's sink, is sent,
Yet, so much in her travail she doth gather,
   That she returns home, wiser than she went;

It pays you well, if it teach you to spare,
   And make you ashamed, to make your hawk's praise yours,
Which when herself she lessens in the air,
   You then first say, that high enough she towers.

However, keep the lively taste you hold
   Of God, love him as now, but fear him more,
And in your afternoons think what you told
40   And promised him, at morning prayer before.

Let falsehood like a discord anger you,
   Else be not froward. But why do I touch
Things, of which none is in your practice new,
   And fables, or fruit-trenchers teach as much;

But thus I make you keep your promise Sir,
   Riding I had you, though you still stayed there,
And in these thoughts, although you never stir,
   You came with me to Mitcham, and are here.

A Letter Written by Sir H. G. and J. D.
alternis vicibus

Since every tree begins to blossom now
Perfuming and enamelling each bough,
Hearts should as well as they, some fruits allow.

For since one old poor sun serves all the rest,
You several suns that warm, and light each breast
Do by that influence all your thoughts digest.

And that you two may so your virtues move,
On better matter than beams from above,
Thus our twin'd souls send forth these buds of love.

10 As in devotions men join both their hands,
We make ours do one act, to seal the bands,
By which we enthral ourselves to your commands.

And each for other's faith and zeal stand bound;
As safe as spirits are from any wound,
So free from impure thoughts they shall be found.

Admit our magic then by which we do
Make you appear to us, and us to you,
Supplying all the Muses in you two.

We do consider no flower that is sweet,
20 *But we your breath in that exhaling meet,*
And as true types of you, them humbly greet.

Here in our nightingales, we hear you sing,
Who so do make the whole year through a spring,
And save us from the fear of autumn's sting.

In Anker's calm face we your smoothness see,
Your minds unmingled, and as clear as she
That keeps untouched her first virginity.

Did all St Edith' Nuns descend again
To honour Polesworth with their cloistered train,
30 Compared with you each would confess some stain.

Or should we more bleed out our thoughts in ink,
No paper (though it would be glad to drink
Those drops) could comprehend what we do think.

For 'twere in us ambition to write
So, that because we two, you two unite,
Our letter should as you, be infinite.

To Sir Henry Wotton

Here's no more news, than virtue, I may as well
Tell you Cadiz' or Saint Michael's tale for news, as tell
That vice doth here habitually dwell.

Yet, as to get stomachs, we walk up and down,
And toil to sweeten rest, so, may God frown,
If, but to loathe both, I haunt Court, or Town.

For here no one is from th' extremity
Of vice, by any other reason free,
But that the next to him, still, is worse than he.

10 In this world's warfare, they whom rugged Fate,
(God's commissary,) doth so throughly hate,
As in the Court's squadron to marshal their state

If they stand armed with silly honesty,
With wishing prayers, and neat integrity,
Like Indian 'gainst Spanish hosts they be.

Suspicious boldness to this place belongs,
And to have as many ears as all have tongues;
Tender to know, tough to acknowledge wrongs.

Believe me Sir, in my youth's giddiest days,
20 When to be like the Court, was a play's praise,
Plays were not so like Courts, as Courts are like plays.

Then let us at these mimic antics jest,
Whose deepest projects, and egregious gests
Are but dull morals of a game at chests.

But now 'tis incongruity to smile,
Therefore I end; and bid farewell a while,
At Court, though from Court, were the better style.

To Sir Henry Wotton

Sir, more than kisses, letters mingle souls;
For, thus friends absent speak. This ease controls
The tediousness of my life: but for these
I could ideate nothing, which could please,
But I should wither in one day, and pass
To a bottle of hay, that am a lock of grass.
Life is a voyage, and in our life's ways
Countries, courts, towns are rocks, or remoras;
They break or stop all ships, yet our state's such,
10   That though than pitch they stain worse, we must touch.
If in the furnace of the even line,
Or under th' adverse icy poles thou pine,
Thou know'st two temperate regions girded in,
Dwell there: But Oh, what refuge canst thou win
Parched in the Court, and in the country frozen?
Shall cities, built of both extremes, be chosen?
Can dung and garlic be a perfume? or can
A scorpion and torpedo cure a man?
Cities are worst of all three; of all three
20   (O knotty riddle) each is worst equally.
Cities are sepulchres; they who dwell there
Are carcases, as if no such there were.
And Courts are theatres, where some men play
Princes, some slaves, all to one end, and of one clay.
The country is a desert, where no good,
Gained (as habits, not born,) is understood.
There men become beasts, and prone to more evils;
In cities blocks, and in a lewd Court, devils.

As in the first Chaos confusedly
30 Each element's qualities were in the other three;
So pride, lust, covetize, being several
To these three places, yet all are in all,
And mingled thus, their issue incestuous.
Falsehood is denizened. Virtue is barbarous.
Let no man say there, 'Virtue's flinty wall
Shall lock vice in me, I'll do none, but know all.'
Men are sponges, which to pour out, receive,
Who know false play, rather than lose, deceive.
For in best understandings, sin began,
40 Angels sinned first, then devils, and then man.
Only perchance beasts sin not; wretched we
Are beasts in all, but white integrity.
I think if men, which in these places live
Durst look for themselves, and themselves retrieve,
They would like strangers greet themselves, seeing then
Utopian youth, grown old Italian.

Be then thine own home, and in thyself dwell;
Inn anywhere, continuance maketh hell.
And seeing the snail, which everywhere doth roam,
50 Carrying his own house still, still is at home,
Follow (for he is easy paced) this snail,
Be thine own palace, or the world 's thy goal.
And in the world's sea, do not like cork sleep
Upon the water's face; nor in the deep
Sink like a lead without a line: but as
Fishes glide, leaving no print where they pass,
Nor making sound, so closely thy course go,
Let men dispute, whether thou breathe, or no.
Only in this one thing, be no Galenist: to make
60 Courts' hot ambitions wholesome, do not take
A dram of country's dullness; do not add
Correctives, but as chemics, purge the bad.
But, Sir, I advise not you, I rather do
Say o'er those lessons, which I learned of you:
Whom, free from German schisms, and lightness
Of France, and fair Italy's faithlessness,

Having from these sucked all they had of worth,
And brought home that faith, which you carried forth,
I throughly love. But if myself, I have won
70 To know my rules, I have, and you have

Donne.

To Sir Henry Wotton, at his going Ambassador to Venice

After those reverend papers, whose soul is
  Our good and great King's loved hand and feared name,
By which to you he derives much of his,
  And (how he may) makes you almost the same,

A taper of his torch, a copy writ
  From his original, and a fair beam
Of the same warm, and dazzling sun, though it
  Must in another sphere his virtue stream:

After those learned papers which your hand
10   Hath stored with notes of use and pleasure too,
From which rich treasury you may command
  Fit matter whether you will write or do:

After those loving papers, where friends send
  With glad grief, to your sea-ward steps, farewell,
Which thicken on you now, as prayers ascend
  To heaven in troops at a good man's passing bell:

Admit this honest paper, and allow
  It such an audience as yourself would ask;
What you must say at Venice this means now,
20   And hath for nature, what you have for task.

To swear much love, not to be changed before
  Honour alone will to your fortune fit;
Nor shall I then honour your fortune, more
  Than I have done your honour wanting it.

But 'tis an easier load (though both oppress)
    To want, than govern greatness, for we are
In that, our own and only business,
    In this, we must for others' vices care;

'Tis therefore well your spirits now are placed
30   In their last furnace, in activity;
Which fits them (schools and Courts and wars o'erpast)
    To touch and test in any best degree.

For me, (if there be such a thing as I)
    Fortune (if there be such a thing as she)
Spies that I bear so well her tyranny,
    That she thinks nothing else so fit for me;

But though she part us, to hear my oft prayers
    For your increase, God is as near me here;
And to send you what I shall beg, his stairs
40   In length and ease are alike everywhere.

H. W. in Hibernia Belligeranti

Went you to conquer? and have so much lost
Yourself, that what in you was best and most,
Respective friendship, should so quickly die?
In public gain my share' is not such that I
Would lose your love for Ireland: better cheap
I pardon death (who though he do not reap
Yet gleans he many of our friends away)
Than that your waking mind should be a prey
To lethargies. Let shot, and bogs, and skeins
10 With bodies deal, as fate bids or restrains;
Ere sicknesses attack, young death is best,
Who pays before his death doth 'scape arrest.
Let not your soul (at first with graces filled,
And since, and thorough crooked limbecs, stilled
In many schools and Courts, which quicken it,)
Itself unto the Irish negligence submit.

I ask not laboured letters which should wear
Long papers out: nor letters which should fear
Dishonest carriage; or a seer's art,
20 Nor such as from the brain come, but the heart.

To Sir Edward Herbert, at Juliers

Man is a lump, where all beasts kneaded be,
   Wisdom makes him an ark where all agree;
The fool, in whom these beasts do live at jar,
   Is sport to others, and a theatre,
Nor 'scapes he so, but is himself their prey;
   All which was man in him, is eat away,
And now his beasts on one another feed,
   Yet couple in anger, and new monsters breed;
How happy is he, which hath due place assigned
10   To his beasts, and disafforested his mind!
Empaled himself to keep them out, not in;
   Can sow, and dares trust corn, where they have been;
Can use his horse, goat, wolf, and every beast,
   And is not ass himself to all the rest.
Else, man not only is the herd of swine,
   But he's those devils too, which did incline
Them to a headlong rage, and made them worse:
   For man can add weight to heaven's heaviest curse.
As souls (they say) by our first touch, take in
20   The poisonous tincture of original sin,
So, to the punishments which God doth fling,
   Our apprehension contributes the sting.
To us, as to his chickens, he doth cast
   Hemlock, and we as men, his hemlock taste.
We do infuse to what he meant for meat,
   Corrosiveness, or intense cold or heat.
For, God no such specific poison hath
   As kills we know not how; his fiercest wrath
Hath no antipathy, but may be good
30   At least for physic, if not for our food.

Thus man, that might be his pleasure, is his rod,
   And is his devil, that might be his God.
Since then our business is, to rectify
   Nature, to what she was, we are led awry
By them, who man to us in little show,
   Greater than due, no form we can bestow
On him; for man into himself can draw
   All, all his faith can swallow, or reason chaw.
All that is filled, and all that which doth fill,
40   All the round world, to man is but a pill;
In all it works not, but it is in all
   Poisonous, or purgative, or cordial,
For, knowledge kindles calentures in some,
   And is to others icy opium.
As brave as true, is that profession then
   Which you do use to make; that you know man.
This makes it credible, you have dwelt upon
   All worthy books, and now are such a one.
Actions are authors, and of those in you
50   Your friends find every day a mart of new.

To Mrs M. H.

Mad paper stay, and grudge not here to burn
   With all those sons whom my brain did create,
At least lie hid with me, till thou return
   To rags again, which is thy native state.

What though thou have enough unworthiness
   To come unto great place as others do,
That's much; emboldens, pulls, thrusts I confess,
   But 'tis not all, thou shouldst be wicked too.

And, that thou canst not learn, or not of me;
10   Yet thou wilt go; go, since thou goest to her
Who lacks but faults to be a prince, for she,
   Truth, whom they dare not pardon, dares prefer.

But when thou com'st to that perplexing eye
    Which equally claims love and reverence,
Thou wilt not long dispute it, thou wilt die;
    And, having little now, have then no sense.

Yet when her warm redeeming hand, which is
    A miracle; and made such to work more,
Doth touch thee, sapless leaf, thou grow'st by this
20   Her creature; glorified more than before.

Then as a mother which delights to hear
    Her early child mis-speak half-uttered words,
Or, because majesty doth never fear
    Ill or bold speech, she audience affords.

And then, cold speechless wretch, thou diest again,
    And wisely; what discourse is left for thee?
From speech of ill, and her thou must abstain,
    And is there any good which is not she?

Yet mayst thou praise her servants, though not her,
30   And wit, and virtue, and honour her attend,
And since they are but her clothes, thou shalt not err
    If thou her shape and beauty and grace commend.

Who knows thy destiny? when thou hast done,
    Perchance her cabinet may harbour thee,
Whither all noble ambitious wits do run,
    A nest almost as full of good as she.

When thou art there, if any, whom we know,
    Were saved before, and did that heaven partake,
When she revolves his papers, mark what show
40   Of favour, she, alone, to them doth make.

Mark, if to get them, she o'erskip the rest,
    Mark, if she read them twice, or kiss the name;
Mark, if she do the same that they protest,
    Mark, if she mark whether her woman came.

Mark, if slight things be objected, and o'erblown.
  Mark, if her oaths against him be not still
Reserved, and that she grieves she's not her own,
  And chides the doctrine that denies freewill.

I bid thee not do this to be my spy;
50   Nor to make myself her familiar;
But so much I do love her choice, that I
  Would fain love him that shall be loved of her.

To the Countess of Bedford at New Year's Tide

This twilight of two years, not past nor next,
  Some emblem is of me, or I of this,
Who (meteor-like, of stuff and form perplexed,
  Whose what, and where, in disputation is,)
  If I should call me anything, should miss.

I sum the years, and me, and find me not
  Debtor to th' old, nor creditor to the new,
That cannot say, my thanks I have forgot,
  Nor trust I this with hopes, and yet scarce true
10   This bravery is, since these times showed me you.

In recompense I would show future times
  What you were, and teach them to urge towards such,
Verse embalms virtue; and tombs, or thrones of rhymes,
  Preserve frail transitory fame, as much
  As spice doth bodies from corrupt air's touch.

Mine are short-lived; the tincture of your name
  Creates in them, but dissipates as fast
New spirits; for, strong agents with the same
  Force that doth warm and cherish, us do waste;
20   Kept hot with strong extracts, no bodies last:

So, my verse built of your just praise, might want
  Reason and likelihood, the firmest base,
And made of miracle, now faith is scant,

Will vanish soon, and so possess no place,
    And you, and it, too much grace might disgrace.

When all (as truth commands assent) confess
    All truth of you, yet they will doubt how I
One corn of one low anthill's dust, and less,
    Should name, know, or express a thing so high,
30   And not an inch, measure infinity.

I cannot tell them, nor myself, nor you,
    But leave, lest truth be endangered by my praise,
And turn to God, who knows I think this true,
    And useth oft, when such a heart mis-says,
    To make it good, for, such a praiser prays.

He will best teach you, how you should lay out
    His stock of beauty, learning, favour, blood,
He will perplex security with doubt,
    And clear those doubts, hide from you, and show you
        good,
40   And so increase your appetite and food;

He will teach you, that good and bad have not
    One latitude in cloisters, and in Court,
Indifferent there the greatest space hath got,
    Some pity is not good there, some vain disport,
    On this side sin, with that place may comport.

Yet he, as he bounds seas, will fix your hours,
    Which pleasure, and delight may not ingress,
And though what none else lost, be truliest yours,
    He will make you, what you did not, possess,
50   By using others', not vice, but weakness.

He will make you speak truths, and credibly,
    And make you doubt, that others do not so:
He will provide you keys, and locks, to spy,
    And 'scape spies, to good ends, and he will show
    What you may not acknowledge, what not know.

For your own conscience, he gives innocence,
    But for your fame, a discreet wariness,
And though to 'scape, than to revenge offence
    Be better, he shows both, and to repress
60   Joy, when your state swells, sadness when 'tis less.

From need of tears he will defend your soul,
    Or make a rebaptizing of one tear;
He cannot, (that 's, he will not) dis-enrol
    Your name; and when with active joy we hear
    This private gospel, then 'tis our New Year.

To the Countess of Bedford

Honour is so sublime perfection,
And so refined; that when God was alone
And creatureless at first, himself had none;

But as of the elements, these which we tread,
Produce all things with which we'are joyed or fed,
And, those are barren both above our head:

So from low persons doth all honour flow;
Kings, whom they would have honoured, to us show,
And but direct our honour, not bestow.

10   For when from herbs the pure parts must be won
From gross, by stilling, this is better done
By despised dung, than by the fire or sun.

Care not then, Madam, how low your praisers lie;
In labourers' ballad, oft more piety
God finds, than in *Te Deum*'s melody.

And, ordnance raised on towers so many mile
Send not their voice, nor last so long a while
As fires from th' earth's low vaults in Sicil Isle.

Should I say I lived darker than were true,
20   Your radiation can all clouds subdue;
But one, 'tis best light to contemplate you.

You, for whose body God made better clay,
Or took soul's stuff such as shall late decay,
Or such as needs small change at the last day.

This, as an amber drop enwraps a bee,
Covering discovers your quick soul; that we
May in your through-shine front your heart's thoughts see.

You teach (though we learn not) a thing unknown
To our late times, the use of specular stone,
30   Through which all things within without were shown.

Of such were temples; so and of such you are;
Being and seeming is your equal care,
And virtue's whole sum is but know and dare.

But as our souls of growth and souls of sense
Have birthright of our reason's soul, yet hence
They fly not from that, nor seek precedence:

Nature's first lesson, so, discretion,
Must not grudge zeal a place, nor yet keep none,
Not banish itself, nor religion.

40   Discretion is a wiseman's soul, and so
Religion is a Christian's, and you know
How these are one, her *yea*, is not her *no*.

Nor may we hope to solder still and knit
These two, and dare to break them; nor must wit
Be colleague to religion, but be it.

In those poor types of God (round circles) so
Religions' types, the pieceless centres flow,
And are in all the lines which all ways go.

If either ever wrought in you alone
50   Or principally, then religion
Wrought your ends, and your ways discretion.

Go thither still, go the same way you went,
Who so would change, do covet or repent;
Neither can reach you, great and innocent.

To the Countess of Bedford

Madam,
Reason is our soul's left hand, Faith her right,
  By these we reach divinity, that's you;
Their loves, who have the blessing of your sight,
  Grew from their reason, mine from fair faith grew.

But as, although a squint lefthandedness
  Be ungracious, yet we cannot want that hand,
So would I, not to increase, but to express
  My faith, as I believe, so understand.

Therefore I study you first in your Saints,
10   Those friends, whom your election glorifies,
Then in your deeds, accesses, and restraints,
  And what you read, and what yourself devise.

But soon, the reasons why you are loved by all,
  Grow infinite, and so pass reason's reach,
Then back again to implicit faith I fall,
  And rest on what the catholic voice doth teach;

That you are good: and not one heretic
  Denies it: if he did, yet you are so.
For, rocks, which high-topped and deep-rooted stick,
20   Waves wash, not undermine, nor overthrow.

In everything there naturally grows
  A balsamum to keep it fresh, and new,
If 'twere not injured by extrinsic blows;
  Your birth and beauty are this balm in you.

But you of learning and religion,
  And virtue, and such ingredients, have made
A mithridate, whose operation
  Keeps off, or cures what can be done or said.

Yet, this is not your physic, but your food,
30   A diet fit for you; for you are here
The first good angel, since the world's frame stood,
    That ever did in woman's shape appear.

Since you are then God's masterpiece, and so
    His factor for our loves; do as you do,
Make your return home gracious; and bestow
    This life on that; so make one life of two.
      For so God help me, I would not miss you there
      For all the good which you can do me here.

To the Countess of Bedford

BEGUN IN FRANCE BUT NEVER PERFECTED

Though I be dead, and buried, yet I have
    (Living in you,) Court enough in my grave,
As oft as there I think myself to be,
    So many resurrections waken me.
That thankfulness your favours have begot
    In me, embalms me, that I do not rot.
This season as 'tis Easter, as 'tis spring,
    Must both to growth and to confession bring
My thoughts disposed unto your influence, so,
10   These verses bud, so these confessions grow;
First I confess I have to others lent
    Your stock, and over prodigally spent
Your treasure, for since I had never known
    Virtue or beauty, but as they are grown
In you, I should not think or say they shine,
    (So as I have) in any other mine;
Next I confess this my confession,
    For, 'tis some fault thus much to touch upon
Your praise to you, where half rights seem too much,
20   And make your mind's sincere complexion blush.
Next I confess my impenitence, for I
    Can scarce repent my first fault, since thereby

Remote low spirits, which shall ne'er read you,
  May in less lessons find enough to do,
By studying copies, not originals,
    Desunt caetera.

To the Countess of Bedford

To have written then, when you writ, seemed to me
  Worst of spiritual vices, simony,
And not to have written then, seems little less
  Than worst of civil vices, thanklessness.
In this, my debt I seemed loth to confess,
  In that, I seemed to shun beholdingness.
But 'tis not so, nothings, as I am, may
  Pay all they have, and yet have all to pay.
Such borrow in their payments, and owe more
10 By having leave to write so, than before.
Yet since rich mines in barren grounds are shown,
  May not I yield (not gold) but coal or stone?
Temples were not demolished, though profane:
  Here Peter Jove's, there Paul hath Dian's fane.
So whether my hymns you admit or choose,
  In me you have hallowed a pagan Muse,
And denizened a stranger, who mistaught
  By blamers of the times they marred, hath sought
Virtues in corners, which now bravely do
20 Shine in the world's best part, or all it; you.
I have been told, that virtue in courtiers' hearts
  Suffers an ostracism, and departs.
Profit, ease, fitness, plenty, bid it go,
  But whither, only knowing you, I know;
Your (or you) virtue, two vast uses serves,
  It ransoms one sex, and one Court preserves;
There's nothing but your worth, which being true,
  Is known to any other, not to you:
And you can never know it; to admit
30 No knowledge of your worth, is some of it.

But since to you, your praises discords be,
   Stoop others' ills to meditate with me.
Oh! to confess we know not what we should,
   Is half excuse; we know not what we would.
Lightness depresseth us, emptiness fills,
   We sweat and faint, yet still go down the hills;
As new philosophy arrests the sun,
   And bids the passive earth about it run,
So we have dulled our mind, it hath no ends;
40   Only the body's busy, and pretends;
As dead low earth eclipses and controls
   The quick high moon: so doth the body, souls.
In none but us, are such mixed engines found,
   As hands of double office: for, the ground
We till with them; and them to heaven we raise;
   Who prayerless labours, or, without this, prays,
Doth but one half, that's none; he which said, *Plough*
   And look not back, to look up doth allow.
Good seed degenerates, and oft obeys
50   The soil's disease, and into cockle strays.
Let the mind's thoughts be but transplanted so,
   Into the body, and bastardly they grow.
What hate could hurt our bodies like our love?
   We, but no foreign tyrants could, remove
These not engraved, but inborn dignities
   Caskets of souls; temples, and palaces:
For, bodies shall from death redeemed be,
   Souls but preserved, not naturally free.
As men to our prisons, new souls to us are sent,
60   Which learn vice there, and come in innocent.
First seeds of every creature are in us,
   Whate'er the world hath bad, or precious,
Man's body can produce, hence hath it been
   That stones, worms, frogs, and snakes in man are seen:
But who e'er saw, though nature can work so,
   That pearl, or gold, or corn in man did grow?
We' have added to the world Virginia, and sent
   Two new stars lately to the firmament;

Why grudge we us (not heaven) the dignity
70   T' increase with ours, those fair souls' company?
But I must end this letter, though it do
    Stand on two truths, neither is true to you.
Virtue hath some perverseness; for she will
    Neither believe her good, nor others' ill.
Even in you, virtue's best paradise,
    Virtue hath some, but wise degrees of vice.
Too many virtues, or too much of one
    Begets in you unjust suspicion.
And ignorance of vice, makes virtue less,
80   Quenching compassion of our wretchedness.
But these are riddles; some aspersion
    Of vice becomes well some complexion.
Statesmen purge vice with vice, and may corrode
    The bad with bad, a spider with a toad:
For so, ill thralls not them, but they tame ill
    And make her do much good against her will,
But in your commonwealth, or world in you,
    Vice hath no office, or good work to do.
Take then no vicious purge, but be content
90   With cordial virtue, your known nourishment.

To the Countess of Bedford

Madam,
You have refined me, and to worthiest things
    (Virtue, art, beauty, fortune,) now I see
Rareness, or use, not nature value brings;
    And such, as they are circumstanced, they be.
      Two ills can ne'er perplex us, sin to excuse;
      But of two good things, we may leave and choose.

Therefore at Court, which is not virtue's clime,
    (Where a transcendent height, (as, lowness me)
Makes her not be, or not show) all my rhyme
10   Your virtues challenge, which there rarest be;

For, as dark texts need notes: there some must be
To usher virtue, and say, *This is she.*

So in the country is beauty; to this place
   You are the season (Madam) you the day,
'Tis but a grave of spices, till your face
   Exhale them, and a thick close bud display.
      Widowed and reclused else, her sweets she enshrines
      As China, when the sun at Brazil dines.

Out from your chariot, morning breaks at night,
20   And falsifies both computations so;
Since a new world doth rise here from your light,
   We your new creatures, by new reckonings go.
      This shows that you from nature loathly stray,
      That suffer not an artificial day.

In this you have made the Court the antipodes,
   And willed your delegate, the vulgar sun,
To do profane autumnal offices,
   Whilst here to you, we sacrificers run;
      And whether priests, or organs, you we obey,
30   We sound your influence, and your dictates say.

Yet to that deity which dwells in you,
   Your virtuous soul, I now not sacrifice;
These are petitions and not hymns; they sue
   But that I may survey the edifice.
      In all religions as much care hath been
      Of temples' frames, and beauty, as rites within.

As all which go to Rome, do not thereby
   Esteem religions, and hold fast the best,
But serve discourse, and curiosity,
40   With that which doth religion but invest,
      And shun th' entangling labyrinths of schools,
      And make it wit, to think the wiser fools:

So in this pilgrimage I would behold
   You as you'are virtue's temple, not as she,

What walls of tender crystal her enfold,
  What eyes, hands, bosom, her pure altars be;
    And after this survey, oppose to all
    Babblers of chapels, you th' Escurial.

Yet not as consecrate, but merely as fair,
50   On these I cast a lay and country eye.
Of past and future stories, which are rare,
  I find you all record, all prophecy.
    Purge but the book of Fate, that it admit
    No sad nor guilty legends, you are it.

If good and lovely were not one, of both
  You were the transcript, and original,
The elements, the parent, and the growth,
  And every piece of you, is both their all:
    So entire are all your deeds, and you, that you
60   Must do the same thing still; you cannot two.

But these (as nice thin school divinity
  Serves heresy to further or repress)
Taste of poetic rage, or flattery,
  And need not, where all hearts one truth profess;
    Oft from new proofs, and new phrase, new doubts grow,
    As strange attire aliens the men we know.

Leaving then busy praise, and all appeal
  To higher courts, sense's decree is true,
The mine, the magazine, the commonweal,
70   The story of beauty, in Twicknam is, and you.
    Who hath seen one, would both; as, who had been
    In Paradise, would seek the cherubin.

To the Lady Bedford

You that are she and you, that's double she,
  In her dead face, half of yourself shall see;
She was the other part, for so they do
  Which build them friendships, become one of two;

So two, that but themselves no third can fit,
    Which were to be so, when they were not yet.
Twins, though their birth Cusco, and Musco take,
    As divers stars one constellation make,
Paired like two eyes, have equal motion, so
10   Both but one means to see, one way to go;
Had you died first, a carcase she had been;
    And we your rich tomb in her face had seen;
She like the soul is gone, and you here stay,
    Not a live friend; but th' other half of clay;
And since you act that part, as men say, 'Here
    Lies such a Prince', when but one part is there,
And do all honour and devotion due
    Unto the whole, so we all reverence you;
For such a friendship who would not adore
20   In you, who are all what both was before,
Not all, as if some perished by this,
    But so, as all in you contracted is;
As of this all, though many parts decay,
    The pure which elemented them shall stay;
And though diffused, and spread in infinite,
    Shall recollect, and in one all unite:
So madam, as her soul to heaven is fled,
    Her flesh rests in the earth, as in a bed;
Her virtues do, as to their proper sphere,
30   Return to dwell with you, of whom they were;
As perfect motions are all circular,
    So they to you, their sea, whence less streams are;
She was all spices, you all metals; so
    In you two we did both rich Indies know;
And as no fire, nor rust can spend or waste
One dram of gold, but what was first shall last,
Though it be forced in water, earth, salt, air,
    Expansed in infinite, none will impair;
So, to yourself you may additions take,
40   But nothing can you less, or changed make.
Seek not in seeking new, to seem to doubt,
    That you can match her, or not be without;

But let some faithful book in her room be,
   Yet but of Judith no such book as she.

Epitaph on Himself

TO THE COUNTESS OF BEDFORD

Madam,
That I might make your cabinet my tomb,
   And for my fame which I love next my soul,
Next to my soul provide the happiest room,
   Admit to that place this last funeral scroll.
      Others by wills give legacies, but I
      Dying, of you do beg a legacy.

OMNIBUS

My fortune and my choice this custom break,
When we are speechless grown, to make stones speak,
Though no stone tell thee what I was, yet thou
In my grave's inside seest what thou art now:
Yet thou'art not yet so good, till death us lay
To ripe and mellow here, we are stubborn clay.
Parents make us earth, and souls dignify
Us to be glass; here to grow gold we lie.
Whilst in our souls sin bred and pampered is,
Our souls become worm-eaten carcases;
So we ourselves miraculously destroy.
Here bodies with less miracle enjoy
Such privileges, enabled here to scale
Heaven, when the trumpet's air shall them exhale.
Hear this, and mend thyself, and thou mend'st me,
By making me being dead, do good to thee,
   And think me well composed, that I could now
   A last-sick hour to syllables allow.

A Letter to the Lady Carey, and
Mistress Essex Rich, from Amiens

Madame,
Here, where by all, all saints invoked are
T'were too much schism to be singular,
And 'gainst a practice general to war;

Yet, turning to saints, should my humility
To other saint, than you, directed be,
That were to make my schism heresy.

Nor would I be a convertite so cold
As not to tell it; if this be too bold,
Pardons are in this market cheaply sold.

10 Where, because faith is in too low degree,
I thought it some apostleship in me,
To speak things which by faith alone I see:

That is, of you; who are a firmament
Of virtues, where no one is grown, nor spent;
They'are your materials, not your ornament.

Others, whom we call virtuous, are not so
In their whole substance, but their virtues grow
But in their humours, and at seasons show.

For when through tasteless flat humility,
20 In dough-baked men, some harmlessness we see,
'Tis but his phlegm that's virtuous, and not he.

So is the blood sometimes; who ever ran
To danger unimportuned, he was then
No better than a sanguine virtuous man.

So cloistral men who in pretence of fear,
All contributions to this life forbear,
Have virtue in melancholy, and only there.

Spiritual choleric critics, which in all
Religions, find faults, and forgive no fall,
30   Have, through this zeal, virtue, but in their gall.

We'are thus but parcel-gilt; to gold we'are grown,
When virtue is our soul's complexion;
Who knows his virtue's name, or place, hath none.

Virtue is but aguish, when 'tis several;
By'occasion waked, and circumstantial;
True virtue is soul, always in all deeds all.

This virtue, thinking to give dignity
To your soul, found there no infirmity;
For your soul was as good virtue as she.

40   She therefore wrought upon that part of you,
Which is scarce less than soul, as she could do,
And so hath made your beauty virtue too;

Hence comes it, that your beauty wounds not hearts
As others, with profane and sensual darts,
But, as an influence, virtuous thoughts imparts.

But if such friends, by the'honour of your sight
Grow capable of this so great a light,
As to partake your virtues, and their might,

What must I think that influence must do,
50   Where it finds sympathy, and matter too,
Virtue, and beauty, of the same stuff, as you:

Which is, your noble worthy sister; she,
Of whom, if what in this my ecstasy
And revelation of you both, I see,

I should write here, as in short galleries
The master at the end large glasses ties,
So to present the room twice to our eyes,

So I should give this letter length, and say
That which I said of you, there is no way
60   From either, but by th' other, not to stray.

May therefore this be'enough to testify
My true devotion, free from flattery.
He that believes himself, doth never lie.

To the Honourable lady
 the lady Carew.

To the Countess of Huntingdon

Madam,
Man to God's image, Eve, to man's was made,
 Nor find we that God breathed a soul in her,
Canons will not Church functions you invade,
 Nor laws to civil office you prefer.

Who vagrant transitory comets sees,
 Wonders, because they are rare; but a new star
Whose motion with the firmament agrees,
 Is miracle; for, there no new things are;

In woman so perchance mild innocence
10 A seldom comet is, but active good
A miracle, which reason 'scapes, and sense;
 For, art and nature this in them withstood.

As such a star, the Magi led to view
 The manger-cradled infant, God below:
By virtue's beams by fame derived from you,
 May apt souls, and the worst may, virtue know.

If the world's age, and death be argued well
 By the sun's fall, which now towards earth doth bend,
Then we might fear that virtue, since she fell
20 So low as woman, should be near her end.

But she's not stooped, but raised; exiled by men
 She fled to heaven, that's heavenly things, that's you,
She was in all men, thinly scattered then,
 But now amassed, contracted in a few.

She gilded us: but you are gold, and she;
   Us she informed, but transubstantiates you;
Soft dispositions which ductile be,
   Elixir-like, she makes not clean, but new.

Though you a wife's and mother's name retain,
30   'Tis not as woman, for all are not so,
But virtue having made you virtue, is fain
   To adhere in these names, her and you to show,

Else, being alike pure, we should neither see,
   As, water being into air rarefied,
Neither appear, till in one cloud they be,
   So, for our sakes you do low names abide;

Taught by great constellations, which being framed
   Of the most stars, take low names, Crab, and Bull,
When single planets by the gods are named,
40   You covet not great names, of great things full.

So you, as woman, one doth comprehend,
   And in the veil of kindred others see;
To some ye are revealed, as in a friend,
   And as a virtuous prince far off, to me.

To whom, because from you all virtues flow,
   And 'tis not none, to dare contemplate you,
I, which do so, as your true subject owe
Some tribute for that, so these lines are due.

If you can think these flatteries, they are,
50   For then your judgement is below my praise,
If they were so, oft, flatteries work as far,
   As counsels, and as far th' endeavour raise.

So my ill reaching you might there grow good,
   But I remain a poisoned fountain still;
But not your beauty, virtue, knowledge, blood
   Are more above all flattery, than my will.

And if I flatter any, 'tis not you
  But my own judgement, who did long ago
Pronounce, that all these praises should be true,
60 And virtue should your beauty, and birth outgrow.

Now that my prophecies are all fulfilled,
  Rather than God should not be honoured too,
And all these gifts confessed, which he instilled,
  Yourself were bound to say that which I do.

So I, but your recorder am in this,
  Or mouth, or speaker of the universe,
A ministerial notary, for 'tis
  Not I, but you and fame, that make this verse;

I was your prophet in your younger days,
70 And now your chaplain, God in you to praise.

To the Countess of Huntingdon

That unripe side of earth, that heavy clime
That gives us man up now, like Adam's time
Before he ate; man's shape, that would yet be
(Knew they not it, and feared beasts' company)
So naked at this day, as though man there
From Paradise so great a distance were,
As yet the news could not arrived be
Of Adam's tasting the forbidden tree;
Deprived of that free state which they were in,
10 And wanting the reward, yet bear the sin.
    But, as from extreme heights who downward looks,
Sees men at children's shapes, rivers at brooks,
And loseth younger forms; so, to your eye
These (Madam) that without your distance lie,
Must either mist, or nothing seem to be,
Who are at home but wit's mere *atomi*.
But, I who can behold them move, and stay,
Have found myself to you, just their midway;

And now must pity them; for, as they do
20 Seem sick to me, just so must I to you.
    Yet neither will I vex your eyes to see
A sighing ode, nor cross-armed elegy.
I come not to call pity from your heart,
Like some white-livered dotard that would part
Else from his slippery soul with a faint groan,
And faithfully, (without you smiled) were gone.
I cannot feel the tempest of a frown,
I may be raised by love, but not thrown down.
Though I can pity those sigh twice a day,
30 I hate that thing whispers itself away.
Yet since all love is fever, who to trees
Doth talk, doth yet in love's cold ague freeze.
'Tis love, but, with such fatal weakness made,
That it destroys itself with its own shade.
Who first looked sad, grieved, pined, and showed his
    pain,
Was he that first taught women to disdain.
    As all things were one nothing, dull and weak,
Until this raw disordered heap did break,
And several desires led parts away,
40 Water declined with earth, the air did stay,
Fire rose, and each from other but untied,
Themselves unprisoned were and purified;
So was love, first in vast confusion hid,
An unripe willingness which nothing did,
A thirst, an appetite which had no ease,
That found a want, but knew not what would please.
What pretty innocence in those days moved!
Man ignorantly walked by her he loved;
Both sighed and interchanged a speaking eye,
50 Both trembled and were sick, both knew not why.
That natural fearfulness that struck man dumb,
Might well (those times considered) man become.
As all discoverers whose first assay
Finds but the place, after, the nearest way:
So passion is to woman's love, about,

Nay, farther off, than when we first set out.
It is not love that sueth, or doth contend;
Love either conquers, or but meets a friend.
Man's better part consists of purer fire,
60   And finds itself allowed, ere it desire.
Love is wise here, keeps home, gives reason sway,
And journeys not till it find summer way.
A weather-beaten lover but once known,
Is sport for every girl to practise on.
Who strives through woman's scorns, women to know,
Is lost, and seeks his shadow to outgo;
It must be sickness, after one disdain,
Though he be called aloud, to look again.
Let others sigh, and grieve; one cunning sleight
70   Shall freeze my love to crystal in a night.
I can love first, and (if I win) love still;
And cannot be removed, unless she will.
It is her fault if I unsure remain,
She only can untie, and bind again.
The honesties of love with ease I do,
But am no porter for a tedious woo.

   But (Madam) I now think on you; and here
Where we are at our heights, you but appear,
We are but clouds you rise from, our noon ray
80   But a foul shadow, not your break of day.
You are at first hand all that's fair and right,
And others' good reflects but back your light.
You are a perfectness, so curious hit,
That youngest flatteries do scandal it.
For, what is more doth what you are restrain,
And though beyond, is down the hill again.
We'have no next way to you, we cross to it:
You are the straight line, thing praised, attribute.
Each good in you's a light; so many a shade
90   You make, and in them are your motions made.
These are your pictures to the life. From far
We see you move, and here your zanies are:
So that no fountain good there is, doth grow

In you, but our dim actions faintly show.
    Then find I, if man's noblest part be love,
Your purest lustre must that shadow move.
The soul with body, is a heaven combined
With earth, and for man's ease, but nearer joined.
Where thoughts the stars of soul we understand,
100 We guess not their large natures, but command.
And love in you, that bounty is of light,
That gives to all, and yet hath infinite,
Whose heat doth force us thither to intend,
But soul we find too earthly to ascend,
'Till slow access hath made it wholly pure,
Able immortal clearness to endure.
Who dare aspire this journey with a stain,
Hath weight will force him headlong back again.
No more can impure man retain and move
110 In that pure region of a worthy love,
Than earthly substance can unforced aspire,
And leave his nature to converse with fire:
Such may have eye, and hand; may sigh, may speak;
But like swoll'n bubbles, when they are high'st they break.
    Though far removed northern fleets scarce find
The sun's comfort; others think him too kind.
There is an equal distance from her eye,
Men perish too far off, and burn too nigh.
But as air takes the sun-beam's equal bright
120 From the first rays, to his last opposite:
So able men, blessed with a virtuous love,
Remote or near, or howsoe'er they move;
'Their virtue breaks all clouds that might annoy,
There is no emptiness, but all is joy.
He much profanes whom violent heats do move
To style his wandering rage of passion, love.
Love that imparts in everything delight,
Is feigned, which only tempts man's appetite.
Why love among the virtues is not known
130 Is, that love is them all contract in one.

To the Countess of Salisbury

AUGUST 1614

Fair, great, and good, since seeing you, we see
What heaven can do, and what any earth can be:
Since now your beauty shines, now when the sun
Grown stale, is to so low a value run,
That his dishevelled beams and scattered fires
Serve but for ladies' periwigs and tires
In lovers' sonnets: you come to repair
God's book of creatures, teaching what is fair;
Since now, when all is withered, shrunk, and dried,
10   All virtue ebbed out to a dead low tide,
All the world's frame being crumbled into sand,
Where every man thinks by himself to stand,
Integrity, friendship, and confidence,
(Cements of greatness) being vapoured hence,
And narrow man being filled with little shares,
Court, city, church, are all shops of small-wares,
All having blown to sparks their noble fire,
And drawn their sound gold-ingot into wire,
All trying by a love of littleness
20   To make abridgements, and to draw to less
Even that nothing, which at first we were;
Since in these times, your greatness doth appear,
And that we learn by it, that man to get
Towards him, that's infinite, must first be great;
Since in an age so ill, as none is fit
So much as to accuse, much less mend it,
(For who can judge, or witness of those times
Where all alike are guilty of the crimes?)
Where he that would be good, is thought by all
30   A monster, or at best fantastical:
Since now you durst be good, and that I do
Discern, by daring to contemplate you,
That there may be degrees of fair, great, good,

Though your light, largeness, virtue understood:
If in this sacrifice of mine, be shown
Any small spark of these, call it your own.
    And if things like these, have been said by me
Of others; call not that idolatry.
For had God made man first, and man had seen
40 The third day's fruits, and flowers, and various green,
He might have said the best that he could say
Of those fair creatures, which were made that day:
And when next day, he had admired the birth
Of sun, moon, stars, fairer than late-praised earth,
He might have said the best that he could say,
And not be chid for praising yesterday:
So though some things are not together true
As, that another is worthiest, and, that you:
Yet, to say so, doth not condemn a man,
50 If when he spoke them, they were both true then.
How fair a proof of this, in our soul grows!
We first have souls of growth, and sense, and those,
When our last soul, our soul immortal came,
Were swallowed into it, and have no name.
Nor doth he injure those souls, which doth cast
The power and praise of both them, on the last;
No more do I wrong any; I adore
The same things now, which I adored before,
The subject changed, and measure; the same thing
60 In a low constable, and in the King
I reverence; his power to work on me:
So did I humbly reverence each degree
Of fair, great, good, but more, now I am come
From having found their walks, to find their home.
    And as I owe my first souls thanks, that they
For my last soul did fit and mould my clay,
So am I debtor unto them, whose worth,
Enabled me to profit, and take forth
This new great lesson, thus to study you;
70 Which none, not reading others, first, could do.
Nor lack I light to read this book, though I

In a dark cave, yea in a grave do lie;
For as your fellow angels, so you do
Illustrate them who come to study you.
   The first whom we in histories do find
To have professed all arts, was one born blind:
He lacked those eyes beasts have as well as we,
Not those, by which angels are seen and see;
So, though I'am born without those eyes to live,
80   Which fortune, who hath none herself, doth give,
Which are, fit means to see bright courts and you,
Yet may I see you thus, as now I do;
I shall by that, all goodness have discerned,
And though I burn my library, be learned.

Epicedes and Obsequies

Upon the Deaths of Sundry Personages

Elegy on the L. C.

Sorrow, who to this house scarce knew the way:
Is, oh, heir of it, our all is his prey.
This strange chance claims strange wonder, and to us
Nothing can be so strange, as to weep thus.
'Tis well his life's loud speaking works deserve,
And give praise too, our cold tongues could not serve:
'Tis well, he kept tears from our eyes before,
That to fit this deep ill, we might have store.
Oh, if a sweet briar climb up by a tree,
10 If to a paradise that transplanted be,
Or felled, and burnt for holy sacrifice,
Yet, that must wither, which by it did rise,
As we for him dead: though no family
E'er rigged a soul for heaven's discovery
With whom more venturers more boldly dare
Venture their states, with him in joy to share.
We lose what all friends loved, him; he gains now
But life by death, which worst foes would allow,
If he could have foes, in whose practice grew
20 All virtues, whose names subtle schoolmen knew;
What ease, can hope that we shall see'him, beget,
When we must die first, and cannot die yet?
His children are his pictures, oh they be
Pictures of him dead, senseless, cold as he,
Here needs no marble tomb, since he is gone,
He, and about him, his, are turned to stone.

Elegy on the Lady Markham

Man is the world, and death the ocean,
    To which God gives the lower parts of man.
This sea environs all, and though as yet
    God hath set marks, and bounds, 'twixt us and it,
Yet doth it roar, and gnaw, and still pretend,
    And breaks our banks, when e'er it takes a friend.

Then our land waters (tears of passion) vent;
   Our waters, then, above our firmament,
(Tears which our soul doth for her sins let fall)
10   Take all a brackish taste, and funeral.
And even these tears, which should wash sin, are sin.
   We, after God's 'No', drown our world again.
Nothing but man of all envenomed things
   Doth work upon itself, with inborn stings.
Tears are false spectacles, we cannot see
   Through passion's mist, what we are, or what she.
In her this sea of death hath made no breach,
   But as the tide doth wash the slimy beach,
And leaves embroidered works upon the sand,
20   So is her flesh refined by death's cold hand.
As men of China, after an age's stay
   Do take up porcelain, where they buried clay;
So at this grave, her limbeck, which refines
   The diamonds, rubies, sapphires, pearls, and mines,
Of which this flesh was, her soul shall inspire
   Flesh of such stuff, as God, when his last fire
Annuls this world, to recompense it, shall,
   Make and name then, th' elixir of this all.
They say, the sea, when it gains, loseth too;
30   If carnal death (the younger brother) do
Usurp the body, our soul, which subject is
   To th' elder death, by sin, is freed by this;
They perish both, when they attempt the just;
   For, graves our trophies are, and both deaths' dust.
So, unobnoxious now, she hath buried both;
   For, none to death sins, that to sin is loth.
Nor do they die, which are not loth to die,
   So hath she this, and that virginity.
Grace was in her extremely diligent,
40   That kept her from sin, yet made her repent.
Of what small spots pure white complains! Alas,
   How little poison cracks a crystal glass!
She sinned, but just enough to let us see
   That God's word must be true, all, sinners be.

So much did zeal her conscience rarefy,
  That, extreme truth lacked little of a lie,
Making omissions, acts; laying the touch
  Of sin, on things that sometimes may be such.
As Moses' cherubins, whose natures do
50   Surpass all speed, by him are winged too:
So would her soul, already in heaven, seem then,
  To climb by tears, the common stairs of men.
How fit she was for God, I am content
  To speak, that death his vain haste may repent.
How fit for us, how even and how sweet,
  How good in all her titles, and how meet,
To have reformed this forward heresy,
  That women can no parts of friendship be;
How moral, how divine shall not be told,
60   Lest they that hear her virtues, think her old:
And lest we take death's part, and make him glad
  Of such a prey, and to his triumph add.

Elegy on Mistress Boulstred

Death I recant, and say, unsaid by me
  Whate'er hath slipped, that might diminish thee.
Spiritual treason, atheism 'tis, to say,
  That any can thy summons disobey.
Th' earth's face is but thy table; there are set
  Plants, cattle, men, dishes for Death to eat.
In a rude hunger now he millions draws
  Into his bloody, or plaguey, or starved jaws.
Now he will seem to spare, and doth more waste,
10   Eating the best first, well preserved to last.
Now wantonly he spoils, and eats us not,
  But breaks off friends, and lets us piecemeal rot.
Nor will this earth serve him; he sinks the deep
  Where harmless fish monastic silence keep,
Who (were Death dead) by roes of living sand,
  Might sponge that element, and make it land.

He rounds the air, and breaks the hymnic notes
    In birds', heaven's choristers, organic throats,
Which (if they did not die) might seem to be
20   A tenth rank in the heavenly hierarchy.
O strong and long-lived death, how cam'st thou in?
    And how without creation didst begin?
Thou hast, and shalt see dead, before thou diest,
    All the four monarchies, and antichrist.
How could I think thee nothing, that see now
    In all this all, nothing else is, but thou.
Our births and lives, vices, and virtues, be
    Wasteful consumptions, and degrees of thee.
For, we to live, our bellows wear, and breath,
30   Nor are we mortal, dying, dead, but death.
And though thou be'st, O mighty bird of prey,
    So much reclaimed by God, that thou must lay
All that thou kill'st at his feet, yet doth he
    Reserve but few, and leaves the most to thee.
And of those few, now thou hast overthrown
    One whom thy blow makes, not ours, nor thine own.
She was more storeys high: hopeless to come
    To her soul, thou hast offered at her lower room.
Her soul and body was a king and court:
40   But thou hast both of captain missed and fort.
As houses fall not, though the king remove,
    Bodies of saints rest for their souls above.
Death gets 'twixt souls and bodies such a place
    As sin insinuates 'twixt just men and grace,
Both work a separation, no divorce.
    Her soul is gone to usher up her corse,
Which shall be almost another soul, for there
    Bodies are purer, than best souls are here.
Because in her, her virtues did outgo
50   Her years, wouldst thou, O emulous death, do so?
And kill her young to thy loss? must the cost
    Of beauty, and wit, apt to do harm, be lost?
What though thou found'st her proof 'gainst sins of youth?
    Oh, every age a diverse sin pursueth.

Thou shouldst have stayed, and taken better hold,
    Shortly ambitious, covetous, when old,
She might have proved: and such devotion
    Might once have strayed to superstition.
If all her virtues must have grown, yet might
60   Abundant virtue'have bred a proud delight.
Had she persevered just, there would have been
    Some that would sin, mis-thinking she did sin.
Such as would call her friendship, love, and feign
    To sociableness, a name profane;
Or sin, by tempting, or, not daring that,
    By wishing, though they never told her what.
Thus mightst thou'have slain more souls, hadst thou not crossed
    Thyself, and to triumph, thine army lost.
Yet though these ways be lost, thou hast left one,
70   Which is, immoderate grief that she is gone.
But we may 'scape that sin, yet weep as much,
    Our tears are due, because we are not such.
Some tears, that knot of friends, her death must cost,
    Because the chain is broke, though no link lost.

An Elegy upon the Death of Mistress Boulstred

Language thou art too narrow, and too weak
    To ease us now; great sorrow cannot speak;
If we could sigh out accents, and weep words,
    Grief wears, and lessens, that tears breath affords.
Sad hearts, the less they seem, the more they are,
    (So guiltiest men stand mutest at the bar)
Not that they know not, feel not their estate,
    But extreme sense hath made them desperate;
Sorrow, to whom we owe all that we be,
10   Tyrant, in the fifth and greatest monarchy,
Was 't, that she did possess all hearts before,
    Thou hast killed her, to make thy empire more?
Knew'st thou some would, that knew her not, lament,

As in a deluge perish th' innocent?
Was 't not enough to have that palace won,
   But thou must raze it too, that was undone?
Hadst thou stayed there, and looked out at her eyes,
   All had adored thee that now from thee flies,
For they let out more light, than they took in,
20   They told not when, but did the day begin;
She was too sapphirine, and clear for thee;
   Clay, flint, and jet now thy fit dwellings be;
Alas, she was too pure, but not too weak;
   Whoe'er saw crystal ordinance but would break?
And if we be thy conquest, by her fall
   Thou'hast lost thy end, for in her perish all;
Or if we live, we live but to rebel,
   They know her better now, that knew her well.
If we should vapour out, or pine, and die,
30   Since, she first went, that were not misery;
She changed our world with hers; now she is gone,
   Mirth and prosperity is oppression;
For of all mortal virtues she was all
   The ethics speak of virtues cardinal.
Her soul was paradise; the cherubin
   Set to keep it was grace, that kept out sin;
She had no more than let in death, for we
   All reap consumption from one fruitful tree;
God took her hence, lest some of us should love
40   Her, like that plant, him and his laws above,
And when we tears, he mercy shed in this,
   To raise our minds to heaven where now she is;
Who if her virtues would have let her stay
   We'had had a saint, have now a holiday;
Her heart was that strange bush, where, sacred fire,
   Religion, did not consume, but inspire
Such piety, so chaste use of God's day,
   That what we turn to feast, she turned to pray,
And did prefigure here, in devout taste,
50   The rest of her high Sabaoth, which shall last.
Angels did hand her up, who next God dwell,

(For she was of that order whence most fell)
Her body left with us, lest some had said,
    She could not die, except they saw her dead;
For from less virtue, and less beauteousness,
    The gentiles framed them gods and goddesses.
The ravenous earth that now woos her to be
    Earth too, will be a lemnia; and the tree
That wraps that crystal in a wooden tomb,
60   Shall be took up spruce, filled with diamond;
And we her sad glad friends all bear a part
    Of grief, for all would waste a stoic's heart.

Elegy upon the untimely death of the incomparable Prince Henry

Look to me faith, and look to my faith, God;
For both my centres feel this period.
Of weight one centre, one of greatness is;
And reason is that centre, faith is this.
For into our reason flow, and there do end,
All that this natural world doth comprehend:
Quotidian things, and equidistant hence,
Shut in, for man, in one circumference.
But, for th' enormous greatnesses, which are
10 So disproportioned, and so angular,
As is God's essence, place, and providence,
Where, how, when, what, souls do, departed hence,
These things (eccentric else) on faith do strike;
Yet neither all, nor upon all alike.
For reason, put to her best extension,
Almost meets faith, and makes both centres one.
And nothing ever came so near to this,
As contemplation of that Prince, we miss.
For, all that faith might credit mankind could,
20 Reason still seconded, that this Prince would.
If then least moving of the centre, make
More, than if whole hell belched, the world to shake,

What must this do, centres distracted so,
That we see not what to believe or know?
Was it not well believed till now, that he,
Whose reputation was an ecstasy
On neighbour States, which knew not why to wake,
Till he discovered what ways he would take;
For whom, what princes angled, when they tried,
30 Met a torpedo, and were stupefied;
And others' studies, how he would be bent;
Was his great father's greatest instrument,
And activest spirit, to convey and tie
This soul of peace, through christianity?
Was it not well believed, that he would make
This general peace, th' eternal overtake,
And that his times might have stretched out so far
As to touch those, of which they emblems are?
For to confirm this just belief, that now
40 The last days came, we saw heaven did allow
That, but from his aspect and exercise,
In peaceful times, rumours of wars did rise.
But now this faith is heresy: we must
Still stay, and vex our great-grandmother, dust.
Oh, is God prodigal? hath he spent his store
Of plagues, on us, and only now, when more
Would ease us much, doth he grudge misery,
And will not let 'us enjoy our curse, to die?
As, for the earth thrown lowest down of all,
50 'Twere an ambition to desire to fall,
So God, in our desire to die, doth know
Our plot for ease, in being wretched so.
Therefore we live: though such a life we have,
As but so many mandrakes on his grave.
    What had his growth, and generation done,
When, what we are, his putrefaction
Sustains in us; earth, which griefs animate?
Nor hath our world now, other soul than that.
And could grief get so high as heaven, that choir
60 Forgetting this their new joy, would desire

(With grief to see him) he had stayed below,
To rectify our errors, they foreknow.
    Is th' other centre, reason, faster then?
Where should we look for that, now we'are not men?
For if our reason be our connexion
Of causes, now to us there can be none.
For, as, if all the substances were spent,
'Twere madness to inquire of accident,
So is 't to look for reason, he being gone,
70   The only subject reason wrought upon.
    If Fate have such a chain, whose divers links
Industrious man discerneth, as he thinks,
When miracle doth come, and so steal in
A new link, man knows not where to begin:
At a much deader fault must reason be,
Death having broke off such a link as he.
But, now, for us with busy proof to come
That we'have no reason, would prove we had some.
So would just lamentations: therefore we
80   May safelier say, that we are dead, than he.
So, if our griefs we do not well declare,
We'have double excuse; he'is not dead; and we are.
Yet I would not die yet; for though I be
Too narrow, to think him, as he is he,
Our soul's best baiting and mid-period
In her long journey of considering God,
Yet (no dishonour) I can reach him thus,
As he embraced the fires of love with us.
Oh may I (since I live) but see, or hear,
90   That she-intelligence which moved this sphere,
I pardon Fate, my life: who e'er thou be
Which hast the noble conscience, thou art she,
I conjure thee by all the charms he spoke,
By th' oaths which only you two never broke,
By all the souls ye sighed, that if you see
These lines, you wish I knew your history.
So much, as you two mutual heavens were here,
I were an angel, singing what you were.

Obsequies to the Lord Harrington, brother to the Lady Lucy, Countess of Bedford

TO THE COUNTESS OF BEDFORD

Madam,
I have learned by those laws wherein I am a little conversant,
that he which bestows any cost upon the dead, obliges him
which is dead, but not the heir; I do not therefore send this
paper to your Ladyship, that you should thank me for it, or
think that I thank you in it; your favours and benefits to me
are so much above my merits, that they are even above my
gratitude, if that were to be judged by words which must
express it: but, Madam, since your noble brother's fortune
being yours, the evidences also concerning it are yours: so his
10 virtue being yours, the evidences concerning it, belong also
to you, of which by your acceptance this may be one piece,
in which quality I humbly present it, and as a testimony how
entirely your family possesseth

Your Ladyship's most humble
and thankful servant
John Donne

Fair soul, which wast, not only, as all souls be,
Then when thou wast infused, harmony,
But didst continue so; and now dost bear
A part in God's great organ, this whole sphere:
If looking up to God; or down to us,
Thou find that any way is pervious,
'Twixt heaven and earth, and that men's actions do
Come to your knowledge, and affections too,
See, and with joy, me to that good degree
10 Of goodness grown, that I can study thee,
And, by these meditations refined,
Can unapparel and enlarge my mind,
And so can make by this soft ecstasy,

This place a map of heaven, myself of thee.
Thou seest me here at midnight, now all rest;
Time's dead-low water; when all minds divest
Tomorrow's business, when the labourers have
Such rest in bed, that their last church-yard grave,
Subject to change, will scarce be'a type of this,
20 Now when the client, whose last hearing is
Tomorrow, sleeps, when the condemned man,
(Who when he opes his eyes, must shut them then
Again by death), although sad watch he keep,
Doth practice dying by a little sleep,
Thou at this midnight seest me, and as soon
As that sun rises to me, midnight's noon,
All the world grows transparent, and I see
Through all, both church and state, in seeing thee;
And I discern by favour of this light,
30 Myself, the hardest object of the sight.
God is the glass; as thou when thou dost see
Him who sees all, seest all concerning thee,
So, yet unglorified, I comprehend
All, in these mirrors of thy ways, and end.
Though God be our true glass, through which we see
All, since the being of all things is he,
Yet are the trunks which do to us derive
Things, in proportion fit, by perspective,
Deeds of good men; for by their living here,
40 Virtues, indeed remote, seem to be near.
But where can I affirm, or where arrest
My thoughts on his deeds? which shall I call best?
For fluid virtue cannot be looked on,
Nor can endure a contemplation;
As bodies change, and as I do not wear
Those spirits, humours, blood I did last year,
And, as if on a stream I fixed mine eye,
That drop, which I looked on, is presently
Pushed with more waters from my sight, and gone,
50 So in this sea of virtues, can no one
Be insisted on; virtues, as rivers, pass,

Yet still remains that virtuous man there was;
And as if man feed on man's flesh, and so
Part of his body to another owe,
Yet at the last two perfect bodies rise,
Because God knows where every atom lies;
So, if one knowledge were made of all those,
Who knew his minutes well, he might dispose
His virtues into names, and ranks; but I
60   Should injure nature, virtue, and destiny,
Should I divide and discontinue so,
Virtue, which did in one entireness grow.
For as, he that would say, spirits are framed
Of all the purest parts that can be named,
Honours not spirits half so much, as he
Which says, they have no parts, but simple be;
So is 't of virtue; for a point and one
Are much entirer than a million.
And had Fate meant to have his virtues told,
70   It would have let him live to have been old,
So, then that virtue in season, and then this,
We might have seen, and said, that now he is
Witty, now wise, now temperate, now just:
In good short lives, virtues are fain to thrust,
And to be sure betimes to get a place,
When they would exercise, lack time, and space.
So was it in this person, forced to be
For lack of time, his own epitome:
So to exhibit in few years as much,
80   As all the long-breathed chronicles can touch.
As when an angel down from heaven doth fly,
Our quick thought cannot keep him company,
We cannot think, now he is at the sun,
Now through the moon, now he through th' air doth run,
Yet when he's come, we know he did repair
To all 'twixt heaven and earth, sun, moon, and air;
And as this angel in an instant knows,
And yet we know, this sudden knowledge grows
By quick amassing several forms of things,

90   Which he successively to order brings;
      When they, whose slow-paced lame thoughts cannot go
      So fast as he, think that he doth not so;
      Just as a perfect reader doth not dwell,
      On every syllable, nor stay to spell,
      Yet without doubt, he doth distinctly see
      And lay together every A, and B;
      So, in short-lived good men, is not understood
      Each several virtue, but the compound good;
      For, they all virtue's paths in that pace tread,
100   As angels go, and know, and as men read.
      O why should then these men, these lumps of balm
      Sent hither, this world's tempests to becalm,
      Before by deeds they are diffused and spread,
      And so make us alive, themselves be dead?
      O soul, O circle, why so quickly be
      Thy ends, thy birth and death closed up in thee?
      Since one foot of thy compass still was placed
      In heaven, the other might securely have paced
      In the most large extent, through every path,
110   Which the whole world, or man the abridgement hath.
      Thou know'st, that though the trópic circles have
      (Yea and those small ones which the poles engrave),
      All the same roundness, evenness, and all
      The endlessness of the equinoctial;
      Yet, when we come to measure distances,
      How here, how there, the sun affected is,
      Where he doth faintly work, and where prevail,
      Only great circles, then, can be our scale:
      So, though thy circle to thyself express
120   All, tending to thy endless happiness,
      And we, by our good use of it may try,
      Both how to live well young, and how to die,
      Yet, since we must be old, and age endures
      His torrid zone at Court, and calentures
      Of hot ambitions, irreligion's ice,
      Zeal's agues, and hydroptic avarice,
      Infirmities which need the scale of truth,

As well, as lust and ignorance of youth;
Why didst thou not for these give medicines too,
130   And by thy doing tell us what to do?
Though as small pocket-clocks, whose every wheel
Doth each mismotion and distemper feel,
Whose hand gets shaking palsies, and whose string
(His sinews) slackens, and whose soul, the spring,
Expires, or languishes, whose pulse, the fly,
Either beats not, or beats unevenly,
Whose voice, the bell, doth rattle, or grow dumb,
Or idle, 'as men, which to their last hours come,
If these clocks be not wound, or be wound still,
140   Or be not set, or set at every will;
So, youth is easiest to destruction,
If then we follow all, or follow none.
Yet, as in great clocks, which in steeples chime,
Placed to inform whole towns, to employ their time,
An error doth more harm, being general,
When, small clocks' faults, only'on the wearer fall;
So work the faults of age, on which the eye
Of children, servants, or the state rely.
Why wouldst not thou then, which hadst such a soul,
150   A clock so true, as might the sun control,
And daily hadst from him, who gave it thee,
Instructions, such as it could never be
Disordered, stay here, as a general
And great sundial, to have set us all?
O why wouldst thou be any instrument
To this unnatural course, or why consent
To this, not miracle, but prodigy
That when the ebbs, longer than flowings be,
Virtue, whose flood did with thy youth begin,
160   Should so much faster ebb out, than flow in?
Though her flood was blown in, by thy first breath,
All is at once sunk in the whirlpool death.
Which word I would not name, but that I see
Death, else a desert, grown a Court by thee.
Now I grow sure, that if a man would have

Good company, his entry is a grave.
Methinks all cities now, but anthills be,
Where, when the several labourers I see,
For children, house, provision, taking pain,
170   They'are all but ants, carrying eggs, straw, and grain;
And churchyards are our cities, unto which
The most repair, that are in goodness rich.
There is the best concourse, and confluence,
There are the holy suburbs, and from thence
Begins God's city, New Jerusalem,
Which doth extend her utmost gates to them.
At that gate then triumphant soul, dost thou
Begin thy triumph; but since laws allow
That at the triumph day, the people may,
180   All that they will, 'gainst the triumpher say,
Let me here use that freedom, and express
My grief, though not to make thy triumph less.
By law, to triumphs none admitted be,
Till they as magistrates get victory;
Though then to thy force, all youth's foes did yield,
Yet till fit time had brought thee to that field,
To which thy rank in this state destined thee,
That there thy counsels might get victory,
And so in that capacity remove
190   All jealousies 'twixt Prince and subject's love,
Thou couldst no title, to this triumph have,
Thou didst intrude on death, usurp'st a grave.
Then (though victoriously) thou hadst fought as yet
But with thine own affections, with the heat
Of youth's desires, and colds of ignorance,
But till thou shouldst successfully advance
Thine arm's 'gainst foreign enemies, which are
Both envy, and acclamations popular,
(For, both these engines equally defeat,
200   Though by a divers mine, those which are great,)
Till then thy war was but a civil war,
For which to triumph, none admitted are;
No more are they, who though with good success,

In a defensive war, their power express.
Before men triumph, the dominion
Must be enlarged and not preserved alone;
Why shouldst thou then, whose battles were to win
Thyself, from those straits nature put thee in,
And to deliver up to God that state,
210   Of which he gave thee the vicariate,
(Which is thy soul and body) as entire
As he, who takes endeavours, doth require,
But didst not stay, to enlarge his kingdom too,
By making others, what thou didst, to do;
Why shouldst thou triumph now, when heaven no more
Hath got, by getting thee, than it had before?
For, heaven and thou, even when thou lived'st here,
Of one another in possession were.
But this from triumph most disables thee,
220   That, that place which is conquered, must be
Left safe from present war, and likely doubt
Of imminent commotions to break out.
And hath he left us so? or can it be
His territory was no more than he?
No, we were all his charge, the diocese
Of every exemplar man, the whole world is,
And he was joined in commission
With tutelar angels, sent to every one.
But though his freedom to upbraid, and chide
230   Him who triumphed, were lawful, it was tied
With this, that it might never reference have
Unto the Senate, who this triumph gave;
Men might at Pompey jest, but they might not
At that authority, by which he got
Leave to triumph, before, by age, he might;
So, though, triumphant soul, I dare to write,
Moved with a reverential anger, thus,
That thou so early wouldst abandon us;
Yet am I far from daring to dispute
240   With that great sovereignty, whose absolute
Prerogative hath thus dispensed for thee,

'Gainst nature's laws, which just impugners be
Of early triumphs; and I (though with pain)
Lessen our loss, to magnify thy gain
Of triumph, when I say, it was more fit,
That all men should lack thee, than thou lack it.
Though then in our time, be not suffered
That testimony of love, unto the dead,
To die with them, and in their graves be hid,
250 As Saxon wives, and French *soldurii* did;
And though in no degree I can express
Grief in great Alexander's great excess,
Who at his friend's death, made whole towns divest
Their walls and bulwarks which became them best:
Do not, fair soul, this sacrifice refuse,
That in thy grave I do inter my Muse,
Who, by my grief, great as thy worth, being cast
Behind hand, yet hath spoke, and spoke her last.

An hymn to the Saints, and to Marquis Hamilton

TO SIR ROBERT CARR

Sir,
I presume you rather try what you can do in me, than what
I can do in verse; you know my uttermost when it was best,
and even then I did best when I had least truth for my sub-
jects. In this present case there is so much truth as it defeats
all poetry. Call therefore this paper by what name you will,
and, if it be not worthy of him, nor of you, nor of me, smother
it, and be that the sacrifice. If you had commanded me to
have waited on his body to Scotland and preached there, I
would have embraced the obligation with more alacrity; but,
10 I thank you that you would command me that which I was
loth to do, for, even that hath given a tincture of merit to the
obedience of
                  Your poor friend and servant in Christ Jesus
                              J. D.

Whether that soul which now comes up to you
Fill any former rank or make a new,
Whether it take a name named there before,
Or be a name itself, and order more
Than was in heaven till now; (for may not he
Be so, if every several angel be
A kind alone?) what ever order grow
Greater by him in heaven, we do not so;
One of your orders grows by his access;
10 But, by his loss grow all our orders less;
The name of father, master, friend, the name
Of subject and of prince, in one are lame;
Fair mirth is damped, and conversation black,
The household widowed, and the garter slack;
The Chapel wants an ear, Council a tongue;
Story, a theme; and music lacks a song.
Blessed order that hath him, the loss of him
Gangrened all orders here; all lost a limb.
Never made body such haste to confess
20 What a soul was; all former comeliness
Fled, in a minute, when the soul was gone,
And, having lost that beauty, would have none:
So fell our monasteries, in one instant grown
Not to less houses, but, to heaps of stone;
So sent this body that fair form it wore,
Unto the sphere of forms, and doth (before
His soul shall fill up his sepulchral stone),
Anticipate a resurrection;
For, as in his fame, now, his soul is here,
30 So, in the form thereof his body's there;
And if, fair soul, not with first innocents
Thy station be, but with the penitents,
(And, who shall dare to ask then when I am
Dyed scarlet in the blood of that pure Lamb,
Whether that colour, which is scarlet then,
Were black or white before in eyes of men?)
When thou rememberest what sins thou didst find
Amongst those many friends now left behind,

And seest such sinners as they are, with thee
40　Got thither by repentance, let it be
Thy wish to wish all there, to wish them clean;
Wish him a David, her a Magdalen.

The Anniversaries

An Anatomy of the World

WHEREIN, BY OCCASION OF THE UNTIMELY
DEATH OF MISTRESS ELIZABETH DRURY, THE
FRAILTY AND THE DECAY OF THIS WHOLE WORLD
IS REPRESENTED

THE FIRST ANNIVERSARY

To the Praise of the Dead, and the Anatomy

Well died the world, that we might live to see
This world of wit, in his Anatomy:
No evil wants his good; so wilder heirs
Bedew their fathers' tombs, with forced tears,
Whose state requites their loss: whiles thus we gain,
Well may we walk in blacks, but not complain.
Yet how can I consent the world is dead
While this Muse lives? which in his spirit's stead
Seems to inform a world; and bids it be,
10 In spite of loss or frail mortality?
And thou the subject of this well-born thought,
Thrice noble maid, couldst not have found nor sought
A fitter time to yield to thy sad fate,
Than whiles this spirit lives, that can relate
Thy worth so well to our last nephews' eyne,
That they shall wonder both at his and thine:
Admired match! where strive in mutual grace
The cunning pencil, and the comely face:
A task which thy fair goodness made too much
20 For the bold pride of vulgar pens to touch;
Enough is us to praise them that praise thee,
And say, that but enough those praises be,
Which hadst thou lived, had hid their fearful head
From th' angry checkings of thy modest red:
Death bars reward and shame: when envy's gone,
And gain, 'tis safe to give the dead their own.
As then the wise Egyptians wont to lay

More on their tombs than houses: these of clay,
But those of brass, or marble were: so we
30 Give more unto thy ghost, than unto thee.
Yet what we give to thee, thou gav'st to us,
And mayst but thank thyself, for being thus:
Yet what thou gav'st, and wert, O happy maid,
Thy grace professed all due, where 'tis repaid.
So these high songs that to thee suited been
Serve but to sound thy maker's praise, in thine,
Which thy dear soul as sweetly sings to him
Amid the choir of saints and seraphim,
As any angel's tongue can sing of thee;
40 The subjects differ, though the skill agree:
For as by infant-years men judge of age,
Thy early love, thy virtues, did presage
What an high part thou bear'st in those best songs,
Whereto no burden, nor no end belongs.
Sing on thou virgin soul, whose lossful gain
Thy lovesick parents have bewailed in vain;
Never may thy name be in our songs forgot,
Till we shall sing thy ditty, and thy note.

An Anatomy of the World

THE FIRST ANNIVERSARY

When that rich soul which to her heaven is gone,   *The*
Whom all they celebrate, who know they have one,   *entry*
(For who is sure he hath a soul, unless   *into the*
It see, and judge, and follow worthiness,   *work*
And by deeds praise it? he who doth not this,
May lodge an inmate soul, but 'tis not his.)
When that Queen ended here her progress time,
And, as to'her standing house, to heaven did climb,
Where, loth to make the saints attend her long,
10 She's now a part both of the choir, and song,
This world, in that great earthquake languished;

For in a common bath of tears it bled,
Which drew the strongest vital spirits out:
But succoured then with a perplexed doubt,
Whether the world did lose, or gain in this,
(Because since now no other way there is
But goodness, to see her, whom all would see,
All must endeavour to be good as she,)
This great consumption to a fever turned,
20 And so the world had fits; it joyed, it mourned.
And, as men think, that agues physic are,
And th' ague being spent, give over care,
So thou, sick world, mistak'st thyself to be
Well, when alas, thou 'rt in a lethargy.
Her death did wound and tame thee then, and then
Thou mightst have better spared the sun, or man.
That wound was deep, but 'tis more misery,
That thou hast lost thy sense and memory.
'Twas heavy then to hear thy voice of moan,
30 But this is worse, that thou art speechless grown.
Thou has forgot thy name, thou hadst; thou wast
Nothing but she, and her thou hast o'erpast.
For as a child kept from the font, until
A prince, expected long, come to fulfil
The ceremonies, thou unnamed hadst laid,
Had not her coming, thee her palace made:
Her name defined thee, gave thee form, and frame,
And thou forget'st to celebrate thy name.
Some months she hath been dead (but being dead,
40 Measures of times are all determined)
But long she'hath been away, long, long, yet none
Offers to tell us who it is that's gone.
But as in states doubtful of future heirs,
When sickness without remedy impairs
The present prince, they'are loth it should be said,
The prince doth languish, or the prince is dead:
So mankind feeling now a general thaw,
A strong example gone, equal to law,
The cement which did faithfully compact

50 And glue all virtues, now resolved, and slacked,
   Thought it some blasphemy to say she'was dead;
   Or that our weakness was discovered
   In that confession; therefore spoke no more
   Than tongues, the soul being gone, the loss deplore.
   But though it be too late to succour thee,
   Sick world, yea dead, yea putrefied, since she
   Thy'intrinsic balm, and thy preservative,
   Can never be renewed, thou never live,
   I (since no man can make thee live) will try,
60 What we may gain by thy anatomy.
   Her death hath taught us dearly, that thou art
   Corrupt and mortal in thy purest part.
   Let no man say, the world itself being dead,
   'Tis labour lost to have discovered
   The world's infirmities, since there is none
   Alive to study this dissection;
   For there's a kind of world remaining still,   *What life
   Though she which did inanimate and fill   the world
   The world, be gone, yet in this last long night,   hath still*
70 Her ghost doth walk; that is, a glimmering light,
   A faint weak love of virtue and of good
   Reflects from her, on them which understood
   Her worth; and though she have shut in all day,
   The twilight of her memory doth stay;
   Which, from the carcase of the old world, free,
   Creates a new world; and new creatures be
   Produced: the matter and the stuff of this,
   Her virtue, and the form our practice is.
   And though to be thus elemented, arm
80 These creatures, from home-born intrinsic harm,
   (For all assumed unto this dignity,
   So many weedless paradises be,
   Which of themselves produce no venomous sin,
   Except some foreign serpent bring it in)
   Yet, because outward storms the strongest break,
   And strength itself by confidence grows weak,
   This new world may be safer, being told

The dangers and diseases of the old: *The sick-*
For with due temper men do then forgo, *nesses of*
90 Or covet things, when they their true worth know. *the world.*
There is no health; physicians say that we *Impossi-*
At best, enjoy but a neutrality. *bility of*
And can there be worse sickness, than to know *health*
That we are never well, nor can be so?
We are born ruinous: poor mothers cry,
That children come not right, nor orderly,
Except they headlong come, and fall upon
An ominous precipitation.
How witty's ruin! how importunate
100 Upon mankind! it laboured to frustrate
Even God's purpose; and made woman, sent
For man's relief, cause of his languishment.
They were to good ends, and they are so still,
But accessory, and principal in ill.
For that first marriage was our funeral:
One woman at one blow, then killed us all,
And singly, one by one, they kill us now.
We do delightfully ourselves allow
To that consumption; and profusely blind,
110 We kill ourselves, to propagate our kind.
And yet we do not that; we are not men:
There is not now that mankind, which was then,
When as the sun, and man, did seem to strive,
(Joint tenants of the world) who should survive. *Shortness*
When stag, and raven, and the long-lived tree, *of life.*
Compared with man, died in minority;
When, if a slow-paced star had stol'n away
From the observer's marking, he might stay
Two or three hundred years to see'it again,
120 And then make up his observation plain;
When, as the age was long, the size was great:
Man's growth confessed, and recompensed the meat:
So spacious and large, that every soul
Did a fair kingdom, and large realm control:
And when the very stature thus erect,

Did that soul a good way towards heaven direct.
Where is this mankind now? who lives to age,
Fit to be made Methusalem his page?
Alas, we scarce live long enough to try
130 Whether a true made clock run right, or lie.
Old grandsires talk of yesterday with sorrow,
And for our children we reserve tomorrow.
So short is life, that every peasant strives,
In a torn house, or field, to have three lives.
And as in lasting, so in length is man
Contracted to an inch, who was a span;   *Smallness of*
For had a man at first in forests strayed,   *stature.*
Or shipwrecked in the sea, one would have laid
A wager, that an elephant, or whale,
140 That met him, would not hastily assail
A thing so equal to him: now alas,
The fairies, and the pygmies well may pass
As credible; mankind decays so soon,
We'are scarce our fathers' shadows cast at noon.
Only death adds to'our length: nor are we grown
In stature to be men, till we are none.
But this were light, did our less volume hold
All the old text; or had we changed to gold
Their silver; or disposed into less glass
150 Spirits of virtue, which then scattered was.
But 'tis not so: we'are not retired, but damped;
And as our bodies, so our minds are cramped:
'Tis shrinking, not close weaving that hath thus,
In mind and body both bedwarfed us.
We seem ambitious, God's whole work to undo;
Of nothing he made us, and we strive too,
To bring ourselves to nothing back; and we
Do what we can, to do 't so soon as he.
With new diseases on ourselves we war,
160 And with new physic, a worse engine far.
Thus man, this world's vice-emperor, in whom
All faculties, all graces are at home;
And if in other creatures they appear,

They're but man's ministers, and legates there,
To work on their rebellions, and reduce
Them to civility, and to man's use.
This man, whom God did woo, and loth t' attend
Till man came up, did down to man descend,
This man, so great, that all that is, is his,
170 Oh what a trifle, and poor thing he is!
If man were anything, he's nothing now:
Help, or at least some time to waste, allow
T' his other wants, yet when he did depart
With her whom we lament, he lost his heart.
She, of whom th' ancients seemed to prophesy,
When they called virtues by the name of *she*;
She in whom virtue was so much refined,
That for allay unto so pure a mind
She took the weaker sex, she that could drive
180 The poisonous tincture, and the stain of Eve,
Out of her thoughts, and deeds; and purify
All, by a true religious alchemy;
She, she is dead; she's dead: when thou know'st this,
Thou know'st how poor a trifling thing man is.
And learn'st thus much by our anatomy,
The heart being perished, no part can be free.
And that except thou feed (not banquet) on
The supernatural food, religion,
Thy better growth grows withered, and scant;
190 Be more than man, or thou'art less than an ant.
Then, as mankind, so is the world's whole frame
Quite out of joint, almost created lame:
For, before God had made up all the rest,
Corruption entered, and depraved the best:
It seized the angels, and then first of all
The world did in her cradle take a fall,
And turned her brains, and took a general maim
Wronging each joint of th' universal frame.
The noblest part, man, felt it first; and then   *Decay of*
200 Both beasts and plants, cursed in the curse of man. *nature*
So did the world from the first hour decay,   *in other*
                                                     parts.

That evening was beginning of the day,
And now the springs and summers which we see,
Like sons of women after fifty be.
And new philosophy calls all in doubt,
The element of fire is quite put out;
The sun is lost, and th' earth, and no man's wit
Can well direct him where to look for it.
And freely men confess that this world's spent,
210 When in the planets, and the firmament
They seek so many new; they see that this
Is crumbled out again to his atomies.
'Tis all in pieces, all coherence gone;
All just supply, and all relation:
Prince, subject, father, son, are things forgot,
For every man alone thinks he hath got
To be a phoenix, and that then can be
None of that kind, of which he is, but he.
This is the world's condition now, and now
220 She that should all parts to reunion bow,
She that had all magnetic force alone,
To draw, and fasten sundered parts in one;
She whom wise nature had invented then
When she observed that every sort of men
Did in their voyage in this world's sea stray,
And needed a new compass for their way;
She that was best, and first original
Of all fair copies; and the general
Steward to Fate; she whose rich eyes, and breast,
230 Gilt the West Indies, and perfumed the East;
Whose having breathed in this world, did bestow
Spice on those isles, and bade them still smell so,
And that rich Indy which doth gold inter,
Is but as single money, coined from her:
She to whom this world must itself refer,
As suburbs, or the microcosm of her,
She, she is dead; she's dead: when thou knows't this,
Thou know'st how lame a cripple this world is.
And learn'st thus much by our anatomy,

240   That this world's general sickness doth not lie
      In any humour, or one certain part;
      But as thou sawest it rotten at the heart,
      Thou seest a hectic fever hath got hold
      Of the whole substance, not to be controlled,
      And that thou hast but one way, not to admit
      The world's infection, to be none of it.
      For the world's subtlest immaterial parts
      Feel this consuming wound, and age's darts.
      For the world's beauty is decayed, or gone,   *Disformity of*
250   Beauty, that's colour, and proportion.   *parts.*
      We think the heavens enjoy their spherical,
      Their round proportion embracing all.
      But yet their various and perplexed course,
      Observed in divers ages, doth enforce
      Men to find out so many eccentric parts,
      Such divers down-right lines, such overthwarts,
      As disproportion that pure form. It tears
      The firmament in eight and forty shares,
      And in these constellations then arise
260   New stars, and old do vanish from our eyes:
      As though heaven suffered earthquakes, peace or war,
      When new towers rise, and old demolished are.
      They have impaled within a zodiac
      The free-born sun, and keep twelve signs awake
      To watch his steps; the goat and crab control,
      And fright him back, who else to either pole
      (Did not these tropics fetter him) might run:
      For his course is not round; nor can the sun
      Perfect a circle, or maintain his way
270   One inch direct; but where he rose today
      He comes no more, but with a cozening line,
      Steals by that point, and so is serpentine:
      And seeming weary with his reeling thus,
      He means to sleep, being now fall'n nearer us.
      So, of the stars which boast that they do run
      In circle still, none ends where he begun.
      All their proportion's lame, it sinks, it swells.

For of meridians, and parallels,
Man hath weaved out a net, and this net thrown
280 Upon the heavens, and now they are his own.
Loth to go up the hill, or labour thus
To go to heaven, we make heaven come to us.
We spur, we rein the stars, and in their race
They're diversely content t' obey our pace.
But keeps the earth her round proportion still?
Doth not a Tenerife, or higher hill
Rise so high like a rock, that one might think
The floating moon would shipwreck there, and sink?
Seas are so deep, that whales being struck today,
290 Perchance tomorrow, scarce at middle way
Of their wished journey's end, the bottom, die.
And men, to sound depths, so much line untie,
As one might justly think that there would rise
At end thereof, one of th' Antipodes:
If under all, a vault infernal be,
(Which sure is spacious, except that we
Invent another torment, that there must
Millions into a strait hot room be thrust)
Then solidness, and roundness have no place.
300 Are these but warts, and pock-holes in the face
Of th' earth? Think so: but yet confess, in this
The world's proportion disfigured is,
That those two legs whereon it doth rely, *Disorder in the*
Reward and punishment are bent awry. *world.*
And, oh, it can no more be questioned,
That beauty's best, proportion, is dead,
Since even grief itself, which now alone
Is left us, is without proportion.
She by whose lines proportion should be
310 Examined, measure of all symmetry,
Whom had that ancient seen, who thought souls made
Of harmony, he would at next have said
That harmony was she, and thence infer,
That souls were but resultances from her,
And did from her into our bodies go,

As to our eyes, the forms from objects flow:
She, who if those great Doctors truly said
That the Ark to man's proportions was made,
Had been a type for that, as that might be
320 A type of her in this, that contrary
Both elements, and passions lived at peace
In her, who caused all civil war to cease.
She, after whom, what form soe'er we see,
Is discord, and rude incongruity;
She, she is dead, she's dead; when thou know'st this
Thou know'st how ugly a monster this world is:
And learn'st thus much by our anatomy,
That here is nothing to enamour thee:
And that, not only faults in inward parts,
330 Corruptions in our brains, or in our hearts,
Poisoning the fountains, whence our actions spring,
Endanger us: but that if everything
Be not done fitly'and in proportion,
To satisfy wise, and good lookers on,
(Since most men be such as most think they be)
They're loathsome too, by this deformity.
For good, and well, must in our actions meet;
Wicked is not much worse than indiscreet.
But beauty's other second element,
340 Colour, and lustre now, is as near spent.
And had the world his just proportion,
Were it a ring still, yet the stone is gone.
As a compassionate turquoise which doth tell
By looking pale, the wearer is not well,
As gold falls sick being stung with mercury,
All the world's parts of such complexion be.
When nature was most busy, the first week,
Swaddling the new born earth, God seemed to like
That she should sport herself sometimes, and play,
350 To mingle, and vary colours every day:
And then, as though she could not make enow,
Himself his various rainbow did allow.
Sight is the noblest sense of any one,

Yet sight hath only colour to feed on,
And colour is decayed: summer's robe grows
Dusky, and like an oft dyed garment shows.
Our blushing red, which used in cheeks to spread,
Is inward sunk, and only our souls are red.
Perchance the world might have recovered,
360 If she whom we lament had not been dead:
But she, in whom all white, and red, and blue
(Beauty's ingredients) voluntary grew,
As in an unvexed paradise; from whom
Did all things verdure, and their lustre come,
Whose composition was miraculous,
Being all colour, all diaphanous,
(For air, and fire but thick gross bodies were,
And liveliest stones but drowsy, and pale to her,)
She, she, is dead; she's dead: when thou know'st this,
370 Thou know'st how wan a ghost this our world is:
And learn'st thus much by our anatomy,
That it should more affright, than pleasure thee.
And that, since all fair colour then did sink,
'Tis now but wicked vanity, to think
To colour vicious deeds with good pretence,   *Weakness in*
Or with bought colours to illude men's sense.   *the want of*
Nor in aught more this world's decay appears,   *correspond-*
Than that her influence the heaven forbears,   *ence of*
Or that the elements do not feel this,   *heaven and*
380 The father, or the mother barren is.   *earth.*
The clouds conceive not rain, or do not pour
In the due birth time, down the balmy shower.
Th' air doth not motherly sit on the earth,
To hatch her seasons, and give all things birth.
Spring-times were common cradles, but are tombs;
And false conceptions fill the general wombs.
Th' air shows such meteors, as none can see,
Not only what they mean, but what they be.
Earth such new worms, as would have troubled much
390 Th' Egyptian Mages to have made more such.
What artist now dares boast that he can bring

Heaven hither, or constellate anything,
So as the influence of those stars may be
Imprisoned in an herb, or charm, or tree,
And do by touch, all which those stars could do?
The art is lost, and correspondence too.
For heaven gives little, and the earth takes less,
And man least knows their trade, and purposes.
If this commerce 'twixt heaven and earth were not
400 Embarred, and all this traffic quite forgot,
She, for whose loss we have lamented thus,
Would work more fully and powerfully on us.
Since herbs, and roots by dying, lose not all,
But they, yea ashes too, are medicinal,
Death could not quench her virtue so, but that
It would be (if not followed) wondered at:
And all the world would be one dying swan,
To sing her funeral praise, and vanish then.
But as some serpents' poison hurteth not,
410 Except it be from the live serpent shot,
So doth her virtue need her here, to fit
That unto us; she working more than it.
But she, in whom to such maturity
Virtue was grown, past growth, that it must die,
She, from whose influence all impressions came,
But, by receivers' impotencies, lame,
Who, though she could not transubstantiate
All states to gold, yet gilded every state,
So that some princes have some temperance;
420 Some counsellors some purpose to advance
The common profit; and some people have
Some stay, no more than kings should give, to crave;
Some women have some taciturnity,
Some nunneries, some grains of chastity.
She that did thus much, and much more could do,
But that our age was iron, and rusty too,
She, she is dead; she 's dead; when thou know'st this,
Thou know'st how dry a cinder this world is.
And learn'st thus much by our anatomy,

430 That 'tis in vain to dew, or mollify
It with thy tears, or sweat, or blood: nothing
Is worth our travail, grief, or perishing,
But those rich joys, which did possess her heart,
Of which she's now partaker, and a part.
But as in cutting up a man that 's dead, *Conclusion.*
The body will not last out to have read
On every part, and therefore men direct
Their speech to parts, that are of most effect;
So the world's carcase would not last, if I
440 Were punctual in this anatomy.
Nor smells it well to hearers, if one tell
Them their disease, who fain would think they're well.
Here therefore be the end: and, blessed maid,
Of whom is meant whatever hath been said,
Or shall be spoken well by any tongue,
Whose name refines coarse lines, and makes prose song,
Accept this tribute, and his first year's rent,
Who till his dark short taper's end be spent,
As oft as thy feast sees this widowed earth,
450 Will yearly celebrate thy second birth,
That is, thy death. For though the soul of man
Be got when man is made, 'tis born but then
When man doth die. Our body 's as the womb,
And as a midwife death directs it home.
And you her creatures, whom she works upon
And have your last, and best concoction
From her example, and her virtue, if you
In reverence to her, do think it due,
That no one should her praises thus rehearse,
460 As matter fit for chronicle, not verse,
Vouchsafe to call to mind, that God did make
A last, and lasting'st piece, a song. He spake
To Moses, to deliver unto all,
That song: because he knew they would let fall
The Law, the prophets, and the history,
But keep the song still in their memory.
Such an opinion (in due measure) made
Me this great office boldly to invade.

Nor could incomprehensibleness deter
470 Me, from thus trying to emprison her.
Which when I saw that a strict grave could do,
I saw not why verse might not do so too.
Verse hath a middle nature: heaven keeps souls,
The grave keeps bodies, verse the fame enrols.

A Funeral Elegy

'Tis lost, to trust a tomb with such a guest,
  Or to confine her in a marble chest.
Alas, what 's marble, jet, or porphyry,
  Prized with the chrysolite of either eye,
Or with those pearls, and rubies which she was?
  Join the two Indies in one tomb, 'tis glass;
And so is all to her materials,
  Though every inch were ten Escurials,
Yet she 's demolished: can we keep her then
10 In works of hands, or of the wits of men?
Can these memorials, rags of paper, give
  Life to that name, by which name they must live?
Sickly, alas, short-lived, aborted be
  Those carcase verses, whose soul is not she.
And can she, who no longer would be she,
  Being such a tabernacle, stoop to be
In paper wrapped; or, when she would not lie
  In such a house, dwell in an elegy?
But 'tis no matter; we may well allow
20 Verse to live so long as the world will now.
For her death wounded it. The world contains
  Princes for arms, and counsellors for brains,
Lawyers for tongues, divines for hearts, and more,
  The rich for stomachs, and for backs, the poor;
The officers for hands, merchants for feet
  By which remote and distant countries meet.
But those fine spirits which do tune and set
  This organ, are those pieces which beget

Wonder and love; and these were she; and she
30   Being spent, the world must needs decrepit be.
For since death will proceed to triumph still,
    He can find nothing, after her, to kill,
Except the world itself, so great as she.
    Thus brave and confident may Nature be,
Death cannot give her such another blow,
    Because she cannot such another show.
But must we say she 's dead? may 't not be said
    That as a sundered clock is piecemeal laid,
Not to be lost, but by the maker's hand
40   Repolished, without error then to stand,
Or as the Afric Niger stream enwombs
    Itself into the earth, and after comes
(Having first made a natural bridge, to pass
    For many leagues) far greater than it was,
May 't not be said, that her grave shall restore
    Her, greater, purer, firmer, than before?
Heaven may say this, and joy in 't; but can we
    Who live, and lack her, here this vantage see?
What is 't to us, alas, if there have been
50   An Angel made a Throne, or Cherubin?
We lose by 't: and as aged men are glad
    Being tasteless grown, to joy in joys they had,
So now the sick starved world must feed upon
    This joy, that we had her, who now is gone.
Rejoice then Nature, and this world, that you,
    Fearing the last fires hastening to subdue
Your force and vigour, ere it were near gone,
    Wisely bestowed and laid it all on one.
One, whose clear body was so pure, and thin,
60   Because it need disguise no thought within.
'Twas but a through-light scarf, her mind to enrol,
    Or exhalation breathed out from her soul.
One, whom all men who durst no more, admired,
    And whom, whoe'er had worth enough, desired;
As when a temple 's built, saints emulate
    To which of them, it shall be consecrate.
But as when heaven looks on us with new eyes,

Those new stars every artist exercise,
What place they should assign to them they doubt,
70   Argue, and agree not till those stars go out:
So the world studied whose this piece should be,
  Till she can be nobody's else, nor she:
But like a lamp of balsamum, desired
  Rather to 'adorn, than last, she soon expired,
Clothed in her virgin white integrity;
  For marriage, though it do not stain, doth dye.
To 'scape th' infirmities which wait upon
  Woman, she went away, before she was one;
And the world's busy noise to overcome,
80   Took so much death, as served for opium.
For though she could not, nor could choose to die,
  She hath yielded to too long an ecstasy.
He which not knowing her sad history,
  Should come to read the book of destiny,
How fair and chaste, humble and high she had been,
  Much promised, much performed, at not fifteen,
And measuring future things by things before,
  Should turn the leaf to read, and read no more,
Would think that either destiny mistook,
90   Or that some leaves were torn out of the book.
But 'tis not so; Fate did but usher her
  To years of reason's use, and then infer
Her destiny to herself; which liberty
  She took but for thus much, thus much to die.
Her modesty not suffering her to be
  Fellow-commissioner with Destiny,
She did no more but die; if after her
  Any shall live, which dare true good prefer,
Every such person is her delegate,
100   T' accomplish that which should have been her fate.
They shall make up that book, and shall have thanks
  Of Fate, and her, for filling up their blanks.
For future virtuous deeds are legacies,
  Which from the gift of her example rise;
And 'tis in heaven part of spiritual mirth,
  To see how well the good play her, on earth.

Of the Progress of the Soul

WHEREIN, BY OCCASION OF THE RELIGIOUS DEATH OF
MISTRESS ELIZABETH DRURY, THE INCOMMODITIES
OF THE SOUL IN THIS LIFE, AND HER EXALTATION
IN THE NEXT, ARE CONTEMPLATED

THE SECOND ANNIVERSARY

The Harbinger to the Progress

Two souls move here, and mine (a third) must move
Paces of admiration and of love;
Thy soul (dear virgin) whose this tribute is,
Moved from this mortal sphere to lively bliss;
And yet moves still, and still aspires to see
The world's last day, thy glory's full degree:
Like as those stars which thou o'erlookest far,
Are in their place, and yet still moved are:
No soul (whiles with the luggage of this clay
10   It clogged is) can follow thee half way;
Or see thy flight, which doth our thoughts outgo
So fast, that now the lightning moves but slow:
But now thou art as high in heaven flown
As heaven's from us; what soul besides thine own
Can tell thy joys, or say he can relate
Thy glorious journals in that blessed state?
I envy thee (rich soul) I envy thee,
Although I cannot yet thy glory see:
And thou (great spirit) which hers followed hast
20   So fast, as none can follow thine so fast;
So far, as none can follow thine so far,
(And if this flesh did not the passage bar
Hadst raught her) let me wonder at thy flight
Which long agone hadst lost the vulgar sight,
And now mak'st proud the better eyes, that they

Can see thee lessened in thine aery way;
So while thou mak'st her soul's high progress known
Thou mak'st a noble progress of thine own,
From this world's carcase having mounted high
30 To that pure life of immortality;
Since thine aspiring thoughts themselves so raise
That more may not beseem a creature's praise,
Yet still thou vow'st her more; and every year
Mak'st a new progress, while thou wanderest here;
Still upwards mount; and let thy maker's praise
Honour thy Laura, and adorn thy lays.
And since thy Muse her head in heaven shrouds,
Oh let her never stoop below the clouds:
And if those glorious sainted souls may know
40 Or what we do, or what we sing below,
Those acts, those songs shall still content them best
Which praise those awful powers that make them blessed.

Of the Progress of the Soul

THE SECOND ANNIVERSARY

Nothing could make me sooner to confess   *The entrance.*
That this world had an everlastingness,
Than to consider, that a year is run,
Since both this lower world's and the sun's sun,
The lustre, and the vigour of this all,
Did set; 'twere blasphemy to say, did fall.
But as a ship which hath struck sail, doth run
By force of that force which before, it won:
Or as sometimes in a beheaded man,
10 Though at those two red seas, which freely ran,
One from the trunk, another from the head,
His soul be sailed, to her eternal bed,
His eyes will twinkle, and his tongue will roll,
As though he beckoned, and called back his soul,

He grasps his hands, and he pulls up his feet,
And seems to reach, and to step forth to meet
His soul; when all these motions which we saw,
Are but as ice, which crackles at a thaw:
Or as a lute, which in moist weather, rings
20   Her knell alone, by cracking of her strings:
So struggles this dead world, now she is gone;
For there is motion in corruption.
As some days are, at the Creation named,
Before the sun, the which framed days, was framed,
So after this sun's set, some show appears,
And orderly vicissitude of years.
Yet a new Deluge, and of Lethe flood,
Hath drowned us all, all have forgot all good,
Forgetting her, the main reserve of all,
30   Yet in this deluge, gross and general,
Thou seest me strive for life; my life shall be,
To be hereafter praised, for praising thee,
Immortal Maid, who though thou would'st refuse
The name of mother, be unto my Muse
A father, since her chaste ambition is,
Yearly to bring forth such a child as this.
These hymns may work on future wits, and so
May great grandchildren of thy praises grow.
And so, though not revive, embalm and spice
40   The world, which else would putrefy with vice.
For thus, man may extend thy progeny,
Until man do but vanish, and not die.
These hymns thy issue, may increase so long,
As till God's great *Venite* change the song.
Thirst for that time, O my insatiate soul,
And serve thy thirst, with God's safe-sealing bowl.   *A just*
Be thirsty still, and drink still till thou go;   *disest-*
'Tis th' only health, to be hydroptic so.   *imation*
Forget this rotten world; and unto thee   *of the*
50   Let thine own times as an old story be.   *world.*
Be not concerned: study not why, nor when;
Do not so much, as not believe a man.

For though to err, be worst, to try truths forth,
Is far more business than this world is worth.
The world is but a carcase; thou art fed
By it, but as a worm, that carcase bred;
And why shouldst thou, poor worm, consider more,
When this world will grow better than before,
Than those thy fellow worms do think upon
60   That carcase's last resurrection.
Forget this world, and scarce think of it so,
As of old clothes, cast off a year ago.
To be thus stupid is alacrity;
Men thus lethargic have best memory.
Look upward; that 's towards her, whose happy state
We now lament not, but congratulate.
She, to whom all this world was but a stage,
Where all sat hearkening how her youthful age
Should be employed, because in all she did,
70   Some figure of the Golden Times was hid;
Who could not lack, whate'er this world could give,
Because she was the form, that made it live;
Nor could complain, that this world was unfit
To be stayed in, then when she was in it;
She that first tried indifferent desires
By virtue, and virtue by religious fires,
She to whose person Paradise adhered,
As Courts to princes, she whose eyes ensphered
Star-light enough, to' have made the south control,
80   (Had she been there) the star-full northern pole,
She, she is gone; she is gone; when thou know'st this,
What fragmentary rubbish this world is   *Contem-*
Thou know'st, and that it is not worth a thought; *plation of*
He honours it too much that thinks it naught.   *our state*
Think then, my soul, that death is but a groom,   *in our*
Which brings a taper to the outward room,   *deathbed.*
Whence thou spiest first a little glimmering light,
And after brings it nearer to thy sight:
For such approaches doth heaven make in death.
90   Think thyself labouring now with broken breath,

And think those broken and soft notes to be
Division, and thy happiest harmony.
Think thee laid on thy death-bed, loose and slack;
And think that, but unbinding of a pack,
To take one precious thing, thy soul, from thence.
Think thyself parched with fever's violence,
Anger thine ague more, by calling it
Thy physic; chide the slackness of the fit.
Think that thou hear'st thy knell, and think no more,
100 But that, as bells called thee to church before,
So this, to the Triumphant Church, calls thee.
Think Satan's sergeants round about thee be,
And think that but for legacies they thrust;
Give one thy pride, to another give thy lust:
Give them those sins which they gave thee before,
And trust th' immaculate blood to wash thy score.
Think thy friends weeping round, and think that they
Weep but because they go not yet thy way.
Think that they close thine eyes, and think in this,
110 That they confess much in the world, amiss,
Who dare not trust a dead man's eye with that,
Which they from God, and angels cover not.
Think that they shroud thee up, and think from thence
They reinvest thee in white innocence.
Think that thy body rots, and (if so low,
Thy soul exalted so, thy thoughts can go),
Think thee a prince, who of themselves create
Worms which insensibly devour their state.
Think that they bury thee, and think that rite
120 Lays thee to sleep but a Saint Lucy's night.
Think these things cheerfully: and if thou be
Drowsy or slack, remember then that she,
She whose complexion was so even made,
That which of her ingredients should invade
The other three, no fear, no art could guess:
So far were all removed from more or less.
But as in mithridate, or just perfumes,
Where all good things being met, no one presumes

To govern, or to triumph on the rest,
130 Only because all were, no part was best.
And as, though all do know, that quantities
Are made of lines, and lines from points arise,
None can these lines or quantities unjoint,
And say this is a line, or this a point,
So though the elements and humours were
In her, one could not say, this governs there.
Whose even constitution might have won
Any disease to venture on the sun,
Rather than her: and make a spirit fear
140 That he to disuniting subject were.
To whose proportions if we would compare
Cubes, they 'are unstable; circles, angular;
She who was such a chain as Fate employs
To bring mankind all fortunes it enjoys,
So fast, so even wrought, as one would think,
No accident could threaten any link;
She, she embraced a sickness, gave it meat,
The purest blood, and breath, that e'er it eat;
And hath taught us, that though a good man hath
150 Title to heaven, and plead it by his faith,
And though he may pretend a conquest, since
Heaven was content to suffer violence,
Yea though he plead a long possession too,
(For they 're in heaven on earth who heaven's works do)
Though he had right, and power, and place before,
Yet death must usher, and unlock the door.
Think further on thy self, my soul, and think   *Incom-*
How thou at first was made but in a sink;   *modities*
Think that it argued some infirmity,   *of the*
                                              soul in
160 That those two souls, which then thou found'st in me,   *the body.*
Thou fed'st upon, and drew'st into thee, both
My second soul of sense, and first of growth.
Think but how poor thou wast, how obnoxious;
Whom a small lump of flesh could poison thus.
This curded milk, this poor unlittered whelp
My body, could, beyond escape or help,

Infect thee with original sin, and thou
Couldst neither then refuse, nor leave it now.
Think that no stubborn sullen anchorite,
170　Which fixed to a pillar, or a grave doth sit
Bedded, and bathed in all his ordures, dwells
So foully as our souls in their first-built cells.
Think in how poor a prison thou didst lie
After, enabled but to suck and cry.
Think, when 'twas grown to most, 'twas a poor inn,
A province packed up in two yards of skin,
And that usurped or threatened with the rage
Of sicknesses, or their true mother, age.
But think that death hath now enfranchised thee, *Her*
180　Thou hast thy expansion now, and liberty;　　*liberty*
Think that a rusty piece, discharged, is flown　*by death.*
In pieces, and the bullet is his own,
And freely flies; this to thy soul allow,
Think thy shell broke, think thy soul hatched but now.
And think this slow-paced soul, which late did cleave
To a body, and went but by the body's leave,
Twenty, perchance, or thirty mile a day,
Dispatches in a minute all the way
'Twixt heaven, and earth: she stays not in the air,
190　To look what meteors there themselves prepare;
She carries no desire to know, nor sense,
Whether th' air's middle region be intense;
For th' element of fire, she doth not know,
Whether she passed by such a place or no;
She baits not at the moon, nor cares to try
Whether in that new world, men live and die.
Venus retards her not, to inquire, how she
Can, (being one star) Hesper, and Vesper be;
He that charmed Argus' eyes, sweet Mercury,
200　Works not on her, who now is grown all eye;
Who, if she meet the body of the sun,
Goes through, not staying till his course be run;
Who finds in Mars his camp, no corps of guard;
Nor is by Jove, nor by his father barred;

But ere she can consider how she went,
At once is at, and through the firmament.
And as these stars were but so many beads
Strung on one string, speed undistinguished leads
Her through those spheres, as through the beads, a string,
210 Whose quick succession makes it still one thing:
As doth the pith, which, lest our bodies slack,
Strings fast the little bones of neck, and back;
So by the soul doth death string heaven and earth;
For when our soul enjoys this her third birth,
(Creation gave her one, a second, grace),
Heaven is as near, and present to her face,
As colours are, and objects, in a room
Where darkness was before, when tapers come.
This must, my soul, thy long-short progress be;
220 To advance these thoughts, remember then, that she,
She, whose fair body no such prison was,
But that a soul might well be pleased to pass
An age in her; she whose rich beauty lent
Mintage to others' beauties, for they went
But for so much as they were like to her;
She, in whose body (if we dare prefer
This low world, to so high a mark as she),
The western treasure, eastern spicery,
Europe, and Afric, and the unknown rest
230 Were easily found, or what in them was best;
And when we'have made this large discovery
Of all in her some one part, then will be
Twenty such parts, whose plenty and riches is
Enough to make twenty such worlds as this;
She, whom had they known who did first betroth
The tutelar angels, and assigned one, both
To nations, cities, and to companies,
To functions, offices, and dignities,
And to each several man, to him, and him,
240 They would have given her one for every limb;
She, of whose soul if we may say, 'twas gold,
Her body was th' electrum, and did hold

Many degrees of that; we understood
Her by her sight, her pure and eloquent blood
Spoke in her cheeks, and so distinctly wrought,
That one might almost say, her body thought;
She, she, thus richly and largely housed, is gone:
And chides us slow-paced snails who crawl upon
Our prison's prison, earth, nor think us well,
250 Longer, than whilst we bear our brittle shell.
But 'twere but little to have changed our room,   *Her ig-*
If, as we were in this our living tomb   *norance*
Oppressed with ignorance, we still were so.   *in this*
Poor soul, in this thy flesh what dost thou know?   *life and*
Thou know'st thyself so little, as thou know'st not,   *know-*
How thou didst die, nor how thou wast begot.   *ledge in*
Thou neither know'st, how thou at first cam'st in,   *the*
Nor how thou took'st the poison of man's sin.   *next.*
Nor dost thou, (though thou know'st, that thou art so)
260 By what way thou art made immortal, know.
Thou art too narrow, wretch, to comprehend
Even thyself; yea though thou wouldst but bend
To know thy body. Have not all souls thought
For many ages, that our body is wrought
Of air, and fire, and other elements?
And now they think of new ingredients,
And one soul thinks one, and another way
Another thinks, and 'tis an even lay.
Know'st thou but how the stone doth enter in
270 The bladder's cave, and never break the skin?
Know'st thou how blood, which to the heart doth flow,
Doth from one ventricle to th' other go?
And for the putrid stuff, which thou dost spit,
Know'st thou how thy lungs have attracted it?
There are no passages, so that there is
(For aught thou know'st) piercing of substances.
And of those many opinions which men raise
Of nails and hairs, dost thou know which to praise?
What hope have we to know our selves, when we
280 Know not the least things, which for our use be?

We see in authors, too stiff to recant,
A hundred controversies of an ant;
And yet one watches, starves, freezes, and sweats,
To know but catechisms and alphabets
Of unconcerning things, matters of fact;
How others on our stage their parts did act;
What Caesar did, yea, and what Cicero said.
Why grass is green, or why our blood is red,
Are mysteries which none have reached unto.
290 In this low form, poor soul, what wilt thou do?
When wilt thou shake off this pedantery,
Of being taught by sense, and fantasy?
Thou look'st through spectacles; small things seem great
Below; but up unto the watch-tower get,
And see all things despoiled of fallacies:
Thou shalt not peep through lattices of eyes,
Nor hear through labyrinths of ears, nor learn
By circuit, or collections to discern.
In heaven thou straight know'st all, concerning it,
300 And what concerns it not, shalt straight forget.
There thou (but in no other school) mayst be
Perchance, as learned, and as full, as she,
She who all libraries had throughly read
At home, in her own thoughts, and practised
So much good as would make as many more:
She whose example they must all implore,
Who would or do, or think well, and confess
That aye the virtuous actions they express,
Are but a new, and worse edition
310 Of her some one thought, or one action:
She, who in th' art of knowing heaven, was grown
Here upon earth, to such perfection,
That she hath, ever since to heaven she came,
(In a far fairer print), but read the same:
She, she not satisfied with all this weight,
(For so much knowledge, as would over-freight
Another, did but ballast her) is gone
As well t' enjoy, as get perfection.

And calls us after her, in that she took,
320 (Taking herself) our best, and worthiest book.
Return not, my soul, from this ecstasy,
And meditation of what thou shalt be,
To earthly thoughts, till it to thee appear,
With whom thy conversation must be there.
With whom wilt thou converse? what station
Canst thou choose out, free from infection,
That will nor give thee theirs, nor drink in thine?
Shalt thou not find a spongy slack divine
Drink and suck in th' instructions of great men,
330 And for the word of God, vent them again?
Are there not some Courts (and then, no things be
So like as Courts) which, in this let us see,
That wits and tongues of libellers are weak,
Because they do more ill, than these can speak?
The poison'is gone through all, poisons affect
Chiefly the chiefest parts, but some effect
In nails, and hairs, yea excrements, will show;
So will the poison of sin in the most low.
Up, up, my drowsy soul, where thy new ear
340 Shall in the angels' songs no discord hear;
Where thou shalt see the blessed mother-maid
Joy in not being that, which men have said.
Where she is exalted more for being good,
Than for her interest of motherhood.
Up to those patriarchs, which did longer sit
Expecting Christ, than they'have enjoyed him yet.
Up to those prophets, which now gladly see
Their prophecies grown to be history.
Up to th' apostles, who did bravely run
350 All the sun's course, with more light than the sun.
Up to those martyrs, who did calmly bleed
Oil to th' apostles' lamps, dew to their seed.
Up to those virgins, who thought that almost
They made joint tenants with the Holy Ghost,
If they to any should his temple give.
Up, up, for in that squadron there doth live

Of our com-
pany in this
life, and in the
next.

She, who hath carried thither new degrees
(As to their number) to their dignities.
She, who being to herself a State, enjoyed
360 All royalties which any State employed;
For she made wars, and triumphed; reason still
Did not o'erthrow, but rectify her will:
And she made peace, for no peace is like this,
That beauty and chastity together kiss:
She did high justice, for she crucified
Every first motion of rebellious pride:
And she gave pardons, and was liberal,
For, only herself except, she pardoned all:
She coined, in this, that her impressions gave
370 To all our actions all the worth they have:
She gave protections; the thoughts of her breast
Satan's rude officers could ne'er arrest.
As these prerogatives being met in one,
Made her a sovereign State, religion
Made her a Church; and these two made her all.
She who was all this all, and could not fall
To worse, by company, (for she was still
More antidote, than all the world was ill,)
She, she doth leave it, and by death, survive
380 All this, in heaven; whither who doth not strive
The more, because she 's there, he doth not know
That accidental joys in heaven do grow.
But pause, my soul, and study ere thou fall
On accidental joys, th' essential.   *Of essential joy*
Still before accessories do abide   *in this life and*
A trial, must the principal be tried.   *in the next.*
And what essential joy canst thou expect
Here upon earth? what permanent effect
Of transitory causes? Dost thou love
390 Beauty? (and beauty worthiest is to move)
Poor cozened cozener, that she, and that thou,
Which did begin to love, are neither now;
You are both fluid, changed since yesterday;
Next day repairs, (but ill) last day's decay.

Nor are, (although the river keep the name)
Yesterday's waters, and today's the same.
So flows her face, and thine eyes, neither now
That saint, nor pilgrim, which your loving vow
Concerned, remains; but whilst you think you be
400   Constant, you'are hourly in inconstancy.
Honour may have pretence unto our love,
Because that God did live so long above
Without this honour, and then loved it so,
That he at last made creatures to bestow
Honour on him; not that he needed it,
But that, to his hands, man might grow more fit.
But since all honours from inferiors flow,
(For they do give it; princes do but show
Whom they would have so honoured) and that this
410   On such opinions, and capacities
Is built, as rise, and fall, to more and less:
Alas, 'tis but a casual happiness.
Hath ever any man to' himself assigned
This or that happiness to arrest his mind,
But that another man, which takes a worse,
Thinks him a fool for having ta'en that course?
They who did labour Babel's tower to erect,
Might have considered, that for that effect,
All this whole solid earth could not allow
420   Nor furnish forth materials enow;
And that this centre, to raise such a place,
Was far too little, to have been the base;
No more affords this world, foundation
To erect true joy, were all the means in one.
But as the heathen made them several gods,
Of all God's benefits, and all his rods,
(For as the wine, and corn, and onions are
Gods unto them, so agues be, and war)
And as by changing that whole precious gold
430   To such small copper coins, they lost the old,
And lost their only God, who ever must
Be sought alone, and not in such a thrust:

So much mankind true happiness mistakes;
No joy enjoys that man, that many makes.
Then, soul, to thy first pitch work up again;
Know that all lines which circles do contain,
For once that they the centre touch, do touch
Twice the circumference; and be thou such;
Double on heaven, thy thoughts on earth employed;
440 All will not serve; only who have enjoyed
The sight of God, in fulness, can think it;
For it is both the object, and the wit.
This is essential joy, where neither he
Can suffer diminution, nor we;
'Tis such a full, and such a filling good;
Had th' angels once looked on him, they had stood.
To fill the place of one of them, or more,
She whom we celebrate, is gone before.
She, who had here so much essential joy,
450 As no chance could distract, much less destroy;
Who with God's presence was acquainted so,
(Hearing, and speaking to him) as to know
His face in any natural stone, or tree,
Better than when in images they be:
Who kept by diligent devotion,
God's image, in such reparation,
Within her heart, that what decay was grown,
Was her first parents' fault, and not her own:
Who being solicited to any act,
460 Still heard God pleading his safe precontract;
Who by a faithful confidence, was here
Betrothed to God, and now is married there;
Whose twilights were more clear, than our midday;
Who dreamed devoutlier, than most use to pray;
Who being here filled with grace, yet strove to be,
Both where more grace, and more capacity
At once is given: she to heaven is gone,
Who made this world in some proportion
A heaven, and here, became unto us all,
470 Joy (as our joys admit) essential.

But could this low world joys essential touch,   *Of acci-*
Heaven's accidental joys would pass them much.   *dental*
How poor and lame, must then our casual be!   *joys in*
If thy prince will his subjects to call thee   *both*
My Lord, and this do swell thee, thou art then,   *places.*
By being a greater, grown to be less man.
When no physician of redress can speak,
A joyful casual violence may break
A dangerous aposteme in thy breast;
480   And whilst thou joyest in this, the dangerous rest,
The bag may rise up, and so strangle thee.
What aye was casual, may ever be.
What should the nature change? Or make the same
Certain, which was but casual, when it came?
All casual joy doth loud and plainly say,
Only by coming, that it can away.
Only in heaven joy's strength is never spent,
And accidental things are permanent.
Joy of a soul's arrival ne'er decays;
490   For that soul ever joys and ever stays.
Joy that their last great consummation
Approaches in the resurrection;
When earthly bodies more celestial
Shall be, than angels were, for they could fall;
This kind of joy doth every day admit
Degrees of growth, but none of losing it.
In this fresh joy, 'tis no small part, that she,
She, in whose goodness, he that names degree,
Doth injure her; ('tis loss to be called best,
500   There where the stuff is not such as the rest)
She, who left such a body, as even she
Only in heaven could learn, how it can be
Made better; for she rather was two souls,
Or like to full, on both sides written rolls,
Where eyes might read upon the outward skin,
As strong records for God, as minds within;
She, who by making full perfection grow,
Pieces a circle, and still keeps it so,

Longed for, and longing for it, to heaven is gone,
510   Where she receives, and gives addition.
Here in a place, where mis-devotion frames   *Con-*
A thousand prayers to saints, whose very names   *clusion.*
The ancient Church knew not, heaven knows not yet,
And where, what laws of poetry admit,
Laws of religion have at least the same,
Immortal maid, I might invoke thy name.
Could any saint provoke that appetite,
Thou here shouldst make me a French convertite.
But thou wouldst not; nor wouldst thou be content,
520   To take this, for my second year's true rent,
Did this coin bear any other stamp, than his,
That gave thee power to do, me, to say this.
Since his will is, that to posterity,
Thou shouldst for life, and death, a pattern be,
And that the world should notice have of this,
The purpose, and th' authority is his;
Thou art the proclamation; and I am
The trumpet, at whose voice the people came.

Divine Poems

To E. of D. with Six Holy Sonnets

See Sir, how as the sun's hot masculine flame
  Begets strange creatures on Nile's dirty slime,
  In me, your fatherly yet lusty rhyme
(For, these songs are their fruits) have wrought the same;
But though the engendering force from whence they came
  Be strong enough, and nature do admit
  Seven to be born at once, I send as yet
But six; they say, the seventh hath still some maim.
  I choose your judgement, which the same degree
10 Doth with her sister, your invention, hold,
As fire these drossy rhymes to purify,
  Or as elixir, to change them to gold;
You are that alchemist which always had
Wit, whose one spark could make good things of bad.

To Mrs Magdalen Herbert: of St Mary Magdalen

Her of your name, whose fair inheritance
  Bethina was, and jointure Magdalo:
An active faith so highly did advance,
  That she once knew, more than the Church did know,
The Resurrection; so much good there is
  Delivered of her, that some Fathers be
Loth to believe one woman could do this;
  But, think these Magdalens were two or three.
Increase their number, Lady, and their fame:
10 To their devotion, add your innocence;
Take so much of th' example, as of the name;
  The latter half; and in some recompense
That they did harbour Christ himself, a guest,
  Harbour these hymns, to his dear name addressed. J.D.

HOLY SONNETS

La Corona

1

Deign at my hands this crown of prayer and praise,
Weaved in my low devout melancholy,
Thou which of good, hast, yea art treasury,
All changing unchanged Ancient of days,
But do not, with a vile crown of frail bays,
Reward my muse's white sincerity,
But what thy thorny crown gained, that give me,
A crown of glory, which doth flower always;
The ends crown our works, but thou crown'st our ends,
For, at our end begins our endless rest,
This first last end, now zealously possessed,
With a strong sober thirst, my soul attends.
'Tis time that heart and voice be lifted high,
Salvation to all that will is nigh.

2 Annunciation

Salvation to all that will is nigh,
That all, which always is all everywhere,
Which cannot sin, and yet all sins must bear,
Which cannot die, yet cannot choose but die,
Lo, faithful Virgin, yields himself to lie
In prison, in thy womb; and though he there
Can take no sin, nor thou give, yet he 'will wear
Taken from thence, flesh, which death's force may try.
Ere by the spheres time was created, thou
Wast in his mind, who is thy son, and brother,
Whom thou conceiv'st, conceived; yea thou art now
Thy maker's maker, and thy father's mother,
Thou' hast light in dark; and shutt'st in little room,
Immensity cloistered in thy dear womb.

3 Nativity

Immensity cloistered in thy dear womb,
Now leaves his well-beloved imprisonment,
There he hath made himself to his intent
Weak enough, now into our world to come;
But oh, for thee, for him, hath th' inn no room?
Yet lay him in this stall, and from the orient,
Stars, and wisemen will travel to prevent
Th' effect of Herod's jealous general doom.
See'st thou, my soul, with thy faith's eyes, how he
10 Which fills all place, yet none holds him, doth lie?
Was not his pity towards thee wondrous high,
That would have need to be pitied by thee?
Kiss him, and with him into Egypt go,
With his kind mother, who partakes thy woe.

4 Temple

With his kind mother who partakes thy woe,
Joseph turn back; see where your child doth sit,
Blowing, yea blowing out those sparks of wit,
Which himself on the Doctors did bestow;
The Word but lately could not speak, and lo
It suddenly speaks wonders, whence comes it,
That all which was, and all which should be writ,
A shallow seeming child, should deeply know?
His godhead was not soul to his manhood,
10 Nor had time mellowed him to this ripeness,
But as for one which hath a long task, 'tis good,
With the sun to begin his business,
He in his age's morning thus began
By miracles exceeding power of man.

5 Crucifying

By miracles exceeding power of man,
He faith in some, envy in some begat,
For, what weak spirits admire, ambitious hate;

In both affections many to him ran,
But oh! the worst are most, they will and can,
Alas, and do, unto the immaculate,
Whose creature Fate is, now prescribe a fate,
Measuring self-life's infinity to a span,
Nay to an inch. Lo, where condemned he
10 Bears his own cross, with pain, yet by and by
When it bears him, he must bear more and die.
Now thou art lifted up, draw me to thee,
And at thy death giving such liberal dole,
Moist, with one drop of thy blood, my dry soul.

6 Resurrection

Moist with one drop of thy blood, my dry soul
Shall (though she now be in extreme degree
Too stony hard, and yet too fleshly,) be
Freed by that drop, from being starved, hard, or foul,
And life, by this death abled, shall control
Death, whom thy death slew; nor shall to me
Fear of first or last death, bring misery,
If in thy little book my name thou enrol,
Flesh in that long sleep is not putrefied,
10 But made that there, of which, and for which 'twas;
Nor can by other means be glorified.
May then sin's sleep, and death's soon from me pass,
That waked from both, I again risen may
Salute the last, and everlasting day.

7 Ascension

Salute the last and everlasting day,
Joy at the uprising of this sun, and son,
Ye whose just tears, or tribulation
Have purely washed, or burnt your drossy clay;
Behold the highest, parting hence away,
Lightens the dark clouds, which he treads upon,
Nor doth he by ascending, show alone,
But first he, and he first enters the way.

O strong ram, which hast battered heaven for me,
10   Mild lamb, which with thy blood, hast marked the path;
Bright torch, which shin'st, that I the way may see,
Oh, with thine own blood quench thine own just wrath,
And if thy holy Spirit, my Muse did raise,
Deign at my hands this crown of prayer and praise.

Divine Meditations

1

Thou hast made me, and shall thy work decay?
Repair me now, for now mine end doth haste,
I run to death, and death meets me as fast,
And all my pleasures are like yesterday,
I dare not move my dim eyes any way,
Despair behind, and death before doth cast
Such terror, and my feeble flesh doth waste
By sin in it, which it towards hell doth weigh;
Only thou art above, and when towards thee
10   By thy leave I can look, I rise again;
But our old subtle foe so tempteth me,
That not one hour I can myself sustain;
Thy Grace may wing me to prevent his art,
And thou like adamant draw mine iron heart.

2

As due by many titles I resign
Myself to thee, O God, first I was made
By thee, and for thee, and when I was decayed
Thy blood bought that, the which before was thine,
I am thy son, made with thy self to shine,
Thy servant, whose pains thou hast still repaid,
Thy sheep, thine image, and, till I betrayed
My self, a temple of thy Spirit divine;
Why doth the devil then usurp on me?
10   Why doth he steal, nay ravish that 's thy right?
Except thou rise and for thine own work fight,
Oh I shall soon despair, when I do see

That thou lov'st mankind well, yet wilt not choose me,
And Satan hates me, yet is loth to lose me.

3

O might those sighs and tears return again
Into my breast and eyes, which I have spent,
That I might in this holy discontent
Mourn with some fruit, as I have mourned in vain;
In mine idolatry what showers of rain
Mine eyes did waste! what griefs my heart did rent!
That sufferance was my sin, now I repent;
Because I did suffer I must suffer pain.
Th' hydroptic drunkard, and night-scouting thief,
10 The itchy lecher, and self tickling proud
Have the remembrance of past joys, for relief
Of coming ills. To poor me is allowed
No ease; for, long, yet vehement grief hath been
The effect and cause, the punishment and sin.

4

Oh my black soul! now thou art summoned
By sickness, death's herald, and champion;
Thou art like a pilgrim, which abroad hath done
Treason, and durst not turn to whence he is fled,
Or like a thief, which till death's doom be read,
Wisheth himself delivered from prison;
But damned and haled to execution,
Wisheth that still he might be imprisoned;
Yet grace, if thou repent, thou canst not lack;
10 But who shall give thee that grace to begin?
Oh make thyself with holy mourning black,
And red with blushing, as thou art with sin;
Or wash thee in Christ's blood, which hath this might
That being red, it dyes red souls to white.

5

I am a little world made cunningly
Of elements, and an angelic sprite,

But black sin hath betrayed to endless night
My world's both parts, and, oh, both parts must die.
You which beyond that heaven which was most high
Have found new spheres, and of new lands can write,
Pour new seas in mine eyes, that so I might
Drown my world with my weeping earnestly,
Or wash it if it must be drowned no more:
10 But oh it must be burnt; alas the fire
Of lust and envy have burnt it heretofore,
And made it fouler; let their flames retire,
And burn me O Lord, with a fiery zeal
Of thee and thy house, which doth in eating heal.

6

This is my play's last scene, here heavens appoint
My pilgrimage's last mile; and my race
Idly, yet quickly run, hath this last pace,
My span's last inch, my minute's latest point,
And gluttonous death, will instantly unjoint
My body, and soul, and I shall sleep a space,
But my'ever-waking part shall see that face,
Whose fear already shakes my every joint:
Then, as my soul, to heaven her first seat, takes flight,
10 And earth-born body, in the earth shall dwell,
So, fall my sins, that all may have their right,
To where they are bred, and would press me, to hell.
Impute me righteous, thus purged of evil,
For thus I leave the world, the flesh, and devil.

7

At the round earth's imagined corners, blow
Your trumpets, angels, and arise, arise
From death, you numberless infinities
Of souls, and to your scattered bodies go,
All whom the flood did, and fire shall o'erthrow,
All whom war, dearth, age, agues, tyrannies,
Despair, law, chance, hath slain, and you whose eyes,
Shall behold God, and never taste death's woe.

But let them sleep, Lord, and me mourn a space,
10   For, if above all these, my sins abound,
'Tis late to ask abundance of thy grace,
When we are there; here on this lowly ground,
Teach me how to repent; for that's as good
As if thou hadst sealed my pardon, with thy blood.

8

If faithful souls be alike glorified
As angels, then my father's soul doth see,
And adds this even to full felicity,
That valiantly I hell's wide mouth o'erstride:
But if our minds to these souls be descried
By circumstances, and by signs that be
Apparent in us, not immediately,
How shall my mind's white truth by them be tried?
They see idolatrous lovers weep and mourn,
10   And vile blasphemous conjurers to call
On Jesus' name, and pharisaical
Dissemblers feign devotion. Then turn
O pensive soul, to God, for he knows best
Thy true grief, for he put it in my breast.

9

If poisonous minerals, and if that tree,
Whose fruit threw death on else immortal us,
If lecherous goats, if serpents envious
Cannot be damned; alas, why should I be?
Why should intent or reason, born in me,
Make sins, else equal, in me more heinous?
And mercy being easy, and glorious
To God, in his stern wrath, why threatens he?
But who am I, that dare dispute with thee
10   O God? Oh! of thine only worthy blood,
And my tears, make a heavenly lethean flood,
And drown in it my sin's black memory;
That thou remember them, some claim as debt,
I think it mercy, if thou wilt forget.

10

Death be not proud, though some have called thee
Mighty and dreadful, for, thou art not so,
For, those, whom thou think'st, thou dost overthrow,
Die not, poor death, nor yet canst thou kill me;
From rest and sleep, which but thy pictures be,
Much pleasure, then from thee, much more must flow,
And soonest our best men with thee do go,
Rest of their bones, and soul's delivery.
Thou art slave to fate, chance, kings, and desperate men,
10 And dost with poison, war, and sickness dwell,
And poppy, or charms can make us sleep as well,
And better than thy stroke; why swell'st thou then?
One short sleep past, we wake eternally,
And death shall be no more, Death thou shalt die.

11

Spit in my face ye Jews, and pierce my side,
Buffet, and scoff, scourge, and crucify me,
For I have sinned, and sinned, and only he,
Who could do no iniquity, hath died:
But by my death can not be satisfied
My sins, which pass the Jews' impiety:
They killed once an inglorious man, but I
Crucify him daily, being now glorified.
Oh let me then, his strange love still admire:
10 Kings pardon, but he bore our punishment.
And Jacob came clothed in vile harsh attire
But to supplant, and with gainful intent:
God clothed himself in vile man's flesh, that so
He might be weak enough to suffer woe.

12

Why are we by all creatures waited on?
Why do the prodigal elements supply
Life and food to me, being more pure than I,
Simple, and further from corruption?
Why brook'st thou, ignorant horse, subjection?

Why dost thou bull, and boar so sillily
Dissemble weakness, and by'one man's stroke die,
Whose whole kind, you might swallow and feed upon?
Weaker I am, woe is me, and worse than you,
10 You have not sinned, nor need be timorous.
But wonder at a greater wonder, for to us
Created nature doth these things subdue,
But their Creator, whom sin, nor nature tied,
For us, his creatures, and his foes, hath died.

13

What if this present were the world's last night?
Mark in my heart, O soul, where thou dost dwell,
The picture of Christ crucified, and tell
Whether that countenance can thee affright,
Tears in his eyes quench the amazing light,
Blood fills his frowns, which from his pierced head fell,
And can that tongue adjudge thee unto hell,
Which prayed forgiveness for his foes' fierce spite?
No, no; but as in my idolatry
10 I said to all my profane mistresses,
Beauty, of pity, foulness only is
A sign of rigour: so I say to thee,
To wicked spirits are horrid shapes assigned,
This beauteous form assures a piteous mind.

14

Batter my heart, three-personed God; for, you
As yet but knock, breathe, shine, and seek to mend;
That I may rise, and stand, o'erthrow me, and bend
Your force, to break, blow, burn, and make me new.
I, like an usurped town, to another due,
Labour to admit you, but oh, to no end,
Reason your viceroy in me, me should defend,
But is captived, and proves weak or untrue,
Yet dearly'I love you, and would be loved fain,
10 But am betrothed unto your enemy,
Divorce me, untie, or break that knot again,

Take me to you, imprison me, for I
Except you enthral me, never shall be free,
Nor ever chaste, except you ravish me.

15
Wilt thou love God, as he thee? then digest,
My soul, this wholesome meditation,
How God the Spirit, by angels waited on
In heaven, doth make his temple in thy breast.
The Father having begot a Son most blessed,
And still begetting, (for he ne'er begun)
Hath deigned to choose thee by adoption,
Coheir to' his glory, 'and Sabbath's endless rest;
And as a robbed man, which by search doth find
10　His stol'n stuff sold, must lose or buy it again:
The Son of glory came down, and was slain,
Us whom he had made, and Satan stol'n, to unbind.
'Twas much, that man was made like God before,
But, that God should be made like man, much more.

16
Father, part of his double interest
Unto thy kingdom, thy Son gives to me,
His jointure in the knotty Trinity
He keeps, and gives me his death's conquest.
This Lamb, whose death, with life the world hath blessed,
Was from the world's beginning slain, and he
Hath made two wills, which with the legacy
Of his and thy kingdom, do thy sons invest.
Yet such are thy laws, that men argue yet
10　Whether a man those statutes can fulfil;
None doth, but thy all-healing grace and Spirit
Revive again what law and letter kill.
Thy law's abridgement, and thy last command
Is all but love; oh let that last will stand!

17

Since she whom I loved hath paid her last debt
To nature, and to hers, and my good is dead,
And her soul early into heaven ravished,
Wholly in heavenly things my mind is set.
Here the admiring her my mind did whet
To seek thee God; so streams do show the head,
But though I have found thee, and thou my thirst hast fed,
A holy thirsty dropsy melts me yet.
But why should I beg more love, when as thou
10   Dost woo my soul for hers; offering all thine:
And dost not only fear lest I allow
My love to saints and angels, things divine,
But in thy tender jealousy dost doubt
Lest the world, flesh, yea Devil put thee out.

18

Show me dear Christ, thy spouse, so bright and clear.
What, is it she, which on the other shore
Goes richly painted? or which robbed and tore
Laments and mourns in Germany and here?
Sleeps she a thousand, then peeps up one year?
Is she self truth and errs? now new, now outwore?
Doth she, and did she, and shall she evermore
On one, on seven, or on no hill appear?
Dwells she with us, or like adventuring knights
10   First travail we to seek and then make love?
Betray kind husband thy spouse to our sights,
And let mine amorous soul court thy mild dove,
Who is most true, and pleasing to thee, then
When she' is embraced and open to most men.

19

Oh, to vex me, contraries meet in one:
Inconstancy unnaturally hath begot
A constant habit; that when I would not
I change in vows, and in devotion.
As humorous is my contrition

As my profane love, and as soon forgot:
As riddlingly distempered, cold and hot,
As praying, as mute; as infinite, as none.
I durst not view heaven yesterday; and today
10 In prayers, and flattering speeches I court God:
Tomorrow I quake with true fear of his rod.
So my devout fits come and go away
Like a fantastic ague: save that here
Those are my best days, when I shake with fear.

A Litany

I
The Father

Father of heaven, and him, by whom
It, and us for it, and all else, for us
   Thou mad'st, and govern'st ever, come
And re-create me, now grown ruinous:
     My heart is by dejection, clay,
     And by self-murder, red.
From this red earth, O Father, purge away
All vicious tinctures, that new fashioned
I may rise up from death, before I am dead.

II
The Son

10   O Son of God, who seeing two things,
Sin, and death crept in, which were never made,
   By bearing one, tried'st with what stings
The other could thine heritage invade;
     O be thou nailed unto my heart,
     And crucified again,
Part not from it, though it from thee would part,
But let it be by applying so thy pain,
Drowned in thy blood, and in thy passion slain.

III
The Holy Ghost

O Holy Ghost, whose temple I
20 Am, but of mud walls, and condensed dust,
And being sacrilegiously
Half wasted with youth's fires, of pride and lust,
Must with new storms be weatherbeat;
Double in my heart thy flame,
Which let devout sad tears intend; and let
(Though this glass lanthorn, flesh, do suffer maim)
Fire, sacrifice, priest, altar be the same.

IV
The Trinity

O Blessed glorious Trinity,
Bones to philosophy, but milk to faith,
30 Which, as wise serpents, diversely
Most slipperiness, yet most entanglings hath,
As you distinguished undistinct
By power, love, knowledge be,
Give me a such self different instinct,
Of these let all me elemented be,
Of power, to love, to know, you unnumbered three.

V
The Virgin Mary

For that fair blessed mother-maid,
Whose flesh redeemed us; that she-cherubin,
Which unlocked Paradise, and made
40 One claim for innocence, and disseized sin,
Whose womb was a strange heaven, for there
God clothed himself, and grew,
Our zealous thanks we pour. As her deeds were
Our helps, so are her prayers; nor can she sue
In vain, who hath such titles unto you.

VI
The Angels

And since this life our nonage is,
And we in wardship to thine angels be,
   Native in heaven's fair palaces,
Where we shall be but denizened by thee,
50   As th' earth conceiving by the sun,
      Yields fair diversity,
Yet never knows which course that light doth run,
So let me study, that mine actions be
Worthy their sight, though blind in how they see.

VII
The Patriarchs

And let thy patriarchs' desire
(Those great grandfathers of thy Church, which saw
   More in the cloud, than we in fire,
Whom Nature cleared more, than us grace and law,
      And now in heaven still pray, that we
60   May use our new helps right,)
Be satisfied, and fructify in me;
Let not my mind be blinder by more light
Nor faith by reason added, lose her sight.

VIII
The Prophets

Thy eagle-sighted prophets too,
Which were thy Church's organs, and did sound
   That harmony, which made of two
One law, and did unite, but not confound;
      Those heavenly poets which did see
      Thy will, and it express
70 In rhythmic feet, in common pray for me,
That I by them excuse not my excess
In seeking secrets, or poeticness.

IX
The Apostles

And thy illustrious zodiac
Of twelve apostles, which engirt this all,
  (From whom whosoever do not take
Their light, to dark deep pits, throw down, and fall,)
        As through their prayers, thou' hast let me know
        That their books are divine;
May they pray still, and be heard, that I go
80 The old broad way in applying; O decline
Me, when my comment would make thy word mine.

X
The Martyrs

And since thou so desirously
Didst long to die, that long before thou couldst,
  And long since thou no more couldst die,
Thou in thy scattered mystic body wouldst
        In Abel die, and ever since
        In thine, let their blood come
To beg for us, a discreet patience
Of death, or of worse life: for oh, to some
90 Not to be martyrs, is a martyrdom.

XI
The Confessors

Therefore with thee triumpheth there
A virgin squadron of white confessors,
  Whose bloods betrothed, not married were;
Tendered, not taken by those ravishers:
        They know, and pray, that we may know,
        In every Christian
Hourly tempestuous persecutions grow,
Temptations martyr us alive; a man
Is to himself a Diocletian.

XII
The Virgins

100   The cold white snowy nunnery,
Which, as thy mother, their high abbess, sent
   Their bodies back again to thee,
As thou hadst lent them, clean and innocent,
      Though they have not obtained of thee,
      That or thy Church, or I,
Should keep, as they, our first integrity;
Divorce thou sin in us, or bid it die,
And call chaste widowhead virginity.

XIII
The Doctors

   Thy sacred academe above
110 Of Doctors, whose pains have unclasped, and taught
   Both books of life to us (for love
To know thy Scriptures tells us, we are wrought
      In thy other book) pray for us there
      That what they have misdone
Or mis-said, we to that may not adhere;
Their zeal may be our sin. Lord let us run
Mean ways, and call them stars, but not the sun.

XIV
   And whilst this universal choir,
That Church in triumph, this in warfare here,
120 Warmed with one all-partaking fire
Of love, that none be lost, which cost thee dear,
      Prays ceaselessly, and thou hearken too,
      (Since to be gracious
Our task is treble, to pray, bear, and do)
Hear this prayer Lord: O Lord deliver us
From trusting in those prayers, though poured out thus.

XV

From being anxious, or secure,
Dead clods of sadness, or light squibs of mirth,
From thinking, that great courts immure
130 All, or no happiness, or that this earth
      Is only for our prison framed,
      Or that thou art covetous
To them whom thou lov'st, or that they are maimed
From reaching this world's sweet, who seek thee thus,
With all their might, Good Lord deliver us.

XVI

From needing danger, to be good,
From owing thee yesterday's tears today,
From trusting so much to thy blood,
That in that hope, we wound our soul away,
140   From bribing thee with alms, to excuse
      Some sin more burdenous,
From light affecting, in religion, news,
From thinking us all soul, neglecting thus
Our mutual duties, Lord deliver us.

XVII

From tempting Satan to tempt us,
By our connivance, or slack company,
From measuring ill by vicious,
Neglecting to choke sin's spawn, vanity,
      From indiscreet humility,
150   Which might be scandalous,
And cast reproach on Christianity,
From being spies, or to spies pervious,
From thirst, or scorn of fame, deliver us.

XVIII

Deliver us for thy descent
Into the Virgin, whose womb was a place
Of middle kind; and thou being sent
To ungracious us, stayed'st at her full of grace,

And through thy poor birth, where first thou
Glorified'st poverty,
160 And yet soon after riches didst allow,
By accepting King's gifts in the Epiphany,
Deliver, and make us, to both ways free.

XIX

And through that bitter agony,
Which is still the agony of pious wits,
Disputing what distorted thee,
And interrupted evenness, with fits,
And through thy free confession
Though thereby they were then
Made blind, so that thou mightst from them have gone,
170 Good Lord deliver us, and teach us when
We may not, and we may blind unjust men.

XX

Through thy submitting all, to blows
Thy face, thy clothes to spoil, thy fame to scorn,
All ways, which rage, or justice knows,
And by which thou couldst show, that thou wast born,
And through thy gallant humbleness
Which thou in death didst show,
Dying before thy soul they could express,
Deliver us from death, by dying so,
180 To this world, ere this world do bid us go.

XXI

When senses, which thy soldiers are,
We arm against thee, and they fight for sin,
When want, sent but to tame, doth war
And work despair a breach to enter in,
When plenty, God's image, and seal
Makes us idolatrous,
And love it, not him, whom it should reveal,
When we are moved to seem religious
Only to vent wit, Lord deliver us.

XXII

190   In churches, when the infirmity
Of him that speaks diminishes the Word,
    When magistrates do mis-apply
To us, as we judge, lay or ghostly sword,
        When plague, which is thine angel, reigns,
        Or wars, thy champions, sway,
When heresy, thy second deluge, gains;
In th' hour of death, th' eve of last judgement day,
Deliver us from the sinister way.

XXIII

    Hear us, O hear us Lord; to thee
200   A sinner is more music, when he prays,
    Than spheres, or angels' praises be,
In panegyric alleluias,
        Hear us, for till thou hear us, Lord
        We know not what to say.
Thine ear to our sighs, tears, thoughts gives voice and word.
O thou who Satan heard'st in Job's sick day,
Hear thyself now, for thou in us dost pray

XXIV

    That we may change to evenness
This intermitting aguish piety,
210   That snatching cramps of wickedness
And apoplexies of fast sin, may die;
        That music of thy promises,
        Not threats in thunder may
Awaken us to our just offices;
What in thy book, thou dost, or creatures say,
That we may hear, Lord hear us, when we pray.

XXV

    That our ears' sickness we may cure,
And rectify those labyrinths aright,
    That we by hearkening, not procure
220   Our praise, nor others' dispraise so invite,

That we get not a slipperiness,
And senselessly decline,
From hearing bold wits jest at kings' excess,
To admit the like of majesty divine,
That we may lock our ears, Lord open thine.

XXVI

That living law, the magistrate,
Which to give us, and make us physic, doth
Our vices often aggravate,
That preachers taxing sin, before her growth,
That Satan, and envenomed men
Which well, if we starve, dine,
When they do most accuse us, may see then
Us, to amendment, hear them; thee decline;
That we may open our ears, Lord lock thine.

XXVII

That learning, thine ambassador,
From thine allegiance we never tempt,
That beauty, paradise's flower
For physic made, from poison be exempt,
That wit, born apt high good to do,
By dwelling lazily
On Nature's nothing, be not nothing too,
That our affections kill us not, nor die,
Hear us, weak echoes, O thou ear, and cry.

XXVII

Son of God hear us, and since thou
By taking our blood, owest it us again,
Gain to thy self, or us allow;
And let not both us and thy self be slain;
O Lamb of God, which took'st our sin
Which could not stick to thee,
O let it not return to us again,
But patient and physician being free,
As sin is nothing, let it no where be.

The Cross

Since Christ embraced the Cross itself, dare I
His image, th' image of his Cross deny?
Would I have profit by the sacrifice,
And dare the chosen altar to despise?
It bore all other sins, but is it fit
That it should bear the sin of scorning it?
Who from the picture would avert his eye,
How would he fly his pains, who there did die?
From me, no pulpit, nor misgrounded law,
10 Nor scandal taken, shall this Cross withdraw,
It shall not, for it cannot; for, the loss
Of this Cross, were to me another cross;
Better were worse, for, no affliction,
No cross is so extreme, as to have none.
Who can blot out the Cross, which th' instrument
Of God, dewed on me in the Sacrament?
Who can deny me power, and liberty
To stretch mine arms, and mine own cross to be?
Swim, and at every stroke, thou art thy cross,
20 The mast and yard make one, where seas do toss.
Look down, thou spiest out crosses in small things;
Look up, thou seest birds raised on crossed wings;
All the globe's frame, and sphere's, is nothing else
But the meridians crossing parallels.
Material crosses then, good physic be,
And yet spiritual have chief dignity.
These for extracted chemic medicine serve,
And cure much better, and as well preserve;
Then are you your own physic, or need none,
30 When stilled, or purged by tribulation.
For when that Cross ungrudged, unto you sticks,
Then are you to yourself, a crucifix.
As perchance, carvers do not faces make,
But that away, which hid them there, do take:

Let crosses, so, take what hid Christ in thee,
And be his image, or not his, but he.
But, as oft alchemists do coiners prove,
So may a self-despising, get self-love.
And then as worst surfeits, of best meats be,
40 So is pride, issued from humility,
For, 'tis no child, but monster; therefore cross
Your joy in crosses, else, 'tis double loss,
And cross thy senses, else, both they, and thou
Must perish soon, and to destruction bow.
For if the'eye seek good objects, and will take
No cross from bad, we cannot 'scape a snake.
So with harsh, hard, sour, stinking, cross the rest,
Make them indifferent; call nothing best.
But most the eye needs crossing, that can roam,
50 And move; to th' others th' objects must come home.
And cross thy heart: for that in man alone
Points downwards, and hath palpitation.
Cross those dejections, when it downward tends,
And when it to forbidden heights pretends.
And as the brain through bony walls doth vent
By sutures, which a cross's form present,
So when thy brain works, ere thou utter it,
Cross and correct concupiscence of wit.
Be covetous of crosses, let none fall.
60 Cross no man else, but cross thyself in all.
Then doth the Cross of Christ work fruitfully
Within our hearts, when we love harmlessly
That Cross's pictures much, and with more care
That Cross's children, which our crosses are.

Resurrection, imperfect

Sleep sleep old sun, thou canst not have repassed
As yet, the wound thou took'st on Friday last;
Sleep then, and rest; the world may bear thy stay,
A better sun rose before thee today,

Who, not content to enlighten all that dwell
On the earth's face, as thou, enlightened hell,
And made the dark fires languish in that vale,
As, at thy presence here, our fires grow pale.
Whose body having walked on earth, and now
10   Hasting to heaven, would, that he might allow
Himself unto all stations, and fill all,
For these three days become a mineral;
He was all gold when he lay down, but rose
All tincture, and doth not alone dispose
Leaden and iron wills to good, but is
Of power to make even sinful flesh like his.
Had one of those, whose credulous piety
Thought, that a soul one might discern and see
Go from a body, at this sepulchre been,
20   And, issuing from the sheet, this body seen,
He would have justly thought this body a soul,
If not of any man, yet of the whole.
    Desunt caetera.

Upon the Annunciation and Passion falling upon one day. 1608

Tamely frail body' abstain today; today
My soul eats twice, Christ hither and away.
She sees him man, so like God made in this,
That of them both a circle emblem is,
Whose first and last concur; this doubtful day
Of feast or fast, Christ came, and went away;
She sees him nothing twice at once, who is all;
She sees a cedar plant itself, and fall,
Her maker put to making, and the head
10   Of life, at once, not yet alive, and dead;
She sees at once the virgin mother stay
Reclused at home, public at Golgotha.
Sad and rejoiced she 's seen at once, and seen
At almost fifty, and at scarce fifteen.

At once a son is promised her, and gone,
Gabriel gives Christ to her, he her to John;
Not fully a mother, she 's in orbity,
At once receiver and the legacy;
All this, and all between, this day hath shown,
20 Th' abridgement of Christ's story, which makes one
(As in plain maps, the furthest west is east)
Of the angels' *Ave*, 'and *Consummatum est*.
How well the Church, God's court of faculties
Deals, in some times, and seldom joining these;
As by the self-fixed pole we never do
Direct our course, but the next star thereto,
Which shows where the'other is, and which we say
(Because it strays not far) doth never stray;
So God by his Church, nearest to him, we know,
30 And stand firm, if we by her motion go;
His Spirit, as his fiery pillar doth
Lead, and his Church, as cloud; to one end both:
This Church, by letting these days join, hath shown
Death and conception in mankind is one.
Or 'twas in him the same humility,
That he would be a man, and leave to be:
Or as creation he had made, as God,
With the last judgement, but one period,
His imitating spouse would join in one
40 Manhood's extremes: he shall come, he is gone:
Or as though one blood drop, which thence did fall,
Accepted, would have served, he yet shed all;
So though the least of his pains, deeds, or words,
Would busy a life, she all this day affords;
This treasure then, in gross, my soul uplay,
And in my life retail it every day.

Good Friday, 1613. Riding Westward

Let man's soul be a sphere, and then, in this,
The intelligence that moves, devotion is,

And as the other spheres, by being grown
Subject to foreign motions, lose their own,
And being by others hurried every day,
Scarce in a year their natural form obey:
Pleasure or business, so, our souls admit
For their first mover, and are whirled by it.
Hence is't, that I am carried towards the west
10 This day, when my soul's form bends toward the east.
There I should see a sun, by rising set,
And by that setting endless day beget;
But that Christ on this Cross, did rise and fall,
Sin had eternally benighted all.
Yet dare I' almost be glad, I do not see
That spectacle of too much weight for me.
Who sees God's face, that is self life, must die;
What a death were it then to see God die?
It made his own lieutenant Nature shrink,
20 It made his footstool crack, and the sun wink.
Could I behold those hands which span the poles,
And turn all spheres at once, pierced with those holes?
Could I behold that endless height which is
Zenith to us, and to'our antipodes,
Humbled below us? or that blood which is
The seat of all our souls, if not of his,
Made dirt of dust, or that flesh which was worn,
By God, for his apparel, ragged, and torn?
If on these things I durst not look, durst I
30 Upon his miserable mother cast mine eye,
Who was God's partner here, and furnished thus
Half of that sacrifice, which ransomed us?
Though these things, as I ride, be from mine eye,
They are present yet unto my memory,
For that looks towards them; and thou look'st towards me,
O Saviour, as thou hang'st upon the tree;
I turn my back to thee, but to receive
Corrections, till thy mercies bid thee leave.
O think me worth thine anger, punish me,
40 Burn off my rusts, and my deformity,

Restore thine image, so much, by thy grace,
That thou mayst know me, and I'll turn my face.

To Mr Tilman after he had taken orders

Thou, whose diviner soul hath caused thee now
To put thy hand unto the holy plough,
Making lay-scornings of the Ministry,
Not an impediment, but victory;
What bringst thou home with thee? how is thy mind
Affected in the vintage? Dost thou find
New thoughts and stirrings in thee? and as steel
Touched with a loadstone, dost new motions feel?
Or, as a ship after much pain and care,
10   For iron and cloth brings home rich Indian ware,
Hast thou thus trafficked, but with far more gain
Of noble goods, and with less time and pain?
Art thou the same materials, as before,
Only the stamp is changed; but no more?
And as new crowned kings alter the face,
But not the money's substance; so hath grace
Changed only God's old image by creation,
To Christ's new stamp, at this thy coronation?
Or, as we paint angels with wings, because
20   They bear God's message, and proclaim his laws,
Since thou must do the like, and so must move,
Art thou new feathered with celestial love?
Dear, tell me where thy purchase lies, and show
What thy advantage is above, below.
But if thy gaining do surmount expression,
Why doth the foolish world scorn that profession,
Whose joys pass speech? Why do they think unfit
That gentry should join families with it?
As if their day were only to be spent
30   In dressing, mistressing and compliment;
Alas poor joys, but poorer men, whose trust
Seems richly placed in refined dust;

(For, such are clothes and beauty, which though gay,
Are, at the best, but as sublimed clay.)
Let then the world thy calling disrespect,
But go thou on, and pity their neglect.
What function is so noble, as to be
Ambassador to God and destiny?
To open life, to give kingdoms to more
40   Than kings give dignities; to keep heaven's door?
Mary's prerogative was to bear Christ, so
'Tis preachers' to convey him, for they do
As angels out of clouds, from pulpits speak;
And bless the poor beneath, the lame, the weak.
If then th' astronomers, whereas they spy
A new-found star, their optics magnify,
How brave are those, who with their engines, can
Bring man to heaven, and heaven again to man?
These are thy titles and pre-eminences,
50   In whom must meet God's graces, men's offences,
And so the heavens which beget all things here,
And the earth our mother, which these things doth bear,
Both these in thee, are in thy calling knit,
And make thee now a blessed hermaphrodite.

Upon the translation of the Psalms by Sir Philip Sidney, and the Countess of Pembroke his sister

Eternal God, (for whom who ever dare
Seek new expressions, do the circle square,
And thrust into strait corners of poor wit
Thee, who art cornerless and infinite)
I would but bless thy name, not name thee now;
(And thy gifts are as infinite as thou:)
Fix we our praises therefore on this one,
That, as thy blessed spirit fell upon
These Psalms' first author in a cloven tongue;
10   (For 'twas a double power by which he sung

The highest matter in the noblest form;)
So thou hast cleft that spirit, to perform
That work again, and shed it, here, upon
Two, by their bloods, and by thy spirit one;
A brother and a sister, made by thee
The organ, where thou art the harmony.
Two that make one John Baptist's holy voice,
And who that psalm, *Now let the Isles rejoice*,
Have both translated, and applied it too,
20 Both told us what, and taught us how to do.
They show us Islanders our joy, our King,
They tell us why, and teach us how to sing;
Make all this all, three choirs, heaven, earth, and spheres;
The first, heaven, hath a song, but no man hears,
The spheres have music, but they have no tongue,
Their harmony is rather danced than sung;
But our third choir, to which the first gives ear,
(For, angels learn by what the church does here)
This choir hath all. The organist is he
30 Who hath tuned God and man, the organ we:
The songs are these, which heaven's high holy Muse
Whispered to David, David to the Jews:
And David's successors, in holy zeal,
In forms of joy and art do re-reveal
To us so sweetly and sincerely too,
That I must not rejoice as I would do
When I behold that these Psalms are become
So well attired abroad, so ill at home,
So well in chambers, in thy church so ill,
40 As I can scarce call that reformed until
This be reformed; would a whole state present
A lesser gift than some one man hath sent?
And shall our church, unto our spouse and king,
More hoarse, more harsh than any other, sing?
For that we pray, we praise thy name for this,
Which, by this Moses and this Miriam, is
Already done; and as those Psalms we call
(Though some have other authors) David's all:

So though some have, some may some psalms translate,
50 We thy Sidneian Psalms shall celebrate,
And, till we come th' extemporal song to sing,
(Learned the first hour, that we see the King,
Who hath translated these translators) may
These their sweet learned labours, all the way
Be as our tuning, that, when hence we part
We may fall in with them, and sing our part.

The Lamentations of Jeremy, for the most part according to Tremellius

CHAPTER I

How sits this city, late most populous,   *1*
    Thus solitary, and like a widow thus!
Amplest of nations, queen of provinces
    She was, who now thus tributary is!

Still in the night she weeps, and her tears fall   *2*
    Down by her cheeks along, and none of all
Her lovers comfort her; perfidiously
    Her friends have dealt, and now are enemy.

Unto great bondage, and afflictions   *3*
10   Judah is captive led; those nations
With whom she dwells, no place of rest afford,
    In straits she meets her persecutor's sword.

Empty are the gates of Sion, and her ways   *4*
    Mourn, because none come to her solemn days.
Her priests do groan, her maids are comfortless,
    And she's unto herself a bitterness.

Her foes are grown her head, and live at peace,   *5*
    Because when her transgressions did increase,
The Lord struck her with sadness: th' enemy
20   Doth drive her children to captivity.

From Sion's daughter is all beauty gone,　　　　　6
　　Like harts, which seek for pasture, and find none,
Her princes are, and now before the foe
　　Which still pursues them, without strength they go.

Now in her days of tears, Jerusalem　　　　　7
　　(Her men slain by the foe, none succouring them)
Remembers what of old, she esteemed most,
　　Whilst her foes laugh at her, for what she hath lost.

Jerusalem hath sinned, therefore is she　　　　　8
30　　Removed, as women in uncleanness be;
Who honoured, scorn her, for her foulness they
　　Have seen; herself doth groan, and turn away.

Her foulness in her skirts was seen, yet she　　　　　9
　　Remembered not her end; miraculously
Therefore she fell, none comforting: behold
　　O Lord my affliction, for the foe grows bold.

Upon all things where her delight hath been,　　　　　10
　　The foe hath stretched his hand, for she hath seen
Heathen, whom thou command'st, should not do so,
40　　Into her holy sanctuary go.

And all her people groan, and seek for bread;　　　　　11
　　And they have given, only to be fed,
All precious things, wherein their pleasure lay:
　　How cheap I am grown, O Lord, behold, and weigh.

All this concerns not you, who pass by me,　　　　　12
　　O see, and mark if any sorrow be
Like to my sorrow, which Jehovah hath
　　Done to me in the day of his fierce wrath?

That fire, which by himself is governed　　　　　13
50　　He hath cast from heaven on my bones, and spread
A net before my feet, and me o'erthrown,
　　And made me languish all the day alone.

His hand hath of my sins framed a yoke   *14*
  Which wreathed, and cast upon my neck, hath broke
My strength. The Lord unto these enemies
  Hath given me, from whom I cannot rise.

He underfoot hath trodden in my sight   *15*
  My strong men; he did company invite
To break my young men; he the winepress hath
60   Trod upon Judah's daughter in his wrath.

For these things do I weep, mine eye, mine eye   *16*
  Casts water out; for he which should be nigh
To comfort me, is now departed far;
  The foe prevails, forlorn my children are.

There's none, though Sion do stretch out her hand,   *17*
  To comfort her, it is the Lord's command
That Jacob's foes girt him. Jerusalem
  Is as an unclean woman amongst them.

But yet the Lord is just, and righteous still,   *18*
70   I have rebelled against his holy will;
O hear all people, and my sorrow see,
  My maids, my young men in captivity.

I called for my lovers then, but they   *19*
  Deceived me, and my priests, and elders lay
Dead in the city; for they sought for meat
  Which should refresh their souls, and none could get.

Because I am in straits, Jehovah see   *20*
  My heart o'erturned, my bowels muddy be,
Because I have rebelled so much, as fast
80   The sword without, as death within, doth waste.

Of all which hear I mourn, none comforts me,   *21*
  My foes have heard my grief, and glad they be,
That thou hast done it; but thy promised day
  Will come, when, as I suffer, so shall they.

Let all their wickedness appear to thee,   22
    Do unto them, as thou hast done to me,
For all my sins: the sighs which I have had
    Are very many, and my heart is sad.

CHAPTER 2

How over Sion's daughter hath God hung   1
90   His wrath's thick cloud! and from heaven hath flung
To earth the beauty of Israel, and hath
    Forgot his foot-stool in the day of wrath!

The Lord unsparingly hath swallowed   2
    All Jacob's dwellings, and demolished
To ground the strengths of Judah, and profaned
    The princes of the kingdom, and the land.

In heat of wrath, the horn of Israel he   3
    Hath clean cut off, and lest the enemy
Be hindered, his right hand he doth retire,
100   But is towards Jacob, all-devouring fire.

Like to an enemy he bent his bow,   4
    His right hand was in posture of a foe,
To kill what Sion's daughter did desire,
    'Gainst whom his wrath, he poured forth, like fire.

For like an enemy Jehovah is,   5
    Devouring Israel, and his palaces,
Destroying holds, giving additions
    To Judah's daughters' lamentations.

Like to a garden hedge he hath cast down   6
110   The place where was his congregation,
And Sion's feasts and sabbaths are forgot;
    Her king, her priest, his wrath regardeth not.

The Lord forsakes his altar, and detests   7
    His sanctuary, and in the foes' hand rests
His palace, and the walls, in which their cries
    Are heard, as in the true solemnities.

The Lord hath cast a line, so to confound   *8*
   And level Sion's walls unto the ground;
He draws not back his hand, which doth o'erturn
120   The wall, and rampart, which together mourn.

Their gates are sunk into the ground, and he   *9*
   Hath broke the bars; their king and princes be
Amongst the heathen, without law, nor there
   Unto their prophets doth the Lord appear.

There Sion's elders on the ground are placed,   *10*
   And silence keep; dust on their heads they cast,
In sackcloth have they girt themselves, and low
   The virgins towards ground, their heads do throw.

My bowels are grown muddy, and mine eyes   *11*
130   Are faint with weeping: and my liver lies
Poured out upon the ground, for misery
   That sucking children in the streets do die.

When they had cried unto their mothers, where   *12*
   Shall we have bread, and drink? they fainted there,
And in the streets like wounded persons lay
   Till 'twixt their mothers' breasts they went away.

Daughter Jerusalem, oh what may be   *13*
   A witness, or comparison for thee?
Sion, to ease thee, what shall I name like thee?
140   Thy breach is like the sea, what help can be?

For thee vain foolish things thy prophets sought,   *14*
   Thee, thine iniquities they have not taught,
Which might disturb thy bondage: but for thee
   False burdens, and false causes they would see.

The passengers do clap their hands, and hiss,   *15*
   And wag their head at thee, and say, Is this
That city, which so many men did call
   Joy of the earth, and perfectest of all?

Thy foes do gape upon thee, and they hiss, 16
150 And gnash their teeth, and say, 'Devour we this,
For this is certainly the day which we
Expected, and which now we find, and see.'

The Lord hath done that which he purposed, 17
Fulfilled his word of old determined;
He hath thrown down, and not spared, and thy foe
Made glad above thee, and advanced him so.

But now, their hearts against the Lord do call, 18
Therefore, O wall of Sion, let tears fall
Down like a river, day and night; take thee
160 No rest, but let thine eye incessant be.

Arise, cry in the night, pour, for thy sins, 19
Thy heart, like water, when the watch begins;
Lift up thy hands to God, lest children die,
Which, faint for hunger, in the streets do lie.

Behold O Lord, consider unto whom 20
Thou hast done this; what, shall the women come
To eat their children of a span? shall thy
Prophet and priest be slain in sanctuary?

On grounds in streets, the young and old do lie, 21
170 My virgins and young men by sword do die;
Them in the day of thy wrath thou hast slain,
Nothing did thee from killing them contain.

As to a solemn feast, all whom I feared 22
Thou call'st about me; when thy wrath appeared,
None did remain or 'scape, for those which I
Brought up, did perish by mine enemy.

CHAPTER 3

I am the man which have affliction seen, 1
Under the rod of God's wrath having been,
He hath led me to darkness, not to light, 2
180 And against me all day, his hand doth fight. 3

He hath broke my bones, worn out my flesh and skin,   *4*
    Built up against me; and hath girt me in   *5*
With hemlock, and with labour; and set me   *6*
    In dark, as they who dead for ever be.

He hath hedged me lest I 'scape, and added more   *7*
    To my steel fetters, heavier than before.
When I cry out, he out shuts my prayer: and hath   *8,9*
    Stopped with hewn stone my way, and turned my path.

And like a lion hid in secrecy,   *10*
190   Or bear which lies in wait, he was to me,
He stops my way, tears me, made desolate,   *11*
    And he makes me the mark he shooteth at.   *12*

He made the children of his quiver pass   *13*
    Into my reins, I with my people was   *14*
All the day long, a song and mockery.
    He hath filled me with bitterness, and he   *15*

Hath made me drunk with wormwood. He hath burst   *16*
    My teeth with stones, and covered me with dust;
And thus my soul far off from peace was set,   *17*
200   And my prosperity I did forget.

My strength, my hope (unto myself I said)   *18*
    Which from the Lord should come, is perished.
But when my mournings I do think upon,   *19*
    My wormwood, hemlock, and affliction,

My soul is humbled in remembering this;   *20*
    My heart considers, therefore, hope there is.   *21*
'Tis God's great mercy we'are not utterly   *22*
    Consumed, for his compassions do not die;

For every morning they renewed be,   *23*
210   For great, O Lord, is thy fidelity.
The Lord is, saith my soul, my portion,   *24*
    And therefore in him will I hope alone.

The Lord is good to them, who on him rely,   25
   And to the soul that seeks him earnestly.
It is both good to trust, and to attend   26
   The Lord's salvation unto the end:

'Tis good for one his yoke in youth to bear;   27
   He sits alone, and doth all speech forbear,   28
Because he hath borne it. And his mouth he lays   29
220   Deep in the dust, yet then in hope he stays.

He gives his cheeks to whosoever will   30
   Strike him, and so he is reproached still.
For, not for ever doth the Lord forsake,   31
   But when he hath struck with sadness, he doth take 32

Compassion, as his mercy'is infinite;
   Nor is it with his heart, that he doth smite; 33
That underfoot the prisoners stamped be,   34
   That a man's right the judge himself doth see 35

To be wrung from him, that he subverted is   36
230   In his just cause; the Lord allows not this.
Who then will say, that aught doth come to pass,   37
   But that which by the Lord commanded was?

Both good and evil from his mouth proceeds;   38
   Why then grieves any man for his misdeeds?   39
Turn we to God, by trying out our ways;   40
   To him in heaven, our hands with hearts upraise. 41

We have rebelled, and fallen away from thee,   42
   Thou pardon'st not; usest no clemency;   43
Pursuest us, kill'st us, coverest us with wrath,
240   Cover'st thyself with clouds, that our prayer hath 44

No power to pass. And thou hast made us fall   45
   As refuse, and off-scouring to them all.
All our foes gape at us. Fear and a snare   46,47
   With ruin, and with waste, upon us are.

With water rivers doth mine eye o'erflow 48
  For ruin of my people's daughter so;
Mine eye doth drop down tears incessantly, 49
  Until the Lord look down from heaven to see. 50

And for my city's daughters' sake, mine eye 51
250 Doth break mine heart. Causeless mine enemy, 52
Like a bird chased me. In a dungeon 53
  They have shut my life, and cast on me a stone.

Waters flowed o'er my head, then thought I, I am 54
  Destroyed; I called Lord, upon thy name 55
Out of the pit. And thou my voice didst hear; 56
  Oh from my sigh, and cry, stop not thine ear.

Then when I called upon thee, thou drew'st near 57
  Unto me, and said'st unto me, 'Do not fear.'
Thou Lord my soul's cause handled hast, and thou 58
260 Rescued'st my life. O Lord do thou judge now, 59

Thou heard'st my wrong. Their vengeance all they have 60
  wrought;
  How they reproached, thou hast heard, and what they 61
  thought,
What their lips uttered, which against me rose, 62
  And what was ever whispered by my foes.

I am their song, whether they rise or sit, 63
  Give them rewards Lord, for their working fit, 64
Sorrow of heart, thy curse. And with thy might 65,66
  Follow, and from under heaven destroy them quite.

CHAPTER 4

How is the gold become so dim? How is 1
270 Purest and finest gold thus changed to this?
The stones which were stones of the Sanctuary,
  Scattered in corners of each street do lie.

The precious sons of Sion, which should be   2
  Valued as purest gold, how do we see
Low rated now, as earthen pitchers, stand,
  Which are the work of a poor potter's hand.

Even the sea-calfs draw their breasts, and give   3
  Suck to their young; my people's daughters live,
By reason of the foes' great cruelness,
280 As do the owls in the vast wilderness.

And when the sucking child doth strive to draw,   4
  His tongue for thirst cleaves to his upper jaw.
And when for bread the little children cry,
  There is no man that doth them satisfy.

They which before were delicately fed,   5
  Now in the streets forlorn have perished,
And they which ever were in scarlet clothed,
  Sit and embrace the dunghills which they loathed.

The daughters of my people have sinned more,   6
290 Than did the town of Sodom sin before;
Which being at once destroyed, there did remain
  No hands amongst them, to vex them again.

But heretofore purer her Nazarite   7
  Was than the snow, and milk was not so white;
As carbuncles did their pure bodies shine,
  And all their polishedness was sapphirine.

They are darker now than blackness, none can know   8
  Them by the face, as through the streets they go,
For now their skin doth cleave unto their bone,
300 And withered, is like to dry wood grown.

Better by sword than famine 'tis to die;   9
  And better through pierced, than by penury.
Women by nature pitiful, have eat   10
  Their children dressed with their own hands for meat.

Jehovah here fully accomplished hath   *11*
  His indignation, and poured forth his wrath,
Kindled a fire in Sion, which hath power
  To eat, and her foundations to devour.

Nor would the kings of the earth, nor all which live   *12*
310 In the inhabitable world believe,
That any adversary, any foe
  Into Jerusalem should enter so.

For the priests' sins, and prophets', which have shed   *13*
  Blood in the streets, and the just murdered:
Which when those men, whom they made blind, did stray   *14*
  Thorough the streets, defiled by the way

With blood, the which impossible it was
  Their garments should 'scape touching, as they pass,
Would cry aloud, 'Depart defiled men,   *15*
320 Depart, depart, and touch us not': and then

They fled, and strayed, and with the Gentiles were,
  Yet told their friends, they should not long dwell there;
For this they are scattered by Jehovah's face   *16*
  Who never will regard them more; no grace

Unto their old men shall the foe afford,
  Nor, that they are priests, redeem them from the sword.
And we as yet, for all these miseries   *17*
  Desiring our vain help, consume our eyes:

And such a nation as cannot save,
330 We in desire and speculation have.
They hunt our steps, that in the streets we fear   *18*
  To go: our end is now approached near,

Our days accomplished are, this the last day.
  Eagles of heaven are not so swift as they   *19*
Which follow us, o'er mountain tops they fly
  At us, and for us in the desert lie.

The anointed Lord, breath of our nostrils, he   *20*
  Of whom we said, 'Under his shadow, we
Shall with more ease under the heathen dwell,'
340   Into the pit which these men digged, fell.

Rejoice O Edom's daughter, joyful be   *21*
  Thou which inhabit'st Huz, for unto thee
This cup shall pass, and thou with drunkenness
  Shalt fill thyself, and show thy nakedness.

And then thy sins O Sion, shall be spent,   *22*
  The Lord will not leave thee in banishment.
Thy sins, O Edom's daughter, he will see,
  And for them, pay thee with captivity.

CHAPTER 5

Remember, O Lord, what is fallen on us;   *1*
350   See, and mark how we are reproached thus,
For unto strangers our possession   *2*
  Is turned, our houses unto aliens gone,

Our mothers are become as widows, we   *3*
  As orphans all, and without father be;
Waters which are our own, we drink, and pay,   *4*
  And upon our own wood a price they lay.

Our persecutors on our necks do sit,   *5*
  They make us travail, and not intermit,
We stretch our hands unto th' Egyptians   *6*
360   To get us bread; and to the Assyrians.

Our fathers did these sins, and are no more,   *7*
  But we do bear the sins they did before.
They are but servants, which do rule us thus,   *8*
  Yet from their hands none would deliver us.

With danger of our life our bread we gat;   *9*
  For in the wilderness, the sword did wait.
The tempests of this famine we lived in,   *10*
  Black as an oven coloured had our skin:

In Judah's cities they the maids abused　　　*11*
370　　By force, and so women in Sion used.
The princes with their hands they hung; no grace　　　*12*
　　Nor honour gave they to the Elder's face.

Unto the mill our young men carried are,　　　*13*
　　And children fall under the wood they bear.
Elders, the gates; youth did their songs forbear,　　　*14*
　　Gone was our joy; our dancings, mournings were.　　　*15*

Now is the crown fall'n from our head; and woe　　　*16*
　　Be unto us, because we'have sinned so.
For this our hearts do languish, and for this　　　*17*
380　　Over our eyes a cloudy dimness is.

Because Mount Sion desolate doth lie,　　　*18*
　　And foxes there do go at liberty:
But thou O Lord art ever, and thy throne　　　*19*
　　From generation, to generation.

Why shouldst thou forget us eternally?　　　*20*
　　Or leave us thus long in this misery?
Restore us Lord to thee, that so we may　　　*21*
　　Return, and as of old, renew our day.

For oughtest thou, O Lord, despise us thus,　　　*22*
390　　And to be utterly enraged at us?

A Hymn to Christ, at the Author's last going into Germany

In what torn ship soever I embark,
That ship shall be my emblem of thy ark;
What sea soever swallow me, that flood
Shall be to me an emblem of thy blood;
Though thou with clouds of anger do disguise
Thy face; yet through that mask I know those eyes,
　　Which, though they turn away sometimes,
　　　　They never will despise.

I sacrifice this Island unto thee,
10 And all whom I loved there, and who loved me;
When I have put our seas 'twixt them and me,
Put thou thy sea betwixt my sins and thee.
As the tree's sap doth seek the root below
In winter, in my winter now I go,
    Where none but thee, th' eternal root
      Of true love I may know.

Nor thou nor thy religion dost control,
The amorousness of an harmonious soul,
But thou wouldst have that love thyself: as thou
20 Art jealous, Lord, so I am jealous now,
Thou lov'st not, till from loving more, thou free
My soul; who ever gives, takes liberty:
    O, if thou car'st not whom I love
      Alas, thou lov'st not me.

Seal then this bill of my divorce to all,
On whom those fainter beams of love did fall;
Marry those loves, which in youth scattered be
On fame, wit, hopes (false mistresses) to thee.
Churches are best for prayer, that have least light:
30 To see God only, I go out of sight:
    And to 'scape stormy days, I choose
      An everlasting night.

Hymn to God my God, in my Sickness

Since I am coming to that holy room,
    Where, with thy choir of saints for evermore,
I shall be made thy music; as I come
    I tune the instrument here at the door,
    And what I must do then, think here before.

Whilst my physicians by their love are grown
    Cosmographers, and I their map, who lie
Flat on this bed, that by them may be shown

That this is my south-west discovery
10   *Per fretum febris*, by these straits to die,

I joy, that in these straits, I see my west;
    For, though their currents yield return to none,
What shall my west hurt me? As west and east
    In all flat maps (and I am one) are one,
    So death doth touch the resurrection.

Is the Pacific Sea my home? Or are
    The eastern riches? Is Jerusalem?
Anyan, and Magellan, and Gibraltar,
    All straits, and none but straits, are ways to them,
20   Whether where Japhet dwelt, or Cham, or Shem.

We think that Paradise and Calvary,
    Christ's Cross, and Adam's tree, stood in one place;
Look Lord, and find both Adams met in me;
    As the first Adam's sweat surrounds my face,
    May the last Adam's blood my soul embrace.

So, in his purple wrapped receive me Lord,
    By these his thorns give me his other crown;
And as to others' souls I preached thy word,
    Be this my text, my sermon to mine own,
30   Therefore that he may raise the Lord throws down.

A Hymn to God the Father

I

Wilt thou forgive that sin where I begun,
    Which was my sin, though it were done before?
Wilt thou forgive that sin, through which I run,
    And do run still: though still I do deplore?
        When thou hast done, thou hast not done,
                For, I have more.

II

Wilt thou forgive that sin which I have won
   Others to sin? and, made my sin their door?
Wilt thou forgive that sin which I did shun
10   A year, or two: but wallowed in, a score?
      When thou hast done, thou hast not done,
        For I have more.

III

I have a sin of fear, that when I have spun
   My last thread, I shall perish on the shore;
But swear by thy self, that at my death thy son
   Shall shine as he shines now, and heretofore;
      And, having done that, thou hast done,
        I fear no more.

Notes

The notes refer to a few important works by the author's name only. These are the editions of Donne's poems by Gardner, Grierson and Milgate, the edition of contemporary musical settings introduced by J. Jacquot, and the Lives by E. Gosse and R. C. Bald. Full references for them are given in the list of further reading. Donne's sermons are quoted from the edition by Potter and Simpson, and his letters from the selections in Gosse's *Life and Letters of John Donne* and Hayward's *John Donne: Complete Poetry and Selected Prose*. Other abbreviations used are:

CE	*College English*
CQ	*Critical Quarterly*
EC	*Essays in Criticism*
ELH	*English Literary History*
HLQ	*Huntington Library Quarterly*
JEGP	*Journal of English and Germanic Philology*
KR	*Kenyon Review*
MLR	*Modern Language Review*
MP	*Modern Philology*
NMLC	*Northern Miscellany of Literary Criticism*
OED	*Oxford English Dictionary*
PQ	*Philological Quarterly*
PMLA	*Publications of the Modern Languages Association of America*
REL	*Review of English Literature*
SEL	*Studies in English Literature* (Rice University)
SP	*Studies in Philology*
SR	*Southern Review*
TLS	*The Times Literary Supplement*

Montaigne's *Essays* are quoted in the translation by J. Florio, 1603. Ben Jonson's *Conversations with William Drummond of Hawthornden* is referred to as 'Jonson *Conversations*', and quoted in the text from *Ben Jonson*, ed. C. H. Herford and Percy Simpson (1925), vol. 1.

Songs and Sonnets

Donne probably wrote his love lyrics over some twenty years of his life, though we cannot certainly date any single one of them. In the first printed edition of his poems, 1633, the love lyrics are scattered in groups through the text and inconspicuously placed. They were first brought together under the title *Songs and Sonnets* in the 1635 edition.

The order of the poems in both these early editions was determined by the manuscript material the editors drew on, and is as good as random. For want of any obvious principle of arrangement almost all modern editors have given the poems in the order of the 1635 edition, which has thus acquired a prescriptive force. Helen Gardner broke decisively with the convention and arranged the poems in two groups, the one group consisting of poems which she thinks were written before 1600, and the other of poems which she thinks were written later than 1602. She finds that the poems can be distinguished in these main groups by the attitudes they suppose between the lovers, and by the more 'philosophical' treatment and greater metrical complexity of the supposedly later pieces. Within each group she brings together poems which strike her as having some connexion in theme, form or style.

I have arranged the poems alphabetically by titles, because that is a neutral order and makes them easy to find. But there is no certainty that the titles themselves are the ones Donne intended, or indeed that he gave the poems any titles.

AIR AND ANGELS

Some recent discussions of the poem are:

Helen Gardner, *The Business of Criticism* (1959), 62–75.
A. J. Smith, 'New Bearings in Donne: *Air and Angels*', in Helen Gardner (ed.), *Twentieth-Century Views: John Donne* (1962).
H. Sykes Davies, 'Text or Context', *REL*, VI (1965), 93–107; and Helen Gardner's reply, 108–10.

5 *Still*] Till *MS*

6 *Some lovely glorious nothing* Renaissance Neoplatonists wrote that lovers could not recognize what it was they sought because the ultimate object of their desire was not this or that body but the divine light shining through bodies, whose splendour amazed and awed them. But Donne's poem concerns the search for a realized love, as distinct

on the one hand from just such an unlocalized worship of beauty, and on the other from an admiration which is all too concretely and bewilderingly fixed in the lady's physical attractions.

7–8 *since my soul . . . / Takes limbs of flesh, and else could nothing do* his soul would be unable to act if it did not work through the senses. See *The Ecstasy* 65–8.

9 *subtle* ethereal, intangible; insidious in its way of working.

13 *assume*] assumes *some MSS*; assures *MS*

17 *wares which would sink admiration* her several physical attractions, which are so numerous that if they alone were the object of his love they would not so much hold his love steady as overwhelm him.

18 *pinnace* a light sailing boat.

21–2 *things / Extreme, and scatt'ring bright* her various physical attributes, extreme embodiments of beauty, which offer love so many scattered lodgements but no one essential home.

22 *inhere* subsist permanently within.

23–4 *as an angel, face and wings / Of air . . . doth wear* Aquinas says that angels, which are insubstantial and therefore invisible, assume a body of air condensed by divine power so that they may appear to men (*Summa Theologica* I.51.2).

24 *as it*] as yet *MS*
not pure as it, yet pure In scholastic metaphysics air is the most pure of elements because it is unmixed, but it necessarily falls short of pure spirit. The reading 'not pure as yet' in one MS suggests that the writer of the MS version was thinking of the air itself as gradually acquiring – wearing towards, as it were – the purity of its wearer. H. Sykes Davies takes 'it' to refer to the condensed air itself rather than to the angel, so that the line then distinguishes between pure air and that thickened air.

25 *my love's*] thy love's *MS*
sphere vehicle or embodiment in which his love can subsist. The heavenly bodies were thought to be made up of a sphere and a controlling intelligence seated within it; and as sphere and intelligence conjoin to make the star, though separately they are nothing, so his love is ineffective or not love at all without her answering love. Separately, his love would have no location and her love no direction; whereas

their mutual love would entail the fit embodiment his love has sought, as the one way to make love effective. See *The Ecstasy* 49–76.

26–8 *Just such disparity* . . . *'Twixt women's love, and men's* . . . the disparity between man's love and woman's love is analogous to that fine difference between pure spirit and the purest of the elements. Some sixteenth-century commentators distinguish between lover and beloved, the man initiating love and the woman responding with love to the love she is offered: 'For women indeed care for nothing but to be loved, and where they assure themselves they are loved, there of their kind and sweet disposition, they bestow love again' (*Orlando Furioso*, trans. Sir J. Harington (1591), XLIII, 373). Donne's distinction is overtly metaphysical, a matter of which of two realized conditions is more essentially love; but he is implicitly asking for her love in return for his and explaining how she may truly love him now though she did not love him at first.

27 *'twixt air and angels' purity* The distinction clinches the argument of the poem by finding the two terms now needed to give their mutual love a whole being as well as a body. Common metaphysical doctrine distinguishes between the parts of our being, celestial, aerial and material: 'The celestial nature differs not in substance from the aerial spirit, but only in degree and complexion; and the aerial spirit differs from the aura, or material part . . . in constitution only, and not in nature; so that these three being but one substantially, may admit of a perfect hypostatic union' (T. Vaughan, *Anima Magica Abscondita* (1650), 12). If the lady returns the poet's love they will thus between them supply love with an embodiment, an aerial spirit, and a celestial nature, to complete the union. They will have created a new joint being of love, far beyond a mere physical coupling, to replace their separate selves. See *The Ecstasy* 33–52.

THE ANNIVERSARY

Title] Ad Liviam *MS*

1–7 *All kings* . . . *Only our love hath no decay* see *The Good Morrow* 19–21, and *The Canonization* 25–7.

3 *they*] these *1635–54*

10 *his*] the *most MSS*

11 *Two graves must hide thine and my corse* because they would otherwise not wish to leave their bodies, so that death would not divorce body from soul as it should.

17 *dwells*   has its own home.

18 *inmates*   lodgers.
prove   experience.

19 *increased there above*   even greater than the love of souls in which nothing dwells but love.
increased   pronounced as three syllables.
there above] then above *MS*

20   *to their graves*] to their grave *1635-9*
souls from their graves ...   when their souls leave their bodies.

22   *we*] now *1633-69*
we no more, than all the rest   their felicity in heaven will be no greater than anybody else's, because all souls there are blessed fully according to their capacity and so are equally content.

23-4   *and none but we / Can be such kings, nor*] and but we / None are such kings and *most MSS*

24   *nor of such subjects be*   nor can be subjects of such kings.

27   *True and false fears let us refrain*   the continuance of love depends upon the lovers' banishing the uncertainties and suspicions that love breeds, whether there is reason for them or not. See *A Lecture upon the Shadow* 14-26.
refrain   restrain, curb.

THE APPARITION

1   *When by thy scorn ...*   Renaissance court poets celebrated a lady's chastity by saying that they were dying of her scornful refusal to yield to them, and some threatened a posthumous revenge or warned her of a frustrated old age.

5   *vestal*   a dedicated virgin. The lady has falsely pleaded her virginity to rebuff the poet's importunings.

11   *aspen*   trembling, as the aspen trembles in the wind.

13   *A verier ghost than I*   her fear will reduce her to a truer ghost than the visitation itself, and the coating of 'cold quicksilver sweat' will make her look more like one.

16–17 *I had rather thou shouldst painfully repent, | Than by my threatenings rest still innocent* he would prefer her to commit her double sin and be forced to an agonizing repentance, than to be put off by his mere threat of revenge and so escape scot-free.

17 *rest still*] keep thee *some MSS*

THE BAIT

In the Dolaucothi MS (in the National Library of Wales) this is one of six poems headed 'Songs which were made to certain airs that were made before', the others being *Community, Confined Love, The Message, Song* (Go, and catch a falling star), and *Song* (Sweetest love, I do not go). Two other MSS have a similar heading but give only three poems under it, *The Bait, The Message* and *Song* (Sweetest love, I do not go). No contemporary setting of *The Bait* is known, but Helen Gardner prints a few bars of a tune which Corkine gives as a lesson for the viol under the caption 'Come live with me, and be my love'; it is presumably a popular song of the time.

The Bait varies Marlowe's *The Passionate Shepherd to his Love*, published in 1599, and Raleigh's *The Nymph's Reply*, published in 1600. Marlowe's piece had already been anonymously parodied in some lines that followed *The Nymph's Reply* in *England's Helicon* (1600):

The seat for your disport shall be
Over some river in a tree,
Where silver sands, and pebbles sing,
Eternal ditties with the spring.

There shall you see the nymphs at play,
And how the satyrs spend the day,
The fishes gliding on the sands:
Offering their bellies to your hands.

In *The Compleat Angler* (1655), Walton has a milkmaid sing Marlowe's lines, her mother sing Raleigh's reply, and Venator give Donne's poem as 'a copy of verses that were made by Doctor Donne, and made to show the world that he could make soft and smooth verses, when he thought fit and worth his labour'.

6 *thy*] thine *1669 and several MSS*

7 *enamoured*] enamelled *Walton*
  stay] play *1669*

9 *live bath* The lady's power to attract the fish when she bathed was a common conceit in the erotic poetry of the time:

Then quickly strip thyself! Lay fear aside!
  For of this dainty prey, which thou shalt take;
  Both sea, fish, and thyself, thou glad shalt make.
(R. Tofte, *Laura* (1597), II, 37)

11] Most amorously to thee will swim *Walton*

15 *myself*] mine eyes *Walton*; my heart *several MSS*

18 *with*] which *1633*

20 *windowy*] winding *1669*

23 *curious* artfully made.
  sleavesilk] sleavesick *1633*
  sleavesilk flies artificial flies made out of the threads of sleaved (unravelled) silk.

24 *Bewitch*] To witch *Walton*

25 *thou need'st*] there needs *several MSS*

THE BLOSSOM

2 *watched* Pronounced as two syllables.

9 *poor heart* Petrarch addressed his heart, lamenting that it had left him to hide itself in Laura's eyes (*Mira quel colle*, *Canzoniere* Sonnet 242).

9-13 *poor heart / . . . bow*] *in brackets 1650-69*

10 *labour'st*] labourest *1635-69*; labours *1633*

12 *forbidden or forbidding* In the ritual of courtly love the lady was married or of superior station, and repulsed the poet.

15 *that sun*] the sun *1635-69*
  that sun the lady, as distinct from 'this sun', the sun in the sky.

23 *tongue*] taste *1633-69*

24 *need you a heart*] need your heart *1633-69*

27-8 *A naked thinking heart . . . / Is to a woman, but a kind of ghost* because a woman has not such a heart herself and can judge of love only by its bodily evidences.

31 *Practice may make her know some other part* A ribald innuendo.

35 *fat* prosperous.

38 *would*] will *1633–69 and MS*

BREAK OF DAY

First printed, with music, in W. Corkine's *Second Book of Airs* (1612). Corkine's setting is given in Jacquot and in Helen Gardner, *John Donne: The Elegies and The Songs and Sonnets*, Appendix B.

1 *'Tis true, 'tis day* The speaker is a woman. The complaint of lovers parted by the dawn was popular with the Provençal poets in the twelfth century, who frequently put speeches or whole lyrics in the mouth of the woman. Donne does it in only one other poem, *Self Love* (if that is his).

12 *him, that had them*] him that hath them *some MSS*; her, that had them *1669*; her that hath them *several MSS*

15 *foul*] fool *MS*

18 *when ... doth*] when ... should *1635–54*; if ... should *some MSS*

THE BROKEN HEART

4 *that it can ten in less space devour* love burns up its victims so fast that it can consume ten of them within the hour.

8 *flask*] flash *1635–69 and some MSS*

14 *chaws* chews.

15 *chain-shot* cannon balls chained together so as to mow down swathes of men.
    chain-shot] chained shot *1633–69 and some MSS*

16 *our hearts*] and we *1669*
    fry young or very small fish, such as a pike might swallow at a gulp.

17 *did*] could *some MSS*; would *several MSS*

21 *thee*] thine *some MSS*

24 *first*] fierce *some MSS*

25–6 *nothing can to nothing fall, | Nor any place be empty quite* no matter can be totally annihilated, nor can there be a complete vacuum.

30 *hundred*] thousand *some MSS*

THE CANONIZATION

Canonization the making saints of love's martyrs after their self-ruin for love.

2–3 *chide my palsy, or my gout, | My five grey hairs, or ruined fortune flout* He ironically anticipates worldly wise objections to an imprudent love, such as that he is too old to fling away his material prospects for an amorous whim.

3 *five*] true *1635–54*

5 *Take you a course* follow out some way of advancing yourself.
place a position at Court.

6 *Observe his Honour, or his Grace* pay court to some Lord or Bishop.

7 *Or the King's*] And the King's *1635–69 and MSS*
real] Royal *several MSS* (both senses are required).

7–8 *Or the King's real, or his stamped face | Contemplate* gaze either upon the king's actual face or upon his image on coins; that is, seek either prestige as a court sycophant, or wealth. He maps the world of ambition from which he and his mistress have deliberately excluded themselves by their love.

8 *approve* try out; commend.
Contemplate The stress falls on the second syllable – contémplate.

11–14 *sighs . . . | . . . colds . . . | . . . heats* Petrarchan lovers con-ceitedly worked out the external effects of their (stereotyped) sufferings. This ironic parody argues that the world should be content to leave the lovers alone since its unedifying traffic goes on unaffected by their love.

14 *veins*] reins *1669*

15 *more*] man *1669 and most MSS*

plaguy bill the bill of mortality issued during outbreaks of plague to list each day's victims.

20–21 *Call her one, me another fly, | We are tapers too, and at our own cost die* they are at once the moths which destroy themselves in the flame of the candle, and the candle itself which consumes its own substance. 'Die', an established figure for orgasm, suggests that they squander their lives as well as their fortunes for love 'since each such act, they say, / Diminisheth the length of life a day' (*Farewell to Love* 24–5).

22 *the eagle and the dove*   symbols of strength and gentleness, the masculine and the feminine qualities which are now united in a perfect whole.

23 *The phoenix*   the mythical bird of which it was said that only one specimen existed. It renewed itself mysteriously from time to time by burning itself on the altar of the temple of the sun at Heliopolis and resurrecting itself out of its own ashes. In sixteenth-century discussions of love the model of a perfect love is usually the hermaphrodite, because it unites the two sexes in one nature which has the characteristics of both. Donne now prefers to re-apply, and thus find more wit in, the already complex riddle of the phoenix.

25 *neutral*] natural *MS*

25–6 *fit*] fit. *1633 and 1669*; fit, *1650–54 and several MSS*

26 *We die and rise the same*   their claim to canonization for love rests in the singularity of a passion which is unaffected by coitus, as by worldly ruin.

26–7 *prove / Mysterious*   show themselves to be beyond the common run of human conduct and the grasp of reason, as saints are.

29 *tombs and*] tomb or *1669*

31 *chronicle*   history.

32 *sonnets*   love lyrics.

33 *a well wrought urn*   H. S. Meller pointed out that some editions of Petrarch's love poems in the sixteenth century showed Petrarch and Laura face to face on a funeral urn which is surmounted by a phoenix in the act of arising from its own burning. A. J. Smith's reply examined the bearing of this representation on the present poem (letters to *The Times Literary Supplement*, 22 April 1965 and 29 April 1965). Cleanth Brooks discusses the images of the poem in *The Well-Wrought Urn* (1947), 10–16.

33–4 *becomes / The greatest ashes*   befits the ashes of the most important people.

38 *hermitage*] pilgrimage *MS*

39 *You, to whom love was peace, that now is rage* The contrast is be-
tween love as it was for these consummate lovers and love as it has now
become for lovers in our later times. S. W. Dawson points out to me
that the poet and his mistress are here addressed by the people of the
future, who will look back on the ideal love attested in such poems as
this one and compare that perfected state with the inadequacies of love
as they know it in their own day. These later lovers will then recognize
that love can be a condition of mutual harmony and peace, though it is
commonly taken for a state of raging frustration. A secondary sense is
that the love of the poet and his mistress, which was formerly peace, is
now 'rage' in that they partake of the bliss of love's saints in heaven, the
highest ecstasy.

40 *contract*] extract *MSS*
  contract the lovers gaze into each other's eyes and see there in
epitome all they thought they had lost. The MSS reading 'extract'
offers a possible alternative, an alchemical image of extraction and
distillation in glass vessels.

40–44 *and drove | Into the glasses ... courts* and drove countries,
towns, courts into the glasses of your eyes, which were thus made such
mirrors and spies that for you they epitomized everything.

44–5 *beg from above | A pattern of your love* intercede on behalf of
later lovers for the blessing of a love patterned on this one, love's
highest condition. The lines suppose that the lovers are true martyrs,
for whom a worldly disaster turns by their death to an eternal triumph.

45 *your*] our *1633–54 and several MSS*

COMMUNITY

3 *there*] these *1633 and some MSS*

5 *prove* try out, experience.

12 *All, all*] All men *1669*
All, all may use all men may use all women.

16–17 *If they were bad, they could not last, | Bad doth itself, and
others waste* In *A Fever* Donne develops the idea that physical decay
follows from moral corruption (lines 17–20).

THE COMPUTATION

1 *For*] From *1669*
  the] my *1635–69 and several MSS*
  For the first twenty years, since yesterday   The poem blows up the twenty-four hours of a separation of lovers to 2400 years.

2 *thou couldst*] thou would'st *MS*; you could *several MSS*; you would *MS*

4 *thou wouldst, they might*] you with they might *several MSS*; you wish they might *MS*; your wish may ever *MS*
  that thou wouldst, they might last   that she would want to continue her favours to him.

6 *neither*] nothing *several MSS*

7 *divide*] deemed *1635–54 and MS*

8 *forgot*] forget *1669 and some MSS*
  forgot that too   in his final torpor of grief his mind cannot even hold the thought of her.

9 *call*] think *several MSS*

10 *by being dead*   she is to suppose that he died when they parted and that his ghost speaks this.

CONFINED LOVE

Title] To the worthiest of all my lovers *MS*; To the worthiest of all my loves my virtuous mistress *MS*

1 *Some man ...*   Helen Gardner assumes that this poem, like *Break of Day*, is spoken by a woman and cites Myrrha's speech in Ovid *Metamorphoses* X, 320–55. Myrrha laments that only human laws, not nature, forbid a woman to mate with her own father: '... piety refuses to condemn such love as this. Other animals mate as they will, nor is it thought base for a heifer to endure her sire, nor for his own offspring to be a horse's mate: the goat goes in among the flocks which he has fathered, and the very birds conceive from those from whom they were conceived. Happy they who have such privilege! Human civilization has made spiteful laws, and what nature allows, the jealous laws forbid ...' (*Metamorphoses*, trans. F. J. Miller (1916), II 87).

6 *should*] might *1633–69*

11 *mate*] meat *1650–69*

12 *do*] did *some MSS*
  jointures   money or property settled upon a widow until she marries again.

13 *choose*] chose *some MSS*

16 *seek new lands*] seek lands *1639–69*
  withal] with all *1635–69*

17 *built*] build *1639–69*

21 *But doth waste with greediness*   but is wasted by the owner's greed in monopolizing what he himself cannot fully use.

THE CURSE

Title] Dirae *several MSS*

The Curse   The anathema, sometimes called *dirae* or invocation of the Furies, was a recognized form in ancient poetry; and the talebearer, Donne's target here, was a familiar enemy of courtly lovers.

3 *His only, and only his*] Him, only for his *1669*; His one and his only *MS*

3–4 *His only, and only his purse | May some dull heart to love dispose*   may the only purse of money he has, and no other reason, dispose some frigid woman to love him.

4 *heart*] whore *1669*

9 *cramps*] cramp *1633–54 and several MSS*

11–13 *may he feel no touch | Of conscience, but of fame, . . . that 'twas she*   may he be aware that everybody knows of his illicit association and feel shame not because it is sinful but because the woman is so foul.

12 *fame*] shame *some MSS*; flame *MS*

14–16] Or may he for her virtue reverence
      One, that hates him only for impotence,
      And equal traitors be she and his sense.
      (*1635–69 and some MSS*)

18 *Meant*] Went *several MSS*

22–3 *may he so long parasites have fed, | That he would fain be theirs, whom he hath bred*   may he ruin himself by pampering hangers-on, to the point where he would be glad to be a hanger-on of his own creatures.

24 *be circumcised for bread*   use circumcision as a meal-ticket, to put himself in the way of sharing in the ritual feasting which is a feature of the Jewish calendar.

32 *out-cursed*   a 'curst' woman was a shrewish or tart one, such as Beatrice in *Much Ado about Nothing* or Katharina in *The Taming of the Shrew*.
   cursed   Pronounced as two syllables.

THE DAMP

4 *your picture in my heart*   The lady's picture in her lover's heart was a common ground of conceited play in Petrarchan love poems.

5 *damp*   a noxious exhalation, a poisonous fume.

6 *through*] thorough *several MSS*

7–8 *prefer | Your murder, to the name of massacre*   promote her murder of the poet to the status of a massacre, by causing many deaths instead of just one.

9 *victories; but*] victories! But *1650–69*
   brave   bold, thorough-going.

11–12 *First kill ... Disdain, | And ... th' enchantress Honour, next be slain*   forgo the ritual defences of the courtly mistress that give women such an unfair advantage over their lovers.

13–14 *like a Goth and Vandal rise, | Deface records, and histories*   the barbarian hordes that overran the decadent Roman Empire all but erased the memory of Roman civilization by destroying the records of its 'arts and triumphs'.

15 *arts*] acts *1669 and several MSS*

21–2 *Kill me ... let me die*   a familiar *double entendre* for orgasm.

23 *Your passive valour*   her sexual mettle, shown in passive feats as distinct from the active audacities of her repudiation of the poet.

24 *Naked*] In that *1633 and several MSS*

THE DISSOLUTION

1 *She is dead*   Following Dante and Petrarch, Renaissance love-poets commonly write of the death of their mistress.

1-2 *all which die | To their first elements resolve* when the soul leaves the body the whole being dissolves back into its constituent elements. The first elements are fire, air, water and earth.

3 *we were mutual elements to us* the two lovers were the elements that made up a single joint being.

5 *My body then doth hers involve* she has resolved into her first elements, him, so that his body now includes hers.

6 *those things whereof I consist* the constituents of his being.

7-8 *In me abundant grow, and burdenous, | And nourish not, but smother* In Galen's medicine an excess of the vital constituents was as dangerous as a deficiency of them.

10 *earthy*] earthly *1633 and some MSS*

12 *near worn out by love's security* their assured love, not calling for the customary supply of passion, sighs, tears and despair, has left him all but empty of the four elements.

   near] ne'er *1633*

13 *repair* replenish.

15 *my fire doth with my fuel grow* his passion feeds on his grief.

18 *soonest break* bankrupt themselves quickest.

20 *store* abundance of materials.

21 *use* consumption of materials.

22 *earnestly* ardently, forcefully.

23-4 *bullets flown before | A latter bullet may o'ertake, the powder being more* a bullet may outspeed one fired before it if the charge of gunpowder is greater.

24 *latter*] later *1669*

THE DREAM

Ovid tells how Corinna came to him as he lay on his couch in the afternoon heat and how he tore her thin tunic away before clasping her in his arms (*Amores*, I. v). The poet's dream or daydream of his mistress became one of the commonplaces of Renaissance love verse. M. Praz cites some Renaissance versions in *A Garland for John Donne*, ed. T. Spencer (1931), 53-6, as does P. Legouis in *Donne the Craftsman* (1928), 75-7.

3-4 *It was a theme | For reason, much too strong for phantasy* the matter of the dream was better fitted to waking reason than to sleeping fancy.

6 *brok'st ... continued'st*] breakest ... continuest *1669 and several MSS*

7 *so true*] so truth *1633 and some MSS*

8 *truths*] truth *some MSS*; true *several MSS*

10 *act*] do *most MSS*

14 *(For thou lov'st truth) an angel*] (Thou lov'st truth) but an angel *some MSS*

15-16 *thou saw'st my heart, | And knew'st my thoughts, beyond an angel's art* God immediately apprehends the thoughts of the heart, but an angel does not.

19 *must*] do *most MSS*
   it] I *some MSS*
   it could not choose but be it was bound to be.

20 *Profane*] Profaneness *most MSS*

24 *fear's as strong*] fears are strong *1669 and some MSS*; fear is strong *some MSS*

25 *pure, and brave* unalloyed and sure of itself.

27-8 *torches which must ready be, | Men light and put out* a used torch flares up more quickly than a new one.
   deal'st] doest *some MSS*

29 *cam'st*] com'st *1669*
   then I] thus I *some MSS*

30 *but*] or *several MSS*
   would] will *several MSS*

THE ECSTASY

An ecstasy is a well-charted experience in devotional writings, occurring 'when as the servants of God were taken up in spirit, separate as it were from the body, and out of the body, that they might see some heavenly mystery revealed unto them' (J. Weemes, *A Treatise of the Four Degenerate Sons* (1636), 72-3). It is the means of an immediate apprehension of truths which are normally inaccessible to us because of our necessary dependence upon sense and discursive reason. Leone Ebreo, one of the best-known Italian theorists of love, speaks of an ecstasy of love in which the lover penetrates the mystery of love itself (*The Philosophy of Love*, trans. F. Friedeberg-Seeley and J. H. Barnes (1937), 62, 199–206).

Some discussions of the poem are:

Helen Gardner, 'The Argument about *The Ecstasy*', in H. Davis and H. Gardner (eds.), *Elizabethan and Jacobean Studies Presented to F. P. Wilson* (1959), 270–306.

M. Y. Hughes, 'The Lineage of *The Ecstasy*', *MLR*, XXVII (1932), 1–5.

M. Y. Hughes, 'Some of Donne's "*Ecstasies*"', *PMLA*, LXXV (1960), 509–18.

A. J. Smith, 'The Metaphysic of Love', *RES*, n.s. LX, 36 (1958), 362–75.

E. M. W. Tillyard, 'A Note on Donne's *Ecstasy*', *RES*, XIX (1943), 67–70.

None of the early editions prints the poem in stanzas, but most MSS divide it so.

1–4 *Where ... | A pregnant bank swelled up ...* A scene of pastoral seclusion was a usual setting for a colloquy of lovers, as in Sidney's *In a grove most rich of shade*, and in Tasso's madrigal *Tirsi, sotto un bel pino* – 'Lying among grass and flowers beneath a beautiful pine tree Thyrsis returned Licori's gaze and sang these words ...'. Such evocations may look back to the spot on the banks of the Ilissus 'with its gentle slope just made for the head to fall back on luxuriously', where Phaedrus read a discourse of love that threw Socrates into an ecstasy as he kept his eye on Phaedrus' face and shared his transports (Plato, *Phaedrus* III, 230–34).

3 *The violet's* The violet is an emblem of faithful love and truth, 'for that blue is the cognisance of truth, and wherein it hath as it were an eye of white, it betokeneth a singular truth without hypocrisy' (H. Goldingham, *The Garden Plot*, 1578, Roxburghe Club, 1825, p. 70). Goldingham says that the violet also represents the virtue of retired humility because 'it groweth low near the ground and commonly under covert of other herbs or flowers', so that it survives unharmed while loftier plants are riven or beaten down.

4 *Sat we two, one another's best*] Sat we on one another's breasts *1669*

6 *With*] By *1635–69*
fast balm a moisture that preserves them steadfast. In Paracelsian medicine balm was the 'natural inborn preservative' (Donne, letter to 'H. G.', 1607) which while our bodies retain it keeps us from decay.

7–8 *Our eye-beams twisted, and did thread / Our eyes, upon one double string* the lovers are gazing fixedly into one another's eyes, in an attitude of mutual absorption – 'For love, all love of other sights controls' (*The Good Morrow* 10).

9 *to' intergraft*] to engraft *1635–69*; to ingraft *some MSS*

10 *our*] the *1633 and some MSS*

11 *in*] on *most MSS*

13–14 *Fate / Suspends uncertain victory* Epic artists sometimes represented the delicately balanced issue between confronting forces by a scales suspended above them. But 'equal armies' suggests that the point of this confrontation is not a victory of one over the other.

15 *Our souls ...* Petrarchan poets sometimes describe debates or contests of souls in erotic terms:

> then bound
> With her enfolded thighs in mine entangled;
> And both in one self-soul placed,
> Made a hermaphrodite, with pleasures ravished
> There, heat for heat's, soul for soul's empire wrangled.
> (B. Barnes, *Parthenophil and Pathenophe* (1593), Madrigal 13)

to advance their state (a) to display their standing, as parleying forces advance their panoplies; (b) to enhance their condition.
their] our *1635–69 and several MSS*

16 *hung*] hangs *several MSS*

22 *he soul's language*] his souls language *MS*

25 *knew*] knows *1633 and several MSS*

25–6 *He (though ... / Because ... the same)*] He though ... / (Because ... the same) *MS*

27 *concoction* the refining of metals by heat; 'the acceleration of anything towards purity and perfection' (Johnson's *Dictionary*).

30 *and tell us what we love* the ecstasy has revealed to them what they previously did not know, the nature of their love itself. See *Negative Love* and *The Relic* 24.

32 *what did move* what their motive was.

33 *several* separate and distinct.

34 *Mixture of things* Aristotelean metaphysicians reasoned that the soul must be a mixture of kinds because it has to perform so many distinct functions.

42 *Interinanimates*] Interanimates *1633–69 and several MSS*

44 *Defects of loneliness controls* the two souls thus united are stronger than either is singly, because they remedy each other's short-comings.

47 *atomies* components.

48 *Are souls*] Are soul *1635–54*
souls, whom no change can invade the soul is distinguished from the body by its exemption from change, and hence its immortality. Their ecstasy thus shows them what their mutual love entails, which is that they are one, united at a level beyond sex or the senses, and unchangeably steadfast.

51 *though they are not*] though not *1633–69*

51-2 *we are | The intelligences, they the sphere* In Aristotelean cosmology an astral body consisted of a sphere or vehicle and an intelligence which controlled it, neither having force without the other. Leone Ebreo speaks of the relationship of soul to body in love as akin to that of an intelligence to its sphere (*The Philosophy of Love*, trans. F. Friedeberg-Seeley and J. H. Barnes (1937), 182–9).

52 *sphere*] spheres *1633–69 and MS*

55 *Yielded their forces, sense, to us* the bodies have relinquished their powers of movement and sense-perception to make possible the communion of souls in ecstasy. But the line supposes a general interdependence of body and soul in which the body yields all its forces to the union, those of sense.
forces, sense] senses' force *1633–69 and MS*; forces, since *several MSS*; forces first *MS*

56 *Nor are dross to us* Transcendental doctrines of love envisaged an

ascent from body to mind and thence to God, in which the body would be discarded as a 'muddy vesture of decay' encumbering the pure spirit. Donne explicitly denied that idea elsewhere: 'You (I think) and I am much of one sect in the Philosophy of love; which though it be directed upon the mind, doth inhere in the body, and find pretty entertainment there' (letter to Sir Henry Wotton, early 1612; Gosse I, 291).

allay alloy, a mixture of base and noble powers.

57–8 *On man heaven's influence works not so, | But that it first imprints the air* (a) an angel has to don a garment of air 'not pure as it, yet pure' *(Air and Angels)* so as to be visible to men and to work upon them'; (b) in hermetic medicine the air mediates the influences of the stars. The argument is that as spiritual forces sometimes need to work through a less pure medium, so a union of souls may require the coupling of bodies.

59 *So*] For *1633–69 and several MSS*

61–4 *As our blood labours to beget | Spirits ... | ... which makes us man* In scholastic metaphysics a man is essentially a complex of unlike components, body and soul, and the necessary link between our body and soul are vapours called spirits produced by the blood.
'In the constitution and making of a natural man, the body is not the man, nor the soul is not the man, but the union of these two makes up the man; the spirits in a man which are the thin and active part of the blood, and so are of a kind of middle nature, between soul and body, those spirits are able to do, and they do the office, to unite and apply the faculties of the soul to the organs of the body, and so there is a man' (Donne, *Sermons* 11, 261–2).

64 *subtle* impalpable; fine; abstruse. Chaucer speaks of 'subtle knittings' in 'the conjunctions of God and of man' which we cannot fully grasp while we are in the flesh (*Boece*, in *Works*, ed. F. N. Robinson (1933), 440b, line 18).

65–7 *So must pure lovers' souls descend | ... reach and apprehend* The analogy turns on the need for mediating elements between soul and body. As blood must strive upwards to produce the purer elements which alone can link sense and soul, and make a man, so pure lovers' souls descend to use some mediating elements that can link them to the agency of sense, without which their love is impotent.

66 *affections* inclinations, feelings.
faculties dispositions, powers of the body.

67 *Which sense may reach and apprehend* sense reaches up to and embraces the immaterial affections and faculties, thus completing the link with the souls and the effective union of the souls themselves.

Helen Gardner emends 'Which' to 'That', a reading not found in any early versions of the poem. She argues that the sense requires a conjunction and not a relative – '*in order that* sense may reach and apprehend'.

68 *Else a great prince in prison lies* a great prince exercises his power over his realm through his officers who are his eyes, ears and arms; and a prince in prison, unable to make contact with the world, loses the effective nature of a prince. So the lovers, however pure and perfect their union of souls, would lose the effective nature of love did not their oneness activate itself in the union of bodies.

70 *Weak men on love revealed may look* men of feeble faith and no experience of love, like religious doubters, require a physical revelation before they can believe.

74 *dialogue of one* 'Because both meant, both spake the same'. From line 29 on the poem reports what they spoke with one voice on this decisive occasion, which is now behind them.

75 *mark*] mock *MS*

75–6 *he shall see | Small change, when we'are to bodies gone* a fellow-initiate in love will recognize how little the essential nature of their love is altered when the souls have returned to the frail bodies.

76 *to bodies gone*] to bodies grown *1635–69 and several MSS*; two bodies grown *several MSS*

THE EXPIRATION

This was the first of Donne's poems to appear in print. It was published with a musical setting in Ferrabosco's *Airs* (1609). Ferrabosco's setting is given in Jacquot and in Helen Gardner, *John Donne: The Elegies and The Songs and Sonnets*, Appendix B.

Title] Valediction *MS*; Valedictio Amoris *MS*
Expiration (a) an exhalation; (b) a breathing away one's life.

1 *break*] leave *most MSS and Ferrabosco*

2 *Which sucks two souls* 'Whereupon, a kiss may be said to be rather a coupling together of the soul, than of the body, because it hath such force in her, that it draweth her unto it, and (as it were) separateth her

from the body' (B. Castiglione, *The Courtier* IV, trans. T. Hoby, 1561).

4 *ourselves*] our souls *some MSS*
happiest] happy *most MSS*

5 *asked*] ask *1633–69 and several MSS*

9 *Oh*] Or *1635–69 and some MSS*
word] words *several MSS*

FAREWELL TO LOVE

First printed in *1635* among poems which are not certainly by Donne. Only four MSS have it, and one of them ascribes it to a 'Mr An. Saintleger'. But no modern editor questions Donne's authorship.

T. Redpath summarizes the controversy over the poem in his note on stanza 3 (*The Songs and Sonnets of John Donne* (1956), 129–31 and Appendix IV). Some contributors to the discussion are Grierson, Hayward and Gardner in their editions, and the following:

H. Gardner, 'A Crux in Donne', *TLS*, 10 June 1949, 318.
L. Hotson, 'A Crux in Donne', *TLS*, 11 April 1949, 249.
A. J. Smith, 'The Dismissal of Love', in A. J. Smith (ed.), *John Donne: Essays in Celebration*, Methuen, 1972, 89–131.
G. Williamson, 'Donne's *Farewell to Love*, *MP*, 1939, 301–3.

Farewell to Love Petrarch renounced his love of Laura for the love of God at one stage in the moral turmoil of his self-destructive obsession with a fellow-creature (*Petrarch's Secret*, trans. W. H. Draper (1911); and *Canzoniere* Sonnets 1, 364 and 365). An abrupt dismissal of love after years of abject devotion became a customary Petrarchan move:

Leave me O love which reachest but to dust,
And thou my mind aspire to higher things:
(Sidney, *Certain Sonnets* 32)

1 *Whilst yet to prove* before putting it to the test of experience.

9 *Our desires give them fashion* they take their character from our desires, of which they are projections.
fashion Pronounced as three syllables.
10 *As they wax lesser, fall, as they size, grow* they diminish or increase in stature as our desires slacken or heighten.
size] rise *MS*

11 *late*] last *several MSS*

12 *His highness sitting in a golden chair* presumably a gilt ginger-
bread effigy of the Pope or Emperor bought or exhibited at a recent
Bartholomew Fair. Such 'fairings' were a noted speciality of the most
celebrated of English fairs, which was held annually in the church-
yard of the Priory of St Bartholomew, Smithfield.

16 *Being had, enjoying it decays* the end once gained, its pleasure
fades or turns to revulsion:

Past reason hunted, and no sooner had
Past reason hated, as a swallowed bait
(Shakespeare, Sonnet 129)

18 *What before pleased them all, takes but one sense* what previously
gratified all the senses now affects only one sense (presumably touch,
a mere awareness of physical contact).

20 *A kind of sorrowing dullness . . .* a tag attributed to Aristotle runs
post coitum triste.

21 *Ah*] Oh *MS*

22 *cocks and lions* Galen says that only cockerels and lions retain their
vitality after coitus. Some writers place them under the government of
the sun, the source of sexual vigour.

23–30 *Unless wise* / *Nature decreed . . .* / *. . . to raise posterity* unless
wise Nature ordained this disillusioning inadequacy of our sexual
experience to stop us killing ourselves in repeated sexual acts, as we
urgently seek to overcome the brevity of our own lives by begetting
children.

24–5 *since each such act, they say* / *Diminisheth the length of life a day*
Aristotle said that sexual acts debilitate, and so shorten life. See *The
First Anniversary* 107–10.

28 *that other curse of being short* the curse of our own brevity
brought on us by the Fall, which makes our pleasures momentary as
well as our lives, and leaves us physically shrunken as in detumescence.
    curse of] curse, of *MS*

28–9 *short,* / *And*] short / And *MS*

28–30 The punctuation of these lines has been much discussed and
emended. The reading in the present text is that of the early editions

and MSS, which agree save for the minor variants noted here. It is not obviously corrupt or in need of emendation.

29 *minute made*] minute, made *MS*

30 *Eager* sentient; virile; sexually keen.
desires to raise posterity prompts the urge to beget children.

31 *Since so* since that is so.

34 *had endamaged me*] had, endamage me *MS*; had endanger me *MS*

35 *moving beauties* beauties which stimulate desire.

36 *the summer's sun* the one kind of hot sun as distinct from the other kind; the sun in the sky rather than a 'moving beauty', both of which have their seasons of greatness when they kindle heat and raise most lust. See *A Nocturnal upon S. Lucy's Day* 38–41.
summer's] summer *1650–69*

38 *their greatness* their provocative power.
heat the desire they provoke.

40 *worm-seed* a harsh anaphrodisiac
the tail the penis

A FEVER

9–12 *Or if, when thou, the world's soul, go'st . . .* Petrarch wrote that the death of his mistress had left the earth without a sun, and destroyed the world for him (*Canzoniere* 268, 326, 338, 352). Donne develops the conceit that a woman can be the sustaining soul of the world in *The First Anniversary* and in Verse Letters to the Countess of Huntingdon and the Countess of Bedford.

13–14 *O wrangling schools, that search what fire / Shall burn this world* the conceit sceptically dismisses those squabbling philosophers who had disputed how the world would end. It was the Stoics who spoke of a general conflagration.

16 *might*] must *MS*

18 *torturing*] tormenting *several MSS*

19 *For much*] For more *1635–69 and MS*; Far more *several MSS*

19–24 *much corruption needful is . . .* Greek medical men held that illnesses are caused by an unequal mixture of the elements, and that fever is like a fire whose best fuel is decayed or corrupt matter, the elements now consuming each other. Donne argues that her fever cannot persist, or cannot touch her real nature, because her essential attributes are of incorruptible substance and not corruptible flesh.

21 *meteors* fireballs or shooting stars which soon consume their own substance; transitory phenomena, peculiar to our sublunary region of imperfectly mixed elements and of change.

24 *firmament* the immutable heavens beyond our world of change.

THE FLEA

This poem was given first of the Songs and Sonnets in early editions from *1635* on. It is sometimes said to have been one of the most celebrated of Donne's poems in the poet's own day, but the only evidence of its popularity is Grierson's reference to some admirers of a Dutch translation of the poem.

Ribald love poems on fleas proliferated in the sixteenth century, in emulation of a medieval piece ascribed to Ovid. The poet commonly envied the flea's free access to his mistress's body, or its death by her hand at the climax of its bliss.

3 *Me it sucked first*] It sucked me first *1633–54 and some MSS*

sucked . . . sucks Mark Roberts suggested that the old form of 's' – ∫ – made it a sensitive letter in such contexts as this, where it could easily be read as 'f' (*EC*, XVI (1966), 309–29). But many of the early manuscripts use the modern form of 's', and we cannot assume that Donne wrote the old form here, whatever the printers did after his death.

4 *our two bloods mingled be* coition was commonly assumed to entail a mingling of bloods, a notion derived from Aristotle.

5 *Confess it*] Thou know'st that *1633–54 and some MSS*

6 *or shame, or loss*] nor shame, nor loss *1633–54 and some MSS*

11 *nay*] yea *1633–54 and several MSS*

21 *In what*] Wherein *1633–54 and some MSS*

THE FUNERAL

Grierson thought it 'probable that the sequence of poems *The Funeral*, *The Blossom*, *The Primrose*, *The Relic*, was addressed to Mrs Herbert in the earlier days of Donne's intimacy with her in Oxford or London'.

Pierre Legouis, H. W. Garrod and Helen Gardner among others contest this view. See P. Legouis, *Donne the Craftsman* (1928), 94–8; H. W. Garrod, 'Donne and Mrs Herbert', *R.E.S.* XXI (1945), 161–73, and John Donne, *Poetry and Prose* (1946), 1115–16; Helen Gardner, *John Donne: The Elegies and The Songs and Sonnets*, Appendix C (ii).

Mrs Magdalen Herbert, mother of the poets Edward Lord Herbert of Cherbury and George Herbert, was widowed in 1596 and lived in Oxford from 1599 to 1601 when she moved to London, marrying again in 1608. She was seven years older than Donne, and their close friendship dates from 1607 or so, when she was in her early forties and he was raising a young family at Mitcham.

1 *to shroud me . . . :* The poet addresses those who will prepare and bury his corpse when he dies of the lady's refusal to yield to him, which she has tempered by sending him a lock of her hair.

3 *subtle* fine; rarified; not readily understood. The wreath of fine hair is a subtler talisman than the wreath of laurel which normally crowns a poet's head and symbolically preserves his fame.

6 *then to*] unto *1633–69*

7 *control* rule; preserve and amend.

9–10 *the sinewy thread my brain lets fall | Through every part* One theory was that the body is held in organic order by skeins of sinews or nerves emanating from the brain to every part.

12 *These*] Those *1633–69 and some MSS*
     grew] grow *1650–69*

12–13 *which upward grew, and strength and art | Have from a better brain* the threads of hair can hold his body whole after his death more effectively than the sinewy thread held it together in life, because these hairs grew upwards (towards heaven and a purer condition) and draw virtue from a brain better endowed to preserve against corruption.

17 *Whate'er* Given as 'what ere' in all the early versions. Both senses of the word seem to be called for – 'Whatever she meant by it earlier, when she gave it . . .'.
     with me] by me *1633*

19–20 *idolatry, | . . . these relics* see *The Relic* 12–22.

21 *humility* modest courtesy.

22 *afford to it all that a soul can do* allow the lock of hair the power of a soul to preserve and integrate.

23 *bravery* defiant pride.

24 *save none of me* keep any part of him alive by satisfying its amorous needs

    save] have *1633–69 and some MSS*

THE GOOD MORROW

Good Morrow the central metaphor of the poem is an awakening to a new life.

2 *were we not weaned till then* He supposes that all their experience before they met and loved each other was infantile, or an immature anticipation of this.

3 *sucked on country pleasures, childishly* In the seventeenth century the infants of well-to-do families were sent to be wet-nursed in the country. 'Country pleasures' would in any case seem simple-minded pastimes to the society of Court or town. Mark Roberts and Helen Gardner see a sexual sense here, as in Hamlet to Ophelia, 'Do you think I meant country matters?' (III. 2. 123); and Roberts finds the innuendo confirmed in some early versions by the old long 's' in 'sucked' (see *The Flea*, note on line 3). Donne's argument would then be that they have both awakened from a juvenile pleasure in sex for its own sake to the adult condition of mutual fidelity.

    on country pleasures, childishly?] on childish pleasures sillily *1669 and some MSS*; one childish pleasure sillily *MS*

4 *snorted*] slumbered *some MSS*
    the seven sleepers' den the cave in which seven Christian youths, walled up alive in the persecution of Decius (A.D. 249), slept miraculously for 187 years.

5 *but this, all pleasures fancies be* all other pleasures than this one are mere fancies.
    but this, all] but as all *MS*

6–7 *If ever any beauty I did see, | Which I desired, and got* The conceit that one's previous mistresses were only shadows or gleams of the lady one addresses is common in Renaissance lyrics, but 'desired, and got' is not.

9 *watch*] watched *MS*

9-10 *Which watch not one another out of fear; | For love, all love of other sights controls* their souls regard each other so absorbedly not out of suspicion but out of love, which inhibits pleasure in any other sight.
fear; | For love, all love] fear / But love; all love *MS*

13 *maps* charts of the heavens.
to others, worlds on worlds] to other, . . . *1633-54*; to other worlds, our worlds *1669*; to other worlds, one world *several MSS*; in studies, worlds *MS*

14 *one world*] our world *many MSS*
each hath one, and is one the one world either wants to possess is the world of the other, and the possession makes them one.

17 *two better hemispheres* either of them is a hemisphere of the world they make up jointly, but together they are without the shortcomings of the geographical hemispheres (see *The Ecstasy* 41-4).
better] fitter *1635-69 and most MSS*

18 *sharp north . . . declining west* bitter bleakness and falling off, the common lapse of human attachments from which their mutual love is exempt.
north] frost *MS*

19 *What ever dies, was not mixed equally* In Galen's medicine disease and death were the consequence of a disproportion in one's constituent elements.
was] is *some MSS*

20 *If our two*] If both our *several MSS*; If our both *MS*
or] as *MS*; and *MS*; both *several MSS*

20-21] . . . both thou and I
Love just alike in all, none of these loves can die.
(*1635-69 and some MSS*)

21 *none can die* neither love will be subject to the alteration and decline which is the general condition of the world they have now awakened from.

THE INDIFFERENT

3 *her who masks and plays* the woman who loves social pleasures best, such as masquerades and plays.

5 *who believes . . . who tries* the woman who takes the poet's avowals

at face value and the woman who questions them or puts them to proof.

12 *Have you old*] Or have you all old *1633–69 and some MSS*

13 *fear*] shame *some MSS*

16 *Rob*] Rack *several MSS*; Reach *MS*
  but] and *MS*

17 *travail*] travel *1635–69*
  came to travail (a) took up with a woman so as to labour – to make love with zest; (b) underwent pain and trouble; (c) took up with her intending to pass on quickly – travel – to some other woman.

18 *fixed subject* permanent thrall, and unrequited victim – the antithesis of the 'travailer / traveller' of line 17.

20 *sweetest part, variety*] sweetest part, sweet variety *MS*

21 *and that it*] it *1635–69 and several MSS*; and it *some MSS*

A JET RING SENT

Given among the Epigrams in one MS

Title] To a Jet Ring sent to me *MS*

1 *Thou art* . . . He addresses a jet ring which a woman has sent him. Jet rings lined with silver for an inscription were a fashionable love token.
  black The colour of mourning, and humility. It was also a token of unvarying constancy since there are no degrees of black.

2 *brittle* frail; light minded.

4 *endless* constant; whereas her property is utter unfaithfulness.

6 *aught less precious* . . . anything less precious than gold, which wedding rings are made of.

7 *loves*] love *MS*

8 *fling me away* colloquially, to jet something was to throw it.

A LECTURE UPON THE SHADOW

First printed in *1635*.

Title] The shadow *several MSS*; Love's Lecture upon the Shadow *MS*; Love's Philosophy *MS*

3 *These*] Those *some MSS*

4 *Walking*] In walking *some MSS*

9 *loves*] love *1699 and some MSS*

10 *Disguises . . . and shadows . . .* pretences and concealments, to keep their love hidden from others.

11 *care*] cares *1635 and several MSS*; ears *several MSS*

12 *high'st*] least *most MSS*; last *MS*

14 *loves*] love *some MSS*

19 *If our loves*] If once love *several MSS*
faint, and westwardly decline see *The Good Morrow* 18.

20–21 *To me thou, falsely, thine, | . . . shall disguise* you will falsely disguise your actions from me, as I will disguise mine from you.

26 *his first minute, after noon, is night* love is as good as finished the moment it goes into decline and the lovers start deceiving each other.
first] short *1635–69*

THE LEGACY

3 *be an*] be but an *1633–69*

4 *lovers' hours be full eternity* 'How infinite a time will it seem till I see you: for lovers' hours are full eternity. Dr Donne said this, but I think it' (Katherine Thimelby writing to her lover in 1635. *Tixall Letters*, ed. A. Clifford (1815), I, 147). This is the earliest known quotation from the *Songs and Sonnets*.

7 *sent*] meant *1635–54*

7–8 *which sent me, I should be | Mine own executor and legacy* which conveyed to me that I should be at once the executor of my own will, and the legacy bequeathed by the terms of the will itself.

10 *'. . . my self', that is you, not I* The poem combines two conceits, the lover's identification with his mistress, and their exchanged hearts.
that is] that's *1633 and some MSS*; that *some MSS*

13–15 *find none, | When I had ripped me . . . lie; | It killed me . . .* The punctuation in the early versions is ambiguous. Some editors have repunctuated so that 'When I had ripped me' relates to 'It killed me again'; thus '... find none. / When I had ... lie, / It killed me again ...'.

14 *ripped me, and*] ripped, and *1635-69 and some MSS*
   hearts should] hearts did *1633*; heart did *some MSS*; hearts do *MS*

14-15 *lie; / It*] lie, / It *1633-69*

16 *cozen* deceive or defraud.

18 *But*] For *1650-69*
   colours it, and corners had it was not a real heart but an ingeniously simulated one, which, however, displayed emblematically its lack of the true characteristics of a heart, pure sincerity and straight dealing.

20 *It was entire to none, and few had part* no one possessed the whole of it, and few had any part of it.

22 *our losses sad*] our loss be sad *1669*; our loss be ye sad *most MSS*
   losses these might be just the lovers' partings; or he may mean that he has lost his heart and she her legacy.

23 *meant*] thought *some MSS*
   this] that *1635-69 and some MSS*

LOVERS' INFINITENESS

Title] Mon Tout *several MSS*. Grierson suggested that the title *Lovers' Infiniteness*, which all the early editions give, is a mistake for *Love's Infiniteness*. Helen Gardner entitles the poem *Love's Infiniteness*.

5 *All my treasure*] And all my treasure *1633-69*

9 *partial*] general *several MSS*

11 *thee*] it *1635-69*

21 *is*] was *1635-54*

25-6] And since my heart doth every day beget
     New love ...
     (MS)

29-30] Except mine come when thine doth part
     And in such giving it, thou savest it:
     (several MSS)
     Perchance mine comes, when thine doth part,
     And by such losing it, thou savest it:
     (MS)

29–30 *Love's riddles are ... / ... and thou with losing sav'st it* The sense is that a heart fixedly given to another person may be lost in one way but is saved in a more important way. See *The Good Morrow* 15–16.

30] And so in giving it, thou savest it *MS*

31 *have*] find *several MSS*

32 *join*] coin *MS*; win *several MSS*

LOVE'S ALCHEMY

Title] Mummy *most MSS*

2 *centric* central or essential.

7 *chemic* alchemist.
the elixir the goal of spiritual alchemy was the elixir of life, a pure quintessence with absolute power to heal and preserve.

10 *Some odoriferous thing, or medicinal* supposed by-products of the search for the elixir or the philosopher's stone – 'Something about the scraping of the shards, / Will cure the itch' (Jonson, *The Alchemist* IV v 91–3) – which alchemists were delighted enough to hit on as an earnest of future success.

12 *a winter-seeming summer's night* at once short and bleak.

13 *our day* our virility and our lives, expended in sexual acts. See *Farewell to Love* 23–30.

15 *my*] any *MS*
my man my servant. Montaigne says of a suffering philosopher: 'He feeleth the same passions that my lackey doth . . . .' (*An Apology of Raymond Sebond, Essays* II, 12). Donne's question reduces love to a natural and humiliating function, and scouts the idea that it is an exalted spiritual state open only to a few choice souls.

17 *short scorn* humiliating brevity. *Farewell to Love* plays on the several senses of 'short' in reference to sexual motives and acts.

19 *marry*] marrow *several MSS*

22 *that day's rude hoarse minstrelsy* Seventeenth-century marriages were consummated to music played by small hired bands, and with much coarse merriment at the door of the marriage chamber. See *An Epithalamion . . . on the Lady Elizabeth, and Count Palatine* 99–112.

the spheres in old astronomy, the concentric globes which revolved round the earth making sublime harmonies by their motion.

23 *women*] woman *several MSS*
at their best] or at best *several MSS*

23-4 *at their best / Sweetness and wit, they are but mummy, possessed.*] at their best, / Sweetness, and wit they are, but, *mummy*, possessed *1633–54*

24 *mummy* Two old senses of the word seem specially relevant – (a) a medicinal preparation of the substance of mummies; hence, an unctuous liquid or gum used medicinally; (b) the jocular use, dead flesh. Donne himself sometimes uses 'mummy' as Paracelsus did, to mean any dead body which retains its preservative balm – 'The later physicians say, that when our natural inborn preservative is corrupted or wasted, and must be restored to a like extracted from other bodies; the chief care is that the mummy have in it no excelling quality, but an equally digested temper' (Letter to Sir H. G., c. 1607). On this Paracelsian theory the best mummy is the fresh corpse of a man killed suddenly, in whom the balm has not been depleted or distempered by illness. The only difference between that and a living being is that the corpse lacks a mind and soul.

possessed (a) owned; (b) enjoyed sexually; (c) moved by a demon spirit. The pointing of these lines in the *1633–54* editions makes them distinguish between women as they are at their best and as they are once one has possessed them – sweetness and wit, or mummy. The MSS reading, followed in this text, completes the figure of alchemy by showing us a lover who anticipates a union of minds, but in possession will find at best only the residual sweetness and wit of animated mummy.

LOVE'S DEITY

2 *before the god of love was born* that is, in the natural state of the first men, when love was at its uninhibited height and an offered love was likely to be returned without cavil.

3 *he, who then loved most* early men, being so much nearer the created condition, realized their human possibilities far more fully than we can do now in our declining times.

5-6 *produced a destiny . . . / . . . custom, lets it be* The god of love has imposed his own arbitrary mode upon lovers, bringing about the present cross-grainedness of love which use makes second nature to us.

8–9 *much, / Nor . . .*] much? / Nor . . . *1635*

9 *young godhead* in his early days as a god.

10 *even* equal.

12 *Actives to passives* lovers, who make advances, and the persons loved who respond with a return of love. Sperone Speroni argued that in love 'the condition of things' is such that 'the lover in loving his beloved, moves her to love him'; for 'although love may be present in a woman's heart, it cannot operate there directly; but in returning to her from her lover in the manner of a victorious captain it achieves its effect with redoubled force' (*Dialogo di Amore* (1542) in *Opere* (1740) I, 33).

12–13 *Correspondency / Only his subject was* the god of love's allotted task was just to match mutual lovers and to supervise their exchanges (whereas now he does nothing but promote one-sided love with its familiar accompaniment of lament and complaint).

13–14 *it cannot be / Love, till I love her, that loves me* a one-sided love is not love at all.

14] Love, if I love, who loves not me *1635–54 and MS*

15 *modern* new; mediocre; commonplace.

17 *To rage, to lust, to write to, to commend . . .* these are the customary ploys of the courtly lover, which have nothing to do with a mutual love and hence are not properly part of love at all.

18 *purlieu* the outlying domain.

21] That I should love, who loves not me *most MSS*

24 *might make*] may make *1633–69 and several MSS*

26 *since she loves before* courtly addresses usually assume that the lady is already married to someone else. See *Twicknam Garden* 26–7.

27–8 *Falsehood is worse than hate; and that must be . . .* it is better that she continue to hate the poet than be false to a prior vow.

LOVE'S DIET

8 *Of which my fortune, and my faults had part* some part of even that one sigh was set aside to lament the poet's fortune and his faults.

11 *feast*] feed *several MSS*

12 *very sound* truly wholesome or genuine.
   meant to me intended for the poet, or prompted by the thought of him.

17 *his meat* the sigh of stanza 2.

18 *For, eyes*] Her eyes *1669*
   which roll towards all which wander round promiscuously, sizing up possible lovers.

19 *Whatever he would dictate, I writ that*] Whate'er might him distaste I still writ that *1650–54*; Whatsoever he would distaste I writ that *some MSS*

20] But burnt her letters when she writ to me *1635–54*
   when] if *several MSS*

21 *that that*] if that *1635–69 and several MSS*

22 *title* right to share in the lady's favour.

24 *entail* the line and order of inheritance.

25 *reclaimed*] redeemed *1633 and MS*
   buzzard love a buzzard wants to gorge itself on its prey, and is not manoeuverable enough for the kind of uncommitted hawking the poet has in mind.

27 *sport*] sports *1633*

27–9 *Now negligent of sport I lie,* | *And now . . .* | *I spring* sometimes unconcerned about the chase and sometimes hotly engaged in it.

29 *spring* start up a bird for his love to hawk after.

30 *and sleep*] or sleep *1635–69 and some MSS*

LOVE'S EXCHANGE

1–2 *any devil else . . .* | *Would for a given soul give something too* the devil strikes specious bargains with men by granting them trivial demonic powers in exchange for their soul.

4 *and*] or *1633–69*

5 *For them who were their own before* courtiers buy control over men's souls with fashionable trifles; the victims are no longer their own men.

who] which *1633–69*

8 *not*] no *1633–69 and some MSS*; but *MS*

dispensation licence from the Pope or king to set aside the law in a particular case.

9 *a tear, or sigh, or vow*] a tear or vow *some MSS*; a tear, a sigh, a vow *MS*; a sigh, a tear, a vow *several MSS*

11 *non obstante* a licence to do a thing notwithstanding any statute to the contrary.

nature's law in this case, the natural inclination to love, which the tyrant god of love allows his minions to thwart with denials, forswearing and the like. As a former rebel against Love's tyranny the poet refuses the licence.

20 *pain*] pains *1633–69*

23 *thy first motions* the first mild incitements to love, which the poet has ignored.

24–5 *which stand stiff, till great shot | Enforce them ... condition not* small towns which refuse to give in to a besieger until they are bombarded into submission have not the right to make conditions of surrender.

27 *article* stipulate by treaty.

30 *the idolatry* the particular religion; but also the worship of a particular woman.

36 *For this Love*] For, this Love *1633–69*

42 *Racked carcases make ill anatomies* the corpses of men who have been stretched on the rack make poor subjects for anatomical dissection.

LOVE'S GROWTH

Title] The Spring *some MSS*

1 *pure* simple and unmixed, hence not subject to change.

3–4 *doth endure | Vicissitude, and season* has its alterations and seasonal fluctuations.

7–8 *which cures all sorrow / With more* Paracelsian doctors sought to cure by the principle of likeness, expelling a disease with the application of a like medicine.

8 *quintessence* the pure essence of anything, which contains all the sustaining virtue.

9 *mixed of all stuffs, paining soul, or sense* compounded of every kind of experience, and hence affecting both soul and the senses.
  paining] vexing *1635–69 and some MSS*

10 *his working vigour* (a) its restorative powers; (b) its motive force, sexual energy.
  working] active *1635–69 and some MSS*

11 *pure, and abstract*] pure an abstract *some MSS*

13–14 *But as all else, being elemented too, / Love sometimes would contemplate, sometimes do* as any other mixture of spirit and matter, love is partly an activity of mind and partly of body.

15 *not*] no *1633–69 and MS*

17–20 *As, in the firmament, / Stars . . . are not enlarged, but shown, / Gentle love deeds . . . / . . . do bud out now* as we would not be able to see the stars were it not for the light which they reflect from the sun, so we would not know of the existence of love were it not for the bodily consequences of the union of souls. See *The Ecstasy* 69–72. There was an old belief that all the heavenly bodies owe their light to the sun.

18–19 *Stars . . . shown, / Gentle love deeds*] Stars . . . shown. / Gentle love deeds *1650–54*; Stars are not by the sun enlarged; but shown / Greater; love's deeds *MS*

23 *like so many spheres* The old astronomers pictured the heavens as a series of concentric hollow globes which revolved round the earth and carried the heavenly bodies with them.
  so many] to many *most MSS*

28 *the*] this *1635–69 and some MSS*

LOVE'S USURY

3 *Usurious . . .* for his freedom now the poet will mortgage his middle years to Love at a twenty-fold rate of interest; but he expects the Faustus-like compact to work to his advantage.

5 *reign*] range *1635–69 and some MSS*

6   *snatch*] match *1635-54*

7   *Resume my last year's relict*   take up his last year's cast-off.
relict   a man's widow; the remains or leavings.

10-11   *at next nine | Keep midnight's promise*   gain at nine a.m. what
the lady had promised his rival at midnight.

11   *mistake*   to take instead of, as well as take for.

12   *tell the Lady*] tell her Lady *MS*

13   *the sport*   the sexual chase itself, which might enslave him as
much as an attachment to one woman.

14-15   *country grass . . . comfitures of Court, | . . . city's quelque-
choses*   the several styles of women. Literally, comfitures are sweet-
meats and quelque-choses or kickshaws are elaborate fancy dishes.

15   *let report*] let not report *1635-54 and some MSS*

19   *or pain*] and pain *1635-54 and MS*

20   *covet, most at that age thou*] covet most, at that age thou *1633-69*;
covet most at that age; thou *MS*
most at that age thou shalt gain   the usurer Love for his part stands
to gain far more by causing the poet to fall in love in middle age than in
his youth

24   *loves*] love *1635-54.*

THE MESSAGE

This was given first of the *Songs and Sonnets* in the *1633* edition. In
some MSS it is one of three poems headed 'Songs which were made to
airs which were made before'.

11   *But if it be taught*] Which if it be taught *1633 and some MSS*;
Yet since there 'tis taught *several MSS*; Yet since it hath learnt *several
MSS*

14   *cross*] break *1633-69*

19   *laugh and joy*] lie and laugh *MS*

NEGATIVE LOVE

Title] The Nothing *several MSS*

5 *sense, and understanding* sense is concerned with the body, and the understanding with the mind or virtue; neither lust for the body nor admiration of the mind is truly love. See *Air and Angels* 15-22.

7 *silly* ignorant.
   more brave bolder, finer.

8 *miss* not gain his end.

10-12 *If that be simply perfectest | Which can by no way be expressed | But negatives* In scholastic metaphysics God is the one absolutely simple and perfect essence, and the schoolmen's attempts to define him ended with their falling back on negatives as the only way of distinguishing divine attributes from human ones.

13 *all, which all love* all those who think that their love is the most perfect because they positively love all the lady's attributes, and not just the partial or exclusive ones set out in stanza 1.

15 *What we know not, ourselves* Our lack of self-knowledge is the final argument of the Christian sceptics of Donne's own day – 'And he who hath no understanding of himself, what can he have understanding of?' (Montaigne, *An Apology of Raymond Sebond*, *Essays* II, 12). Montaigne's disciple Charron added that the only certainty we can reach is negative, a knowledge of what God is not (*Les Trois Veritez* (1593), 29).

18 *Though I speed not, I cannot miss* though he does not gain any end, he cannot lose his end either. Dante wrote of a love whose nature and end passed his human comprehension; and the following court poets trivialized his idea to the conceit that the lady's beauty defied definition. But Donne's demur is empirical, and sceptical. He supposes that to define his love by some end it seeks would merely spell out our own self-ignorance and prove our inability to grasp anything. Genuine love is precisely what we cannot limit thus by an arbitrary definition; it is a condition or relationship and not a desire to realize some given end.

A NOCTURNAL UPON S. LUCY'S DAY

St Lucy's Day is 13 December, which was formerly the shortest day and the winter solstice when the sun entered the sign of the goat. The name Lucy itself betokens light, and suggests the light shining in darkness: 'But Christ was *fons lucis*, the fountain of all their light' (Donne, *Sermons* III, 353-4).

Lucy was the name of Donne's patroness the Countess of Bedford, and commentators from Grierson on have argued that the poem was written for her in some serious illness, such as she had in 1612–13, or even on her death in 1627. Donne wrote elegies on the deaths of several people associated with her, her brother Lord Harrington who died in 1612, her first cousin Lady Markham and her cousin Cecilia Boulstred who both died at her home, Twickenham Park, during 1609. Some MSS suggest a peculiar poetic link between Donne and the Countess in the mourning for these ladies, assigning to 'L. C. of B.' herself the funeral elegy *Death be not proud, thy hand gave not this blow*, which was printed in all the early editions as Donne's further tribute to Lady Markham or Mrs Boulstred.

Donne's wife Ann has also been proposed for the subject of this *Nocturnal* (see J. T. Shawcross, 'Donne's *A Nocturnal upon S. Lucy's Day*', *Explicator*, XXIII (1965), no. 56). She died in 1617, but Walton tells how Donne believed her dead in childbirth in 1612 while he was visiting Paris; however, the stillbirth to which Walton's anecdote refers actually took place late in January 1612 and Donne himself knew nothing of the event some months later. Donne's daughter Lucy, named after the Countess of Bedford, died in 1627.

3 *flasks* the stars, which store up the sun's energy as flasks store gunpowder.

4 *light squibs* weak flashes.

5–6 *sap . . . / . . . balm* lifegiving and life-preserving essences, which have sunk or been sucked down into the earth leaving organic life desiccated. Current medical theory supposed that every living body contains a 'natural inborn preservative' or balm, whose wastage brings decay and death (see the note on line 24 of *Love's Alchemy*; and *Sermons* V, 347–8).

6 *hydroptic* immoderately thirsty, as dropsical people were thought to be.

7 *Whither, as to the bed's-feet, life is shrunk* Two senses seem possible: (a) the sap and balm have sunk from the dying world, as the preserving moisture of a dying man drains from him back towards the earth via the feet of the bed; (b) the scope of life has shrunk to the briefest bound, as a dying man's concern contracts to the limit of his own bed.

9 *me, who am their epitaph* he sums up in himself the general debility.

11 *At the next world . . . the next spring* for other lovers the coming spring will be a resurrection into a new life after the dead time of love, but not for the poet.

12 *every*] a very *1635-69*

13 *love wrought new alchemy* love has reversed the normal process of alchemy by working to produce more intense degrees of negativeness, so as to arrive at an elixir of death or of nothing.

14 *express* distil by crushing out.

16-17 *From ... emptiness / He ruined me*] From ... emptiness, / He ruined me *1669*; From ... emptiness; / He ruined me *1719*, Grierson and Gardner.

16-18 *From dull privations, and lean emptiness / He ruined me, and I am re-begot / Of absence, darkness, death ; things which are not* love has annihilated the poet comprehensively by starting with the usual deprivations of a thwarted lover and ruining him further from there, so that he is now reborn into a wholly negative existence.

19-20 *All others, from all things, draw all that's good, / Life, soul, form, spirit, whence they being have* the essential constituents of a person's being derive from, and are sustained by, the vitalizing elements present in all created nature.

21 *limbeck* alembic, a chemical apparatus used for distilling.

24 *Drowned the whole world, us two* they themselves were the world which their mutual grief drowned. See *A Valediction : of Weeping* 14-20.

25 *two chaoses* chaos is a state in which things go their own way without due regard for their place in the whole scheme. These lovers fell into chaos the moment they showed concern for anything besides each other because either of them was the other's true place in the scheme.

26 *absences* separations, which parted their bodies but not their souls, so that the bodies were mere shells. See *A Valediction : forbidding Mourning* 17-24.

29 *the first nothing* as the alchemists strove for the quintessence or first principle of life, so love has worked towards the essence of death, the first principle of nothing.

30-31 *that I were one, / I needs must know* it is a characteristic of man to know that he is a man; and the poet, not knowing this, cannot then be a man.

31-3 *I should prefer, / If I were any beast, / Some ends, some means* beasts characteristically elect means and ends, and the poet's inability to do this proves him less than a beast.

33-4 *yea plants, yea stones detest, / And love* Early naturalists inter-preted all physical events in terms of attraction or repulsion, sympathy or antipathy. Pliny speaks of desire and marriage between trees, and of sexual forces at work between precious stones: 'And I pray you, hath not God so knit all things together with certain links, that one ever seemeth to have need of an other?' (T. Wilson, *The Art of Rhetorique* (1560), ed. G. H. Mair (1909), 46). Since the poet now finds himself without motions of attraction or repulsion, he must be lower than vege-tables and mineral nature.

34-5 *invest; / If*] invest, / If *1633*; invest / If *1635-69*

35-6 *an ordinary nothing ... / As shadow* he is also less than in-substantial phenomena such as shadows, for something has to produce a shadow.

38-40 *lovers, for whose sake, the lesser sun / At this time to the Goat is run / To fetch new lust.* The sun enters the constellation of Capricorn at the winter solstice, the agent of our life thus replenishing itself at the source of sexual energy. Donne's point is that while the 'lesser sun' will ultimately revive the world's life and the virility of lovers, for him there can be no renewal since his greater sun is now dead, but only a self-dedication to night after St Lucy's Day.

THE PARADOX

3 *that else none can* that nobody else is capable of loving.

3-4 *else none can, nor will agree / That*] else none can or will agree, / That *1633-69*; else none can nor will agree / That *MS*

7 *Love with* love kills with.

8 *Death kills with too much cold* death's victims are chiefly old men whose blood has lost its heat.

12 *doth the sense beguile* it deceives our eyes.

14 *light's life*] life's light *1633-69 and some MSS*
light's life the sun, the source of light.

20 *lie*] die *1633-69 and some MSS*

THE PRIMROSE

In editions from *1635* on, the poem is subtitled 'being at Montgomery Castle, upon the hill, on which it is situate'. Montgomery Castle was the seat of the Herbert family and the home of Sir Edward Herbert (later Lord Herbert of Cherbury). Donne stayed there in the spring of 1613, for he wrote to Sir Robert Harley from Montgomery on 7 April (Hayward 464–5; see also *Goodfriday, 1613. Riding Westward*). If he did write *The Primrose* at or about Montgomery Castle then 1613 is the likely date of the poem.

1 *primrose hill* John Aubrey, who quotes this poem in his *Life of Edward Herbert Lord Herbert of Cherbury*, writes 'In the park' against the first line and says that there is a 'Prim-rose hill' standing 'southwards, without the castle'. The hill now called Town Hill which stands against Montgomery Castle was formerly known as Primrose Hill, and is still covered with primroses in April.

4 *manna* (a) the small yellowish drops of juice exuded from the manna ash; (b) nourishment from heaven, as 'the small round thing, small as the hoar frost on the ground' with which God fed the Israelites in the wilderness (Exodus xvi 14–35).

6 *a terrestrial galaxy* C. M. Coffin takes this as evidence that the poem was written after Galileo's demonstration in *Sidereus Nuncius* (1610) that the Milky Way is made up of countless small stars (*John Donne and the New Philosophy* (1937), 151–4). Donne does mention Galileo's work with the telescope (*Ignatius his Conclave* (1611)), but the idea itself is ancient.

8 *to find a true love* to see by examining the flowers what kind of woman he may love, as children count the petals of daisies. In the country lore of the time both six-petalled flowers and four-petalled flowers were sometimes called true-loves, because they looked like true-love knots; but the name was proper to the primrose – 'my primrose sweet is lo a truelove rare' (H. Goldingham, *The Garden Plot*, 1578, Roxburghe Club, 1825).

In this common lore the primrose stood for several qualities which might be relevant to Donne's poem: 'How well the primrose being the first flower of the spring which representeth youth may well be alluded to a truelove I leave for to consider who by comparing them together shall find their budding flourishing and fading all alike and yet notwithstanding, the choice thereof so good as when the beauty fadeth there resteth a virtue behind, which the shape of the flower doth signify, leaving a kind of commendation to the chooser who though he desire to have it youthful, yet regardeth so far as his age permitteth to have it also fruitful so that as outwardly it seemeth goodly, it inwardly may be also thought godly' (Goldingham, p. 28).

9–10 *a mere woman ... / ... or more, or less than woman* The true-love primroses he finds, either having more petals than is common in primroses, or less, give him a choice between a true love who is more than a woman and one who is less than a woman.

12 *a six, or four* a six-petalled flower or a four-petalled one.

17 *study her, not*] study her, and not *1633 and several MSS*

22 *with thy true number, five* primroses commonly have five petals.
number, five] number five *1633–69*

24 *this mysterious number* five, which was traditionally a magic number. One occult writer says that five is particularly potent because it consists of the first odd number and the first even number (not counting one as a number), symbolizing male and female respectively; and that being the 'just middle' of the universal number, ten, it is the number of justice and of wedlock (C. Agrippa, *Of Occult Philosophy* (1531), trans. 'J.F.' (1651), 188). Ben Jonson uses five as the number of wedlock in the *Masque of Hymen*, performed at Court in 1606 for the marriage of the Earl of Essex and Lady Frances Howard (see the introductory note to the Epithalamion *Eclogue 1613. December 26*). He has Reason speak as follows:

For five the special number is,
Whence hallowed union claims her bliss.
As being all the sum, that grows
From the united strengths, of those
Which male and female numbers we
Do style, and are first two, and three.
Which, joined thus, you cannot sever
In equal parts, but one will ever
Remain as common; so we see
The binding force of unity:
For which alone, the peaceful gods
In number, always, love the odds
And even parts as much despise,
Since out of them all discords rise.

25 *Ten is the farthest number* ten is the universal number, which takes in everything. It is also the complete or perfect number and is thus the number of the male, who is complete in himself as the female was supposed not to be until she united herself with a man (see the *Epithalamion made at Lincoln's Inn*).

25–7 *if half ten | Belong unto each woman, then | Each woman may take half us men*   if a woman is a five and a man is a ten then each woman may perfect herself by taking half of each man, and thus making up ten.

26 *Belong*] Belongs *1633–69 and MS*

28 *if this will not serve their turn*   if this does not meet women's ends.

29 *and*] since *1635–69*

29–30 *and they fall | First into this, five*   since five is the first number that consists of an odd number and an even number.

30 *into this, five, women*] into this five, women *1633 and most MSS*; into five, women *1635–69 and several MSS*

woman may take us all   then each odd (or female) number may complete itself by taking all of each even (or male) number: 3 plus 2 equals 5.

In point of fact however no early version reads 'first into this, five', the crucial comma being Grierson's generally accepted emendation. The *1633* and *MSS* reading 'first into this five' does make sense. It suggests that since women have already preempted the five of the primrose, out of a possible ten, the remaining five must comprehend all men; hence to make the odds into evens and complete a whole number 'women may take us all'.

The distinction between 'may take half us men' and 'may take us all' has been variously interpreted. The likelier suggestions are: (a) that a woman united with a man will be half of a perfect life; or that a woman may wholly include and absorb a man so as to rob him of his will (Grierson); (b) that a woman is imperfect without a man; or that men and women are equal or complementary, though different (Gardner); (c) that each woman may take on sexually half the race of men; or that a woman may take on all the men in the world, counting herself wholly free to encounter whom she pleases (P. Legouis, *Donne the Craftsman* (1928), 94–7). Otherwise the lines might distinguish between limitations of men's liberty – we half-belong to one woman, or we belong wholly to one – or between the kinds of love, whether of the soul only, or of both the soul and body.

THE PROHIBITION

2 *forbade*] forbid *several MSS*

3–4 *repair my unthrifty waste | Of breath and blood*   make good the breath and blood he has wasted in lamenting her obduracy, by feeding upon the sighs and tears she will then spend for him.

5] By being to me then that which thou wast *1633*; *not in some MSS*

11 *officer* instrument of revenge.

13 *style of conqueror* the title or reputation of a conqueror, which depends upon her displaying the victim as a proof of a conquest.

17-24 *A number of MSS omit the last stanza. One MS which gives it heads the first two stanzas J.D. and the last stanza T.R.; another MS makes the last stanza an Answer to the other two stanzas*

18 *neither's*] neither *several MSS*; ne'er their *1633-69 and MS*

19 *die the gentler way* in sexual orgasm.

20 *thy love's*] my love's *1633*

21 *themselves, not me decay* wear each other away and not the poet.

22 *So shall I live thy stage, not triumph be* he will survive as a living celebrant of all her qualities rather than as a mere proof of her conquering power.
  stage] stay *1633 and several MSS*
  not triumph] and triumph *MS*

23-4] Then lest thou thy love hate, and me thou undo
      O let me live, yet love and hate me too.
            (*1635-54 and most MSS*)

      Lest thou thy love, and hate, and me thou undo,
      O let me live, yet love and hate me too.
            (*1669*)

THE RELIC

This is another of the poems which Grierson thought was probably addressed to Mrs Magdalen Herbert. See the introductory note to *The Funeral* (p. 376).

1 *my grave* The poem picks up the situation of *The Funeral* some decades on, with the re-opening of the poet's grave and discovery of the lock of hair that he had tied about his arm. Both poems assume a gift of this lock of hair as their starting point.

3 *woman-head* womanishness; an ironic analogue with maidenhead.

6 *bright* fair.

9 *thought . . . some way*] hoped . . . a way *most MSS*
  this device The sympathetic gravedigger of some future time will

suppose that his customary token of love is a clever device of lovers to exploit the circumstances of the Resurrection, when our souls will have to scurry about the earth gathering in our scattered members. With a bit of both of them together in the grave they have some chance of a snatched meeting of souls there, even at that hour.

13 *mis-devotion*] mass-devotion *1669*
  mis-devotion In *The Second Anniversary* Donne calls prayers to saints mis-devotion (line 511) because they ought to be addressed to God. Here the lovers' remains will command the devotion that is rightly due to love itself.

14 *Then, he that digs us up*] He that doth dig it up *most MSS*

17 *a Mary Magdalen* Renaissance painters depict Mary Magdalen with long golden hair.

18 *A something else* possibly 'a Jesus Christ', if the 'mis-devotion' denies his resurrection; but more probably one of Mary Magdalen's lovers in her riotous youth. Christopher Ricks points out that 'a Jesus Christ' and 'a something else' are metrically equivalent.

20 *time*] times *most MSS*

21 *would have that age*] would that age were *several MSS*
  this paper the present poem.

22 *harmless lovers* loving without blame, a condition so rare as to be miraculous in itself.

24 *Yet knew not what we loved, nor why* see *Negative Love*.

25-6 *Difference of sex no more we knew, / Than our guardian angels do* angels have no sexual nature, and the claim is that this was an ideal spiritual love between equal souls. It is thus different in kind from the love of such poems as *The Ecstasy*, *The Canonization* and *The Good Morrow*.
  no more we knew, / Than our] we never knew, / No more than *1635-69 and several MSS*; we never knew, / More than our *some MSS*

27 *Coming and going* arriving or taking leave.

29-30 *the seals, / Which nature, injured by late law, sets free* the restrictions on love which did not operate in the original free condition of created nature, but came in when that state degenerated into the cramping rule of law.

30 *sets*] set *1669*

31 *These miracles* not the kind the mis-devotionists look for, but true miracles none the less in that they escape the normal laws of love.

SELF LOVE

First printed in 1650 as one of two appended poems, and in following editions pushed in among the funeral tributes to Donne. Few MSS have it, and modern editors have not felt confident that it is Donne's.

Title] E. K. Chambers called the poem *Self Love*. It has no title in the early editions and *MSS*

1 *He that* ... the speaker is a woman.

6] And cannot pleasure choose *1650–69*; And can all pleasure choose *MS*

11 *he that can for foul ones care* the man who can love ugly women. *foul ones*] foulness *MS*

15–16] *These lines are incomplete in the early versions.*

17 *pays*] prays *1650–69*

18 *thralled* enslaved.

20 *Within* the real woman beneath the outside appearance; sexually.

22 *freely prove* enjoy without reservation.

23 *vent that humour* indulge that particular fancy.

SONG (GO, AND CATCH A FALLING STAR)

In some MSS this is one of several poems headed 'Songs which were made to certain airs that were made before'. See the introductory note to *The Bait* (p. 357).

An anonymous setting of the poem survives in a seventeenth-century MS. It is given in Jacquot and in Helen Gardner, *John Donne: The Elegies and The Songs and Sonnets*, Appendix B.

1–9 *Go, and catch a falling star,* / ... *an honest mind* Lists of impossible tasks figure in Petrarchan love poems as rhetorical devices of emphasis or hyperbole:

He that can count the candles of the sky,
  reckon the sands whereon Pactolus flows,
Or number numberless small atomies,
  what strange and hideous monsters Nilus shows,

What mis-shaped beasts vast Africa doth yield,
　　what rare-formed fishes live in the ocean,
What coloured flowers do grow in Tempe's field,
　　how many hours are since the world began:
Let him, none else, give judgement of my grief!
　　let him declare the beauties of my Love!
(R. Linche, *Diella* (1596), Sonnet 30)

2　*mandrake*　a fork-rooted plant, supposed to have human qualities.

3　*past years*] past times *MS*; times past *1669*; past hours *MS*

4　*cleft*] clove *MS*

11　*to see*] go see *1669 and several MSS*; see *most MSS*

12　*Ride ten thousand days and nights*　Spenser's Squire of Dames went on a country-wide search for a chaste woman (*The Faerie Queene* III vii 54–61). Harington says of him that he 'could in three years' travel find but three women that denied his lewd desire: of which three, one was a courtesan, that rejected him because he wanted coin for her; the second a Nun, who refused him because he would not swear secrecy; the third a plain country gentlewoman, that of good honest simplicity denied him . . .' (*Orlando Furioso*, trans. Sir John Harington (1591), XLIII 373).

18　*Lives a woman true, and fair*　the unlikeliest of all wonders would be the combination of the two qualities, a beautiful woman who is faithful too.

24　*last, till*] last so till *several MSS*

27　*False, ere I come, to two, or three*] False, ere she come to two or three *1669*

SONG (SWEETEST LOVE, I DO NOT GO)

Walton imputes several expressions in this poem to Donne's wife and implies that Donne wrote it for her, with *A Valediction: forbidding Mourning*, when he left for the continent in 1611. But this may be conjecture.

In some MSS the poem appears as one of a group of 'Songs which were made to certain airs which were made before' (see the introductory note to *The Bait*, p. 357). Contemporary music for the poem survives in several seventeenth-century MSS, but it may be a later setting of Donne's words and not a tune to which he wrote them. It is given in

Jacquot and in Helen Gardner, *John Donne: The Elegies and The Songs and Sonnets*, Appendix B.

In most MSS the opening of each stanza is written as two long lines, not four short ones.

6–8] At the last must part 'tis best
      Thus to use my self in jest
        By fained deaths to die;
    (*1635–54 and MS*)

8 *deaths*] death *several MSS*

15 *journeys, since I*] return, since I do *several MSS*; journeys and do *MS*

21–4 *come bad chance, ... to advance* if misfortune strikes us we are all too ready to feed it by our misery, and to show it subtle and drawn-out ways of putting us down.

22 *join*] add *several MSS*

25 *not wind*] no wind *1635–69*

32] Thou art not fond of me *MS*
   Thou] That *1635–69 and several MSS*
   Thou art the best of me the two of them are interinvolved and in thus expending her body and spirit in grief she wastes the life and soul of her lover.

33 *divining* foreseeing, anticipating the future.

34 *Forethink me any ill* feel grief now for the misfortune it intuitively anticipates.

38 *Are but turned*] Are turned *MS*

SONNET. THE TOKEN

First printed in 1649 as a stray piece at the tail-end of Donne's secular poems. Helen Gardner among others doubts if it is by Donne, and few commentators have discussed it as his.

1 *token*] tokens *1649–69 and several MSS*

4 *my passions* his sufferings for love.
   passions] passion *several MSS*

5 *no*] nor *1649–69*

6-7 *the fantastic strain | Of new-touched youth* the fanciful ways in which first youthful love displays itself.

7 *stands* condition, standards.

11 *in*] with *several MSS*

12 *in the same hold* immovably at one.

14 *because best like the best*] 'cause 'tis like thee best *1649-54*; 'cause 'tis like the best *1669*

15 *most*]] more *MS*

17 *store*] score *1649-69*

THE SUN RISING

Title] To the Sun *some MSS*
The Sun Rising Love poets traditionally invoked the sun or the dawn, and Ovid and Petrarch offer celebrated examples (*Amores* I. xiii; *Almo sol, Canzoniere* 188). But these morning songs commonly address their subject with reverence as a flushed young goddess or a life-giving god.

1 *Busy old fool, unruly* unmannerly foolish old busybody.

6 *sour*] slow *some MSS*

7 *court-huntsmen* sycophantic courtiers who hunt office by falling in with the monarch's enthusiasms, in this case early morning stag-chasing. King James's passion for the sport was a byword, and the reference indicates that the poem was written when he was on the English throne, that is, after 1603.

8 *country ants to harvest offices* slavish farmers to the routines of harvesting.

9 *all alike* the same at all times.

10 *rags of time* our divisions or changes of time, as against the timeless condition which is the true reality known to God. See *The Anniversary* 9-10.

11-14]   Thy beams so reverend, and strong
                  Dost thou not think
       I could eclipse and cloud them with a wink,
       But that I would not lose her sight so long?
       (*1635-69*)

17 *both th' Indias of spice and mine* the East Indies and the West

Indies, one of them the great repository of spice and the other of gold.
  both th' Indias] both Indies *MS*

24   *alchemy*   a flashy pretence.

25   *Thou sun art half as happy as we*   because the sun is single whereas
either lover enjoys the other's happiness.

30   *This bed thy centre is, these walls, thy sphere*   the bed is the earth
around which the sun is to revolve, and the walls mark the limit of his
revolution. The sun, as the source of sexual vigour and of life, is invited
to focus all his powers on the activity of the lovers.

THE TRIPLE FOOL

The poem turns on the performance of some settings of the poet's love
verses, which renews his grief and shame and compounds his folly. A
number of Donne's lyrics were in fact set to music by his contemporaries
(see the introductory note to *Break of Day*, p. 359).

6   *lanes*] veins *several MSS*

6-7   *Then as th' earth's inward narrow crooked lanes* / *Do purge sea
water's fretful salt away*   One topsyturvy reason proposed in antiquity
for the freshness of river water was that the tortuous courses of rivers
filtered out the salt in the seawater which rushed into them from the
ocean. Donne's point is that this did not work, even by analogy, for his
salt tears.

14   *set*] sit *most MSS*

19   *increased*   Pronounced as three syllables.

20   *published*   Pronounced as three syllables.
  triumphs] trials *some MSS*; tortures *MS*

TWICKNAM GARDEN

Twicknam Garden   Twickenham Park was the home from 1607 to 1618
of Donne's patroness, Lucy Countess of Bedford. If this poem was
addressed to her then it must have been written in those years.

1   *Blasted with sighs*   stricken by the withering air of his own sighs.
  surrounded   inundated. The stress falls on the first syllable – súr-
rounded.

2-4   *to seek the spring,* / *. . . Receive such balms*   Petrach tells how his
amorous grief made a barren waste of the rejuvenated nature that sur-
rounded him in springtime (*Zefiro torna, Canzoniere* 310).

4 *balms* healing influences, such as might restore nature to its first state and make the garden a paradise.

6–7 *spider love, which transubstantiates all, | And can convert manna to gall* Spiders were supposed to turn everything they eat into poison; 'transubstantiates' and 'manna' evoke the eucharistic transformation of bread into the body of Christ. The poet's love works a kind of counter-miracle, transforming into deadly bitterness what ought to sustain and save.

12 *grave*] gray *some MSS*

14 *But that I*] But I *several MSS*

14–18 *that I may not this disgrace | Endure, nor yet leave loving . . . | . . . weeping out my year* his difficulty is that he cannot love and express love's pain without also feeling love's shame. This dilemma Love may resolve (and incidentally establish him in the garden) by transforming him into some perpetually lamenting vegetable or stone.

15 *nor yet leave loving*] nor leave this garden *1635–69 and many MSS. Not in some MSS*

16 *piece*] part *some MSS*

17 *a mandrake, so I may groan* mandrakes were supposed to cry out in agony when molested in the ground.
  groan] grow *1633–69 and some MSS*

18 *my year*] the year *1635–54 and some MSS*

19 *crystal vials* lachrymatories or tear-vessels, such as the ancients were thought to put in tombs for mourning tributes.

20 *love's*] lovers' *1639*

20–22 *my tears, which are love's wine. | . . . | For all are false . . .* Petrarchan poets wrote that true lovers' sighs and tears are love's meat and drink, whereas false tears are unpalatable – 'What had you then to drink? Unfeigned lover's tears' (Earl of Oxford, *Of the Birth and Bringing up of desire* (1591)).

24 *woman's*] women's *1633–69 and several MSS*

26–7 *O perverse sex . . . | Who's therefore true . . . kills me* she demonstrates the perverseness of her sex by remaining true to her present lover, or her husband, simply so as to destroy the poet.

THE UNDERTAKING

Title] Platonic love *some MSS*

1 *braver* more remarkable.

2 *the Worthies* the nine most celebrated warriors from Hector to Geoffrey of Boulogne. They were often represented in pageants announcing their prodigious deeds, as in *Love's Labours Lost* V. 2; hence the superior 'bravery' of the poet's keeping his deed secret.

6 *specular stone* supposedly, a transparent stone used by the ancients in building, but lost in modern times. Cutting it into strips for use was said to call for great art. Helen Gardner suggests that Donne learned of specular stone from a book published at Hamburg in 1599, which would make the poem later than that.

16 *their*] her *MS*

18 *Virtue attired in*] Virtue in *1635–69*

21 *placed* Pronounced as two syllables.

22 *profane men* men who are too low minded to credit a refined condition of love based in something other than sexual satisfaction.

A VALEDICTION: FORBIDDING MOURNING

Walton quoted a version of this poem in his *Life of Dr John Donne* (1640) and described it as a copy of verses that Donne gave to his wife when he left for France with the Drury family in 1611. Most modern commentators have taken that as conjecture. Walton says of the verses, 'I beg leave to tell, that I have heard some critics, learned, both in languages and poetry, say, that none of the Greek or Latin poets did ever equal them.'

Parting and absence were recognized occasions of love poetry, and Donne had many illustrious predecessors to emulate.

Title] Upon the parting from his Mistress *some MSS*; To his Love upon his departure from her *MS*; A Valediction, forbidding to Mourn *Walton*. Early versions of the title, as of Donne's other Valediction titles, have light pointing or none; the colon is a modern clarification.

6 *tear-floods . . . sigh-tempests* Petrarch made these the stock conceits of love poets (*Passa la nave mia, Canzoniere* 189). Donne takes them up again in *The Canonization* and *A Valediction: of Weeping*.

8 *the laity* those who do not understand such love and will profane it if they know of it.

laity our] laity of our *some MSS*

9–12 *Moving of th'earth ... | But trepidation of the spheres, | ... is innocent* movements of our world, such as earthquakes, do damage and provoke frightened speculation about what they have caused and portend; whereas the far greater oscillations of the heavenly spheres have no such violent consequences. In old astronomy, the spheres were the concentric hollow globes that moved round the earth.

13 *Dull sublunary lovers' love* the love of the common run of lovers, which depends upon physical proximity and shares the fleeting condition of all things beneath the inconstant moon.

16 *Those things which elemented it* the bodies of these ordinary lovers, whose senses are the whole substance of their love.

18 *That our selves know not what it is* See *Negative Love* and *The Ecstasy* 29–48. Donne regularly makes it a condition of a truly mutual love that the lovers are unable to locate their love in some particular feature or activity, or define it in terms of some goal to be achieved.

19 *assured* Pronounced as three syllables.

20 *Care less*] Careless *1639–54*
lips, and hands] lips, hands *1633*

24 *Like gold to aery thinness beat* gold was beaten out fine to make gold leaf. But the terms of Donne's simile intimate that their love will be so refined by absence as to pass beyond the highest condition of material nature to the still more exalted quality of air or spirit.
beat written as bett *in some MSS*

26 *stiff* firm, stable.
twin compasses dividers. Compasses were a common emblem of constancy in change. Guarini used them to figure a lover who is fixedly centred upon his mistress even while he travels away from her (*Con voi sempre son'io, Madrigali* 96); but Guarini's madrigal was not published until 1598 and there is no evidence that Donne knew it or wrote his poem after that date.

32 *that*] it *some MSS*; mine *Walton*

34 *obliquely* deviating from the strict course.

35 *firmness* fixed constancy.
makes] draws *several MSS*; make *MS*
makes my circle just makes me complete a true circle. The circle was an emblem of perfection and unbroken continuity.
circle] centre *MS*

36 *makes*] make *MS*; me to *Walton*

A VALEDICTION: OF THE BOOK

Title] A Valediction of this book *MS*; A Valediction of a book left in a window *MS*; Valediction to his book *1633–69 and MS*

3 *esloign* remove to a distance.

6 *Sibyl's glory* A Sibyl was a prophetess whose ecstatic utterances were put into Greek verse and collected in the Sibylline Books for consultation. One such collection is said to have been placed in the charge of a special college of priests, who consulted and interpreted it only at the command of the Roman Senate.

7 *Her who from Pindar could allure* The story went that as a youth Pindar was defeated in a poetical contest by the Theban poetess Corinna, who afterwards told him that he would attract more readers if he used mythological embellishment sparingly.

8 *her, through whose help Lucan is not lame* Lucan's wife is supposed to have helped him with the versification of his *Pharsalia*.

9 *her, whose book (they say) Homer did find, and name* There was a remote story that the *Iliad* and the *Odyssey* were written in Egypt by a woman called Phantasia, and that Homer found them and published them as his own.

13 *subliming* purifying, by an alchemical process which calls for great heat.

15–16 *There, the faith of any ground | No schismatic will dare to wound* no dissident will dare to cast doubt on any article in the doctrine of love these letters make up, because it is clear that the lovers have their authority from Love himself.

18 *to be these his records* One seventeenth-century sense of 'records' was witnesses.

   records The stress falls on the second syllable – recórds.

18–19 *records. | This book*] recórds, / This Book *1635*

19–22] This book, as long-lived as the elements,
    Or as the world's form, this all-gravèd tome
      In cipher writ, or new made idiom;
    We for love's clergy only are instruments,
    (*1633–69 and most MSS*)

This is syntactically obscure, but two early readings offer possible alternatives. *1635* makes the sense of stanza 2 run straight on into stanza 3, whose first three lines thus amplify 'records' in line 18. Harleian MS 4064 supplies the missing main verb twice over by rendering line 21 as 'In Cipher write, or new make idiom', which presumably means 'Either write it in some established system of occult characters or devise an altogether new cryptic code for it.'

19-20 *elements, | Or as the world's form*   the unformed original materials, or the form imposed upon them to make the world.

20 *all-graved*   engraved throughout and therefore enduring, as are Egyptian hieroglyphics.
   graved   Pronounced as two syllables.
   tome] to me *1639-54*; tomb *1669 and some MS S*

21 *write*] writ *1633-69 and most MS S*
   made] make *MS*

21-2 *idiom; | We*] idiom. | We *MS*

22 *We for Love's clergy only are instruments*   they are the sole means of which priests of love will be able to gain access, through these hieroglyphic writings, to the elemental truths and universal knowledge that love comprehends.

25 *Vandals and Goths*   the barbarian peoples whose invasions of the Roman Empire in the fourth and fifth centuries AD brought about its fall, and the loss of ancient learning which plunged Western civilization into the Dark Ages. The recovery of Roman manuscripts and the idea of Roman civil order they enshrined gave the prime impetus to Renaissance humanists.
   Goths inundate us] the Goths invade us *1633-54 and MS*; Goths invade us *1669 and several MS S*

26 *universe*   repository of universal truth.

27 *Schools might learn sciences*   learned academies might acquire knowledge of the various disciplines they profess.
   spheres music   the music made by the cosmic bodies in their turning is the perfect concord, which our earthly music imperfectly echoes.
   angels verse   angelic hymns in praise of God are the type of perfect poetry.

31 *exhaled*   drawn out of their bodies.

32-3 *amuse | Faith's infirmity*   puzzle or mislead our infirm faith which always requires tangible evidence of things.

34 *Something which they may see and use* physical acts of love, which are the outward evidence of 'abstract spiritual love'. See *The Ecstasy* 60–70.

36 *Beauty a convenient type may be to figure it* Plato held that sensible beauty is a shadow of the intelligible beauty which is the divine essence. In Dante and the Florentine Neoplatonists the notion led on to a transcendental metaphysic of love ironically distant from the understanding of love Donne expresses here in their very language.

38–9 *titles . . . / . . . states* legal rights or entitlements to the possession of property.

39 *prerogative* a peculiar right or privilege beyond the common course of law, such as a monarch enjoys. Women evade men's rightful claim on them by usurping the arbitary powers of exemption which really belong only to Love himself.
  states] rites *several MSS*

43 *Forsake* deny or refuse.
  who on them relies who is bound to them and serves them.

46 *statesmen*] tradesmen *several MSS*

48–9 *Love and their art alike it deadly wounds, | If to consider what 'tis, one proceed* it is fatal to statesmanship, as to love, if one stops and considers what it amounts to. Both are pragmatic arts whose good management calls for a blind commitment to the present action without thought of its inevitable inadequacy.

53 *their nothing*] there something *1633, 1669 and MS*; there nothing *several MSS*

53–4 *such will their nothing see, | As in the Bible some can find out alchemy* (a) politicians will find here the ground of their profession, which is really an art of nothing; (b) politicians will imagine that they find a political system in these letters, though it is not really there. Spiritual alchemists commonly found the basis of their system in the Bible, which they read as a secret language.

56 *takes* measures.

61 *At their brightest* at their zenith.

61–2 *to conclude | Of* to determine.

62 *longitudes* the duration of lovers' love.

63 *eclipses* lovers' separations, which test the stability of love. Ways of calculating longitudes by observing eclipses were known from ancient times.

A VALEDICTION: OF MY NAME IN THE WINDOW

Title] Upon the engraving of his name with a diamond in his mistress' window when he was to travel *several MSS*

3 *that charm* the magical power of the name, which makes the window a talisman.

5 *eye*] eyes *many MSS*
  price value.

6 *either rock* Helen Gardner quotes a seventeenth-century authority on precious stones who distinguishes between diamonds which come from old rock and diamonds which come from new rock. Diamonds from new rock may be rock crystal, used then as now for the finest cut glass; but in any case Donne's point is that her eye will by its own alchemy transform plain window glass into something beyond price.

8 *through-shine* transparent.

14 *accessory*] accessories *1633–69*

17 *entireness* settled constancy, of which the engraved name is the type.

21 *a given death's head* a representation of a skull given as a *memento mori*, possibly in a ring.

22 *Lovers' mortality* their separation, which is a death to them.

24 *My ruinous anatomy* his anatomized corpse, or disordered skeleton.

25 *all my souls* the vegetable, sensitive, and intellectual souls, which control our faculties of growth, perception and understanding. The conceited argument is that since she thus retains his soul, his faculties and his bones, there needs only the muscle, sinews and veins to make the whole man again.

29–32]   . . . the muscle, sinew, and vein,
                  Which tile this house, will come again,

> Till my return repair
> And recompact my scattered body so.
> (*MS*)

31-2
> Till my return, repair
> And recompact my scattered body so.
> (*1633-35*)

32-6 *so,* / ... *supremacy,*] so, / ... supremacy, *1650-69*

33-6 *As all the virtuous powers ... supremacy* Writers on magic held that a hieroglyphic inscription might work as a talisman and transmit the influence of the stars which were in the ascendant when it was cut. Donne assumes conceitedly that since love and grief were at their height when his name was cut in the window, then the name will have power to move those passions.

Stanzas 6 and 7 together argue that she should open herself to the power of the name, and so mourn lovingly for him every day until his return reunites the scattered parts of his body.

35 *graved* Pronounced as two syllables.

42 *Since I die daily* every day of his absence from her is a new death (from which his return will be the resurrection).

44 *ope*] out *most MSS*

48 *Genius* his tutelary spirit; his distinctive quality.

50 *and*] or *1669 and some MSS*

52 *Disputed it, and tamed thy rage* the maid pleads the suitor's cause, with some success.

55 *go*] grow *several MSS*

57 *superscribing* addressing the letter.

58 *pane*] pen, *1635-69 and several MSS*

62 *No means our firm substantial love to keep* in the end a few mere scratches on glass cannot be the means of safeguarding the firm love of flesh and blood people.

63 *lethargy* coma.

64 *this*] thus *several MSS*

65 *Impute this idle talk, to that I go*   he asks her to take the poem itself, spoken at the point of leaving, as the babble of a dying man.

A VALEDICTION: OF WEEPING

Title] A Valediction of Tears *several MSS*

2 *whilst I stay here*   while I am still with you here; while I pause for a moment here before leaving you. The lover is shortly to embark on a sea journey, leaving his mistress behind.

3 *thy face coins them*   (a) her face causes or produces them; (b) they bear her image, which gives them value.

7 *emblems of more*   his tear bearing her likeness falls and shatters on the ground, so foretelling the undoing of the lovers when they are in separate countries.

8 *thou falls*] thou falst *1633–69 and some MSS*

9 *thou and I are nothing then*   as mutual lovers they are one being who exist only in each other. Their separation thus annihilates them.
  on a divers shore   (a) in separate countries; (b) in an alien element, as the tear is when it strikes the ground.

13 *quickly make that, which was nothing, all*   it was nothing because it was a big O, and becomes all because it has the whole world represented upon it. Presumably the workman quickly transfers to the globe one of the copies he has by, either by drawing it or pasting it on.

14–16 *So doth each tear | . . . | A globe, yea world by that impression grow*   her image makes each of his tears a world (since she is his world), as the workman makes a blank ball into the world by drawing the map upon it.

18 *my heaven dissolved so*   the lady (the poet's heaven) drowns the tear-world with her tears as heaven drowned the world in the Deluge.
  dissolved   Pronounced as three syllables.

20 *up seas*] thy seas *1669*
  to drown me in thy sphere   the sphere of an astral body was its outer limit, and an attractive power exceeding the moon's pull might draw up seas as far as itself.

THE WILL

Title] Love's Will *MS*; Love's legacies *several MSS*; His Last Will and Testament *MS*

3 *Argus* in Greek myth, a giant whom the gods used as a spy because he had eyes all over his body. He was killed while spying on one of Jove's mistresses, for Hera.

5 *fame* common report or rumour.

8 *serve her*] love her *1669*

9 *That . . . as*] Only to give to those that *several MSS*

12 *ingenuity* ingenuousness, candour.

13 *Jesuits* members of the Jesuit Order had a reputation for subtly disguising the truth without actually telling lies.
   buffoons jesters and clowns.
   pensiveness thoughtfulness; melancholy.

15 *Capuchin* the Capuchins were a sixteenth-century offshoot of the Franciscan Order, who were vowed to absolute poverty.

18 *an incapacity*] no good capacity *1669*

19–27 *Stanza 3 is not in most MSS, and has plainly been added later in several of the MSS that do have it.*

20–21 *the schismatics / Of Amsteram* The Amsterdam brethren were an extreme Puritan sect, and were therefore most hostile to the idea of salvation by good works.

22 *courtship* courtliness; courtesy.

26 *disparity* unequal to her, beneath her.

30 *schoolmen* academic metaphysicians, whose hairsplitting contradictions of each other only raise doubt or scepticism.

31 *physicians, or excess* he bequeathes his sickness to what caused it, his doctors or his excesses. A current medical theory attributed illness to an excess of some element, and the consequent imbalance of one's constitution.

36 *did*] do *1635–69 and MS*

38 *physic* medical.

40 *brazen medals* old bronze coins, not current money.

45 *disproportion* make inappropriate. The poet's love is no use to her because she wants young lovers, not an older poet.

48 *Then all your beauties will be no more worth* her beauty has worth

only while there are lovers to admire it, and will have none if she kills them or their love by refusing them.

52 *making*] appointing *several MSS*

53 *neglect both me and thee* she neglects Love in that she does not want faithful love but pleasure, got by sharing her friendship with younger lovers.

54 *all three* the poet, his mistress and Love himself.

WITCHCRAFT BY A PICTURE

2 *my picture* A picture in the eyes, tears or heart was one of the commonest properties of conceited love poetry.

6 *By pictures made and marred, to kill* Witches pierce effigies or pictures of their victims to kill them.

8 *now I have drunk thy sweet salt tears* This is an act of counter-witchcraft as well as a recovery of the picture, since sweet tears betokened love and hers give away her real feelings (see *Twicknam Garden* 19–22 and note).
  sweet salt] sweetest *some MSS*

9 *though thou pour more I'll depart*] though thou therefore pour more will depart *several MSS*

11 *that art*] thy art *several MSS*

14 *all malice*] thy malice *several MSS*

WOMAN'S CONSTANCY

5 *We are not just those persons, which we were?* will you say that we are not now exactly the same persons as we were? 'Epicarmus avoucheth, that who ere while borrowed any money, doth not now owe it; and that he who yesternight was bidden to dinner this day, cometh today unbidden; since they are no more themselves, but are become others' (Montaigne, *An Apology of Raymond Sebond, Essays* II, 12).

8 *Or*] For *1635–54*

12 *falsehood, you*] falsehood; you *1633–69*

14 *'scapes* escapes from a contract; extravagant special pleadings

Elegies

The evidence is that most of Donne's Elegies are early poems, written in the mid-1590s. But they were not all printed together at first, and neither early nor modern editors have agreed upon the canon. Thirteen Elegies were to have been published in 1633, but five were refused a licence then – *The Bracelet, On his Mistress, Love's Progress, Going to Bed* and *Love's War*. The licensing system established by Henry VIII gave effective power of censorship to a panel of ecclesiastics, which presumably deemed these five poems licentious. The edition of 1635 printed seventeen Elegies, and the remainder were added one at a time in subsequent editions, save for *Love's War* which did not get printed until 1802.

Some MSS and early editions give with the Elegies poems which might go better elsewhere – such as the funeral *Elegy on the L.C., The Autumnal, The Dream* ('Image of her whom I love') – and poems which may not be Donne's. Helen Gardner excludes from the acceptable canon five Elegies that Grierson printed as Donne's, *Variety, Julia, A Tale of a Citizen and his Wife, His parting from Her* and *The Expostulation*; and she excludes with them the Ovidean poem *Sappho to Philaenis*.

The order and numbering of the Elegies in Grierson's edition substantially followed that of the edition of 1635, and is arbitrary. But the poems have been so long known now by those numbers that there is no point in re-ordering them.

None of the Elegies had titles in the 1633 edition, or in most of the MSS. The familiar titles first appeared in *1635*.

ELEGY I   JEALOUSY

4   *sere-bark*] sere-cloth *1669 and several MSS*; sore bark *some MSS*
    sere-bark   an encrustation of dry sores such as some poisons were assumed to cause.

9   *poor*] pure *several MSS*

14   *death, heart's-bane*] bane, deathful *MS*
    heart's-bane   that which poisons the heart.

18   *deformity*   ugliness.

21   *great fare*] high fear *MS*; high fare *several MSS*; his fare *MS*

30   ] We into some third place retired were *several MSS*
    another] another's *1669*

32 *silly* simple, naïve.
pensionary paid.

33-4 *Thames' right side | ... London's Mayor* The only part of the South Bank that fell under the Lord Mayor's jurisdiction was Southwark, the disorderly quarter, which disputed the City's control over it.

34 *Mayor*] Major *1633-54*
Germans, the Pope's pride From Luther's time on the German states were foremost in opposing the Pope.

In one MS the poem goes on for another twenty lines. The added lines have some obscene wit but are clumsy and superfluous; it is not likely that Donne wrote them.

ELEGY 2 THE ANAGRAM

Helen Gardner notes that this was a favourite poem in MS miscellanies. Poems praising extreme ugliness had a vogue in sixteenth-century Europe; there are well-known examples by Berni, Tasso and others.

5 *light* wanton.

6 *hair fall*] hair's foul *1669*
rough] tough *1635-54*

13 *perfumed* The stress falls on the second syllable – perfúmed.

18 *words*] letters *several MSS*

19 *gamut* the entire musical scale.

22 *simply good* good in themselves.

29 *fair*] fairer *several MSS*

35 *husbands* (a) tillers of land; (b) married men (with a sexual innuendo).

37 *sovereign plaster* effective remedy.

40 *marmoset* weasel (supposedly a very lecherous creature).

41] Like Belgia's cities when the country is drowned *1669*
round] low *MS*; foul *several MSS*

41-2 *When Belgia's cities, the round countries drown, | That dirty foulness guards, and arms the town* the surrounding countries which try to inundate the Belgian cities fail because of the mounds of refuse that act as a city wall.

46 *mightier than the sea, makes Moors seem white*   the sea itself cannot wash Negroes white, but they look white alongside her.

47 *stews*   brothels.

49 *childbed's*] childbirth's *some MSS*

50 *tympany*   a swelling of the stomach.

53 *dildoes, bedstaves, . . . velvet glass*   instruments of female masturbation.

53–4] *not in 1633–54*

54 *as Joseph was*   Potiphar's wife repeatedly asked Joseph to lie with her, but he refused and fled (Genesis xxxix 7–20).

ELEGY 3 CHANGE

1 *hand . . . faith . . . good works*   the evidences of religious devotion, given a sexual sense as proofs of love.
   works] word *1669*

3 *apostasy*   a lapse from the true faith, such as might sometimes witness sincere religious devotion rather than the reverse. But she falls back literally, to confirm her love in sexual acts.

5 *forced unto*] forbid to *MS*

12 *women, more hot, wily, wild*   Helen Gardner cites Montaigne, who says that women 'are much more capable and violent in love's effects than we' (*Upon Some Verses of Virgil, Essays* III, 5).

13 *did*] bid *1669*

15 *clogs*   encumbrances.
   and their own] not their own *1633–69*
   and their own   they belong only to themselves; hence they encumber us, but are themselves free.

17 *plough-land*   a single piece of land; formally, the area capable of being tilled by a ploughteam of eight oxen in the year.

18 *corn*] seed *MS*

21 *By nature, which gave it, this liberty*   In the Golden Age, when behaviour was entirely natural, love was unrestricted.

23 *Likeness glues love*   'Everywhere similarity is the reason for love. We see that clearly in the stars and elements, in plants and animals' (M. Ficino, *Opera omnia* (1561), 861).

24 *like* (a) be fond of each other; (b) be alike. He asks if the fact that she causes them to 'like and love' means that they must behave alike too.

27-8 *so not teach, but force my opinion ... | ... nor every one* He is forced by the circumstances, rather than persuaded by reason, to the compromise opinion that one should neither love just one woman nor love every woman.

32 *worse putrefied*] more putrefied *1633-9*; more purified *1655-54*; worse purified *1669*; worst putrefied *several MSS*

ELEGY 4 THE PERFUME

Title] Discovered by a Perfume *MS*

2 *escapes* amorous escapades.

6 *hydroptic* dropsical.

7-8] *Not in 1633 and several MSS*
to search with glazed eyes | As though he came to kill a cockatrice The cockatrice (or basilisk) was supposed to kill by its stare, which could however be turned back upon itself. Her father's 'glazed eyes' may be thick with rheum; or possibly he wears glasses.
glazed Pronounced as two syllables.

21 *To try if thou long* to see if she longs for some unusual delicacy. Like all these symptoms this was an old wives' test of pregnancy.

23 *politicly* craftily, to worm out an answering confession.

26 *gull* deceive.

29 *ingled*] dandled *1669*
ingled fondled and coaxed.

34 *the great Rhodian Colossus* The Colossus of Rhodes, one of the seven wonders of the ancient world, is said to have stood seventy cubits high and spanned the harbour with its legs.

41 *perfume* The stress falls on the second syllable – perfúme.

44 *shivered* Pronounced as three syllables.

47 *imprisoned* Pronounced as four syllables.

49 *The precious unicorns* The mythical unicorn was thought to be infinitely precious because its horn possessed magical and medicinal properties. But unicorns were commonly confused with rhinoceroses, whose horns were sought for aphrodisiacal preparations and as an antidote against poisons.

50 *good*] sweet *1669*

52 *my oppressed shoes*   pressing was a torture used to make stubborn prisoners talk.

57-8 *confound / Sense*   confuse one's sense of smell, so that one does not know what is rotten and what is wholesome.

64 *substantial*   having substance; real. Pronounced as four syllables, with a heavy stress on the second and fourth syllable – sub-stán-ti-ál.

67 *simply*] single *MS*
    simply   by its separate constituents.

69 *decay*   fade.

70 *rare*   good is immutable and common, whereas perfume is neither.

ELEGY 5 HIS PICTURE

Title] Travelling, he leaves his picture with his mistress *MS*

1 *take my picture*   miniature portraits were much in fashion as gifts in absence.

4 *shadows both*   the two shadows are the picture, and the ghost of the dead poet.

6 *Perhaps*] Perchance *several MSS*

8 *hoariness*] storms, being *1633 and several MSS*; cruel storms *MS*
   o'erspread] o'erpressed *several MSS*

10 *powder's*   gunpowder's.

12 *then written* than *in the early editions and MSS*

14-15 *reach ... / ... reach*   affect; extend to.

16 *now love less*] like and love less *some MSS*

19 *nurse*] nourish *several MSS*

20 *disused*] weak *1650-69*
    disused   unaccustomed.
    tough] rough *MS*

ELEGY 6 OH, LET ME NOT SERVE SO

1 *those men* the hangers-on of great men; courtiers.

1 *honours' smokes* the empty shams of titles and dignities, which blow a man up in self-importance but do not feed him.
   fatten] flatter *1669 and some MSS*

6 *prince's styles, with many realms fulfil* flatteringly swell out their monarch's titles with the names of many countries supposedly subject to him.
   styles] style *several MSS*
   with] which *1633–69*
   realms] names *1669*

7 *where*] bear *1669*

9 *dead names* empty titles, carrying no practical rights.

10 *in ordinary* the regular performer of an office, as distinct from a man who might extraordinarily bear its title.

18 *fly* moth.

24 *then*] there *1635–69 and some MSS*

26 *to*] of *1633 and MS*
   upmost] utmost *1635–69 and MS*

33 *the*] her *1635–69 and several MSS*
   who] which *1635–69 and MS*

35 *bitterness* cruelty, severity.

36 *Careless* no longer caring.

41 *bred*] breed *1635–69 and most MSS*

45 *recusant* one who refuses to serve some particular religion or cause, especially a Roman Catholic who refuses to attend the services of the Church of England.

ELEGY 7 NATURE'S LAY IDIOT

1 *Nature's lay idiot* ignorant uninitiate in the workings of nature.

2 *sophistry* cunning art.

6 *sounds* expresses.

7 *by the'eye's water* as a doctor diagnoses a bodily condition by the

patient's urine, so the initiate diagnoses a condition of love by the lover's tears.

call] know *1635–69*

10   *they devisefully being set*] their devise in being set *several MSS devisefully* emblematically.

13   *Remember since*   call to mind the time when.

15   *household charms, thy husband's name to teach*   homely magic, the games girls play on certain saints' days to learn who their husband will be.

19   *sentences*   common sayings.

22   *Inlaid*   hid her away.

23   *who*] which *most MSS*

24   *Refined thee into*   made her into, by such refinements.

25   *words*] works *1669 and some MSS*

26   *knowledge and life's tree*   the final attributes of a blissful paradise, which he bestows upon her by sexual penetration.

28   *Frame and enamel plate*   fashion goblets of gold or silver plate and decorate them with enamel.

29   *Chafe*   (a) heat; (b) rub. He melts her for someone else to set their imprint upon her, arouses her for the sexual consummation others will have.

ELEGY 8   THE COMPARISON

Grotesque descriptions of people, full of coarse comparisons, are common in medieval poetry. But sixteenth-century Italian poets travestied the Petrarchan convention of hyperbolic praise by celebrating hideous women in scabrous analogies; and mock love poems became a European fashion.

1   *sweat of roses in a still*   distilled attar of roses.

2   *musk cat's*] muskets *1669*
   musk cat's   the musk cat is the musk deer, which secretes a sweet smelling substance used to make perfume.
   trill   trickle.

3 *the almighty balm of th' early east* the morning dew, which was assumed to have great powers of healing and nourishing life.

4 *of*] on *some MSS*

6 *carcanets*] coronets *1633–69 and some MSS*
carcanets jewelled necklaces.

8 *boils* written biles *or* byles *in the MSS*

10 *Sanserra's starved men* the Protestant inhabitants of Sancerre were beseiged in the city for nine months in 1573. Reports of how they boiled down for sustenance skins, clothes, books and the like made them a byword for endurance in the Protestant countries.
starved Pronounced as two syllables.

12 *sovereign fatness* sustaining juiciness

13 *lying stones in saffroned tin* fake jewels in a fake setting of gilded tin.
lying stones] stones lying *1633–69*

14 *they hang*] it hangs *1633–69*

15 *Round as the world's her head* roundness implies a harmony and perfection which the two following similes at once belie.

16 *the fatal ball which fell on Ide* the golden apple which Eris, to stir up discord, tossed among the guests at the wedding of Thetis and Peleus on Mount Ida. It led to the judgement of Paris, and hence to the Trojan War.

17–18 *that whereof God had such jealousy* the forbidden apple that Eve plucked.

21 *the first Chaos* the original unordered state of the universe.

22 *Cynthia, when th' earth's shadows her embrace* the thin moon in its early phases.

23 *Prosperpine's white beauty-keeping chest* the box containing the ointment of beauty, that Psyche took from Proserpina (Apuleius, *The Golden Ass* VI); but also Proserpina's bosom.

24 *Jove's best fortune's urn* 'On the floor of Jove's palace there stand two urns, the one filled with evil gifts, and the other with good ones. He for whom Jove the lord of thunder mixes the gifts he sends, will meet now with good and now with evil fortune' (Homer, *Iliad* XXIV,

526–7, trans. Samuel Butler). Jove's urn of good fortune was some-
times represented as a vessel of harmony or beauty.

26   *dust*] dirt *most MSS*

26–9   ] *Not in some MSS*

31   *quarters*   quartered bodies of malefactors, impaled above the
city's gates.

34   *thy gouty*] her gouty *1633 and several MSS*; thy mistress' *1669*

35   *chemic's*   alchemist's.
  masculine   alchemical operations were often paralleled to sexual
processes.
  equal   equable, an even heat such as was supposed to be necessary to
change base metals into gold.

36   *limbeck*   alembic, the vessel in which base materials were heated
for projection into gold.

37   *dirt*] part *1633*; dust *MS*

46   *fears*] feared *some MSS*

48   *when*] where *1633*

  rent   rend.

49   *turtles*   turtle-doves.

50   *Are priests in*] A priest is in his *1669*

51   *such*] nice *1633–69*

54   *comparisons are odious*   an old proverb, which Dogberry mangles
(*Much Ado About Nothing*, III v 18).

ELEGY 9   THE AUTUMNAL

Some MSS give this poem with the Songs and Sonnets; *1633* calls it
an Elegy but puts it with a small group separated from the main set of
Elegies. It became *Elegy 9* in *1635*.

Title] An autumnal face.   On the Lady Sir Edward Herbert's mother
Lady Danvers *MS*; On the Lady Herbert afterwards Danvers *MS*;
Elegy Autumnal on the Lady Shandoys *MS*; A Paradox of an old
woman *MS*; Widow *several MSS*

2 *one autumnal face* Many Renaissance authors argued the superiority of mature beauty; some, such as Bacon, used the analogy of the seasons, claiming that autumn is the most beautiful (essay *Of Beauty*),

3 *your love*] our loves *1669*; our love *1633 and several MSS*

6 *Affection here takes reverence's name* passion here becomes reverence.
   Affection ... takes] Affections ... take *1633–69 and several MSS*

7 *Were her first years* her first years were.

7–8 *the Golden Age* ... / *But now she's gold oft tried, and ever new* the Golden Age was the age of innocence, as her first years were; but now she is gold repeatedly proved in experience yet (as gold) untouched by age.
   she's] they are *1633*

9–10 *torrid and inflaming* ... / ... *tolerable tropic clime* the torrid zones are the fiercely hot regions about the equator, whereas a tropic with a tolerable climate is still hot but supportable.
   tolerable] habitable *1633 and some MSS*

12 *in a fever wishes pestilence* wishes to have his fever intensify into plague.

13 *graves* (a) pits or trenches; (b) burial places.

14 *for*] or *1635–69*

16 *anachorit* anchorite, one who pledged himself to a particular spot such as a shrine.

18 *build a tomb* a tomb is a monument to a dead person, whereas a grave merely effaces him.

19 *dwells* resides permanently, as in one's 'standing house'.

19–20 *sojourn* ... / *In Progress* lodge temporarily, as a monarch stays at various houses on a formal progress through his domain.

23 *unto all hearers fit* she suits her conversation decorously to her company.

24 *revels* ... *council* she can be festive or deliberate seriously as the occasion demands.

25 *underwood* brushwood, which flares up quickly and soon burns itself out.

26 *enrages*] brings *several MSS*; breeds *MS*

27-8 *seasonabliest, when our taste | . . . to other things is past* the most seasonable time for love, as wine, is when we have lost our appetite for other things.
   taste given as tast *in the early versions.*

29 *Xerxes' strange Lydian love* Herodotus tells how Xerxes passionately admired the beauty of a plane tree which he found in Lydia.

30 *Was loved for age, none being so large* Later writers say that it was the size of the tree which appealed to Xerxes, this being a sign of its age.
   large] old *1635-69*

31-2 *being young, nature did bless | . . . age's glory, barrenness* Donne paradoxically makes barrenness a blessing, rather than conception, because it is a desirable quality in one's mistress; he suggests that if she is young too then she offers one the best of both worlds.

36 *Age must be loveliest at the latest day* because it will then have no rivals, having outlasted all other objects of love.

37 *winter-faces* old women, as distinct from middle-aged women.

38 *unthrift's* a spendthrift's.
   soul's] fool's *1635-54*

43 *death's-heads*] death-shades *MS*

44 *ancient, but antiques*] ancients, but antiques *1635-54 and severa MSS*
   antiques] antique *1633, 1669 and several MSS*

47 *natural lation*] motion natural *1633*; natural station *1635-69 and several MSS*
   lation an astrological term for the movement of a body from one place to another.

48-50 *My love descend . . .* a subdued sexual innuendo, continued in the final lines so as to distinguish between an immature and a mature concern with women's bodies, the one 'panting' upwards 'after growing beauties' and the other going downwards to find its home and consummate its arrival there in an ebbing-out.

50 *ebb out*] ebb on *1635-69 and MSS*

ELEGY 10 THE DREAM

Helen Gardner puts this poem with the Songs and Sonnets. In the early editions and MSS it was given without division into stanzas; R. E. Bennett first printed it in stanzas in *The Complete Poems of John Donne* (1942).

1 *Image of her whom I love*   the lady, as his love idealizes her.
  more than she   the image is more truly she than the reality itself.

2 *fair*   (a) accurate and clear-cut; (b) beautiful.

3 *Makes me her medal*   A notorious conceit of the Italian court poet Cariteo turned on the stamping of his mistress's image on the gold medallions to which Cupid's best arrows had been melted in the furnace of his heart.

8 *the more, the less we see*   the stronger the impact upon our sense the less we can make out, as when an object is 'Dark with excessive bright' (*Paradise Lost* III, 380).

9 *and reason gone with you*   reason is seated in the heart and works upon real things; in their absence and its own it resigns the government of our being to fancy, as the queen rules in the king's absence.

11 *meaner*   less extreme, nearer a mean.

12 *Convenient*   congruous, more fitting.

14 *all our joys are but fantastical*   since all our pleasures are merely imagined, then the pleasure of a dream is as real as the pleasure of an actual event.

15 *for pain is true*   unlike pleasure, pain has real substance.

16 *out*] up *several MSS*

21 *dearest heart*   (a) his own heart, which bears the impression of her image; (b) the lady herself.

23 *Though you stay here you pass too fast away*   because we change and decline moment by moment. See *Woman's Constancy* 5 and note.

24 *snuff*   the expired part of the wick of a candle, which is cut off as the candle burns down.

26 *idiot*   lacking reason and contact with reality.

ELEGY II THE BRACELET

This is one of the poems which was refused a licence for *1633*. It was first printed in *1635*.

Drummond said that Jonson instanced this poem and a passage in *The Calm* when he praised Donne as 'the first poet in the world in some things'; Jonson told him that he knew the 'verses of the lost chain' by heart (Jonson, *Conversations* 135).

The references to current politics in the poem suggest that it was written about 1593.

Title] Armilla. To a lady whose chain was lost. *MS*

6   *those*] these *1635–69*
    are tied] were tied *MS*; were knit *1635–69*
    love] loves *some MSS*; hearts *several MSS*

7   *sevenfold*   having seven loops; but also, very strong and difficult to sever, as Anthony's 'seven-fold shield of Ajax' (*Anthony and Cleopatra* IV 1438).

8   *the luck sake*   the bad fortune of losing it, or the bad luck which that loss will bring.

9   *angels*   gold coins which bore the figure of an angel. Their name is played on tiresomely in the writings of the time. The double status of angels, metaphysical and commercial, is the basis of the wit in this poem.

10   *solder*   (a) metal used to repair mutilated coins; (b) the taint of pride which corrupted the angels who followed Satan.

11   *way*] taint *several MSS*; fault *most MSS*

17–18   *Shall these twelve innocents . . . / . . . my sins' great burden bear?*   She has demanded that he give twelve gold angels to be melted down for a new bracelet to replace the lost one.

19   *damned*] burnt *MS*

23   *cared*   Pronounced as two syllables.

24   *their natural country rot*   syphilis, which was commonly associated with France and known as the French disease or French crown, and which is contracted by sexual contact ('country' pertaining to the vagina).
    natural country] country's natural *1635–54 and MS*; natural country's *several MSS*

26 *pale ... lame ... lean ... ruinous* Terms which describe the several debasements and deficiencies of the French coinage of the day.

28 *Their crowns are circumcised* (a) their gold coins are clipped; (b) their royal headgear is skimpy; (c) they have had surgery for syphilis.

29 *stamps* coins which had a design stamped upon them.

29–30 *still travelling, | That are become as Catholic* In the late sixteenth century Spanish gold was as pervasive and powerful as the American dollar is now.

31 *unlicked bear-whelps* New-born bears were assumed to have no regular form until their mothers licked them into shape.
  pistolets Spanish gold coins of about the present value of a dollar.

32 *avails or lets* opens or bars access.

39–42 *Visit all countries ... | ... seventeen-headed Belgia* These lines describe the intrusive and corrupting power of Spanish gold in the European politics of Donne's day. It financed rebellion or sedition, paid invading armies, and played havoc with national currencies. Spanish intrigue in Scotland and France was notorious, as was the military intervention in the Low Countries.

40 *Gorgeous France, ruined* Helen Gardner suggests that this reference would have lost its point by 1595, when France's recovery from her ruinous wars of religion was well under way.

41 *Scotland, which knew no State, proud in one day* The Scottish monarchy was too poor to sustain the machinery and style of central rule, and there were constant fears in the early 1590s that it had been bought and suddenly puffed up with Spanish gold.

42 *seventeen-headed Belgia* The seventeen heads were the United Provinces of the north, the Protestant Netherlands, whose separation from Belgium was confirmed when Farnese reconquered the southern provinces for Spain in the early 1580s and systematically Catholicized them.

44 *chemics* alchemists.

45 *a soul out-pulled* As the essential step towards turning base minerals into gold, alchemists sought to extract from them by heat their common 'first matter' or 'mercuric soul'.

46 *gulled* deceived, tricked.

47 *they were in*] they are in *1635–69*; therein *several MSS*

48 *they are guilty of much heinous sin*   they would be corrupted angels, the cause of the alchemist's self-deceit or his deceiving others.

52 *lustihead*   virility.

53 *if thou love*] if thou Love *1650–69*

54–5 *gone. / Oh*] gone, / And *1635–69 and several MSS*

55 *crier*   Criers were commonly employed to advertise wares or offer rewards for the recovery of lost property.

58 *they*] he *1635–54 and several MSS*

59 *conjuror*   an astrologer or diviner, whose art might disclose the whereabouts of missing objects.

60 *schemes*] scenes *1635–69 and several MSS*; sheaves *MS*
schemes   zodiacal calculations

61 *divided heaven in tenements*   Astrologers compartmentalized the heavens by squaring off the seven planets against the twelve houses or zodiacal signs. Each compartment thus represented a certain state of a planet, which might be propitious for particular transactions or trades, and the fortunate trades were sometimes indicated in the compartments.

62 *his*] her *some MSS*; their *MS*
rents   (a) rented tenements; (b) gaping holes. Donne's charge is that for profit, and to repair the holes in their clothes, the astrologers had prostituted heaven to commercial gain or squalid self-interest, filling the compartments with the trades of whore, thief, murderer.

64 *He leaves himself no room to enter in*   Astrologers did not need a place in their own schemes since they conducted their affairs by commercial cunning, not by the stars.

73 *these*   the gold angels, whose power of purchasing good will be turned to evil, a barren cause of pride, if they are made into a chain.

76 *form gives being*   In Aristotelean metaphysics it is the form imposed upon inchoate matter which gives a thing its distinctive being.

77 *angels yet;*] angels; yet *most MSS*

78 *Virtues, Powers, and Principalities*   (a) high angelic orders much above the standing of ordinary angels; (b) the highest earthly distinctions and offices. Donne's claim is a paradox if it is taken in the first sense, but it is true in the second sense. All angels are superior to men and these gold angels, while they stay as money, are more powerful than earthly dignities.

92   *So, that*] So much that *most MSS*

95–110   ] *not in one MS*

98   *that*] it *MSS*

101–2   *Or libels, or some interdicted thing, | Which negligently kept, thy ruin bring*   Helen Gardner cites the notorious case of Thomas Kyd, the searching of whose rooms in May 1593 when he was suspected of a political libel yielded a document that laid him open to the dangerous charge of atheism. He said that it was an old fragment by Marlowe which had got mixed up with his own rough papers when they shared a room two years before.

104   *Itchy*] Itching *1635 and MS*

105   *evils*] hurt *most MSS*

108   *love and marriage*] love, marriage *1635–54 and several MSS*

109   *latest*] last *1635 and some MSS*

111   *thee*] then *some MSS*; thou *some MSS*

112   *restorative*   potable gold was thought to restore failing health.

113   *But if from*] Or if with *some MSS*

114   *Because 'tis cordial*   Chaucer's Doctor of Physic 'loved gold in special' because 'gold in physic is a cordial' *Canterbury Tales, General Prologue* 443–4). A cordial is a medicine that works upon the heart.
    would 'twere at thy heart   'I wish it would kill you'.

ELEGY 12   HIS PARTING FROM HER

Helen Gardner thinks that this poem may not be by Donne and places it among the pieces whose authorship is in doubt. It was first printed in full in *1669*, though *1635–54* have a short version of forty-two lines.

Title   At his Mistress' departure *MS*

4   *love*] soul *1635–54*

5–44   ] *Not in 1635–54 and several MSS*

6   *to boot are*] are nought but *several MSS*

7   *Cynthia*   the moon.

9   *I could lend thee obscureness*   he could lend night darkness, so that it might cover the day as well.

10   *Out of my self*   by his own doing, out of his own resources.

11   *felt want*] self-want *1669*

14   *Or*] Are *MS*; And *MS*

18   *old chaos*   the original chaos, in which nothing made sense.

20   ] That thus with parting thou seek'st us to spite? *1669*

23   *(since I loved for form before)*] (since I loved) for me before *1669 and several MSS*; since I loved in jest before *MS*
      for form   he professed a love he did not feel, for some ulterior end.

26   *the golden fruit*   The punishment of Tantalus in Hades was to have luscious fruits glistening before his eyes, which the wind moved out of reach when he stretched his hand to take them.
      rapt] wrapped *1669*

30   *my amiss*   his transgression (presumably she has been sent away from him for a misdemeanour that he has committed, which also offended Love).

31   *own glad*] one sad *1669*
      glad truth   eager fidelity.

33   *blinded*] blindest *MS*

34   *their house*   their family and dynasty.
      followers] favourites *1669 and several MSS*

37   *glow*] blow *1669*

38   *thy self into our flame didst turn?*   their love consumes them in its own insubstantial heat, after offering them the prospect of a physical consummation.

40   *so dangerous*] and dangerous *1669*

42   *thy husband's towering*] the towered husband's *MS*; the loured husband's *MS*; thy husband's towered *several MSS*. Two quite different readings of the line seem possible. The version in Harleian MS 4064, 'the towered husband's eyes', completes the military metaphor with a picture of the lady's husband overseeing his spying oper-

ation from a watchtower. But in *1669* ('thy husband's towering eyes') the reference cannot be to the lady's husband at all, for she is not being addressed here, but to Love's husband. Love must then be Venus at this point, and the husband Vulcan, whose fires ignite the oily sweat of his own jealous frustration to transform his eyes into torches that expose the lovers' concealments. This version of the line does not ask one to suppose that the lady is already married, and plainly allows a different reading of the situation in the poem.

towering (a) standing at a great height, as a tower; (b) hovering to swoop, as a hawk; (c) rising to a high pitch of violence or intensity, as in 'a towering passion'.

43 *That flamed with oily*] Inflamed with the ugly *1669*

45 *not kept our*] we for this kept *1669*
kept our guards, like spy on spy kept wary watch, as spies upon the spies.
on] o'er *1635-54*

46 *had correspondence* exchanged messages.

49 *Shadowed with negligence our most respects* covered up with a show of indifference our warmest expressions of love.
most] best *1669*

51 *becks* nods.
under-boards under the table.

52 *from our words*] from words *1635-54*

53 *proved* tried out in experience.
thy art] our art *1669 and most MSS*

54 *thy pale inwards, and thy panting heart*] thy pale colours inward as thy heart *most MSS*
pale inwards the dim interior, as of a church which enshrines Love's secrets.

panting heart the altar or inmost sanctuary of Love. The MSS reading offers a less coherent alternative; it suggests that the dissimulations or 'colours' of love 'are inconspicuous, making no outward show' (Helen Gardner).

55 *passed purgatory* purgatory through which they have now passed.
passed Pronounced as two syllables.

56 *sad*] rude *several MSS*
the vulgar story a popular legend.

57-66] *Not in 1635-54 and several MSS*

57-8 *let our eyes be riveted quite through / Our turning brains* such a riveting would confirm their customary attitude as lovers, whose eye-beams look right through each other's eyes into the brain (see *The Ecstasy* 7-8).
brains] beams *MS*

61 *rive*] ruin *1669*; reave *MS*
rive split apart.

62 *Strain her eyes open, and it make them bleed* Fortune is depicted blind because she acts at random. Donne wants her not only to see what she is about but to feel compassion, and so spare them.
her] his *1669*
it] yet *1669*

65 *exclaim* complaint, protest.

66 *shame*] name *1669*

67 *Do thy great worst*] Fortune, do thy worst *1635-54*
arms] charms *MS*

69 *Rend*] Bend *1635-54*

72 *shifts* resources, devices, ways and means.

73 *quickening* (a) rising, growing bright; (b) lifegiving, arousing.

76 *suggest her clear* imply that she is pure, and beautiful.

77 *our passages* their amorous interchanges; the transitions of their love.

78] Shall tell our love was fresh in the beginning *MS*; How fresh our love was in the beginning *1669*

79 *ripened in the ear*] ripened in the year *1635*; enripened the year *1639-69*

81 *winter* the barren season of love, such as their coming absence will be.

83-94] *not in 1635-54 and several MSS*

86 *Phoebus* the sun.

87 *he*] we *1669*
portions] proportion *MS*

87–8 *what he cannot in like portions pay, / The world enjoys in mass* since the sun cannot illuminate the whole globe equally it compensates in one place for its falling short in another, and the world over all enjoys its full measure of light.

so we may if they are a world, then their deprivation now cannot be a final loss but will be made up later on.

enjoys] yet joys *MS*
mass] Mass *1669*

89 *ever yourself*] your fairest self *several MSS*

92 *by your contempt than constancy*] be your contempt then constancy *several MSS*; be your contempt then her inconstancy *1669*

94 *there reflected*] here neglected *1669*; there neglected *MS*

95–104] *not in one MS*

96 *words*] deeds *1635–69 and several MSS*; thoughts *MS*

97 *poles*] Pole *several MSS*
poles The poles are 'each of the two points in the celestial sphere ... about which as fixed points the stars seem to revolve; being the points at which the earth's axis produced meets the celestial sphere' (*OED*).

to teach me to show him what he would not otherwise know, give him example for what he would not otherwise dream of doing.

start deviate, change allegiance.

100 *motion* (a) the movements of the heavenly bodies; (b) desire, passion.
fire (a) one of the four elements; (b) passion.

102 *would*] most *1669*; could *MS*

ELEGY 13 JULIA

First printed in *1635*. Helen Gardner thinks that it is not by Donne and puts it among the poems of doubtful authorship. Giles Oldisworth, who annotated a copy of Donne in the seventeenth century, wrote 'Not licensed nor Dr Donne's' against both this poem and the following one, *A Tale of a Citizen and his Wife*.

1 *descried* made public.

6 *opinion* a private estimation of someone, which would do damage if maliciously made known.

7 *vilde*] vile *1635–69*

'Vilde' was a common form of the word, which the MSS have; it is needed here for the rhyme.

8 *Sticks jealousy* plants suspicions that stir up jealousy.

in wedlock] in the sheets of wedlock *MS*

11 *reputation* one's good name or honour.

14 *That female-mastix, to limn*] That foemall mastix to limn *1639–69*.

female-mastix a scourge of women. Mantuan's fourth Eclogue satirized woman's nature and earned him the reputation of a woman-hater.

limn depict, paint.

15 *chimera* a fire-breathing female monster, part lion, part goat, part serpent.

17 *night-crow* a bird of ill-omen, possibly the owl or nightjar.

18 *Give out for nothing but new injuries* the night-crow croaks only when calamities portend; so she opens her mouth only to cause disasters.

19–20 *the juice in Tenarus | That blasts the springs* Hercules dragged Cerberus up from the underworld through a cave on Cape Taenarus in Laconia. Cerberus spat on encountering the light, and his saliva produced a plant called *aconitum* whose juice was a blasting poison much sought for its power of destruction.

springs] Spring *MS*

23 *Orcus* In Roman mythology, the lower world of shadows and abortive shapes.

24 *mischiefs*] mischief *1635–69*

27 *cavils* hair-splitting objections and fault-findings.

untroths untruths, breaches of faith.

28 *Inevitable errors* devious schemes and falsehoods whose consequences one cannot avoid.

self-accusing loaths hatreds, which really condemn the hater.

loaths] oaths *MS*

29 *atoms swarming in the sun* In presocratic physics the sun and stars are made up of inchoate conglomerations of atoms, which move at random until some force gives them form and distinct being.

31 *give her half*] give but half *MS*; give half *MS*

ELEGY 14   A TALE OF A CITIZEN AND HIS WIFE

First printed in *1635*. Helen Gardner thinks that it is not by Donne – as did the seventeenth-century annotator Giles Oldisworth – and gives it among the poems whose authorship is uncertain.

The poem refers to affairs of the year 1609 and was probably written then.

1   *wight*   person.

4   *reformed . . . reduced*   Each pronounced as three syllables.

5   *juggler*] judge *1650–69*
   juggler   a trickster.

6   *touch no fat sow's grease*   question no rich man's side-pickings.

9   *ore tenus*   in law, sentence by word of mouth.

10   *will red*] will look red *1635–54*; shall red *MS*

13   *peat*   a fetching girl.

16   *steal*] seal *MS*

17   *kind*   natural, proper.

21   *Plaguy*] Plaguing *1635–54*
   Plaguy Bill   the latest bill of mortality, listing plague victims.

22   *Asked if*] Whether *several MSS*
   Custom Farmers   men who collected custom duties on imported goods. Having paid heavily for the right, they held out against the merchants for the full amounts due.

23   *the Virginian plot*   the settlement and planting of Virginia as an English colony, which was in the hands of a group of merchants and others forming a limited company. The enterprise, begun by Gilbert and Raleigh, was reconstituted in 1609 and stocks were offered in the City.

23   *Ward*   a notorious pirate who preyed on the Venetian trade in the Mediterranean in the first decade of the seventeenth century.

24   *Midland*] Island *1635–54*; the land, the seas *MS*

25   *the Britain Bourse*   'Britain's Burse', a stock exchange opened in 1609 as a rival to Gresham's Royal Exchange.

27   *new-built Aldgate*   the city gate at Aldgate was pulled down in 1606 and rebuilt in 1609.
   the Moorfield crosses   crosses were transverse or intersecting ways.

Grierson conjectures that these were the 'most fair and royal walks' (Stowe) which were built across the marshy fields of Moorfield after 1606.

29 *urged* Pronounced as two syllables.

32 *fit*] hit *MSS*

34 *no doing* no trading, business is slack. The lady and the poet both give 'doing' a sexual sense in which, evidently, business was not slack.

39 *frayed* frightened.

40 *Essex' days* Essex was executed in 1601.

41 *those*] that *1635–54*
   quoth he] quoth I *1635–54*

42 *itch of bravery* lust for heroic action.

43 *heat of taking up, but cold lay down* eager bravado in starting enterprises, which fizzle out miserably.
   lay down] good done *several MSS*

44 *push of pay* the test of action.

46 *Bawd ... scrivener*] *All the traders are in the plural in 1635–54, and the first two are in the plural in 1669.*
   scrivener a moneylenders' broker.

47 *privileged kingsmen* people whom the king rewarded for service or support with a grant of monopolies or trading privileges.
   kingsmen, and the store] kinsmen, and store *1635–54*

48 *protections* exemptions from being sued, which MPs among others could grant to their followers. Tradesmen lost heavily by such grants since the debts of protected people could not be recovered at law.

49 *In the first state of their creation* when they are first given these privileges.

50 *stoutly stand* make a fine flourish of equity.

50–51 *yet proves not one | A righteous paymaster* none of them turns out to be a just dealer in money matters.

58 *him off*] off him *1669*; him *1635–54*

61 *have been*] had been *1635–9. In some MSS* been *is written in the colloquial form* bin *for the rhyme.*

62 *Well used* well entertained; though the suggestion is that the wives have been 'well used and often' there in a sexual sense too.

64–5 *he . . . that hid the gold* The anecdote of the man who found a halter to hang himself where he had buried his gold goes back to the Greek Anthology (Book IX, Epigram 45, ascribed to Stabyllius Flaccus; Loeb edition, ed. W. R. Paton (1917) III, 27).

65 *at*] at's *1669*

66 *on*] at *1635–54*

67 *day*] stay *1635–54*

68 *found my miss* saw that the plan had failed.
shook] struck *1635–69*
yet] and *1635–69*

71 *the very sign* (a) the precise name or signboard of the house; (b) a covert invitation.

ELEGY 15 THE EXPOSTULATION

This poem was printed as Ben Jonson's in Jonson's *Underwoods* (1640), though it is in all the early editions of Donne from *1633*. Helen Gardner suggests that the author was neither Donne nor Jonson but Sir Thomas Roe; and she gives it with the poems of doubtful authorship.

1 *make the doubt clear* settle the well-known question.

2 *strong*] full *Underwoods*

3 *breathed* Pronounced as two syllables.
purest] the purer *Underwoods*

6 *your perfection* her maturity as a woman.

8 *hath, smile*] has, wink *Underwoods*

9–10 *the matter | Whereof they are made* the subject of the vows, fidelity in love.

12 *(Both hot and cold) at once*] (Both hot and cold at once) *MS*; Both heat and cool at once *MS*
make] threat *Underwoods*

14 *Formed into*] Tuned to our *Underwoods*

15 *As*] Blown *Underwoods*

16 *sweeter*] sweetened *1635-69 and several MSS*

17 *impression* imprint, stamp.

19 *draw bonds to forfeit* draw up a binding agreement just to forfeit one's pledge by breaking it.
 sign to break seal an attestation of faith just to break the seal and one's faith together.

20 *quite from* take what she says as the opposite of what she means.

21-2 *must | He first desire you false, would wish you just?* must her lover assume that she does everything perversely, by contraries, so that he can get her to be true to him only by telling her that he wants her to be false?
 wish] have *MS*

24 *This kind of beast*] The common monster *Underwoods*

25 *though froward*] however *MS and Underwoods*
 froward malicious.

26 *circumstance* details of her alleged infidelity.
 [*thy inconstancy*] the contrary *Underwoods*

36 *cast* condemn.

39 *love*] loves *MS*

40 *wretched as Cain*] as wretched Cain *MS*; as cursed Cain *MS*; wretched on the earth, as Cain *Underwoods*

44 *noisome* foul-smelling.

46 *on his soul's price* though the fate of his soul is at stake.

51-2 *a longer feast | To the King's dogs* Possibly the King's dogs were more fierce or ravenous than other beasts, or perhaps the poet wished them poisoned. King James was notoriously fond of hunting, and the reference would seem to date the poem firmly as later than 1603.

53 *I have*] have I *1633-54 and MS*
 revive] receive *Underwoods*

58 *Delight, not in made work*] Not in made works delight *several MSS*

60 *the law* the rule and right.

64 *officious*   zealous in attentions.
  be] grow *Underwoods*
  impertinent   forward, presumptuous.

65 *soft*] lost *Underwoods*

ELEGY 16   ON HIS MISTRESS

This is one of the poems which was refused a licence for the edition of *1633*. It was first printed, without authority, in *1635*.

Title] His wife would have gone as his page *MS*; On his Mistress' desire to be disguised and to go on like a Page with him *MS*

1 *strange*   when they were strangers to one another.
  interview   meeting.

3 *starving*] striving *1669 and several MSS*; starveling *several MSS*
  remorse   compassion, tender feeling.

7 *father's*] parents' *most MSS*

8 *want and divorcement*   the lack of one another, and separation.

12 *ways*] means *1669 and most MSS*

18 *From other lands my soul towards thee*] My soul from other lands to thee *1635–69 and MS*

19 *move*   take away.

21 *Boreas*   the god of the north wind in Greek mythology.
  harshness] rashness *MS*

23 *Orithea*   The god Boreas carried off Orithyia from the banks of the Ilissus when her father refused her to him in marriage. Some versions of the myth say that she then lived with him happily and bore him several children; but Plato reduces the story to an incident of a girl blown over a cliff by Boreas and killed (*Phaedrus* 229c–d).

24 *Fall*] Full *MS*

24–5 *proved | Dangers unurged*   undergone dangers when one was not compelled to.

26 *lovers*] friends *MS*

27 *Dissemble nothing*   (a) do not practise concealments or deceits

such as wreck love; (b) do not put on a feigned character, as an actor does.

not a boy   least of all is she to put on a character which would impute so perverse a motive to their love.

28   *mind's*] mind *1635–69 and some MSS*

28–9   *be not strange | To thy self only*   if she dressed up as a boy she would be a stranger only to herself, since everyone else would see through the disguise.

31   *apes*   people who ape others.

31–2   *as soon | Eclipsed as bright*   the moon is no less the moon when it is in eclipse than when it is at its brightest.

34   *Spitals*   hospitals, especially those treating venereal diseases.

35   *Love's*] Lives' *1669 and some MSS*
fuellers   inflamers of their own passion.

37   ] Will quickly know thee, and no less, alas! *1635–54*; Will too too quickly know thee; and alas *1669*; Will quickly know thee, and thee, and alas *MS*; Will quickly know thee, and alas *some MSS*
know thee, and know thee   see through her disguise and then ravish her.

38   *indifferent*   equally ready to take his pleasure with a man or a woman.

39   *well*] will *MS*

40   *hunt*] haunt *most MSS*

41   *Lot's fair guests*   Lot entertained two angels at his house in Sodom but the house was beseiged by lustful Sodomites demanding the youths within (as they thought them) and threatening to use Lot himself as a substitute (Genesis xix 4).

42   *spongy hydroptic*   soaking up drink insatiably, like a man with dropsy.

44   *only a worthy*   the only worthy.
gallery   the long ante-room in which suitors waited to be called into the royal presence.

46   *greatest*] great *some MSS*
call] do call *several MSS*
to] in to *several MSS*

49   *me, nor bless*] me; bless *some MSS*

51   *midnight's*] midnight *some MSS*

55   *except*   unless.

ELEGY 17 VARIETY

First printed as an appended poem in *1650*; few MSS have it. Helen Gardner doubts if Donne wrote it and gives it with poems of uncertain authorship.

Title] *Untitled in all the early versions. Grierson first called the poem* Variety

1   *motion, why*] motion why *1650–69*

2   *so much loved*] so beloved *several MSS*

3   *love divide?*] loved divide? *1650–69*
   divide   share.

5   *chair*   throne, source.

6   *ever else seems*] else seems *MS*; else is not so *MS*; else so ever doth seem *1650 and several MSS*

7   *at one sign to inn*   to lodge at only one hostelry.

12   *fair spreading*] broad silver *MS*
    far] clear *1650–69*; fair *MS*

13   *bank*] banks *MS*; bark *1650 and some MSS*
    that no strange bank doth greet   see *Elegy 3, 33–4.*

14   *itself and*] itself, kills *MS*

16   ] And only worthy to be past compare *MS*

19   *aver*] ever *1650–69*

20   *Him*] He is *MS*
    humane   human; civil, obliging.
    would turn back from] could not fancy *MS*; would return from *MS*; would turn from *MS*

23–4   ] Of other beauties, and in change rejoice? *MS*

25–36   ] *Not in one MS*

25   *The last . . . in all extremes*   the very latest.

27 *agreements* agreeable qualities.

28 *grave* a bawdy double entendre turning on the obsolete sense of 'grave', a pit or trench.

30 *takes* ravishes.

31 *well descended* (a) coming of a noble family; (b) they are good on their backs.
   are] were *1650–69*

34 *degree* (a) social standing; (b) the measure or worth of their performance.

37–48 *How happy were our sires ... | ... such reverence held* see *The Progress of the Soul* 191–210, *The Relic* 30, *Love's Deity* 8–14.

40 *stir up race* beget children.

41 *bands* sexual unions.

42 *still in usage* is still the custom.

43 *asked*] wooed *MS*

45 *title*] little *1650–69*

47 *The golden laws of nature* the laws operating in the Golden Age, which gave scope to our natural impulses instead of running counter to them.

48 *first Fathers*] great grandsires *MS*

49 *liberty's*] liberty *1650–69 and MS*
   our] and *1650–69 and MS*

50 *we*] we are *MS*
   opinion common repute.

51 *in no certain shape attired* popular belief alters with place and time.

52 *whose original*] one whose origin *MS*
   whose original is much desired people would very much like to know what its origin or birth is.

53 *growing on it*] going on it *MS*; growing on its *1650–69*
   growing on it fashions it takes on this or that shape as fashion changes.

54 *manners and laws to*] laws, manners, unto *MS*

57 *is*] of *MS*

60 *bruise*] wound *MS*

62 *seeds of ancient*] seed of pristine *MS*

63 *that part*   the party or faction; the particular office.
  although depressed   though it now has few active followers or champions.

69 *subjection of his hand*   the dominion his hand exercises.
  of his] under's *MS*; to his *MS*

70 *Nor ever did decline*] Never declining from *MS*

71-8] *Not in one MS*

72 *flame*] same *1650 69*

74 *loved*   Pronounced as two syllables.

77 *we reposed*   we are settled.

79 *Nor to the art of several eyes obeying*   not responding to the blandishments of this woman and that one.

80 *securely*] unpartially *MS*; sincerely *MS*

81 *being*] having *MS*

82 *We'll love her ever*] We'll leave her ever *1650-69*; Would love for ever *MS*

ELEGY 18 LOVE'S PROGRESS

This is one of the poems which was refused a licence in 1633. It was first printed in *1654* in *The Harmony of the Muses: or, The Gentlemans and Ladies Choisest Recreation* and first included in an edition of Donne's poems in *1669*.

Title] *Untitled in the early printed versions. Love's Progress is the title in some MSS*

4 *And love's a*] Love is a *1669 and several MSS*
  bear-whelp   newly born bears were supposed to be mere lumps of malleable flesh until their mother licked them into shape.

5 *strange*] strong *1669*

8 *though better than his own*   though a man's face in itself is better than a calf's.

9 *prefer*   choose.

12 *application*   the use gold is put to.

13 *wholesomeness*   medicinal power.
  ingenuity   noble quality (*OED*); skilful contrivance (of things made from gold).

14 *from soil*   from being tarnished.
  ever] for ever *several MSS*

16 *use*   custom or habit.

17 *these*] this *1661 and several MSS*

18 *and*] but *most MSS*

20 *they' are*] they're *1669*

26 *From her to hers*   from the essential woman to her mere properties.

27–8 *Search every sphere / And firmament, our Cupid is not there*   Cupid cannot be a heavenly deity because one finds no planet or constellation called by his name.

30 *where gold and fire abound*   money and destructive heat are the conditions of love. *Pluto* means 'the rich one' and the conflation of Plutus, the symbol of wealth, with Pluto, the king of the Underworld, yielded the common notion of a hell much like a Nibelheim or Cave of Mammon.

32 *in*] on *1669 and MS*
  pits and holes   offerings to the infernal gods were supposed to be thrown into deep trenches.

32–6 *pits and holes . . . / . . . the earth we till and love: / . . . the centric part*   Continued double entendre in a fabric of wittily sophistical argument was a feature of erotic poems following Marlowe's *Hero and Leander*.

34 *till*] fill *MS*

35 *airs*   (a) rarified heights; (b) manners and appearance.
  contemplate   The stress falls on the second syllable – contémplate.

36   *centric part*   the earth could still be spoken of as the centre of the universe.

38   *this, as infinite as it*   a woman's 'centric part' is as infinite as the soul. The argument plays upon two senses of 'infinite': (a) not bound by time; (b) of unlimited capacity and variety.
   it] yet *MS*

40   *stray*] err *1669 and several MSS*

42   *springes*   nooses for trapping small game.

46   *and*] but *1669*
   our] a *1669*

47   *the first meridian*   the first circle of longitude, which divides the eastern hemisphere from the western.
   first] sweet *1669*

48   *two suns*   her eyes.

51   *the Islands Fortunate*   an old name for the Canary Isles, through which the first meridian was conventionally assumed to pass.

52   *(Not faint Canary, but ambrosial)*   canary is a light dessert wine whereas ambrosia is the heady food and drink of the gods.
   Canary] Canaries *1669 and some MSS*

53   ] Unto her swelling lips when we are come *1669*

55   *seem all: there*] sing all their *1661 and several MSS*

57   *There*] Then *1669 and several MSS*; Here *MS*
   where] when *several MSS*

58   *remora*   a sucking-fish, which was supposed to stop ships by attaching itself to them with it's mouth or tongue.
   cleaving   (a) cleft; (b) holding on to things. Her tongue seduces one into staying there instead of sailing on to one's proper port.

60   *O'erpast; and the strait Hellespont*] Being past the Straits of Hellespont *1669*

62   *two lovers*   Hero and Leander. They lived on opposite shores of the Hellespont, the one in Sestos and the other in Abydos.
   two loves   Petrarchan poets commonly spoke of their mistress's breasts as the nests of love.

63   *yet*] that *some MSS*

65 *India* A generic name for all the countries of the East, which were just being opened up for trade with Europe in Donne's day. India replaced Cathay as a token of ultimate wealth.

66 *navel*] Naval *1669*

67 *thence*] there *1661-9*; hence *MS*
the current be thy pilot made one is guided on by the flow of the stream.
thy] the *1661-9*

68 *wouldst*] shouldst *1669*
embayed (a) in harbour; (b) shut in; (c) bathed or drenched.

70 *many*] some do *MSS*

73 *my*] thine *several MSS*

74 *symmetry* correspondence, likeness.

78 *the Devil never can change his* the devil cannot disguise his cloven foot.

80 *Firmness* stability; constancy; health.

81-2] Civility we see refined: the kiss / Which at the face began
transplanted is *1669 and several MSS*
Civility politeness; decency. The descent of the kiss from face to hand to knee to foot marks a progression from equality to absolute subservience, which is presumably what a refinement of civility amounts to.

83 *the imperial knee* kissing the emperor's knee was a token of feudal fealty.

84 *the papal foot* kissing the Pope's toe is the sign of a total submission to Rome.

85 *If kings think that the nearer way* if kings think that they can better gain their ends by starting with an act of submission and then working up towards independence.

87 *free spheres* the heavenly bodies move unimpeded and so travel much faster even than birds, which have to meet the resistance of the air.

89 *ethereal* (a) unimpeded; (b) the way to heaven.

90 *elements*] enemies *1669*
elements essential constituents or principles.

92 *Two purses* the mouth and the vulva. A purse was a small leather bag with a string threaded round its mouth to draw it shut.

aversely lying different ways, at an angle to one another.

93 *tribute* a due offering of submission or esteem; a tax or rent paid into a prince's exchequer by a subject realm.

94 *looks*] books *MS*: opes *MS*

96 *clyster* an enema.
clyster gave] glister gives *1669 and some MSS*

ELEGY 19 TO HIS MISTRESS GOING TO BED

This is one of the poems which was refused a licence for the edition of 1633. Many MSS have it, but it was first printed in *1654* in *The Harmony of the Muses: or, The Gentlemans and Ladies Choisest Recreation* and first included in an edition of Donne's poems in *1669*.

1 *all rest my powers defy* his virile powers defy inaction or sleep.

2 *in labour* in impatient anticipation.

4 *standing* (a) standing to, in expectation of action; (b) standing erect, as a tumid penis.
they] he *some MSS*

5 *heaven's zone* the belt of Orion; or the furthest circle of the universe with its inlay of fixed stars.
zone] zones *several MSS*
glistering] glittering *1669 and MS*

7 *spangled breastplate* the stomacher, an ornamental covering for the chest which was worn under the lacing of the bodice and often covered with jewels.

8] That I may see my shrine that shines so fair *several MSS*
busy fools prying people, who will be so taken up with the ornaments that they will look no further.

9 *harmonious chime* ladies sometimes wore a chiming watch on their stomachers. But the phrase also suggests that she is in accord with him here and has started to undress as he asks her.

10 *'tis your*] it is *1669*; is your *several MSS*; 'tis full *MS*

11 *busk* corset.
which] whom *some MSS*

12 *stand* see the note on *standing*, line 4.

13 *gown*] gowns *some MSS*

14 *from*] through *1669*
   hill's shadow] hills' shadows *1669*

15 *that*] your *some MSS*
   coronet a band of metal worn round the brow.

16 *on you*] on your head *1669*

17 *Now off with those shoes*] Off with those shoes *several MSS*; Off
   with those hose and shoes *MS*; Off with those shoes you wear and
   several MS
   safely] softly *1669 and some MSS*

20 *Received by*] Revealed to *1669*

21 *Mahomet's paradise* a heaven of sensual blisses.

21–2 *though* | *Ill spirits walk in white* 'even if ill spirits should walk
   in white, yet . . .'. Evil spirits sometimes masquerade as angels to de-
   ceive men.
   Ill] All *several MSS*
   spirits] angels *several MSS*

23 *these angels* women.

24 *Those*] They *most MSS*
   our] the *several MSS*
   set . . . our flesh upright give us an erection.

26] Behind, before, above, between, *most MSS*; Above, behind,
   before, beneath *MS*

28 *kingdom*] Kingdom's *1669 and several MSS*
   safeliest] safest *1669 and several MSS*
   manned (a) inhabited; (b) supplied with and used by a man.

29 *empery* an emperor's territory.

30 *How blessed am I*] How am I blest *1669*
   this] thus *1669 and several MSS*
   discovering] discovery *several MSS*
   discovering uncovering (dis-covering); finding her hidden riches.

31 *bonds*] bands MS
   bonds binding commitments; fetters (her arms).

32   *Then*] There *several MSS*; That *MS*
where my hand is set, my seal shall be   (a) he has signed the compact
between them and will now make it legally binding with his seal; (b) he
has put his hand where he will soon consummate their love.

32-3   *shall be. / Full nakedness*] shall be, / Full nakedness *1669*

34-5   *As souls unbodied, bodies unclothed must be, / To taste whole joys*
just as souls must divest themselves of their bodies before they can enjoy
total bliss, so the bodies must shed their clothes.

36   *like*] as *some MSS*
Atlanta's balls   Atalanta said that she would marry only a suitor who
could beat her in a foot-race; no one could, until Hippomenes got three
golden apples from Aphrodite and threw them down as he ran, so that
Atalanta forgot the race and picked them up. But Donne's simile makes
women the distracting agents and men the gross dupes.
balls] ball *1669*

38   *covet*] court *1669 and several MSS*
theirs] those *MS*; that *1669 and several MSS*

40   *laymen*   (a) the laity; (b) unschooled outsiders who are capable of
grasping things only through pictures or the decorated covers of books.

41   ] Themselves are only mystic books, which we *1669 and MS*
mystic books]   music books *MS*
we   the few initiates or priests of love who are worthy to have love's
mysteries (their mistress's body) revealed to them.

42   *imputed grace*   In Calvinist doctrine, Christ imputes grace to a
few elect in order to save them since men cannot acquire it for themselves
or gain salvation by any merit of their own. The suggestion here is that
a man cannot gain by merit the revelation and bliss he seeks but depends
for it upon the arbitrary election of the woman, who imputes to him, and
loves him for, her own qualities.

43   *see*] be *several MSS*
since] since that *1669 and several MSS*; sweet that *several MSS*;
(sweet) since *MS*

44   *a midwife*] thy midwife *1669*

46   *Here is no penance, much less innocence*] There is no penance due
to innocence *1669 and some MSS*
White is the garb of a penitent and of innocence; nakedness also be-
tokens innocence, as before the Fall. Either version of the line makes

good sense. The reading of *1669* and some MSS asks her to throw off her white linen because that will leave her innocent and not in need of penitential white. The reading of the other MSS plays on the equivocal force of whiteness, asking her to throw the linen off because in this situation neither the garb of penitence nor that of virginity is appropriate. The textual evidence for the *1669* reading is weaker, and I print the other one for that reason alone.

48 *more covering than a man* (a) more clothes on than the poet himself; (b) anything else to cover her than a man.

ELEGY 20 LOVE'S WAR

This is one of the poems which was refused a licence for the edition of *1633*. It was first printed by F. G. Waldron in *A Collection of Miscellaneous Poetry* (1802), though many early MSS have it.

Title] Making of Men *MS; untitled in the remaining MSS* F. G. Waldron first called the poem *Love's War*, and Grierson gave the title currency. The issue between the wars of love and the wars of arms was a commonplace in Roman and Renaissance writing.

3 *scrupulous* the rights and wrongs of them are in doubt.

4 *free city* she can make her own choice of attachment without provoking an international wrangle.

5 *Flanders* the Low Countries, which were in continuous ferment under the Spaniards in the 1590s. Donne puts the troubles in terms of the domestic conflict between a master and his apprentices, where the fault may lie with a tyrannical regime or with insubordinate underlings.

7 *all*] most *MS*
  idiots common unlearned men.

9 *giddiness* bewildering inconstancy. French policy changed about rapidly with the death of the Catholic Henri III, the accession of the Protestant Henri de Navarre, and then the conversion of Henri to Catholicism in 1593.

9–10 *did hate / Ever our men, yea and our God of late* The feud between English and French soldiers went back to Henry V's invasion of France, but from the 1580s Protestants were persecuted in France.

11 *our angels* Elizabeth backed Henri de Navarre with large sums of English gold, which looked as though they had gone for good when Henri turned Catholic on ascending the throne.

13–16 *Sick Ireland* ... / ... *let blood* The Irish question was the bugbear of Elizabeth's reign and rebellion flared up there recurrently. Tyrone's rising in 1594 ended a long lull and opened a phase of utter disaster for English policy.

16 *purged* (a) given a cathartic or emetic to remove impurities from the body; (b) cleared by force of dissident factions.

her head-vein let blood (a) having excess blood drawn off from the head to relieve pressure; (b) having the heads of her leaders cut off.

17 *our Spanish journeys* English privateering raids upon the Spanish gold traffic with South America and the treasure houses there. The raiders might undergo extreme hardship during an expedition or in their overland treks, though they had immense wealth within their grasp.

19 *should*] shall *several MSS*
that hot] the hot *some MSS*

20 *before my time* before he is dead.

21 *mew* coop up.
enthral enslave.

22 *that were like to fall* that is likely to yield itself to an enemy, or to collapse in ruins.

24 *swaggering* (a) blustering; (b) lurching or swaying.

25 *consumptions* wasting deprivations and diseases.

31 *Thine*] Thy *some MSS*

37 *engines* long-range weapons.

38 *Near*] Ne'er *MS*

39 *uprightly* flat on her back.

SAPPHO TO PHILAENIS

Printed as Donne's in *1633*, and from *1635* on put with the *Letters to Several Personages*. Grierson placed it immediately after the Elegies, calling it a 'Heroical Epistle'. Helen Gardner doubts if Donne wrote it and gives it with poems whose authorship is in question.

Sappho to Philaenis Ovid's *Heroides* or heroical epistles are wittily erotic poems purporting to be letters between famous lovers. Sappho is the celebrated woman poet of Lesbos (b. 612 BC) whose poems to other women made 'lesbian' a synonym for female homosexuality.

3 *Verse, that draws Nature's works, from Nature's law* the verse of Orpheus, the archetypal poet, worked so powerfully upon its hearers that inanimate as well as animate things suspended their natural function to pay him homage or follow him.

4 *her work* Nature's work is love.

10 *fires environ*] fire environs *several MSS*

15–17 *thou art so fair, | As, gods . . . | Are graced thereby* you are so fair that when I compare you with gods it is the gods who are graced by the comparison.

19 *silly* ordinary.

20 *then?*] *written as* than? *in the early versions.*

22 *down*] doves *MS*

25 *Phao* Sappho is supposed to have loved a certain Phaon, and an apocryphal story, evidently discounted here, says that she threw herself to her death in the sea for love of Phaon.

26 *mayst thou be*] mayst be *1633*; shalt be for *MS*; mayst thou be for *MS*

29–30 *yet I grieve the less, lest grief remove | My beauty* she tries to moderate her grief in case it should spoil her beauty and so cause Philaenis to stop loving her.

31–54] *Not in some MSS*

36 *unmanured* untilled; unfertilized.

37 *perfection* a woman was supposed to need the complement of a man to perfect her. See the *Epithalamion made at Lincoln's Inn.*

58 *thee*] she *1633*
  half] heart *several MSS*

59–60] So may thy cheeks outwear all scarlet dye
  May bliss and thee be one eternally.
  (*MS*)

59–62 *So may thy cheeks' red outwear scarlet dye . . .* presumably Sappho's verse will perpetuate her lover's beauty. The real Sappho is in fact the first known poet who claims to bestow an eternity of fame upon her subject.

61 *mighty*] almighty *MS*

Epithalamions or Marriage Songs

EPITHALAMION MADE AT LINCOLN'S INN

The occasion of this poem is not known. Presumably Donne wrote it when he was a student at Lincoln's Inn, between 1592 and 1594. D. Novarr thinks that it was written for a mock-wedding, which was part of the summer revels at Lincoln's Inn ('Donne's *Epithalamion made at Lincoln's Inn*, Context and Date', *RES*, n.s., VII (1956), 250–63). But there is no record of such revels.

Title] Epithalamion on a Citizen *some MSS*; Epithalamion of the Lady Elizabeth *MS*

4   *body's*] body *1633*

12   *Today*] Tonight *MS*
   put on perfection, and a woman's name   a woman was said to be per-fected by union with a man, and to fall short of full womanhood until then. See *The Primrose* 25 and note, and Shakespeare, *Twelfth Night* –
                        alas, that they are so;
To die, even when they to perfection grow!
(II iv 41–2)

14   *Our golden mines, and furnished treasury*   they brought rich dowries with them. 'Mines' has a sexual sense.
   furnished   amply supplied.

16   *angels*   gold coins.

17   *device*   inventiveness.

19   *Conceitedly dress her*   ingeniously adorn her with nuptial emblems.

22   *Flora*   a Roman goddess of flowers, whose dedication day in late April was celebrated with great sexual licence.
   Ind   India, which was proverbially opulent.

23   *fair and rich, in*] fair, rich, glad, and in *some MSS*
   lame   deficient, imperfect.

24   *Today put on*] Put on *MS*

25   *frolic*   liberal; merry.

26   ] Some of these senators wealth's deep oceans *1633 and several MSS*; Sons of these senators, wealth's deep oceans *MS*; Sons of those

senators, wealth's deep oceans *1635–69 and several MSS*; Sons of those senators wealths deep ocean *MS*

Sons of these senators' wealth's deep oceans   Grierson thinks that the patricians are young noblemen who accompany the bridegroom, and have their eye on the daughters of rich city merchants – 'senators'; they seek to make themselves sons, and suns, of the deep oceans of the wealth of these senators. But a simpler reading is that the patricians are the play-boy sons of wealthy merchants, possibly with bought titles, who suck up their fathers' wealth and disburse it like rain. They are the suns/sons of the deep oceans of their fathers' wealth.

27   *painted*   ostentatious; artificial, and not what they seem.

29   *Ye of those fellowships*   the Inns of Court.
those fellowships] that fellowship *MS*

30   *hermaphrodites*   combining opposite functions in one nature, that is, study and play. (Written 'hermaphrodits' in the early versions.)

31   *Temple*   possibly the Temple Church in Fleet Street, which had close associations with the Inns of Court.

32   *Lo*] See *MS*
of strewed flowers] of strowed flowers *1669*; of flowers *MS*

35   *shame*] blame *MS*

40   *starved*   Pronounced as two syllables.

43   *elder claims*   previous claims on the affections of either.

46   ] Always th' each other may the each one possess *MS*.
Always] All ways *MS* (*both senses are required*)

49   *Oh winter*] Winter *1633–69 and several MSS*
winter days   evidently the wedding took place in summer.

54   *that*] if *MS*

57   *nill*] will *1633–69 and most MSS*
nill   will not.

59   *run*] come *1633 and several MSS*
the world's] the heaven's *1635–69 and MS*

60   *Tonight put*] Put *MS*

61   *The amorous evening star*   Venus.

62 *our amorous star* the bride.

64 *truce* respite.

68 *duly; at night*] duly at night *MS*
 dispensed dispensed with, relinquished.

71 *who, lest*] but lest *MS*
 turn return

73 *Thy virgin's*] The virgin *several MSS*; Thy virgin *MS*

76 *were*] we *some copies of 1633*

81–2 *thou wast but able | To be what now thou art* she had not
reached the perfection she has now attained but was merely capable of
reaching it; she has now fully realized what was previously only possible
to her.

85 *faithful* full of faith.

86 *spent* extinguished, and exchanged.

87 *style* name and status.

90 *t'embowel* to disembowel, as for a paschal sacrifice.

91 *watch* remain awake.
 joy; and O light] joy, or light *MS*

93 *This sun* the bride.

95–6 *Wonders are wrought . . . | . . . puts on perfection* the wonder is
a paradox, that what was previously without fault now becomes perfect.

95 *which had no maim* she was a virgin.
 maim] name *1633–69 and most MSS*

AN EPITHALAMION, OR MARRIAGE SONG ON THE LADY
ELIZABETH AND COUNT PALATINE BEING MARRIED ON
ST VALENTINE'S DAY

Elizabeth Stuart (1596–1622), eldest daughter of James I, married
Frederick the Elector Palatine on 14 February 1613. The marriage was
a major ceremonial event for it was designed to strengthen James's
alliance with the Protestant powers in Germany, which was a keystone
of his policy. Donne's poem is one of many pieces written to celebrate
the occasion in verse.

1 *Bishop Valentine* one of the nebulous St Valentines whose feast-day falls on 14 February was a martyred bishop.

2 *All the air is thy diocese* the idea that St Valentine has a special care of flying things arises from an old belief that birds begin to pair on St Valentine's day.

5 *Thou marriest every year* see previous note.

7 *The sparrow that neglects his life for love* not out of faithful devotion, but because they kill themselves with lechery.

8 *stomacher* waistcoat.

9 *speed* prosper. Black was generally held to be a foul colour, and the sense is that by St Valentine's agency ugly things get husbands as soon as golden ones.

10 *halcyon* the kingfisher, which was fabled to have the power of stilling the waves so that it could breed in peace.

11 *straight*] soon *MS*
sped matched, satisfied.

14 *enflame* stimulate sexually.

18 *phoenixes* there was supposed to be only one phoenix in the world at a time, which reproduced itself by setting itself afire and arising again out of its own ashes.

25 *such fires* Donne draws on the sexual sense implicit in the image of the phoenix. See *The Canonization* 23–7.

27 *courage* sexual vitality.

37 *by their blazing, signify* the appearance of a blazing comet was believed to portend the death of a prince.
their blazing] this blazing *most MSS*

38 *falls, but doth not die* 'falls' has its sexual sense and 'die' its literal sense.

42 *this day*] this day *1669 and several MSS*

46 *grow*] go *1633–69 and MS*

48 *on such things as*] one such things, as *MS*
infinite their greatness has no limits.

52 *his way* the way of the Church, as distinct from the ways of affection and of sexual love.

55 *one way* that of sexual consummation.

56 *this Bishop's knot, or Bishop Valentine* beside the agency of others, whether the Bishop who marries them now or Bishop Valentine who brought them together.
knot, or Bishop] knot O Bishop *1633–54*; knot of Bishop *1669*

60 *store*] stars *1633–69 and MSS*
store abundance.

61 *you two walk*] you two go walk *MS*

64 *be to others*] to be others' *MS*

67 *come late*] come too late *1633 and some MSS*

70 *O Valentine?*] old Valentine? *1669*

75 *nicely* delicately, meticulously.

81 *sphere after sphere* as a celestial body passes through the concentric zones or globes of the heavens to encounter another star.

83 *Let not this day, then*] O let not this day *MS*

84 *Thy day*] This day *MS*

85 *the sun . . . he moon* male and female exchange natures, and merge.
here] there *1650–69 and several MSS*

86 *the best light to his sphere* she is now the sun who shares her light with the sphere of the moon.

90 *that coin* sexual pleasure, their own bodies.

94 *acquittances*] acquittance *1633 and MS*

95-6 *and so let fall | No such occasion to be liberal* they lose no opportunity to please each other.

98 *turtles* turtle doves, types of true love.
sparrows types of 'courage', or sexual vitality.

99 *And*] Now *MS*

100 *Nature again restored is* the larger sense is that this miraculous union has put right the ruin caused by Adam and Eve.
restored Pronounced as three syllables.

102] There is but one phoenix as before *MS*

103-4 *we | As satyrs watch* satyrs were rustic spirits who loved wine and amorous sport. They were associated with Dionysus, whose marriage feast was celebrated in February or March.

105 *when your eyes opened, let out day*   the day does not break until their eyes open and light the world.

108 *at which side*   they are lying in a curtained four-poster bed.

112 *we*] all *MS*
  enlarge   extend as far as that, by celebrating the marriage and keeping the vigil.

ECLOGUE 1613. DECEMBER 26

The occasion of this poem was the marriage of the divorced Countess of Essex to Robert Carr, newly created Earl of Somerset, in 1613. The marriage caused scandal since it followed shortly upon the decree of nullity that wound up a shabby divorce action between the Countess and Earl of Essex. But Somerset's standing with King James made him a man worth pleasing; hence the present poem. Within three years the Somersets went to prison for the murder of Sir Thomas Overbury, whom they had committed to the Tower on a trumped-up charge in April 1613 because he opposed their marriage.

Allophanes   one who has the appearance of another. Grierson conjectured that Donne meant Sir Robert Ker, a friend of his and a protégé of Somerset's, who bore the same name as the bridegroom.

Idios   a private man, one who has no part in public affairs. Grierson took this to be Donne himself.

in Christmas time] this Christmas *MS*

absence from court] absence thence *1633*; actions there *1635-69 and some MSS*; absence then *several MSS*

the marriage] this marriage *MS*

2   *country's*] country *several MSS*

5   *small*] smaller *1635-69*

8   *frieze*   (a) a bare coarse cloth; (b) frozen.

11   *Thy madness from thee*] Thee from this madness *MS*

12   *Have*] Having *1635-69*
  murmur] murmurs *1633-69*

16 *The sun* the king.

21 *that early light* God ordained light on the first day of the creation, but set the sun and moon in place on the fourth day. The light that precedes sun and moon here is the king himself, or his favour.

24 *From which all fortunes, names, and natures fall* the king's favour creates a world as God created the world at first, giving things their fortunes, titles and distinctive characters.

27 *prevent* outstrip, exceed.

34 *plots*] places *1633*, *1669* and *MS*
plots (a) places, corners; (b) conspiracies.

37 *digest*] disgest *1633–39*
digest disperse.

38 *our*] one *MS*

39–41] No, I am there / As heaven ... is everywhere: / So *1633–69* (*1633 has a comma after* everywhere)

40 *to men disposed* to men who are fitly disposed for heaven, or capable of apprehending it.

43 *full* having all they want.

44 *pattern* the origin of their authority and the model for the exercise of it.

47 *they* the kings.

50–52 *As man is of the world ... / Of creatures* as man is an epitome of the world, so man's heart is an epitome of God's book of creatures.

53 *the country'of Courts* the country is an epitome of Courts.

54 *one*] own *1635–69* and *MS*

55 *I am not then from Court.*] And am I then from Court? *1635–69*

57 *East-Indian*] Indian *1633–69*

61 *inward*] inner *1633–69*

62 *well disposed, and which would fain be gold* In the qualitative physics all minerals aspired to the pure harmony of gold, but might attain it only if they were inherently well disposed and encountered some subliming power.

63   *except*] unless *MS*

64   *that heaven gild it with his eye*   (a) that the sun's rays transmute it to gold; (b) that God refines earthy flesh to pure spirit; (c) that the king's favour elevates ordinary mortals to nobility.

66   *tinctures*   the pure quintessences of things.

68   *the use*   the nature, functions, customary practice.

72   *abroad, to honest actions come*   (a) acts honestly away from his home; (b) takes part in the honourable ceremonies of the world of public affairs.

74   *bewray*   disclose.

75   *present*] represent *several MSS*

76   *affections*   motives, sentiments, wills.

77   *and that, that King's are just*   and in which that king's affections are just (as his choice of confidant is – see lines 89-90).

78   *trust.*] trust, *1650-69*

83   *To them, in him*   in favouring one he favours all, because he prospers what they all aspire to and seek to share in.

84   *pretend*   aspire to.

85   *Thou hast no such*   you cannot point to any such history, since there have been no other courts like this.

86   *An earnest lover, wise then, and before*   the bridegroom is not an infatuated boy who is no more wise in marrying than he was in wooing.

87   *hath sued livery*   has sought service with a great man.

92   *only therefore*   for this reason only.

95   *therefore*   for this following reason.

101   *dead, and buried*   the state of men in the country, away from the Court.

EPITHALAMION

Epithalamion] *No title given in 1633-69*

108   *by*] from *1635-69*

110 *When he doth in his largest circle run* In northern skies the sun reaches the highest point of his largest circle, his summer solstice, in late June.

111 *west or east*] East or West *MS*

113 *Promethean* Prometheus brought down fire from heaven and gave it to men.

120 *then*] *written* than *in the early versions*

123–4 *Which scorns unjust opinion ... / ... chance or envy's art* the circumstances of this marriage gave ample scope to scandalmongers.

124 *or*] our *1669*

126 *both th' inflaming eyes*] th' inflaming eye *1633–69*

128 *Singly*] Single *1633–69 and MS*

129 *Yet let*] Let *1633–69*
   contemplate The stress falls on the second syllable – contémplate.

131 *prevent'st* anticipate.

133 *breast* confidential care.

134 *reinvest* take them up again.

136 *who doth the like impart* who kindles a like fire in you.

138 *it is some*] it were some *MS*

142 *Powder thy radiant hair* Brides commonly powdered their hair for the wedding day – 'Ha, ha, ha. Her hair is sprinkled with arras powder, / That makes her look as if she had sinned in the pastry' (John Webster, *The White Devil*, V iii 117–18).

145 *Art*] Are *1633 and some MSS*; Wert *1635–69 and MS*
   Phoebus the sun, Apollo the giver of light.

   Phaëton the boy who all but set the world on fire when he lost control of the chariot of the sun.

146 *unusual*] universal *MS*

148 *thy inflaming*] th' inflaming *MS*

149 *our infirmity* we cannot look upon the sun directly.

152 *cloud'st*] cloth'est *MS*

154 *the fruits of worms and dust* silk and gold.

156 *stars are not so pure, as their spheres are*   The spheres in which the stars rotated were sometimes said to be composed of the same celestial stuff as the heavenly bodies themselves, but purer; the crystalline sphere, for example, was held to be of exceptional purity.

157 *stoop*   condescend to the level of our senses and understanding.
  in part   as much as we are capable of gazing on, and understanding.

158 *entirely*   the whole, her qualities at full.

164 *that veil*   the impediment of our sight, by which we see them as two distinct beings.

167 *the Militant doth strive no more*   the Church Militant, champion of the faith and moral law, now has no office here since these two people are made one by a sacrament of the Church.

171 *swans*   Swans were emblems of purity and nobility, as in Spenser's marriage poem *Prothalamion*.

172 *never sing*   Swans were said to sing only at point of death.

177-8 *may here, to the world's end, live | Heirs from this King, to take thanks, yours, to give*   may there live here until the end of the world descendants of this king to receive thanks, and your descendants to offer those thanks for the benefits they have enjoyed.

178 *from this King*] for this, King *MS*; from the King *MS*
  yours] you *1633-69 and some MSS*

179 *Nature and grace do all, and nothing art*   and in this continuing interchange of benefits and courtesies may everything be the natural and gracious outcome of the relationship itself, and may nothing be due to crafty self-interest and policy.

180 *overthwart*   place counter to.

181 *west*   decline, fading.
  north   coldness, barrenness.

186-7 *the doctrine ... | That the earth moved*   this is Copernicus' theory that the earth moves round the sun.

189 *fall not where they rose*   as the sun or other cosmic bodies, whose dance of joy these revellers reproduce.

192 *a centre to this heart*   a single focus, the centre of a planet's orbit (see *The Sun Rising* 30).

199–200 *if sun and moon together do | Rise in one point, they do not set so too* she may go off to bed before he does even if they got up at the same time that morning.

202 *being gone, where e'er*] being gone where e'er *1650–69*

205–7 *a jelly ... | ... finds her such* he finds something which has quite changed its appearance, having lost its brilliant external glitter and fire; also, perhaps, something chaste (gelid) or fear-struck, yet soft and yielding.

214 *eye*] hand *1650–69*.

215 *Tullia's tomb* Tullia was Cicero's daughter. There was a legend that her body was found after 1500 years in a monument on the Appian way, with a lamp still burning beside it; but contact with the air reduced both body and lamp to dust.

219 *aspire* seek to rise upwards.

220 *like itself*] like to itself *MS*

222 *these*] them *MS*
  but fire too neither of them is merely fuel to the other's fire; both are themselves fire. Hence neither can reduce the other to ashes.

230 *of all* it belongs to all.

231 *festival*] nuptial *MS*

235 *Such altars* Probably he proposes to lay the poem before the bridegroom, or the king himself.

Epigrams

Few of the Epigrams can be dated. Several of them refer to events of 1596, and one to a publication of 1602. Presumably they were written over a period of some years.

HERO AND LEANDER

1–2 *air ... ground, | ... fire ... water* these are the four elements.

2 *one fire* love.

PYRAMUS AND THISBE

Pyramus and Thisbe were lovers in a story in Ovid's *Metamorphoses*. When their parents sought to separate them they resolved to run away together; but a lion frightened Thisbe away from their agreed meeting place and Pyramus, believing her killed, stabbed himself. Thisbe came back to find Pyramus dying, and took her own life. Their parents buried them together.

1-2 The main verbs are 'slain' and 'have joined'. 'Cruel friends by parting them have here joined two who were slain by themselves, each other, love, and fear.'

NIOBE

Niobe's twelve children were killed by Apollo and Artemis, the two children of Leto, after Niobe had boasted that she was at least Leto's equal. Wearied with shedding tears, Niobe became a stone.

1 *birth*] births *1633*

2 *So dry* (a) the dry humour in the body predominates, as happens with age or long suffering; (b) she has wept herself dry of tears.
  made mine own] made my own *MS*; mine own *MS*; mine own sad *1633*

A BURNT SHIP

R. C. Bald refers to the burning of the Spanish flagship *San Felipe* on the Cadiz raid in June 1596.

4 *decay* die, wither away.

FALL OF A WALL

3 *brave* magnificent (in that he had such a splendid tomb).

4 *town*] tower *1635-69*
  bones] corpse *some MSS*

CALES AND GUIANA

First printed in Gosse.
  After the sack of Cadiz in 1596 some English leaders were for sailing west to attack the Spanish treasure fleets and follow up Raleigh's

survey of Guiana. In that summer of 1597 there were hopes of diverting the Azores' expedition westward, but the Queen objected.

1 *spoil* the sack of Cadiz.
  th'old world's farthest end Cadiz lies west of Gibraltar, towards the south-westerly tip of the Spanish Peninsula.

SIR JOHN WINGFIELD

First printed in Gosse.
  Sir John Wingfield served with great gallantry under Essex in the Cadiz raid and was killed when the town had already fallen, the only English loss of note.

Title] On Cavallero Wingfield *MS* (Sir John Wingfield *is Grierson's title*)

1 *th'old Pillars* the Pillars of Hercules, the two mountains at the western entrance to the Mediterranean which were regarded as the limits of the old world.
  travelled Pronounced as three syllables.

2 *the sun's cradle* westward.
  throne] grave *MS*

3 *A fitter pillar* a memorial or tombstone.
  our Earl Essex.

4 *that late island* Cadiz which had a single link with the mainland. It was 'late' in that it had been lately in the news, and perhaps in that the town no longer existed after the English raid.
  late] Lady *MS*

A SELF ACCUSER

Title] A mistress *MS*

2] 'Tis strange that she should thus confess it, though it be true *1633*
confess it] confess *several MSS*

A LICENTIOUS PERSON

Title] Whore *MS*

1 *Thy sins and hairs* 'mine iniquities have taken hold upon me . . . they are more than the hairs of mine head' (Psalm xl).

1-2 *Thy ... / ... thy ... thy*] His ... / ... his ... his *MS*

2 *thy hairs do fall* it was an old joke that people with syphilis lose their hair.

ANTIQUARY

Title] Hammon *MS*

1 *he hath so much*] he have such *several MSS*; Hamon hath such *most MSS*

DISINHERITED

2 *good title* a good legal claim to the legacy.

AN OBSCURE WRITER

1-2 *hath been grieved | To be understood* it grieves him when people understand his writings, for he counts himself so learned as to be beyond the grasp of most readers.

KLOCKIUS

1 *Klockius*] Rawlings *MS*
   so deeply hath sworn, ne'er more] hath sworn so deep never *MS*
   sworn] vowed *most MSS*

RADERUS

Title] Randerus *MS*

1 *gelded Martial* Matthew Rader, a German Jesuit, published an expurgated edition of Martial in 1602.

2 *Except himself alone his tricks would use* unless Rader wanted to keep all Martial's licentious devices for his own exclusive use.

3 *As Katherine ... put down stews* presumably the reference is to some Queen Catherine who suppressed the public brothels, but no one has identified her.
   for the Court's sake (a) so as to benefit the morals of the Court; (b) so that the Court could have a monopoly of sexual licence.

MERCURIUS GALLO-BELGICUS

Mercurius Gallo-Belgicus was a Latin register of news, published annually at first and then half-yearly between 1588 and 1654. It had a name for hearsay report.

1 *Aesop's fellow-slaves* Aesop and two fellow-slaves were all asked by a prospective buyer what they were good at; the other two said that they were good at everything. Aesop answered that he was good at nothing because his companions left him no scope.

2 *faith* credulity.

5 *credit ... credit* your credulousness cost you our trust.

8 *stealing* filching scraps of news from all quarters without acknowledgement, as Mercury stole Apollo's cattle and denied it. Mercury was patron of thieves.
   but] and *several MSS*
   but liest like a Greek The ancient Greeks had a name for deviousness and lies in politics. Balancing a Roman title – Mercury – against Greek, the line suggests a combination of the vices of both ancient peoples.

RALPHIUS

2 *the broker keeps his bed* several readings seem possible, depending upon the sense of 'keeps'. (a) Ralphius is the broker, who now has to stay in bed and thus allows compassion to return to the world in his absence; (b) the broker is holding Ralphius's bed as security, so that when Ralphius is sick the broker 'keeps' his bed – stays by it as a solicitous attendant.

THE LIAR

First printed by J. Simeon in *Miscellanies of the Philobiblon Society* (1857).

2 *swear'st*] say'st *several MSS*

3 *Nebuchadnezzar* King Nebuchadnezzar told how for his sins 'he was driven from men, and did eat grass as oxen' (Daniel iv 33).

4 *Spanish dieting* The common people in Spain were assumed to live like animals, on grass and water.

MANLINESS

First printed in R. E. Bennett, *Complete Poems of John Donne* (1942). Only two MSS have it.

Title] The Juggler *MS*. *R.E. Bennett called the epigram* Manliness.

1 *joys*] toys *MS*

Satires

The Satires were probably written over the period 1593 to 1598. With Joseph Hall's *Virgidemiarum* (1597) they are the first formal satires written in English and owe something to Roman satiric writers, especially Horace, Juvenal and Persius.

Donne's five Satires were at first refused a licence for the edition of 1633, with five of the Elegies, but the ban on the Satires was lifted before the volume went to press and they appeared in it. A few blanks in the Satires in *1633* may indicate cuts made to meet the Licenser's objections.

Pope took the roughness of these Satires for a sign of the relative barbarousness of Donne's times, and rewrote two of them in elegant Augustan couplets as *The Second Satire of Dr John Donne, Dean of St Paul's, Versified* and *The Fourth Satire ... Versified*. But modern commentators agree that Donne wrote harshly by design, because he knew a tradition that satire ought to be harsh. A. Davenport speaks of a cult of the obscure deriving from the satires of Juvenal and Persius – 'The obscurity arising from the difficult and glancing allusions, the sudden and abrupt transitions of thought, the unexpected insertion of conversation not clearly divided between the speakers' (*The Collected Poems of Joseph Hall* (1949), xxv). He adds that Roman satirists cultivated ambiguity and darkness as safeguards in the dangerous business of 'threatening powerful men, and making risky attacks on vice in high places'. C. S. Lewis says that 'Donne ... writes under the influence of the old blunder which connected *satira* with *satyros* and concluded that the one should be as shaggy and "salvage" as the other. Everything that might make his lines come smoothly off the tongue is deliberately avoided. Accents are violently misplaced (ii. 7), extra syllables are thrust in (ii. 49), and some lines defy scansion altogether (i. 13, ii. 103). The thought develops in unexpected and even tormented fashion ...' (*English Literature in the Sixteenth Century excluding Drama* (1954), 469).

See also A. Stein, 'Donne and the Satiric Spirit', *ELH*, XI (1944), 266–82, and 'Donne's Obscurity and the Elizabethan Tradition', *ELH*, XIII (1946), 96–118.

SATIRE I   AWAY THOU FONDLING MOTLEY HUMOURIST

1 *Away thou ... humourist* the poem leaves us to guess who Donne's companion is and what he stands for. He may be an aspect of the poet's

own nature, the active man of the world in him as against the retired contemplative man his profession makes him.

fondling] changeling *1635–69 and most MSS*
fondling motley humourist foolish changeable zany.

2 *standing wooden chest* a study, such as those for the students in Lincoln's Inn.
chest] Christ *MS*

5 *God's conduits, grave divines*] God's conduits; grave Divines, *1633–9.*
conduits pipes, channels.

6 *Nature's*] Is Nature's *1669 and MS*
Nature's secretary, the Philosopher Aristotle was spoken of as 'the philosopher'. But a 'philosopher' might be a natural scientist or even an alchemist, who would be nature's secretary because he handled nature's secrets.

7 *jolly*] wily *1635–69 and MS*
jolly presumptuous, showy.

8 *mystic body* the civic organism as distinct from the physical fact.

9 *gathering* scavenging.

10 *Giddy* light, capricious.
fantastic dealing in unrealities; extravagant.

12 *follow headlong, wild*] follow headlong wild *1635–69. The comma in 1633 may be an attempt to make* headlong *an adverb modifying* follow *rather than an adjective qualifying* thee.

13 *love in earnest*] love, here, in earnest *1635–69 and MS*
earnest Pronounced as three syllables.

16 *dost meet*] do meet *several MSS*

18 *parcel gilt* (a) partly gilded, as figuratively with money or literally with showy armour; (b) partly guilty.
with forty dead men's pay swindling officers might continue to collect the pay of their dead soldiers and keep it for themselves.

19 *Nor*] Not *1633–69 and several MSS*
pert] neat *MS*

20 *courtesy*] curtsies *several MSS*

22 *blue coats* servants wore blue coats; but so did minor officials of the law, such as beadles.

23 *Wilt*] Shalt *most MSS*

25 *or worse*] and worse *some MSS*; or for worse *MS*; and for worse *MS*

27 *Oh monstrous*] Ah monster *several MSS*

27-8 *superstitious puritan, / Of refined manners* punctilious purist of courtly etiquette (like Osric in *Hamlet*).

28 *yet ceremonial man* he stands on ceremony, whereas the puritans abhorred it.

30 *broker* shopkeeper; pedlar.
prize appraise.

32 *raise*] vail *some MSS* (To vail *is to doff*)
hat] hate *1633*

33 *consort none*] consort with none *some MSS*

36 *Jointures* property held jointly between husband and wife or to provide for the wife in widowhood.

37-40 *(that ... / ... boy)*] *No brackets in 1633-9*

39 *barrenness*] bareness *some MSS*

40 *plump* coarse, dull; fat.
muddy foul, gross.

43 *unapparelled* Pronounced as five syllables.

44 *banished* Pronounced as three syllables.

45 *blessed*] best *some MSS*

46 *yet*] *Not in 1635-69 and some MSS*

47 *this coarse attire* the garb of a scholar or contemplative.
I now] now I *several MSS*

50 *warned*] warmed *1633*

53 *that*] who *1633 and MS*

54 *Worn by*] Worn out by *1650-69*

55 *black feathers, or musk-colour hose* fashions of the day. Musk is a reddish brown or dark purple colour.

56 *right true father, 'mongst*] true father amongst *several MSS*

58] The infant ... India *1635-54 and most MSS*; The Infantry of London, hence to India *1669*

The Infanta of London, heir to an India Strictly, the Infanta is the eldest daughter of the king and queen of Spain who is not heir to the throne, just as the Infante is the second son and not the heir. But the word was popularly used to mean any young daughter of a noble house and here may just refer to the best marriage-prospect then going in London. 'Heir to an India' simply means that she stands to inherit vast wealth. No one has been able to suggest a particular person whom Donne might have had in mind.

59 *a gulling weather spy* a cheating astrologer.

60 *scheme*] schemes *several MSS*; scenes *1633 and some MSS*; scene *MS*

heaven's scheme a diagram of the positions of the heavenly bodies, used for prediction; a horoscope.

62 *subtle-witted*] subtle wittied *1633-54 and several MSS*; supple-witted *several MSS*; giddy-headed *1669*
   antic fantastic.
   youths] youth *1669*

63 *from me*] from hence *several MSS*; hence *several MSS*
   canst] can *1633-69 and most MSS*

64 *when*] where *MS*

68 *the wall* the inside position on the pavement, against the wall, where conditions were less foul and hazardous. It was a point of courtesy to yield the wall to men of higher social standing.

70 *state*] room *MS*
   state status, prestige.
   his] high *1633*

73 *them*] then *1633*

77 *stop lowest* stop the string at the lowest fret.

78 *brave* splendid, showy.
   stoops] stoopeth *several MSS*; stooped *1633 and some MSS*
   nigh'st the ground] nighest ground *several MSS*

80 *the wise politic horse* In the 1590s a showman called Banks exhibited a horse which supposedly responded to the audience's requests, or refused to respond if it did not approve.

81-2] *Not in 1633*
    O elephant or ape The performing elephant and ape also seem to
have been London sights in the 1590s and many writers allude to them.
Ben Jonson has his Stage-keeper lament the absence from *Bartholomew
Fair* of 'a juggler with a well-educated ape, to come over the chain for a
king of England, and back again for the prince, and sit still on his arse
for the pope and the king of Spain' (The Induction).

85 *Oh*] Yea *some MSS*

86 *here*] so *MS*

88 *drinking his tobacco well* Tobacco was introduced into England in
1565 but not smoked until Raleigh acquired an Indian pipe in 1586.
Its proper use was for years a matter of avant-garde dispute, and writers
speak more often of drinking tobacco than of smoking it.

89 *whispered, 'Let us go*] whispered (let's go) *MS*

94 *goes on the way,*] goes, on the way *several MSS*
    on] in *several MSS*

95 *all repute*] is all repute *1633 and MS*

96 *device* invention.
    handsoming adorning, embellishing.

97 *pink* a decorative eyehole or piece of scalloping.
    panes decorative strips or slashes.
    print the crimping of the pleats of a ruff.
    cut a slash.
    pleat] plight *several MSS*

98 *conceit* idea, conception.

99 *dull comedians* comic actors who relied on outlandish clothes for
laughs.

100 *stoop'st*] stop'st *1635-54 and MS*
    stoop'st bow and scrape.

101] Why, he hath travelled long? no, but to me *1633-9*; Why hath he
travelled long? no, but to me *1650-54 and MS*; Why: he hath travelled.
Long? No: but to me *MS*; Why, he hath travelled. Long? no. But to
me *MS*; Why he hath travelled; Long? No: but to me *MS*; Why.
He hath travelled long; no, but to me *1669*

102 *(Which understand none,)*] No brackets in *1633–69 and most MSS*
understand] understood *1669*

104 *pox* syphilis, often called the French or Italian disease and
assumed to be native to those countries.

105 *and qualities*] of qualities *several MSS*

108 *lechery*] liberty *1633*

109 *were there*] there were *1650–69*
command have her at his disposal.

112 *constantly a while must keep his bed* the 'motley humourist' of
the streets himself finishes up in a course of retired constancy.

SATIRE 2 SIR; THOUGH (I THANK GOD FOR IT) I DO HATE

The butt of this Satire is a bad poet who becomes a worse lawyer and
then viciously misuses the law to enrich himself.

Title] Law Satire *MS*; Against Poets and Lawyers *MS*

2 *Perfectly* thoroughly

2–3] All this town perfectly yet in every state
There are some found so villainously best
(*MS*)
All this town perfectly yet every state
Hath in't one found so villainously best
(*MS*)

3 *excellently best* most nearly perfect in evil.

4 *hate, towards them, breeds pity towards the rest* other things by com-
parison are so much less evil that one pities rather than hates them.
them] that *MS*

6 *As I think that*] As I'am afraid brings *MS*
dearths famines.

7–8 *like the pestilence and old fashioned love, | Riddlingly it catch men*
men catch poetry mysteriously, as they catch the plague or caught love
in old romances.

8 *Riddingly it*] It riddlingly *most MSS*

9 *starved out* starvation cures a man of the itch to earn his living by
poetry, as it supposedly cures the plague and love.

10 *like papists* Roman Catholics were so discriminated against in late sixteenth-century England that – Donne implies – there was no point in persecuting them since they could not injure the State.

11 *at Bar judged as dead* condemned to death at the Bar.

12–13 *prompts him which stands next, and cannot read, | And saves his life* Criminals could in some circumstances escape execution by pleading benefit of clergy and giving proof of literacy. They were set to read their Latin 'neck-verse', which was usually the beginning of Psalm li, a plea for God's mercy.
  cannot] could not *most MSS*

13 *idiot* ignorant.

15 *organ*] organs *1669 and most MSS*

17 *move love* provoke or cause love.
  rhymes] rhythms *1633–69 and several MSS*

17–18 *witchcraft's charms | Bring not now their old fears, nor their old harms* trying to win love by poems is now as old-fashioned and superstitious as trying to harm people by spells.

19 *Rams* battering rams.
  slings] songs *MS*
  silly battery feeble and ineffectual weapons of assault.

20 *Pistolets* (a) small firearms; (b) foreign gold coins. Women are now won by bullets (see *Elegy 20 Love's War 38*) or gold.

21 *they who write to lords* poets who dedicate their writings to noble patrons.

22 *singers at doors*] boys singing at door *most MSS*; singers at men's doors *MS*

25 *chaw* chew.

26 *Others' wits' fruits* the fruits of the wits of others, other writers' works.

27 *Rankly*] Rawly *several MSS*

31–2 *use | To* habitually.

32 *outdo*] outswive *some MSS*

32 *dildoes*] *Word replaced by a dash in 1633.*

outdo dildoes dildoes were artificial phalluses and to outdo – or outswive – them might in the poet's view be a prodigious feat indeed.

33 *outswear the Litany* take God's name in oaths more than the Litany invokes it in supplication.

Litany] gallant, he *1650-54*

34 *sins' all kinds*] sins of all kinds *1633 and several MSS*

36 *Schoolmen* Aristotelean theologians, who subtly categorized sins and their punishment.

37 *canonists* legal theologians, who judge issues by reference to ecclesiastical law.

38 *receipt* receptacle, accommodation, scope. The sins they claim are so strange that canon lawyers, schooled in the task, would have the greatest difficulty in deciding just which ample commandment of the ten actually covers them.

39 *insolence* arrogance.

40 *just*] great *most MSS*; heart's *MS*
just offence offence he justly feels.

41 *botches* boils or rashes.
pox eruptive skin diseases; syphilis.

43 *was alas of late*] which, (alas) of late *1635-69*

44 *But a scarce poet* scarcely a poet; a feeble poet.
a scarce] scarce a *1633-69 and several MSS*
jollier of this state more puffed-up with his new status as a lawyer.
this] that *some MSS*; his *some MSS*

46 *nets, or lime-twigs* devices for snaring birds.
wheresoe'er] wheresoever *1633-69*; where ere *MS*

48 *Pleas* actions at law; the Courts of Common Pleas.
Bench the Queen's Bench.

49-57 Legal wooing in verse had a fashion in the 1590s and there are many instances and burlesques of it. The unknown poet of the *Zepheriah* sequence of sonnets, 1594, is barbarously like Donne's Coscus:

How often hath my pen (mine heart's solicitor)
Instructed thee in breviat of my case! . . .
How have my sonnets (faithful counsellors)
Thee without ceasing moved for Day of Hearing!

While they, my Plaintive Cause (my faith's revealers)
Thy long delay, my patience, in thine ear ring.
(Sonnet 20)

49 *motion* application to commence a legal action.

50 tricesimo *of the Queen* the thirtieth year of the Queen's reign, 1588.

51 *Continual claims* in law, claims formally repeated at intervals.
injunctions orders from Chancery to stay proceedings.

53 *Hilary term* the first term of the English legal year, running from early January to early April.

54 *returned*] return *1633*
next 'size] this 'size *most MSS*
next 'size next assize.

55 *in remitter of your grace* entitled to her grace retrospectively, by his former claim rather than the later one.

56–7 *should take place / Of affadavits* serve as sworn statements in his absence.

58 *soft maid's ear*] maid's soft ear *1669*

59 *Sclavonians* Slavs, whose language, not being understood, was a by-word for noisy outlandishness.
scolding brawling.

63 *gain, bold soul, repute*] gain; bold soul repute *1633–69 and some MSS*; gain (bold soul) repute; *MS*; gain, bold souls repute *1719*; gain, hold soul repute *some MS*
bold soul the poet's own resolute soul; or the person to whom the whole Satire is addressed, the 'Sir' of line 1.

63–4 *repute / Worse than* . . . Think of them as worse than . . .

64 *Worse than embrothelled strumpets prostitute* more corrupt than embrothelled strumpets.

66 *His hand still at* (a) clutching; (b) signing, putting his hand to.
bill (a) a watchman's halberd; (b) a legal statement or petition; (c) an order to pay.

66–7 *talk / Idly* speak deliberately beside the point, to play for time or confuse the issue.

68 *suretyship* standing surety for someone, who then defaults leaving one to pay the penalty.

69–70] *Not in 1633, but the omission is indicated by dashes*

70 *yea*] or *1635–69*

71–2 *Like a wedge in a block, wring to the bar, | Bearing like asses* force one's way to the Bar as a wedge cleaves a block of wood, pressing back one's fellow asses who are trying to claim attention, or borne down by huge piles of documents.

73 *carted whores* convicted whores were carried through the streets in a cart to be whipped, but often just brazened it out.

74–5] *Not in 1633, but the omission is indicated by dashes*

74 *kings' titles* lines of descent, their claim to the throne, which might be founded in legitimate descent but usually is not.

77 *compass* encompass, get into his own possession.
  our land] the land *1633–69 and MS*

78 *Mount* St Michael's Mount, off Land's End.

79 *spying heirs melting with luxury* spying out heirs who are dwindling away with debauchery (and whose early deaths may thus leave their inheritance open to legal chicanery and pocket-lining).
  luxury] gluttony *some MSS*

80 *will*] would *several MSS*

82 *barrelling* storing up.

84 *Relic-like*] Relicly *1633–69 and some MSS*
  gear] cheer *1669*

86 *Wringing* extorting by trickery or force (as by a confession under threat or torture).
  men] maids *1669*
  pulling prime drawing for the winning hand at the fashionable card game of primero, where the stakes were often high.

87 *parchments*] parchment *1633–69 and some MSS*

88 *Assurances* deeds of conveyance.
  glossed civil laws commentaries upon the civil law, which were usually voluminous.

89 *our time's forwardness* this advanced time of ours.

90 *Fathers of the Church* Patristic writings are notoriously vast.

91-2 *These he writes not ... / Therefore spares no length* not having to write these himself or pay a scribe to write them, he finds it to his legal advantage to make the documents unreadably long.

93 *was professed* had taken the vows of a religious order.

93-6 *he did desire / Short Pater nosters ... / ... the power and glory clause* While young Luther professed monastic vows he wanted short prayers, since a friar has to repeat every day a prayer for each bead. But having renounced his order he lengthened the 'Our father' by appending to it the doxology, which he had not used as a friar because it is not in the Vulgate.

When Luther translated the New Testament into German in 1521 he took from Erasmus's Latin translation (1516) the clause 'For thine is the kingdom, the power and the glory'. The analogy offers a notable instance of a profession of principle that really just glosses petty self-interest.

97 *changes* exchanges.
impairs abbreviates, so as to diminish his own legal obligation.

98 *unwatched* if one does not keep a sharp eye on him.
ses heires the phrase which ensures that property passes to a man's heirs after his death. By omitting the words from the deed of conveyance the landgrabber thinks to recover the land himself when the buyer dies.
ses] his *some MSS*

99 *As*] And *1669*
any commenter commentators upon difficult authors (such authors as Donne) notoriously sidestep passages they cannot make sense of.

100 *Hard words, or sense* harsh conditions and penalizing clauses in a legal document, which the trickster craftily conceals.

101 *controverters* controversialists.
vouched texts texts cited as authoritative.

102 *Shrewd* awkward, or difficult to get round; sharp.
which might against them clear the doubt which might settle the controversy in favour of their opponents.

104 *Those*] These *several MSS*
not built, nor burnt within door the woods are not now drawn on

sparingly for building or heating on the estate, but hewn down whole-sale for quick profit.

105 *troops, and alms* the throngs of people to whom the great estates gave a centre and employment; and the charity dispensed by the head of the house.

    alms? In great halls] alms, great halls? *1633 and some MSS*; alms? In halls *1635–69 and several MSS*; alms in halls *MS*; alms? great halls *several MSS*

    great halls great houses; the dining halls of those houses.

106 *Carthusian fasts* extreme austerity of fare.
    fulsome bacchanals gross orgies.

107 *Equally I hate*] Equally hate *MS*
    means bless] mean's blessed *1635 and several MSS*
    means bless moderate courses bring prosperity.

108 *no*] not *several MSS*
    hecatombs a wholesale slaughter of animals as a sacrifice.

109–10 *we allow, | Good works as good, but out of fashion now* we concede that good works are good but disregard them because they are not now in fashion.

111 *old rich wardrobes* luxurious stocks of clothes of a bygone day, still good in their substance but not now the fashion.

111–12 *my words none draws | Within the vast reach of the huge statute laws* no one can bring the satirist's charges within the scope of Acts of Parliament, even though those laws now encroach so far upon one's liberty to speak and act.

    statute laws] statute's jaws *1669*

SATIRE 3   KIND PITY CHOKES MY SPLEEN

Title] Of Religion *MS*

1–2 *Kind pity chokes my spleen; brave scorn forbids | Those tears to issue* he turns now to an evidence of human folly which equally evokes his derisive anger and his fellow-feeling of pity, so that the two impulses frustrate each other.

    chokes] checks *1635–54*; cheeks *1669*

2 *Those*] These *several MSS*

3 *not*] nor *several MSS*
    sins] sin *several MSS*
    and] but *1669*

and be wise   the wise course is neither to laugh at sins nor to weep over them.

4   *Can*] May *some MSS*
railing   abusing, inveighing against them.
worn   long-standing; ingrained.

7   *As virtue was to the first blinded age*   the early pagan philosophers, who lived perforce in blind ignorance of Christ and true religion, none the less gave their devotion to the abstract idea of virtue.
to] in *1633 and several MSS*
blinded] blind *several MSS*

8   *valiant*   powerful.

9   *as earth's honour was to them*   pagan devotees of virtue, knowing nothing of an after life, made earthly honour the focus of their moral code.
honour was] honours were *several MSS*

10–11   *As we do them in means, shall they surpass | Us in the end*   as we surpass the pagans in the means of getting to heaven (for we have the revelation of Christ in the New Testament) may they not surpass us in that end itself, and get there while we go to hell?

12   *blind philosophers*   pagan moralists, such as the Stoics.

12–13   *whose merit | Of strict life may be imputed faith*   the merit of whose strict moral conduct of their lives may be credited to them to make up for the faith they necessarily lacked, and so earn them Christ's redeeming grace.

14   *so easy ways and near*] ways easy and near *some MSS*; ways so easy and near *MS*
near   direct ways of getting to heaven.

17   *mutinous Dutch*   in the last twenty years of the century many English soldiers of fortune went off to fight in the Low Countries against the Spanish conquerors.
Dutch, and dar'st] Dutch? dar'st *most MSS*

22   *frozen north discoveries*   the search for the north-west passage to the Pacific was one of the great sea-going enterprises of Donne's day.

23   *salamanders*   lizard-like creatures, popularly supposed to be able to live comfortably in fire.

23-4 *divine / Children in th'oven* Shadrach, Meshach and Abednego, whom Nebuchadnezzar threw into the burning fiery furnace for refusing to worship a golden idol as he commanded them.

24 *fires of Spain* the Spanish Inquisition handed over heretics to be burned.
and the line the fiery heat of the equatorial regions.

25 *limbecks to our bodies* those regions are like alembics in which the bodies of northern Protestants are heated up.

26 *for gain bear* endure hardships for mere monetary gain.

27-8 *Which cries not 'Goddess!' to thy mistress, draw, / Or eat thy poisonous words?* must every man who does not hail one's mistress as a goddess either draw his sword and fight or suffer any insults one chooses to thrust down his throat?

30 *and his* God's.

31 *Sentinel*] Soldier *some MSS*
his] this *1669 and several MSS*

32 *forbidden wars* wars whose ends are worldly and not holy.
th'appointed field the moral battlefield of this world, in which Christians are God's soldiers.

33] Know thy foes; the foul Devil, whom thou *many MSS* Know thy foe, the foul devil h'is, whom thou *1633 and several MSS*
Devil, he,] devil is *MS*; devil, his *MS*

34-5 *would allow / Thee fain, his whole realm to be quit* the devil would willingly give you for your service his whole kingdom of hell, to be rid of it, though out of hate not love.
quit] rid *some MSS*

38 *her decrepit wane* the world was thought to be running down fast and nearing its end. See the two *Anniversaries, passim.*

40 *Flesh (itself's death)* the sins of the flesh brought in and bring on death, which destroys the flesh.
(itself's death)] it self death *1633 and several MSS*

43 *Mirreus* Myrrheus, the incense-scented man (myrrh gives incense its cloying smell).

44 *here* in Protestant Britain.

47 *He*] And *1635–54*
her] the *1633–69 and several MSS*
rags the few shreds of the original truth that Rome retains; the ostentatious trappings that Rome substitutes for truth and worship.

48 *statecloth* the canopy over the throne or chair of state. In England the throne itself was reverenced even in the monarch's absence.

49 *Crants*] Grants *1669 and several MSS*; Crantz *MS*; Grant *several MSS*; Crates *MS*
Crants a garland or wreath. Possibly the only point here is the German or Dutch associations of the name.
brave splendid, showy.
enthralled enslaved.

50 *Geneva* the home of Calvin and the most rigorous Puritanism.

51 *sullen*] solemn *several MSS*
sullen obstinate; dismal.

53 *Lecherous humours* tastes in lechery.

55 *Graius* a Greek.

56 *ambitious bawds* pimps who seek their own preferment by selling their mistress to all comers.

56–7 *laws / Still new like fashions* devotion in England under Elizabeth was regulated by a multiplicity of laws, which were meant to uphold the Anglican settlement.

57 *bid*] bids *1633–69*

58 *is only perfect* is alone perfect.

59 *godfathers* (a) sponsors at baptism; (b) spiritual guides – 'fathers in God' (among whom might be those who make the laws that bind him).

60 *Tender to him* offer him.
being tender because he is young, weak, impressionable.

62 *Pay values* pay the fine imposed upon wards who refused a marriage which their guardians had arranged for them. The Act of Uniformity of 1559 imposed fines upon people who did not attend their parish church.
Careless caring for none of the alternatives open to him; free.
Phrygius] Prigas *MS*; Phrygas *MS*; Prigias *MS*
Phrygius a Phrygian. Possibly Donne alludes to the multiplicity of

gods which confronted the ancient Phrygians as a consequence of their subjection to several different peoples in turn.

65 *Gracchus* one of the Gracchi, a Roman family renowned for its enlightened liberalism.

all as one every one of them equally.

66 *divers countries* various different countries.

67 *diver habits* various costumes.

one kind of one nature of species.

68 *so doth, so is religion* religion may go in a variety of garbs from country to country but is essentially one and the same.

68-9 *this blind- | ness too much light breeds* this blindness is caused by too much light. Thinking that everything has the light of truth, he cannot tell true from false and is blinded to the one real truth.

69 *unmoved* not swayed by other motives than the search for the one right religion.

70 *Of force must one, and forced but one allow* you must necessarily recognize only one religion as true (for there is only one final truth), and even under force you must not admit any other.

force must one ... forced but one] force but one ... forced must one *MS*

71 *ask thy father which is she* 'ask thy father, and he will show thee; thy elders and they will tell thee' (Deuteronomy xxxii 7). Donne is appealing to the primitive state of the Church, and then of mankind altogether; he assumes that we fall further and further short of this state as time runs on.

75 *He's not of none, nor worst, that seeks the best* he is not of no religion or the worst religion who seeks the best religion.

76 *To adore, or scorn an image, or protest* to be a Roman Catholic, or an anti-Catholic, or a Protestant.

77 *May all be bad* easy certainties may be vicious in themselves in a situation where the truth is not simple or easily come by.

78 *stray*] stay *some MSS*

79 *To sleep, or run wrong is* being indifferent or unreflectingly taking a wrong course is, in fact, to stray, whereas to inquire or doubt may not be.

huge] high *some MSS*

80 *Cragged*] Ragged *some MSS*; Rugged *several MSS*
stands] dwells *some MSS*

81 *her*] it *several MSS*
about must, and about this way and that, round about.
about must go] about it go *1669*; about go *most MSS*

82 *what the hill's suddenness resists, win so* overcome in this way the resistance that the hill's abruptness offers to your ascent.

84 *soul*] mind *some MSS*
none can work in that night 'the night cometh when no man can work' (John ix 4).
that night] the night *1635–54*

85–6 *now do. / Hard deeds*] now do / Hard deeds *1633*
now do now actively begin your efforts to find truth.

86–7 *Hard deeds, the body's pains … / The mind's endeavours reach* as one accomplishes hard deeds by the pains of the body, so one gains hard knowledge by the endeavours of the mind.
too] to *1633–69 and most MSS*

87–8 *mysteries / Are like the sun, dazzling, yet plain to all eyes* the fact that there are central truths that our minds cannot grasp – religious mysteries – need not stop us seeking truth, for we can plainly see that the truth is there and aim towards it.

90 *In so ill case here* in such an evil condition here on earth, or in matters of the salvation of one's soul.
ill] evil *MS*
here] Not in *1633–69 and several MSS*

91 *Signed kings blank-charters* given kings a free hand and moral right.

92 *vicars* proxies. Kings do not take over the function of Fate but are merely Fate's instruments; they cannot kill anyone whom God has not marked for martyrdom.

94 *man's*] men's *some MSS*
shall not be tried] shall be tried *1635–54*

95 *Or will*] Oh will *some MSS*; Will *1633 and some MSS*
boot] serve *some MSS*
boot thee do you any good.

96-7 *Philip ... Gregory, | ... Harry ... Martin* Philip II of Spain;
Pope Gregory VII (who established the papal claim to infallibility and
to final power over secular rulers), or the then Pope, Gregory XIV;
Henry VIII, the originator of the English Church; Martin Luther.

97 *thee*] me *1669*

98-9 *Is not this excuse for mere contraries, | Equally strong* does not
the same excuse that one must perforce obey authority hold equally for
directly opposite religious factions, who cannot both be right?

101 *Those past* once power oversteps its proper limits.
   is] are *1669*

104 *At the rough stream's calm head* the ultimate source of earthly
power is God himself, and those who root themselves around the source
itself prosper.
   prove] do *1633-69 and several MSS*

105-6 *themselves given | To the stream's tyrannous rage* yielding
themselves not to God's power but to the will of earthly tyrants, which
is the more violent and arbitrary the further it moves from God.

107 *mills, and rocks*] mills, rocks *1635-69 and most MSS*

SATIRE 4 WELL; I MAY NOW RECEIVE, AND DIE

The compiler of an early MS, the poet Drummond of Hawthornden,
wrote 'anno 1594' beside this poem. But one event mentioned in the
poem occurred in March 1597 (line 114) and seems to have been current
news when Donne was writing.

1 *receive* receive the last sacrament. He accounts himself thoroughly
shriven by the purgatory he has been through.

2 *but I*] but yet I *1635-69 and some MSS*

4 *recreation, and scant*] recreation to, and scarce *MS*
   recreation, and scant map of this All the early versions save one
make hell a mere re-creation and inadequate map of the torment the
poet had just endured. But the reading 'recreation to, and scarce map'
suggests that the hell we fear is just a pleasant entertainment compared
to the torment he has lately endured, and a poor shadow of it.

5 *neither*] not *MS*; nor *several MSS*

7 *no suit ... nor new suit* no petition ... nor new costume.

8 *Glaze*] Glare *1635–69 and some MSS*

9 *To a Mass*] To Mass *1633–69 and several MSS*
catched arrested for participating in a prohibited ceremony.

10 *the Statute's curse* The penalty decreed by the Statute of the year 1580 was a hundred marks for attending Mass, two hundred marks and a year in prison for presiding at Mass. A hundred marks represented something over £65 at the value of the day.

12 *(Guilty of my sin of going)* since the poet stood guilty of the sin of going to Court at all he must expect to suffer for all the sins that being a courtier comprehends, and his punishment is to endure the conversation of a courtier.
of going] in going *1633–54 and several MSS*
14 *proud, as lustful*] proud, lustful *1635–69 and some MSS*

16 *at Court*] in Court *1633–69 and MS*

18 *Nile's*] Nilus' *some MSS*

18–19 *than on Nile's slime the sun / E'er bred* The Egyptian sun generated strange living creatures out of the mud of the Nile, according to Pliny.

20 *posed* nonplussed.

21 *seven* many.

22 *Guiana's rarities* Raleigh described these in 1596. They included strange people, such as the Amazons and Anthropophagi, as well as monstrous animals.

23 *strangers*] strangest *several MSS*
strangers foreigners.

24 *the Danes' Massacre* The Danish settlers were massacred throughout England in the year 1012 at the order of King Ethelred the Unready.

26 *When next the 'prentices 'gainst strangers rise* The London apprentices took the lead in expressing the City's hostility to foreign traders, and were always threatening a renewal of the riots of the previous reign.

27–9 *One, whom the watch ... / ... the examining Justice sure would cry, / 'Sir, by your priesthood ... what you are.'* the Justice to whom the noonday watch brings him for examination would think him a Jesuit or seminarist in disguise, and as such, liable to execution.

32   *much ground*] much the ground *MS*
 ground   the fabric itself.

33   *tufftaffaty*   taffeta with a pile arranged in tufts.

34   *rash*   smooth fabric – silk, serge, or worsted.

35   *This*] The *1635–69*
 saith] faith *1669*

36   *only knoweth what to all states belongs*   he alone understands the
several conditions of men and of politics everywhere.

37   *th' accents*] the ancient *MS*; the ancients *MS*
 accents   The stress falls on the second syllable – accénts

38   *one language*] no language *several MSS*
 speaks one language   he speaks none of the languages he affects to
know but only one language made up of scraps of each of them.

41   *Mountebank's drugtongue*   a quack-doctor's sales talk.
 terms of law   legal jargon.

42   *enough preparatives*] preparatives enough *several MSS*

43   *bear*] hear *1669*

44   *compliment*   the jargon of courtly address.

45   *widows*   presumably rich and gullible widows.
 pay scores   settle bills.

46   *cozen*   cheat.

47   *or*] and *some MSS*

48   *Jovius, or Surius*   Paolo Giovio and Laurentius Surius, Counter-
Reformation historians and hagiologists, whose rendering of the religious
upheavals of the earlier sixteenth century outraged Protestants.
 Surius] Sleydan *several MSS*; Snodons *MS*

50   *thy wrath's furious rod*   the courtier, who afflicts the poet as
God's scourge might do.

51   *chooseth*] chaseth *several MSS*

53   *the best linguist*   the speaker means the man who knows most
languages; the poet wilfully takes him to mean the most learned lexico-
grapher or philologist.
 sillily   innocently.

54 *Calepine's Dictionary* the polyglot dictionary covering eleven languages developed out of a Latin Dictionary by A. Calepine, 1502.

55 *Beza* a Calvinist theologian who translated the Greek New Testament into Latin, 1556, and wrote copiously in Latin and French.

56 *Some other*] Some *1633-69 and most MSS*

57 *our two Academies* Oxford and Cambridge. A marginal note in one early MS identifies the two reverend men as 'Dr Reynolds and Dr Andrewes', that is, John Reynolds of Corpus Christi and Lancelot Andrewes of Pembroke Hall, both of whom later had a hand in the Authorized Version.
  There] here *1635-69*

58 *Apostles* they spoke with the gift of tongues at Pentecost (Acts ii 4, 6).

59 *Good pretty*] Pretty good *some MSS*
  Panurge a character in Rabelais's *Gargantua and Pantagruel* who knew a dozen languages.

60 *gentleman, all*] gentleman; all *1633-69*

62 *wonders*] words *1633 and several MSS*

65 *Babel's bricklayers* God confounded the language of the builders of the city and tower of Babel so that they could not understand one another and abandoned the enterprise.
  the] that *several MSS*

67-8 *loneness ... / ... loneness*] loneliness ... / ... loneliness *1633 and several MSS*

67-8 *not alone / My loneness is* 'I am never less alone than when I am alone' (Cicero, *De Officiis* III i 1).

68 *Spartan's fashion* Plutarch says that the Spartans warned young warriors against drunkenness by showing them disgustingly drunken serfs.

69 *last*] taste *1635-54 and several MSS*

70 *Aretine's pictures* a celebrated set of erotic paintings by Giulio Romano, generally ascribed in England to Pietro Aretino who in fact wrote the obscene sonnets that accompanied them.

80 *King Street* Stowe's *Survey of London* (1603) shows that King's

Street led up to the bridge over Long Ditch that gave access to the city of Westminster.

81 *smacked* clapped his hands.
mechanic low.

82–3 *'your Englishmen ... / ... your Frenchmen ....' 'Mine? ...'* the poet again wilfully misunderstands, taking as possessive the fashionable idiom 'your' which at most indicates a typical case.
Mine?] Fine *1633*; Mine *1669*

84 *I have but one Frenchman* References in his letters suggest that Donne did have a French servant at some point in his career.
Frenchman] Sir *1635–69 and MS*; here *MS*

86 *Your only wearing is your grogaram* grosgrain is the only material worth wearing. The poet's reply again takes the idiom literally, as if it meant that he has no clothes made of other material.
your grogaram] this grogaram *most MSS*; the grogaram *MS*

87–8 *Under this pitch | He would not fly* he would not pitch his speech lower than this highflown style.

91 *Crossing* running counter to his meaning, crossing him.

92 *dress*] address *1633 and several MSS*

94 *still* an apparatus for distilling.

97 *Holinsheads ... Halls ... Stows* sixteenth-century chroniclers of British history and life, who give much the same importance to domestic gossip and old wives' tales as to affairs of state.
or ... or] and ... and *several MSS*

98 *trash he knows; he knows*] trash. He knows; he knows *1635–69*

102 *an office's reversion* the succession to some important position of state.

103 *who hath*] who *several MSS*

104 *A licence* Some courtiers had power to grant licences and monopolies for commercial enterprises, and feathered their nests thereby. The point here though is that the man on the make sells real substance, his land, for the price of a bribe which will get him the licence to make a quick profit out of trash.
and] or *some MSS*

105 *transport* import and export.

106   *span-counter*   a variant of marbles.
   blow-point   another forfeit game, played with and for the 'points'
or tags which fastened the hose to the doublet.
   they pay] shall pay *1633-69 and MS*

108   *what*] which *most MSS*

109   *home-meats*   domestic gossip.
   tries] cloys *1635-69 and several MSS*: tires *several MSS*

111   *thrusts on more*] thrusts more *some MSS*; thrusts me more *some
MSS*; thrusts me *MS*
   he undertook] he had undertook *1635-69 and some MSS*

112   *Gallo-Belgicus*   *Mercurius Gallo-Belgicus* was the title of a Latin
register of current events. See Donne's Epigram on it, and my note.

113-14   *since | The Spaniards came*   1588, the year of the Armada.

114   *the loss of Amiens*   Amiens fell to the Spaniards in March 1597,
and the French recaptured it in the following September.

115   *a big wife*   a pregnant woman.

116   *sigh*] belch *several MSS*

117   *this*] his *some MSS*
   Macaron   a foolish fop.
   talk: in vain] talk in vain *1633 and MS*; talk, in vain *1635-69*

119   *a privileged spy*   an informer, who draws people on and entraps
them by himself uttering libels and treason.

122   *delayed*   impeded by political connivance and corruption.

123-4   *offices are entailed, and that there are | Perpetuities of them*   the
line of succession to the chief offices of state has been settled in per-
petuity.
   and that there] and there *1635-54*

125   *great officers*   high authorities.

126   *pirates ... Dunkirkers*   Dunkirk was the headquarters of the
channel pirates.

130   *turn*] turned *MS*

132   *giant Statutes*   the statutory enactments against treason, which
were both comprehensive and menacing.
   Statutes] Statues *1639*

134-6] *Replaced by dashes in 1633.*

134 *burnt venomed lechers* lechers covered with the poisonous sores of syphilis. They were supposed to be able to cure themselves by passing the disease on to somebody else.
  venomed] venomous *1669*; venom *1635-54*

139 *to my power* to the limit of my power.

141 *mercy now*] my redemption *several MSS*; redemption now *several MSS*

143 *can you spare me* can you spare me money? The poet affects to misunderstand, taking the phrase to mean 'Can you now spare my company?'

145 *Gave*] Give *several MSS*

148 *complimental* full of courtly compliment.

150 *the prerogative of my crown* (a) the special power of the poet's money has bought the man off; (b) the poet exercises his sovereign choice in getting rid of him.
  scant hardly.

152 *more strange things than*] such strange things as *1669*

154 *actions* lawsuits against him.
  make] haste *1633-69 and several MSS*

156 *precious*] piteous *1635-69 and some MSS*
  precious fastidious.

158 *his, who dreamed he saw hell* Dante.

159 *on*] o'er *1635-69 and some MSS*
  me, such] me; and such *several MSS*

161 *Becomes* befits.

162 *raised* men raised to noble rank, not born into it.

164 *huffing braggart*] huffing, braggart *1635-54 and several MSS*

166 *the whole world*] the world *several MSS*

169 *your*] yon *some MSS*; the *some MSS*
  waxen garden the lines suggest that an artificial garden of wax, made in Italy, was exhibited in London; but nothing is known of it.

170 *Transported*] Transplanted *some MSS*
  to stand] to Strand *several MSS*

171 *flouts* mocks.
our Presence] our Court here *some MSS*; our Courtiers *1635–69 and MS*
our Presence (a) our Royal Court or the people who attend the Queen there; (b) our demeanour.

174 *stocks* (a) tree trunks or stems; (b) lines of descent.
fruits issues, actions. 'A good tree cannot bring forth evil fruit; neither can a corrupt tree bring forth good fruit. ... Wherefore by their fruits ye shall know them' (Matthew vii 18, 20).

175 *mews* stables or riding schools.

176 *Balloon* a game like handball.
diet (a) a council of state; (b) a course of aphrodisiacal food in preparation for a visit to the brothel, or of curative food in consequence of recent visits.
stews brothels.

178 *made ready* costumed.
are found] were found *1635–54*

180 *their apparels*] th'apparels *some MSS*

182 *cry the flatterers*] cry his flatterers *1635–54*; cries his flatterers *some MSS*; cries the flatterer *1669 and MS*

184 *Wants reach all states* great and small alike are hard up and living on borrowed goods.
me seems] me thinks *several MSS*

186 *o'er*] in *several MSS*
Cheapside books the ledgers of the Cheapside tailors from whom these courtiers have had their clothes on account, and whom they thus dare not go near for fear of being dunned for payment.

188 *do know*] did know *some MSS*

189 *cochineal* spelled 'cutchannel' in early versions. Cochineal brought from South America was used for making scarlet dye, and highly prized. Evidently the court ladies are highly rouged.

192–4 *Why goods wits ne'er wear scarlet gowns ... / ... which scarlets dye* the reason that good wits never win the scarlet robes of high office is that courtiers buy up their wit to embellish fine speeches, and court ladies buy up all the scarlet dye for cosmetics.

193 *these*] those *several MSS*

194 *scarlets*] scarlet *some MSS*

195 *called*] calls *some MSS*
   lime-twigs . . . net traps for birds, a bathetic compliment.

196 *drugs ill laid* make-up unevenly laid on.

197 *Heraclitus* known as the weeping philosopher because he made transience the condition of all being.

198 *refine* make elegant.

199 *As if the Presence were a moschite*] As the Queen's Presence were a meschite *several MSS*
   moschite mosque.

199–200 *lift / His skirts and hose* straighten his hems and stockings.

200 *shrift* confession.

202 *venial* pardonable or reparable sins, such as their 'fornication' with feathers and dust which can be amended by brushing them down.

203 *wherewith*] with which *several MSS*

204 *Dürer's rules* Durer's *Of Human Proportion* (1582) sets out the rules of proportion for representing the human body.

205 *odds* proportions.

209 *his*] the *several MSS*

211 *he arrests*] straight arrests *most MSS*
   arrests buttonholes.

212 *protests* protests his love.

213 *at Rome* such a deal of protestation as would suffice to have ten Cardinals condemned as Protestants.

215 *whispered*] whispers *1635–69*

216] Topcliffe would have ravished him quite away *several MSS*
   Pursuivant an officer who executes warrants of state, in this case by hunting out covert Roman Catholics. The courtier's oath 'by Jesu' would lay him under suspicion in this country as his protesting would, for the opposite reason, in Rome.
   The Topcliffe named in some MSS was in fact the most notorious pursuivant of the day, a kind of head of secret police.

217 *saying of our*] saying our *some MSS*
our Lady's] Jesus' *MS*

220–21 *only doth* / *Call* ... *good fashion* calls nothing else good fashion but a rough carelessness.

222 *whom*] or whom *1635–69 and MS*

223 *not, his*] not he. His *1633–69*

225 *meant*] came *some MSS*

226 *theirs which in old hangings whip Christ* the villainous faces of the men who scourge Christ, as the scene is depicted in old tapestries.
still] yet still *1633 and several MSS*

229 *I leave*] I'll leave *some MSS*

230 *men which from*] men from *1633–69*

231–2 *hung* / *With the seven deadly sins* seven Flemish tapestries representing the seven deadly sins did hang at Hampton Court, and still do.

232–6] sins) being ... / ... wine. *1633–39*; sins?) being ... / ... wine *1650–69*

233 *Ascaparts* Ascapart was a giant, thirty feet tall, in the old romance of Bevis of Hampton. The poet has now moved into the Guard Chamber where the Queen's bodyguard scrutinize the traffic in and out of the Presence.

234 *Charing Cross* the cross set up by Edward I.
for a bar Throwing the bar was a sport much like tossing the caber. But the yeomen warders carried a halberd or bar, and to throw the bar may simply have been to manage this weapon.

235–6 *fine* / *Living, barrels*] fine / Living barrels *1633–54*
barrels of beef, flagons of wine the guard – the original beef-eaters – resemble the viands they consume in vast quantities.
beef, flagons] beef, and flagons *1669*

237 *spied* espied, detected.

238 *Seas of wit and arts*] Seas of wits and arts *1633 and some MSS*; Seas of wit and art *several MSS*; Great seas of wit and art *several MSS*

238 *you can, then dare* you have the power, then have the courage to use it against the Court too.

239 *Drown*] To drown *several MSS*
Drowns the sins   as God drowned the sinful world at the Flood.

240 *Which am but a scarce brook*] Which am but a scant brook *1635–69*;
Who am a scant brook *some MSS*; Who am a shallow brook *some MSS*
scarce   meagre, inadequate.

241 *the*] their *most MSS*; these *several MSS*

242 *Maccabees' modesty*   The apocryphal Books of the Maccabees end
with a humble submission to the reader's judgement: 'And if I have
done well, and as is fitting the story, it is that which I desired; but if
slenderly and meanly, it is that which I could attain unto' (2 Maccabees
xv 38).
the known merit] the merit *some MSS*

243 *man*] men *1650–69 and some MSS*

244 *canonical*   (a) orthodox; falling within the accepted canon as
Maccabees does not, or falling within the law; (b) authoritative, because
what they say is true; (c) meriting approval (or reward) by the accepted
canons of judgement.

SATIRE 5   THOU SHALT NOT LAUGH IN THIS LEAF, MUSE

This poem as it stands could not have been written before 1592 (line 85)
or later than 1603 (line 28). If the person Donne addresses in lines 31–4
is Sir Thomas Egerton, the Lord Keeper, then he must have written the
poem while he was Egerton's secretary, between 1598 and 1601/2. In
that case 1598 seems the likely date.

Title] Satire 5. Of the misery of the poor suitors at Court *MS*

2–6 *he which did lay / Rules to make courtiers*   Castiglione in *Il
Cortegiano* (1528) says that 'it provoketh no laughter to mock and scorn
a silly soul in misery and calamity, nor yet a naughty knave and common
ribald, because a man would think that these men deserved to be other-
wise punished, than in jesting at' (*The Courtier*, trans. T. Hoby (1561),
II).

7 *Charity and liberty give me*   charity to pity the wretched and liberty
to accuse the wicked.

8 *officers' ... suitors'*   high officials of state or the law; and those who
petition them for justice or favours.

9 *and*] in *1669*
If all things be in all   if every part of the natural creation reproduces
in little the constitution of the whole.

12 *implies*] employs *1633 and some MSS*

13 *man* the human race.

14 *ravishing*] ravenous *MS*; ravening *several MSS*

16 *self* same.

24 *wasteful* destructive; consuming; useless.

25 *and you fight it* suitors fight against themselves by sustaining the people who destroy them.

25-6 *they | Adulterate law* great officers falsify law by prostituting it to their interests, when its true duty is the protection of their suitors.

26 *their*] the *1635-69 and several MSS*

27 *wittols* husbands who connive at their wife's adultery.
   issue outcome; children illicitly begotten, who ruin their legal father by devouring his goods or inheriting what would otherwise be his.

28 *Empress* Queen Elizabeth.

31 *You Sir, whose righteousness she loves* possibly Sir Thomas Egerton, who became Lord Keeper of England in 1596 and made Donne his secretary in 1598. He stood for justice and legal reform in the last years of the Queen's reign, and under James I became Lord Chancellor.

31-3 *whom I | . . . authorized* the privilege of serving a righteous man in itself richly repays the poet's labours and justifies his attack on injustices.

33 *now begin* he enjoins this person to start a campaign against the legal corruptions which the poem exposes. From 1597 on Egerton led a struggle to reform the Star Chamber.

37-9]   was sold (now
       Injustice is sold dearer) did allow
       All claimed fees and duties. Gamesters anon
       (*1635-54 and several MSS*)

38-41 *allow | . . . other hands* suitors are gamblers with the law who will find that by the time they have allowed for all the demands, fees and duties that a lawsuit entails, they themselves have nothing left for their efforts (Dickens made the same point in *Bleak House* over two hundred and fifty years later).

39 *All demands, fees*] All claimed fees *some MSS*

40 *swear for* take oaths for (which will imperil your soul if they are perjured).

41 *controverted* disputed.

42 *'Scape, like Angelica* In Ariosto's *Orlando Furioso* the heroine Angelica several times escapes from rival suitors for her love and body while they are fighting over her.

43 *If law be in the judge's heart* if law is merely the judge's personal inclincation.

44 *letter, or fee* influence or bribe.

45 *the courts below* magistrates' courts and the like, whose power draws from the courts above them and ultimately from the central judiciary, so that if the source is tainted one has no appeal from the corruptions of the lower branches.

46 *Flow*] Flows *MS*

50 *when upwards* when swimming upstream means also moving upwards, complaining from the lesser to the greater.

52 *the*] thy *1635–69*

54 *Forced to make golden bridges* compelled to get over by bribes.

57 *Judges are gods* 'I have said, Ye are gods' (Psalm lxxxii). The Psalm calls upon temporal authorities to 'Defend the poor and fatherless' and 'see that such as are in need and necessity have right'.
  he who made and said them so] and he who made them so *1669*
  said] called *MS*
  said them so declared them so.

59 *angels* gold coins.

60–61 *Dominations, / Powers, Cherubins* the orders of angels.

61 *courts*] Court *1635 and some MSS*

63 *so 'tis* this is how things are.

65–8 *To see a pursuivant come in ... / And ask a fee for coming?* Pursuivants rooting out Roman Catholics looked for the evidence of Catholic observances, such as vestments, liturgical utensils, and manuals of devotion. The legalized witch-hunt laid anyone who owned old books or plate open to blackmail and the loss of their possessions, sometimes at the hands of frauds posing as pursuivants.

65 *call* name as prohibited instruments.

67 *mistake* mis-take, take away by fraud.

68 *ask*] lack *1633-54 and MS*

72 *and but tells us who*] and tells who *1633-69 and some MSS*

73 *chairs* high offices.

76 *th'extremities*] extremities *1633-69*

78 *comes to*] can come to *MS*

79 *barest* take your hat off, bare your head.

80 *which erst men*] which men *1633 and some MSS*; which men erst *several MSS*

82 *dole* good fortune; just share.
    these corrupt officers of the law.

83 *Urim and Thummim* certain mysterious objects worn by the Jewish High Priest which empowered him to speak as the will of Jehovah (see Deuteronomy xxxiii 8). The Hebrew words mean 'doctrine and truth' or 'light and integrity'.

84 *for all hast paper* the suitor seeking to recover his goods is furnished with vast quantities of documents concerning them.

85 *clothe* wrap in small twists, as pepper was commonly sold.
    the Great Carrack's pepper the *Great Carrack* was a huge Spanish merchant vessel captured in 1592 with a cargo of hundreds of tons of pepper.

86 *Sell that . . . more shalt leese* if the suitor sells the documents for their value as paper, that is all that he will get out of his going to law.
    leese lose.

87 *Haman*] Hammon *1635-69 and MS*; Hammond *some MSS*
    when] if *1635-54 and some MSS*
    Haman, when he sold his antiquities Haman is named in some *MSS* versions of the Epigram *Antiquary*. The suggestion is that his collection is so much junk.

88 *moralize* afford the moral for.

89 *make tales, prophecies* make Aesop's fables a prophecy of your fortunes.

90 *the swimming dog* trying to snatch the meat from the mouth of his own reflected image, the dog released and lost the real meat he held.
    cozened] cozeneth *1669*
    cozened Pronounced as three syllables.

91 *And*] Which *1635–69*; Who *MS*
    div'st] div'dst *several MSS*; div'd *some MSS*
    what vanished] what vanisheth *1669*; what's vanished *MS*
    vanished Pronounced as three syllables.

UPON MR THOMAS CORYAT'S CRUDITIES

First printed in *Coryat's Crudities hastily gobbled up in five months' travels* (1611); first given in an edition of Donne's poems in 1649.

Thomas Coryate (?1577–1617) was a learned eccentric who served Prince Henry. His *Crudities* give a diverting account of a European journey he made in 1608, but some Court wag thought to make sport of it by getting all the wits of the day to write mock-panegyrics which were printed with the book as prefatory commendations. Donne's poem is one of these, and alludes closely to episodes in the book.

2 *leavened*] learned *1649–69*
    leavened puffed-up.
    sesqui-superlative superlative, and half as much again.

3 *Venice' vast lake* the Lagoon.

4 *Some vaster thing . . . a courtesan* An obscene innuendo. Venetian courtesans were famous, and Coryate wrote about them admiringly.

6 *A cellar gulf* the Great Tun of Heidelberg, which in Coryate's reckoning held some 28,000 gallons of wine. Donne's point is that Coryate has made a rake's progress in gulfs in passing from Venice to her courtesans, thence to this sea of wine, and may now sail to hell in drink.

10 *study it to any end* (a) find a proper ending in it; (b) finish it; (c) read it with profit.

14–16 *thy book doth half make man. | . . . never touch* it makes people laugh, though it does not call for a use of reason having no reason in it.

17 *lunatic* (a) madman, governed by the changes of the moon; (b)

moon-like being, who is still waxing and may write at still greater length when he is at full.

22 *Munster* Sebastian Munster, to whose *Cosmographia Universalis* (1541) Coryate acknowledged a debt.

Gesner Konrad von Gesner, who listed authors in his *Bibliotheca Universalis* (1545).

23 *Gallo-Belgicus* See note on the Epigram *Mercurius Gallo-Belgicus*.

24 *gazetteer*] garretteir *1649-69*

gazetteer a journalist, one who writes in a gazette of the kind said to have been first devised in Venice in the sixteenth century.

26 *Prester Jack* Prester John was the mythical priest-king of Ethiopia or the Orient, who was supposed to guard fabulous wealth.

29 *both Indies* the 'Indias of spice and mine' (*The Sun Rising* 17).

31 *upon the press* on getting his vast tome into print; though without any prospect of recovering the money he spent on it.

33 *thy leaves must embrace what comes from thence* the pages of the book will be used to wrap spices.

35 *magnifies* makes them more splendid and important.

36 *neighbour* adjacent.

39 *tons*] tomes *1611*

41 *a better method* if they reduce these huge quantities to small packages for sale.

43 *vent* vend; issue.

44 *Home-manufactures* home-made confectioneries.
thick crowded.

45-6 *omni-pregnant . . . / . . . the buyer calls* wrapping up every sort of goods for sale and hatching the appropriate kind, as if by the heat of the stall, when the buyer asks for it.

48 *all kind of matter comprehend* the book will be in this literal way a universal compendium of matter.

50 *pandect* a complete body of the laws of any country or system; a treatise covering the whole of a subject.

53 *prize* prey and victims, as ships are the prize of pirates who loot and destroy them.

54 *cut in anatomies* cut up for lessons in anatomy, as the bodies of executed felons sometimes were.

55-7 *for a lord | Which casts at portescues . . . | Provide whole books* Coryate's pages will provide whole books of counters for lords and the whole school of gamesters who play for high stakes. (A gold portague was worth over £4.)

57-8 *each leaf enough will be | For friends to pass time, and keep company* one leaf will suffice for counters when friends play cards for pastime and company.

59 *carouse up thee* drink your health.

59-60 *fit/Measures* fit the quantity of drink to the occasion.

60 *fill out for the half-pint wit* fill the glasses only so far as will meet the half-pint of wit they are toasting.

62 *stop muskets* Early cartridges were just charges of powder wrapped in paper.

64 *at once their hunger to assuage* to satisfy at one go their hunger to read you (they will instead have the trouble of running around reading him in fragments, a bit here and a bit there).

65 *wit-pirates* thieves of others' wit, plagiarizing hacks.

66 *in one bottom* in one ship, as it were, which a wit-pirate might capture intact. Literally, in one book.

67 *paste strings there in other books* Bookbinders pasted paper from unwanted stock over the strings that tied the quires of a book together.

68 *which on another looks* who is reading a work by somebody else, pasted up with scraps of Coryate's book.

70 *But hardly much* he will be hard put to it to get much wit out of Coryate's book in any case.

71-2 *As Sibyl's was, your book is mystical, | For every piece is as much worth as all* The Cumaean Sibyl offered to sell Tarquinius Superbus nine books of prophecy; when he refused her high price she burned all but three of the books and demanded the same price again under threat of burning the rest. He paid. But presumably Coryate's book is mystical in that the whole is worth as *little* as any part.

73-4 *mine impotency I confess . . . | . . . be far less* he is impotent to honour Coryate's book as it deserves for his brain will not bear such heady draughts of compliment as are in order.

74 *healths* salutations; toasts drunk in honour of Coryate.

75 *Thy giant wit o'erthrows me* he cannot cope with the sheer bulk of Coryate's display of wit.

In eundem macaronicon in the macaronic manner. Macaronic verses are strictly a mixture of the vernacular and Latin in which the vernacular words take Latin forms; but the term can mean any poem written in a jumble of languages.

77–80 *Quot, dos haec ... / ... n'estre creduto, tibi* your book will make as many prudent statesmen as these two distichs make perfect linguists. To me the honour of being understood in this is sufficient; for I leave to you the honour of being believed by no one.

Explicit finished. ..

The Progress of the Soul (Metempsychosis)

THE PROGRESS OF THE SOUL (METEMPSYCHOSIS)

This is the first poem in the edition of *1633*. Most early versions bear the date 16 August 1601.

Commentators in general have found this poem puzzling, partly because it is unfinished, so that we do not know certainly who was to receive the migratory soul in the end and what Donne would have made of the whole progress. As it stands, the power of the satire lies in the picture of the world that emerges as the soul activates now this, now that kind of body, showing us a telling similarity of behaviour in the diverse conditions of being. In one way the poem offers an allegory of civil society, stripping away the mask of morality or dignity to expose a ravening jungle of self-interest. In another way it ironically marks our degeneracy at this distance from the Fall, for its characters are at once far more virile than we, standing so much nearer the created state of things, and exactly like us in their motives as fallen creatures; with their original capacities still very little diminished, and without our restraint of law, they are as we would be.

Infinitati Sacrum sacred to infinity. There seems to be a play on the Pythagorean notion of an endless cycle of transmigration, and on the fact that the poem is unfinished or unfinishable. Donne may be suggesting that however far the poem followed the progress of the soul around the several orders of being, the same pattern of conduct would emerge.

Metempsychosis transmigration of the soul, the 'passage of the soul of a human being or animal at or after death into a new body of the same or a different species' (*OED*). It was thought to be a tenet of the Pythagoreans.

Poëma Satyricon a satiric poem.

EPISTLE

3 *through light* (a) transparent; (b) wholly frivolous.

5 *tax* challenge, question.

9 *sine talione* without retaliation. The *lex talionis* is the law of an eye for an eye, a tooth for a tooth.

11 *Trent Council* The Council of Trent (1542) instituted an index of prohibited books. But it did not in fact ban authors rather than their particular writings.

22 *would*] will *1633–69*

27 *mushroom*] maccron *1635–69 and MS* mucheron *1633 and several MSS*

27–8 *no unreadiness in the soul, but an indisposition in the organs* the soul in itself is fit to occupy any living body, human, animal or vegetable; but its capacities in the body are limited by the body's faculties.

30 *and now*] and can now *1635–69*

33 *who used it for poison* spiders were thought to convert food to poison in their bodies (see *Twicknam Garden* 6 and note).
   dignity rank, office.

36 *her relation* her own telling.

37 *making* what she did; making headway, success.

38 *she is he*] she is she *1635–69 and MS*

38–9 *he, whose life you shall find in the end of this book* since the poem was not finished we do not know who this ultimate recipient of the soul was to be. Ben Jonson told Drummond of Hawthorden that it was to have occupied the bodies of all the heretics from Cain and finished up in Calvin (*Conversations* 136). Gosse and Grierson assumed that it was to be Queen Elizabeth herself, chiefly on the evidence of lines 61–70. W. Milgate argues that it could not be either Calvin or Queen Elizabeth since both their lives overlap one of the named recipients of the soul, Luther.

THE PROGRESS OF THE SOUL

2 *control* restrain, check.

3 *the law* the law given to Moses in the Ten Commandments.

7 *gold*] cold *1635–54*

7–8 *gold Chaldee ... silver Persian ... / Greek brass ... Roman iron* the successive civilizations of the world, progressively deteriorating from gold to iron.

9 *Seth's pillars, brick and stone* Josephus tells how the children of Seth (who was Adam's son) set up inscribed pillars of brick and stone to perpetuate for mankind their discovery of the cosmic sciences.

10 *writ*] writs *1633 and several MSS*

11 *eye of heaven* the sun.

12 *thy male force* the sun was assumed to be the source of procreative power and the begetter of life.

16 *Danow*] Danon *1633*
   Danow Danube.

17 *western land of mine* the West Indies, reputed to be rich in gold.

19 *before thee, one day*] one day before thee *MS*
   before thee, one day the soul came into being with the vegetable life on the third day of creation, the sun when God decreed light on the fourth day.

21 *Nor, holy Janus*] Nor holy Janus *1633–69*
   holy Janus Noah, who like Janus looked two ways, to the world before the flood and the world after it. Noah was accounted the first priest.
   sovereign all-saving.

22 *The Church, and all the monarchies* the Ark was a type of the Church; but it also carried with it the entire destiny of ensuing mankind, all the kingdoms to come.

23 *college* (a) company, society; (b) centre of learning in which Noah passed on the wisdom of the times before the Flood.
   hospital (a) sanctuary; (b) place of healing.

24 *vivary* vivarium, a place in which living animals are kept.

26 *latest nephews* most recent descendants.

27 *From thence*] For, thence *MS*

30 *informed by this heavenly spark* occupied by the 'deathless soul' whose transmigrations the poem describes.

33 *where we offspring took* where our actions have consequences that we cannot foresee or control.

35 *Knot of all causes* resolver of all actions or purposes.

36 *vouch thou safe*] vouch safe thou *1633-69*

41 *six lustres* a lustre was five years, and Donne was thus nearly thirty years old when he wrote this poem.

43 *lets* hindrances.

47 *calls from this* lures him from the business of writing the poem.
t'other] to other *1633 and MS*

49 *Th' expense* the expenditure.

52 *this sea* the task of writing.

54 *shall*] hold *1635-69*
lone] love *1633 and some MSS*

55 *dark heavy ... light, and light* one 'light' is the opposite of 'dark', the other of 'heavy'.

57 *launch at paradise ... sail towards home* he begins with Eden and moves towards the England of his own day.

60 *Tigris, and Euphrates* traditionally, the two rivers of Paradise.

61 *For the*] For this *several MSS*; For that *MS*

62-3 *that hand, and tongue, and brow, | Which as the moon the sea, moves us* Presumably this is the latest host of the soul and it is plainly not Calvin. Whatever happens in the rest of the poem this reference seems to fit no one but Queen Elizabeth, whom Raleigh had celebrated as the moon in *The Ocean to Cynthia*.

68 *wracks* injuries, ruins.
th' Empire, and late Rome the Holy Roman Empire, and the Church of Rome in recent times, both of them torn apart by heresies and then mended again by heresy.

69 *when*] where *some MSS*

71 *room* relative standing, position.

73-8 *That Cross ... | Stood in the self same room in Calvary, | Where* *first grew the forbidden learned tree* This idea occurs elsewhere in Donne as a received hypothesis, though it seems to be peculiar to him (see the *Hymn to God my God, in my Sickness* 21–2).

80 *from pulling free* exempt from plucking.

82 *the law* God's edict forbidding Adam and Eve to pluck the fruit.

87 *her*] whose *MS*
  only forbiddings drive one can get them to do something only by forbidding them to do it.

90 *treason taints the blood* the descendants of a man convicted of treason were held to be tainted by his crime, and could not inherit from him or recover the property he forfeited.

94 *corrupt us, rivulets*] corrupt as rivulets *MS*; corrupt us nothing lets *MS*

96 *thrust*] thrusts *1633*

97 *from turning to whence we are fled* from returning to Paradise.

98–9 *Were prisoners judges . . . / She sinned, we bear* if we were the judges instead of the condemned men we might think it a harsh judgement that we should suffer for Eve's sin.

99 *bear*] here *1633*; hear *several MSS*

100 *them* women.

103 *curious* improperly inquisitive; sophistical.

112 *vanities*] vanity *1635–69*

114 *good mind* good intention.
  reasons] reason's *1635–69*

121 *the serpent's gripe* Some versions of the story of the Fall had the serpent pluck the apple and give it to Eve.

125 *old, one and another day* two days old.

127 *proof*] proofs *MS*

130 *earth's pores*] earth-pores *1633–50*

131 *abled* given strength.

134 *thronged* pressed, forced.

137 *the Prince, and have so filled*] the Princess, and so filled *1633*; the

Prince, and so fill up *1635-69*; the Prince, and so filled *several MSS*

141-50 *His right arm ... / ... conception kill* the plant has grown into a mandrake, a vegetable which is supposed to have had human shape and some human propensities.

142 *digest* divide, separate.

147 *middle parts*] middle part *1635-69*; mid-part *several MSS*

148-50 *in love's business he should still / A dealer be ... / His apples kindle, his leaves, force of conception kill* the fruits of the mandrake were reputed to kindle sexual desire, its leaves to abort conception.

150 *kindle*] kind *1633 and some MSS*

159-60 *the guest, / This living*] the guest / This living *1633-69*.

165 *moist red eyes* the name Cain was wrongly thought to mean 'perpetual weeping'.

169 *Unvirtuous* without medicinal properties or 'virtues'.

180 *enclosed*] enclothed *several MSS*; unclothed *1633*
picked] pecked *several MSS*; pricked *MS*; poked *MS*

185 *a new downy*] downy a new *1633*

194 *his next hen* the hen nearest him. Sparrows were reputed to be very lecherous.

195 *taste*] last *MS*

197 *pule* whine.

198 *change* transfer his sexual allegiance.

200 *Where store is of both kinds* where both male and female offer an abundance of sexual opportunity.

201 *till they took laws which made freedom less* before they allowed the sexual freedom of the Golden Age to give way to the rule of law (see *The Relic* 30 and note).

202 *ingress* enter.

203-5] Till now unlawful, therefore ill; 'twas not
       So jolly, that it can move this soul; is
       The body so free of his kindnesses,
                              (*1633 and 1669*)

> Till now, unlawful, therefore ill 'twas not
> So jolly, that it can move this soul. Is
> The body, so free of his kindnesses.
>
> *(1635-54)*

204 *jolly* sprightly; bold; lustful.

205 *free of* lavish with.

208 *straitens* tightens.

209 *blood, and spirit, pith, and marrow spends* sexual acts were assumed to shorten life. See *Farewell to Love* 24-5.

212 *gummy blood* the sticky sap of the holly, used to make bird-lime.

214 *hid*] his *1633-69 and several MSS*

217 *roots . . . cock-sparrows* some root-plants and the flesh or dung of the male sparrow were supposed to kindle desire and help conception.

219 *straitened* restricted; in privation.

220 *his race*] *Not in 1633*

227 *informed* occupied, gave form and life to.
  abled gave it power.

241 *a prison in a prison* the fish imprisoned the soul and the swan the fish.

249 *gone* lost, as an easy prey.

251 *her*] the *1633-69*

254 *windows* apertures.

257 *but few, and fit for use to get* nets were not made to catch everything but to catch only a few fish which were fit for eating.

260 *hardly* with difficulty.

266 *limbecks* alembics, stills.

267 *water*] weather *1633 and several MSS*

267-8 *faith / Cares not* how fishes breathe is not an article of faith.

270 *board* tack, as a ship against the wind.

274 *sea pie* oystercatcher.

276 *silly* harmless, foolish.
  disputing debating with itself.

291 *self* same.

294 *orator* advocate, representative.

296 *many leagues at sea*] leagues o'er past at sea *1633–69*; leagues at sea *some MSS*

298 *The soul's no longer foes* the soul's former foes who are so no longer.
  err wander.

300 *he lives yet in some great officer* some great state official still typically embodies the bird's nature as the best advocate of gluttony, who seizes small fry for more sport when he is not hungry.

301 *our*] this *MS*

302 *thrown out* put forth, extended.

304 *Morea* the Peloponnesus.

306 *severed* Pronounced as three syllables.

307 *the hopeful promontory's head* the tip of the Cape of Good Hope.

309 *overset* capsized.

310 *Hulling* floating along without sail.

315 *bark* outer covering, skin.

320 *seas above the firmament* The old cosmologists conjectured that there were waters beyond the zone of the fixed stars as there are seas here.

321 *officer*] favourite *MS*

322–3 *Stays in his court, as his own net, and there / All*] Lies still at Court, and is him self a net / Where *MS*

322 *Stays in his court, as his own net* like an officer of state he does not need to hunt but stays in his place (or his court) and waits for petitioners to enslave themselves to him.
  as] at *1633–69*; in *MS*

327 *Flyer and follower* pursued and pursuer.

328 *states* conditions of people; realms.

333 *roomful* roomy.

334-5 *like a Prince ... | ... distant as provinces* see *The Ecstasy* 65-8.

336-7 *The sun hath twenty times both crab and goat | Parched* twenty years have gone by, the sun has twenty times passed through the zodiacal divisions of Cancer and Capricorn.

337 *this*] his *1635-69*

339 *there's no pause at perfection* human affairs do not stay still; having reached perfection one cannot arrest the movement there.

340 *a period* a time when it is at its height; an end.

342-3 *not throughly armed | With hope that they could kill him* not wholly fortified by the hope of killing the vastly bigger fish.

344 *did not*] do not *several MSS*

345 *outstreat* exude.

346-7 *it might undo | The plot of all, that the plotters were two* the fact that there were two plotters might have wrecked the plot altogether because in the normal way of human affairs they would seek to betray one another.

349-50 *How shall a tyrant wise strong projects break, | ... the common anger wreak?* how may a despotic ruler hope to thwart shrewd and powerful plots against him when miserable wretches can so easily revenge the petty grievances of the common people upon him!

351 *thresher* the fox-shark, which lashes its opponent with its long tail.

353 *to beat* to lash the whale with its tail.

358 *well the*] were the *1633 and several MSS*; weareth *MS*

360 *his own dole* (a) he distributes rewards or alms still as a great being should, but the alms now is his own substance; (b) he is his own grief, no one else mourns for him.

365 *they, revenge*] they revenge, *1633*

366-8 *Nor will against such men the people go, | ... Love in that act.* there is no point now in their displaying their love for him by avenging his death, because he is dead and cannot appreciate the gesture.

368 *Some*] And *MS*

369–70 *that of their own | They think they lose* they think that love shown for a dead ruler diminishes the love which they themselves should have from their subjects.

371 *and passion* the passion of the individual being, from which the soul escapes when it leaves the body.

375 *strait cloister* narrow confine.

378 *reposed* settled.

383 *thought, no more had gone, to make one*] thought none had, to make him *1635–69*; thought nor had gone, to make one *MS*; had been King but that too *MS*

384 *But to be just, and thankful*] He was, just, thankful *MS*

385 *Yet*] For *MS*
  no knees to bend There was a popular but discredited belief that elephants have no knees; and they were also supposed to be the noblest of beasts. The point here is their innocence, in that they have not learned to crawl to great men for advancement.

388 *fantasy* imagination.

390 *remissly* negligently, slackly.

394 *life cords* All the body's nerves and sinews were assumed to emanate from the controlling brain (see *The Funeral* 9–11).

397 *meant*] went *several MSS*

398 *room* rank or station.

399 *his foe, his*] him for his *MS*

400 *Who cares not to turn back, may any whither come* a desperado who has no care for his own life may accomplish anything.

405–6 *in that trade of Church, and kingdoms . . . | Was the first type* Abel was traditionally a shepherd, hence the earliest type or figure of the Church. Some authorities also saw him as a type of the ruler because of the charge he had over his sheep.

406 *still infested* continually plagued.

411 *course*] way *MS*

416 *Attached her with strait grips* seized tight hold of her.

419 *Nor much resist*] Now must resist *MS*; now much resist *several MSS*; Resistance much *MS*
 straiten confine, hold tightly.

420 *nor bark*] not bark *1650–69 and several MSS*

421 *engaged* won her over to him.
 wholly] only *several MSS*
 bides remains.

422 *none*] no *several MSS*

427 *ends all*] ended *several MSS*; end and *several MSS*; ending *MS*

429–30 *that mass / Of blood in Abel's bitch* the embryonic offspring of the wolf. Physiologists of Donne's day supposed that sperm is the quintessence of the parents' blood, and that the foetus itself is at first just a lump of blood.

432 *lives of emperors*] life of Princes *MS*

434–6 *begot himself* since the soul has passed from the father to the offspring the offspring is at once the father and the son.

437 *A riddling lust* a form of sexual perversity that finds excitement in an enigma.

437–8 *schoolmen would miss / A proper name* even the medieval theologians would not be able to categorize so strange a sin.

439 *Moaba* The names of Adam's other children come from rabbinical tradition, not scripture. One Hebrew chronicle speaks of Seth's wife Nōba or Noaba, who is presumably Donne's Moaba.

443 *field. Being*] field, being *1633–69*
 kinds thus made] kinds made *1633*

446 *cozened* cheated, juggled.

447 *hopeless that his faults were hid* having no hope of keeping up the deceit.

448 *followed* Pronounced as three syllables.

450 *perished* Pronounced as three syllables.

451 *toyful* sportive, amorous.

452 *Gamesome* playful.

457 *Siphatecia* The tradition is that Adam's other daughters were

called Zifath and Hekhiah, names which (as Milgate points out) Donne seems to have telescoped here.

459 *fruits*] fruit *several MSS*

460 *of*] in *MS*

465 *vaulter's somersaults* feats such as people perform on the vaulting horse.

466 *hoiting gambols* frolicsome caperings.

468 *anger*] angers *several MSS*
  kind one's own nature; human nature altogether.

471 *proved* tried, experienced.

473 *through-vain* thoroughly vain.

475 *would*] could *MS*

476 *toys* amorous triflings.

479 *or awe*] of awe *1669*

480 *Nature hath no gaol, though she have law* one can go against the law of nature – behave unnaturally, as the ape does – without punishment.
  she have] she hath *1633 and MS*

481 *silly* naïve, innocent.

484 *now*] nor *1635-69*; then *several MSS*

485 *loth*] tooth *1633 and MS*; wroth *1635-69*

486 *outright* openly.

487 *Tethlemite*] Tethelemite *1633*; Thelemite *1635-69*
  Tethlemite the known sources give no name like this. Donne may have invented it.

488 *entered*] enters *several MSS*

489 *prevented* forestalled.

492 *where the ape would have gone in* from that part of a woman's body; not Siphatecia's body, in fact, but Eve's.

493 *mingled bloods* conception was supposed to follow from the mingling of bloods in coition (see *The Flea* 4).

494 *chemics' equal fires* the even heat of the fires by which alchemists sought to produce the philosopher's stone. Alchemical operations commonly paralleled the gestatory processes and were spoken of in the same way.

her Eve's.

496–8 *A spongy liver ... / ... unto every part* the liver was thought to control the supply of moisture to the body, and to make the blood.

499 *a thicker heart* thicker than the liver. The heart was assumed to be fleshy and thick because it had to kindle and preserve the body's heat.

500 *life's spirits* the substances that were supposed to permeate the blood and chief organs of the body, activating the vital functions.

503 *Those sinewy strings which do our bodies tie* See the note on line 194.

sinewy] sinew *1669*

504 *fast there by one end* the soul waits at the controlling centre in the brain for the sinews to link it to the limbs, as the limbs await the vital link with the soul.

505 *attend* await.

506–7 *some quality / Of every past shape* some part of the character of every being the soul had already inhabited.

508 *enow* enough.

509 *Themech* in Hebrew chronicle Cain's wife is called Téméd.

510 *Cain that first did plough* 'And Abel was a keeper of sheep, but Cain was a tiller of the ground' (Genesis iv 2).

511 *sullen* sombre; unaccommodating.

516 *Cain's race* in Genesis iv 17–22 various descendants of Cain are credited with the building of cities or are said to be the 'fathers' of particular crafts and arts.

517 *blessed Seth* Eve bore Seth after Abel's death and looked upon him as a second Abel; some commentators thus see him as a resurrected Abel, and a type of Christ. Noah descended from him.

astronomy astrology, the art concerned with prediction and with the occult influences of the stars. Some authorities say that Seth discovered astronomy, and some that Adam taught him it.

518 *There's nothing simply good, nor ill alone* nothing in this world is purely good (as God is) or purely evil (as the devil is). So bad men may benefit the human race and good men may simply cause it pain.

519-20 *comparison, | The only measure is* since there is nothing absolutely good or bad we can assess things only relatively, that is, as more good or less good in comparison with each other. But a world of relative values cannot be the object of certain knowledge. At best we can arrive at opinion, the 'middle station between ignorance and knowledge' (Donne, *Sermons* VI, 317), and rest our judgement on that.

Verse Letters

Humanist poets exchanged Latin letters in verse, or passed them around as rhetorical showpieces. Donne's verse letters amount to the first considerable body of such writing in English. That they were actually sent as letters now seems certain, for we have one of them in Donne's hand, just as he dispatched it from France early in 1612. He had written the poem out carefully on either side of a thin sheet of gilt-edged quarto notepaper, then folded the manuscript into a small packet and put the recipient's name on the outside, presumably for inclusion in a bag of mail to be delivered by courier in London. We have it now because it arrived safely, and was passed down in the family of one of the two ladies it addresses. One assumes that Donne disposed of all his verse letters in much the same way; but it is a vain hope that any more of them will emerge from neglected family archives.

THE STORM

To Mr Christopher Brooke

Christopher Brooke (1570-1628) was Donne's enduring friend from the time they shared a study at Lincoln's Inn in the early 1590s. Brooke gave away the bride at Donne's clandestine marriage in 1602 and was imprisoned for it. He served in six Parliaments between 1604 and 1626.

The Storm and *The Calm* describe incidents in the 'Islands Expedition' to the Azores under Essex, Howard and Raleigh, in the summer of 1597. Donne went with the fleet as did many other young adventurers. Some ten ships put out from Plymouth on 5 July 1597 but were beaten back after a few days by the storm described in the poem.

Jonson told Drummond that he had by heart 'that passage of the calm, that dust and feathers do not stir, all was so quiet' (*Conversations* 135).

Subtitled from the Island Voyage with the Earl of Essex *in 1635–69 and several MSS*

2 *these*] this *1635–69 and several MSS*

4 *Hilliard* Nicholas Hilliard (1547–1619) was the best-known Court artist of the day, and had particular renown as a painter of miniature portraits.

12 *and way*] one way *1635–54*

14 *th' air's middle marble room* the middle region of the air was assumed to be intensely cold, and presumably might be frozen hard as marble.

17 *leese* lose.

18 *lie but for fees* prisoners who had served their sentence had to pay the jailer's fees before they were released.

22 *Sara* Sarah laughed when she found that she was pregnant with Isaac in her old age (Genesis xviii 12 and xxi 6–7).

24 *Which*] Who *several MSS*

33 *Jonas* Jonah tried to escape from God by taking ship to Tarshish, but God struck the ship with a mighty tempest while Jonah slept; the mariners woke him in their search for the cause of the storm.

38 *I, and*] Yea, and *MS*

39 *could only say*] could but say *most MSS*; could then but say *MS*; could say *several MSS*; should say *MS*

40 *lasted, now*] lasted, yet *1635–54*; lasted yet *MS*

42 *his*] this *1669*

47 *graves*] grave *1633–54 and MS*

49 *tremblingly*] trembling *1635–69 and some MSS*

50 *Like*] As *1635–69*

53 *Then*] There *1669*

54 *this*] an *1635–69*
   waist amidships. *Given as* wast *in the early versions.*

55 *salt dropsy* they were awash with sea-water.

56 *too high stretched*] too too high stretched *1635-54*; to too high stretched *1669*

57 *tottered* tattered.

59 *Even*] Yea even *1635-69*

60 *Strive*] Strives *1635-69*; Strived *several MSS*

64 *knows*] knew *several MSS*

66 *Hell*] Hell's *MS*
  lightsome] light *several MSS*
  and the Bermuda] and the Bermudas *some MSS*; the Bermudas *1635-54 and MS*
  the Bermuda The 'still-vexed Bermoothes. (*The Tempest* I 2 229) were notoriously tempestuous.

67 *elder*] eldest *1633-69 and several MSS*

68 *Claims*] Claimed *1633*
  this] the *1635-69 and some MSS*

69 *none* nothing.

70 *deformity* absence of form. In the darkness everything is reduced to one thing in that men cannot tell one thing from another; and this one thing is nothing, since the darkness uniformly robs all things of their form which gives them their being.

72 *Another* Fiat *Fiat lux*, 'Let there be light', the words with which God began the creation of the world (Genesis i 3).

74 *starve* deprive, kill.
  I wish not thee I do not wish you here.

THE CALM

The English fleet divided on its way to the Azores, and parts of it were becalmed while they sought in vain for Spanish shipping to harry. The dead calm on 9 and 10 September prevented Raleigh's squadron from re-establishing contact with Essex.

3-4 *The fable is inverted ... / ... than a stork before* In Aesop's fable of King Log and King Stork the frogs asked Zeus for a king and he gave them a log. Dissatisfied, they importuned him again and he sent them a stork which ate them all.

4 *A block afflicts* the becalmed ship is just a motionless block of wood in which they are exposed to the parching heat.
  stork] stroke *1639*

6 *heaven laughs*] heavens laugh *MS*

7 *can wish, that my*] could wish that my *MS*; could wish my *1635–69*

9 *those Isles*] these Isles *several MSS*; the Isles *1633–69*

14 *ended*] ending *1669*

15 *seamen's rags* Presumably the sailors had hung out their washing in the forward area where, in action, hand-to-hand fighting took place.
  rags] rage *1669*

16 *frippery* an old-clothes shop.

17 *No use of lanthorns* ships in a fleet maintained contact at night by watching the lantern in the stern of the flagship. But these ships are not moving.

19–20 *Earth's hollownesses . . . / . . . upper vault of air* it was assumed that winds were generated in hollows in the earth's interior, as wind in a man's belly. The 'upper vault of air' was a completely calm region.

21 *lost*] left *some MSS*
  lost friends . . . recover find the other squadrons of the fleet.

23 *calenture* a tropical madness that caused sailors to throw themselves into the sea, taking the waves for pleasant meadows.

24 *jaws*] maws *1635–69 and several MSS*

28 *walkers in hot ovens* Shadrach, Meshach and Abednego walked unharmed in Nebuchadnezzar's burning fiery furnace.

29 *these*] this *several MSS*
  these the great fishes of line 24.

30 *our*] a *1635–69 and several MSS*
  our brimstone bath possibly sulphur baths used in the treatment of syphilis.

33 *Bajazet . . . the shepherd's scoff* the Emperor of the Turks in Marlowe's *Tamburlaine the Great*, Part 1. Tamburlaine, the erstwhile shepherd of Scythia, conquers him and puts him in a cage to be mocked.

34 *Or*] And *some MSS*
slack-sinewed Samson Samson lost his strength when his hair was shaved off; and he languished in prison in Gaza as a blind slave.

35-6 *a myriad | Of ants, durst th'Emperor's loved snake invade* ants ate the pet snake of the Emperor Tiberius, presenting him with an omen of his fate if he flouted the power of the people.

37 *The crawling galleys* galleys were propelled by oars, and so were slow and cumbrous.
sea-gaols] sea gulls *1635-54 and MS*; sea snails *several MSS*
sea-gaols the oarsmen were chained prisoners, convicted of crimes and sentenced to the galleys.
finny chips small slivers of wood with fins.

38 *Might brave* might get the better of, since the galleys are not dependent upon the wind.
pinnaces] venices *1633 and some MSS*
pinnaces light scouting vessels, often carried on big men of war.
bed-rid ships the pinnaces remain fast to their parent ships as helpless as bed-ridden patients.

39 *and*] or *several MSS*

40 *disuse* accustom him to do without, free him from.
queasy nauseous; uncertain, ticklish; hurtful.

44 *and a coward*] and coward *1635-69*; a coward *several MSS*

45 *all*] each *several MSS*

48 *'gainst which we all forget to pray* Fate commonly catches us out by visiting upon us the one scourge we had not thought to guard against with our prayers.
forget] forgot *1669 and some MSS*

49 *He that at sea prays for more wind* sailors are so buffeted by storms that it would seem absurd, in general, for them to pray for wind.

50 *poles*] pole *several MSS*

52-3 *he was! he was | Nothing; for us, we are for nothing fit*] he was, he was? Nothing for us, we are for nothing fit *1669 and some MSS*

54 *Chance, or ourselves still disproportion it* by ill chance or by our own shortcomings our means never match our intentions.

55 *no power, no will*] no will, no power *several MSS*; no will nor power *MS*; nor will, nor power *several MSS*
no sense] nor sense *several MSS*

TO MR B. B.

We do not know who B. B. was but R. C. Bald thinks that he might have been one Beaupré Bell, who stayed on at Cambridge after graduating in 1591 and moved to Lincoln's Inn in 1594 ('Donne's Early Verse Letters., *HLQ*, XV (1952), 283–9). Donne and Bell must have known each other, but there is nothing to connect them save that Bell's circumstances fit this poem. If B. B. is Bell then the poem must have been written before his move to Lincoln's Inn in May 1594.

3 *Fulfilled* filled full.

4 *spirits and ... quintessence* the pure and enduring essence of learning. The 'spirits' of a substance was its distilled essence, and the 'quintessence' of anything was its essential nature purged of impurities and mortal corruptions.

7 *Here* presumably at one of the Inns of Court.

8 *our*] the *MS*

12 *giddy* thoughtless, foolish.

13 *stray*] stay *MS*

14 *ride post* gallop furiously to make good lost time.

15 *married* Pronounced as three syllables.

16] Embrace her still: increase and multiply *MS*
ever multiply never stop writing poetry.

18 *widowhead*] widowhood *1633–69*

19 *Muse*] nurse *1633–69*

20–22 *the cause being in me, / ... power doth withhold* since it was Donne's own coldness that caused the Muse to divorce him, and it persists, he has not now the will or the power to espouse another Muse, as it were bigamously. Hence the badness of his present verses.

24–5 *matter ... / ... form* lacking a mother (the Muse) his verses lack poetic substance and have only the external form of poetry, which Donne himself gives them.

28 *confirmed* (a) approved as true poetry; (b) admitted to the name or communion of poems.
bishoped sealed, as by the laying on of hands in confirmation. Pronounced as three syllables.

TO MR C. B.

C. B. is probably Christopher Brooke. See the introductory note to *The Storm*. R. C. Bald thinks that this poem and the epistle *To Mr I. L.* presumably mark Donne's first authentic appearance in the role of a lover' (*John Donne: A Life*, p. 75).

2 *inexcusable*] unexcusable *1633–69*
inexcusable unavoidable; he cannot excuse himself from going.

3 *the saint of his affection* the poet's mistress.

4 *both wants* his separation from both C. B. and the lady.

9 *thyself*] myself *1669*

10 *Heaven's liberal, and earth's thrice-fairer sun* the real sun in the sky; and the lady who is three times as beautiful as that. The poet is presumably travelling north, to the cold and dark regions.
earth's] the *1635–54*; the earth's *MS*
thrice-fairer] thrice-fair *1633–69 and several MSS*

11 *stern*] starved *1635–69 and MS* (spelled sterved).
aye doth won dwells perpetually.

13 *forth*] out *several MSS*

TO MR S. B.

S. B. is probably Samuel Brooke (?1575–1631), the younger brother of Donne's friend Christopher Brooke. Samuel Brooke was at Cambridge through the 1590s and took orders in 1599. He married Donne to Ann More, and was thrown into prison for it with the rest; but he subsequently had a distinguished career in the Church and in academic life. This verse letter evidently addresses a young man who had just entered upon academic life, and its probable date is thus the early 1590s.

3 *advice* judgement, wisdom (*written* advise *in early versions*).

5 *travailing* (a) labouring; (b) voyaging.

7–8 *take / Fresh water at the Heliconian spring* drink at the fountain of poetic inspiration and refresh your mind by writing poetry.

9 *siren like* the singing of the sirens drew ravished mariners to their destruction upon the rocks (*Odyssey* XII).

10 *those schismatics with you* some dissident Cambridge faction that was then gaining a large following. R. C. Bald suggests that Donne meant Gabriel Harvey and his supporters ('Donne's Early Verse Letters', *HLQ*, XV (1952), 283–9).

12 *seeing*] seen *several MSS*; seem *MS*

13] I thought I brought no fuel, but desire *1650–54*
no fuel the present verse letter has no substance, only wind.

TO MR E. G.

First printed in Gosse. Only the Westmoreland MS has it.

E. G. was probably Everard Guilpin, a minor poet who was at Gray's Inn in the early 1950s and lived for some time in Highgate (line 5); he came of a Suffolk family (lines 19–20).

2 *slimy* the sun's heat was supposed to breed living creatures out of the slime of the Nile.

14 *retrieve* spelled retrive *in the MS*

17 *Russian merchants* merchants trading with Russia loaded their vessels there in summer when the waters were navigable, and moved south to sell the goods in winter.

19 *that* Suffolk.

20 *this* the place from which E. G. oversees London – presumably Highgate.

TO MR I. L. (BLESS'D ARE YOUR NORTH PARTS)

We do not know who I. L. was. The poem speaks of a summer of unusual weather, such as occurred in 1594 (see R. C. Bald, 'Donne's Early Verse Letters', *HLQ*, XV (1952), 283–9); it may have been written in the autumn of that year.

Title] To Mr T. L. *MS*; To M. I. P. *1633–69*; To M. J. L. *several MSS*

2 *My sun* a woman the poet professes to love, who was staying with I. L. in the north.

3 *Heaven's sun* the sun in the sky.

6 *chafes*] burns *MS*
pestilence the plague.

9 *my kind and unkind heart* the poet's heart is kind in that it runs to bridge the distance between him and his friends, unkind in that it abandons him.

11-12 *These lines are given only in the Westmoreland MS. They were first printed in Grierson.*

12 *help thy friend to save* help to save your friend by pleading his case with the lady.

14 *suddenly as lard* so quick and rich in growth as to fatten cattle like fat itself.

15 *polled* (a) having the branches cut back to produce a thick close growth; (b) having the hair cut short.

16 *when thee list*] (when she list) *1635-69 and MS*; when thou wilt *MS*

   when thee list when you wish it
   golden hair the leaves in autumn.

19 *courage* vigour.

20 *Thy son ne'er ward* the wish is double, that I. L. should live to see his son reach his majority, and that the boy himself should never fall into the hands of some courtly guardian who will fleece him.

   loved] fair *MS*; young *MS*

22 *her* Donne's lady.

TO MR I. L. (OF THAT SHORT ROLL OF FRIENDS)

Title] To Mr J. L. *several MSS*; to Mr T. L. *MS*

4 *Sequan* the Seine.

6 *Lethe* the river of forgetfulness in the underworld of Greek mythology. The traveller who passed over it and drank its water forgot all his previous life.

13 *both we* Donne and Mr I. L.'s Muse.

TO MR R. W. (IF, AS MINE IS, THY LIFE A SLUMBER BE)

This letter appears to relate to events of 1596 and early 1597, when English hopes of exploiting Raleigh's discovery of Guiana were frustrated by the Queen's reluctance to act. The English fleet, assembled in Plymouth in the summer of 1597 for the Islands expedition (see the introductory note to *The Storm*), stood ready to sail for Guiana if sanction were given. But the Queen held to the original plan of an attack on Ferrol, where a new Spanish Armada was fitting out, and then a raid in the Spanish Main.

3 *Morpheus nor his brother* Morpheus, the god of sleep, could assume the shapes of men when he wished, and one of his brothers could assume the shapes of animals.

brother] brethren *MS*

6 *hand*] hands *several MSS*

9 *thy retirings* presumably R. W. has retired from town society to meditate in 'a wise melancholy'.

13 *patient* one who suffers for love.

17 *gospel* (a) news from the larger world; (b) divine messages and truths, such as missionaries carried to the heathen.

18 *Guiana's harvest* Raleigh went to Guiana in 1595 and his *Discovery of Guiana* was published in 1596. Hopes of colonizing the earthly paradise Raleigh described then ran high for a time.

20 *the Jews' guide* Moses (Numbers xx 12; Deuteronomy xxiv 1-5).

22 *Oh*] Our *1633-69*

23 *these Spanish business* presumably the projected embroilment with Spain at Ferrol and in the Azores, which distracted the Government from the colonizing of Guiana.

business] businesses *1635-69 and several MSS*

27 *all th'all* the whole of everything, the entire creation.

28 *an India* a source of greatest wealth in itself.

30 *to answer* to correspond to.

31-2 *this / Virtue, our form's form and our soul's soul, is* virtue in good men is the quintessence, the principle of riches itself; it informs their informing spirit and is the soul of their soul.

TO MR R. W. (KINDLY I ENVY THY SONG'S PERFECTION)

First published in Grierson. Only the Westmoreland MS has it. Since that was Roland Woodward's MS the likelihood is that R. W. is Woodward.

1 *Kindly I envy* his envy is friendly.

2 *all th'elements* the elements are earth, fire, water and air.

6 *Grief* tears of grief.

8 *for now I admire thee* admiring R. W., he scorns all inferior beings.

10 *fulfil* fill full.

11 *this sound* the present poem.

14 *thy creature* R. W.'s poem.

TO MR R. W. (MUSE NOT THAT BY THY MIND THY BODY IS LED)

First printed in Grierson. Only two *MSS* have it, one of them the Westmoreland MS.

2 *by thy mind* R. W.'s mind is presumably expressed in some verses he had written.
   distempered Pronounced as four syllables.

5 *intermission* Pronounced as five syllables.

7 *a lay man's genius* the tutelary deity which guides the body and mind of ordinary men, those men who are not poets.

9 *that methinks* the Muse, poetry itself, which ought to ease the anguish of poets whatever their state of body or mind.

12 *charming sovereign melody* as R. W.'s earlier writings have communicated his pain to Donne, now Donne asks for a cure of that pain by a new and happier writing which will charm with all-powerful harmony.

TO MR R. W. (ZEALOUSLY MY MUSE DOTH SALUTE ALL THEE)

First printed in Gosse. The poem is given in two MSS only, one of them the Westmoreland MS.

1 *all thee* all three parts of the mystic trinity that make up R. W. the poet.

4 *Like fire* similar poetic power.

5 *Dost thou recover sickness ...?* are you recovering from sickness ... ?
   or prevent? or are you keeping out of the way of infection?

6 *travailed* (a) journeyed; (b) exercised, troubled.

TO MR ROWLAND WOODWARD

Rowland Woodward (1573–1636/7) was Donne's close friend from the time they were at Lincoln's Inn together in the early 1590s. He served in official posts on the continent and at home, and was with another of Donne's friends, Sir Henry Wotton, in Venice from 1605 to 1607. He evidently tried to gather Donne's poems together, and the Westmoreland MS is in his hand.

Title] A letter of Dr Donne to one that desired some of his papers *MS*; To Mr R. W. *MS*

2 *tied*] tired *several MSS*

3 *fallowness*] holiness *several MSS*

4 *too*] so *MS*
shown] flown *1635–54*

5 *How love-song weeds*] How long love's weeds *1635–54 and MS*

9 *Omissions of good, ill, as ill deeds be* omitting to do good is as wrong as actively doing bad.

10 *to us it*] to use it *several MSS*
seem, and be light] seem but light *1635–69 and several MSS*

11 *faithful* accurate, delicate.

12 *vanity* trivialness, the pursuit of vain ends.

14 *honesty*] integrity *some MSS*

15 *imputes, as native purity* God imputes faith and uprightness to us as if they were the original innocence which we have lost.

17–18 *are names, which none / Want, which want not vice-covering discretion* religion is the only true virtue, for the rest are mere names; anyone can be called wise, valiant, sober, just, who is discreet enough to cover up his vice.

19 *ourselves in ourselves* 'I had rather understand myself well in myself than in Cicero' (Montaigne, *Of Experience, Essays* III, 13, trans. J. Florio (1603)).

21 *crystal glass* a magnifying glass.

23 *our*] the *several MSS*
   sparks] spark *1669 and several MSS*
   outburn burn out, destroy.

24 *straw* rubbish, vanities.
   sojourn The stress falls on the second syllable – sojoúrn.

25 *physicians* physicists, alchemists.

25-6 *when they would infuse / Into any oil, the soul of simples* an alchemical process for purifying base metals. One sought to infuse the essence or spirit of a pure simple substance into the liquid form of a metal (the 'oil') by mixing the two components in a glass container and burying it in some warm dark place where the transformation might proceed.

26 *soul*] souls *1633–69 and several MSS*

30 *a banishment* the world's distractions banish us from our true selves as the pursuit of a vanity banished us from Eden.

31 *but farmers of our selves* we are tenant farmers who have to cultivate ourselves and make account of our stewardship to God.
   farmers] termers *1633*

32 *and thrive*] and there *several MSS*

32-3 *uplay / Much, much dear treasure* 'Lay up for yourselves treasures in heaven' (Matthew vi 20).

33 *dear*] good *1635–69 and some MSS*
   the great rent day the day of reckoning, when we settle up finally with God according to what we have made of the material he has given us.

34 *to thy self be approved* make your life such as you yourself can approve, regardless of how the world judges you.
   approved] improved *1669 and MS*

36 *loved*] beloved *some MSS*

TO MR T. W. (ALL HAIL, SWEET POET)

T. W. may have been Thomas Woodward, brother of Donne's friend Rowland Woodward. But there is no evidence one way or the other.

Title] Ad amicum *MS*; to M. I. W. *1633–69 and some MSS*

1 *more full*] and full *1669*

2 *any spirit*] my dull spirit *1635–69 and several MSS*

3 *this merit*] thy merit *1635–69 and several MSS*

6 *laboured* Pronounced as three syllables.

13 *ever was*] never was *several MSS*

14–15] In fortunes, nor in nature's gifts alas,
        But by thy grace . . .
                              (*several MSS*)

15 *Before*] But for *1635–69 and MS*
  Before thy grace (a) compared to your grace, and graciousness;
(b) before you bestowed your grace upon me by sending me these verses.

16 *A monster and a beggar* in respect of nature he was an unnatural
monster, and in respect of fortune, a beggar.
  an now a fool] am a fool *1633–69 and some MSS*
  am now a fool T. W.'s verses show up Donne's own poetic efforts as
foolish.

20 *surquedry* presumption.

23 *worth*] work *1633–54 and several MSS*

26 *bad god* badly executed god.

27–8 *'Twill be good prose . . . | If thou forget the rhyme as thou dost
pass* if you overlook the rhyme as you read you can at least take this
for good prose, though it is bad verse.

29 *that I*] then I *1633–54 and several MSS*

30 *zany* buffoon, comic hanger-on.

TO MR T. W. (AT ONCE, FROM HENCE)

Title] An Old Letter *several MSS*

1 *At once* together.

2 *my soft still walks* his melancholy solitude.
  to my heart to T. W., who has the poet's heart.

3 *the nurse . . . of art* his solitary meditations.

6 *his*] the *several MSS*

7 *pressed* oppressed.

8 *strict* exact, rigorously drawn; tightly restricted.

11 *things happy* the verses are fortunate in that they will see T. W. and outlive the poet.

12 *a picture* a representation of the poet himself.
 bare sacrament a naked sign of the poet himself.

13–14 *if in them there be | Merit of love* if the lines themselves merit love then in loving them T. W. will be bestowing love upon the poet, whose picture or sacrament they are.

TO MR T. W. (HASTE THEE HARSH VERSE)

2–3 *to him, my pain and pleasure. | I have given thee*] to him; my pain and pleasure / I have given thee *1633–69*

5–6] *These lines are given in the Westmoreland MS only.*

11–12 *in every street | Infections follow* presumably the plague was raging in London.

14 *And you'are*] You are *1635–69 and MS*
 my pawns, or else my testament the verses are the pledges of his love if he survives and the testament of it, his will, if he does.

TO MR T. W. (PREGNANT AGAIN WITH TH' OLD TWINS)

5 *Watch*] Mark *MS*
 and eye] or eye *1633–69*

13 *gluttons* a glutton's love devours its object, and T. W.'s love kills the poet by keeping him so starved of letters.

TO SIR HENRY GOODYER

Sir Henry Goodyer (1571–1628) was in Donne's later life his closest friend and regular correspondent. He inherited the estate of Polesworth in the Forest of Arden, and held office in the Court for some years; Essex knighted him in 1599, possibly in the Irish campaign. Goodyer was noted both for his hospitality to writers and his extravagance, which left him perpetually short of money. The present poem suggests that he was also fonder of sport than of husbandry. Donne wrote it from Mitcham (line 48), his home between 1605 and 1610.

Title] To Sir Henry Goodyer moving him to travel *several MSS*

1 *past*] last *1669*

2 *things*] thing *several MSS*

4 *pair* a string.

8 *upward*] upwards *MS*
fortune] fortunes *several MSS*

11 *guest* the soul

13 *lustier* more youthful and strong.

16–17 *women's milk, and pap … / … manlier diet* 'For every one
that useth milk, is unskilful in the word of righteousness: for he is a
babe. But strong meat belongeth to them that are full of age, even
those who by reason of use have their senses exercised to discern both
good and evil' (Hebrews v 13–14).
the end] her end *several MSS*

18 *All libraries, which are schools, camps, and courts* Goodyer's career
had left him well read in the library of life, taking him around various
centres of learning, battlefields and courts.

19–20 *ask your garners if you have not been / In harvests, too indulgent
to your sports* Goodyer's garners, of wheat and of wisdom alike, were
less full than they might have been because he neglected the harvest
for gaming and other such diversions.

20 *harvests*] harvest *1669 and some MSS*

22 *outlandish* foreign, overseas.

23 *no*] not *several MSS*

28 *prescribe* gain authority over us, by the prescriptive right that
Adam's fall gave to sin.
in us] to us *1635–69 and several MSS*

33 *to spare* to be sparing, thrifty; to avoid excess.

34 *your hawk's praise* that it flies higher than the rest.

35 *when herself she lessens* when she goes higher and so looks smaller,
diminishes herself as Goodyer diminishes his estate by his unthriftiness.

36 *towers* soars at the highest point.

37 *However*] Howsoever *some MSS*
taste apprehension, sense of.

38   *him as now*] him now *1639–69*

42   *Else be not froward*   do not otherwise be irascible.

44   *fables*] tables *1633 and MS*
  fables   moralized fables. *The* tables *of 1633 is a possible reading, since* tables *could be moral emblems.*
  or] and *several MSS*
  fruit-trenchers   wooden platters for fruit, usually decorated with moral texts.

45   *make*] made *several MSS*
  your promise   Goodyer may have promised to spend some time with Donne.

46   *Riding I had you*   he enjoyed Goodyer's company as if they rode together, or Goodyer had ridden to join him. In a prose letter Donne told Goodyer that he often composed letters to him while he rode between Mitcham and London.

48   *with me to*] to me at *several MSS*

A LETTER WRITTEN BY SIR H. G. AND J. D. ALTERNIS VICIBUS

First printed in E. K. Chambers, *Poems of John Donne* (1896). Only one MS has it.

alternis vicibus   by turn and turn about. Goodyer wrote the first stanza, Donne the second, and so on alternately. The poem makes it clear that Donne was staying with Goodyer at Polesworth when they wrote it.

5   *You several suns*   presumably the letter was written to two ladies.

6   *digest*   (a) at once disperse their thoughts to other people, and concentrate them in each person; (b) bring to maturity by heat.

9   *twin'd*   The MS spelling keeps the sense both of 'twined' and 'twinned'.

16   *our magic*   the two poets appear before the ladies in this letter; and they make the ladies appear before them by seeing their beauties in the natural delights around Goodyer's home.

18   *Supplying*   making up the number, finding all nine Muses in the two ladies.

21   *them*   the flowers.

25 *Anker* a Warwickshire river that flowed through Goodyer's estate at Polesworth.

26 *unmingled* unmixed with impure thoughts and passions.

28 *St Edith' Nuns* Goodyer's estate was formerly the land of a Benedictine convent whose second Abbess was the ninth-century St Edith.

35 *because we two, you two unite* even though one letter brings both ladies together it cannot comprehend their qualities or the poet's wonder at them.

36 *be infinite* go on any longer.

TO SIR HENRY WOTTON (HERE'S NO MORE NEWS)

Title] A Letter to Sir Henry Wotton from the Court *several MSS*; To Mr H. W. 20 July 1598 at Court *several MSS*

2 *Cadiz' or Saint Michael's tale* the story of the expeditions to Cadiz and the Azores in 1596 and 1597, stale news indeed to men such as Donne and Wotton who had been on the two voyages. The Azores were popularly known as the Islands of St Michael.

Tell you Calis' or Saint Michael's tales, as tell *1635-54*; Tell Calis, or Saint Michael's Mount, as tell *1669*; Tell you Calais, or Saint Michael's Mount as tell *1719*

Cadiz given as Cales *or* Calis *in the seventeenth-century editions and MSS*

4 *stomachs* appetites.

9 *But that the next to him, still, is worse than he* the only reason that any courtier can claim to fall short of the extreme of vice is that he can be sure his neighbour is worse than he is.

12 *marshal their state* (a) assemble their panoply of power; (b) follow their calling.

13 *silly* simple, innocent.

14 *wishing prayers*] wishing, prayers *1669*; wishes, prayers *1635-54 and some MSS*

wishing prayers entreaties that their rights or needs should be respected.

neat pure.

17 *tongues* readiness to speak malice of others.

18 *Tender to know* quick to see slights to oneself.

tough to acknowledge unready to admit that one has wronged others.

19 *youth's*] young'st *several MSS*

20 *play's*] player's *1639-69*

21 *Courts are like*] Courts are now like *several MSS*; Courts like *1635-69 and several MSS*

22 *these mimic antics* grotesquely posturing courtiers.

23 *projects* plots.
and egregious gests] are egregious guests *1669*
egregious gests ostentatious acts.

24 *Are but*] And but *1669*
dull morals of a game at chests chess was commonly moralized as a model of war or of power politics.
of a game at] at a game of *1669*
chests the common name for chess.

25 *now 'tis*] 'tis an *1669*

26 *Therefore*] Wherefore *MS*

27 At Court, *though from Court, were the better style*] *At Court*; though *From Court,* were the better style *MS*
At Court, *though from Court were the better style* (a) he subscribes his letter with his present address 'at Court', though it would be more formally accurate to subscribe it 'from Court' since it comes from there; (b) he gives his present location, at Court, but he would be better off if he could say that he was far from the Court.

TO SIR HENRY WOTTON (SIR, MORE THAN KISSES)

Wotton and Donne were at Oxford together and remained close friends thereafter. Sir Henry Wotton was a lawyer who became a courtier, and then a distinguished diplomat. His early career parallels Donne's; he was agent and secretary to the Earl of Essex and, like Donne, went on the Cadiz and Islands expeditions in 1596-7. The present poem seems to arise out of a literary exchange among members of the Essex circle over the question of where the best life is to be led, in Court, city, or the country; poems taking one or other side passed among Wotton, Bacon, Donne and lesser writers, and some MSS give what appears to be Wotton's reply to Donne's poem headed 'To Mr J. D. from Mr H. W.' A minor poet, Thomas Bastard, refers to the debate in a book which was entered in the Stationers' Register in 1598; so that the likely date of Donne's poem is 1597 or early 1598. Wotton was not knighted until 1603.

Title] To Mr H. W. *MS*; To Sir H. W. many years since *MS*

2 *controls* limits, relieves.

6 *bottle* bundle.

8 *remoras* impediments. The remora, a small sucking fish, was supposed to be able to stop any ship to which it attached itself.

11 *even*] raging *1633–54*; other *MS*; over *MS*
even line the equator, which evenly divides the globe, the northern hemisphere from the southern hemisphere, and where the day and night are of equal length.

12 *adverse* opposite.
poles] pole *1633–69 and several MSS*

16 *cities, built ... extremes, be*] cities built ... extremes be *1633–69*

17 *dung and garlic*] dung, or garlic *1635–69 and some MSS*
dung and garlic can a combination of two foul-smelling things make a sweet-smelling thing?

18 *and torpedo*] or torpedo *1633–69 and some MSS*
torpedo the electric ray, whose sting is numbing whereas the scorpion's sting is maddening.

22 *no such*] none such *1635–69 and several MSS*
there were] they were *1633 and MS*; then were *several MSS*

24 *and of one clay*] of one clay *1639–69*; of one day *1650–54*; and at one day *MS*; and all end in one day *1669*

25–6] The country is a desert, where the good,
     Gained inhabits not, borne, is not understood.
     (*1635–54 and several MSS*)

     The country is a desert, where no good
     Gained doth inhabit, nor born's understood.
                    (MS)

where no good, / *Gained (as habits, not born)* where men do not appreciate acquired good, such as civilized habits, but are simply content to stay as they were born. The underlying sense is that all men are born into sin and can acquire virtue only by their reason and deliberate choice thereafter.

27 *prone to more evils* men are free moral agents and can sin, whereas beasts merely follow out their natural dispositions.
more] mere *some MSS*; all *1635–69*; men *MS*

30 *Each element's qualities were in the other three* the separation of confused matter into four distinct elements was a critical stage in the coming of order out of chaos.

31–2 *being several* / *To these three places* presumably pride belongs to the Court, lust to the country and covetousness to the city.

32 *all are in all*] are all, in all *several MSS*

33 *issue incestuous*] issue is incestuous *1635–69 and several MSS*; issue's monstrous *MS*

34 *denizened* naturalized, accommodated as if it were native.
Virtue is barbarous virtue owes nothing to society but can be cultivated only in solitude.

35 *there*] then *MS*

42 *intregrity* innocence.

44 *for themselves, and themselves*] in themselves, and themselves *1633–69*; into themselves, themselves *several MSS*
retrieve Spelled *retrive in the early versions.*

45–6 *then* / ... *Italian*] than / ... Italian *1635–69 and most MSS*; that / ... Italianate *several MSS*

46 *old Italian* crafty and corrupt.

47 *Be then*] Be thou *1633 and MS*

48 *Inn* lodge for a short while.

50 *his*] her *several MSS*

57 *so closely*] so, closely *1633–69*

59 *in this one thing, be*] in this be *1635–69*
no Galenist Galenists worked to cure by contraries, correcting an excess of some bodily humour by making up the deficiency in its opposite humour so as to restore a balance.

62 *chemics* alchemists, who sought to arrive at the purified quintessence of substances.

65 *German*] Germany's *1635–69*

65–6 *German* ... / ... *France* ... *Italy* Wotton had travelled on the continent between 1589 and 1594.

69 *throughly* wholly.

70 *my rules* the precepts set out in the poem.

TO SIR HENRY WOTTON, AT HIS GOING AMBASSADOR TO VENICE

Wotton sailed for Venice to become British Ambassador on 19 July 1604, having just been knighted by the king. Walton gives the poem in his *Life of Sir Henry Wotton* (1670) as 'a letter sent by him [Donne] to Sir Henry Wotton, the morning before he left England'.

1 *those reverend papers* Wotton's commission as ambassador.

3 *derives* delegates.
  his the king's soul (line 1), or kingly power.

4 *how he may* as far as he can impart to a layman the powers of his own sacred office.

8 *his virtue* the king's power.

10 *pleasure*] pleasures *1633*

13 *where*] which *1635-69, MS and Walton*

17-18 *allow | It such an audenice as yourself would ask* receive this letter as warmly as you wish your diplomatic hosts to receive you.

19 *must*] would *MS and Walton*
  means] says *Walton*

20 *hath for nature* . . . the nature of this letter is the same as the task Wotton will have in Venice, that is, 'To swear much love. . . .'

21 *not*] nor *Walton*

21-2 *not to be changed before | Honour alone will to your fortune fit* the poet's friendly love will change only when Wotton's status becomes so great as to demand honour rather than love.

24 *Than I have done your honour wanting it* than he has respected Wotton's honour when Wotton lacked advancement.
  honour wanting it] noble-wanting wit *1635-69 and MS*; honour-wanting-wit *Walton*; noble wanting it *some MSS*

26 *To want, than govern greatness* it is easier to bear the lack of advancement than it is to bear great office.

29-30 *your spirits now are placed | In their last furnace* in alchemy substances are progressively refined and purified by heat until one has their spirits or essence, and the final process – 'their last furnace' – produces the elixir or touchstone.

31 *wars*] tents *MS*

32 *To touch and test in any best degree* as a touchstone, to inspire virtue in others and to test others' qualities up to the highest degree of worth.
 test] taste *1669 and Walton*

35 *Spies*] Finds *Walton*
 her tyranny his continued ill fortune.

38 *increase* prosperity.
 God is as near me here the distance now opening between the two friends does not affect their proximity to God, so that Donne's prayers for Wotton's prosperity will avail no less than before.

39–40 *his stairs | In length and ease are alike everywhere* God's blessings can reach us in just the same way wherever we are on the earth. In Genesis xxviii 12–15, Jacob 'dreamed, and behold a ladder set upon the earth, and the top of it reached to heaven; and behold, the angels of God ascending and descending on it. And behold, the Lord stood above it, and said ... "behold I am with thee, and will keep thee in all places whither thou goest, and will bring thee again into this land".'

H. W. IN HIBERNIA BELLIGERANTI

First printed in Grierson. The poem was given in only one MS, Wotton's common place book, which has itself been destroyed since Grierson copied the poem from it. The initials 'J. D.' in the MS are the only external evidence that Donne wrote it, though a letter Wotton sent to Donne from Ireland in 1599 is plainly a reply to just such a complaint of Wotton's failure to write to his friend (see L. P. Smith, *The Life and Letters of Sir Henry Wotton* (1907) I, 308).

in Hibernia Belligeranti fighting in Ireland. Wotton went with the Earl of Essex on the botched Irish campaign of mid-1599, and the poem was evidently written to him while he was there.

3 *Respective* considerate.

4 *In public gain my share' is not such ...* whether or not there is any public gain in England's conquering the Irish, the poet himself does not stand to win so much that he would forfeit Wotton's friendship for it.

He would sooner that England should let Ireland go than that the war should alienate friends.

5–6 *better cheap | I pardon death* he would sooner accept Wotton's death, as a cheaper and more pardonable loss, than that his friend should fall into a dangerous torpor.

6–7 *though he do not reap | Yet gleans he many of our friends away* (a) death merely gathers up what the enemy has reaped; (b) even if death does not slaughter people in masses yet he picks off many of their friends one by one.

9 *skeins* Irish daggers.

12 *pays* discharges his spiritual obligations and debts.
doth 'scape arrest is not taken by surprise but dies prepared.

14 *thorough crooked limbecs, stilled* distilled through crooked alembics, such as were used to refine and purify the essence of a substance.

15 *schools and Courts* these are 'crooked limbecs' in the sense that their tortuous dealings have added worldly wisdom to Wotton's natural graces of spirit.
quicken stimulate to sharper life.

16 *Irish negligence* dullness or indifference of spirit.

18–19 *which should fear | Dishonest carriage* something containing dangerous secrets, such as would put the writer at the mercy of the man who carried it.

19 *a seer's art* (a) the art of someone skilled in unsealing letters and seeing the contents; (b) the art of an interpreter of cryptic messages or a breaker of codes.

TO SIR EDWARD HERBERT, AT JULIERS

Edward Herbert (1583–1648) was George Herbert's brother and the eldest son of Mrs Magdalen Herbert. James I knighted him in 1603, and he became Lord Herbert of Cherbury in 1629. He was a philosopher, and a considerable poet; indeed Donne's verse letter to him seems to be a response to a long poem of his own called *The State-Progress of Ill* (1608) which concludes with an image of the world as Noah's Ark, 'few men and many beasts'.

Herbert was with an English force which helped the Prince of Orange to beseige Juliers in the summer of 1610, in the war between the

Protestant Princes and the Emperor. 1610 is thus the date of this poem.

Title] To Sir Edward Herbert, now Lord Herbert of Cherbury, being at the siege of Juliers *1635–69*

4 *theatre* a wild-beast show.

10 *disafforested* uprooted the jungle and made the soil fit for cultivation.

11 *Empaled* fenced around, stockaded.

15 *the herd of swine* in the country of the Gadarenes Jesus healed a man by casting out the devils that possessed him into a herd of swine, which then ran dementedly down a slope into the sea (Matthew viii 30–4; Mark v 2–14; Luke viii 27–33).

19 *our first touch* the first encounter of our soul with our body.

20 *tincture* tinge; the quintessence of corruption, as the elixir is the universal tincture of healing.

22 *Our apprehension* our awareness that we have merited God's punishments.

23 *chickens* any small birds.

24 *Hemlock* hemlock was supposed to nourish birds, though it kills men.
   we as men God provides for us as for his birds, and we eat as men; he gives us food and we make it poisonous to us.

25 *infuse* change by introducing some quality of our own.

26 *Corrosiveness, or intense cold or heat* these are the three supposed effects of poison, which made it lethal.

27–8 *no such specific poison . . . / As kills we know not how* Contemporary accounts of poisons supposed that there is one type of poison which kills not by some accidental effect upon our constitution but by its own specific malignity, whose working is a mystery to us.

28 *we know*] men know *1635–69*

30 *physic* medicine.

31 *his pleasure . . . his rod* men, who might be the means of their own well-being, are in fact their own punishment.

32 *is his devil* men are devils to themselves.

33-4 *to rectify | Nature, to what she was* to recover our natural selves as God created us in the first place, before we fell.

35 *them, who man to us in little show* those who speak of man as a microcosm, a little world.

36-7 *Greater than due . . . | On him* we cannot possibly speak more of man than is his due, or ascribe to him more than he is capable of.

37-8 *man into himself can draw | All* man contains in his own being the properties or qualities of everything else in the world.
Chaw chew.

41 *In all it works not* the pill of wordly knowledge, which is also self-knowledge, does not have a like effect upon everybody.

43 *calentures* feverish delusions that drive men to their deaths (see *The Calm* 23 and note).

44 *icy opium* a cold deadly lethargy.

48 *such a one* Herbert is now a worthy book in himself.

49 *Actions are authors* actions speak as well as words.

50 *mart* a whole market or emporium.

TO MRS M. H.

Mrs M. H. is presumably Mrs Magdalen Herbert, mother of Sir Edward Herbert and George Herbert (see the introductory note to *The Funeral*). Donne first met her about 1600 but his close friendship with her developed some years later, about 1607. She was widowed in 1596 and remarried in 1608. H. W. Garrod suggests that the latter part of the present poem refers to her impending second marriage ('Donne and Mrs Herbert', *RES*, XXI (1945), 161–73). If that is so then Donne wrote it in 1607 or 1608.

1 *Mad paper stay* the poet addresses his poem.

2 *sons*] suns *several MSS*
sons (a) offspring; (b) suns, sources of heat.
my] thy *1635–69*

4 *is*] was *MS*

6 *come unto* (a) gain the presence of; (b) advance to, and occupy.

7 *That's much; emboldens*] That's much emboldness *1669*; That's much, it emboldens *several MSS*
  emboldens, pulls, thrusts unworthiness is a necessary qualification for great office because it emboldens men, and pulls and thrusts aside the more worthy.

8 *'tis*] that's *several MSS*

10 *go; go*] go, Go *1633–69*

12 *they* princes.
  not] to *several MSS*

13 *perplexing* bewildering, dazzling (like the presence of God).

15 *dispute it* argue your case.

19 *sapless*] shapeless *several MSS*
  sapless without life.

20 *Her creature* her creation, the life she has newly created.

27 *From*] For *1633*
  speech of ill, and her thou must abstain since it would be indecorous to speak to her of bad things, or of her own qualities, the entire range of evil and of good is closed to the poem.

33 *Who knows thy destiny?*] We know thy destiny *several MSS*

37 *any, whom we know* someone whose letters she particularly favours, possibly Sir John Sanvers, her prospective second husband.

38 *saved* (a) preserved, not discarded; (b) fitted for heaven.

40 *she, alone* mark what favour she shows only to them.

41 *get them*] get to them *several MSS*
  o'erskip] do skip *several MSS*; skip o'er *several MSS*; skip *several MSS*

43 *Mark, if she do the same that they protest* observe if she herself carries out the devotions to love which the letters avow.

44 *whether*] whither *1635–69*

45 *if slight things be objected, and o'erblown* if trifling difficulties are made and then brushed aside.

47 *Reserved* qualified with exceptions, so that she does not really reject him although she swears not to remarry.
grieves] grieve *1635–69*

48 *chides the doctrine that denies freewill* (a) she wants to feel herself free to remarry; (b) she reproves what she most desires, the loss of her independence of mind.

50 *familiar* confidant.

51 *I do*] do I *several MSS*

TO THE COUNTESS OF BEDFORD AT NEW YEAR'S TIDE

Title] To ... Bedford. On New-year's day *1633–69*

3 *of stuff and form perplexed* whose matter and form are so confusedly intertwined.

8 *That cannot say, my thanks I have forgot* The sense of lines 6–9 turns upon an antithesis between 'the'old years and 'the new' year – 'That' and 'this'. The old years cannot accuse the poet of having to thank them; and he does not trust the new year with hopes. He has nothing to thank his past years for and expects nothing from what is to come.

10 *bravery* bold defiant assertion.

16 *Mine* his verses.
tincture the quintessential quality that regenerates and transforms everything.

18 *spirits*] spirit *1633*.
strong agents the most powerful chemical or alchemical agents, which benefit life in small doses but will destroy it if they are left to work.

19 *cherish, us do*] cherish us, do *1635–69*

20 *extracts* The stress falls on the second syllable – extrácts.

25 *too much grace might disgrace* her virtues are so great that no one will credit what he says in celebration of them, and thus she and his verse will be alike disgraced.

28 *corn* grain of dust.

30 *not an inch* they will fail to see how one who is himself so insignificant – less than an inch – could measure infinity.

35 *To make it good* to overlook and amend the shortcoming.
    such a praiser prays praise of virtue is itself a kind of prayer, and an implicit plea for grace to amend its inevitable human inadequacy.
    praiser prays] prayer prays *1633*; prayer praise *MS*

37 *favour* comeliness.

38 *perplex* intermingle; disturb.

39 *and show you good* and then afterwards show favour to you.

42 *One latitude* a like position, and degree of freedom.

43 *Indifferent there the greatest space hath got* most things to do with the Court are morally indifferent.

44 *Some pity is not good* to pity vice would be wrong if it led one to tolerate it.

45 *this side sin,*] this side, sin; *1633*; this side, sin, *1635-69*

47 *Which*] with *1633*
    ingress trespass upon.

48 *what none else lost* she possesses virtue in her own right, and not because she has acquired what someone else has lost.

49-50 *He will make you, what you did not, possess, / ... but weakness* God will make her gain what she did not have before, by allowing her to benefit from the shortcomings – though not the vice – of others.

55 *may*] will *1669*

60 *when your state swells* when her fortunes prosper.

61 *need of tears* whatever might oblige her to weep, such as sins or misfortunes.

62 *a rebaptizing* God will make a regenerating sacrament of the one tear of penitence she may need to shed.

63 *dis-enrol* remove her name from the roll of the saved, the Book of Life.

65 *This private gospel* the assurance of our own redemption and entry into a new life.
    New Year] new year *1633*

TO THE COUNTESS OF BEDFORD (HONOUR IS SO SUBLIME
PERFECTION)

Lucy Countess of Bedford (died 1627) became Donne's friend and
patroness about 1608. She was prominent at the Court of James I,
where she sponsored the best poets of the day, and her home at Twick-
enham had some note as a centre of culture. She herself wrote verse
and may have essayed poetic exchanges with Donne. The poems he
wrote to her which can be dated belong to the years 1609-14 or so.

1-2   *sublime ... / ... refined*   These are alchemical terms indicating
the highest degree of purity.
  perfection   Pronounced as four syllables.

3   *himself had none*   honour depends upon other people's attitude to
one, so that an unknown or a sole being could not have honour.

4   *these which we tread*   earth and water.

6   *barren both*   barren of both. Nothing grows in air or fire.

9   *but direct our honour*   since honour depends upon our attitude to a
person, kings cannot bestow honour upon people directly but can only
indicate the people whom they want us to honour.

10   *parts*] part *1633-69*

11   *stilling*   distilling, refining.

12   *dung*   alchemists supposed that the even warmth of dung was a
better purifying agent than the unequal heat of fire or the sun.
  or sun] of sun *1635-54*

13   *Madam*] Lady *several MSS*
  praisers] praises *1633-69*; prayer *MS*

18   *Sicil Isle*   Sicily. The line alludes to the subterranean caverns of
Mount Etna.

19   *darker*   more obscurely and humbly.

20-21   *subdue; / But one*] subdue, / But one *1633-69*

21   *But one*   save for God.
  contemplete   The stress falls on the second syllable – contémplate.

23   *Or took soul's stuff*   possibly God made her body of the material
of souls, which will long outlive normal bodies.

26   *Covering discovers*] Coverings discover *1669*
  quick   lively, alert; essentially alive.

27 *through-shine* transparent.
front] face *several MSS*
your heart's] our hearts' *1633–69*

29 *the use of specular stone* The ancients were supposed to have had the art and use of specular stone, now lost (see the notes on *The Undertaking* 5–12 and R. N. Ringler, 'Donne's Specular Stone', *MLR*, LX (1965)). Nero is said to have built a temple of it, which was thus perfectly transparent.

31 *and of such*] and such *1633–69 and several MSS*

33 *know and dare* to know good and to dare to do it.

34–5 *souls of growth . . . souls of sense | . . . reason's soul* In Aristotelean and scholastic metaphysics men have three souls, the vegetative, sensible and rational. The vegetative and sensible souls exist in an infant before he gains his rational soul, but they neither resign their offices when this later soul arrives nor seek to dominate it.

36 *precedence*] presidence *1633–54.*

37–9 *so, discretion, | . . . nor religion* in the same way, though discretion is first acquired it must neither keep out zeal nor itself remain untempered by it; nor again must discretion give place to zeal altogether, or keep out religion.

40–42] *These lines precede 34–9 in 1635–69 and some MSS. One MS omits them altogether.*

42 *her yea, is not her no* discretion and religion are not at odds, the one saying yes and the other saying no; they are one soul, and say the same thing.

44 *dare to break them* by putting discretion before religious faith, or being religious without discretion.

44–5 *not must wit | Be colleague to religion, but be it* intelligence must not just help out faith, but must be part of it.

46 *types of God* the circle was a traditional type or emblem of God.

47 *Religion's types* the general forms or characters of religion; the central religious truths.
pieceless centres the indivisible central points of our lives.

47–8 *flow, | And are in all the lines which all ways go* the central truths of religion flow into every aspect of all our lives as the centre of a circle flows into every radius.

48   *all ways*] always *1633–69*

49   *either ever*] ever either *several MSS*
  either   religion, and discretion.

50–51   *then religion / Wrought your ends, and your ways discretion*]
'*twas religion, / Yet you neglected not discretion MS*

51   *ways*   means.

53   *Who so would change, do covet or repent*   people alter their lives
either out of envy for someone else, or in repentance for their past sins;
and the Countess has neither motive for change.
  so] ere *several MSS*
  do covet] doth covet *1669 and several MSS*

54   *great and innocent*   her singularity lies in this conjunction of two
qualities normally incompatible, greatness and innocence.

TO THE COUNTESS OF BEDFORD
(REASON IS OUR SOUL'S LEFT HAND)

3   *blessing*] blessings *1633 and several MSS*
  sight] light *1633–69*

4   *fair*] far *some MSS*

5   *a squint lefthandedness*   (a) a perverse awkwardness or contrari-
ness; (b) a one-sided adherence to reason only.

6   *want that hand*   do without reason in attaining truth.

7   *express*   define, make clear.

8   *as I believe, so understand*   as he already believes in the Countess's
divinity, so he would now understand it too.

10   *election*   choice.

11   *accesses, and restraints*   what she admits to her favour and what
she refuses to admit.

12   *what yourself devise*   what she herself writes or thinks.

16   *catholic*   universal; what everyone believes and says.
  voice] faith *1633 and several MSS*

19   *high-topped and*] high to sense *1635–54 and MS*; high to sense and
MS; high to sun and *several MSS*; high do seem *1669 and MS*; high
to some, and *several MSS*; high to seem, and *MS*

22 *balsamum* In Paracelsian medicine every living body contains a balm which preserves and heals it. The body decays and dies only when some part of it has been deprived of the balm by an external means, or when the balm is depleted in old age. (See the note on *Love's Alchemy* 24, and on *A Nocturnal upon S. Lucy's Day* 5-6.)

27 *mithridate* a universal antidote against poison and infection. The Countess has added this to the natural qualities she was born with, by her acquired learning, religion and virtue.

29 *physic* medicine.

34 *His factor for our loves* God's agent or deputy, who gains men's love on God's behalf.
  do as you do go on towards heaven just in the same way.

35 *your return home* her return to her home in heaven, which she will make gracious by carrying with her the souls of those who loved her here.

35-6 *bestow | This life on that* make one life of your existence here and your existence in heaven, since you have lived here as if you were in heaven all the time.

36 *This*] Thy *1633*
  make one life of two (a) add your life here to the next life and make one unbroken existence of them; (b) make one life of your own being and that of the creature you have saved (the poet himself).

37 *miss* (a) be deprived of; (b) fail to reach, by not getting to heaven.

38 *all the good* (a) the moral benefit of her example and divinity; (b) the material help she can give him as his patroness.

TO THE COUNTESS OF BEDFORD (THOUGH I BE DEAD)

Donne was in France with Sir Robert Drury from November 1611 until April 1612. This poem may relate to the two Anniversaries written for the death of Elizabeth Drury, the second of which was finished in France on this trip. Donne had been censured for extravagance in his praises of the dead girl, as his letters show, and had left himself little to say of other ladies whom he might wish to praise. The latter part of the present poem seems to be an attempt to put things right with his patroness of long standing.

1 *dead, and buried* he is out of England, and so cut off from the source of his life.

5   *begot*] forgot *1633*

8   *growth ... confession*   the natural growth of spring, and the confession that precedes his Easter Communion.

11-13   *to others lent / Your stock ... / Your treasure*   he presents himself as an ill steward of his patroness's qualities.

14   *or*] and *1650-69*

16   *any other mine*   any other lady whom he has praised; possibly Elizabeth Drury.

19   *half rights seem too much*   to be just to only half her qualities would seem an excessive praise.

23   *read*   see and understand her, or read her praises, which would not be published as the poems for Elizabeth Drury had been.

24-5   *less lessons ... / ... copies*   his praises of lesser people offered lessons to those who were too low to grasp the original of which those others were only copies, the Countess herself.

26   *Desunt caetera*   the rest is missing.

TO THE COUNTESS OF BEDORD
(TO HAVE WRITTEN THEN)

The reference to Virginia in line 67 suggests that the poem was written between 1607 and 1609, when the Virginia Company's efforts to recolonize Virginia stirred up much interest among speculators and adventurers. If the 'two new stars' in line 68 are two friends lately dead, then they may well be Cecilia Bulstrode and Lady Markham who both died in 1609, and the likely date of the poem is late 1609.

2   *simony*   offering payment for something sacred.

5   *debt*] doubt *1633-54*

5-6   *In this ... / In that*   in not writing at once, or in writing at once.

6   *beholdingness*   obligation, something due.

7   *nothings*] nothing *1633 and several MSS*

9   *borrow in their payments*   the honour of writing in grateful acknowledgement is itself so great that it puts them still further in the recipient's debt.

14 *Peter Jove's ... Paul hath Dian's fane* St Peter's in Rome was supposed to have been built on the site of a pagan temple to Jove, and St Paul's in London on the site of a temple to Diana.

fane temple.

16 *hallowed a pagan Muse* she has turned his profane writing to sacred writing.

17 *denizened a stranger* made him at home in a country alien to him.

18 *blamers of the times they marred* people whose railing against the times merely covered up their own guilt, and was itself one of the things that ruined the times.

20 *or all it; you*] or all, in you *1633*
all it all the world.

22 *ostracism* banishment.

23 *fitness* concern for what is fit, nice points of Court precedence and etiquette.

25 *Your (or you) virtue*] Your, or you virtue *1633-54*; You, or you virtue *1669*
or you she is virtue itself.

26 *ransoms one sex* redeems all women.
one Court the English Court, which the Countess attends.

28 *not to you* one sign of true worth is that it is not aware that it is worthy.

32 *Stoop*] Stop *1633*

35 *Lightness ... emptiness* frivolous and shallow occupations, which damn men by taking up their whole attention.

37 *new philosophy* Copernican astronomy, which showed that the earth is not the fixed centre of the universe but moves around the sun.

39 *hath no ends* our mind has lost its sovereign purposes, and so remains inactive while the body moves.

40 *pretends* presumes to rights it does not properly have; seeks to further its own ends.

42 *so doth the body, souls* our bodies eclipse and control our souls.

43 *engines* instruments.

46 *without this* without labouring.
  this] these *1669*

47–8 *he which said*, Plough / And look not back 'And Jesus said unto him, No man, having put his hand to the plough, and looking back, is fit for the kingdom of God' (Luke ix 62).

50 *cockle* a weed that grows in cornfields.

53 *our love* love that becomes a mere matter of bodily satisfaction ruins the body itself (see *Farewell to Love*).

54–5 *We, but no foreign tyrants could* we do to ourselves what no outside agent could force upon us, destroy the native dignity of our own bodies.

55 *not engraved* not imposed from without but inherent.

56 *Caskets ... temples ... palaces* our bodies, as they might be if we did not corrupt them.

57 *redeemed* Pronounced as three syllables.

58 *Souls but preserved, not naturally free* souls are not by their nature exempt from death but are preserved from it by God. They are thus not naturally superior to bodies, which God redeems from death.
  not naturally free] born naturally free *1635–69 and MS*

59 *prisons, new souls*] prisons now, souls *1635–69 and MS*; prisons, now souls *several MSS*

60 *Which learn vice there* the body, which ought to be the temple and palace of the soul, now corrupts the innocent soul.
  vice] it *1633 and several MSS*

66 *pearl, or gold, or corn* man's body can and ought to produce precious things but in fact produces only squalid things.

67 *Virginia* the region was discovered late in the reign of Elizabeth by Sir Humphrey Gilbert and Sir Walter Raleigh, and successfully colonized by the Virginia Company after 1607.

68 *Two new stars* several new stars had been observed since the 1570s. But the following couplet points the reference to two people who had lately died, possibly Cecilia Bulstrode and Lady Markham who were both close to the Countess of Bedford (see the Funeral Elegies on them).

69 *Why grudge we us (not heaven) . . .?* why do we grudge ourselves (for we do not impair heaven's dignity thereby) the dignity of going to heaven?

70 *T' increase with ours . . . company?* to add ourselves to the company those fair souls have in heaven.

72 *two truths* the Countess's virtue, and the evil of the world.
 neither is true to you the Countess will not accept either truth.

75 *you,*] your *1633*

77 *too much of one* humility.

78 *unjust suspicion* she wrongly mistrusts her own virtue.

81 *aspersion* sprinkling. Pronounced as four syllables.

82 *complexion* temperament; state of affairs. Pronounced as four syllables.

85 *thralls* enslaves.

89 *vicious purge* (a) a violent expulsive; (b) a process that drives out some part of her virtue and replaces it with vice.

90 *cordial* a medicine that restores and preserves.

TO THE COUNTESS OF BEDFORD
(YOU HAVE REFINED ME)

Title] To the Countess of Bedford. Twitnam. *MS*

1–3 *and to worthiest things | . . . Rareness, or use, not nature value brings* because she has refined his understanding, he now sees that the best things have their value from their rareness or their usefulness, and not from their own intrinsic nature.

4 *such, as they are circumstanced* such things owe their qualities to their circumstances.

5 *Two ills can ne'er perplex us . . .* we are never put into a situation where we are obliged to choose between two evils, and so have an excuse for sin.

6 *leave and choose* pass over one and choose the other.
 and] or *1669*

7 *at Court* ... her virtue has extreme value at Court by reason of its rarity there.

8-9 *(Where ... / ... show)*] (Where ... / ... show: *1633*; Where ... / ... show: *1639-54*
a transcendent height, (as, lowness me) | *Makes her not be, or not show* the Countess transcends the Court and so is never there, or at any rate is never observed there; whereas if the poet is not at Court or not noticed there it is because he is too low.

9 *not be, or not show) all*] not see, or not show. All *1669*

9-10 *all my rhyme* | *Your virtues challenge, which there rarest be* at Court her virtues test the full extent of his poetic powers to describe them, because they are rarest there, more truly transcendent.

11 *notes: there some*] notes some: there *1669*

12 *usher* announce and identify.

13 *So in the country is beauty* her beauty gives value to the country as her virtue to the Court.
this place Twickenham Park (see line 70).

16 *Exhale them, and a thick close bud display* her face, like the sun, causes the flowers to exhale their scents and the buds to unfold.

17 *reclused* The stress falls on the first syllable – réclused.
her sweets she enshrines when the Countess is absent the country shuts up its treasures and goes into solitary mourning.

20 *falsifies both computations* One can compute the day artificially, by the length of time the sun is above the horizon, or naturally, by the full orbit of twenty-four hours. When the Countess's coach arrives at night it is like the arrival of the chariot of the sun, and day breaks then, falsifying our normal calculations.

21 *light*] sight *several MSS*

23 *you from nature loathly stray* the conceit proves that she is loath to depart from nature, in that day shines perpetually wherever she is and she has no truck with our short artificial day.

25 *the antipodes* the Court lacks the sun while Twickenham enjoys it, and has its autumn while Twickenham enjoys the spring.

26 *the vulgar sun* our common everyday sun.

27 *profane autumnal offices* the ordinary sun, doing the humdrum secular work of the world, brings autumn to the Court.

29 *priests, or organs* whether they serve her ends in the world or merely celebrate her.

30 *sound your influence ... your dictates say* the organs sound, and the priests expound her words.

34 *survey the edifice* visit the Countess.

38 *Esteem* estimate, assess.

39 *serve discourse* provide matter for conversation.

40 *invest* dress, the mere external mode of religious observance.

41 *schools* theological disputants.

42 *make it wit* consider it witty.

44 *she* virtue herself.

48 *Babblers*] Bablers *1633*; Builders *1669*
Babblers of chapels chattering connoisseurs of mere minor places of devotion.
th'Escurial the Escorial, near Madrid, built by Philip II as the royal pantheon and the centre of Spanish religious life. It is one of the largest religious establishments in the world.

50 *a lay and country eye* he now looks at her beauties as a practical layman rather than as an interpreter of religious mysteries.

51 *stories* histories.
rare choice, singular.

52 *record* The stress falls on the second syllable – recórd.
all prophecy] and prophecy *1633–69*

57 *parent*] parents *1669*

58 *both*] worth *1635–69 and MS*
both their all the whole of goodness, and of loveliness.

59 *entire* so much of a piece; manifesting such complete integrity.

60 *do the same thing* follow the one right course, be wholly true to herself.
thing] things *1633–69 and MS*
you cannot two she is incapable of doing anything that falls short of her own standard.

61 *these* these lines, and praises.
nice thin school divinity academic theology, full of hair-splitting abstractions.

62 *Serves heresy to further or repress* can be used just as well to promote heresy as to suppress it.

64 *one truth* the Countess's worth.

66 *aliens*] alters *1635–54*
aliens the men we know makes familiar acquaintance seem strange.

67 *busy* elaborate; impertinent.
and] end *1669*

68 *higher courts* higher faculties than the senses, such as reason.
sense's decree what our senses assert, the testimony of sight in particular.

70 *story* history; the sum of all past beauty.

71 *would both* would wish to see both Twickenham and the Countess.
had been] hath been *1639–69 (but given as* bin *in all the early versions)*.

72 *cherubin* members of one of the highest orders of angels, noted especially for their knowledge and beauty.

TO THE LADY BEDFORD

This poem evidently relates to the death of some lady who stood close to the Countess of Bedford, and its placing in many early collections suggests that that was either Cecilia Bulstrode or Lady Markham. Both ladies died at the Countess's home in the summer of 1609. Most of the early collections give the piece as a funeral poem; though one MS puts it with the Elegies and another with the Verse Letters. Grierson placed the poem with the Verse Letters, conjecturing that it was a covering letter to the funeral elegy *Death*) 'Language thou art too narrow, and too weak') which it adjoins in *1633* and most of the MSS.

Title] Elegy to the Lady Bedford *1633 and most MSS*

1 *You that are she and you, that's double she*] You that are she, and you that's double she *1633–69*
You that are she and you the Countess and the dead lady were so close to each other as to be one, so that the Countess as the survivor is now both of them – at once 'she and you' and 'double she'. Lady Mark-

ham's particular closeness to her cousin, the Countess, was recorded
on her tombstone – '*amicitia propinquissima*'.

5 *but themselves no third can fit* the only possible match for the one
was the other; no third person can fit them.

6 *Which were to be so* . . . even before they existed they were intended
to match each other thus, as two halves of the same thing.

6–7 *not yet. / Twins* . . .] not yet / Twins *1633–39*

7 *Cusco, and Musco* Cuzco (in Peru) and Moscow. Though such
twins are born at opposite ends of the earth they still belong together in
one constellation (such as Gemini).

15 *since you act that part* the Countess's grief for the dead lady makes
her seem as a dead body herself.

15–16 *as men say, ' Here / Lies such a Prince', when but one part is there*
as people talk of a monarch's lying in this or that tomb when only a
part of his body is buried there, such as his heart.

17 *honour and devotion due*] honour: and devotion due; *1633*

20 *what both was* the single being that was made up of both of them.
was] were *MS*

21 *as if some perished* as if something of their combined qualities
were lost.
perished pronounced as three syllables

22 *as all in you*] as in you all *MS*; that in you all *most MSS*

23 *this all* the whole creation.

24 *The pure which elemented them shall stay* the pure elements which
gave things their distinctive being will not decay but endure.

25 *spread is infinite* infinitely scattered.

26 *recollect* reassemble, collect together in one.
one all one unified whole, from which nothing essential has been lost.

27–8 *So madam* . . . / . . . *as in a bed* as with the general case so in
the particular instance, the pure parts of the dead lady will not perish
but be preserved against a final reuniting.

28 *a bed*] the bed *1633–69*; her bed *MS*

30 *of whom they were* (a) in whom they had part; (b) from whom she had them.

31. *circular* The circle figured eternity and was an emblem of God; hence the perfect motion was circular, as in the final return of things to their source.

32 *their sea, whence less streams are* all virtues draw from the Countess and return to her; as the waters drawn up in clouds from the sea fall as rain and ultimately return to the sea in rivers.
  less streams virtuous people, who owe their virtues to the Countess.

34 *both rich Indies* the East Indies and the West Indies, the region of spice and the region of precious metals (see *The Sun Rising* 17 and note, and *The Progress of the Soul* 17 and note).

36 *dram*] dream *1633*

37 *forced* forcibly constricted.

38 *Expansed in infinite* infinitely expanded or spread.

41 *in seeking new* in looking for new friends.

41-2 *to seem to doubt, / That you can match her* to entertain the possibility of finding someone who will match her.

42 *or not be without* or think that you can replace her with someone else, and so not feel her loss.

44 *Judith* The apocryphal *Book of Judeth* describes how Judeth, a beautiful young widow, saved the Israelites from their Assyrian besiegers by beguiling the enemy general Holofernes and then cutting off his head. She combined great piety with great beauty and intelligence, which may be Donne's point here; but the account makes much of her lasting fidelity to her dead husband, and one of the possible subjects of Donne's poem, Lady Markham, was a widow.

EPITAPH ON HIMSELF

First printed in *1635*. This poem is an odd man out in the early collections of Donne's poetry. No single edition or MS has all the parts of the title as it is given here; some give only a part of the poem; and all the early compilers and editors seem uncertain where the piece belongs. Editions from 1635 to 1654 give a part of the poem (the introductory epistle and the first ten lines of the epitaph itself) among the funeral poems with the title *Elegy*; then they give the complete epitaph, without the epistle, among the Divine Poems entitled *On himself*. *1669* also prints *Elegy* and *On himself* as two poems – though again the first ten lines of the epitaph are common to both – but puts them side by side among the funeral poems. Some MSS give the six-line epistle only; one MS gives the epistle and the epitaph as separate poems; another MS gives a version of the epistle as a love poem.

There is thus no accepted place for the poem or version of it. Grierson gives it as an *Epitaph* after the funeral poems. Milgate puts it with the Verse Letters. I give the full version of the epitaph, called *On himself* in *1635–69*, and have noted the differences between that and the incomplete version called *Elegy*.

Title] Epitaph *some MSS*; To the Countess of Bedford *several MSS*; Elegy *(epistle and first ten lines of the epitaph) 1635–54*; On himself *(epitaph only) 1635–69*

3 *Next to my soul* his soul is already with the Countess.

5 *Others by wills*] Others by testaments *some MSS*; Men by testament *MS*; Then by testament *MS*; O then by testament *several MSS*

Omnibus] To all *several MSS*; On himself *1635–69*
   Omnibus to all.

7 *My fortune and my choice* both by his poor fortune and by his choice he has no monument on his grave, thus breaking the custom of having a stone to speak for one after one's death.
   choice] will *Elegy in 1635–54 and MS*

8 *speechless*] senseless *Elegy in 1635–54 and MS*

9 *yet thou* He addresses all who read the poem.

10 *seest*] see *Elegy in 1635–54 and MS*

11 Yet] Nay *MS*
not yet so good we who are alive are not just living corpses but worse off than corpses; we have to die before we can improve.
   death us lay] us death lay *MSS*

12 *here*] there *Elegy in 1635–54 and several MSS*

13–14 *earth . . . / . . . glass . . . gold* Occult writers commonly parallel spiritual growth with alchemical transmutation, by which base minerals were refined up the hierarchy of qualities to the sublimity of gold. But Donne makes death itself no more than the last necessary stage in the process, the final transforming incubation.

17 *miraculously* because we thus kill something immortal.

18 *less miracle* because mortal bodies thus become immortal.

20 *them*] then *1669*
   exhale (a) blow them out of their graves; (b) hale them from their graves.

22 *to thee*] for thee *1635-69*

23 *well composed* (a) the poet is well prepared for death, his mind is composed; (b) he is already well tempered in spirit, able to resist decomposition and move up towards the condition of gold; (c) the epitaph itself is well composed.

A LETTER TO THE LADY CAREY, AND MISTRESS ESSEX RICH, FROM AMIENS

Lady Carey and Mistress Essex Rich were sisters, the daughters of Robert Lord Rich and his first wife Penelope Devereux (Sidney's Stella). Donne may not have known them when he wrote this verse letter. The instigator of the poem was probably their brother Sir Robert Rich, who passed through Amiens in late January 1612 while Donne was staying there with the Drury party. He might well have suggested that Donne write something in praise of his sisters, and taken the completed poem away with him to deliver it in person when he left Amiens a few days later.

At all events we now have the verse letter itself as Donne sent it, the only English poem of his which survives in his own hand. Its discovery was announced in June 1970 after it had passed to Sotheby's for auction, unidentified among the papers of the Duke of Manchester. It appears to have come into the possession of the Duke's family in the seventeenth century when the second Duke married in succession the niece, the daughter and the sister-in-law of the Essex Rich whom Donne addresses here; and it was deposited in the Public Records Office in the nineteenth century with the rest of the Manchester papers.

Donne wrote out the poem on either side of a thin sheet of gilt-edged quarto paper, which he then folded into a narrow packet and addressed on the blank front panel 'To the Honourable lady / the lady Carew'. If Rich himself did not carry the document to England then it probably came with a bundle of letters Donne wrote on 7 February 1612, when he had the rare chance of a reliable messenger. A letter to Sir Robert More from Amiens bearing that date (Gosse I, 287–9) appears to be written on just the same kind of watermarked paper as Donne used for the verse letter, though it is not folded and addressed in the same way.

The real value of our possessing Donne's autograph text of the poem is that we can now see in this one instance exactly how Donne set out his verse, and what relation his own copy bears to the MSS and early editions we have. Neither the *1633* edition nor any of the early MSS give the poem just as Donne wrote it. His text challenges our accepted grouping of the early versions, for they all have a seemingly unpredictable scatter of incorrect and correct readings. The verbal differences between the original copy and the version in *1633* are slight, as the notes below show. Moreover *1633*, with all the other early versions, gives the correct final reading of line 41, which Donne evidently changed from his early draft as he was writing out the copy to be sent, for he has first written 'Which is but little' then crossed out 'but little' and put 'scarce' above it.

But the striking difference between Donne's copy and any other version is in the punctuation. Donne pointed the poem far more meticulously and subtly than his scribes and editors convey, so as to control its movement and intonation. Thus in *1633* the first line reads 'Here where by All All Saints invoked are,' where Donne actually wrote 'Here, where by all, all Saints invoked are,'. Again, *1633* gives the second stanza as follows:

Yet turning to saints, should my humility
To other Saint than you directed be,
That were to make my schism, heresy.

Donne's own pointing is incomparably sharper:

Yet, turning to Saints, should my humility
To other saint, than you, directed be,
That were to make my schism heresy.

Pause and elision, so delicately placed, become part of the dramatic syntax of the poem, sensitively articulating the argument for the speaking voice. Donne seems to have sought his own way, too, of conveying the sense of the onward sweep of the argument in a tight dialectical progression; for he sets out the poem in stanzas which are marked off by oblique strokes in the margin rather than by a wide gap between them.

4 *humility* devotion.

7 *would*] could *several MSS*
convertite so cold such a lukewarm convert.

9 *this market* in Roman Catholic countries. The sale of pardons and indulgences was a standing offence to Protestant consciences.

10–12 *faith ... / ... faith alone* Protestants argued that faith alone might save one, whereas Catholics held that good works are also necessary; hence either side accused the other of undervaluing an essential means of grace. Donne's point here is that he believes by faith what he cannot know by proof.

13 *are*] is *1633*

13–14 *a firmament / ... where no one is grown, nor spent* the firmament was a zone of fixed stars set beyond the alterations of the lower heavens.

17 *In their whole substance* in their essential being; through and through.

18 *in their humours* in their physical dispositions or temperaments according to which humour predominates, the phlegmatic, sanguine, melancholy, or choleric.

19 *tasteless* insipid.
humility] humidity *1669*

20 *dough-baked* heavy, stodgy.

21 *phlegm* the phlegmatic man was too stolid and unresponsive, and might refrain from a sin simply out of indifference.

23 *then* Donne wrote it *as* than.

24 *sanguine* the sanguine man acted rashly, with more vain hope than due caution.

25 *cloistral men* retired men such as monks and recluses.
fear the fear of being contaminated by the world.

28 *choleric* choleric men were explosive-tempered and biting.
which] who *several MSS*

29 *no fall* no error or sin.

30 *this zeal*] their zeal *1633 and several MSS*

31 *parcel-gilt* partly gilded, a mere patchy gloss of virtue.
gold] golds *1633*

32 *complexion* (a) the inherent quality of the soul itself; (b) an exactly even temper of the elements, such as gold was supposed to have. Pronounced as four syllables.

33 *hath none* the truly virtuous do not know that they are virtuous.

34 *aguish*] anguish *1650-54*
   aguish fitful.
   several when it shows itself in isolated actions now and again, rather than in a settled disposition to act virtuously.

35 *By 'occasion waked, and circumstantial* when it is evoked merely by some chance occasion or circumstance.

39 *as she* as virtue herself.

40-41 *that part of you, | Which is scarce less than soul* her body.

47 *capable* able to receive her virtuous influence and be affected by it.

50 *Where*] When *several MSS*
   sympathy, and matter a soul and body wholly sympathetic to her influence, whereas the friends and others, 'parcel gilt' at best, are initially resistant to it.

53 *my ecstasy* he has a revelatory vision of them while they are far distant from him.

56 *glasses* mirrors.

57 *our*] your *several MSS*

59-60 *there is no way | . . . not to stray* anything one says about one sister which does not apply to the other too must be wrong.

TO THE COUNTESS OF HUNTINGDON (MAN TO GOD'S IMAGE)

1 *Eve, to man's* Genesis ii does not in fact say this.

2 *Nor find we that God breathed a soul in her* Donne debated the question whether women have souls in his *Paradoxes and Problems*, and pronounced on it in several sermons.

3 *Canons will not Church functions you invade* the canons of the Church prohibit women from holding ecclesiastical office.

6-7 *a new star | Whose motion with the firmament agrees* the stars were assumed to be fixed in the unchangeable firmament and to move with it; hence the advent of a new star there would be miraculous, denoting a change in the unchangeable.

10 *A seldom comet* a rare wonder.

12 *this in them withstood* art and nature denied active good to women, though some few may be passively innocent.

13 *the Magi*] which Magi *1633*

15 *fame* reputation, celebrity.

17 *the world's age, and death* there was a common belief that the world was in its decline and would soon come to an end.

18 *the sun's fall* variation in the arc of the sun's path persuaded some thinkers that the sun was coming nearer the earth year by year.

20 *So low as woman* so low as to be represented by a woman.

23 *then* before the Fall.

24 *amassed*] a mass *1635-69*
   amassed, contracted brought together, summed up.

25 *She* virtue.
   gilded . . . gold the distinction is that between a veneer and a solid metal.

25-6 *gold, and she; / Us she informed*] gold, and she, / Us she informed *1633*; gold; and she, / Informed us *1633-69*
   and she the Countess is not just wholly virtuous, she is virtue itself.

26 *informed* gave form to; stamped; animated.
   transubstantiates transforms her to something beyond mere human nature.

28 *Elixir-like* in spiritual alchemy the quest for the elixir which transforms base metals to gold figured the progress towards personal regeneration, the purifying of the old Adam.
   not clean, but new not just innocent, as in the first state, but re-generate and hence transformed.

32 *adhere in* dwell in, take the form of.

33 *being alike pure, we should neither see* we should then see neither virtue not the Countess, since they are equally pure.

34 *water ... into air rarefied* vaporized, as in mist. But 'rarefied' here indicates a moral ascent from an impure to a pure order of being.

35 *Neither appear* neither water nor air is visible.

37–9 *great constellations ... / ... gods are named* the more populous the constellation the baser its name, whereas single planets get the names of gods.
  which being framed / ... named] in brackets in 1635–69

41 *one doth comprehend* one person knows her fully as a woman, her husband.

42 *in the veil of kindred others see* others, her relatives, see her obscurely in the aspect of a kinswoman.
  veil] spelled *vail* in the early versions; vale 1669

46 *'tis not none* to dare to contemplate her is a virtue in itself.
  contemplate The stress falls on the second syllable – contémplate.

47 *which do so* contemplate her.
  do so] do *several MSS*; to you 1633

48 *so these lines are due* the poem is the tribute he owes her as her true subject, in recompense for the privilege of contemplating her.

49–50 *If you can think these flatteries, they are, / For then your judgement is below my praise* if this seems like flattery to her then it is flattery, for in that case he will have overpraised her judgement.

50 *below* fall short of.

52 *counsels* advice, moral guidance.
  as far th'endeavour raise people try to live up to what has been flatteringly said of them.

53–4 *my ill reaching you might there grow good* his overpraising her thus might spur her to merit his claims after all, and so turn to good in her although the source would be tainted.

55 *But*] And 1635–69
  But not were it not that, save that.

56 *than my will* than his will or capacity to praise them.

58 *long ago* possibly when she was a child; or in an earlier poem.

63 *confessed* made manifest.

64 *Yourself were bound to say that which I do* she herself would be compelled to say what he says now, in her own praise.

66 *or speaker*] and speaker *1635–69*

67 *ministerial notary* a scribe of the divine power.

68 *fame* public knowledge.

69 *your prophet* he foretold what was to come.

70 *your chaplain* he assumes the office of a chaplain in that he now praises God in her.

TO THE COUNTESS OF HUNTINGDON (THAT UNRIPE SIDE OF EARTH)

In the MSS this poem is headed 'Sir Walter Ashton to the Countess of Huntingdon'. It was first printed in *1635*, as Donne's. Grierson thought that it is not by Donne, and gave it among the poems attributed to him; Milgate is sure Donne wrote it.

Lady Elizabeth Stanley became Countess of Huntingdon when her husband succeeded to the earldom in 1605. Donne would then have known her for some time, for her mother, the Countess of Derby, married Sir Thomas Egerton in 1600 and brought the three Stanley sisters into Sir Thomas's household. But J. Yoklavich argues that Donne wrote the poem to her soon after her marriage in 1603, when she was thirteen years old ('Donne and the Countess of Huntingdon', *PQ*, XLIII (1964), 283–8).

1–10 The sense of these lines is incomplete. Milgate suggests that some opening lines were lost before the Countess allowed the poem to be copied, and that they likened those people who did not know the Countess to the savages beyond civilized influence.

1 *unripe . . . heavy* It was generally believed that people's manners and temperaments are formed by the air of the region in which they grow up. So the naked savages of South America and the tropics altogether are the immature product of their torpid climate.

2 *man*] men *MS*

4 *Knew they not it, and feared beasts' company* if men were not aware of their nakedness, and afraid of being taken for beasts.

9 *that free state* the natural condition of freedom before the Fall.

10 *wanting the reward* not having acquired the knowledge of good

and evil that Adam and Eve gained at the Fall; and not knowing of Christ's redemption of mankind.

bear the sin   bear the consequences of Eve's sin.

11   *downward*] inward *MS*

13   *younger forms*   the forms of smaller objects.

14   *These ... that without your distance lie*   people who are outside the Countess's circle, particularly those who address trite poems of praise to her.

16   *at home but wit's mere atomi*   mere poetic minnows in their own spheres.

17   *who can behold them move, and stay*   who can see them clearly enough to know when they move or stand still.

18   *just their midway*   halfway between them and her.

21   *neither*] never *MS*

22   *cross-armed*   the posture of a lover.

24   *white-livered*   thin-blooded with age.

26   *faithfully*] finally *several MSS*
   faithfully, (without you smiled) were gone   if she did not smile at him he would faithfully die of love.
   you smiled] your smile *1669 and MSS*

28   *raised by love*   (a) elevated; (b) sexually stimulated.

30   *whispers*] whispered *MS*; vapours *MS*

31-2   *who to trees | Doth talk*   the orthodox courtly lover, who complains to the trees when he should be making love.

32   *ague*] fever *MS*

34   *with its own shade*   the lover is killed by the mere shadow of love, his solitary sufferings, and not by the reality.

36   *women*] woman *MS*

37   *were one*] were but one *1669*

38   *raw disordered heap*   the original chaos, which first began to give way to order when the several elements separated out, each following its own nature and desire.

41 *but*] once *MS*

47 *those days*] that day *1669*

50 *both*] but *several MSS*; yet *1669*

52 *man become*   be fitting to man.

53-4 *whose . . . / Finds*] who . . . / Find *MS*

54 *Finds but the place, after, the nearest way*   one is at first content just to locate the place, but then one looks for the nearest way to it.

55 *passion is to woman's love, about*   a mere display of passion, as in love poetry, is an impossibly roundabout way of getting a woman's love.

57 *sueth, or*] sues and *MS*
   sueth, or doth contend   pleads or debates for her love.

58 *but meets a friend*   finds mere friendship instead of an answering love.

59 *Man's better part*   what is better than mere passion, as the spirit and reason are.

60 *allowed*   admitted, favourably received.

62 *till it find summer way*   discreet love does not venture anything until it sees that the ice has thawed, and that it is likely to succeed.

63 *weather-beaten*   much refused, buffeted by his mistress's scorn.

64 *every girl*   every mere novice in the art of repudiating lovers.

65-6 *Who strives through woman's scorns . . . / . . . his shadow to outgo*   a woman's scorn is only the reflection of the lover himself, and to strive to know her by that is to seek to run faster than one's own shadow.
   woman's] women's *MS*
   scorns, women] scorn, woman *MS*

67 *It must be*] It is mere *1669*

69 *sigh*] sin *1633-69*

73 *unsure*   not securely attached.

74 *can untie, and bind*   as Christ vested in Peter the power to loose or to bind souls (Matthew xvi 19).
   and bind] I bind *1635-69 and MS*

76 *porter* one who is permanently installed at the gate and never admitted beyond that.
  woo] woe *1635–69*

79 *clouds you rise from, our noon ray*] clouds, you rise from our noon ray *1635–69 and MS*

80 *not your break of day* compared to her brightness their noon ray is not even a daybreak but a foul shadow.

81 *right*] bright *MS*

83 *a perfectness*] all perfections *MS*; all perfectness *MS*
  curious finely, delicately.

84 *youngest*] quaintest *MS*
  youngest flatteries do scandal it even the least flatteries misrepresent her perfection.
  flatteries] flatterers *some MSS*

85 *what is more* what overshoots the truth about her.
  restrain limit.

86 *though*] what's *MS*
  down the hill overshoots the peak of her perfection and goes down the other side, still coming short of her.

87 *next* near, direct, parallel.
  we cross to it we cannot take the direct path of her perfection but cross to it obliquely from our own way, to encounter it at some one point only.

88 *straight line, thing praised, attribute* she is at once perfection and rectitude itself, the object of all praise and the attribute of any good thing.
  line] lace *MS*

89–90 *many a shade / You make* people strive to follow her.

90 *in them are your motions made* (a) the light and shade show up her qualities in clear relief; (b) her imitators enact her qualities.

92 *zanies* parasitic imitators, aping her virtues.

98 *for man's ease, but nearer joined* for man's well-being the soul is still more closely joined to the body than heaven could be joined to earth.

99 *thoughts*] through *MS*

99–100 *Where thoughts the stars of soul ... / ... but command* where we understand some thoughts to rule and guide our soul, as the stars in heaven influence things on earth, we cannot comprehend their large natures but recognize their authority.

101 *that bounty is of light* her love is as the sun, whose bounty of light is universal and inexhaustible.

103 *thither to intend* it draws us towards her, as the sun draws up vapours from the earth.

105 *access* approach.
wholly] holy *MS*

106 *clearness* pure brightness and perfection.

107 *dare*] dares *MSS*
stain some moral impurity.

108 *weight*] weights *several MSS*

109 *impure*] vapour *MS*
retain continue, remain.

111 *unforced* unassisted by some refining process.

112 *converse* live in, mingle with.

113 *eye, and hand*] eyes and hands *MSS*

114 *high'st they*] highest *MSS*

115 *Though far removed*] Through far remoteness *MS*
removed Pronounced as three syllables.
fleets] isles *1669 and MS*

116 *sun's comfort*] sun's sweet comfort *1669*
others] yet some *1669*

117 *equal* a mean between the extremes: equable.

119 *as air*] as the air *MS*
the sun-beam's] all sunbeams *MS*
the sun-beam's equal bright the uniform brightness of the sun's beam, which illuminates all the air equally.

120 *the first rays*] the rays' first *1669 and MS*; the rise first *MS*
his last opposite the sunset in the west.

121 *able men*] able man *1635–54*; happy man *1669*
able men men who are fit to receive love.

122 *Remote or near, or howso'er they move*   distant from their mistress
or near her, or whether they move further from or back towards her
(see *A Valediction: forbidding Mourning*, 25–36).

123 *Their*] There *1635–54*

125 *violent*] valiant *1635–69*

126 *wandering rage*   sensual lust, which is necessarily unfixed and
unstable.

127 *imparts*] imports *1669 and MS*

128] Is thought the mansion of sweet appetite *MS*; Is fancied *(rest
of the line left blank) 1635–39*; Is fancied in the soul, not in the sight
1650–54; Is fancied by the soul, not appetite *1669*

129 *Why love among the virtues is not known*   The cardinal virtues of
the pagan moralists were wisdom, courage, temperance and justice.

130 *Is, that*] Is 'cause *MS*
   contract in] contracted *1635–39 and MS*
   contract   contracted, summed up.

TO THE COUNTESS OF SALISBURY

The Countess of Salisbury was the Lady Catherine Howard, who mar-
ried the Earl of Salisbury in 1608. Donne's connexion with her is not
known, but he wrote an epithalamion for her sister in 1613 (the *Eclogue
1613. December 26*), and one of his friends, George Garrard, was in the
service of the Salisburys by 1614. In an undated prose letter Donne
thanks Garrard for commending him to 'that noble lady in whose pres-
ence you are', and pleads that he is inadequate to the task of praising
her fitly in verse (Gosse I, 294–5).

6 *tires*   attires, clothes. Petrarch's sonnet *Chiome d'oro* lay behind the
fashion of praising one's mistress's hair as so many nets to catch the
sun's golden rays.

9–14 See *The First Anniversary* for the terms of this account of the
world's subsidence towards chaos. The two poems plainly have much
in common.

10 *virtue*] virtues *1633–69 and MS*

15 *little shares*   mere small portions of the qualities men might have.

30 *best*] least *several MSS*

32 *contemplate* The stress falls on the second syllable – contémplate.

33-4 *there may be degrees of fair, great, good . . . / . . . virtue understood*
her light, amplitude and virtue enable us to understand that there may
be degrees of fair, great and good (for we can see how far all other
things that have such qualities fall short of her). See lines 52-4 of this
poem.

35 *this sacrifice* the present poem, his devout offering to her.

38 *idolatry*] adultery *several MSS*

48 *and, that you* that there are two people who are worthiest, the
Countess and somebody else.

50 *then* given as than *in the early versions.*

52 *souls of growth, and sense* the vegetable soul, and the sensible soul.

53 *our soul immortal* the reasonable soul, which makes us human.

57 *any; I adore*] any, if I adore *1635-69 and MS*

59 *measure* the amount.

64 *their walks . . . their home* the distinction is between the occasional
resorts of these qualities, and their permanent dwelling or centre.

67 *them* the people he has praised previously.

70 *Which none, not reading others, first, could do* which no one could
do who had not first read other (lesser) people.

74 *Illustrate* give them light and understanding. The stress falls on
the second syllable – illústrate.

76 *one born blind* presumably Homer. It was a Renaissance common-
place that his two epic poems comprehended all arts and sciences.

77-8] *Several MSS omit these lines*

79 *though I'am born without those eyes* fortune has deprived him of
the means to use his eyes where he wants to.

82 *see you thus* he contemplates her with the eyes of his mind.

Epicedes and Obsequies
Upon the deaths of Sundry Personages

ELEGY ON THE L.C.

The 1633 edition and most of the MSS place this poem among the Elegies, as does Helen Gardner.

The title 'the L.C.' occurs only in *1635–69* and may not be authentic. As it stands it could refer to the Lord Chancellor, Donne's old employer Sir Thomas Egerton, who died in 1617; but little in the poem fits his circumstances. A more likely conjecture is that 'the L.C.' stands for the Lord Chamberlain, Henry Cary the first Baron Hunsdon, who died in 1596; and in fact one seventeenth-century annotator of Donne expanded the title in his copy of *1639* to 'Lord Cary' (see J. Sampson, 'A Contemporary Light upon John Donne' in *Essays and Studies by Members of the English Association*, VII (1921)). But again the domestic emphasis of the poem seems incommensurate with the mourning for a major public figure who was a kinsman of the Queen. Helen Gardner suggests that the editor of *1635* misunderstood a heading 'To L.C.' which he found in a MS now lost, and that the poem was written to one Lionel Cranfield on the death of his father, a merchant, in 1595. Donne and Cranfield were on friendly terms many years later, and it is possible that they knew each other at this time though there is no evidence of it. Cranfield (1575–1645) was an apprentice who rose to be a privy councillor, and became the first Earl of Middlesex in 1622.

6 *serve*] starve *(written* sterve*) MS*

8 *store* plenty.

10 *that* the tree.

11 *felled*] filled *MS*

12 *which by it*] by which it *MS*

15 *venturers*] venturous *MS*
venturers merchant venturers, such as those who formed companies to exploit the resources of Virginia and the East Indies.

16 *Venture their states*] Venture estates *MS*
states (a) estates, possessions; (b) spiritual well-being.

16-17 *with him in joy to share. / We lose what*] with him in joy to share / We lose what *1633*; ... share, / We lose *1635-69*

20 *names*] name *1635-69*

22 *die first* die in order to be able to see him again.

24 *dead, senseless* stunned with grief.

ELEGY ON THE LADY MARKHAM

Lady Markham, widow of Sir Anthony Markham, was a first cousin and close friend of the Countess of Bedford. She died at Twickenham on 4 May 1609. Several poets wrote verses on her death; indeed Lady Bedford herself may have done so, for some MSS ascribe to her the funeral elegy *Death be not proud, thy hand gave not this blow.*

1 *ocean* pronounced as three syllables.

2 *the lower parts* the body.

5 *pretend* claim; threaten; foreshadow.

6 *And breaks*] To break *1669*
banks] bounds *MS*; bank *1633-69*

7 *vent* issue forth.

7-8 *vent; / Our waters*] vent / Our waters *several MSS*

8 *above our firmament* There was supposed to be a region of waters in the pure zone above the firmament of heaven. 'And God made the firmament; and divided the waters which were under the firmament, from the waters which were above the firmament. ... And God called the firmament Heaven' (Genesis i 7-8). In Donne's figure these waters correspond to our most spiritual tears.

9 *sins*] sin *MS*

10 *brackish ... funeral* our purest tears are tainted by mortal passion and fear.

11 *these*] those *1633-69*

12 *God's 'No'*] God's Noe *1633 and MS*; God, new *1669*
God's 'No' the 'Noe' in some early versions points the reference to Noah. But the sense is that we now sinfully drown ourselves out of despairing grief, although God has forbidden us to take our own lives.
our world] the world *1633-54 and some MSS*

16 *mist*] mists *several MSS*
what she] what we *MS*

21-2 *As men of China, after an age's stay | Do take up porcelain, where they buried clay* there was a common belief that the Chinese obtained porcelain simply by burying clay in the earth for a hundred years.
porcelain] procelane *MS*; purse lend *MS*
where they buried] when they burned *MS*

23 *limbeck* alembic, a vessel used in alchemy for purifying minerals.

24 *mines* rich deposits of precious metals.

25 *inspire* infuse and animate.

27 *to recompense it* to make up for the destruction of the world by fire.

28 *then*] them *1650-69 and MS*
th'elixir of this all her flesh was already so pure that when it has thus been transmuted by death God need look no further for the elixir which will complete the purging work of the last fire, and bring what remains of the material world to pure gold and eternal life.

29 *the sea, when it gains, loseth too* the common belief was that any gain the sea made had to be compensated by a loss somewhere else.

30-32 *the younger brother ... | ... th'elder death* the two brothers are the death of the body and the death of the soul. If one gains, the other loses; for our body's death is the liberation of our soul from sin.

33 *when they*] who *MS*

34 *and both deaths' dust*] and both, death's dust *1633*; and both death's dust *1635-69*; and both dead dust *most MSS*
both deaths' dust the dust of the two deaths, for neither of them has power over a just person.

35 *unobnoxious now* no longer exposed to harm.

36 *none to death sins* no one sins mortally.
to sin] to death *MS*

37 *do*] did *MS*

38 *this, and that virginity* being loth to sin and not loth to die, she was exempt from mortal sin and from death.

42 *cracks*] cracked *MS*; breaks *most MSS*

45 *rarefy*] rectify *some MSS*

46 *lacked little of a lie*   made a lie of whatever fell slightly short of absolute truth.

49 *Moses' cherubins*   God commanded Moses to have an ark made, with a mercy-seat flanked by two winged cherubim of gold (Exodus xxv 18–21).

50 *winged*   pronounced as two syllables.

52 *tears, the common stairs*   tears of penitence such as are a necessary means of our getting to heaven, since all men have cause to shed them and cannot gain God's grace without them.

54 *vain*] rash *MS*

55 *even*   consistent in her behaviour.

56 *good in all her titles*   worthy of her standing and high repute.

57 *reformed*   corrected.
forward   recent, modern.

58 *That women can no parts of friendship be*   that women cannot be party to a friendship. Grierson cites Montaigne on this opinion: 'her mind shall one day be capable of many notable things, and amongst other of the perfection of this thrice-sacred amity, whereunto we read not, her sex could yet attain' *(Of Presumption, Essays* II, 17*)*. But its origin may be Ficino's Neoplatonic assumption that friendship between men is the ideal expression of love, far removed from the vulgar love between men and women *(Opera omnia* (1561), 613, 795 and many other places).
women] woman *1633 and MS*
parts] part *several MSS*

60 *virtues*] virtue *1639–54*
Lest they . . . think her old   it would seem to them that a short life could not accommodate so many virtues.

62 *triumph*] triumphs *most MSS*

ELEGY ON MISTRESS BOULSTRED

Cecilia Boulstred, or Bulstrode, a kinswoman of the Countess of Bedford, died at Twickenham on 4 August 1609 aged twenty-five. A number of poets wrote verses on her death, among them Ben Jonson who in an epigram referred to her as the Court *pucelle* and in an epitaph praised her virgin virtue.

In several MSS this elegy is followed immediately by a funeral elegy for Cecilia Bulstrode, *Death be not proud, thy hand gave not this blow*. Editors have generally agreed that the second poem is not by Donne. Two MSS attribute it to the Countess of Bedford herself.

1 *Death I recant* the opening address suggests a palinode, as though the poet here takes back an earlier disparagement of death. This is presumably why some compilers gave the poem with the elegy, *Death be not proud*.

5 *there are set*] and the meat *some MSS*

6 *dishes*] dished *1635–39 and some MSS*

10 *best first*] best fruit(s) *some MSS*; first fruit *MS*
well preserved to last virtuous people were thought to keep their preserving balm better than others, whose sin erodes it.

13 *Nor will this earth serve him* nor is he content to prey on land creatures only.

15 *were Death dead* if there were no more death.
by roes] the roes *1635–54*; the rows *1669*; by rows *some MSS*

17 *rounds* encompasses, takes all its inhabitants into his sweep.

18 *organic* like Church organs.

20 *A tenth rank in the heavenly hierarchy* Pseudo-Dionysius described the chain of angelic beings as divided into three groups, each with three sub-divisions, making nine orders of angels in all.

24 *the four monarchies* Babylon, Persia, Greece, Rome.
antichrist the early Church took a reference in Isaiah as a prophecy of Christ's ultimate destruction of antichrist: 'and with the breath of his lips he shall slay the wicked' (xi 4).

26 *this all* the entire creation.
nothing else is] nothing is else *MS*

27 *lives*] life *1633 and some MSS*

30 *Nor are we mortal, dying, dead, but death* we are not merely subject to death, we are death itself.

34 *but few* the saved.
to thee] for thee *1635–69*

35 *thou hast*] hast thou *MS*

37 *more storeys high* her moral stature put her beyond death's reach.

38 *her lower room* her body.
  lower] low *MS*

40 *both of captain missed and fort* death has failed to capture either the captain or the stronghold, her soul or her body.

41 *king*] Kings *1635-69*
  remove moves on, departs.

42 *rest for* wait to be rejoined with their souls in heaven.

45 *work*] works *some MSS*; makes *several MSS*

50 *do so* do what you have done (kill her young).

51 *to thy loss* to the disadvantage of death itself.

51-2 *the cost | Of beauty, and wit* what beauty and wit cost other people, the havoc they wreak.

52 *apt to do harm* (a) peculiarly fit and willing to do harm; (b) prone to do harm.

54 *Oh*] Of *MS*

57 *devotion* pronounced as four syllables.

58 *once* one day; at some future time.
  superstition pronounced as five syllables.

59 *must*] might *MS*

61 *persevered* The stress falls on the second syllable – persévered.
  there] then *MS*
  been given as bin *in the early versions*

62 *mis-thinking*] mistaking *several MSS*

63-4 *feign | To sociableness, a name profane* affect to see something vicious in her love of company.

65 *by tempting* by tempting her to sin.

66 *By wishing* by covertly wishing that she would fall into sin, or would sin with them; by putting the thought of sin in her mind, without naming particular sins.

67 *crossed* (a) thwarted; (b) inadvertently saved her (by allowing her a virtuous death and the benefit of Christ's cross).

68   *triumph*   The stress falls on the second syllable – triúmph.
   thine army   all those virtues in her that might have drawn others to sin, and so made them a prey to death.
   army] armies *MS*; armour *MS*

71   *weep as much*   weep as much as if we grieved immoderately.

72   *because we are not such*   because we are not dead ourselves.

73   *knot*   (a) small group; (b) tightly linked company.

74   *the chain is broke, though no link lost*   although the circle of friends has been broken here, as it must be because we are mortal and finite, yet it will be perfectly remade in heaven.
   though] but *1633 and some MSS*

AN ELEGY UPON THE DEATH OF MISTRESS BOULSTRED

Title   ] Elegy *1633*; Elegy XI. Death *1635–54 (where it is placed among the Elegies)*

2   *sorrow*] sorrows *1635–69 and several MSS*

4   *Grief wears, and lessens, that tears breath affords*   grief wears away and grows less if tears give it utterance.

7   *estate*   condition, circumstances.

8   *extreme*   The stress falls on the first syllable – éxtreme.
   sense   awareness.

10   *the fifth and greatest monarchy*   the four monarchies were Babylon, Persia, Greece and Rome. Presumably the fifth monarchy is death, which sorrow rules over.
   fifth] first *MS*

15–16   *that palace won, / But thou must raze it too, that was undone?*   the figure suggests that the lady had been thrown into a prolonged grief and had then died of it.

20   *told not when, but did the day begin*   they did not just announce the beginning of the day but began it themselves.

21   *sapphirine*   transparent, because morally pure and precious.

24   *crystal ordinance*   chemical apparatus made of crystal, for the purest work.
   ordinance] ordance *MS*

26 *Thou'hast lost thy end* the end of conquest is to subdue other peoples, not to exterminate them or oppress them so savagely that they rebel.
  for in her] in her we *1635–69*

27 *to rebel* (a) to call in question the final power of sorrow or death; (b) to find that this was no conquest after all but a benefit.

28 *They ... that*] That ... who ... *1635–69 and some MSS*
  They know her better now they now have the certain knowledge of her blissful condition in heaven.

29 *or pine, and*] and pine, and *1633–69 and several MSS*; or pine or *some MSS*

30 *not*] no *MS*

31 *our world with hers; now*] our word with hers now *MS*

33–4] For all moral virtues she was all
      That ethics speak of virtues cardinal.
      (MS)

  all | The ethics speak she personified all that pagan writings on ethics say of the cardinal virtues.

34 *The ethics*] That Ethics *1635–69 and several MSS*; The ethnics spake *MS*
  virtues cardinal the four cardinal virtues are justice, prudence, temperance and fortitude.

36 *keep* guard.
  that kept out] to keep out *several MSS*

37] She had no more; then let in death for we *1669*

40 *him and his laws above* more than God and his laws.

41–2 *tears, he mercy shed in this, | To*] see his mercy shown in this / 'Twill *MS*

44 *holiday* the anniversary of her death.

45 *that strange bush* 'And the Angel of the Lord appeared unto [Moses] in a flame of fire out of the midst of a bush; and he looked, and behold, the bush burned with fire, and the bush was not consumed' (Exodus iii 2).

48 *That what*] That when *MS*

what we turn to feast, she turned to pray   what we make a religious festival of, she took as a prompting to prayer.

turn] turned *some MSS*

feast] feasts *some MSS*

50   *The rest*   the quiet repose.

52   *that order whence most fell*   seraphim, who stand next to God and attend upon him.

53   *Her body left*] Her body's left *1635–69*

54   *except*] unless *MS*

56   *framed*] fained *several MSS*; formed *several MSS*
them] their *MS*

57   *moas*] woes *1633*

58   *lemnia   terra lemnia*, specifically a medicinal earth found in Lemnos. But alchemists used the term to mean a clay which aided the process of transmutation from non-precious substances to precious.

59   *crystal*   a substance of transparent purity which is nonetheless not yet precious.

60   *took up spruce*   raised from the grave as an evergreen, rejuvenated into perpetual life.
diamond   our earthly flesh transformed into the most precious jewel, pure and unchanging.

61   *sad glad*] glad sad *most MSS*
all] each *MS*
bear a part   each accepts a share.

62   *all would waste a stoic's heart*   to bear all the grief would be too much for one person; it would wear away the heart even of someone who professes indifference to human fortunes and passions.
waste] break *1635–69 and several MSS*

ELEGY UPON THE UNTIMELY DEATH OF THE
INCOMPARABLE PRINCE HENRY

First published in *Lachrymae Lachrymarum, or the Spirit of Tears distilled from the untimely Death of the Incomparable Prince Panaretus*, edited by J. Sylvester (1613).

Prince Henry, James I's eldest son and the heir to the throne, died on 6 November 1612 aged eighteen. Much had been hoped of him as a patron of the arts and a leader of the Protestant cause in Europe, so that his death came as a real public shock. Grierson says that it 'evoked more elegiac poetry in Latin and English than the death of any single man has probably ever done' (II, 204). Donne's poem appeared in one of several collections of mourning tributes, along with poems by some of his friends. Jonson told Drummond of Hawthornden that 'Donne said to him, he wrote that epitaph on Prince Henry *Look to me Faith* to match Edward Herbert in obscureness' (*Conversations* 136).

Title] Elegy on Prince Henry *1633–54 and some MSS*

2–16 *both my centres ... / ... both centres one* These are at once the focal points of reference in the poet's understanding of the universal scheme, and the faculties which fix those points for him, reason and faith. In our dislocated understanding these centres do not coincide, as they should and may (since reason and faith are concentric circles), but control two distinct areas of our experience. The field of reason is wholly circumscribed and finite, because we can resolve by discursive reason only what pertains to life in the world; the operation of reason may thus be represented by a circle whose circumference marks the limit of reason's grasp. Faith on the other hand has a centre but no limiting circumference, for 'the nature of God is a circle of which the centre is everywhere and the circumference is nowhere' (St Bonaventura quotes this celebrated dictum in the thirteenth century but its author is unknown).

If we try to grasp the matters of faith with our ordinary reason alone then they seem repugnant to reason; they have no order or focus but strike us as so many divergent lines and angles in an eccentric chaos. Yet our elevated understanding may all but close the gap between reason and faith so that we glimpse the absolute reasonableness of the universal order. Such an event as Prince Henry's death, however, disturbs both centres by its apparent unreasonableness; it shakes our faith in a reasonable universe and in a divine providence.

2 *feel this period* are disturbed by this end or completion (see lines 23–4).

3 *weight* finite mass, everything we can know and understand.
 greatness non-finite extension, everything that goes beyond the evidence of our senses.

5 *there do end* we can understand them fully, there is nothing about them that reason cannot grasp.

7 *Quotidian things* the things pertaining to the everyday life of the world.

equidistant hence they are equidistant from each other and from the centre, in that we can grasp them all equally well and that they are of equal standing; so that it is a matter of final indifference which of such things we know and which we do not know.

8 *Shut in . . . in one circumference* they do not go beyond the reach of our finite reason.

man] men *1613*

10 *disproportioned . . . angular* they escape our finite categories of order; our reason cannot fit them into any coherent pattern, make any sense of them or grasp them.

13 *eccentric else* they would otherwise seem to have no centre, symmetry, or relation to each other.

14 *neither all, nor upon all alike* not all of them are matters for faith alone, nor do they all demand a like degree of faith.

15-16 *put to her best extension, / Almost meets faith* our reason used properly at its furthest stretch is almost capable of reaching to these non-finite matters and thus seconding faith.

18 *that*] the *1613*
we miss we now lack.

19 *might*] could *1613*

20 *would* would perform it.

21 *moving*] movings *1613*
the centre the centre of the earth, the world's axis.

23-4 *centres distracted so* faith and reason alike are shaken, thrown off balance by an event which seems to confound both of them.

26 *was an ecstasy* put them in a trance; showed them a vision of something beyond their ordinary understanding.

28 *discovered* disclosed.

29 *angled* tried to gain his support for their policy by guile.

30 *torpedo* the electric ray, whose sting can numb.

31 *others' studies* he was others' studies. Those who were not actively seeking his support for some policy of their own were trying to align their policy with his.

34 *This soul of peace*   King James himself (see *The Ecstasy* 65–8), and his present policy of peacemaking.

  through] to *1635–69*

38 *those, of which they emblems are*   the new order presided over by Christ after the world has passed away.

40 *The last days came*   that the end of the world was at hand. This was a common belief in the seventeenth century.

41 *aspect*   The stress falls on the second syllable – aspéct.

42 *rumours of war*   'And as he sat upon the mount of Olives, the disciples came unto him privately, saying "Tell us . . . what shall be the sign of thy coming, and of the end of the world?" And Jesus answered and said unto them ". . . ye shall hear of wars and rumours of wars . . . but the end is not yet"' (Matthew xxiv 6).

  did] should *1613, 1635–69*

43 *this faith*   specifically, the belief that the world would shortly end, and that Prince Henry was a type of Christ. In the larger sense, faith altogether (see line 63).

44 *vex our great-grandmother, dust*   (a) we must still go on dying and being buried in the dust from which we drew in the first place; (b) we have to go on providing the evidence of our mortal descent from Eve's flesh, and lengthening out Eve's guilt; (c) we are thrown back on our old uncertainties, and can only interrogate the dust (*OED* 'vex' II, 2).

  great-grandmother] great grand mother *1633*; great grand-mother *1635–69*

48 *to die?*] to die. *1633*; to die *1669*; to die! *1635–54*

49–50 *As, for the earth . . . | . . . to desire to fall*   in the same way as the lowest of low things would be ambitious if it merely wished to fall still further.

52 *Our plot for ease*   our plan to gain relief from our misery by the still greater wretchedness of dying.

54 *so many mandrakes*   they are rooted, shrieking, in Prince Henry's grave.

55 *What had his growth, and generation done*   what would his live growth and fertility have achieved . . .?

56-7 *what we are, his putrefaction | Sustains in us; earth, which griefs animate* when his very putrefaction sustains what being we have – for we are no more than earth animated by our griefs.

58 *other soul than that* than our grief for Prince Henry. There is a play on 'animate', which Donne here takes in the sense of 'provides with a soul' (*anima*).

60 *this their new joy* Prince Henry's ascent to heaven.

62 *they foreknow* the errors which they foreknow we will commit.

63 *faster* more secure.

65-6 *our connexion | Of causes* discursive reason proceeds by steps, connecting cause to effect and cause to cause.

66 *Of*] With *1613*

67-8 *substances ... | ... accident* In Aristotelean physics substances are the basic natures of material things and accidents are their variable properties.

71 *Fate*] faith *1613*
such a chain such a connexion of causes and effects as we assume when we reason.

73 *come*] join *1613*
so] to *1613*

74 *A new link* some circumstance that baffles us because it lies outside our finite 'laws' of cause and effect, which are in fact only inductions from our previous experience.

75 *deader fault* more serious error; total loss.

77 *busy* officious; ingeniously elaborate.
proof] proofs *1613*

80 *May safelier say, that we are dead* because we cannot now either reason or lament his death.

81 *well declare* adequately express.

82 *and we are*] we are *1613*

83 *I would not*] would not I *1669*

84 *as he is he* as he really is in himself.

85-6 *Our soul's ... | ... God,*] *In brackets in 1633*

85–6 *Our soul's best baiting* ... / ... *considering God* meditating upon Prince Henry is our best help to considering God himself, a kind of halfway stage for our finite understandings.

baiting a staging post, where travellers stop for refreshment on a long journey.

mid-period a halfway stage.

87 *no dishonour* it is no dishonour to his memory to consider him under a purely human aspect, that of love.

89 *since I live* since his understanding is thus restricted to human experience.

90 *That she-intelligence which moved this sphere* in a cosmic body, the intelligence is the directing spirit seated within the larger orb.

moved (a) impelled; (b) provoked amorous passion.

91 *I pardon Fate, my life* he forgives Fate for condemning him to go on living now.

92 *conscience* tenderness of feeling; awareness of Prince Henry's love and of the fact that these lines are addressed to her now.

93 *charms* (a) spells used in conjuration; (b) amorous words.

94 *only you two* you two alone, of all lovers.

95 *souls ye sighed* see *Song (Sweetest love, I do not go)* 25–6 and *The Expiration* 1–2.

96 *you wish I knew your history* so that he might celebrate her too, or celebrate the two lovers together.

97–8 *So much, as you two* ... / ... *what you were* if he did know something of her, then he would celebrate the two lovers as an angel hymns the joys of heaven.

two mutual heavens they were a heaven to each other.

OBSEQUIES TO THE LORD HARRINGTON,
BROTHER TO THE LADY LUCY, COUNTESS OF BEDFORD

Lord Harrington, second Baron of Exton, died at Twickenham in February 1614 aged twenty-two, a year after succeeding to his father's title. He had been a close friend of Prince Henry, was noted for his humane learning, and gave promise of a spectacular public career; but he was taken suddenly ill on a continental journey (some spoke of poison) and came home to his sister's house to die. Donne's poem reflects the young man's interests and studies.

Title] Obsequies to the Lord Harrington's brother. To the Countess of Bedford. *1633-54*

Letter

1 *I am a little conversant*] I am little conversant *1669*

3 *the heir*] his heir *1669*

10 *virtue*] virtues *1635-69*
concerning it] concerning that *1635-69*

Poem

1-2 *which wast, not only ... | Then when thou wast infused, harmony* which was harmony not only when it was first infused into his body, as all souls are then, but throughout his life.
infused Pronounced as three syllables.

3-4 *bear | A part* he contributes his own music to the harmony of the whole.

4 *sphere* the entire creation.

6 *pervious* passable; affording a passage; open to communication.

7 *men's*] man's *1633 and several MSS*

8 *affections* feelings, especially joy.

11 *these*] those *most MSS*
meditations Pronounced as five syllables.

12 *unapparel and enlarge* throw off the limitations of flesh.

13 *soft ecstasy* a tranquil and easy way to a revelation of truth while his mind is outside his body (see *The Ecstasy*, and the note on the title).

16 *when*] where *MS*

19 *Subject to change* they are subject to change in the grave, but not in their beds.

22 *then* given as than *in the early versions*

26 *that sun*] this sun *several MSS*
that sun the thought of Harrington.

30 *the hardest object* one finds most difficulty in seeing oneself.

34 *mirrors of thy ways, and end* Harrington's life and death reflect all we need to know for our good.

37 *trunks* derivatives.

37–9 *which do to us derive | . . . good men* good men's deeds reflect God, showing us in reduced perspective such a view or proportion of him as is fitting.

39 *their* good men.

40 *near*] more *MS*

43 *fluid* not limited to one circumstance but flowing through all.

44 *contemplation* Pronounced as five syllables.

45–9 *As bodies change . . . | . . . and gone* see *Woman's Constancy* and note.

57 *all those* all Harrington's virtues.

58 *Who knew his minutes well* someone who was closely acquainted with his particular circumstances.

61 *discontinue* separate.

66 *simple* one indivisible whole, as is God's essence.

67 *of virtue*] in virtue *MS*
a point and one a single indivisible whole.

69 *told* separately listed.

76] When they would, exercised, lack room and space *MS*
lack time, and space so many virtues seek to exercise their force that none has time and space to display itself at length.
lack] last *1669*

80 *the long-breathed chronicles*] our long lived chronicles *MS*
long-breathed chronicles chronicle histories, that tell anecdotes of early times as though their compiler were himself alive then.

85 *repair* call at, or pass close to.

87 *in an instant knows* angels are said to apprehend not by reason but by immediate intuition; though Donne suggests here that this angelic intuition is just a swift process of discursive thought.

95–6 *The order of these two lines is reversed in one MS*

99 *in that pace* at a like speed.

101 *balm* a restorative and preservative substance which every living body was assumed to contain, but whose powers were impaired at the Fall and still further weakened by subsequent sins.

102 *this*] the *1633–69*
    tempests] tempest *1633–69 and several MSS*
    becalm] be calm *MS*

104 *be dead?*] being dead? *MS*

106 *closed up* the circle was a figure of eternity.

110 *man the abridgement* man the epitome or microcosm of the whole world.

111 *know'st*] knewst *MS*

114 *the equinoctial* a circle which exactly bisects the earth's sphere, as the sun's supposed path does.

117 *Where … where*] When … when *1633–69 and several MSS*

118 *great circles* meridians, circles of longitude which run through the poles and whose planes pass through the centre of the earth. Donne distinguishes them from the circles running parallel to the equator, which diminish in size as they approach the poles.

119–30 *though thy circle to thy self express | All … | … what to do?* though the small circle of Lord Harrington's existence was perfect in itself, it offers us a model only for youthful living and dying; we still have no guide in all the large area of our experience which lies beyond that and makes up the great circle of a full human life.

121 *it*] that *some MSS*

122 *Both how*] How both *MS*

124 *torrid zone* the equatorial region of raging heat and madness.
    calentures tropical fevers in which men are subject to self-destructive delirium.

125 *ambitions*] ambition *1669*

126 *Zeal's agues*] Zeals, agues *MS*
    hydroptic immoderately thirsty.

127 *scale* yardstick.

130 *tell us*] set us *1635–54 and several MSS*

132 *distemper* irregularity, loss of equilibrium.

133 *hand gets*] hands get *1633–54*

134 *sinews*] sins *MS*

135 *fly*] flee *1635–69*

138 *idle* foolish, prattling.
  hours come] hour come *1669*

139 *be wound still* are wound too often, overwound.

140 *set at every will* altered to suit every fresh opinion of the correct time.

141 *is easiest to* brings us most easily to.

142 *follow all ... follow none* if we try to follow every fashion of conduct that presents itself, or if we refuse to follow any good example.

150 *control* regulate.

152 *such as it* such that it.

154 *great*] grave *several MSS*

155 *any*] an *1639–69*

157 *not miracle, but prodigy* it is an event that runs strikingly counter to what we normally expect in nature, but not a marvellous act of God for our benefit.

158 *That when the ebbs, longer than flowings be* that whereas the tide normally takes longer to ebb than to reach the point of high water.
  when] where *most MSS*; whereas *MS*

159 *flood* incoming tide, high water.

161 *was*] were *1635–69*

164 *grown*] is *MS*

165 *grow sure*] am sure *1635–69*

170 *and*] or *most MSS*

179–235 *at the triumph day ... / ... by age, he might* A triumph was the highest honour bestowed in Rome upon a victorious general; but it was granted only when certain stringent conditions were met.

184 *as magistrates* In Rome only those who held the office of dictator, consul or praetor were entitled to a triumph.

186 *brought*] wrought *1639*

186-7 *that field, / . . . destined thee* high office of state, such as membership of the king's privy council

192 *usurp'st*] usurp'dst *some MSS*; usurp *1635-69 and several MSS*

193 *Then*] That *1633*

197 *foreign enemies* Another condition of a triumph was that the victory must have been gained over a foreign enemy.

198 *acclamations*] acclamation *1633-54*

199 *engines* destructive means.

200 *by a divers mine* by two distinct ways of undermining their moral standing.

205-6 *the dominion / Must be enlarged* A Roman triumph was granted only for a war which resulted in an extension of the boundaries of the state.

208 *those straits nature put thee in* our sinful state, the consequences of the corruption of our nature at the Fall.

212 *who takes endeavours* who counts such attempts in our favour.
endeavours] indentures *1669*

221 *Left safe from present war* Another condition of a triumph was that the war must have been brought to a definite conclusion with no likelihood of insurrection.

224 *His*] This *1669*
than] but *most MSS*

227 *joined* Pronounced as two syllables.
commission Pronounced as four syllables.

231-2 *it might never reference have / Unto the Senate* the Roman people might speak ill of a triumphant leader only so far as they did not question his right to a triumph, or the authority of the Senate which granted it to him.
reference] reverence *1650-54*

235 *before, by age, he might* Gnaeus Pompey claimed and was granted a triumph in 81 BC after he had defeated the forces of Marius

in Sicily and Africa, though he was only twenty-five and still un-qualified to be a magistrate. The unconstitutional act was forced upon the Senate by the dictator Sulla, whom Pompey's victories had con-firmed in power.

239   *am I*] I am *1633-69*

241   *for*] with *1633-69 and MS*

242-3   *which just impugners be | Of early triumphs*   (a) it is not the natural law that someone dies young, and so triumphs; (b) by nature, young people have not usually merited a triumph; (c) our decisive triumph over our own sinful nature is not likely to be early and easily won.
  early] earthly *MS*

244   *magnify*   (a) increase; (b) praise.

246   *lack it*   the triumph.

247   *time*] times *1669 and most MSS*
  suffered   pronounced as three syllables.

249   *To die with them*   Many primitive peoples had a custom that when men of rank died their wives and bondmen killed themselves at the grave.

250   *French* soldurii   Caesar tells how the forces of Crassus were attacked in Aquitaine by a body of *soldurii*, men who had taken a vow to share all the fortunes of life with a chosen friend, and to share his fate too or kill themselves forthwith when he died (*De Bello Gallico* III, 22).
  soldurii] soldarii *1633-69*; solary *MS*

252   *in great Alexander's great excess*   in the excessive degree of mourning which Alexander the Great showed for his favourite Hephaes-tion, who died at Ecbatana on Alexander's last Middle Eastern expedi-tion in 324 BC.

253-4   *made whole towns divest | Their walls and bulwarks*   The de-fences of subject towns were pillaged to provide materials for the monument and temples erected to Hephaestion in Babylon.

254   *which became them best*   which were better suited to defend the towns than to be the materials of a tomb.

257   *Who*] Which *1639-69*

257–8 *being cast | Behind hand* Presumably Donne sent the poem to the Countess of Bedford some little time after her brother's death.

AN HYMN TO THE SAINTS, AND TO MARQUIS HAMILTON

This piece was placed with the Divine Poems in all the early editions.

James Hamilton the second Marquis died on 2 March 1625 aged thirty-six, at the height of a glittering career in the Scots and English Courts. Donne was then Dean of St Paul's, and the prefixed letter intimates that he wrote this funeral poem reluctantly at the behest of an old friend. R. C. Bald thinks that it is almost certainly Donne's last poem.

Letter

Sir Robert Carr an old friend of Donne, who became Earl of Ancrum in 1633. Carr may have been the 'Allophanes' of Donne's *Epithalamion Eclogue 1613*.

Poem

1 *Whether*] Whither *1633*

4 *order more* a further order of angels or saints.

6–7 *if every several angel be | A kind alone* Aquinas says that each angel is a unique species (*Summa Theologica* Ia. 50.4).

9 *access* arrival thither.

10 *orders* relationships, dignities and ranks. Hamilton was a Privy Councillor and held several high offices in the royal household.

14 *the garter* Hamilton was made a Knight of the Garter in 1623.

20 *What a soul was* how all his worldly qualities depended upon his soul.

23 *So fell our monasteries* The English monasteries fell to ruins within years of Henry VIII's order dissolving them, in the late 1530s.
  one instant] an instant *1635–69*

25 *this*] his *1635–69*

26 *the sphere of forms* a celestial region where the ideal forms of earthly bodies await the resurrection of the material bodies (see *The Faerie Queene* III, vi, 33–6).

26–30 *before | His soul shall fill up his sepulchral stone, | . . . his body's there* These lines paradoxically reverse the commonplace that the body rests in the grave while the soul ascends to heaven. The Marquis's bodily form ascends to heaven while his soul – his worldly fame (line 29) – fills out his tomb and monumental stone.

28 *resurrection* pronounced as five syllables.

29 *as in*] as it *1650–54*; as it is *1669*

31 *first innocents* those who died before they reached the years of experience and of wilful sin.

36 *in eyes*] in the eyes *several MSS*

42 *a David . . . a Magdalen* penitent sinners who became saints. David, among other things, used his kingly power to get Bathsheba for himself and have her husband murdered (2 Samuel xi). Mary Magdalen was the erstwhile sinner who washed Jesus's feet with her tears (Luke vii 37–50) and out of whom went seven devils (Luke viii 2).

The Anniversaries

The two Anniversaries form complementary meditations upon death, moving from an estimation of our life and experience in this world to a celebration of the joys of the liberated soul in heaven. They are best approached through Donne's other celebratory and funeral poems.

The shaping fiction of the two poems is that a young girl, by her very innocence, may stand for and ideally embody all those perfections that man and woman forfeited with their innocence at the Fall: virtue, true apprehension, beauty, vitality itself. It is Donne's means of expressing the sense of a possible human sublimity which we have utterly betrayed. Death came in with the Fall, and in the young girl's death Donne chooses to see an enactment of the consequences of the first sin and of the withdrawal from the world of those vital qualities. That withdrawal poses us the choice of clinging to the body of our decaying world, or turning away from it altogether to make ourselves anew after the pattern of the dead girl; who is dead, in any case, only by our perverse worldly reckoning.

AN ANATOMY OF THE WORLD

First published in 1611. Reprinted with *The Second Anniversary* in 1612, 1621 and 1625; then given in the editions of Donne's poems from

1633 on. One of the six surviving copies of the 1612 printing has an errata slip pasted into it which amends readings in both Anniversary poems. But there is no knowing who drafted it, or why no following edition made use of it, and its corrections cannot be taken as authoritative. I give them where they seem worth considering.

Elizabeth Drury, the only surviving child of a wealthy London landowner, died in December 1610 aged fourteen. Donne had not known her, and may not then have known her parents. The circumstances in which he wrote this poem are not clear, but there were several possible links between him and Sir Robert Drury: they had friends in common, and Donne's sister Anne had lived in the Drury household some years before. The likelihood is that through one of these common acquaintances Sir Robert commissioned the best funeral poet of the day to commemorate his daughter in verse. Donne probably also wrote the Latin epitaph for the girl's tomb in Hawstead Church.

The poem evidently established Donne's friendship with the Drurys for he accompanied them on a tour of the Continent in 1611–12, and he rented a house on Sir Robert's estate in Drury Lane until he moved to the Deanery of St Paul's in 1621. Otherwise the two Anniversaries seem to have met more blame than praise in Donne's day. He wrote from France in April 1612:

'I hear from England of many censures of my book of Mistress Drury; if any of those censures do but pardon me my descent in printing anything in verse (which if they do they are more charitable than myself; for I do not pardon myself, but confess that I did it against my conscience, that is, against my own opinion, that I should not have done so), I doubt not but they will soon give over that other part of that indictment, which is that I have said so much; for nobody can imagine that I who never saw her, could have any other purpose in that, than that when I had received so very good testimony of her worthiness, and was gone down to print verses, it became me to say, not what I was sure was just truth, but the best that I could conceive; for that had been a new weakness in me, to have praised anybody in printed verses, that had not been capable of the best praise that I could give' (Gosse I, 305–6). Drummond of Hawthornden reported Ben Jonson as saying that 'Donne's Anniversary was profane and full of blasphemies; that he told Mr Donne, if it had been written of the Virgin Mary it had been something; to which he answered, that he described the Idea of a Woman, and not as she was' (*Conversations* 133).

R. C. Bald traces Donne's connexion with the Drury family in *Donne and the Drurys* (1959). L. L. Martz examines the structure of the two

Anniversaries in *The Poetry of Meditation* (1954), as does G. Williamson, 'The Design of Donne's Anniversaries', *MP*, LX (1963), 183-91; R. L. Colie analyses their movement in 'The Rhetoric of Transcendence', *PQ*, XLIII (1964), 145-70.

TO THE PRAISE OF THE DEAD, AND THE ANATOMY

To the Praise ... Anatomy   The author of this commendatory poem is not known. But Ben Jonson said that Joseph Hall wrote the preliminary poem for *The Second Anniversary, The Harbinger to the Progress*, and Hall had known the Drurys for years; he may well have written this poem too.

4 *forced*   Pronounced as two syllables.

35 *been   given as* bin *in the early versions.*

36 *in thine*] and thine *1633-69*

44 *burden*   (a) formal refrain; (b) bass accompaniment or undersong.

AN ANATOMY OF THE WORLD

The First Anniversary

The entry into the work] *Not in 1611. All the marginal glosses were added in 1612 and reproduced in subsequent editions*

2 *all they ... who know they have one*   all those who know that they have a soul.
   they celebrate] do celebrate *1621-69*

6 *inmate*   a temporary guest, a lodger.

7 *progress*   a ceremonial journey made by the monarch and Court.

8 *standing house*   permanent dwelling, the chief royal residence.

11 *languished*   pronounced as three syllables.

12 *bath of tears.*   Bleeding into a warm bath, as Seneca did, is an imperceptible way of losing one's vitality and life.

14 *then*] them *1650-69*

25 *then, and then*] *Written* than, and than *in the early versions*

32 *o'erpast*   outlived.

33 *font*] fount *1612-69*

40 *times*] time *1635-69*
determined ceased; we can no longer measure time. Pronounced as four syllables.

48 *equal to law* her example should have been as good as law to us.

49 *cement* The stress falls on the first syllable.
compact hold together.

50 *glue*] give *1650-69*
resolved melted.

52 *discovered* disclosed, displayed. Pronounced as four syllables.

57 *intrinsic balm* inherent preservative (see *To the Countess of Bedford* (Reason is our soul's left hand) 21-3 and note).

59 *try* seek to see.

64 *discovered* pronounced as four syllables.

66 *dissection* pronounced as four syllables.

73 *shut in all day* enclosed all light within herself, and so denied it to the world.

75 *from the carcase* the sun was supposed to breed life out of dead bodies, and mud.
free freely, in the sense that the new creatures do not share the corruptness of the carcass from which they are bred.

76 *a new world; and new creatures* a regenerate world of virtuous beings.

79 *though*] thought *1621-33*
elemented constituted, properly made up of matter and form.

84 *foreign* from outside.

89 *due temper* a fit temperateness.
then] them *1650-69*

92 *a neutrality* (a) a balance of humours; (b) we are at best neither well nor ill.

98 *precipitation* (a) falling head first; (b) moving faster and faster. Pronounced as six syllables.

103-4 *They were to good ends, and they are so still, | But accessory, and* *principal in ill*   they were and still are merely accessory to good ends, whereas they are principal in working evil.

107-10   *singly, one by one, they kill us now*   There was a common belief that coitus shortens life. See *Farewell to Love* 24-5 and note.

115   *stag, and raven*   Pliny says that deer live four times longer than ravens, and ravens four times longer than men.
   the long-lived tree   probably the oak.

120   *make up*   complete.

122   *confessed, and recompensed the meat*   men's growth showed in itself how good the food was before the Flood; and moreover, men grew by as much as they ate of it.

123   *spacious*   Pronounced as three syllables.

128   *Methusalem*   Methuselah lived 969 years, according to the literal sense of Genesis v 27.

130   *true*] new *1611*. J. Sparrow discussed these readings in *TLS*, 29 June 1946; H. J. C. Grierson replied to him in *TLS*, 20 July 1946.
   true made   accurately made.

134   *to have three lives*   to contract for a long tenure (say ninety-nine years).

136   *a span*   (a) about nine inches, the span of one's extended hand; (b) the full extent of a human life; (c) an arch that joins two widely separated points, as earth and heaven.

142   *pygmies*   accounts of pygmies were though to be travellers' tales.

145   *death adds to'our length*   (a) we are laid out on the ground long-wise then; (b) we cast longest shadows as the sun declines farthest; (c) we are transfigured in death, and only then make good what we lost at the Fall.

147   *this were light*   this would be unimportant.
   our less volume   (a) our reduced bulk or capacity; (b) our smaller book.

149-50   *disposed into less glass / Spirits of virtue*   if we had brought together in a single small phial the concentrated essence of virtue, which had previously been dispersed at large.

151   *retired*   concentrated.
   damped   dulled, quenched; shrunken, as damp wool shrinks.

153 *close weaving*] close-weaning *1611–62*; close weaning *1621–5*

154 *bedwarfed* Pronounced as three syllables.

159 *new diseases* syphilis came into Europe in the fifteenth century; and men warred on themselves in that they knowingly risked contracting it by sexual indulgence.

160 *new physic* specifically, the medicine of Paracelsus, who had written on the cure of syphilis in the 1520s. But the treatments attempted by his traditionalist opponents were far more barbaric than his. In *Biathanatos* Donne talks of syphilis as God's punishment of our general licentiousness, and of the 'second worse affliction' which God sent upon us when that failed, 'which was ignorant, and torturing physicians' (introd. J. W. Hebel (1930), 215).

161 *Thus man*] This man *1635–69*
    vice-emperor God gave man dominion over all earthly creatures (Genesis i 26–8).

164 *legates* (a) delegates; (b) legacies, bequests.

172-3 *Help, or at least some time to waste, allow | T'his other wants* even if one allows that man's other deficient faculties may be helped, or that at least it will be some time before they waste away altogether, yet . . .

173-4 *depart | With* part with, relinquish.

176 *When they called virtues by the name of she* in Greek and Latin the names of virtues are feminine.

178 *allay* alloy, as a pure metal needs to be tempered with a less pure one for everyday use.

180 *tincture* tinge; but in alchemy, the essential principle of a substance. Donne shifts between these two senses in offering us a descendant of Eve who could none the less rid herself of so much of woman's nature.

181 *thoughts*] thought *1621–33*

187 *feed (not banquet)* make it one's everyday fare, not one's infrequent public excess.

188 *religion* Pronounced as four syllables.

189 *withered* Pronounced as three syllables.

190 *Be more than man* 'Oh what a vile and abject thing is man ... unless he raise himself above humanity!' (Montaigne, *An Apology of Raymond Sebond, Essays* II, 12).

192 *lame* defective.

199 *then written* than *in the early versions.*

205 *new philosophy* the latest theories of the nature of the universe, such as the ideas of Copernicus, Tycho Brahe, Kepler, Galileo.

206 *The element of fire* the outermost of the concentric spheres of the elements whose centre was the earth. Copernicus's theory of a heliocentric universe denied such an arrangement, though some 'new philosophers' continued to argue that the element of fire exists.

207 *The sun is lost, and th'earth* Men had assumed from Ptolemy's time that the earth was the centre of the universe and that all the heavenly bodies move round it; Copernicus had recently argued that in fact the earth moves round the sun. Donne's sceptical conclusion is that in fact we cannot know which is true, or where we are.

211 *They seek so many new* Galileo's first accounts of his work with the telescope were published in 1610. They revived an old question, whether there are other worlds than ours in the universe.

212 *atomies* atoms, smallest constituents.

213 *coherence* connectedness; the proper order of things.

214 *just supply* (a) mutual support between the parts; (b) fair distribution of goods.
relation right relationship.

217 *a phoenix* only one phoenix was supposed to exist in the world at a time, rebegetting itself in fire out of its own ashes.
then] there *1612 errata slip*

220 *bow* (a) bring into a circle of harmony; (b) bend their stiff self-will in humble acknowledgement of each other and of God.

228-9 *the general / Steward to Fate* she saw to it that everything happened in the world as Fate decreed, that is, as God had willed.

230 *Gilt* gilded.
perfumed The stress falls on the second syllable – perfúmed.
the East the East Indies, which commonly stood for scent and spice, as the West Indies stood for gold.

232 *those isles* the East Indies.

234 *single money* loose coins, small change.

236 *microcosm* miniature version.

243 *hectic* consumptive.

250 *proportion* Pronounced as four syllables.

251 *their spherical* their spherical shape.

252 *proportion* Pronounced as four syllables.

253 *perplexed* (a) involved, tangled; (b) bewildered, lost. Pronounced as three syllables.

255 *eccentric* (a) not concentric with other circles or with the earth; (b) not having reference to a fixed centre, irregular. Ptolemaic astronomers had used the idea of eccentric circles or 'moveable eccentrics' to account for the varying brightness and devious movement of heavenly bodies.

256 *down-right lines* lines running straight downwards.
     overthwarts transverse lines.

257 *that pure form* the form of a circle, which the heavens really do have. Presumably the vertical and horizontal lines are those on a reticulated map of the heavens.

258 *eight and forty shares* Ptolemy divided the stars into forty-eight constellations.

259 *then*] there *1612 errata slip*

259-60 *then arise / New stars, and old do vanish* The traditional understanding was that the heavens are not subject to change. But several astronomers had recently announced the discovery of new stars, or had discarded stars whose existence had been taken for granted from ancient times. Donne points to a double lapse into chaos, in the heavens themselves, and in our understanding of them.

263 *zodiac* a great circle of twelve star-groups through which the sun passes in its annual movement, relative to the earth, from west to east and north to south.

265 *the goat and crab* The Tropic of Capricorn stands at the sun's winter solstice and the Tropic of Cancer at its summer solstice, the

solstices being the points furthest north and furthest south in the sun's yearly journey, where it seems to pause and then reverse its direction.

267 *Did not these tropics fetter him* F. Manley (*John Donne: The Anniversaries* (1963)) suggests that Donne here shifts ground from the signs of the ancient zodiac to the modern Tropics of Capricorn and Cancer, which run north and south of the equator and parallel to it and touch the sun's path at its most northerly and southerly points.

268 *For his course is not round* The angle of the sun's supposed path around the earth constantly shifts so that relative to us the sun appears to slip from west to east and north to south during the year. Moreover the sun's path cuts the equator at a point slightly further on each year, in the so-called 'precession of the equinoxes' (which is actually caused by the slow wobble upon its axis of the earth itself).

271 *cozening* deceiving.

272 *serpentine* (a) moving in a spiral; (b) having more to do with the infernal serpent than with God, the perfect circle.

273 *with*] of *1635–69*

274 *being now fall'n nearer us* It was widely argued that the sun must be nearer the earth than it was in former ages, because Ptolemy's estimate of its distance was so much greater than more recent estimates. But the opinion was contested.

276–7 *none ends where he begun* The ancients noted that the planets appeared to oscillate in their movements relative to the sun and the other stars, and that their brightness is not constant. Some supposed that their paths are 'moveable eccentrics', that is, that a planet moves in a circle whose centre shifts in relation to the earth. Others held that their paths are large circles concentric to the earth upon which they themselves move in small circles called epicycles. Either theory would account for the sinking and swelling which Donne notes; but he concludes that the motion of the stars is not circular at all.

278 *meridians, and parallels* the lines of celestial longitude and latitude.

284 *pace*] peace *1612–33*

286 *Tenerife*] Tenarus *1633–69*
  Tenerife The reference is to the double topped volcanic peak on the island of Tenerife, the Pico de Teyde, which rises sharply to some 12,000 feet.

295 *under all* at the centre of the earth.

296 *spacious* Pronounced as three syllables.

298 *strait*] straight *1633-69*
strait narrow.

302, 306, 308, 309, 318, 333 *proportion[s]* Pronounced as four syllables.

305 *questioned* Pronounced as three syllables.

310 *Examined* tried, verified.

311-12 *that ancient ... who thought souls made | Of harmony* Galen thought that the soul is a harmony of the elements; Aristoxenus regarded the soul as a 'tuning' of the body; Pythagoras interpreted all metaphysical phenomena in terms of musical intervals.

314 *resultances* derivatives.

316 *the forms from objects* A theory ascribed to Aristotle supposed that we see because objects emit rays which imprint the forms of the objects upon our minds, by way of our eyes.

317-18 *those great Doctors ... | ... the Ark to man's proportions was made* St Augustine and St Ambrose both make Noah's ark a figure of the human body. St Ambrose depicts the just man's situation, alone amidst a sea of sin. St Augustine sees the ark as a type of the Church, made in the proportions of Christ who saved us by wood from the deluge: 'For the dimensions of the length, depth, and breadth of the ark do signify man's body, in which the Saviour was prophesied to come, and did so' (*The City of God* XV, 26, trans. J. Healey (1610)).

337 *well* what is seemly.

341 *proportion* Pronounced as four syllables.

343-4 *a compassionate turquoise ... | ... is not well* the turquoise was commonly believed to lose or gain lustre according to its wearer's state of health.

345 *gold falls sick being stung with mercury* a gold amalgam has a much paler colour and much less value than pure gold.

351 *enow*] enough *1633*
enow enough.

353 *Sight is the noblest sense* It was a commonplace in scholastic and

Neoplatonic writings that sight is the highest of the senses and touch the lowest.

357-8 *Our blushing red . . . | Is inward sunk, and only our souls are red* we have moved from transparent innocence to covert, and damning, guilt.

359 *recovered* pronounced as four syllables.

361 *white* the colour of innocence, purity and holiness.
red the colour of love.
blue the colour of heavenly love, of truth, and of the Virgin.

365 *Whose composition was miraculous* the miracle lies in the paradox that something was at once all colour yet perfectly diaphanous.

376 *illude* deceive.

378-80 *Than that her influence the heaven forbears, | . . . or the mother barren is* either because heaven witholds its influence, or because our elements no longer feel this influence, all our natural processes are abortive or unproductive – one or other party, the male or the female, is always barren.

382 *balmy* balm was supposed to preserve and heal (see *To the Countess of Bedford* (Reason is our soul's left hand) 21-4).

386 *false conceptions* (a) imaginary pregnancies; (b) abortive monsters; (c) mistaken ideas of things.

387 *meteors* (a) atmospheric phenomena in general, such as rain, snow, hail, dew; (b) comets, whose appearance was thought to portend general disaster.

389 *new worms* (a) maggots, bred from the decaying body of the world; (b) serpents, new species of which had lately been discovered in America and Africa.

390 *Th'Egyptian Mages* Aaron 'cast down his rod before Pharaoh . . . and it became a serpent', and 'the magicians of Egypt, they also did in like manner . . . For they cast down every man his rod, and they became serpents' (Exodus vii 10-12).

391 *artist* an astrologer or alchemist.

392 *constellate* (a) to judge when to perform a task under a favourable constellation; (b) to bring stars together or join their powers. The stress falls on the second syllable – constéllate.

395 *by touch* Paracelsus thought that men might heal by touch, as they were supposed to have done in the earliest times, if they knew how to draw upon the natural virtues of things and were morally fit to use them.

396 *correspondence* the correspondence and free traffic between heaven and earth, that gave us access to the magical virtues of things as God created them.

399 *commerce* The stress falls on the second syllable – commérce.

400 *Embarred* arrested, stopped.

404 *yea ashes too, are medicinal* the ashes of some herbs and other things were thought to have power to heal, because they had been purified by fire so that only the essence of their particular virtue remained.
    medicinal Pronounced as three syllables – med'cinal.

407 *one dying swan* the swan was supposed to be mute until just before its death, when it sang its own dirge.

408 *then* given as than *in the early versions*

415 *impressions*] impression *1612-69*

418 *gilded* covered with a layer of gold; impregnated with gold.

422 *Some stay, no more than kings should give, to crave* some restraint in their demands, so that they ask no more than kings should give them.

430 *mollify* (a) soften, relieve, (b) appease.

440 *punctual* punctilious.

452 *then* given as than *in the early versions.*

456 *concoction* progress towards purity and perfection, under the pressure of alchemical forces. Pronounced as four syllables.

462-6 *He spake / To Moses ... / ... still in their memory* God told Moses to write a song before his death and teach it to the children of Israel, so that they would have a perpetual reminder of God's mercy to them and threat of vengeance against them if they abandoned him (Deuteronomy xxxi 19 and xxxii 1-43).

469 *incomprehensibleness* (a) she cannot be contained within limits, (b) she cannot be grasped by our understanding.

474 *fame*] same *1611-25*

A FUNERAL ELEGY

Some modern editors have assumed that Donne wrote *A Funeral Elegy* first of all and then developed it into the two Anniversaries. But there is no evidence that this is what happened.

1   *lost*] loss *1635-69*

4   *chrysolite*   green gems such as topaz, often cited as a figure of pure perfection.

6   *the two Indies*   the gold of the West Indies and the spices and scents of the East Indies.

8   *Escurials*   The Escorial, near Madrid, is one of the largest and most handsome religious establishments in the world. Philip II had it built between 1563 and 1584 as the official centre of Spanish devotional life; its vast complex of buildings takes in a church, a royal palace and mausoleum, a rich art collection, a library, and a museum.

13   *aborted*] abortive *1635-69*

16   *tabernacle*   a temporary dwelling for her soul and for God.

27   *spirits*   those choice spirits which harmonize the parts of civil society, as the spirits of music give the music its life and the spirits in the blood link body and soul (see *The Ecstasy* 61-4 and note).

33   *as she*] was she *1633-69*

40   *Repolished*   reassembled and perfected.

41-4   *the Afric Niger ... / ... far greater than it was*   Donne follows the common opinion in the sixteenth century that the Niger flows eastward into the Nile, partly above ground and partly underground.

48   *her, here*] her here, *1635-69*

50   *An Angel made a Throne, or Cherubin*   Angels are the lowest of the nine celestial orders, thrones and cherubim nearly the highest.

51   *We lose by't*   Angels have care of human affairs; thrones and cherubim serve or contemplate God.

52   *tasteless*   having dulled senses.

59   *thin*   fine, as thin porcelain or glass.

61   *a through-light scarf*   a covering of transparent gauze.
    enrol   register, record.

64 *worth*] work *1633*

65 *emulate* vie with each other.

67 *when heaven looks on us with new eyes* when new stars disclose themselves.

68 *artist* astronomer.

71 *whose this piece should be* who would marry her.

72 *nor she* nor herself.

73 *a lamp of balsamum* Balsam or balm was an aromatic mixture of oil and resins which was supposed to have healing powers and to be very precious. In Paracelsian medicine and in alchemy balm is the preservative essence which all organic bodies have but whose force is impaired by the Fall (see *A Nocturnal upon S. Lucy's Day* 6 and note).

75 *integrity* wholeness, innocence, uncorrupted virtue.

76 *it do*] it doth *1633-69*

80 *opium* a temporary sleep.

81 *she could not, nor could choose to die* she could not die, even if she wanted to.

82 *esctasy* a state in which the soul leaves the body to have a revelation of final truth (see *The Ecstasy*).

83 *sad*] said *1612-33 and MS*

92-3 *infer | Her destiny to herself* put her destiny in her own hands.

94 *She took but for thus much, thus much to die* she exercised the liberty Fate had newly bestowed upon her only thus far, to die as far as she has died.

95-7 *Her modesty not suffering her . . . | She did no more but die* since her destiny was now in her own hands she could have executed God's commissions in the world alongside Destiny itself, but she was too modest to do more with her power than die.

103-4 *legacies, | Which from the gift of her example rise* the example she gave us is like the gift of a piece of property or capital sum, which entails continued side-benefits (such as rent, or interest) upon the heirs.

106 *play her* mimic her, play the part of Elizabeth Drury.

OF THE PROGRESS OF THE SOUL

First published in 1612. Lines 511–18 show that the poem was written in France, or at least finished there.

Donne left for the Continent with the Drurys in November 1611. The party was in Amiens from late November 1611 to March 1612, spent a month in Paris, and then went on to Frankfurt. The anniversary of Elizabeth Drury's death, which was the specific occasion of the poem, fell in December 1611. By April 1612 Donne was writing to friends in England about the censures they had heard of 'my book of Mistress Drury' which contained the two Anniversaries, so that *The Second Anniversary* must have been finished and sent to England for publication well before that.

THE HARBINGER TO THE PROGRESS

Ben Jonson told Drummond of Hawthornden that Joseph Hall wrote 'the Harbinger to Donne's Anniversary' (*Conversations* 149). Hall was a former rector of Hawstead, the Drurys' family church, and must have known the dead girl well.

The Harbinger to the Progress   A harbinger was an official who went on ahead of an army or a royal progress to make preliminary arrangements.

7   *o'erlookest*   outgo; survey from a superior position.

10   *clogged*   Pronounced as two syllables.

16   *journals*   daily movements or concerns; the record of these movements.

19   *thou (great spirit)*   Donne.

23   *raught*] caught *1621–69*
     raught   reached (the obsolete past tense of 'reach').

27   *soul's high*] souls by *1612*

36   *Laura*   Laura was Petrarch's poetic mistress.

OF THE PROGRESS OF THE SOUL

The Second Anniversary

The entrance] Not in *1625–33*. There are no rubric glosses in *1635–69*

10   *Though*] Through *1612–25*

12 *be sailed*] he sailed *1621-33*

23-4 *some days are, at the Creation named, / Before the sun ... was framed* Genesis i speaks of the passage of three days before God created the sun and moon.

27 *Lethe* in classical mythology, a river of Hades from which the souls of the dead drink oblivion of all their former existence.

29 *reserve* store, capital.

34-5 *be unto my Muse / A father* her asks her to impregnate his Muse, and so work heaven's ends through his poetic gift.

37-8 *These hymns ... / ... thy praises grow* the present poems may play the male part in begetting more such poems upon the wits of future poets.

43 *thy*] they *1621-25*

44 *God's great* Venite the time when God finally calls all the creation to himself.

46 *safe-sealing*] safe-feeling *1621-39*
safe-sealing bowl the cup of Christ's blood, which safely seals our salvation.
A just disestimation] A just estimation *1625*

48 *'Tis*] To *1612*
hydroptic dropsical, and hence insatiably thirsty.

49 *unto thee* the poet is addressing himself.

53 *try truths forth* test them thoroughly.

60 *resurrection* Pronounced as five syllables.

66 *congratulate* rejoice with, share the joy of.

70 *The Golden Times* The times of innocence and naturalness before the Fall.

72 *the form* the principle of life and individuality.

75 *tried* tested.
indifferent morally neutral, or uncertain.

78 *ensphered* enclosed as in a sphere.

79 *control* dominate, surpass.

80 *the star-full northern pole* The northern hemisphere was assumed to have far more stars than the southern.

82–3 *this world is | Thou knowest*] this world is. / Thou knowest *1612–25*

92 *Division* (a) in music, a melody made up of short notes; (b) the dividing of the soul from the body.

96 *parched*] patched *1613–35*

98 *physic* medicine.
slackness mildness.

103 *that but for legacies they thrust* that they are merely jostling for legacies, like greedy heirs around a deathbed.
thrust] trust *1669*

115–7 *if so low, | Thy soul exalted so, thy thoughts can go* if your thoughts can sink so low as to imagine yourself a prince, when your soul is so exalted.

117–8 *a prince, who of themselves create | Worms which insensibly devour their state* the power rulers have begets parasites, who imperceptibly eat away the wealth of the realm and the ruler's own standing.

118 *state* (a) the prosperity of the realm; (b) status, pomp; (c) human condition.

119 *rite*] right *1612–69*

120 *a Saint Lucy's night* the longest night of the year (see *A Nocturnal upon S. Lucy's Day*).

123 *whose complexion was so even* whose constitution was so evenly balanced.

124–5 *which of her ingredients should invade | The other three* which of her four humours should gain upon the rest (and so make her ill and kill her).

125 *no fear, no art* such as the fear of her parents, and the art of her doctors.

127 *mithridate* an ancient antidote against all poisons, which was made up of many ingredients.
just exactly blended.
perfumes The stress falls on the second syllable – perfúmes.

130   *all were*   all the parts were best.

137   *won*] worn *1612-25*
won   persuaded.

138   *to venture on the sun*   the sun was supposed to be made up of celestial matter, which is exempt from change or disease.

140   *That he to disuniting subject were*   spirits were supposed to be simple essences and not therefore subject to division. Donne's point is that the girl's blend of unlike humours was so perfect as to make even uncompounded beings feel inferior.
to] too *1633-69*

142   *unstable*   irregular.

143-4   *such a chain . . . / . . . it enjoys*   the inevitable connection of causes and effects.

144   *enjoys*   experiences.

146   *accident*   (a) any event that might take place; (b) mishap, something that Fate itself has not provided for.

150   *Title*   legal right.

151   *pretend*   claim in law.

152   *Heaven was content to suffer violence*   Grierson quotes Matthew xi 12 – 'And from the days of John the Baptist until now the kingdom of heaven suffereth violence, and the violent take it by force.'

157   *Incommodities . . . body*] *Not in 1625-33*

160   *those two souls*   in scholastic metaphysics, the soul of growth and the soul of sense, which our immortal soul absorbs into itself in the womb.

161   *thee, both*] thee both *1633-69*

163   *obnoxious*   The stress falls on the first syllable – óbnoxious.

169   *anchorite*   a stationary hermit. *Written* anchorit *in the early versions*

173   *didst*] dost *1669*

177   *the rage*] a rage *1633-69*

181   *piece*   firearm.

182   *his own*   its own master.

190   *meteors*   atmospheric phenomena of the lower air. Higher up, they would be called comets.

192   *intense*   thick.

193   *th'element of fire*   See *The First Anniversary* 206 and note.

195   *baits*   pauses for rest.
      try   find out.

197   *retards*] recards *1612-25*

198   *Hesper and Vesper*   the two names of Venus, when she appears as the morning star and as the evening star.

199   *He that charmed Argus' eyes*   Mercury sent all Argus's eyes to sleep by means of a magic wand and a flute, and then cut his head off.
      Mercury   (a) Hermes, the messenger of the gods; (b) the planet Mercury.

200   *grown all eye*   souls perceive directly once they are free of the organs of sense.

202   *staying*   delaying.

204   *his father*   Saturn.

208   *undistinguished*   too fast to be distinguished.

209   *the beads*] those beads *1669*

219-20   ] This must, my soul, thy long-short progress be,
         To'advance these thoughts; remember then that she
                                                    (1633-69)

219   *long-short*   a long distance in a short time.

224   *others'*] other *1633-69*

226   *prefer*   raise in order to compare.

232-3   *in her some one part ... / Twenty such parts*   in any one part of her there will be twenty such parts.

234   *make*] wake *1635-69*

235-6   *they ... who did first betroth / The tutelar angels*   medieval theologians developed the notion that guardian angels are assigned (or betrothed) to particular human beings.

236–9 *assigned one, both | To nations ... | And to each several man*
Catholic devotional writers in Donne's day argued that every Christian
institution has its guardian angel, in addition to the angel assigned to
each human being.

242 *th'electrum* an alloy of gold and silver; something higher than
base metal, but not yet the purest metal.

244 *her sight* her appearance.

245 *wrought* worked.

249 *Our prison's prison* the prison of our flesh, which is the prison of
our soul.

249–50 *nor think us well, | ... our brittle shell* and who consider our-
selves well only as long as we are in the frail body and able to bear it
about.

251 *Her ignorance in this life and knowledge in the next*] *Not in 1633*

255 *Thou know'st thyself so little* 'If man know not himself, how can
he know his functions and forces?' (Montaigne, *An Apology of Raymond
Sebond*, *Essays* II, 12). This essay bears closely upon Donne's argument
here, as does Montaigne's essay *Of Experience* (*Essays* III, 13).

266 *new ingredients* Paracelsus thought that these were sulphur,
mercury and salts. He denied the theory of the balanced elements on
which Galenist medicine was based.

277–8 *opinions ... | Of nails and hairs* Authorities debated whether
nails and hair were to be classed as bones, skin, organic substance, or
waste matter.

282 *controversies* The stress falls on the third syllable – contravérsies.

285 *unconcerning* of no concern, trivial.

290 *low form* (a) base condition; (b) state of simple ignorance, as
that of pupils who sit in the lower forms of a grammar school.

291 *pedantery* given so in the early versions. Pronounced as four
syllables, with the stress on the second syllable – pedántery.

292 *taught*] thought *1612–25*
  sense, and fantasy Scholastic philosophers argued that we are able to
know the outside world only mediately, because our senses convey im-
pressions to a part of the mind called the fantasy which interprets them
and submits them to the intellect.

298 *circuit* roundabout processes.
collections inferences.

299 *concerning it* concerning heaven itself.

304 *practised* Pronounced as three syllables.

307 *or do, or think well* either do well, or think well.

308 *aye*] are *1625*; all *1633–69*

309 *edition* Pronounced as four syllables.

310 *action* Pronounced as three syllables.

312 and 318 *perfection* Pronounced as four syllables.

314 *print*] point *1612–33*

321 *ecstasy* see *The First Anniversary, A Funeral Elegy* 82 and note.

323 *earthly*] early *1625*

324 *conversation* society, company.

325 *With whom wilt thou converse?* where in this world will you find fit company?
station pronounced as three syllables.

326 *infection* pronounced as four syllables.

327 *will nor*] will not *1625–69*

330 *vent* discharge; utter.

334 *they do more ill, than these can speak* courts do more ill than libellers can speak.

336 *some effect*] some, effect *1633*

338 *will*] wise *1612–25*; lies *1633–69*

341 *mother-maid* the Virgin Mary.

342 *not being that, which men have said* theologians – mere men – have declared her free from the taint of original sin; and she rejoices that she was not free of it, but through her son's sacrifice and her own virtue is in glory none the less.

344 *for her interest of motherhood* merely because she was Christ's mother.

345–6 *patriarchs, which did longer sit*   Genesis v records the great ages of Adam and his descendants down to Noah.

350 *All the sun's course*   (a) they went everywhere in the world; (b) they followed Jesus wherever he went, and then followed out the pattern of his life and death.

354 *joint tenants*   fellow-lodgers.

355 *his temple*   their bodies.

357–8 *new degrees* / (*As to their number*) *to their dignities*   she has brought them new dignities, and fresh degrees of dignity.

360 *royalties*   sovereign powers and rights.

366 *rebellious*] rebellion's *1635–69*

369 *impressions*] impression *1633–69*
  impressions   (a) stamped effigies, as of the king's head on coins which gives them their worth; (b) shaping influences.

371 *protections*   immunities from legal arrest, such as the king could grant in certain cases.

382 *accidental joys*   accessory joys; all other joys than the essential one.

384 *essential*   Pronounced as four syllables.

385–6 *before accessories do abide* / *A trial, must the principal be tried*   in law, accessories to an offence could not be tried for it if the principal had not been accused.

391 *cozened cozener*   deceived deceiver.

391–400 *that she, and that thou,* / *Which did begin to love, are neither now*   Montaigne quotes the Stoic philosophers on the transience of all things to support his argument that we are not the same people today as we were yesterday, and that having no constant existence we can have no constant identity either – 'what admitteth alterations, continueth not the same; and if it be not the same, then is it not' (*An Apology of Raymond Sebond, Essays* II, 12).

398 *saint . . . pilgrim*   Petrarchan terms for a mistress and her lover.
  vow] row *1612–25*

400 *hourly in inconstancy*   see *Woman's Constancy* 2–5 and note.

402–3 *God did live so long . . .* / *Without this honour*   honour is not inherent in a person but an attitude others take. When God was alone he had no honour (see *To the Countess of Bedford* (Honour is so sublime perfection) 2–3 and note).

412 *casual* arbitrary, dependent upon chance.

415 *takes a worse* follows a worse course.

416 *Thinks*] Think *1612–25*

418 *for that effect* to build a tower as high as they intended, 'whose top may reach unto heaven' (Genesis xi 4).

420 *enow*] enough *1633*

421 *this*] his *1621–69*
 this centre the earth.

423 *world*] world's *1612–25*
 foundation Pronounced as four syllables.

426 *rods* afflictions, punishments.

429–30 *changing that whole precious gold | To such small copper coins* breaking down the one true God into many minor gods.
 that] the *1625*

432 *thrust* throng.

436 *which circles do contain* which are bounded by circles.

439 *Double on heaven, thy thoughts on earth employed* (a) think twice as much about heaven as you think about earth; (b) refer every earthly concern to its beginning and its end in God, as a line through the centre (earth) touches the circumference of the circle (God) at two opposite points.

440 *All will not serve* even to devote all one's thought to heaven will not suffice, while one is still on earth.

441 *can think it* can think the sight of God.

442 *it is both the object, and the wit* God is both the object of thought and the thought itself.

444 *diminution* Pronounced as five syllables.

446 *Had th' angels once looked on him* There is a traditional idea that the angels who fell never looked upon God but fixed their love upon themselves in the first moments of their creation.
 they had stood they had not fallen.

455 *devotion* Pronounced as four syllables.

456 *reparation* good repair. Pronounced as five syllables.

460 *safe precontract* (a) a binding contract made before she existed on earth; (b) a prior betrothal, which kept her from any other attachment.

461 *confidence* trust; assured expectation.

463 *clear*] clean *1635*

464 *use to* do habitually.

468 *proportion* Pronounced as four syllables.

470 *as our joys admit* as far as our joys can go on earth.
essential pronounced as four syllables.

473 *casual* accidental; by chance.

475 *swell*] smell *1669*
swell thee puff you up.

476 *being a greater*] being greater *1625-69*

477 *redress* remedy.

479 *aposteme* an internal abscess, thought to be caused by a gathering and boiling of some superfluous humour.

480-81 *the dangerous rest, | The bag* presumably the remains of the abscess, the sac that contained the putrefied humour.

482 *What aye was casual, may ever be* what always was fortuitous is likely to continue so always.
aye] eye *1621-25*; e'er *1633-69*

486 *that it can away* that it can leave us again.

491-2 *consummation / . . . resurrection* Each pronounced as five syllables.

498 *degree* rank, place in the hierarchy of heaven.

499-500 *'tis loss to be called best, | There where the stuff is not such as the rest* it is pointless to speak of a best or a worst in heaven, for where every being is unique there is no way of comparing it with any other.

501 *even*] ever *1625*

504 *full, on both sides written rolls* rolls of parchment filled with writing on both sides.

506 *records* The stress falls on the second syllable – recórds.

507 *making full perfection grow* making what was already wholly perfect grow still more perfect.

508 *Pieces a circle, and still keeps it so* perfects a circle and yet keeps it as it was.

509 *Longed for* heaven longed to have her there (as in Dante's *Vita Nuova* the angels and saints call upon God to have Beatrice with them in heaven – XIX, *Donne, ch'avete intelletto d'amore*).

510 *addition* Pronounced as four syllables.

511 *a place where mis-devotion frames* France.

514 *what laws of poetry admit* such things as invocations of the Muses and of pagan deities.

517 *Could any saint provoke that appetite* if any saint could stir him to invoke the name of that saint instead of God.

518 *a French convertite* a convert to the religion of France; one who would readily invoke a saint.

520 *rent* an offering in return for the moral benefits she has bestowed upon him.

527 *the proclamation* (a) the king's proclamation of a new ordinance; (b) the open manifestation of final truth.

528 *The trumpet* (a) the herald of a royal proclamation; (b) the 'preacher of the word, the watchman, *Tuba Domini*' who in feeble anticipation of the Last Trump calls the people 'to rise together in this resurrection of grace' (Donne, *Sermons* III, 133); (c) the poem itself, as it will speak to its own time and to posterity.

Divine Poems

TO E. OF D. WITH SIX HOLY SONNETS

Given with the Verse Letters in *1633–69*. Few MSS have it.

We do not know who 'E. of D.' was or which sonnets accompanied this poem. A. B. Grosart suggested that Donne is addressing the Earl of Doncaster, who received the title of Viscount Doncaster (not Earl) from James I in 1618 (*The Complete Poems of John Donne*, 1872.)

Grierson rejected this identification and proposed the Earl of Dorset, who succeeded to his title in 1609 aged nineteen. Both Grosart and Grierson thought that the 'six holy Sonnets' were six of the *La Corona* set. Helen Gardner argues that they could not be the same poems as those sent to Mrs Herbert in 1607 (see the introductory note to the following poem) but might well have been six of the *Divine Meditations*, making up in themselves a sequence on the Last Things. She thinks that these were the first six sonnets in *1633*, numbers 2, 4, 6, 7, 9, 10 in the present text. So she prints the present poem at the head of these six sonnets.

2 *Begets strange creatures on Nile's dirty slime* Pliny says that the sun generates living creatures from the mud of the Nile.

3 *your fatherly yet lusty rhyme* poems written by the person addressed, which Donne professes to acknowledge as the seed of his own six sonnets.

4 *their fruits*] the fruit *MS*

6–7 *nature do admit | Seven to be born at once* Pliny mentions cases of septuplets in Egypt, where people are fecund because they drink from the Nile.

9 *choose*] chose *MS*

9–10 *the same degree | Doth with her sister, your invention, hold* invention and judgement were thought to be the two essential faculties of composition, which in a true artist would be exactly proportioned to each other.

TO MRS MAGDALEN HERBERT: OF ST MARY MAGDALEN

First printed in Walton's *Life of Mr George Herbert* (1670). Walton attaches the poem to a letter Donne wrote to Mrs Herbert in July 1607, which ends: 'by this messenger, and on this good day, I commit the enclosed Holy Hymns and Sonnets (which for the matter, not the workmanship, have yet escaped the fire) to your judgement, and to your protection too, if you think them worthy of it; and I have appointed this enclosed Sonnet to usher them to your happy hand.' Walton adds 'These Hymns are now lost to us'; but Grierson conjectured that they were the *La Corona* sonnets.

1 *Her of your name* Church tradition identified St Mary Magdalene with the woman 'which was a sinner' of Luke vii, and Mary of Bethany the sister of Martha and Lazarus (Luke x, John xi).

1-2 *whose fair inheritance / Bethina was* Bethany was the family home of Mary, Martha and Lazarus. In the gospel narrative Martha appears to be the eldest child, and she, not Mary, would thus have inherited the family estate. But Mrs Herbert was a Newport, whose family inheritance was an ancestral estate in Shropshire.

2 *jointure Magdalo* in the tradition of the Western Church Mary Magdalene's family owned great estates at Magdala and Bethany, to which Mary herself was part heir. A jointure is strictly a property settled on a wife for use after her husband's death, and Donne is again looking to Mrs Herbert whose first husband had died in 1599 leaving her the use of Montgomery Castle, the Herbert family home.

5 *The Resurrection* Mary Magdalene first saw the risen Christ (John xx).

8 *think these Magdalens were two or three* Origen among others argued that the actions sometimes assigned to Mary Magdalene were those of several distinct women called Mary. But some commentators took it that there were in fact two Mary Magdalenes involved in the events of the Resurrection as Luke xvi describes them.

11-12 *Take so much of th'example, as of the name; / The latter half* since Mrs Herbert bears the latter half of the saint's name, Magdalene, she can take as her example the latter half of Mary Magdalene's life, the devout part. She thus adds another Magdalen to the number, though one whose life is a record not of sin then penitent devotion but of innocence and devotion.

12 *some recompense* some action which will go at least a little way to match or compensate their harbouring Christ himself.

13 *they did harbour Christ* Christ was a guest in the house of Mary of Bethany after he had raised up Lazarus from the dead (John xii). The sinful woman anointed his feet with ointment while he was a guest in the house of Simon the Leper (Matthew xxvi, Mark xiv, Luke vii).

HOLY SONNETS

La Corona

If these were the 'Holy Hymns and Sonnets' which Donne sent to Mrs Herbert in July 1607 then he probably wrote the sequence earlier in that year. But D. Novarr argues that it is more likely to have been written in 1608 or early 1609 ('The Dating of Donne's *La Corona*', *PQ*, XXVI (1957), 259-65).

Holy Sonnets] *This is the general title of the two groups of sonnets in 1633–69,* La Corona *and the* Divine Meditations. Holy Sonnets written twenty years since *M S*

La Corona] The Crown *several M S S*

La Corona   Isaiah xxviii contrasts a 'crown of pride' and the 'fading flower' of its beauty, which 'shall be trodden underfoot', with the 'crown of glory' and 'diadem of beauty' with which the Lord will reward the just.

I

1   *Deign at my hands*   Helen Gardner points out that some of the ideas and phrases in this Advent sonnet derive from the Advent offices in the Roman Breviary, the only Breviary then current.

   this crown   the sequence of sonnets itself, which comes full circle by ending just where it began, with this line.

2   *Weaved*] Weaned *M S*
   low] lone *1635–69 and several M S S*; love's *M S*

2   *melancholy*   The stress falls on the second syllable – meláncholy.

3   *yea*] yet *M S*
   art treasury] art a treasury *some M S S*

4   *Ancient*   Pronounced as three syllables.

5   *bays*   laurel leaves, the traditional garland of poetic or military glory.

9   *ends crown*] end crown *several M S S*
   our ends] our days *several M S S*

11   *This*] The *1633 and M S*
   first last end   the first death, that of the body, will for the just man also be the last.
   zealously] soberly *several M S S*

11–12   *possessed, / With a strong sober thirst, my soul attends*   his soul, zealously possessed with a strong sober thirst, awaits the 'first, last end'.

12   *a strong sober thirst*   Isaiah repeatedly contrasts a pious thirst with the drunkard's thirst of self-glory – 'behold my servants shall drink, but ye shall be thirsty' (lxv 13), 'they that have brought it [thy wine] together, shall drink it in the courts of my holiness' (lxii 9).

13 *heart and voice*] voice and heart *some MSS*

14 *Salvation to all that will is nigh* 'Hearken unto me, my people, and give ear unto me ... My righteousness is near; my salvation is gone forth ...' (Isaiah li 4–5).
Salvation Pronounced as four syllables.

2 Annunciation

1 *to*] unto *MS*

2–4 *That all, which always is all ... | ... yet cannot choose but die* these lines are repeated, with a change of tense, in *The Progress of the Soul* 74–6.

8 *try* attempt to conquer.

9 *Ere by the spheres time was created* Aristotle and other ancient cosmologers say that time is a consequence of the movement of the heavens.
the spheres] thy spheres *MS*
created] begotten *some MSS*

10–12 *thy son, and brother, | ... conceiv'st, conceived ... | Thy maker's maker, and thy father's mother* The writings of some of the Church Fathers make much of the paradoxes inherent in Christian doctrine. St Augustine for example spoke of Mary as physically the Mother of Christ, but spiritually his sister and his mother together.

3 Nativity

4 *our*] the *several MSS*

6 *this*] his *1669*

7 *will*] shall *some MSS*
prevent anticipate, forestall.

8 *Th'effect of Herod's jealous general doom* the Massacre of the Innocents, from which the infant Christ was saved by the appearance to Joseph in a dream of the angel of the Lord.
effect] effects *1635–54 and several MSS*
jealous] dire and *some MSS*; zealous *several MSS*

9 *eyes*] eye *1635–69 and several MSS*

10 *yet none holds him* the whole world is too small to contain Christ.

12 *by*] of *several MSS*

13 *with him into Egypt* into exile and hardship, to save oneself from the world.

14 *kind* sharing our nature, and therefore our condition.

4 Temple

Temple] Flight. Temple *MS*

3 *yea blowing out* baffling the learned men with searching questions, after astonishing them with 'his understanding and answers' (Luke ii).

4 *the*] those *most MSS*

5 *The Word but lately could not speak* 'Verbum infans, the Word without a word; the eternal word not able to speak a word' (Lancelot Andrewes, Christmas Day Sermon 1618). The quibble derives from St Bernard.

9 *His godhead was not soul to his manhood* Christ was not a god in a human body but had a human soul.

10 *Nor had time mellowed him* his understanding was not something that had matured with time.

11 *for one*] one *MS*; some one *MS*; to one *MS*
    a long task] long tasks *some MSS*; long task *several MSS*
    'tis] thinks *several MSS*; thinks it *MS*

5 Crucifying

3 *weak*] meek *some MSS*
    weak the humble and poor in spirit, who realize their own insufficiency.

4 *both affections* both dispositions, the weak and the ambitious.
    ran] came *MS*

7] whose face is now prescribed a Fate [*sic*] *MS*

8 *to a span*] to span *1633-69 and several MSS*

8-9 *Measuring self-life's infinity to a span, | Nay to an inch* (a) narrowing down to the mere span of a human life, or much less than the full span, the infinite principle of life itself; (b) limiting the infinity of existence itself to a mere spread of human limbs upon the cross; (c) attempting to measure infinity by finite feet and inches.

9 *condemned* pronounced as three syllables.

13 *dole* (a) pain; (b) sustenance.

6 Resurrection

3 *Too stony hard* impervious to Christ or to its own condition.
too fleshly too much occupied with the world and the flesh.

4 *starved* withered, deprived, killed with cold.

5 *this*] thy *some MSS*
abled enabled, given the power.
control restrain, overcome.

6 *shall to*] shall now to *several MSS*; shall move to *MS*

7 *first or last death* the death of the body or the damnation of th
soul.

8 *little book*] life-book *1635–69 and some MSS*; little books *MS*
little book there is room for few names in it; or few will fit themselve:
to be entered in it.

9 *that long sleep*] that last long sleep *some MSS*; that sleep *MS*
that steeped *MS*

10 *of which, and for which 'twas* the flesh returns to the dust of which
it was made; and it puts on that immortality for which man was created
in the first place.

11 *glorified*] purified *some MSS*

12 *death's*] death *1633–69 and some MSS*

7 Ascension

2 *this sun, and son* 'Then shall the righteous shine forth as the sun
in the kingdom of their father' (Matthew xiii 43). Donne repeatedly
uses this play on words to make an identity between the sources of life in
the universe. See, for example, *Resurrection, imperfect* 4–8 and *A
Hymn to God the Father* 15–16.

3 *just*] true *1635–69 and several MSS*
tribulation Pronounced as five syllables.

7 *show alone* display only his own triumphant ascent to heaven.

8 *first he, and he first* he leads the way for us, and is the first to
open that way.

9 *ram*   (a) battering ram; (b) male sheep, the leader of the flock.
which hast battered] which battered *MS*

11   *the way*] thy ways *some MSS*; thee *several MSS*

12   *thine ... thine*] thy ... thy *1633 and several MSS*

13   *raise*   exalt above its usual capacity.

DIVINE MEDITATIONS

Twelve of these sonnets were printed in *1633* and another four in *1635*; the remaining three sonnets appear only in the Westmoreland MS and were not printed until 1899 when Gosse found them there.

Walton implied that Donne wrote his devout poetry in later life, long after he was ordained in 1615; and following readers have naturally assumed that the Divine Meditations belong together as the private record of the inquietude that underlay Donne's formal ministry. Certainly one of the three sonnets in the Westmoreland MS, 'Since she whom I love', must have been written when Donne was already a priest, for it relates to the death of his wife which occurred in 1617. But there is nothing to suggest that the nineteen sonnets make up a single body of work written over a short period of time. Indeed Helen Gardner argues on circumstantial evidence that Donne wrote all save the three poems in the Westmoreland MS well before his ordination, possibly between 1609 and 1611. She assumes that Donne sent a set of six of the Divine Meditations to the Earl of Dorset in 1609 (see *To E. of D. with Six Holy Sonnets* and note).

1635 printed four more of these sonnets than *1633*, sixteen in all, interspersing the four additional poems among the other twelve. All following editors save Helen Gardner have given the poems in the order of the *1635* edition with the three poems from the Westmoreland MS at the end, as I do here. But Professor Gardner thinks that the order of the twelve poems in *1633* is Donne's order, which the *1635* editor destroyed. She argues that the twelve sonnets make up two distinct sets of six meditations, and that the four sonnets added in *1635* also belong together. She would group the sonnets thus:

Poems given in *1633*

(i)

As due by many titles
Oh my black soul!
This is my play's last scene

At the round earth's imagined corners
If poisonous minerals
Death be not proud

(ii)

Spit in my face ye Jews
Why are we by all creatures waited on?
What if this present were the world's last night?
Batter my heart, three-personed God
Wilt thou love God, as he thee?
Father, part of his double interest

Poems added in *1635*

Thou has made me
I am a little world
O might those sighs and tears
If faithful souls be alike glorified

Poems in the Westmoreland MS only

Since she whom I loved
Show me dear Christ
Oh, to vex me

In Professor Gardner's view the first set of six sonnets makes up a
sequence on the Last Things, death and judgement. The second set of
six, she thinks, treats of two complementary aspects of love, Christ's love
for us as the Atonement shows it, and then the love man owes to God
and his neighbour. The four sonnets added in *1635* are penitential,
emphasizing sin and tears for sin. But the remaining three sonnets,
from the Westmoreland MS, are unconnected with each other.

My reason for printing the sonnets here in the order of *1635* is that
the groupings Professor Gardner finds do not seem sufficiently differ-
entiated in the poems themselves to help the reader of an edition such as
this. To congeal such writings in a set mould may be to prejudge the
critical question of what the point of a particular poem really is. Until
we are clear about that then a neutral ordering seems preferable.

Helen Gardner discusses the doctrinal standing of the sonnets in the
Introduction to her *Divine Poems*, as does D. L. Peterson in 'John
Donne's "Holy Sonnets.' and the Anglican Doctrine of Contrition',
SP, LVI (1959), 504–18. There is discussion of particular sonnets by
J. E. Parish, 'Donne's Holy Sonnet XIII', *Explicator*, XXII (1963),

no. 13, and 'Donne's Holy Sonnet XIV', *CE*, XXIV (1963), 299–302;
by D. Cornelius, 'Donne's Holy Sonnet XIV', *Explicator*, XXIV
(1965), no. 25; by A. J. Smith, 'Two Notes on Donne', *MLR*, LI
(1956), 405–7; and by Helen Gardner, 'Another Note on Donne:
"Since she whom I loved",' *MLR*, LII (1957), 564–5.

I THOU HAST MADE ME

First printed in *1635*.

7 *feeble*] feebled *MSS*

11 *so tempteth me* Satan tempts him to despair, in this extremity.

12 *I can myself*] my self I can *1635–69*

13 *prevent* forestall, frustrate.

14 *thou . . . draw* God may if he chooses draw the poet's heart to
him.
   adamant (a) lodestone, a magnetic stone; (b) adamantine rock, a pro-
verbially hard stone which here figures the unyielding determination
God might show in drawing the poet's heart to him.

2 AS DUE BY MANY TITLES

1 *titles* legal rights or entitlements.

2 *O God, first*] O God. First *1635–69*

3 *decayed* corrupted by sin.

5 *thy son, made with thy self to shine* this is another variant of the
play on son / sun.

9 *usurp on*] usurp in *some MSS*

10 *that's*] what's *several MSS*

12 *do*] shall *1635–69 and several MSS*

3 O MIGHT THOSE SIGHS AND TEARS

First printed in *1635*.

1–2 *those sighs and tears . . . / . . . which I have spent* He presents
himself as a former Petrarchan lover.

3 *holy discontent* He contrasts his pious grief now with the profane
discontents and vain mourning of his earlier love of women.

5 *idolatry* worship of women, or of erotic love itself.

6 *rent* rend.

7 *sin, now I*] sin I now *1635-69*

9 *hydroptic* insatiably thirsty.
night-scouting (a) spying at night; (b) flouting the night by working then as other people do in the day.

4 OH MY BLACK SOUL!

1 *summoned* Pronounced as three syllables.

4 *turn* return.

5 *death's doom* sentence of death.

7 *damned* condemned.
execution Pronounced as five syllables.

13 *in*] with *MS*

5 I AM A LITTLE WORLD

First printed in *1635*.

1 *a little world* It is a Renaissance commonplace that man is a microcosm.

2 *elements, and an angelic sprite* matter and spirit. The four elements of material substance are coupled with an angel-like intelligence or soul.

5-6 *You which . . . | Have found new spheres* (a) recent astronomers; (b) the blessed, who have ascended to a heaven beyond our apprehension.
that heaven which was most high what men formerly took to be the extent of heaven.

6 *new spheres, and . . . new lands* (a) the discoveries of recent astronomy; (b) the true domains of heaven, unimagined by us here below.
lands] land *1635-69 and MS*

7 *new seas* heavenly seas yielding penitential tears, instead of the terrestrial seas which supplied his amorous grief. Renaissance cosmographers conjectured that there is a region of seas in the heavens beyond the fixed stars, the 'waters . . . above the firmament' of Genesis i 7.
I] he *1669*

8–10 *Drown my world . . . / But oh it must be burnt* It was widely held that the world would end either in a new flood or by fire.

12 *their*] those *MS*

13 *Lord*] God *MS*

6 THIS IS MY PLAY'S LAST SCENE

6 *and soul*] and my soul *1633*

7] Or presently, I know not, see that face *some MSS*
ever-waking] everlasting *MS*

13 *Impute me righteous* Protestant theologians supposed that even after the soul had been purged of its actual sins by penitence it still bore the imputed guilt of Adam, and needed to be imputed righteous by the merit of Christ.
righteous Pronounced as three syllables.

14 *and devil*] the devil *1633–69*

7 AT THE ROUND EARTH'S IMAGINED CORNERS

1 *the round earth's imagined corners* 'And after these things I saw four angels standing on the four corners of the earth, holding the four winds of the earth' (Revelation vii 1). Maps showing the earth as round go back to the sixth century BC

4 *scattered bodies* bodies dispersed about the earth as dust and bones. See *The Relic* 10–11.

5 *fire* the fire that will end the world. See *I am a little world* 8–10 and *A Fever* 13–16. Revelation vi–xii rehearses the several modes of final destruction.
o'erthrow] overthrow *1669*

6 *dearth*] death *1633–69 and most MSS*

8 *and never taste death's woe* 'We shall not all sleep, but we shall all be changed, in a moment, in the twinkling of an eye, at the last trump' (1 Corinthians xv 51–2).
woe] owe *1669*

12 *lowly*] holy *1669*

14 *sealed* (a) authorized with the necessary imprint; (b) pledged, confirmed.

my pardon   true repentance can earn for the poet the general pardon that Christ's sacrifice offered to mankind.

thy] my *1669*

8 IF FAITHFUL SOULS BE ALIKE GLORIFIED

First printed in *1635*.

1-2   *be alike glorified | As angels*   be blessed equally with angels, so that all have full angelic apprehension. Angels are said to apprehend by immediate intuition, whereas men reason by inference.

6   *circumstances ... signs*   outward appearances, such as human reason has to go by.

7   *in us, not immediately*] in us not immediately *1635-69*

8   *by*] to *several MSS*

9   *idolatrous lovers*   lovers whose god is their mistress, or love itself.

10   *vile*] style *1635-69*
conjurers   magicians.

14   *Thy true grief*] Thy grief *1635-69 and several MSS*
in] into *1635-69 and several MSS*
my] thy *several MSS*

9 IF POISONOUS MINERALS

1   *poisonous*] poisons *1639-54*
and if that] or if the *several MSS*

4   *Cannot be damned*   only creatures having the power of reasoned choice can incur damnation.

5   *or*] and *several MSS*

7-8   *mercy being easy, and glorious | To God*   why does God threaten in anger when it is easy for him to show mercy and his doing so redounds to his glory?

9   *dare*] dares *MS*

9-10   *thee | O God?*] thee? / O God *1633-69*

10   *thine only worthy blood*   Christ's blood which alone is worthy to drown the memory of our sins.

11 *lethean* Lethe in ancient myth is a river of Hades, out of which the souls of the departed drink oblivion of all their early existence.

13 *That thou remember them, some claim as debt* some people entreat God to remember their sins and so forgive them as part of the general debt Christ discharged.
   some claim] no more *several MSS*

14 *if thou wilt forget* 'for I will forgive their iniquity, and their sin will I remember no more' (Jeremiah xxxi 34).

10 DEATH BE NOT PROUD

5 *pictures*] picture *1635–69*

5–6 *From rest and sleep . . . / Much pleasure . . . more must flow* since much pleasure flows from rest and sleep, which are only pictures of death, then much more pleasure must flow from death itself.

7 *soonest our best men with thee do go* (a) the best men die young; (b) good men make least fuss in dying (see *A Valediction: forbidding mourning* 1–4).

8 *Rest of their bones, and soul's delivery* death is a rest of their bodies and a birth or liberation of their souls.
   bones] bodies *several MSS*

10 *dost*] doth *1633*

11 *poppy* the juice of the poppy is a narcotic. See *Othello* III iii 330–33.

12 *better*] easier *several MSS*
   swell'st thou puff yourself up in pride.

13 *wake*] live *several MSS*

14 *Death thou shalt die* 'The last enemy that shall be destroyed is death. . . . Death is swallowed up in victory' (1 Corinthians xv 26, 54).

11 SPIT IN MY FACE YE JEWS

1 *ye*] you *1633–69 and several MSS*

2 *scoff* scoff at.

3 *only*] humbly *MS*

4 *Who*] Which *MS*
no] none *several MSS*

5 *satisfied* atoned for, settled.

6 *impiety*] iniquity *several MSS*

7 *inglorious* (a) an unknown wretched malefactor; (b) not yet ascended in glory.

8 *Crucify him daily* every fresh sin, knowingly indulged in, is a fresh crucifixion of Christ. 'They crucify to themselves the Son of God afresh' (Hebrews vi 6).
being now glorified now he is in his state of glory.

9 *admire* wonder at.

10 *Kings pardon, but he bore our punishment* at best kings pardon our crimes whereas Christ, the king of kings, bore the punishment of our sins for us.

11–12 *Jacob came ... / But to supplant, and with gainful intent* Jacob took the place of his elder brother Esau, clad in the skins of goats to disguise the smoothness of his own skin. He thus deceived their blind father Isaac and supplanted Esau, gaining the blessing that rightly belonged to the firstborn son (Genesis xxvii 1–36).

12–13 *intent: / God*] intent / God *1633*

13–14 *God clothed himself in vile man's flesh ... / ... to suffer woe* whereas Jacob put on a vile harsh garb wholly for his own gain, Christ put on our vile flesh so as to be weak enough to suffer pain for us.

12 WHY ARE WE BY ALL CREATURES WAITED ON?

1 *are we*] am I *MS*

3–4 *being more pure than I, / Simple, and further from corruption* Man is a compound of the four simple elements held in balance, and corruption sets in when the balance is disturbed; he is thus much more prone to corruption than are the simple and pure elements themselves. Further, since the elements and creatures were not the prime agent in the Fall but partake of its consequences only through man's action, they are so much nearer the original state of created innocence than men are.

4 *Simple*] Simpler *1635–69 and some MSS*

4–5 *corruption ... subjection* Both pronounced as four syllables.

5 *Why brook'st thou ... subjection?*   why do you put up with man's making a slave of you?

6 *sillily*   meekly, naïvely.

7 *by 'one man's stroke*   (a) the slaughterman's blow; (b) Adam's sin, for which the whole creation suffers death.

9 *Weaker I am*] Alas I am weaker *MS*

10 *timorous*   fearful.

11 *a greater wonder, for*] a greater, for *1635-69*

13-14 *But their Creator ... / ... hath died*   The paradoxical progression of the argument is that the creatures are less guilty than man but have to serve men, while the Creator himself, who is not guilty at all, abases himself to serve men infinitely more.

   tied   (a) constricted, as men are by their frailty and death; (b) assigned to a definite place in the natural order.

13 WHAT IF THIS PRESENT WERE THE WORLD'S LAST NIGHT?

2 *Mark*] Look *MS*
   O soul, where thou dost dwell   Some scholastic metaphysicians thought that the heart is the seat of the soul.

3 *The picture of Christ crucified*   The crucifix replaces the image of a mistress that secular lovers found in their hearts (see *Elegy 10, The Dream 1-5*).

4 *that*] his *1633-69 and several MSS*

5 *amazing*   overwhelming, terrifying.

8 *fierce*] rank *MS*

9 *my*] mine *MS*

9 *idolatry*   amorous devotion to women, and worship of love.

10 *profane*   secular; blasphemous (because he worshipped women as goddesses).

11-12 *Beauty, of pity, foulness only is / A sign of rigour*   beauty is a sign of compassion, and it is only ugly women who never relent towards their lovers.

12 *to thee*   to his soul (reassuring it).

14 *assures*] assumes *1633–69*
  assures assures one of, guarantees.

14 BATTER MY HEART, THREE-PERSONED GOD

5 *to another due* owing duty to somebody other than its usurping occupier.

7 *me should*] we should *1669*

8 *captived* the stress falls on the second syllable – captíved.

9 *would be loved fain* he eagerly wishes to be loved.

11 *Divorce me, untie, or break that knot again* dissolve the attachment, annul it, or separate the parties by force.

13 *enthral* make a slave or prisoner of.

15 WILT THOU LOVE GOD, AS HE THEE?

1 *digest* reflect on methodically.

6 *for he ne'er begun* God begets Christ eternally, not in time where things have a beginning and an end.

7 *adoption* Pronounced as four syllables.

8 *Coheir* 'We are the children of God: and if children, then heirs; heirs of God, and joint-heirs with Christ; if so be that we suffer with him, that we may be also glorified together' (Romans viii 30; the Rheims New Testament has 'co-heirs', translating the Vulgate *coheredes*).

9–10 *And as a robbed man . . . / . . . must lose or buy it again* As the law stood, a man whose property was stolen and then sold lost his right in it to the purchaser, and could only recover it by buying it back again if the purchaser was willing to sell. In the same way, Christ has to pay with his life to recover his own property – us – from Satan.

10 *stuff*] steed *several MSS*

11 *Son*] Sun *1635–69*

12 *stol'n*] stole *1635–69 and some MSS*

13–14 *'Twas much . . . / . . . much more* The comparison in degree suggests that the Fall had its fortunate aspect in that it evoked this surpassing demonstration of God's love for us.

16 FATHER, PART OF HIS DOUBLE INTEREST

1 *double interest* twofold right or claim.

3 *jointure* joint part or share. A jointure is a tenancy held jointly between two or more persons.
  knotty (9) inextricably intertwined; (b) difficult for the mind to grasp.

4 *gives me*] gives to me *most MSS*
  his death's conquest what he won by his death.

6 *from the world's beginning slain* 'the Lamb slain from the foundation of the world' (Revelation xiii 8).

7 *two wills* the Old Testament and the New Testament.

8 *do*] doth MSS; *not in 1635–69*

9 *thy*] these *1633–69*; those *some MSS*

10 *those statutes* God's laws, such as the Ten Commandments, that set down the conditions on which men can inherit Christ's bequest to them in the Testaments.

11 *but thy all-healing*] but all-healing *some MSS*

11–12 *thy all-healing grace and Spirit / Revive again what law and letter kill* by the law and letter of the Old Testament we merit death, but the grace of Christ and the operation of the Holy Spirit (Christ's bequest to us) offer us life.
  Revive again] Revive and quicken *some MSS*

13 *Thy law's abridgement* the Ten Commandments, which epitomize God's law.

14 *Is all but love* The Ten Commandments rest upon the notion of a just reward for obedience rather than upon love. Christ himself added a commandment when he enjoined us to love one another – 'A new commandment I give unto you, that ye love one another' (John xiii 34). But it is upon Christ's mercy and love for us that our salvation depends, since in strict justice we stand condemned.
  oh let that last will stand! uphold the New Testament and put aside the Old Testament; let our salvation stand upon love and mercy, not upon justice.
  that last] thy last *several MSS*; this last *1633–69*

17 SINCE SHE WHOM I LOVED

In the Westmoreland MS only. First printed in E. Gosse, *Jacobean Poets* (1894).

1 *she whom I loved* Donne's wife Ann died in August 1617 at the age of thirty-three, after giving birth to their twelfth child.

1-2 *her last debt / To nature* 'to pay one's debt to nature' was a common way of referring to events that brought home one's human frailty or mortality.

2 *and to hers . . .* the syntax is ambiguous here in that one can take this phrase either with the preceding words or with what follows. If one reads 'To nature, and to hers' the phrase means (a) and to her nature specifically; (b) and to her family and kindred, to whom she can now owe nothing. If one reads 'to hers, and my good is dead' then the sense is that she is dead to the poet's good and her own, beyond worldly concerns in that (a) she can now no longer do good to herself and her husband; (b) she has died – gone to heaven so early – for her own good and for his. The following lines show how her death has worked for his good.

3 *And her soul . . . ravished* The line is perhaps best scanned with heavy slurring on 'early into heaven' – éarly into héaven ravished.
   ravished Pronounced as three syllables.

6 *show the head* reveal their source.

8 *dropsy* immoderate desire for more.

9-10 *when as thou / Dost woo my soul for hers; offering all thine* God woos the poet's soul on behalf of the soul now in heaven, to reunite and marry them there, as a father might plead his daughter's case with a desirable young man; and the offered dowry or ransom is Christ himself, God's only son.

14 *put thee out* exclude God by claiming the poet's allegiance. The lines may carry the secondary sense that God has deliberately thwarted the poet in this world so as to preserve his allegiance, not only removing loved ones whose origin was divine (saints and angels) but frustrating worldly ambitions or well-being.

18 SHOW ME DEAR CHRIST

In the Westmoreland MS only. First printed in Gosse.
   Some commentators have coupled this sonnet with *Satire 3* and

assigned it to a period before Donne's ordination in 1615, on the ground that it shows him still seeking for the true Church among the several contenders. Grierson assumed that it belonged to the same period as its fellow in the Westmoreland M S, *Since she whom I loved*, and thus shows an Anglican priest of some three years' standing still uncertain whether or not he is in the right communion. But Evelyn Simpson and Helen Gardner have argued, rightly in my view, that the sonnet is not an expression of doubt but a comment on the distance between the actuality and the ideal, the present state of Christendom and the condition of the true Church as it must be. Professor Gardner thinks that lines 3 and 4 refer to specific circumstances of the year 1620.

1 *thy spouse* 'the marriage of the Lamb is come, and his wife hath made herself ready' (Revelation xix 7).

so bright and clear pure and free from error or guilt. 'And to her was granted that she should be arrayed in fine linen, clean and white' (Revelation xix 8).

2–3 *she, which on the other shore / Goes richly painted* the Church of Rome.

3–4 *or which robbed and tore / Laments and mourns in Germany and here?* Grierson took this to be the Church at Geneva 'made to include Germany' (II, 235). But Helen Gardner sees a reference to the ravished Jerusalem of Lamentations, and suggests that Donne was paralleling the captivity of Israel with the collapse of the Protestant cause in Bohemia after the defeat of the Elector of Hanover outside Prague in October 1620. English interests were deeply involved in the Elector's cause and there was general dismay here at his defeat.

5 *Sleeps she a thousand, then peeps up one year?* The claims of some Protestant sects implied that the true Church had disappeared from the earth for a thousand years, but has now emerged afresh.

6 *Is she self truth and errs?* can the true Church be an institution which claims to be truth itself and yet is in continual error?

now new, now outwore can truth, or the true Church, be a matter of fashion, to be accepted while it is new and discarded when it is not?

8 *On one* Mount Moriah, where Solomon built 'the house of the Lord at Jerusalem' (2 Chronicles iii 1) as the temple of the Jews. Alternatively perhaps, Ludgate Hill on which St Paul's stood.

on seven the seven hills of Rome.

or on no hill Geneva, the centre of Calvinism.

12 *court thy mild dove* 'Open to me, my sister, my love, my dove, my undefiled' (Song of Solomon v 2). The Authorized Version glosses this 'Christ awaketh the church with his calling', and reads the whole erotic dialogue in the traditional way as expressing 'the mutual love of Christ and his Church' (rubric to ii 1).

14 *open to most men* open to the generality of mankind (with a glance at the paradoxical sense 'available to the largest number of males'). Universality, not division or exclusiveness, is a note of the true Church.

19 OH, TO VEX ME

In the Westmoreland MS only. First printed in Gosse.

1 *vex* trouble; agitate or shake.

4-5 *devotion . . . contrition* Both pronounced as four syllables.

5 *humorous* changeable, subject to whim.

7 *riddlingly distempered* enigmatically disproportioned or unbalanced, now one extreme, now the other.

8 *As praying, as mute* as full of rapid alternations of petition and dumbness as the customary behaviour of a lover.
as infinite, as none now infinitely contrite, now not contrite at all.

13 *fantastic* capricious, extravagant.
ague a fever, with paroxysms of hot and cold and fits of trembling.

A LITANY

Donne wrote to Sir Henry Goodyer from his sickbed saying that he had just made 'a meditation in verse, which I call a Litany'; but the letter bears no date. He does however excuse himself 'as a lay man, and a private' for taking 'such divine and public names, to his own little thoughts'. So the poem must have been written before his ordination in 1615. R. C. Bald thinks that Donne wrote it during a severe and prolonged attack of neuritis in the winter of 1608-9.

Title] The Litany *1633-69*

Litany 'A form of public prayer, usually penitential, consisting of a series of petitions, in which the clergy lead and the people respond' (*OED*).

5 *dejection* debasement; reduction to excrement.

7 *red earth* The name 'Adam' was assumed to mean 'red earth', being derived from the Hebrew word for red, 'adom'.

8 *vicious tinctures* the corrupting blemishes which have to be purged away before one arrives at the true tincture, or spiritual quintessence.
  fashioned Pronounced as three syllables.

9 *I may rise up from death, before I am dead* the regenerate man has already imitated Christ, having died to the world and risen again as a new being.
  before] ere *several MSS*

13 *could*] did *MS*
  thine] thy *several MSS*

20 *condensed* Pronounced as three syllables.

23 *new storms* illnesses.

25 *intend* intensify (as the sacrilegious tears of Petrarchan lovers intensified their amorous flames instead of quenching them).

26 *glass*] dark *MS*

27 *Fire, sacrifice, priest, altar be the same* however storm-wrecked the frail temple itself, let the observances within be unaffected. He asks that his devout zeal may be unquenched though fevers waste his body.

29 *Bones to philosophy, but milk to faith* the Trinity is at once the hard irreduceable bedrock of thought and the mild nourishment of belief.

30–31 *wise serpents . . . / Most slipperiness, yet most entanglings hath* Serpents could be emblems of wisdom, and of Christ himself. But Donne likens them to the Trinity here in their disparate qualities of elusiveness and involvedness.
  slipperiness . . . entanglings (a) relationships which elude or entangle our finite understandings; (b) a relationship which our minds misapprehend in diverse ways, either separating the persons altogether or failing to distinguish between them at all.

32 *distinguished undistinct* separate and yet not separate.

33 *power, love, knowledge* The characters of the Father, the Son and the Holy Ghost.

34 *a such*] such *1635–69*; such a *most MSS*
  a such self different instinct an impulse like that, which is made up of diverse elements and yet has one nature and end.

35   *these*] thee *several MSS*; all these *several MSS*
let all me elemented be   let my whole being be composed of.

36   *you*] your *MS*
The Virgin Mary] Our Lady *MS*

40   *One claim for innocence*   she committed no sin herself, whether or not she was free of the taint of original sin.
disseized   dispossessed (her innocence robs sin of its prey).

45   *titles unto*   claims upon.

46   *nonage*   minority, infancy.

47   *thine*] thy *several MSS*

48   *Native*] Natives *several MSS*
heaven's fair palaces] heaven's palaces *1650-69*

49   *denizened*   naturalized, as an alien admitted to citizenship.

50   *th'earth conceiving by the sun*   The sun was thought to impregnate the earth and make it fruitful.

52   *which*] what *1635-69*
which course that light doth run   how the sun's light actually works that end.

53   *me . . . mine*] us . . . our *several MSS*

54   *blind in how they see*   ignorant of how the angels apprehend our actions.
how] what *several MSS*

55   *patriarchs*   the Old Testament fathers of the Jewish race such as Abraham, Isaac and Jacob.

56   *great grandfathers of thy Church*   they are the fathers of the apostles, who are themselves the fathers of the Church Fathers.

56-7   *which saw / More in the cloud, than we in fire*   they saw better in the Old Testament darkness than we do in the light of the New Testament. God guided the Israelites out of Egypt as a pillar of cloud by day and a pillar of fire by night; and the two pillars were traditionally interpreted as the Old Testament and the New Testament.

58   *cleared*   (a) enlightened; (b) absolved of guilt. The Patriarchs saw better and did better by the light of nature than we do with the help of grace and the law, the New Testament and the Old Testament.
and law] or law *several MSS*

61 *satisfied*] sanctified *1633*
   fructify] fructified *several MSS*

62-3 *more light | . . . faith by reason added*   we have had the revelation of Christ to assure us, a ground of reason rather than faith.

66-7 *That harmony, which made of two | One law*   the Prophets fore-told the coming of Christ, and so made one law of the two Testaments as of the different natures of God and man.

71 *excuse*] execute *MS*

72 *In*] Of *several MSS*
   seeking secrets, or poeticness   activities of human wit which become excessive and improper when indulged in for their own sake.
   or] in *MS*

73 *thy*] the *MS*
   zodiac   the belt of the celestial sphere, divided into twelve parts, which encircled the universe.

74 *engirt*   encompassed, travelled around. The Apostles' journeyings took in the whole world, as the zodiac encircled the universe.

75 *whosoever*] whoever *most MSS*

76 *throw down, and fall*   throw down their followers into dark deep pits and fall into them themselves.
   and fall] do fall *1635-69*

78 *books*] works *several MSS*

80 *The old broad way in applying*   the straightforward traditional way of interpreting the Scriptures.
   decline   humble; refuse to accept, disown.

81 *make thy word mine*   when he would seek more to show his own ingenuity than to expound God's word.

85 *thy scattered mystic body*   the Church is the mystic body of Christ.

86 *In Abel*] An Able *MS*
   Abel   as a keeper of sheep, Abel was the first type of the Church.

87 *In thine*   in Christ's followers, the Christian martyrs.

88 *patience*   Pronounced as three syllables.

89 *or of worse life*   or in the endurance of a life which is worse than death.

92 *squadron* a comparatively large number of people.

confessors those who avow and adhere to their faith under persecution and torture, but do not suffer martyrdom. In Donne's conceit they are therefore not married but betrothed, virgin and white. The stress falls on the first syllable – cónfessors.

94 *Tendered* offered.

99 *a Diocletian* a persecutor. The Emperor Diocletian began a direct persecution of the Christian Church in AD 303, which continued throughout the Empire until his abdication in AD 305.

100 *The*] Thy *most MSS*

104–5 *they have not obtained of thee, | That or thy Church, or I, | Should keep . . . integrity* they have not obtained from Christ the grace that would have preserved either his Church or the poet in their native singleness, or purity (for the Church was divided and sullied, and the poet a sinner and married).

108 *chaste widowhead* the state of one whom Christ has separated from sin.

109 *Thy*] The *1635–69*
academe] academy *1633 and some MSS*

110 *Doctors* the great Christian theologians.

111 *Both books of life* the Scriptures and God's register of the saved.

112 *thy*] the *1650–69*
Scriptures tells us] Scripture tells us *1669*; Scriptures, tell us *MS*
wrought (a) wrote, written down in; (b) made fit to be in.

117 *Mean ways* middle courses.

118–125 *whilst this universal choir, | . . . | Prays ceaselessly, and thou hearken too, | . . . | Hear this prayer* The construction runs, 'and even though this universal choir prays ceaselessly, and you listen to those prayers, hear this prayer as well . . .'.

119 *That Church . . . , this . . . here* the Church in heaven and the Church here upon earth.

122 *Prays ceaselessly*] Pray ceaselessly *some MSS*; Ceaselessly prays *several MSS*

123 *to be gracious* (a) to be courteous; (b) to receive grace.

124 *Our task is treble* (a) we sing the treble part in the universal choir; (b) the task of Christians in the world is threefold, to pray, suffer and act.

125 *this prayer* this particular addition to the universal prayer.

126 *From trusting in those prayers* from relying on the Church's universal prayers, so that we neglect our own testimony of suffering and action here.

127 *secure* over-confident, and hence spiritually careless.

128 *clods*] clouds *1635-69 and several MSS*

132-3 *that thou art covetous | To them whom thou lov'st* that God would resent their esteeming any worldly thing (because he would jealously want all their love for himself).

133 *To them whom thou*] To them thou *several MSS*; To whom thou *several MSS*

133-4 *maimed | From reaching this world's sweet* cut off from enjoying this world.
sweet] sweets *1635-69 and some MSS*

139 *soul*] souls *1669 and several MSS*

142 *light affecting, in religion, news* lightly taking up new fashions in religion.

144 *Our mutual duties* the obligations we owe to each other as human beings who are flesh and blood as well as spirit.

147 *measuring ill by vicious* thinking that our minor offences are not really bad because some sins are much worse.
vicious Pronounced as three syllables.

150-51 *Which might be scandalous, | And cast reproach on Christianity* if Christians depreciate themselves indiscreetly then Christianity itself might be brought into contempt as a religion of no-goods.

152 *spies* religious busybodies.
pervious open, either because our conduct makes us vulnerable or because we are too ready to listen to what does not concern us.

153 *From thirst, or scorn of fame* from the thirst for fame, or the scorn of fame.
fame] flame *1633*

154 *for*] through *1635–69 and several MSS*

156 *middle kind* between godly and human.

157 *her full of grace* (a) her entireness of grace; (b) her advanced pregnancy, when she was full with Christ.

162 *to both ways free* free from thinking that being poor, or being rich, has in itself anything to do with one's salvation.

163 *that*] thy *some MSS*

164 *is still*] still is *1635–69*
   agony (a) anguish; (b) contest or struggle. Christ's agony is still the subject of the anguished disputes of pious theologians.

166 *And*] An *MS*
   interrupted evenness, with fits (a) broke up Christ's equableness with spasms of pain; (b) left us a legacy of illness by substituting fevered fits of hot and cold for the even temper of health; (c) threw creation itself into discontinuity by disrupting the very principle of harmony.

167–9 *through thy free confession* / *Though thereby they were then* / *Made blind* 'Jesus saith unto them, I am he . . .' (John xviii 5). The soldiers' falling to the ground at these words was commonly taken to mean that they had been struck blind, so that Jesus could have escaped from them had he wished.
   confession Pronounced as four syllables.
   thereby they were] they were thereby *several MSS*

171 *blind unjust men* deliberately deceive men who act against the truth.

173 *clothes*] robes *1635–69 and several MSS*

175 *And*] Or *several MSS*
   that thou wast born that you were a man born of woman, like us.

178 *express* expel. Christ died of his own free will before the tortures of his foes could kill him.

182 *sin*] him *MS*

188 *religious* Pronounced as four syllables.

189 *to vent wit* to show off our own cleverness, discharge our superfluous ingenuity.

190 *when*] where *some MSS*
   infirmity unworthiness.

191   *that*] which *1633*

192–3   *magistrates do mis-apply | To us, as we judge, lay or ghostly sword*   when we think that judges unjustly condemn us by secular or spiritual law.

195   *Or*] When *several MSS*

196   *When*] Where *most MSS*

197   *last judgement*] the last *several MSS*; God's judgement *MS*

198   *the sinister way*   the left-hand way, the misjudgement of God's purposes that leads to hell.
   sinister   The stress falls on the second syllable – siníster.

202   *alleluias*   Pronounced as five syllables.

206   *who*] which *MS*
   who Satan heard'st in Job's sick day   'And Satan answered the Lord and said . . . put forth thine hand now, and touch his bone and his flesh, and he will curse thee to thy face. And the Lord said unto Satan, Behold, he is in thine hand; but save his life. So went Satan forth from the presence of the Lord, and smote Job with sore boils, from the sole of his foot unto his crown' (Job ii 4–7).

208   *evenness*   steady unfluctuating devotion, as the even temperature of a healthy body. The stanza puts the disquiets of a devout life in terms of his present illness.

210   *snatching*   seizing us suddenly, and claiming us.

211   *fast*   (a) sudden in its attack; (b) tenacious.

212–13   *music of thy promises, | Not threats in thunder*   our ability to respond to the harmony of music is another expression of an even temper and of a spirit lifted above our physical limitations—

Such harmony is in immortal souls;
But whilst this muddy vesture of decay
Doth grossly close it in, we cannot hear it.
(*The Merchant of Venice* V i 63–5)

217   *we*] me *1635–69*

218   *labyrinths*   the convolutions of our ear-passages, in which the true sounds easily get lost or distorted.

219–20   *by hearkening, not procure | Our praise, nor others' dispraise*   by our mere willingness to listen to malicious talk, inviting praise of our-selves and dispraise of others.

221 *slipperiness* a laxity of judgement that puts one on the slippery slope from bad to worse.

222 *senselessly* without being aware of it.

223 *excess* greatness, pre-eminent power.

227 *to give us, and make us physic* to give us corrective medicine and make us an example to others.

229 *taxing sin, before her growth* accusing us of sin and censuring it before we even perform it.

231 *Which well*] Which will *1635–69 and M S*; That will *several M S S*
  Which well, if we starve, dine who dine the better as they cause us to starve.
  starve (a) go short of food; (b) die; lose our souls to Satan and suffer in hell.

232–3 *may see then | Us, to amendment, hear them; thee decline* may these exaggerating accusers see us listen to them only so as to amend our-selves, and God decline to hear them.
  hear them] hearken *several M S S*
  thee decline] then decline *M S*

234 *lock*] stop *several M S S*

236 *From thine allegiance* . . . that we never put learning to any other end than God's service.
  thine] his *M S*

238 *For physic made, from*] Nor physic made from *M S*
  physic healing.

240–41 *dwelling lazily | On Nature's nothing* frivolously occupying itself with trifles; investigating natural circumstances without reference to final causes, and God.

242 *affections* human feelings, which might lead us to hell but are also our saving impulses.

243 *Hear us, weak echoes, O thou ear, and cry* in calling thus upon God we are only weak echoes of God himself, who is at once the invoca-tory cry and the ear that listens to it (see line 207).
  echoes] wretches *several M S S*
  cry] eye *several M S S*

245 *By taking our blood* (a) by taking on our human nature, and so incurring a debt to it; (b) by shedding our blood, which you should now restore to us.

246 *or us*] and us *1635–69 and several M.S.S*

246–7 *Gain to thy self, or us allow; | And let not both us and thy self be slain* since Christ was slain for us, the gain of his death is our eternal life; if we perish then our loss is his also.

251 *patient and physician being free* when we, the patients, are as free of sin as Christ, the physician.

252 *sin is nothing* In scholastic theology sin is said to have no positive nature but to be a perversion of good or a mere absence of it.

let it no where be not subsisting in its own right, sin can have no being when we are no longer sinful.

THE CROSS

This poem bears upon a Church controversy of the early years of King James 1st's reign. In the so-called Millenary Petition of 1603 Puritan ministers called for the abolition of the sign of the cross in baptism, among other things; but James I rejected their demands at the Hampton Court conference in 1604: 'Another scruple was, concerning the Crosse in Baptisme, which Doctor *Reynolds* confessed to have ever been used since the Apostles time, at going abroad, or entering into the Church, or at their Prayers and Benedictions; but doubted of the ancient use of it in Baptisme: to which the Bishop of *Winchester*, answered that in *Constantines* time it was used in Baptisme, and the Deane of *Westminster* shewed out of *Tertullian, Cyprian, Origen* and others; that in their time it was used *In Immortali lavachro*: which could be nothing but Baptisme: and this the King Judged to be antiquity enough to warrant the continuance of it still. . . . Doctor *Reynolds* added; that the Crosse should be abandoned, because in the time of Popery; It had been superstitiously abused. To which his Majesty answered, that his very reason was an inducement to him to have it reteyned still: For in asmuch as it was abused (so you say) to superstition in time of Popery, it doth plainly imply, that it was well used before Popery' (Sir Richard Baker, *A Chronicle of the Kings of England*, 1643, 148).

Donne's advocacy of the Cross in this poem is an argument against that Puritan policy, as well as a reprobation of those unregenerates who do not want to concern themselves with Christ at all.

Title] Of the Cross *MS*

6 *sin*] sins *MS*

8 *pains*] pangs *MS*

9–10 *no pulpit, nor misgrounded law, / Nor scandal taken* Puritans abhorred representations of the Cross; they preached against them, sought legislation to prohibit them, and took it as a scandal when people crossed themselves.

12 *another cross* another burden to bear. The poem plays on several senses of cross: (a) Christ's Cross; (b) any crossed pieces, or attitudes of things crossing at right angles; (c) a burden or weight of suffering, which one willingly bears; (d) a deliberate thwarting of one's own impulses or ends.

13 *Better were worse* not to have to bear that Cross is worse than having to bear it.
   affliction Pronounced as four syllables.

15 *instrument* (a) a means by which something is done, in this case the sacramental bread and wine; (b) a legal enactment confirming an agreement, an undertaking or the like.

16 *dewed on me* 'pour upon them the continual dew of thy blessing' (*The Book of Common Prayer*, A Prayer for the Clergy and People). God in the Sacrament bestows upon the poet thus refreshingly the blessing of the body and blood of Christ.

20 *yard* yardarm.

21 *out*] our *1669*

23 *is*] are *several MSS*

25 *good*] and *MS*
   physic medicine.

26 *And yet*] But yet *1633 and some MSS*

27 *extracted chemic medicine* the quintessence of a remedial substance, arrived at by chemical extraction. Such extractions of the 'virtues' of plants and minerals were supposed to have preservative powers.

30 *stilled* distilled, sublimed; transformed.
   purged purified.
   tribulation Pronounced as five syllables.

31 *ungrudged* uncomplained of, welcomed.

33–4 *As perchance, carvers do not faces make, | But that away, which hid them there, do take* In a celebrated sonnet, *Non ha l'ottimo artista*, Michelangelo says that even the finest sculptor has no conceit which is not already hidden in the block of marble waiting to be uncovered.

37 *as oft alchemists do coiners prove* alchemists' inability to make gold legitimately, forces them to the antithetical activity of forging money; the one extreme begets its opposite extreme.

38–40 *So may a self-despising, get self-love. | . . . pride, issued from humility* Puritans were commonly charged with a proud self-love or self-righteousness, begotten of their professed self-contempt and excessive humility (see Ben Jonson, *The Alchemist* III 2).

41–2 *cross | Your joy in crosses* frustrate the pleasure you take in humbling or denying yourself.

44 *destruction*] corruption *MS*

45 *seek*] see *1650–69*

46 *a snake* the deceitfulness of outward beauty, as instanced in Eve's admiration of the serpent.

47 *the rest* the other senses, each of which is to be mortified by having to endure things repugnant to it.

48 *indifferent; call nothing best*] indifferent; all, nothing best *1635–69*

50 *move; to th'others th'objects*] move to the others, the objects *MS*
      to th'others th'objects] to th'other th'objects *1633*; to th'others objects *1635–69*
      to th'others the other senses, which unlike the eye cannot move to find or select gratifying objects.

51–2 *cross thy heart: for that in man alone | Points downwards, and hath palpitation* Aristotle said that man is practically the only animal whose heart jumps, because he alone has hope and anticipation of the future. 'O man, which . . . hast thy head erected to heaven, and all others to the centre; that yet only thy heart of all others, points downwards, and only trembles' (Donne, *Essays in Divinity*, ed. E. M. Simpson (1952), 30). Donne finds a moral in the heart's physical character as his age understood it, seeing here the force that pulls men down towards hell and betrays them to worldly preoccupations.
      Points] Pants *1633–69 and some MSS*

53 *dejections*] detorsions *1635-69 and MS*; defections *MS*
dejections downward impulses; abasements.
it the heart.

55 *the*] thy *some MSS*
vent find an outlet, discharge; express itself.

56 *sutures, which a cross's form present* the upper cranial bones meet
at the crown of the head in the form of a cross.

58 *concupiscence of wit* the lust to show ingenuity, or pursue profitless
speculation for its own sake. 'Picus Earl of Mirandola . . . being a man
of an incontinent wit, and subject to the concupiscence of inaccessible
knowledge and transcendencies . . .' (*Essays in Divinity* 13).

59 *let none fall* let no opportunities ecape you.

61 *fruitfully*] faithfully *1633-69*

63 *That*] The *1633-69*
That Cross's pictures much,] That Cross's Pictures; much, *MS*

64 *That Cross's children* the consequences of Christ's crucifixion;
or the continual re-enactments of it that his followers have to undergo
in the world.

RESURRECTION, IMPERFECT

imperfect the poem is incomplete.

1 *Sleep, sleep old sun* the time of the poem is before sunrise on Easter
Monday.
repassed recovered from. The wound was presumably the eclipse of
light from the sixth to the ninth hour which accompanied the death of
Christ, who is the ultimate source of all light.

4 *A better sun* Christ, the son and the sun.

6 *enlightened*] enlightenedst *MS*

10-11 *that he might allow / Himself unto all stations* so that he might
put himself in every earthly condition of being.

12 *a mineral* earth in the earth; but also in the sense set out in the
following lines.

13 *all gold* In the qualitative physics gold is the perfect metal to whose condition all baser metals strive in the earth. The sense here is that the grave itself is an alchemical alembic, in which good men's bodies are refined from dross to gold ready for their resurrection. But Christ was pure gold already.

13-14 *but rose / All tincture* tincture is the essence of gold which has the power to transform other metals to itself. Christ gains this power to regenerate sinful humanity through his own human mortification and regeneration in the crucifixion and burial.

15 *Leaden and iron wills*, spiritually apathetic people and obdurate sinners.

21 *this body*] his body *MS*

22 *of the whole* the soul of all mankind, and of the whole creation.
Desunt caetera the rest is lacking.

UPON THE ANNUNCIATION AND PASSION FALLING UPON
ONE DAY. 1608

Title] Upon the Annunciation, when Good Friday fell upon the same day *several MSS*
falling upon one day The Feast of the Annunciation falls upon 25 March, which was in fact Good Friday in 1608. 1608 is thus confirmed as the date of the poem.

1 *Tamely* meekly, not rebelling against the fast.
body] flesh *1635-69 and several MSS*

2 *hither and away* Christ's impending birth, and his death. The entire poem is a meditation upon the paradox of this simultaneous birth and death of God himself.

4 *of them both*] of both them *MS*
a circle emblem is The circle was the emblem of God, perfection and infinity. It belongs to Christ as man in that his beginning and his end thus meet on this day.

7 *She sees him nothing twice at once* A man is as nothing before his birth, and again after his death, but here Christ was both nothings simultaneously.

8 *a cedar* The cedar is a symbol of Christ and of his kingdom. 'I will also take of the highest branch of the high cedar ... and will plant it upon an high mountain and eminent' (Ezekiel xvii 22).

9 *put to making* submitted to the process of being made.

10 *and dead*] yet dead *1633 and several MSS*

12 *Reclused* secluded, solitary; in religious retirement, as an anchoress.

16 *he her to John* 'When Jesus therefore saw his mother, and the disciple standing by, whom he loved, he saith unto his mother, Woman, behold thy son' (John xix 26).

17 *orbity* bereavement of her child.

19 *hath*] is *several MSS*

21 *plain* flat, not a globe.

21-2 *east)* / ... est] east / ... est). *MS*
   Ave ... Consummatum est 'Hail!' the angel's greeting to Mary at the Annunciation; and 'It is perfected', the last words of Christ upon the Cross.

23 *court of faculties* the body of learned authorities empowered to administer God's affairs here.

24 *in some times, and seldom joining these* the Church's wisdom is shown in that it sometimes joins the Annunciation and the Passion, but does it rarely.

25 *the self-fixed pole* the fixed pole itself.

26 *the next star thereto* the pole star, which is not fixed and does not always stand right above the pole, but is none the less our best guide to the location of the pole.

28 *not far)* ... stray] not far ... stray) *MS*

29 *So God by his Church, nearest to him, we know* so we know God by his Church, which of all the things that we can fix on stands nearest to him.

31 *His Spirit* the Holy Ghost, third part of the Trinity, which Christ bequeathed to the world as guide after his own departure.
   as] and *1635-69*

31-2 *his fiery pillar doth* / *Lead* God guided the Israelites out of Egypt in a pillar of cloud and a pillar of fire. 'And the Lord went before them by day in a pillar of cloud, to lead them the way, and by night in a pillar of fire, to give them light' (Exodus xiii 21).

32 *and his Church, as cloud* 'And the Lord said unto Moses, Lo, I come unto thee in a thick cloud, that the people may hear when I speak with thee, and believe thee for ever. (Exodus xix 9). Moses was traditionally taken as the forerunner of Christ, and a figure of the Church which revives its people from the rock (see Exodus xvii 5–6).

as cloud] a cloud *MS*

33 *these*] those *1633–69*
days] feasts *1635–69 and some MSS*

34 *is one*] are one *1635–69 and MS*

35 *Or 'twas in him the same*] And that in him 'twas one *MS*

37 *had*] hath *1633–69 and several MSS*
as God Christ in his nature as God.

38 *the*] his *several MSS*
but one period just one point of time, the same moment (for being outside time God sees the beginning and the end together).

39 *His imitating spouse* the Church, the bride of Christ.

42 *Accepted* (a) if God had accepted this as sufficient; (b) if we would then have accepted this as our saving means, and devoted ourselves to Christ.

44 *Would busy a life* would preoccupy one for an entire lifetime.
she all this day affords the Church gives us all Christ's 'pains, deeds, or words' on this one day.

45 *in gross* whole, as a capital sum.
uplay lay up, store for future need, as in 'lay up for yourselves treasures in heaven ... for where your treasure is, there will your heart be also' (Matthew vi 20–1).

46 *my*] thy *several MSS*
retail impart in small quantities; recount, or testify to.

GOOD FRIDAY, 1613. RIDING WESTWARD

Title] Good Friday. 1613. Riding towards Wales *several MSS*; Good Friday. 1613. Riding to Sir Edward Herbert in Wales *MS*; Mr J. Dun going from Sir H. G. on good friday sent him back this meditation, on the way *MS*; Good Friday / made as I was riding Westward that day *MS*

Riding Westward Donne stayed with Sir Henry Goodyer at Polesworth in Warwickshire in the early spring of 1613, and then went on to visit Sir Edward Herbert at Montgomery, some seventy miles due west. He had reached Montgomery by 7 April for he wrote a letter from there on that day. The several versions of the subtitle thus agree in implying that Donne composed this poem during the journey from Polesworth to Montgomery on 3 April – Good Friday – 1613.

1-2 *Let man's soul be a sphere ... / ... devotion is* as a sphere is moved by the intelligence within it, so devotion moves a man's soul.

3-4 *And as the other spheres ... / ... lose their own* as the heavenly spheres lose their own proper motion or impulse under the influence of external forces acting upon them.

4 *motions*] motion *1633–69*

5 *by others hurried every day* The cosmologists of the day did in fact suppose that the spheres were subject to a number of cosmic forces which deflected them out of their natural orbit from west to east, or might actually impel them in the opposite direction.

6 *their natural form* their true moving principle, the guiding intelligence.

7-8 *our souls admit / For their first mover* devotion ought to move and guide our souls on their true path towards the east and Christ, but we let ourselves be distracted hither and thither by pleasure or business, and lose sight of our natural goal.

8 *are whirled* (a) are giddily distracted; (b) are made 'world'.

10 *my soul's form bends* his body goes one way while his devotion impels his soul another way, humbling itself towards Christ.
    toward] to *1633–69 and MS*

11 *a sun* Christ, the son and sun.
    by rising by coming to the world; by being raised on the Cross; by rising from the flesh, and then from the tomb.

13 *on*] an *MS*
    this Cross] his Cross *1635–69 and some MSS*

16 *too*] two *1635–69*

17 *Who sees God's face ... must die* God told Moses 'Thou canst not see my face: for there shall no man see me, and live' (Exodus xxxiii 20).
    that is self life which is the principle of life itself.

19 *lieutenant* deputy, vicegerent.
    Nature shrink Matthew xxvii 51-4 recounts the perturbations in nature at the moment when Christ died on the Cross. Nature shrank, too, in the original sin of Adam that necessitated Christ's death.

20 *his footstool crack* 'Thus saith the Lord, The heaven is my throne, and the earth is my footstool' (Isaiah lxvi 1). Matthew xxvii 51 tells of an earthquake at the moment of Christ's death.

the sun wink (a) darkness covered the land from the sixth to the ninth hour; (b) the son and sun himself suffered a three-day eclipse from his death to his resurrection.

22 *turn*] tune *1633–69 and some MSS*

turn all spheres at once Modern editors are divided between 'turn' and 'tune', as are the early versions. 'Tune' presents Christ as 'the Wisdom which "sweetly ordereth all things" ' (Helen Gardner), 'turn' as the all-powerful first mover. Grierson pointed out that the notions are interdependent, since the turning of the spheres and their tune are the same thing.

Roma Gill tells me that medieval artists sometimes represented God in the act of turning all spheres at once. A fourteenth-century fresco she photographed on the north arm of the Camposanto at Pisa shows the universe as a series of concentric circles, which moves out from the earth at the centre through the spheres of the four elements, of the planets, and of the celestial hierarchies, to the highest order of creation. God appears at the top as First Mover, with his arms spread wide to encompass the whole and his hands clearly gripping the entire system of spheres at either side. His attitude is just that of Christ on the Cross. The artist is Piero di Puccio da Orvieto.

24 *Zenith to us, and to' our antipodes* God is at the same time the highest point to us and to the people who live on the other side of the world.

and to] and *1633–69 and some MSS*

25–6 *that blood which is* | *The seat of all our souls* Some metaphysicians argued that our soul resides in the blood; and Donne elsewhere calls the blood *'sedes animae*, the seat and residence of the soul. (*Sermons* IV, 294). But Christ's blood saves and sustains all our souls.

26 *if not of his* whether or not Christ's blood was the seat of his own soul.

27 *Made*] Make *some MSS*

Made dirt of dust (a) mingled with the dust, and so made into muddy dirt; (b) made still less than the dust of its human incarnation, lower than the low.

28 *ragged* Pronounced as one syllable.

30 *Upon his miserable*] On his distressed *1635–69*

32 *Half of that sacrifice ...* (a) in bearing Christ Mary shared with God himself the sacrifice of a son to ransom us; (b) she shared in her son's saving sacrifice by her grief at his sufferings on the cross.

33 *be from mine eye* he looks westward, not to the east.

36 *tree;*] tree. *MS*

38 *Corrections* correcting punishments.

40 *rusts*] rust *1635–69 and some MSS*

41 *Restore thine image* (a) show me the image of your sufferings again, which is now concealed from me; (b) make me look like you again, restore me to your own likeness by burning away the deforming cankers of sin.

42 *That thou mayst know me* (a) that you may recognize me by seeing yourself in me again; (b) that you may acknowledge me as your own.

TO MR TILMAN AFTER HE HAD TAKEN ORDERS

First published in *1635*; only three MSS have it.

Edward Tilman took deacon's orders in December 1618 and the poem must have been written after that. It is a reply to some verses of Tilman's which express their author's reluctance to take orders because he feels himself unworthy. Tilman's poem is given in H. Harvey Wood, 'A Seventeenth-Century Manuscript of Poems by Donne and Others', in *Essays and Studies by Members of the English Association*, XVI (1930), 179–90.

3 *lay-scornings* laymen's scorn for the Christian ministry.

5 *What bringst thou home ...?* what harvest have you garnered?

6 *in*] since *1635 and MS*
in the vintage in the coming to maturity and perfecting of your purpose.
vintage] voyage *MS*

10 *For* in exchange for.

13–14 *Art thou ... / ... more?*] Thou art ... / ... more. *1635*

14 *changed* Pronounced as two syllables.

15 *crowned* Pronounced as two syllables.

17 *God's old image by creation* man as he was first created in the likeness of God.

18 *new stamp*] new birth *MS*
  coronation?] coronation; *1635*

22 *new feathered with celestial love?* has celestial love completely transformed you and not just put a different stamp upon the old material?

23 *thy purchase* your gain or profit.

24 *above, below* show here on earth what advantage you have now gained in heaven.

25 *gaining*] gainings *1635 and MS*
  surmount expression go beyond what you can express.

28 *That gentry should join families with it?* that gentlemen should become clergymen?

29] Would they think it well if the day were spent . . .? *several MSS*; Would they think you that the whole day were spent . . .? *MS*

32 *placed* Pronounced as two syllables.
  refined] sublimed *1635*
  refined Pronounced as three syllables.

33 *beauty*] beauties *several MSS*

34 *as*] of *1635*
  sublimed elevated, superior; as in alchemy a base substance might be transmuted into something slightly less base, or ostensibly changed but not materially. Pronounced as three syllables.

39 *to more* to more people.

40 *dignities* honours and titles.
  keep guard.

42 *convey* communicate, impart, express.

43 *As angels out of clouds* This analogy appears to involve two traditional ideas: (a) as angels and God himself sometimes speak to men out of clouds, that is, stoop to communicate with us from a zone dark to our mere human vision; (b) as angels take on bodies of air or cloud so as to be visible to men with whom they communicate.

The double analogy in lines 41–3, with Mary and with angels, suggests that like them preachers are vehicles of divine purpose, doing spiritual offices through material bodies.

45 *whereas* when it happens that.

46 *optics magnify* praise their telescopes.

47 *engines*] engine *1635*
   engines the instruments of the priest, such as preaching and the sacraments.

50 *must meet* must coexist.
   men's offences the affronts men give to priests; the stumbling-blocks and difficulties men find in religion (*OED* 2).

52 *bear* (a) give birth to; (b) sustain.

54 *hermaphrodite* a being who combines the natures of both sexes; a uniting of unlikes or opposites. In this case Tilman's priestly calling marries and makes fruitful the element of heaven and the element of earth in man.

UPON THE TRANSLATION OF THE PSALMS BY SIR PHILIP SIDNEY, AND THE COUNTESS OF PEMBROKE HIS SISTER

First printed in *1635*, and given in only one MS. Lines 52-3 must mean that the poem was written after the Countess of Pembroke's death in 1621.
   The Sidneys' version of the Psalms was not published until 1823, though it was well known in manuscript. A note in one such manuscript indicates that much of the translation was the work of Mary Sidney alone, since Philip Sidney died early on in the project; but Donne attributes it to both of them equally.

2 *do the circle square* attempt something absurdly unlikely.

3 *strait corners of poor wit* the narrow confines of man's feeble intelligence.

4 *cornerless and infinite* the circle was the emblem of God.

7 *this one* this particular gift.

9 *in a cloven tongue* (a) in a twofold form, being made up of words and music together; (b) with a double force, a literal sense and a Messianic application.

17 *John Baptist's holy voice* John the Baptist 'came for a witness, to bear witness of the light. . . . He said, I am the voice of one crying in the wilderness, make straight the way of the Lord' (John i 7, 23).

18 *Now let the Isles rejoice* Psalm 97.

19 *and applied it too* by making these islands rejoice.

23 *Make all this all, three choirs* the entire creation is made up of three choirs.

29 *he | Who hath tuned God and man* Christ, who reconciled man to God in his atonement and in his own person.

38 *abroad* outside the churches, in private chambers where people might reach such 'well attired' versions of the Psalms as this one by the Sidneys, instead of the poor rendering the churches used then.

40 *call that reformed* the Church of England, which claimed to have reformed the errors of Rome.

45 *For that we pray* for a reformation of the psalter used in Anglican churches.

we praise thy name for this for this version by the Sidneys.

46 *this Moses*] thy Moses *1635-69*

this Moses ... this Miriam In Exodus xv Moses sings a song of praise to the Lord after the overthrow of the Egyptians in the crossing of the Red Sea, and his sister Miriam takes up his exultation with a short song of her own.

51 *th'extemporal song* (a) the unpremeditated song, which our life here has not prepared us to sing; (b) the song beyond time.

53 *translated* taken them to a life beyond this one.

these] those *1635-69*

54 *learned* Pronounced as two syllables.

56 *fall in with them* (a) join in their song; (b) encounter them; (c) join them in heaven.

THE LAMENTATIONS OF JEREMY, FOR THE MOST PART ACCORDING TO TREMELLIUS

The poem is a paraphrase of the Lamentations of Jeremiah from the Latin Old Testament of Tremellius and Junius, which was published in 1575-9, and at times from the Vulgate. Tremellius (1510-80) was an Italian Jew who became a Calvinist and, with Junius, gave European Protestants their standard Latin Old Testament.

Helen Gardner suggests that the poem may reflect the situation of German Protestants after the defeat of the Elector Palatine in November 1620, when the Catholic League overran Bohemia and handed the Elector's territories over to the Emperor Maximilian.

4 *tributary* enslaved; owing tribute to another nation.

17 *grown her head* become her ruler.

25 *her*] their *1633-69 and several MSS*; the *MS*

31 *Who honoured, scorn her*   those who honoured her now scorn her.

41 *her*] the *MS*

43 *pleasure*] pleasures *MS*

44 *O Lord, behold*] behold O Lord *MS*

49 *governed*   Pronounced as three syllables.

53 *hand*] hands *1650-69*
framed   Pronounced as two syllables.

54 *hath*] have *MS*

56 *whom*] whence *1633*

58 *company* 'an assembly' (Authorized Version).
invite] accite *1635-69 and several MSS*

59-60 *the winepress hath | Trod upon Judah's daughter* 'the Lord hath trodden the virgin, the daughter of Judah, as in a wine-press' (Authorized Version).

73 *called*   Pronounced as two syllables.

75 *they*] there *MS*

76 *and none could get*] they could not get *1633*; they could none get *MS*

78 *o'erturned*] returned *1633*

80 *waste*   given as wast *in the early versions*

81 *hear I mourn*] hear me mourn *MS*
which hear I mourn   which hear that I mourn.

87 *sighs*] sights *1669*

93 *swallowed*   Pronounced as three syllables.

94 *demolished*   Pronounced as four syllables.

95 *strengths*] strength *1635-69 and several MSS*

97 *horn*   military power, means of defence or resistance.

104 *poured*   Pronounced as two syllables.
like fire] like a fire *MS*

107 *holds*   strongholds.

110 *where*] which *several MSS*
congregation   Pronounced as five syllables.

112 *regardeth*] regarded *1669*

114 *hand*] hands *1633–69*

116 *as in the true solemnities* 'as in the day of a solemn feast' (Authorized Version). The enemies' festive shouts replace the sounds of the true religious solemnities in the temple.

121 *Their gates*] The gates *1635–69*

122 *bars*] bar *1633–69 and several MSS*

124 *their*] the *1669*

135 *streets*] street *1633–69 and several MSS*

141 *For thee*] For, the *1633*; For the *1669*

143 *disturn*] dis-urn *1669*
     disturn   turn away, avert.

144 *False burdens, and false causes* 'but have seen for thee false burdens, and causes of banishment' (Authorized Version).

145 *passengers*   passers by.

153 *purposed*   Pronounced as three syllables.

154 *determined*   Pronounced as four syllables.

157 *against*] unto *1635–69 and MSS*

158 *wall*] walls *1633 and several MSS*

161 *pour, for*] pour out *1635–69*; pour forth *MS*

166 *this*] thus *MS*

167 *of a span*   young.

174 *thy*] his *1633*

182 *girt*] hemmed *several MSS*

182–3 *girt me in | With hemlock, and with labour* 'compassed me with gall and travail' (Authorized Version).

193–4 *He made the children of his quiver pass | Into my reins* 'He hath caused the arrows of his quiver to enter into my reins' (Authorized Version).
     reins   the kidneys or loins used figuratively in the Bible for the seat of the feelings.

202 *perished*   Pronounced as three syllables.

203 *mournings*] mourning *MS*

204 *affliction*   Pronounced as four syllables.

209 *renewed*   Pronounced as three syllables.

211 *portion*   Pronounced as three syllables.

215 *It*] He *MS*

216 *salvation*   Pronounced as four syllables.

220 *yet then*] yet *MS*; yet there *several MSS*

222 *reproached*   Pronounced as three syllables.

227 *stamped*   Pronounced as two syllables.

228 *doth*] might *MS*

229 *wrung*] wrong *1633*

231 *doth*] will *several MSS*

239 *us with wrath*] with thy wrath *several MSS*

245 *water*] watery *several MSS*

246 *daughter*] daughters *1633-69*

249 *city's*] city *1633-69*

251 *dungeon*   Pronounced as three syllables.

252 *on me*] me on *1633-69*

254 *called*   Pronounced as two syllables.

256 *sigh*] sight *1650-69*
    sigh, and cry, stop] Sigh. And cry stop *MS*

258 *said'st*] sayst *MS*

260 *Rescued'st*] Rescuest *1633-69 and several MSS*

260-61 *now, / Thou*] now. / Thou *1650-69*

262 *heard*] hard *MS*

274 *as*] at *1633-39*

286 *perished*   Pronounced as three syllables.

295 *carbuncles*   rubies (Authorized Version).

296 *sapphirine*] seraphine *1633*
    sapphirine   as sapphire.

298 *streets*] street *1633-69 and several MSS*

299 *their bone*] the bone *several MSS*

300 *withered* Pronounced as three syllables.

302 *by penury*] through penury *several MSS*

303 *nature pitiful*] Nature, pitifully, *MS*

304 *hands*] hand *1633-69*; hand, *MS*

313-20 *for the priests' sins, and prophets' ... / ... depart, and touch us not* 'For the sins of her prophets, and the iniquities of her priests, that have shed the blood of the just in the midst of her; they have wandered as blind men in the streets, they have polluted themselves with blood, so that men could not touch their garments. They cried unto them, Depart ye, it is unclean, depart, depart, touch not, when they fled away and wandered. . . .' (Authorized Version).

314 *murdered* Pronounced as three syllables.

316 and **319** *defiled* Pronounced as three syllables.

318 *garments*] garment *1635-69*

325 *their old men shall the foe*] the old men shall their foe *1650-69*

329-30 *And such a nation as cannot save, / We in desire and speculation have* 'in our watching we have watched for a nation that could not save us' (Authorized Version).
nation Pronounced as three syllables.

332 *approached* Pronounced as three syllables.

337-40 *The anointed Lord ... / Into the pit which these men digged, fell* In a sermon of 1622 on this text Donne takes the fallen hero to be a king of Israel. But the Vulgate and the Authorized Version render the passage as foretelling Christ's fate: 'the anointed of the Lord was taken in their pits . . .' (Authorized Version).
digged pronounced as two syllables.

341 *joyful*] joyfully *MS*

342 *which*] that *1635-69*
Huz] Hus *several MSS*; her *1633*; Uz *1635-69*
Huz 'the land of Uz' (Authorized Version).

350 *reproached* Pronounced as three syllables.

351 *possession* Pronounced as four syllables.

354 *father*] fathers *1633–69*

355 *drink*] drunk *1633 and MSS*

359 *Egyptians* Pronounced as four syllables.

368 *Black as an oven coloured had our skin* had coloured our skin black as an oven.
   oven] ocean *1633*

371 *with their hands they hung* 'are hanged up by their hand' (Authorized Version).

374 *fall . . . bear*] fell . . . bare *1633 and MS*

375 *Elders, the gates* In Old Testament times the city gates were places of public resort where people met for business, to discuss news, and to see justice administered.

378 *sinned* Pronounced as two syllables.

389–90 *thus, / . . . us?*] thus? / . . . us. *MS*

A HYMN TO CHRIST, AT THE AUTHOR'S LAST GOING INTO GERMANY

Donne was in Germany as chaplain to the Earl of Doncaster's diplomatic mission from May 1619 to January 1620.

In the MSS the last two lines of each stanza are written as one line.
Title] At his going with my Lord of Doncaster 1619 *some MSS*; At his departure with my Lord of Doncaster 1619 *MS*; At the seaside going over with the Lord of Doncaster 1619 *MS*

2 *my . . . thy*] an . . . the *MS*

3 *soever swallow me*] soe'er swallows me up *several MSS*

5 *with*] in *several MSS*

10 *I loved there*] I love here *1635–69*; I love there *MS*
   who loved me] who love me *1635–69 and some MSS*

11 *our seas*] this flood *1635–69*; these seas *several MSS*; those seas *several MSS*

12 *sea*] seas *1633 and MS*; blood *1635–69*
   sea Christ's blood.

15 *thee, th'eternal root*] thy eternal work *several MSS*

17 *control* restrain, check. Christ and Christianity stand for love, which is itself a condition of spiritual harmony; they would not then seek to inhibit the love of a harmonious soul.

20 *I am*] am I *several MSS*

21-2 *from loving more* (a) from excessive love of things in the world; (b) from loving anyone other than Christ.

22 *who ever gives, takes liberty* (a) giving one's love to somebody else is a licence which may not be justified; (b) Christ's gift to us is such as takes away our liberty to love anyone else.

26 *those fainter beams of love* the love given to other things than Christ.

28 *fame*] face *1635-69 and some MSS*
hopes expectations of advancement.

29 *prayer*] prayers *several MSS*

30 *To see God only* (a) only to see God; (b) to see no one else but God.
go out of sight (a) go a long way from this country; (b) go where human sight fails, that is, to death.

32 *An everlasting night* death, which had to be reckoned with in his undertaking such a voyage, and for which the entire poem is a preparation.

HYMN TO GOD MY GOD, IN MY SICKNESS

First printed in *1635*. Walton quoted this poem in his *Life of Dr John Donne* (1640) and said that Donne wrote it on his deathbed. In a later edition of the *Life* he added to the title of the poem the date 23 March 1630, which by our reckoning is 23 March 1631, eight days before Donne died. But the judge Sir Julius Caesar, who died in 1636, wrote on a manuscript copy of the poem that these were Donne's 'verses in his great sickness in Decemb. 1623'. Donne did have a serious illness in the winter of 1623 and recorded its stages in the *Devotions upon Emergent Occasions*, published shortly after. Modern scholars are divided over whose testimony and which date to accept, but both Helen Gardner and R. C. Bald argue for 1623.

1 *that holy room* heaven.

2 *thy*] the *1639-69*

4 *the instrument*] my instrument *Walton*
the instrument the poetic faculty, tuned in the making of this poem.

5 *here*] now *MSS*

6 *Whilst . . . love*] Since . . . loves *Walton*
by their love   by their loving attention to his diseased body.

7 *Cosmographers*   geographers, men skilled in mapping the features of the heavens and the earth.

9 *this is my south-west discovery*   the south is the zone of heat, or fever, the west the region of decline. He sees his death of fever as the discovery of a passage to a new world.

10 *Per fretum febris*   by the heart, and strait, of fever.
to die,] to die. *1635–54*

11 *straits*   (a) sufferings, rigours; (b) narrow difficult ways; narrow channels of water.
my west   his death, or ultimate destination.

12 *their*] those *1635–69*

13–15 *As west and east / . . . are one, / So death doth touch the resurrection*   our west is death and our east is Christ; hence death is merely the prelude to resurrection, and our end is our beginning (see *Upon the Annunciation and Passion* 21).

16–17 *the Pacific Sea . . . / The eastern riches . . . Jerusalem*   Topographical metaphors for the peace and joys of heaven.

18 *Anyan*   probably modern Annam, then called 'Anian' and located on the west coast of America. It gave its name to the strait that supposedly divided America from Asia. But some commentators think that the Mozambique Channel is meant, which has an island called Anyouam at its northern entrance.

19 *none but straits*   (a) one can get to the Pacific and the East by going through the straits (though by other ways as well); (b) all the ways of getting to the Pacific, the East, and the Holy Land put one to straits, that is, ardours and hazards.

20 *Japhet . . . Cham . . . Shem*   the sons of Noah, between whom the world was divided. Europe was Japhet's portion, Africa was Ham's, and Asia was Shem's.

21–2 *We think that Paradise and Calvary, / . . . stood in one place*   Donne has the same idea in *The Progress of the Soul* 71–80. 'Place' here and 'room' in *The Progress of the Soul* may mean just the country or region, as Helen Gardner argues (*The Divine Poems*, Appendix F). The accepted view was that Paradise stood in Mesopotamia, near Damascus; but the Golden Legend says that Christ died 'in the same place' where

Adam was buried, and a gloss in the fourteenth century *Stanzaic Life of Christ* adds that Christ's Cross and Adam's tree stood '*in loco singulari*' too.

23 *both Adams*　Christ is the second Adam.

26 *his purple*　(a) Christ's saving blood; (b) Christ's imperial cloak, that commends a soul to God and assures its salvation; (c) the flush of the poet's fever.

27 *these his thorns*　the poet's sufferings, which re-enact Christ's.

28 *others' souls*] other souls *Walton and MS*

29 *to mine own*　to his own soul.

30 *Therefore that he may raise*] That, he may raise; therefore *Walton*
   Therefore that　in order that, to the end that.

A HYMN TO GOD THE FATHER

There are in effect two distinct versions of this poem, one given in the early editions and the other in the MSS. The version in the present text is that of *1633–69*. Here is the version in the MSS:

TO CHRIST

Wilt thou forgive that sin, where I begun,
　Which is my sin, though it were done before?
Wilt thou forgive those sins through which I run
　And do them still, though still I do deplore?
　　When thou hast done, thou hast not done, 　　　　5
　　　For I have more.

Wilt thou forgive that sin, by which I won
　Others to sin, and made my sin their door?
Wilt thou forgive that sin which I did shun
　A year or two, but wallowed in a score? 　　　　10
　　When thou hast done, thou hast not done,
　　　For I have more.

I have a sin of fear that when I have spun
　My last thread, I shall perish on the shore;
Swear by thy self that at my death, thy sun 　　　　15
　Shall shine as it shines now, and heretofore;
　　And having done that, thou hast done,
　　　I have no more.

To Christ   Christo Salvatori *MS*

2   *were*] was *several MSS*

7   *by which I won*] by which I have won *MS*

18   *I have*] I ask *MS*; I'll ask *MS*; I need *MS*

Walton gave the poem in full in the first edition of his *Life of Donne* (1640) and said that Donne wrote it during a serious illness in 1623. In the 1658 edition of the *Life* he added that Donne himself had the poem set to music. A contemporary setting by John Hilton survives; it is given in Jacquot.

1   *that sin where I begun*   original sin, the corruption into which man is born as a consequence of Adam's sin.

5   *thou hast not done*   (a) you have not finished yet; (b) you have not yet gained Donne. The pun on the poet's own name runs through the poem and resolves it – 'thou hast done' (line 17).

8   *my sin*] my sins *1639-69*

15   *thy son*   God's son and his sun are the same being, whose light of mercy draws the sinning poet from the darkness of hell.

Index of Titles

A Burnt Ship 149
A Fever 57
A Funeral Elegy (An Anatomy of the World: The First Anniversary) 283
A Hymn to Christ, at the Author's last going into Germany 346
A Hymn to God the Father 348
A Jet Ring Sent 61
A Lame Beggar 150
A Lecture upon the Shadows 62
A Letter to the Lady Carey, and Mistress Essex Rich, from Amiens 234
A Letter Written by Sir H. G. and J. D. *alternis vicibus* 212
A Licentious Person 150
A Nocturnal upon S. Lucy's Day, being the shortest day 72
A Self Accuser 150
A Tale of a Citizen and his Wife (Elegy 14) 114
A Valediction: forbidding Mourning 84
A Valediction of my Name in the Window 87
A Valediction: of the Book 85
A Valediction: of Weeping 89
Air and Angels 41
An Anatomy of the World: The First Anniversary 269
An Anatomy of the World (An Anatomy of the World:
  The First Anniversary) 270
An Elegy upon the Death of Mistress Boulstred 251
An Epithalamion or Marriage Song on the Lady Elizabeth and
  Count Palatine being married on St Valentine's Day 135
An Hymn to the Saints, and to Marquis Hamilton 263
An Obscure Writer 151
Annunciation (La Corona 2) 306
Antiquary 151
As due by many titles (Divine Meditations 2) 309
Ascension (La Carona 7) 308
At the round earth's imagined corners (Divine Meditations 7) 311
Away thou fondling motley humourist (Satire 1) 155

Batter my heart, three-personed God (Divine Meditations 14) 314
Break of Day 45

Cales and Guiana 150

Change (Elegy 3)   97
Community   48
Confined Love   49
Crucifying (La Corona 5)   307

Death be not proud (Divine Meditations 10)   313
Disinherited   151
Divine Meditations   309

Eclogue   1613. December 26   139
Elegy 6   101
Elegy 7   102
Elegy on Mistress Boulstred   249
Elegy on the Lady Markham   247
Elegy on the L.C.   247
Elegy upon the untimely death of the incomparable Prince Henry   253
Epitaph on Himself   233
Epithalamion Made at Lincoln's Inn   133

Fall of a Wall   149
Farewell to Love   56
Father, part of his double interest (Divine Meditations 16)   315
First Song (The Progress of the Soul)   177

Good Friday, 1613. Riding Westward   329

Hero and Leander   149
His Parting from Her (Elegy 12)   110
His Picture (Elegy 5)   100
Holy Sonnets   306
H. W. *in Hibernia Belligeranti*   217
Hymn to God my God, in my sickness   347

I am a little world (Divine Meditations 5)   310
If faithful souls be alike glorified (Divine Meditations 8)   312
If poisonous minerals (Divine Meditations 9)   312

Jealousy (Elegy 1)   95
Julia (Elegy 13)   113

Kind pity chokes my spleen (Satire 3)   161
Klockius   151

La Corona   306
Lovers' Infiniteness   64
Love's Alchemy   65

Love's Deity 65
Love's Diet 66
Love's Exchange 67
Love's Growth 69
Love's Progress (Elegy 18) 122
Love's Usury 69
Love's War (Elegy 20) 126

Manliness 152
Mercurius Gallo Belgicus 152

Nativity (La Corona 3) 307
Negative Love 71
Niobe 149

O might those sighs and tears (Divine Meditations 3) 310
Obsequies to the Lord Harrington, brother to the Lady Lucy,
  Countess of Bedford 256
Of the Progress of the Soul: The Second Anniversary 286
Of the Progress of the Soul (Of the Progress of the Soul:
  The Second Anniversary) 287
Oh my black soul! (Divine Meditations 4) 310
Oh, to vex me (Divine Meditations 19) 316
On his Mistress (Elegy 16) 116

Phryne 151
Pyramus and Thisbe 149

Raderus 151
Ralphius 152
Resurrection (La Corona 6) 308
Resurrection, imperfect 327

Sappho to Philaenis 127
Self Love 76
Show me dear Christ (Divine Meditations 18) 316
Since she whom I loved (Divine Meditations 17) 316
Sir John Wingfield 150
Sir; though (I thank God for it) I do hate (Satire 2) 158
Song (Go, and catch a falling star) 77
Song (Sweetest love, I do not go) 78
Sonnet. The Token 79
Spit in my face ye Jews (Divine Meditations 11) 313

Temple (La Corona 4) 307
The Anagram (Elegy 2) 96

The Anniversary 41
The Apparition 42
The Autumnal (Elegy 9) 105
The Bait 43
The Blossom 44
The Bracelet (Elegy 11) 107
The Broken Heart 46
The Calm 199
The Canonization 47
The Comparison (Elegy 8) 103
The Computation 49
The Cross 326
The Curse 50
The Damp 51
The Dissolution 52
The Dream 52
The Dream (Elegy 10) 106
The Ecstasy 53
The Expiration 56
The Expostulation (Elegy 15) 116
The Flea 58
The Funeral 59
The Good Morrow 60
The Harbinger to Progress (Of the Progress of the Soul:
 The Second Anniversary) 286
The Indifferent 61
The Lamentations of Jeremy, for the most part according to
 Tremellius 334
The Legacy 63
The Liar 152
The Litany 317
The Message 70
The Paradox 73
The Perfume (Elegy 4) 98
The Primrose 74
The Progress of the Soul (Metempsychosis) 176
The Prohibition 75
The Relic 75
The Storm 197
The Sun Rising 80
The Triple Fool 81
The Undertaking 83
The Will 90
This is my play's last scene (Divine Meditations 6) 311
Thou hast made me (Divine Meditations 1) 309
Thou shalt laugh in this leaf, Muse (Satire 5) 170

To E. of D. with Six Holy Sonnets 305
To his Mistress Going to Bed (Elegy 19) 124
To Mr B. B. 200
To Mr C. B. 201
To Mr E. G. 202
To Mr I. L. (Blessed are your north parts) 203
To Mr I. L. (Of that short roll of friends) 203
To Mr Roland Woodward 206
To Mr R. W. (If, as mine is, thy life a slumber be) 204
To Mr R. W. (Kindly I envy thy song's perfection) 205
To Mr R. W. (Muse not that by thy mind the body is led) 205
To Mr R. W. (Zealously my Muse doth salute all thee) 206
To Mr S. B. 202
To Mr Tilman after he had taken orders 331
To Mr T. W. (All hail, sweet poet) 207
To Mr T. W. (At once, from hence) 208
To Mr T. W. (Haste thee harsh verse) 209
To Mr T. W. (Pregnant again with th' old twins) 209
To Mrs Magdalen Herbert: of St Mary Magdalen 305
To Mrs M. H. 219
To Sir Edward Herbert, at Juliers 218
To Sir Henry Goodyer 210
To Sir Henry Wotton (Here's no more news) 213
To Sir Henry Wotton (Sir, more than kisses) 214
To Sir Henry Wotton, at his going Ambassador to Venice 216
To the Countess of Bedford (Honour is so sublime perfection) 223
To the Countess of Bedford (Madam, Reason is our soul's left hand) 225
To the Countess of Bedford (Madam, You have refined me) 229
To the Countess of Bedford (Though I be dead) 226
To the Countess of Bedford (To have written then) 227
To the Countess of Bedford at New Year's Tide 221
To the Countess of Huntingdon (Madam, Man to God's image) 236
To the Countess of Huntingdon (That unripe side of earth) 238
To the Countess of Salisbury 242
To the Lady Bedford 231
To the Praise of the Dead and the Anatomy (An Anatomy of the World: The First Anniversary) 269
Twicknam Gardens 82

Upon Mr Thomas Coryat's Crudities 173
Upon the Annunciation and Passion falling upon one day. 1608 328
Upon the translation of the Psalms by Sir Philip Sidney, and the Countess of Pembroke his Sister 332

Variety (Elegy 17) 119

Well; I may now receive and die (Satire 4) 164
What if this present were the world's last night? (Divine
  Meditations 13) 314
Why are we by all creatures waited on? (Divine Meditations 12) 313
Wilt thou love God, as he thee? (Divine Meditations 15) 315
Witchcraft by a Picture 91
Woman's Constancy 92

After those reverend papers, whose soul is 216
All hail, sweet poet, more full of more strong fire, 207
All kings, and all their favourites, 41
Although thy hand and faith, and good works too, 97
As due by many titles I resign 309
As the sweet sweat of roses in a still, 103
As virtuous men pass mildly away, 84
At once, from hence, my lines and I depart, 208
At the round earth's imagined corners, blow 311
Away thou fondling motley humourist, 155

Batter my heart, three-personed God; for, you 314
Before I sigh my last gasp, let me breathe, 90
Beyond th' old Pillars many have travelled 150
Blasted with sighs and surrounded with tears, 82
Blessed are your north parts, for all this long time 203
Both robbed of air, we both lie in one ground, 149
Busy old fool, unruly sun, 80
By children's birth and death, I am become 149
By miracles exceeding power of man, 307
By our first strange and fatal interview, 118

Come live with me, and be my love, 43
Come, Madam, come, all rest my powers defy, 124
Compassion in the world again is bred: 152

Dear love, for nothing less than thee 52
Death be not proud, though some have called thee 313
Death I recant, and say, unsaid by me 249
Deign at my hands this crown of prayer and praise, 306

Eternal God (for whom who ever dare 332
Even as lame things thirst their perfection, so 202

Fair, great, and good, since seeing you, we see 242
Fair soul, which wast, not only, as all souls be, 256
Father of heaven, and him, by whom 317
Father, part of his double interest 315

Fond woman, which wouldst have thy husband die, 95
For every hour that thou wilt spare me now, 69
For God's sake hold your tongue, and let me love, 47
For the first twenty years, since yesterday, 49

Go, and catch a falling star, 77
Good we must love, and must hate ill, 48

Hail Bishop Valentine, whose day this is, 135
Hark news, O envy, thou shalt hear descried 113
Haste thee harsh verse as fast as thy lame measure 209
He is stark mad, who ever says, 46
He that cannot choose but love, 76
Her of your name, whose fair inheritance 305
Here take my picture, though I bid farewell, 100
Here's no more news, than virtue, I may as well 213
Honour is so sublime perfection, 223
How sits this city, late most populous, 334

I am a little world made cunningly 310
I am two fools, I know, 81
I am unable, yonder beggar cries, 150
I can love both fair and brown, 61
I fix mine eye on thine, and there 91
I have done one braver thing 83
I long to talk with some old lover's ghost, 65
I never stooped so low, as they 71
I scarce believe my love to be so pure 69
I sing no harm good sooth to any wight, 114
I sing the progress of a deathless soul, 177
I wonder, by my troth, what thou, and I 60
If, as mine is, thy life a slumber be, 204
If faithful souls be alike glorified 312
If in his study he hath so much care 151
If poisonous minerals, and if that tree, 312
If yet I have not all thy love, 64
If you from spoil of th' old world's farthest end 150
I'll tell thee now (dear love) what thou shalt do 85
Image of her whom I love, more than she, 106
Immensity cloistered in thy dear womb, 307
In what torn ship soever I embark, 346
Is not thy sacred hunger of science 200

Kind pity chokes my spleen; brave scorn forbids 161
Kindly I envy thy song's perfection 205
Klockius so deeply hath sworn, ne'er more to come 151

Language thou art too narrow, and too weak 251
Let man's soul be a sphere, and then, in this, 329
Let me pour forth 89
Like Aesop's fellow-slaves, O Mercury, 152
Like one who in her third widowhood doth profess 206
Little think'st thou, poor flower, 44
Look to me faith, and look to my faith, God; 253
Love, any devil else but you, 67

Mad paper stay, and grudge not here to burn 219
Madame, Here, where by all, all Saints invoked are 234
Madam, Man to God's image, Eve, to man's was made, 236
Madam, Reason is our soul's left hand Faith her right, 225
Madam, That I might make your cabinet my tomb, 233
Madam, You have refined me, and to worthiest things 229
Man is a lump, where all beasts kneaded be, 218
Man is the world, and death the ocean, 247
Mark but this flea, and mark in this, 58
Marry, and love thy Flavia, for, she 96
Moist with one drop of thy blood, my dry soul 308
Muse not that by thy mind thy body is led: 205
My name engraved herein, 87

Nature's lay idiot, I taught thee to love, 102
No lover saith, I love, nor any other 73
No spring, nor summer beauty hath such grace, 105
Not that in colour it was like thy hair, 107
Nothing could make me sooner to confess 287
Now thou hast loved me one whole day, 92

O might those sighs and tears return again 310
O thou which to search out the secret parts 202
Of that short roll of friends writ in my heart 203
Oh do not die, for I shall hate 57
Oh, let me not serve so, as those men serve 101
Oh my black soul! now thou art summoned 310
Oh, to vex me, contraries meet in one: 316
Oh to what height will love of greatness drive 173
Once, and but once found in thy company, 98
Our storm is past, and that storm's tyrannous rage, 199
Out of a fired ship, which, by no way 149

Philo, with twelve year's study, hath been grieved 151
Pregnant again with th' old twins hope, and fear, 209
Salute the last and everlasting day, 308

Salvation to all that will is nigh, 306
See Sir, how as the sun's hot masculine flame 305
Send home my long strayed eyes to me, 70
Send me some token, that my hope may live, 79
She is dead; and all which die 52
Show me dear Christ, thy spouse, so bright and clear. 316
Since Christ embraced the Cross itself, dare I 326
Since every tree begins to blossom now 212
Since I am coming to that holy room, 347
Since she must go, and I must mourn, come night, 110
Since she whom I loved hath paid her last debt 316
Sir, more than kisses, letters mingle souls; 214
Sir; though (I thank God for it) I do hate 158
Sleep sleep old sun, thou canst not have repassed 327
So, so, break off this last lamenting kiss, 56
Some man unworthy to be possessor, 49
Some that have deeper digged love's mine than I, 65
Sorrow, who to this house scarce knew the way: 247
Spit in my face ye Jews, and pierce my side 313
Stand still, and I will read to thee 62
Sweetest love, I do not go, 78

Take heed of loving me, 75
Tamely frail body''abstain today; today 328
That unripe side of earth, that heavy clime 238
The heavens rejoice in motion, why should I 119
The sun-beams in the east are spread, 133
This is my play's last scene, here heavens appoint 311
This twilight of two years, not past nor next, 221
Thou art not so black, as my heart, 61
Thou call'st me effeminate, for I love women's joys; 152
Thou hast made me, and shall thy work decay? 309
Thou in the fields walk'st out thy supping hours 152
Thou shalt not laugh in this leaf, Muse, nor they 170
Thou which art I, ('tis nothing to be so), 197
Thou, whose diviner soul hath caused thee now 331
Though I be dead, and buried, yet I have 226
Thy friend, whom thy deserts to thee enchain, 201
Thy father all from thee, by his last will, 151
Thy flattering picture, Phryne, is like thee, 152
Thy sins and hairs may no man equal call, 150
Till I have peace with thee, war other men, 126
'Tis lost, to trust a tomb with such a guest, 283
'Tis the year's midnight, and it is the day's, 72
'Tis true, 'tis day, what though it be? 45
To have written then, when you writ, seemed to me 227

To make the doubt clear, that no woman's true, 116
To what a cumbersome inwieldiness 66
Twice or thrice had I loved thee, 41
Two, by themselves, each other, love and fear 149
Two souls move here, and mine (a third) must move 286

Under an undermined, and shot-bruised wall 149
Unseasonable man, statue of ice, 139
Upon this primrose hill, 74

Well died the world, that we might live to see 269
Well; I may now receive and die; my sin 164
Went you to conquer? and have so much lost 217
What if this present were the world's last night? 314
When by thy scorn, O murderess, I am dead, 42
When I am dead, and doctors know not why, 51
When I died last, and, dear, I die 63
When my grave is broke up again 75
When that rich soul which to her heaven is gone, 270
Where is that holy fire, which verse is said 127
Where, like a pillow on a bed, 53
Whether that soul which now comes up to you 264
Whilst yet to prove, 56
Who makes the past, a pattern for next year, 210
Whoever comes to shroud me, do not harm 59
Whoever guesses, thinks, or dreams he knows 50
Whoever loves, if he do not propose 122
Why are we by all creatures waited on? 313
Why this man gelded Martial I muse, 151
Wilt thou forgive that sin where I begun, 348
Wilt thou love God, as he thee? then digest, 315
With his kind mother who partakes thy woe, 307

You that are she and you, that's double she, 231
Your mistress, that you follow whores, still taxeth you: 150

Zealously my Muse doth salute all thee 206

PENGUIN ONLINE

READ MORE IN PENGUIN

In every corner of the world, on every subject under the sun, Penguin represents quality and variety – the very best in publishing today.

For complete information about books available from Penguin – including Puffins, Penguin Classics and Arkana – and how to order them, write to us at the appropriate address below. Please note that for copyright reasons the selection of books varies from country to country.

In the United Kingdom: Please write to *Dept. EP, Penguin Books Ltd, Bath Road, Harmondsworth, West Drayton, Middlesex UB7 0DA*

In the United States: Please write to *Consumer Services, Penguin Putnam Inc., 405 Murray Hill Parkway, East Rutherford, New Jersey 07073-2136.* VISA and MasterCard holders call 1-800-631-8571 to order Penguin titles

In Canada: Please write to *Penguin Books Canada Ltd, 10 Alcorn Avenue, Suite 300, Toronto, Ontario M4V 3B2*

In Australia: Please write to *Penguin Books Australia Ltd, 487 Maroondah Highway, Ringwood, Victoria 3134*

In New Zealand: Please write to *Penguin Books (NZ) Ltd, Private Bag 102902, North Shore Mail Centre, Auckland 10*

In India: Please write to *Penguin Books India Pvt Ltd, 11 Community Centre, Panchsheel Park, New Delhi 110017*

In the Netherlands: Please write to *Penguin Books Netherlands bv, Postbus 3507, NL-1001 AH Amsterdam*

In Germany: Please write to *Penguin Books Deutschland GmbH, Metzlerstrasse 26, 60594 Frankfurt am Main*

In Spain: Please write to *Penguin Books S. A., Bravo Murillo 19, 1°B, 28015 Madrid*

In Italy: Please write to *Penguin Italia s.r.l., Via Vittorio Emanuele 45/a, 20094 Corsico, Milano*

In France: Please write to *Penguin France, 12, Rue Prosper Ferradou, 31700 Blagnac*

In Japan: Please write to *Penguin Books Japan Ltd, Iidabashi KM-Bldg, 2-23-9 Koraku, Bunkyo-Ku, Tokyo 112-0004*

In South Africa: Please write to *Penguin Books South Africa (Pty) Ltd, P.O. Box 751093, Gardenview, 2047 Johannesburg*